PREHISTORIC TEXTILES

PREHISTORIC
TEXTILES

THE DEVELOPMENT OF
CLOTH IN THE
NEOLITHIC AND
BRONZE AGES

*with Special Reference to
the Aegean*

BY E. J. W. BARBER

PRINCETON UNIVERSITY PRESS

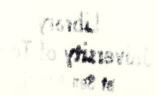

Copyright © 1991 by Princeton University Press
Published by Princeton University Press, 41 William Street,
Princeton, New Jersey 08540
In the United Kingdom: Princeton University Press, Oxford

Library of Congress Cataloging-in-Publication Data

Barber, E.J.W., 1940–
Prehistoric textiles : the development of cloth in the
Neolithic and Bronze Ages with special reference to
the Aegean / E.J.W. Barber.
    p.   cm.
Bibliography: p.
Includes index.
ISBN 0-691-03597-0
ISBN 0-691-00224-X (pbk.)
1. Textile fabrics, Prehistoric—Europe. 2. Textile fabrics,
Prehistoric—Middle East. 3. Neolithic period—Europe.
4. Bronze age—Middle East. 5. Neolithic period—Middle East.
6. Bronze age—Europe. 7. Europe—Antiquities.
8. Middle East—Antiquities. I. Title.
GN776.2.A1B37 1990

Third printing, for the Princeton Paperback edition, 1992

We are very grateful to the Publications Program of the
National Endowment for the Humanities, an
independent Federal agency, for its support

Published with the assistance of the Getty Grant Program

This book has been composed in Linotron Caledonia

Princeton University Press books are printed on
acid-free paper, and meet the guidelines for permanence
and durability of the Committee on
Production Guidelines for Book Longevity
of the Council on Library Resources

Printed in the United States of America

10   9   8   7   6   5   4   3

TO MY FAMILY

to Virginia
who taught me how to weave
and to appreciate color,
form and texture;

and to Harold, Ann, and Paul
who also supported me, each
from a different set of
disciplines,
and all with patience.

CONTENTS

List of Illustrations and Tables   ix

Preface   xxi

Site Maps   xxiv

Chronology (in Logarithmic Scale) of Main
    Eras Mentioned, 20,000–400 B.C.   xxx

Chronology of Later Cultures Mentioned,
    3000–400 B.C.   xxxi

Introduction   3

PART I: THE BASIC TEXTILE CRAFTS —
THE DATA

1. The Domestication of Fibers   9
   Flax   11
   Hemp   15
   Nettle and Other Bast Fibers   19
   Wool   20
   Other Hair Fibers   30
   Silk   30
   Cotton   32
   Esparto   33
   Appendix to Chapter 1:
      The Archaeolinguistics of Hemp   36

2. Spinning   39
   Twisted Thread   39
   Spinning, Drafting, and Splicing   41
   The Evidence for Spindles and Whorls   51
   Other Accoutrements   68

3. Looms and Weaving   79
   The Ground-Loom   83
   The Warp-Weighted Loom   91

The Vertical Two-Beam Loom   113
Band Looms   116
Tablet-Weaving   118
Sprang   122
Conclusions   124

4. The Textile Weaves: (1) The Beginnings   126
   The Earliest Remains   126
   Neolithic Europe   133

5. The Textile Weaves: (2) Egypt   145
   Early Techniques   145
   The Later (18th Dynasty) Techniques   156

6. The Textile Weaves: (3) The Bronze Age   163
   Mesopotamia   164
   The Levant   165
   Anatolia, the Caucasus, and the Aegean   166
   Italy, France, and Spain   174
   Denmark   176
   Germany, Holland, and Britain   184

7. The Textile Weaves: (4) The Iron Age   186
   Hallstatt, North, and South   186
   Greece, Anatolia, and the Steppes   196

8. The Textile Weaves: (5) An Overall View   210

9. Felt and Felting   215

10. Dyes   223
   Survey of the Artifacts   223
   Dye Processes   225
   Some Dyes   227
   Some Colors   229
   Mordants   235
   Dye-Works   239

PART II: DISCUSSIONS

Introduction to Part II   247

11. Beginnings Revisited   249
    A new analysis, in light of Part I, of the
    origins of spinning and weaving

12. Word Excavation   260
    A pilot study, from a base of ancient
    Greek, in how to use linguistic analysis
    and reconstruction to fill out and clarify
    the archaeological findings, as well as
    how to use archaeology to facilitate lin-
    guistic reconstruction—applied to textiles

13. Women's Work   283
    An assessment of the role of women in
    textile production

14. The Weight Chase   299
    A discussion of why textile artifacts are
    uniquely useful to the archaeologist in
    tracing migrations, with considerable
    comment on three interesting cases

15. Minoans, Mycenaeans, and Keftiu   311
    An inquiry into the Bronze Age textile
    export from the Aegean to Egypt, and the
    nature of Aegean textiles

16. And Penelope?   358
    An investigation of a possible Mycenaean
    legacy of monumental textile art to early
    Classical Greece

Coda   383

APPENDICES

A. The Loom Weights: Data Table and Its
   Bibliography for Chapter 3   387

B. The Hollow Whorls: List and Its Bibliography for Chapter 14   391

C. Aegean Representations of Cloth: List and
   Its Bibliography for Chapter 15   394

D. Egyptian Tombs with Aegean Data: List
   and Its Bibliography for Chapter 15   396

Bibliography   397

Index   431

LIST OF ILLUSTRATIONS

MAPS

A Europe and the Near East, with inset of
   Asia   xxiv
B Denmark   xxvi
C Egypt and Palestine   xxvi
D Southern Greece and Crete   xxviii

COLOR PLATES   Opposite p. 160

1 Linen fragments from the tomb of Thutmose
   IV; early 15th century B.C.: tapestry-woven
   fragments with name of Thutmose III, and
   fragment decorated with inwoven pink and
   green rosettes and stripes. (Cairo; Carter and
   Newberry 1904, pl. 28)
2 Fresco figure of a woman dancing(?) in a
   garden, wearing dress with quatrefoil
   interlock pattern; Hagia Triada, Crete; mid-
   2nd millennium B.C. (Late Minoan I).
   (Halbherr 1903, pl. 10)
3 Egyptian ceiling patterns (18th Dynasty)
   probably copied from contemporary Aegean
   weavings. Quatrefoil interlock pattern
   decorating the soffit of a doorway in the tomb
   of Amenemhet (Th 82); early 15th century
   B.C. (After Nina Davies and A. Gardiner
   1915, pl. 32D; courtesy of the Committee of
   the Egypt Exploration Society) "Wrought-
   iron fence" motif and two meander-based
   patterns from the ceiling of the tomb of
   Hatshepsut's herald Antef (Th 155); early
   15th century B.C. (After Säve-Söderbergh
   1957, pl. 19) Ceiling pattern from the tomb of
   Menkheperraseneb (Th 86); mid-15th century
   B.C. (After Davies and Davies 1933, pl. 30B;
   courtesy of the Committee of the Egypt
   Exploration Society) (Redrawn by M. Stone)
4 Woolen cloths from the frozen tombs at
   Pazyryk in the Altai Mountains, mid-1st
   millennium B.C.: woolen *shabrak* (saddle
   cloth) pieced together from tapestry
   apparently woven in Iran, from Kurgan 5;
   polychrome spirals woven in slit-tapestry
   technique and sewn to strips of plain red
   woolen twill, from Kurgan 2. (Hermitage
   Museum, Leningrad)

FIGURES

0.1 Woodblock (17th century) showing
     Balkan women spinning while doing
     other things. (Valvasor 1689, 321)   4
1.1 Theban papyrus of the Book of the
     Dead (18th Dynasty), showing the
     growing of flax. (Courtesy of Trustees of
     the British Museum)   12
1.2 Swiss Neolithic flax-working
     implements. (After E. Vogt 1937, fig.
     72; courtesy of Swiss National Museum)   14
1.3 Hemp being grown for rope fiber,
     eastern Romania, 1979   16
1.4 Diagrams of the structures of wool,
     hair, and kemp   21
1.5 *Ovis orientalis*: wild Persian Red
     Sheep (female)   23
1.6 Fleece from a modern sheep bred for
     wool compared with the kempy coat of
     Ovis orientalis   24
1.7 Middle Kingdom Egyptian
     heiroglyphic painting of hairy sheep,
     from Beni Hasan, ca. 2000 B.C.
     (Griffith 1896, pl. 3.35)   25
1.8 Map of principal fibers used for
     weaving in prehistoric times   34
1.9 Minoan bowl containing clay models of
     a shepherd and his flock of sheep; from
     Palaikastro, Crete, early 2nd
     millennium B.C. (Iraklion Museum, no.
     2903; Bosanquet and Dawkins 1923, pl.
     7)   35
2.1 Palaeolithic "Venus" figure, wearing a
     skirt of twisted string; Lespugue,

France; ca. 20,000 B.C. (Courtesy of
Musée de l'Homme, Paris)   40

2.2 Restored design, showing three
spinners(?), on an Early Dynastic vase
from Tell Agrab in Mesopotamia; early
3rd millennium. (After Delougaz 1952,
pl. 12)   42

2.3 Modern Greek peasant woman
spinning with a low-whorl drop-
spindle. (Drawing by M. Stone, after
photos by author)   43

2.4 Bedouin woman spinning with a hand-
held spindle. (Pencil sketch by F.
Goodall, ca. 1858; courtesy of Trustees
of the British Museum)   44

2.5 Egyptian wall painting of women
spinning thread and weaving cloth, and
men washing cloth and spinning cord.
Middle Kingdom tomb of Baqt at Beni
Hasan (No. 15). (Newberry 1894, pl. 4)   45

2.6 Women working flax, from a wall of
the Middle Kingdom tomb of Daga at
Thebes (No. 103). (Davies 1913, pl. 37;
courtesy of the Committee of the Egypt
Exploration Society)   45

2.7 Eighteenth Dynasty Egyptian spindle,
shown upside-down. (British Museum
no. 4677; photo courtesy of Trustees of
the British Museum)   46

2.8 Magnified photo of splices in typical
dynastic Egyptian linen   47

2.9 Schematic representation of a linen
splice   47

2.10 Spinner with two spindles and four
threads; from a wall of the Middle
Kingdom tomb of Khety at Beni Hasan
(No. 17). (Roth and Crowfoot 1921,
cover; courtesy of Department of
Egyptology, University College
London)   48

2.11 Egyptian hieroglyphics for "spin"
showing a high-whorl spindle. (After
Budge 1920, 563; and Gardiner 1957,
520)   53

2.12 Late Neolithic spindle of wood with
antler whorl, from Meilen Rohrenhaab,
Switzerland; ca. 3000 B.C. (Courtesy of
Swiss National Museum)   55

2.13 Late Neolithic spindle of wood with a
clay whorl, from Switzerland. (After
Staub 1864, pl. 4.7)   55

2.14 Two typical Terremare spindle
whorls, one with a bit of spindle shaft
remaining. Northern Italy, Bronze
Age. (After Gastaldi 1865, 45 fig. 25)   55

2.15 Urn from Sopron (Ödenburg) in
western Hungary, showing women
spinning and weaving. Hallstatt period,
early 1st millennium B.C. (Photo
courtesy of Naturhistorisches Museum,
Vienna)   56

2.16 Seal from Choga Mish, in Khuzistan,
showing a spinner seated on a platform;
4th millennium. (Delougaz and Kantor
1972, 32 pl. X.a; courtesy of the
Oriental Institute of the University of
Chicago. Drawing by H. J. Kantor)   57

2.17 Seal from the Newell collection
(NCBS 31), showing spinning and
warping. (After von der Osten 1934, pl.
4.31; Amiet 1961, pl. 19.319; Buchanan
1981, fig. 153; courtesy of Yale
Babylonian Collection. Drawing by
M. Stone)   57

2.18 Part of a mosaic panel from Mari:
spinner skeining off onto the hands of a
seated woman; early 2nd millennium
B.C. (After Parrot 1962, pl. 11)   57

2.19 Two "distaffs" and a spindle from
Kish, in Mesopotamia; late 3rd
millennium. (After Mackay 1925, pl.
58.1–3)   58

2.20 Copper spindle with two whorls and
a thread groove, from Hissar II,
northern Iran; 3rd millennium. (After
E. F. Schmidt 1937, pl. 29, no. H2171;
courtesy of the University Museum,
University of Pennsylvania)   58

2.21 Neo-Elamite relief of a lady spinning,
from Susa; early 1st millennium B.C.
(Courtesy of Musée du Louvre: Sb
2834)   58

2.22 Metal spindle with thread-groove,
from Marlik in northern Iran; early 1st
millennium B.C. (After Negahban 1964,
fig. 43)   59

2.23 Neo-Hittite relief from Maraş,
showing seated lady with spindle.
(After Bossert 1942, pl. 814)   59

2.24 Silver and gold or electrum spindle
from Tomb L at Alaca Höyük, in
Turkey. Early Bronze Age: mid-3rd
millennium. (After Koşay 1951, pl. 197
fig. 1)   60

2.25 Early Bronze Age metal spindles from Horoztepe, in Turkey. (Özgüç and Akok 1958, figs. 25–26)   61

2.26 Contents of royal Tomb H, Alaca Höyük, with a spindle in precious metal. (Koşay 1951, pl. 124)   61

2.27 Bronze spindle with two whorls, from Karataş, in southwest Turkey. Early Bronze Age. (After Mellink 1969, pl. 74 fig. 23; courtesy of *American Journal of Archaeology*)   62

2.28 Probable spindles of ivory from Megiddo, in northern Israel. Late Bronze Age; mid-2nd millennium B.C. (After Guy 1938, fig. 175.6, pl. 84.1, 95.50)   62

2.29 Late Bronze Age clay spindle from Vounous, Cyprus, ornamented to imitate ivory ones. (After E. Stewart and J. Stewart 1950, pl. 100.d)   63

2.30 Imported ivory spindle found at Peratí, in Attica, Greece. Late Bronze Age. (National Museum, Athens)   64

2.31 Bronze spindles from Iron Age Deve Hüyük, in eastern Turkey. (After Moorey 1980, figs. 16.399–400)   64

2.32 Spindle from Grave 11 at Gurob, in the Faiyum, and typical Middle Kingdom Egyptian spindle for comparison. (After Brunton and Engelbach 1927, pl. 13.8, courtesy of Department of Egyptology, University College London; and British Museum no. 50980, courtesy of Trustees of the British Museum)   65

2.33 "S" and "Z" directions of twisting threads   66

2.34 Bronze hooks from the Dictaean cave, Crete, possibly for spindles; and bronze spindle-hooks from Olynthus, Classical era. (After Hogarth 1899–1900, 112 fig. 46; D. M. Robinson 1941, pl. 119 nos. 1884, 1891, 1886; courtesy of Johns Hopkins University Press)   69

2.35 Early representation of a distaff, which a girl holds with her spindle, on an Archaic stele from Priniás, Crete. (Pernier 1910, pl. 4.9)   70

2.36 Greek girl spinning with her thread in her mouth. Center of vase found at Orvieto; early 5th century B.C. (Blümner 1877, pl. 6)   70

2.37 Clay bowls with internal loops worn by thread, from Egypt and Palestine. Late Bronze Age. (After Dothan 1963, figs. 1, 3)   71

2.38 Scenes of spinning and weaving on an Attic Greek lekythos, ca. 560 B.C. (The Metropolitan Museum of Art; Fletcher Fund, 1931: no. 31.11.10)   72

2.39 Modern Japanese fiber-wetting bowl. (After Tsuboi 1984)   73

2.40 Wall painting of a Middle Kingdom Egyptian textile shop, from the tomb of Khnumhotep at Beni Hasan (No. 3); 12th Dynasty, early 2nd millennium B.C. (Photography courtesy of the Metropolitan Museum of Art; Rogers Fund, 1933: no. 33.8.16)   74

2.41 Looped bowl, probably for wetting linen thread, from an Early Bronze II village at Myrtos, Crete. (Photo courtesy of P. Warren)   75

2.42 Looped bowl, from Drakones, Crete; Middle Bronze Age. (After Xanthoudides 1924, pl. 42 no. 5033)   75

2.43 Man spinning string; fragment of a 6th Dynasty Egyptian relief. (Firth and Gunn 1926, 36)   76

2.44 Late Minoan pottery vessel of uncertain use ("Ariadne's clew-box"), possibly for winding bobbins; found in the "House of the Sacrificed Oxen" at Knossos, Crete. (Courtesy of Iraklion Museum: no. 7742)   77

2.45 Knee guard or *epinētron*, used in preparing roves of wool for spinning. Attic; 6th–5th century B.C. (The Metropolitan Museum of Art; Rogers Fund, 1910: no. 10.210.13)   78

3.1 Bronze figurine of a woman weaving on a backstrap loom with tension controlled by the toes. Yunnan, China; early Han Dynasty (late 1st millennium B.C.). (After no. 176 of the travelling Exhibition of Archaeological Finds from the People's Republic of China)   81

3.2 Diagram of an Egyptian ground-loom in use. (Winlock 1922, fig. 2; Courtesy of Department of Egyptology, University College London)   82

3.3 Neolithic Egyptian dish showing a ground-loom, from Badari; early 4th millennium. (Photo courtesy of Petrie Museum, University College London: UC 9547) 83

3.4 Early cylinder seal designs from Susa, 4th millennium (drawings courtesy of Dominique Collon): ground-loom with a weaver crouching on either side, and someone warping (GS 673; Le Breton 1957, 106 fig. 20.20; Amiet 1961, pl. 16.275); warping-frame viewed from side (GS 674; Amiet 1961, pl. 16.273) 84

3.5 Egyptian horizontal ground-loom depicted in the Middle Kingdom tomb of Khnumhotep, at Beni Hasan. (Drawing by Norman de Garis Davies: Roth [1913] 1951, fig. 6; courtesy of Calderdale Museums Service: Bankfield Museum, Halifax) 84

3.6 Egyptian funerary model of female textile workers, from the Middle Kingdom tomb of Meketre, showing splicers, spinners, weavers operating two looms, and women warping on wall pegs. (Egyptian Museum, Cairo. Photography by the Egyptian Expedition, the Metropolitan Museum of Art) 85

3.7 Egyptian heddle jacks from Kahun (Middle Kingdom), now in the Petrie Museum, London. (After Roth and Crowfoot 1921, 100 fig. 4; courtesy of Department of Egyptology, University College London) 87

3.8 Textile manufacture depicted in the Middle Kingdom Egyptian tomb of Djehutihetep at el-Bersheh, including women warping on pegs on the wall, and removing the warp to the loom. Early 2nd millennium B.C. (Newberry n.d., pl. 26) 90

3.9 Painting of warping and weaving in the Middle Kingdom tomb of Daga at Thebes (No. 103). (Davies 1913, pl. 37; courtesy of Committee of the Egypt Exploration Society) 91

3.10 Egyptian hieroglyphs, depicting "warp stretched between two uprights," "netting needle; reel," and "netting needle filled with twine." (After Gardiner 1957, 520, 525; Hayes 1953, 292) 91

3.11 Probable representations of warp-weighted looms carved on the Great Rock at Naquane, in northern Italy. Mid-2nd millennium B.C. (Nos. 225, 165, 102, 103, 128, 182; after Anati 1960a, fig. 5) 91

3.12 Sealing with a Cretan Linear Script A sign, apparently representing warp-weighted loom; mid-2nd millennium B.C. (Iraklion Museum, no. 73) 92

3.13 Women weaving on a warp-weighted loom. Greek lekythos, ca. 560 B.C. (The Metropolitan Museum of Art; Fletcher Fund, 1931: no. 31.11.10) 92

3.14 Room 206 at Troy, Level IIg, with remains of a loom extending out from a wall. (Blegen et al. 1950, fig. 461; courtesy of Princeton University Press) 93

3.15 Plan of an Early Bronze II–III room at Aphrodisias, with fallen loom weights along the side of the excavation trench. (Kadish 1971, fig. 11; courtesy of *American Journal of Archaeology*) 94

3.16 Plan of an Early Neolithic house at Tiszajenő, Hungary, with probable remains of an upright loom facing the doorway; ca. 5000 B.C. (After Selmeczi 1969, 18) 94

3.17 Neolithic weights for looms and for a fishnet, from the Tisza valley in Hungary. (Damjanich János Museum, Szolnok) 95

3.18 Neolithic loom weights among other artifacts on a house floor at Utoquai-Färberstrasse, Zurich, Switzerland. (Photo courtesy of Swiss National Museum, Zurich) 96

3.19 Dumbbell-shaped loom weight from Slatina, Bulgaria; Early Neolithic. (After Petkov 1965, fig. 2∂) 98

3.20 Cylindrical loom weight from Gródek Nadbużny, Poland; Late Neolithic. (After Kowalczyk 1956, pl. 2.18) 100

3.21 Crescentic weight from Lagozza, in northern Italy; Late Neolithic. (After Barfield 1971, fig. 23) 100

3.22 Conical and donut-shaped loom weights from Hradčany, Czechoslovakia; Bronze Age, Unětice Culture. (After Červinka 1946, 141 nos. 1, 6, 9) 101

3.23 Small, disc-shaped clay loom weights from a Minoan village at Myrtos, southern Crete. Early Bronze Age; mid- to late 3rd millennium B.C.

(Warren 1972, 243 fig. 96)   104

3.24 Small vase (aryballos) from Corinth, Greece, showing weavers wearing platform clogs, and probably depicting the weaving contest between Arachne and Athena. (Weinberg and Weinberg 1956, fig. 1)   106

3.25 Classical Greek relief from Thessaly, showing Penelope weaving with a raised bobbin, while her nurse washes the disguised Odysseus's feet. (After Robert 1900, pl. 14)   108

3.26 Greek vase found at Chiusi, Italy, depicting Penelope in front of her warp-weighted loom, which is shown with a roller beam, and with tapestry images on the cloth. (Furtwängler 1932, pl. 142; by permission fee)   108

3.27 Comparative diagrams of the versions of the warp-weighted loom as used in Scandinavia in this century (Hoffmann [1964] 1974, fig. 2) and as used in Classical Greece (inked by M. Stone)   111

3.28 Side view of a warp-weighted loom, on an early 5th-century Greek vase found at Pisticci, Italy, showing deflection of the warp by both shed and heddle bars. (Quagliati 1904, 199 fig. 4)   111

3.29 Weavers and spinners working in the basement(?) of a townhouse of the 18th Dynasty nobleman Thutnofer, at Thebes (earliest known Egyptian representation of vertical two-beam looms). From a wall painting in Thutnofer's tomb (No. 104) at Thebes, reign of Amenhotep II or Thutmose IV; late 15th century B.C. (Davies 1929, fig. 1; courtesy of the Metropolitan Museum of Art)   114

3.30 Weaving workshop showing four vertical two-beam looms, two warping frames, and a doorman chasing away children. Tomb of Neferronpet (No. 133) at Thebes; reign of Rameses II, 13th century B.C. (Davies 1948, pl. 35; courtesy of Committee of the Egypt Exploration Society)   114

3.31 Diagram showing construction of a tubular warp, as found on a few textiles from Denmark in the Bronze Age, late 2nd millennium B.C. (Munksgaard 1974a, fig. 13; courtesy of National Museum, Copenhagen)   116

3.32 Scene from an Etruscan pendant of bronze, showing two women producing a warp; ca. 600 B.C. (After Govi 1971, pl. 53–54)   116

3.33 Diagram of tablet-weaving or card-weaving, with four-holed cards   118

3.34 Tablet-woven girdle of Rameses III; ca. 1200 B.C. (Courtesy of Liverpool Museum, Merseyside County Museums)   120

3.35 Bronze pin cast from a mold decorated with impressions of what appear to be card-woven textiles. From Nalchik, in the northern Caucasus; early 3rd millennium. (Degen 1941, pl. 16.1)   121

3.36 Bronze Age hairnet done in sprang (twisted thread) technique, from Borum Eshøj, Denmark. Late 2nd millennium B.C. (Photo courtesy of National Museum, Copenhagen)   123

4.1 Diagrams of the simplest weaves: plain weave, basket weave, and triple basket weave   127

4.2 Earliest direct proof of weaving yet known: impressions of textiles (in plain weave and basket weave) from Jarmo in northeastern Iraq, ca. 7000 B.C. (Adovasio 1983, figs. 169.9–10; photos courtesy of the Oriental Institute of the University of Chicago)   127

4.3 Narrow tapes in warp-faced weave, from Çatal Hüyük, in south central Turkey. Early Neolithic, ca. 6000 B.C. (Photo courtesy of J. Mellaart)   128

4.4 Varieties of plain-weave created by different densities of warp and weft: balanced plain weave, warp-faced plain weave (warp covers weft), and weft-faced plain weave (weft covers warp)   128

4.5 Diagrams of twining techniques used at Çatal Hüyük; ca. 6000 B.C. (Burnham 1965, figs. 1–2)   128

4.6 Enlargement of weft-twined fabric from Çatal Hüyük; ca. 6000 B.C. (Photo courtesy of J. Mellaart)   129

4.7 Diagram of the structure of the edge—possibly the heading band—of a textile from Çatal Hüyük; ca. 6000 B.C. (Burnham 1965, fig. 3)   129

4.8 Weft-twined linen cloth from Naḥal Ḥemar, in Israel. Early Neolithic, ca. 6500 B.C. (Israel Museum; photo

courtesy of the Israel Department of
Antiquities and Museums)   131

4.9 Remains of texture-striped cloth
preserved on a copper axe-head. Susa;
4th millennium. (Lacaisne 1912, pl. 43)   133

4.10 Late Neolithic linen cloth No. 11,
from Robenhausen, Switzerland; ca.
3000 B.C. (Photo courtesy of the Swiss
National Museum)   134

4.11 Diagram of the construction of a
typical heading band and warp, for the
warp-weighted loom   135

4.12 Diagram of the construction of the
selvedge and heading band of linen
cloth No. 1, from Robenhausen,
Switzerland; ca. 3000 B.C. (E. Vogt
1937, fig. 82)   135

4.13 Diagram of the elaborate closing
border of linen cloth No. 5, from
Schaffis, Switzerland; ca. 3000 B.C.
(E. Vogt 1937, fig. 92)   136

4.14 Diagram of striped cloth and
elaborate closing border: linen cloth
No. 9, from Lüscherz, Switzerland; ca.
3000 B.C. (E. Vogt 1937, fig. 104)   136

4.15 Late Neolithic linen cloth No. 10,
from Robenhausen, Switzerland; ca.
3000 B.C. (Photo courtesy of Swiss
National Museum)   137

4.16 Photograph and constructional
diagram of the heading band and
supplementary weft stripes on linen
cloth No. 3, from Robenhausen,
Switzerland; ca. 3000 B.C. (E. Vogt
1937, fig. 86; photo courtesy of Swiss
National Museum)   138

4.17 Remains of Late Neolithic linen cloth
heavily decorated in a sort of "brocade"
done with supplementary weft, from
Irgenhausen, Switzerland; ca. 3000
B.C. (Photo courtesy of Swiss National
Museum)   138

4.18 Irgenhausen "brocade" reconstructed
in a modern reweaving. (Photo
courtesy of Swiss National Museum)   139

4.19 Diagram of some of the
supplementary weft techniques found
on the Irgenhausen "brocade." (E. Vogt
1937, fig. 138)   140

4.20 Neolithic linen fragment composed of
two woven sections joined with knotted
netting; the lower piece is ornamented
with beads and woven stripes. From
Murten, Switzerland; ca. 3000 B.C.
(Photo courtesy of Swiss National
Museum)   140

4.21 Drawings, made at the time of
discovery, of now-lost patterned
fragments of cloth from Spitzes Hoch,
in north-central Germany. Late
Neolithic. (Schlabow 1959, 112 fig. 3)   143

5.1 Earliest known piece of linen cloth
from Egypt; Faiyum, 5th millennium
B.C. (Courtesy of Petrie Museum,
University College London: UC 2943)   146

5.2 Pleated and fringed Egyptian shirt of
fine spliced linen, from the 1st
Dynasty. Tarkhan; ca. 3000 B.C.
(Courtesy of Petrie Museum,
University College London, UC
28614B')   147

5.3 White linen sheet patterned with weft-
looping, from the 11th Dynasty. Deir
el-Bahari; ca. 2000 B.C. (Egyptian
Museum, Cairo. Photography by the
Egyptian Expedition, the Metropolitan
Museum of Art)   150

5.4 Diagram of a tiny patch of gauze
weave, found as a "weaver's mark"
among linens from the Middle
Kingdom burial of Wah. (The
Metropolitan Museum of Art, no.
20.3.249)   151

5.5 Diagram of three closely related types
of Egyptian "inlaid" fringe, done with
supplementary weft   152

5.6 Diagram of extra weft laid into the
shed, then turned to become warp   152

5.7 Weaver's mark inlaid with stained
thread, on a linen sheet from the
Middle Kingdom mummy of Wah.
(Photo courtesy of the Metropolitan
Museum of Art; Rogers Fund, 1920:
no. 40.3.51)   153

5.8 Tunic decorated with blue and brown
woven stripes and inlaid hieroglyphs.
Tomb of Tutankhamon; mid-14th
century B.C. (Courtesy of Egyptian
Museum, Cairo)   154

5.9 Detail of warp-faced band sewn onto a
linen horsecloth, from a horse mummy
in the 18th Dynasty tomb of Senmut at
Thebes. Early 15th century B.C.
(Egyptian Museum, Cairo.

Photography by the Egyptian Expedition, the Metropolitan Museum of Art) 157

5.10 Linen tunic belonging to Tutankhamon, embroidered with his name, and decorated with warp-faced bands and embroidered hem-panels. Mid-14th century B.C. (Egyptian Museum, Cairo; Crowfoot and Davies 1941, pl. 14; courtesy of Committee of the Egypt Exploration Society) 160

5.11 Detail and schematic drawing of embroidered hem-panels from Tutankhamon's tunic. (Crowfoot and Davies 1941, pl. 20.3–8; courtesy of Committee of the Egypt Exploration Society) 161

6.1 Fragments of a 2/2 twill cloth from burial L4.e.x14 at Alishar, Turkey; late 4th millennium. (Photo courtesy of the Oriental Institute of the University of Chicago) 167

6.2 Black-and-yellow plaid cloth from a kurgan at Tsarskaja (Novosvobodnaja), just north of the Caucasus; 3rd millennium. (Veselovskij 1898, 37 fig. 56) 169

6.3 Impression of a patterned rug beside the burial pit in Kurgan 9 at Tri Brata near Elista, west of the Lower Volga; 3rd millennium. (Sinitsyn 1948, 152 fig. 16) 170

6.4 End of a 6-foot-long linen cloth, showing a woven pattern, from Lago di Ledro, northern Italy. Early Bronze Age; 3rd millennium. (Perini 1967–69, 226–27 figs. 2–3; courtesy of Museo Tridentino di Scienze Naturali) 175

6.5 Diagram of a "weaving wedge" 177

6.6 Diagram of the passage of weft, in a blanket from Trindhøj, Denmark, showing by the crossings that three weft bobbins were being used by three weavers working simultaneously. Late 2nd millennium B.C. (Broholm and Hald 1935, 242 fig. 31; courtesy of National Museum, Copenhagen) 178

6.7 Woolen belt from Borum Eshøj, Denmark, with the end fringed in the manner of a string skirt; late 2nd millennium B.C. (Photo courtesy of National Museum, Copenhagen) 179

6.8 Manner of producing the apparent zigzag in the Borum Eshøj belt, by alternating groups of S- and Z-spun threads ("shadow striping") 180

6.9 String skirt from Egtved, Denmark, of wool woven at the waistband and knotted at the bottom; late 2nd millennium B.C. (Photo courtesy of National Museum, Copenhagen) 181

6.10 Diagrams of a tubular side-selvedge and a plaited heading band, as found on Danish Bronze Age fabrics; late 2nd millennium B.C. (Broholm and Hald 1935, fig. 37.2–3; courtesy of National Museum, Copenhagen) 182

6.11 Diagram of netted "embroidery" built out from the edge of a woman's woolen blouse from Skrydstrup, Denmark; late 2nd millennium B.C. (Broholm and Hald 1939, fig. 39; courtesy of National Museum, Copenhagen) 183

7.1 Some basic types of twill weave: 2/2 diagonal twill, herringbone twill, pointed twill, and diamond twill 187

7.2 Woolen twills from the salt mines at Hallstatt, Austria; early 1st millennium B.C. (Photo courtesy of Naturhistorisches Museum, Vienna) 188

7.3 Reconstruction of designs on the bottom of a woman's garment, done in silk on wool; from Hallstatt tomb No. VI at Hohmichele, in southwest Germany; 6th century B.C. (Hundt 1969, color plate) 189

7.4 Scrap of polychrome woolen cloth with stripes and float-weave designs, used to seat a Late Bronze Age axe blade, found in the salt-works at Hallein, Austria; ca. 1000 B.C. (After Klose 1926, 347 fig. 1) 191

7.5 Twill pattern of the woolen mantle from Gerumsberg, Sweden, including a row of offset lozenges ("goose-eye twill"). Late 2nd millennium B.C.? (Post et al. 1925, 28 fig. 6; courtesy of the Royal Academy of Letters, History, and Antiquities, Stockholm) 193

7.6 Remains of a black horsehair sash, done in twill with elaborate fringes, from a bog at Armoy, County Antrim, northern Ireland. Late Bronze Age;

early 1st millennium B.C. (Coffey 1907, pl. 12) 196

7.7 Lozenge, warp-stripe, and meander patterns among numerous textile scraps from Gordion, Turkey, a Phrygian city destroyed about 690 B.C. (Ellis 1981, pl. 101 C–D; courtesy of the University Museum, University of Pennsylvania) 198

7.8 Analysis of the lozenge pattern shown in Fig. 7.7: repeated error in the complementary-warp design, suggesting that pattern heddles were being used; probable completion of the pattern. (Ellis 1981, fig. 147; courtesy of the University Museum, University of Pennsylvania) 199

7.9 Knotted pile rug from the frozen Kurgan 5 at Pazyryk, in the Altai Mountains; mid-1st millennium B.C. (Rudenko 1953, pl. CXV [1970, pl. 174]) 201

7.10 Diagram of the principal knots used in pile carpets: the symmetrical, Turkish, or Ghiördes knot; and the asymmetrical, Persian, or Sehna knot 202

7.11 Reconstruction of part of a resist-painted cloth, used as a sarcophagus cover, from Kurgan 6 of the Seven Brothers, Taman', east of Kertch. Early 4th century B.C. (Gertsiger [1972] 1975, pl. 24) 207

7.12 Woolen fragments from the body in Kurgan 6, Seven Brothers, Taman': tapestry-woven ducks and stag heads on cherry-red woolen ground; and geometric designs. (Stephani 1878–79, pl. 5) 208

7.13 Embroidered fragments from the Pavlovskij kurgan, south of Kertch, depicting a horse, rider, and waves. Early 4th century B.C. (Stephani 1878–79, pl. 3; inset by M. Stone) 209

8.1 Part of a design from the shoulder of a funerary urn of the Hallstatt era, from Rabensburg in Lower Austria, showing a woman, a square frame (thought to be a two-beam loom) with a checkered cloth, and perhaps a warping stand. (After Rosenfeld 1958, fig. 58; and Franz 1927, 97 fig. 1) 213

9.1 Felt *shabrak* decorated with felt cutouts. From Kurgan 5, Pazyryk. Mid-1st millennium B.C. (Rudenko 1953, pl.

CI [1970, pl. 160]) 219

10.1 Dye-works installation of four large stone vats at Tell Beit Mirsim, in Israel; ca. 700 B.C. (After Albright 1941–43, pl. 11b) 241

10.2 Dye vat from Tell Beit Mirsim, ca. 700 B.C., with a flat top, a channel, and a small hole near the edge for salvaging excess dye. (After Albright 1941–43, pl. 52–53; composite drawing by D. Keast and M. Stone) 242

11.1 Map of the major prehistoric textile zones, seen by plotting loom type against fiber type 250

11.2 Map showing the distribution of direct evidence for types of looms, prior to ca. 2000 B.C., and the location of the two earliest sites yet known with true weaving 252

11.3 Bronze figurines of girls wearing string skirts; from Grevensvænge, Denmark, and Itzehoe, Schleswig. Late Bronze Age; early 1st millennium B.C. (Photos courtesy of National Museum, Copenhagen) 256

11.4 Neolithic clay statuette of a woman wearing a string skirt; from Šipintsi, in the Ukraine. (Naturhistorisches Museum, Vienna) 256

11.5 Palaeolithic "Venus" figure wearing a string skirt; from Gagarino, on the upper Don. (After Tarasov 1965, fig. 14) 257

11.6 Girl from eastern Serbia dancing, wearing heavily fringed woolen front- and back-aprons, the woven part being decorated with "hooked lozenges." (After Belgrade State Folk Ensemble) 258

12.1 *Talasiourgein*: preparing the wool and spinning it. Etruscan bronze pendant; Bologna, ca. 600 B.C. (Govi 1971, pl. 52) 265

12.2 *Histourgein*: making the cloth by warping and weaving. Etruscan bronze pendant (reverse of Fig. 12.1). (Govi 1971, pl. 54) 269

12.3 Diagram of ancient Greek type of warp-weighted loom, with parts labeled in Greek 270

12.4 *Exastis*: ribbed heading band visible on cloth over the left arm of figures on the Parthenon frieze. 5th century B.C. (Courtesy of Trustees of the British Museum) 272

12.5 *Termioeis*: "thrummed" or warp-fringed. Mycenaean soldier wearing a fringed tunic; Warrior Vase, from Mycenae, ca. 1200 B.C. (National Museum, Athens) 274

13.1 Scenes from Middle Kingdom tomb of Khety at Beni Hasan (No. 17): men laundering, spinning cord, and weaving mats; women preparing flax; a young boy and two women spinning thread; women weaving. (Newberry 1894, pl. 13) 286

13.2 Clay statuettes from Cîrna, Romania. Bronze Age; 2nd millennium B.C. (After Dumitrescu 1961, pl. 152–53) 294

13.3 Design on vase from Sopron (Ödenburg), Hungary, showing women spinning and weaving while being entertained. Hallstatt culture; early 1st millennium B.C. (Courtesy of Naturhistorisches Museum, Vienna) 295

13.4 Modern Ukranian costume. (Ethnographic Museum, Leningrad) 296

13.5 Female statuette of clay, from Kličevac in northeastern Jugoslavia. Bronze Age. (M. Hoernes 1898, pl. 4) 296

14.1 Typical clay loom weights from Megiddo in the Middle Bronze II period; early 2nd millennium B.C. (After Loud 1948, pl. 169 nos. 2, 5, 11, 13) 300

14.2 Typical clay loom weights from Early Bronze Age Anatolia: from Alishar (after von der Osten 1937, vol. 1 fig. 99 no. e2103c–d) and from Mersin (after Garstang 1953, 173 fig. 112) 300

14.3 Map of the distribution of similar loom weights in Early Bronze Age Anatolia and Middle Bronze Age Palestine 301

14.4 Clay spindle whorls from Neolithic levels I–II at Anau, in Turkestan. (After Pumpelly 1908, 163 figs. 341, 346, 348, 342, 349, 350) 303

14.5 Clay spindle whorls from level III at Anau, in Turkestan. (After Pumpelly 1908, 165 figs. 370–71, 375, 374, 379, 377) 304

14.6 Map of hollow and "sand-dollar" whorls, in the Neolithic and Bronze Ages, showing direction of influx where ascertainable 306

14.7 Late Neolithic spindle whorls from Gródek Nadbużny and Ćmielów in southeast Poland, and from Rajki and Gorodsk in the Ukraine. (After Poklewski 1958, pl. 15.9; Kowalczyk 1956, pl. 2.6, 2.4; Podkowińska 1950, pl. 35.7, 35.11; Passek 1949, figs. 86.2, 86.9, and 84.11) 307

14.8 Bronze Age whorls dug up at Troy by Schliemann. (After Schliemann [1875] 1968, pl. 33, 40, 31) 307

14.9 Early Bronze Age whorls dug up at Troy I–III by Blegen. (After C. Blegen 1963, figs. 9, 16, 21) 308

14.10 Late Bronze Age whorls from Switzerland. (Photo courtesy of Swiss National Museum) 309

15.1 Clay figurine of a woman, from Petsofá, Crete; early 2nd millennium B.C. (Middle Minoan II). (Myres 1902–3, pl. 8) 314

15.2 Rapport pattern composed of either four-pointed stars inside circles, or four-petaled flowers 317

15.3 Simple "yo-yo" pattern with oval fillers, and a rapport pattern therefrom 317

15.4 Relief fresco depicting a seated woman; island of Pseira, north of Crete; mid-2nd millennium B.C. (Late Minoan I). (Seager 1910, pl. 5; courtesy of the University Museum, University of Pennsylvania) 318

15.5 Acrobat with kilt, engraved on a sword pommel, from the Old Palace at Mallia, Crete; mid-2nd millennium B.C. (Middle Minoan III). (Iraklion Museum, no. 636; drawing by M. Stone) 320

15.6 Faience plaques of dresses and belts, decorated with crocuses and a yo-yo pattern, from the Temple Repository, Knossos, Crete; mid-2nd millennium B.C. (Evans 1921, 506 fig. 364; by permission of Mark Paterson on behalf of the Sir Arthur Evans Trust) 320

15.7 Miniature ornaments, including sphinxes, griffins, and bulls' heads, apparently adorning women's clothing. Fresco from Knossos; mid-2nd millennium B.C. (Late Minoan I). (Evans 1930, 41 fig. 25; by permission of Mark Paterson on behalf of the Sir Arthur Evans Trust) 321

15.8 Person holding a fishnet(?) and wearing a skirt decorated with birds and rocks. Phylakopí, island of Melos; mid-2nd millennium B.C. (Based on Atkinson et al. 1904, fig. 61)   322

15.9 Fresco of a cupbearer wearing a pointed kilt with a pattern of interlocking quatrefoils; tassel and other cloth patterns (in boxes) drawn from similar kilts in the Procession Fresco. Knossos; mid-2nd millennium B.C. (Composite drawing by M. Stone around photo; courtesy of Iraklion Museum)   323

15.10 Fresco fragment of a woman's skirt, from Mycenae, Greece; mid- to late 2nd millennium B.C. (Late Helladic III). (Rodenwaldt 1919, pl. 9)   324

15.11 Fresco of ladies wearing chemises and driving a chariot. Tiryns, Greece; late 2nd millennium B.C. (Late Helladic IIIB). (Rodenwaldt 1912, 98 fig. 40)   324

15.12 Simplest form of the four-color barred band, a common Mycenaean edge pattern   325

15.13 Lappish woman making a warp and its heading band for her warp-weighted loom, in 1955. (Hoffmann [1964] 1974, 66 fig. 26)   326

15.14 Representations of Minoan "sacred knots": fresco of a girl ("La Parisienne") wearing a knot, from the palace at Knossos (after Evans, Cameron, and Hood 1967, back cover; courtesy of Gregg International Publishers); ivory carving, from the Southeast House, Knossos (courtesy of Iraklion Museum); faience pieces from Shaft Grave IV, Mycenae (courtesy of National Museum, Athens); fresco fragment from Mycenae (after Rodenwaldt 1921, fig. 26); and fresco fragments from Nirou Khani, Crete (after Xanthoudides 1922, 11 fig. 9) (Drawings by M. Stone)   327

15.15 Fresco of the "priestess" from the West House at Akrotiri, showing reversal of pattern on sleeves and earring. Thera; mid-2nd millennium B.C. (Courtesy of National Museum, Athens)   329

15.16 Minoan ambassadors to the Egyptian court at Thebes, from the tomb of Senmut (Thebes No. 71); early 15th century B.C. (Davies 1926, fig. 2; courtesy of the Metropolitan Museum of Art)   332

15.17 Loincloth on the 12th porter, tomb of Useramon (Thebes No. 131); early 15th century B.C. (After Vercoutter 1956, pl. 16.137)   333

15.18 Kilts of two Aegean ambassadors to the Egyptian court at Thebes (with traces of original codpieces). Tomb of Rekhmire (Thebes No. 100); early 15th century B.C. (Vercoutter 1956, pl. 21.162 and 19.156)   334

15.19 First five Aegean ambassadors to the Theban court, from the tomb of Menkheperraseneb (Thebes No. 86); mid-15th century B.C. (Davies and Davies 1933, pl. 5; courtesy of the Committee of the Egypt Exploration Society)   335

15.20 Kilt worn by male in martial dress, from a Hittite relief on the King's Gate at Boğazköy, in central Turkey; 3rd quarter of the 2nd millennium B.C. (Museum of Anatolian Civilizations, Ankara)   337

15.21 Ceiling pattern from the tomb of Hapuseneb (Thebes No. 67), composed of spirals ending in a vertical "bud"; early 15th century B.C. (After Jéquier 1911, pl. 28.43; and Kantor 1947, pl. 11B)   343

15.22 Fragments of fresco depicting wind-shelters (ikria) covered with patterned cloth, for the deck of a boat. Mycenae; mid- to late 2nd millennium B.C. (Late Helladic III). (Shaw 1980, fig. 4; courtesy of American Journal of Archaeology)   344

15.23 Painted ceiling in the 12th Dynasty tomb of Hepzefa, at Assiut, showing "wrought-iron fence" motif; early 2nd millennium B.C. (Photo of an early drawing by Baroness von Bissing; courtesy of Hans-Wolfgang Müller)   346

15.24 Ceiling fresco from the robing-room of the palace of Amenhotep III at Malkata, Thebes, showing a spiral rapport and bulls' heads; early 14th century B.C. (Photograph courtesy of the Metropolitan Museum of Art; Rogers Fund, 1911: no. 11.215.451)   349

15.25 Fragments of faience tiles of
foreigners, from a 20th Dynasty
Egyptian palace at Tell el-Yahudiyeh;
12th century B.C. (After Wallis 1900,
pl. 5–6) 353
15.26 Fragments of faience tile depicting a
red-skinned captive wearing a friezed
kilt; from the palace of Rameses II at
Kantir; 13th century B.C. (Hayes 1937,
pl. 8; courtesy of the Metropolitan
Museum of Art) 356
16.1 Folded peplos of Athena, on the
Parthenon frieze; mid-5th century B.C.
(Photo courtesy of Trustees of the
British Museum) 361
16.2 Demeter wearing a cloak with friezes
of dolphins, chariots, and winged
runners. Cup by Makron, ca. 490 B.C.
(Photo courtesy of Trustees of the
British Museum; no. E-140) 363
16.3 Detail of the François vase, showing
goddesses attending a wedding,
including a dress friezed with scenes.
(Furtwängler 1904, pl. 1–2; by
permission fee) 364
16.4 François vase, by Athenians Kleitias
and Ergotimos; ca. 570 B.C.
(Archaeological Museum, Florence; no.
4209. Courtesy of Gabinetto
Fotografico Soprintendenza
Archeologica della Toscana) 365
16.5 East Greek vase of "wild goat" style,
from Rhodes, ca. 630–620 B.C. (Photo
courtesy of Museum of Fine Arts,
Boston; no. 03.90; gift of Mrs. S. T.
Morse) 366
16.6 Late Geometric Attic funerary vase,
showing mourning scene, animals, and
chariots and warriors. (Walters Art
Gallery, Baltimore; no. 48.2231) 367
16.7 Attic Geometric funeral crater, with
friezes of mourning and chariot-riding.
(The Metropolitan Museum of Art;
Rogers Fund, 1914: no. 14.130.14) 368
16.8 "Warrior Vase" from Mycenae, ca.
1200 B.C. (National Museum, Athens) 369
16.9 Painted grave stele from Mycenae,

ca. 1200 B.C., showing friezes of
animals, soldiers, and a throne scene.
(National Museum, Athens) 369
16.10 "Chariot crater" found in Cyprus,
but made in Greece; late 13th century
B.C. (Late Cypriot III). (Courtesy of
Trustees of the British Museum; no.
1925.11-1.3) 369
16.11 Pithos from Tomb II at Fortetsa,
near Knossos, painted in red and blue
on white; early 1st millennium B.C.
(Brock 1957, pl. 119 no. 1021) 371
16.12 Tampan (ceremonial cloth) from
Indonesia, South Sumatra: a so-called
ship cloth, woven in supplementary-
weft technique; late 19th to early 20th
century A.D. (Courtesy of the Los
Angeles County Museum of Art;
Costume Council Fund) 374
16.13 Prothesis scene from an Attic
Geometric funeral pitcher. (Photo
courtesy of Trustees of the British
Museum; no. 1912.5-22.1) 375
16.14 Lip of a Clazomenian sarcophagus,
from the east coast of the Aegean; ca.
500 B.C. (Photo courtesy of Kestner
Museum, Hanover; no. 1897.12) 378
16.15 Detail of a frieze from the resist-
painted pall found in Kurgan 6 of the
Seven Brothers, near Kertch in the
Crimea; early 4th century B.C.
(Gertsiger 1973, fig. 3) 379

TABLES

1.1 Sheep's Typical Age at Death/
Slaughter, According to Use of Sheep 27
12.1 Greek Double Vocabulary, Divided
by Type of Etymology 278
12.2 Further Division of the Greek
Double Vocabulary for Textiles, by
Etymology 279
12.3 Non-Double Greek Textile Terms,
Divided by Etymology 280
12.4 Greek Weaving Terms, Divided by
Etymology 280
15.1 Egyptian Tombs with Spiral Decor 339

When I began this research project some thirteen years ago, I intended to study only the Aegean. In particular, I intended to explore the possibility that, despite the paucity of material remains, textiles formed an industry of great cultural and economic importance in the Aegean throughout most of the Bronze and early Iron Ages. And when I began to study the Aegean textile industry, I thought I would be able to search out what little was determinable about it, discover whatever patterns were in it, and write up the subject, all in a short space of time.

As I worked, however, three things became abundantly clear: (1) that the Aegean, while clearly not the best, was in fact one of the worst possible places in the Old World for the survival of textiles; (2) that the list of ways I could think of for obtaining indirect evidence for textiles was long and getting longer the more I put my mind to it; and (3) that the Aegean evidence, and indeed the evidence from every other small area or time-span, was impossible to assess adequately by itself. In every case, the context of the large time-frame and the entire cultural world to which it belonged was needed for a sound interpretation. Yet virtually no one who had dealt with early textiles—and such people were very few—had looked beyond his or her little bailiwick. With reluctance in the face of the immensity of the project, coupled with eagerness and delight as the pieces of the puzzle began falling into place, I had to expand my research back to the very invention of both weaving and the related crafts, 7000 B.C. and earlier, and to an area stretching roughly from Iran to Britain, with an occasional glance at India and across Asia even to China.

The result was rather like the problem of viewing a *pointilliste* painting: each dot or little patch of data scrutinized closely by itself makes no sense, but when one takes an overview of a great many of these dots, the larger picture becomes remarkably clear. Hence I learned far more about ancient Aegean textiles by going outside the area and period than by staying within it.

The immense span of time and space covered has caused innumerable problems of both research and presentation. As I dug deeper and deeper, I found that a good deal of error has been generated and perpetuated in the general literature. But as I learned, the hard way, to trust no one this side of the original sources (and even they are not always trustworthy!), the task of documentation became fearsome, extending by now into some 25 languages, with more waiting to be tackled.

In some sense I do not even trust myself, for the more I learn, the more I come to re-understand material already dealt with, in a never-ending spiral. But a book must be finite. For this reason I adopted a thorough, if at times burdensome, documentation of sources throughout, making it my guideline that the source of each detail should be quickly and readily recoverable by anyone wishing to pursue it. And there are a thousand things left to pursue. Where I have quoted directly, I have used the original language for accuracy, while providing a translation on the spot for the general reader. I have purposely chosen to use the year-date as part of each reference, and to put it right into the text, because in archaeology one necessarily assesses an excavation report from 1875 very differently than one from 1975 or even 1925. For those not interested in this level of detail, it is not difficult to learn to let the eye skip past everything in parentheses—much easier than for the interested to keep looking down to the bottom of the page or to the end of the book. There is no perfect solution, but I have worked hard to construct one with a minimum of evils for my purposes.

There have been other problems in finding viable limits to set for this book. Not least has been the definition of what I would consider a textile—or rather, a cloth. I have chosen, as I say in the Introduction, to concentrate on those techniques which produced large, floppy coverings of the sort typically used for clothing, regardless of technique. Hence I have included felt—which can be made from loose as well as woven fibers—but I have excluded basketry and mats. Others might have made a different choice, but there is a certain unity to this one.

Another problem has been setting the lower limits of time. As I explain at the beginning of Chapter 6, I cover a much longer period in the west than in the east, partly because of my area of interest but partly because one must switch from primarily archaeological to primarily literary sources much earlier in the east. This book—and here is another limit—draws primarily from archaeological and linguistic (i.e., language structure) sources, not from literary sources. The latter need experts of their own for interpretation; and the literary experts need the "hard" archaeological data on which to build their deductions.

I am an Aegeanist at heart, and the bias will be clear in many of the choices I have made, especially in the second half of the book. But I am also at heart an interdisciplinarian. It is not possible to know everything about everything; and at times I have deliberately chosen, in Part II, to sacrifice depth for breadth, in order to throw important tie-lines from one field to another. Thus the Syrian archaeologist may complain that I missed some sites or some texts, and the Celticist may complain at my Celtic word forms (or lack of them); the economist and the ethnographer may carp at other details. But my challenge to each specialist is to pitch in and strengthen his or her section of the broad framework that I have begun, and not to forget that there is much to be learned from the specialist of another field, who may be holding up the other end of a particular plank. There are many potential thesis topics lying about in these pages, waiting to be dealt with adequately.

The book has been written with various readers in mind, from the archaeologist who needs to know how to interpret the basic finds (but knows nothing about cloth or weaving) to the handweaver who wants to know in detail about the history of the craft (but knows little archaeology). I trust that linguists, classicists, historians, art historians, economists, and enthusiastic students of any of these fields will find the discussions understandable: I have tried, without dwelling on it, to provide in passing the information necessary for a non-expert to follow the main lines of argument, if not every last detail.

But most of all, and for the sake of all these, I hope the framework laid out in this book will induce the excavators who dig up the basic material to take more seriously an industry which, as the data will show, is older than pottery or metallurgy and perhaps even than agriculture and stock-breeding, and which sometimes took more time than all these put together. How can we claim to make balanced assessments of ancient economic systems when we ignore completely such a time-consuming industry, as most books do? (Most don't even have an index entry for textiles.) Because the product is so perishable, cloth does not obtrude itself on our attention the way metal-work, ceramics, and carved stone do. But that is no good reason to ignore the subject.

Nor is the fact that textiles have traditionally been "women's work" a good reason to cast them aside. Unfortunately, this traditional bias in the division of labor and therefore of interest and awareness has cost us dearly. For the most part, people untrained and uninterested in textiles (and in our culture, all sexism aside, this includes most men) have done the excavating, and have ignored or even thrown out the artifacts that relate to cloth; nor did the museum curators of the more distant past do better, when they scrubbed the oxide casts of textiles off their bronzes so as to present a handsome surface to the paying public. And perhaps predictably, it has generally (though not always!) been the few women in the field who have salvaged any remains, analyzed them, and carefully published them. The bias will be clear in the bibliography. But to all those people who have rescued or pulled together *any* information about ancient textiles I am indebted; for it is on the foundation of fact that they have laid that I have built my edifice, and have tried to fill to some extent the millennia-long gap at the beginning of the standard handbooks of textile history.

IN PARTICULAR, I would like to thank the following people for their assistance with this project.

For reading and criticizing sizable sections of the manuscript at one stage or another: Paul Barber, Richard Ellis, Bette Hochberg,

Henry Hoenigswald, Sara Immerwahr, Ann Peters, Jaan Puhvel, Brunilde Ridgway, Tamar Schick, and Virginia Wayland.

For lengthy technical discussions along the way: Rosalind Hall, Hans-Jürgen Hundt, Nobuko Kajitani, Roger Moorey, Elisabeth Munksgaard, Jerry Norman, Sebastian Payne, Pal Raczky, Michael Ryder, Richard Schultes, Andrew Sherratt, Michael Vickers, and Susan Wadlow.

For interpreting and inking my maps and drawings: Mark Stone.

For word-processing help, often far beyond the call of duty: Robert Seal, Barbara Kennard, Julie Eby-McKenzie, Chuck Grieve, Ben Squire, and Missy Sprague.

For other kinds of help and support: Earleen Ahrens, Patty Anawalt, Ernestine Elster, Marija Gimbutas, Dale Gluckman, Joanna Hitchcock, Donna Keast, Frank Kierman, Mabel Lang, Scott Littleton, Edward Maeder, Machteld Mellink, Andrew Sherratt, Harold Wayland, Mary Zirin, and the staff of the American School of Classical Studies in Athens.

The help of many others has been noted in footnotes throughout the text.

I wish to thank the Louis and Hermione Brown Humanities Support Fund for paying for the inking of the maps and drawings, and the J. Paul Getty Trust for subsidizing the publication of this book, making possible its extensive illustrations. I would also like to thank the following foundations for their generous and much-needed support of various phases of this research: the Haynes Foundation (Summer 1975); the Wenner-Gren Foundation (Spring 1984); and most especially the John Simon Guggenheim Memorial Foundation (1979–80), whose major support at a critical point made possible a much broader and deeper approach to this subject.

—August 1987

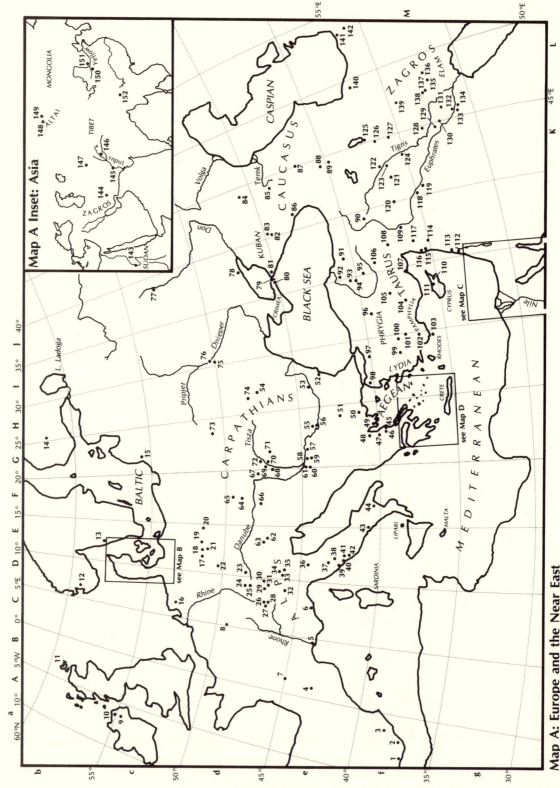

Map A: Europe and the Near East

KEY TO MAP A

SPAIN

1 Cueva de los Murciélagos, Andalucia
2 El Argar
3 Cigarralejo

FRANCE

4 Lespugue
5 Adaouste
6 Grotte des Enfants
7 Lascaux
8 Apremont

BRITAIN

9 Island MacHugh, County Tyrone
10 Armoy, County Antrim
11 Skara Brae, Orkney

SCANDINAVIA/BALTIC (for Denmark, see Map B)

12 Tegle, Norway
13 Gerumsberg, Sweden
14 Korpilahti, Finland
15 Šventoji, Lithuania

NETHERLANDS

16 Roswinkel

GERMANY (for northernmost Germany, see Map B)

17 Kreienkopp bei Ditfurt, Kr. Quedlinburg
18 Spitzes Hoch bei Latdorf, Kr. Bernburg
19 Rietzmeck, Kr. Rosslau
20 Niemitz(sch), Kr. Gubin
21 Unterteutschenthal
22 Schwarza, Thuringia
23 Goldberg bei Nördlingen
24 Hochdorf
25 Hohmichele

SWITZERLAND

26 Lüscherz am Bielersee
26 Schaffis am Bielersee
27 La Tène
28 Murten
29 Zurich
30 Irgenhausen am Pfäffikersee
30 Robenhausen am Pfäffikersee
31 Meilen Rohrenhaab

ITALY

32 Lagozza
33 Borno
34 Naquane, Camonica Valley
35 Lago di Ledro
36 Bologna
37 Chiusi
38 Orvieto
39 Tarquinia
40 Sasso di Furbara
41 Veii
42 Rome
42 Decima, near Rome
43 Pompeii
44 Pisticci

GREECE (for southern Greece and Crete, see Map D)

45 Dimini
46 Sesklo
47 Argissa Magula
48 Nea Nikomedeia
49 Olynthus
50 Sitagroi

BULGARIA

51 Slatina
52 Varna

ROMANIA

53 Căsioarele
54 Cucuteni
55 Salcuţa
56 Cîrna

JUGOSLAVIA

57 Kličevac
58 Vinča
59 Selevac
60 Gomolava
61 Vučedol

AUSTRIA

62 Hallstatt
63 Hallein
64 Rabensburg

CZECHOSLOVAKIA

65 Hradčany, Moravia

HUNGARY

66 Sopron (Ödenburg)
67 Aszód
68 Tiszajenő
69 Szolnok
70 Szolnok-Szanda
71 Dévaványa-Sártó
72 Kisköre

POLAND

73 Gródek Nadbużny

SOVIET UNION

74 Šipintsi (Schipenitz; now Zaval'e), Ukraine
75 Tripolye, Ukraine
76 Kiev, Ukraine
77 Gagarino, Upper Don
78 Mariupol (Marijupil'), Ukraine
79 Kertch (Pantikapaion), Crimea
80 Pavlovskii Kurgans, Crimea
81 Seven Brothers (Sem' Brat'ev), Taman'
82 Maikop, Kuban
83 Tsarskaja (now Novosvobodnaja), Kuban
84 Tri Brata, Lower Volga Basin
85 Nalchik, Kabardino-Balkaria

TRANSCAUCASIA

86 Ochamchira, Georgia
87 Martkopi, Georgia
88 Karmir-Blur, Armenia
89 Ararat, Armenia

ANATOLIA

90 Çayönü Tepesi
91 Horoztepe
92 Merzifon
93 Alaca Höyük
94 Boğazköy
95 Alishar
96 Gordion
97 Dorak
98 Troy
99 Aphrodisias

100 Beycesultan
101 Hacılar
102 Karataş
103 Ulu Burun
104 Çatal Hüyük
105 Acemhöyük
106 Kanesh (Kültepe)
107 Mersin
108 Maraş
109 Deve Hüyük, near Carchemish

CYPRUS

110 Enkomi
111 Vounous

SYRIA

112 Tyre
113 Sidon
114 Hama
115 Latakia
116 Ugarit (Ras Shamra)
116 Minet el Beida
117 Ebla

MESOPOTAMIA

118 Terqa
119 Mari
120 Tell Halaf
121 Karana (Tell al Rimah)
122 Nineveh
123 Hassuna
124 Aššur
125 Hasanlu
126 Shimshara
127 Jarmo
128 Tell Agrab
129 Ras al 'Amiya
130 Kish
131 Lagash
132 Uruk
133 Abu Salabikh
134 Ur

IRAN

135 Susa
136 Choga Mish
137 Tepe Sabz

138 Ali Kosh
139 Tepe Sarab
140 Marlik
141 Belt Cave
142 (Tepe) Hissar

INSET TO MAP A

143 Kerma, Sudan
144 Tepe Yahyā, Iran
145 Mohenjo-Daro, Pakistan
146 Harappa, Pakistan
147 Sapalli-tepa, Uzbekistan
148 Bash-Adar, Altai
149 Pazyryk, Altai
150 Pan-p'o, China
151 Hsi-yin-ts'un, Shansi, China
152 Ka Ruo, Chang-du County, Tibet

KEY TO MAP B

NORTHERN GERMANY

153 Behringen
154 Wiepenkathen, Kr. Hamburg
155 Itzehoe

DENMARK

156 Lille Dragshøj
157 Skrydstrup
158 Trindhøj
159 Egtved
160 Deibjerg
161 Muldbjerg
162 Stubdrup
163 Store Arden
164 Borum Eshøj
165 Voldtofte
166 Haastrup
167 Hagendrup
168 Ølby
169 Grevensvænge

KEY TO MAP C

PALESTINE

170 Akko (Acre)
171 Megiddo (Armageddon)
172 Tell Ta'anach

173 Nir David
174 Beth Shan (Shean)
175 Tell Jerishe
176 Tell Qasileh
177 Gezer
178 Jericho
179 Teleilat Ghassul
180 Haḥal Mishmar
181 Haḥal Ḥemar
182 Tell Beit Mirsim
183 Lachish
184 Tell el-'Ajjul
185 Tell Jemmeh
186 Beer Sheba

EGYPT

187 Kantir
188 Tell el-Yahudiyeh
189 el-Omari
190 Saqqara
191 Lisht
192 Tarkhan
192 Kafr Ammar
193 Meydum
194 el-Lahun, Faiyum
195 Kahun, Faiyum
196 Gurob, Faiyum
197 Beni Hasan
198 el-Bersheh
199 Amarna
200 Meir
201 Mostagedda
202 Assiut
203 Badari
204 Qau
205 Abydos
206 Balabish
207 Deir el-Balas
208–14 Thebes, Egypt
208 Valley of the Kings
209 Deir el-Bahari
210 Theban tombs (nobles)
211 Deir el-Medineh
212 Valley of the Queens
213 Malkata
214 Luxor
215 el-Gebelein

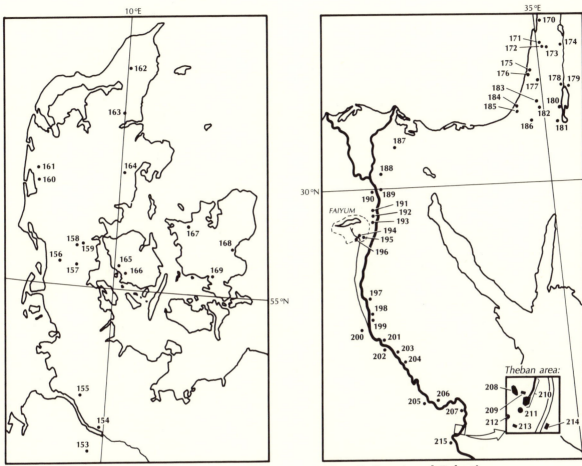

Map B: Denmark

Map C: Egypt and Palestine

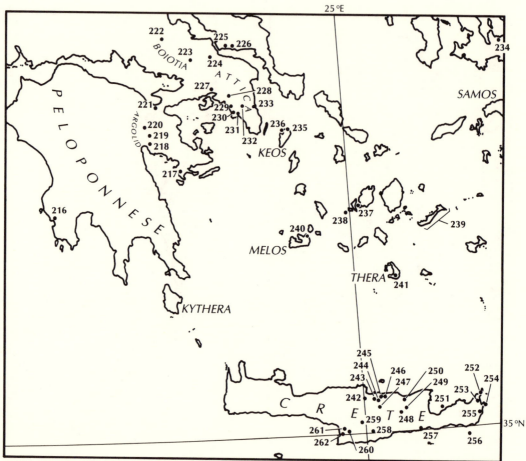

Map D: Southern Greece and Crete

KEY TO MAP D

GREECE

Peloponnese:
216 Pylos
216 Routsi, near Pylos
217 Franchthi Cave

Argolid:
218 Tiryns
219 Dendra
220 Mycenae

Isthmus:
221 Corinth

Boiotia:
222 Orchomenos
223 Thebes, Greece
224 Tanagra

Euboia:
225 Lefkandi

226 Eretria

Attica:
227 Eleusis
228 Athens
229 Trakhones
230 Voula
231 Vari
232 Koropi
233 Perati

Ionia:
234 Clazomenae

Islands:
235 Kephala, Keos (Kea)
236 Aghia Irini, Keos (Kea)
237 Saliagos
238 Strongylos
239 Amorgos
240 Phylakopi, Melos
241 Akrotiri, Thera

CRETE

242 Tylissos
243 Fortetsa
244 Knossos
245 Zafer Papoura
246 Nirou Khani
247 Arkhanes
248 Dictaean Cave
249 Karphi
250 Mallia
251 Pseira
252 Itanos
253 Palaikastro
254 Petsofa
255 Kato Zakro
256 Kouphonisi (Leuke)
257 Myrtos
258 Drakones
259 Prinias
260 Phaistos
261 Hagia Triada
262 Kommos

Chronology (in Logarithmic Scale) of Main Eras Mentioned, 20,000–400 B.C.

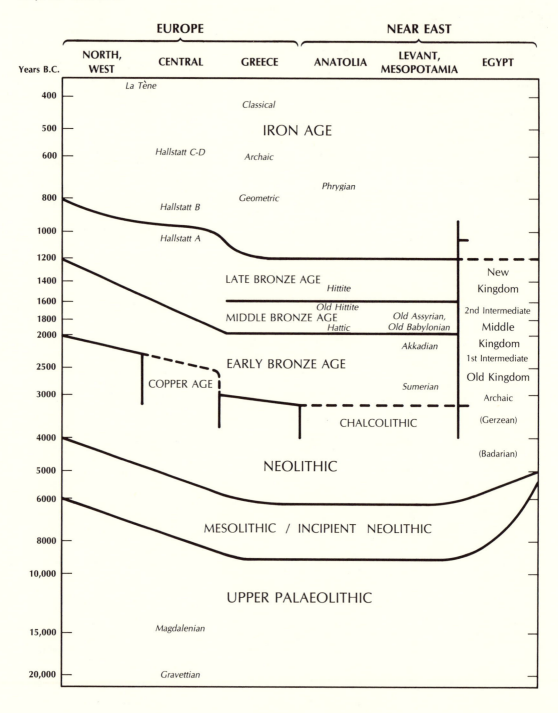

CHRONOLOGY OF LATER CULTURES MENTIONED,
3000–400 B.C.

	Greece		Crete	Anatolia	Mesopotamia
400					
	Classical				
600					
	Archaic				Neo-Babylonian, Neo-Assyrian
800				Phrygian	
	Geometric				
1000				Neo-Hittite	
	Sub-Mycenaean				
1200	—	M	—		
	Late	Y C	Late		
1400	Helladic	E N A E A N	Minoan	Hittite	
1600	—		—		
	Middle		Middle	Old Hittite	
1800	Helladic		Minoan		Old Babylonian, Old Assyrian
2000	—		—	Hattic	
					Neo-Sumerian, Akkadian
2500	Early Helladic		Early Minoan	Early Bronze	
					Sumerian
3000					

PREHISTORIC TEXTILES

The Twelfth day is much better than the Eleventh,
For on that day, you know, the airborne spider spins its web
In full day, when the wise [ant] gathers up a heap:
On that day a woman should set up her loom and get on with her work.

—Hesiod, *Works and Days* 776–79

INTRODUCTION

In a group of mounds known as the Seven Brothers, some Russian noblemen stationed in the Crimea in 1875 were hunting for *schast'e*—the word in Russian means simultaneously "happiness" and "treasure." They found what they sought: gold treasure, marble art works, and an exploit to talk about back in St. Petersburg. But they also discovered something rarer by far than any of those commodities: pieces of ancient figured textiles.

Cloth seldom survives the millennia. Where it does, it has had the advantage of unusual conditions, such as freezing, or anaerobic waterlogging, or, as evidently in this case, desiccation. These particular fragments came from burials associated with the nearby Greek colony of Pantikapaion (modern Kertch), founded in the 6th or 7th century B.C. The largest cloth (Figs. 7.11, 16.15; Stephani 1878–79, 121–22) was found draped like a flag over a wooden sarcophagus: it consisted of at least a dozen friezes, one above the other, of mythological, animal, and geometric figures, with floral borders, in black, red, and buff. The tomb's contents dated its deposition securely to the 4th century B.C.—although the fact that the cloth had been carefully mended in antiquity implies that it was not new when put into the tomb. Other scraps of textile from the Kertch tombs depict birds, stag heads, horses and riders, palmettes, etc., in a variety of colors and techniques, including tapestry and embroidery (see Figs. 7.12–13).

Fragmentary though they were, these finds should still have sufficed to show that the absence of ornate Classical Greek cloth was an archaeological deficit, not a cultural one. Just because Egypt was blessed with a climate that preserved fabrics to a remarkable extent did not mean that other people had not been busy weaving. Unfortunately, the Kertch fragments were published over a century ago in a Russian journal that is hard to find in Western libraries, and very little else of Classical Greek fabric has been unearthed since. And so people still tend to forget about pre-Roman textile industries, other than that of Egypt, and to start histories of textiles with the turn of the era. We still perpetuate the notion that the Classical Greeks had just climbed out of a cave, sartorially speaking.

The complex variety of Kertch fragments warns us, however, that textile technique had already undergone a very long period of development. It had done so, moreover, on looms that historians have often branded as primitive and incapable of refined work: yet 3rd-millennium Trojans used the same loom as 4th-century Greeks. If the latter could produce such elaborate fabrics, why not the former? Indeed, we now know that Troy II was nearer the middle than the beginning of the history of weaving, for we have high-quality cloth from Anatolia and Palestine from the 7th and early 6th millennia B.C., and clay impressions of woven goods back to 7000 B.C., proving the antiquity of weaving to that date and implying a considerably longer history.

The textile industry, in fact, is older than pottery and perhaps even than agriculture and stock-breeding, and it probably consumed far more hours of labor per year, in the temperate climates, than pottery and food production put together. Up until the Industrial Revolution, and into this century in many peasant societies, women spent every available moment spinning, weaving, and sewing, and even had men helping them (in Europe shearing sheep, curing and hackling flax, occasionally also spinning or weaving)—or at least entertaining them while they worked late into the evenings. The women spun while they tended the flocks, fetched water, or walked to market (Fig. 0.1); they wove while they tended the children, the oven, and the cooking pot. Men could rest when the crops were in; but where making the cloth was the woman's chore, as it generally was, woman's work was never done. Indeed, when Homeric Greeks raided, we are told, they killed off the men but brought the women home as captives to help with the spinning and weaving. We may justly surmise from all available data that not only did a woman spend far more hours per year working at the cloth industry than a man did at any one of the men's tasks, but the women also formed considerably more than half the work force in not a few of these societies. It was the Industrial Revolution that finally changed all this, with its power loom, cotton gin, spinning jenny, and great

0.1 Woodblock (17th century) showing Balkan women spinning while doing other things, a common sight until the Industrial Revolution. (Valvasor 1689, 321)

cloth mills. But by now, a few generations later, we have forgotten that this was once the most time-consuming single industry.

Because, as a culture, we no longer know about textiles in detail, we must start from the beginning. We must come to understand in detail what cloth is, how it is constructed, and the resources and processes needed to produce it. Let us begin, then, by defining the domain of our subject.

I have chosen to write this book about those objects which come under the broad category of cloth—large, thin sheets of material made from fiber, which are soft and floppy enough to be used as coverings for people and things. Technically the word *textile*, which comes to us from the Latin *texere* 'to weave,' refers exclusively to woven cloth. But I also wish to include those large and floppy coverings, like felt or tapa cloth, which are used for much the same purposes (and are often hard to distinguish at first glance from woven cloth), but which are constructed from fibers that have been made to cohere by some means other than weaving.

On the other hand, I shall exclude mats and baskets, although they typically display a woven structure. First, these objects are relatively stiff and self-shaped, and hence quite different from cloth in their range of uses. Second, despite the similarities of final structure, the techniques of manufacture are of-ten quite different, as are the materials used for each. In fact, it is the choice of materials that differentiates cloth from matting and basketry at almost every point.

As long as one is interlacing somewhat stiff materials, which will stay put during the process of manufacture, it is unnecessary to use a loom, or even to differentiate "warp" from "weft" since each element can be manipulated independently. Such an interlacing process is known as *plaiting*. The limp yarns used for making cloth, however, cannot be worked without some sort of tension on some of them—a mechanical replacement for stiffness—so that they will stay put while the remainder are being interlaced among them. The tensioned set of threads, which must be set up first, constitute the *warp*, while the threads introduced by interlacing constitute the *weft*. This interlacing process is true *weaving*, in the narrow sense, and the device that provides the tension is the *loom*.[1]

In Part I of this book we shall look in detail at the basic data associated with ancient cloth and its manufacture: the acquisition of the raw fibers, the making of fibers into weavable thread, the looms, the weaves of cloth, the process of felting, and the art of dyeing. On these data, in turn, the interpretive discussions that comprise Part II are and must be based.

---

[1] The waters are muddied, of course, by two considerations: mats are sometimes constructed on a loom, with a soft warp and stiff weft; and small numbers of soft threads alone can be plaited by hand. In this latter case, tension is still quite necessary, but there is no differentiation of warp and weft. In general I will mention these products, where they have survived, without attempting to be comprehensive.

PART I

THE BASIC TEXTILE
CRAFTS—
THE DATA

CHAPTER 1

THE DOMESTICATION
OF FIBERS

Weaving requires suitable materials; without them the craft cannot exist. And so we must start our exploration by asking what textile materials were known to ancient weavers. Given that a particular fiber was available at all, how familiar was it—how available? That is, how long can we ascertain that it was physically present, how long known to and used by the local people, how long even domesticated? We must also know what special properties the various fibers have or had that might have affected their use in textile production, and hence in the development of the industry.

Technically, as we have said, true weaving involves two operationally different sets of elements: a pre-arranged and more or less fixed set, the *warp*; and a second, inserted set, the *weft* (the word is derived from the same root as *weave*). Anyone who tries inserting row after row of weft into a warp will quickly discover that, unless the substance inserted is stiff enough to hold its place, it is much easier and more effective to work with a long weft that continues from one row to the next. It is easier because you don't have to keep reaching for new material, and it is more effective because each time the weft turns from one row to the next it binds the edge (the "self-edge" or *selvedge*), keeping the finished work from slipping out of place. We could say then, depending upon the

point of view, either that the technique of weaving with long or "continuous" elements solves the problem of how to interlace highly flexible materials, or that "true weaving" differs in a practical way from matting and basketry in using very long and very flexible materials and in creating products that tend toward the soft and floppy rather than toward the stiff and self-shaped. Length and flexibility are thus key qualities in the raw materials of textiles.

No filament produced by nature, however, is long, strong, and flexible enough to qualify outright. Reeds, grasses, and strips of bark, although long enough to go a few rows perhaps, are still too stiff: we classify their products, in general, as mats or baskets. The wonderfully flexible wool fibers, hairs, and most individual vegetable fibers, on the other hand, are too short and breakable to be used very practically without somehow being combined; and the longest natural filament known to weavers, silk, is too fragile to be used singly. In practice, then, the art of weaving generally follows that of spinning: the process by which several single and usually short, pliable filaments are twisted into one long, strong thread. Such a thread, in addition to its greater strength, has all the flexibility of the individual fibers of which it is composed, the flexibility that we associate with textiles.

For an initial idea of the fibers used in ancient times, we can look at the oldest known fragments of weaving, which date from the Neolithic period. The first to be dug up were those found in the mid-19th century in the Swiss "lake dwellings," some now dated as far back as 3000 B.C. These fragments proved to be of flax, that is, linen, and excellently made, of fine quality and with varied techniques, including "brocaded" (technically, supplementary weft) patterns and elaborately fringed edges (E. Vogt 1937; see Chapter 4 below). Wondering in a letter of September 2, 1860, whether these cloths were locally made or imported, the excavator, Ferdinand Keller, cited in favor of local production the fact that he had also found on the site quantities of flax both as unworked fibers and as hanks of spun thread; and against it he expressed the astonishment of antiquarians everywhere: "How are we to imagine a loom, which even in its simple form is a rather complicated instrument, among people who don't even know metal?" (Messikommer 1913, 25–26).

But local Neolithic cloths they were, and more Neolithic textiles were to come presently from Egypt. In a 5th-millennium layer of a site in the Faiyum, Caton-Thompson and Gardner found a swatch of coarse linen in a small cooking pot, along with two flints and a fish vertebra. The piece, they reported, "is flax, though not necessarily *Linum usitatissimum*" (Caton-Thompson and Gardner 1934, 46). The find was further supported at the site by the presence of spindle whorls and of flax seeds—this time reportedly *Linum usitatissimum*, or common domestic flax (ibid., 33, 49).

Since it is rather coarse, and lies among the earliest strata in the cultural sequences leading towards the civilization of Dynastic Egypt, the Faiyum linen looks rather like the beginning of the line of development. And perhaps it was, within Egypt. But if Keller was surprised to find looms and weaving among "pre-metallic" people in Europe, archaeologists were even more surprised, almost exactly a century later, to see fine fabrics turning up among virtually pre-ceramic people in Anatolia.

In 1962, digging into Level VI at the Turkish site of Çatal Hüyük,[1] James Mellaart and his staff palaeobotanist Hans Helbaek uncovered the carbonized remains of a variety of textiles (Mellaart 1963a). The date was set by the radiocarbon analysis of other artifacts as falling at the beginning of the 6th millennium B.C. (Mellaart 1967, 52)—better than a millennium earlier than the Faiyum linen, and nearly three millennia before the ornate Swiss cloth. The fiber of these Anatolian fabrics continued to elude positive identification for some time, however, because of the heavy carbonization that, ironically, had preserved the fabrics to begin with.

The course of the argument over identification is highly instructive to us. In the initial report, Mellaart (1963b) assumes that the fibers are wool and cites the presence of sheep bones in the settlement. In his later, retrospective write-up of the site (1967, but penned considerably earlier), Mellaart continues to suggest wool, this time supporting

---

[1] Where variant spellings exist for names of sites, persons, etc., I have in general adopted the spelling used in the chief publication(s) and in the sources that I have cited, so as not to confuse the lay reader any more than necessary, on the assumption that the expert already knows how to sort things out. Where particularly unrecognizable or irreconcilable variants exist, I have tried to provide the alternate forms at first mention. The problem is especially difficult with ancient Egyptian names—for instance, with the nobleman who turns up as Anherkhawi in one prestigious publication and as Khai-inheret in another (see Chapter 15). My purpose in this book is not to engage in arguments over how these names are to be read or spelled, but to help the reader through the literature on textiles as easily as possible.

his argument with palaeobotanical evidence of a sort published earlier by Helbaek (1959; 1960), the expert in ancient flax. Mellaart states (1967, 219), "The possibility that the material was linen, i.e. flax fibre, can be discarded as flax was not grown at Çatal Hüyük, nor anywhere else before *c.* 5000 B.C." Harold Burnham, too, in his special report as a textile expert, leans toward the wool hypothesis, mentioning what appear to be scales—wool is scaly, flax is smooth—in one photomicrograph, and the presence of nitrogen, a chemical signalling animal substances. He carefully remarks, though, that the identification is still open to doubt (Burnham 1965, 170 and pl. 31a). Finally, however, the wool expert M. L. Ryder put a sample of the fibers through a masterfully constructed battery of tests, most of which either favored flax slightly or came out quite inconclusive. Even the nitrogen, since it occurred without sulfur, seemed inconclusive to him, because it could well have infiltrated from the human bones that the textiles had encased. As a final drastic measure, a co-worker "then boiled the material with dilute alkali, a treatment which would have destroyed wool, but which in this instance removed the black colour and revealed the characteristic cross-striations of

flax when viewed under the microscope through crossed polaroids. This almost unrecognizable material is therefore conclusively identified as flax" (Ryder 1965, 176).

So once again the early textiles turned out to be of plant fiber, specifically of some sort of linen—an interesting fact in itself. But the grounds on which flax had earlier been discarded as a candidate, namely that we have no evidence for the plant being *domesticated* there or anywhere else that early, provide an equally interesting moral to the story. For the logic may have gone astray in either of two ways. We may simply not have been lucky enough to find other evidence for the earliest domestication of flax.[2] Or it may be that the flax first used for textiles was not domesticated, but was gathered wild. Archaeologists have discovered elsewhere too that although domestication implies use—some sort of use—lack of domestication does not in itself imply non-use; and so we must look at our few pitiful scraps of evidence for textiles within a much wider, palaeobiological world: the range of habitats of the wild as well as domestic species of fiber-bearing plants and animals, at given points of time in antiquity. Let us now look at each of the fibers in turn.

FLAX

Domestic flax (*Linum usitatissimum*) provides the fiber we know as linen (Fig. 1.1). In recent times it has been the most important bast fiber (woody plant fiber) for textiles, and, as we have seen, it has been extremely important as far back as our direct evidence for textiles goes.

According to Helbaek, who has done the most definitive work on the history of flax, the most likely of the various wild species to be the progenitor of domestic flax is *Linum bienne* (formerly called *Linum angustifolium*) (Helbaek 1959; 1960, 115–18), which, he reports, occurs as a perennial along the Medi-

---

[2] A recent analysis of seeds salvaged by flotation shows a fair number of flax seeds in the early levels of Çayönü Tepesi, a Turkish site east of Çatal Hüyük dated to about 7000 B.C. (R. B. Stewart 1976, 219, 221). Since an abrupt fall-off of all the oil-bearing seeds, including

flax, coincides with a sudden rise in the number of animal bones, the analyst feels he has strong evidence here that the flax seeds had been used for oil (ibid., 223). It is not clear whether the flax was domestic or wild, but it is clear that it was locally available and being used.

1.1 Theban papyrus of the Book of the Dead (18th Dynasty), showing the growing of flax. The flax has been sown close together to force it to grow tall and straight, for better linen fiber. The seed-tops show that it is ready to harvest. (Courtesy of Trustees of the British Museum)

terranean and Atlantic coastal areas, and as a winter annual in the foothills of Iran and Iraq-Kurdistan (Helbaek 1959, 105–7). The earliest definite evidence yet located for the domestication of flax comes from sites in northwestern Iraq dated close to 5000 B.C., in the form of improved seeds (Helbaek 1969, 417–18; 1970, 211), and in eastern Iraq ca. 5500, in the form of clearly imported stock (Helbaek 1969, 397). The improved seeds should remind us that flax might have been domesticated originally for its oil-bearing seeds (linseed oil is still important today, and linseed bread can still be found in Central European bakeries), instead of or as well as for its fibrous stem. Thus, although the presence of the domestic plant implies use, it does not guarantee textile use. On the other hand, neither does it always guarantee use for food. The lack of seed remains for flax in Anatolian sites, which puzzled Helbaek (1970, 211–13), could be explained this way: the Anatolians, who, as we now can demonstrate, used flax for textiles well before 5000 B.C., might have raised or collected their flax chiefly for fiber rather than for seed. The flax stem yields the nicest fiber, incidentally, before the seed develops.

Very recently, another trove of textiles turned up at a pre-pottery Neolithic site, in a small cave at Nahal Ḥemar in the Judaean desert, in Israel. The artifacts, which have been dated to the 7th millennium B.C. both by radiocarbon and by the nature of the as-semblage, include twined, knotted, and needle-made fabrics, although no early pieces in true plain weave (Bar-Yosef 1985; Tamar Schick, pers. comm. 1985; see Chapter 4). Once again we see flax in abundant use long before 5000 B.C.; but whether it was domestic or gathered wild we can't yet say.

In any case, the domestication as well as use of flax must have started in or at the edge of locations where it grew wild. The domesticant must then have spread from such places to lower altitudes and drier locations, where it could thrive if humans watered it (Helbaek 1959, 117; 1969, 397; 1970, 211–13). The presence of *Linum usitatissimum* itself can be charted in northern Iraq (a home area for the wild ancestor) and southwestern Iran before 5000 B.C., and in southern Iraq, Syria, Egypt, Switzerland, and Germany between 5000 and 3000 B.C. (Helbaek 1959, 118–19; J. Renfrew 1973, 120). As it spread into widely different environments, it diversified in form to adapt to local conditions. Thus in Egypt it turns up as a large-seeded, summer-annual type with a single stem (though sown in Egypt in October or November to avoid the scorching heat there), whereas in Switzerland it appears as a small-seeded, multiple-stemmed winter annual (Helbaek 1959, 105). When assessing the domain of flax, however, we must not forget to include the wild varieties, for it was possible to collect these also, wherever they occurred.

The physical and chemical properties of flax fibers have much to do with their use. The fibers originate inside the stem of the plant, where their function is to protect and support the channels that carry nutrients along the length of the plant. These fibers, known as *bast*, occur in bundles of overlapping strands among the sieve (food-carrying) cells. They form a ring around the woody core, and are in turn surrounded by a sort of skin or rind. The "ultimate fibers" of bast, which are long, thin cells that reach a few centimeters in length and are joined end to end in long strands, are held together in these bundles by a matrix of pectinous substances (Kirby 1963, 3, 22–23; Durrant 1976, 190). In order to obtain the bast fibers, then, all of these other parts, with the exception of some of the matrix found within the bundles, must somehow be stripped or eaten away.

The age-old way of doing this—and we have both ancient Egyptian representations and Swiss Neolithic tool complexes proving the antiquity of the method—consists basically of the following steps. First, the flax is pulled up by the roots at the desired stage of growth: the younger the plant is, the finer and paler the fibers will be; the older it is, the coarser and stronger (Geijer [1972] 1979, 6; Hess 1958, 286). In Egypt apparently some growers pulled their flax early, whereas others waited until the seeds were ripe (Fig. 1.1), sacrificing fineness of linen in favor of being able to collect the valuable linseeds (Montet 1925, 192–99). (Pliny the Elder, who describes the entire process in the first century A.D., says people leaned the stalks in a circle with their heads toward the center, so that as the plants dried the seeds fell into a heap in the middle for easy collection [Pliny, *Natural History* 19.3.16].) Next, the plants are dried or "cured" to the right point, then put in a place calculated to rot out most of the plant material that binds the bast fibers in the stem. Called *retting* (an old causative form of the verb *rot*, i.e., "to make rot"), this step can be done slowly with the dew, in fields or on roof-tops (cf. Joshua 2:6), in which case the flax is said to come out rather brittle and silvery grey, like weathered wood (Bellinger 1962, 7); or it can be done quickly by submerging the flax in rivers or ponds, in which case the flax will usually come out supple and golden blond—whence the poetic image of "flaxen hair." Considerable care and experience are needed at this stage, however, to keep from staining the fibers and particularly to avoid either over-retting—in which case the bast fibers too are weakened—or under-retting—which makes the fibers hard to separate (Hess 1958, 288–89).

After retting, the flax is dried, and further processed at leisure. The remaining unwanted pieces of stem material need to be broken up (a process called *breaking* or *braking*) and beaten free (*scutching*), processes that are normally carried out with large wooden implements. The scutched flax is then *hackled* or *heckled*, that is, combed to remove the last fragments (see Hess 1958, 290–91, or Hammond 1845, 390–91 for more about these processes). During scutching and hackling, the short, broken fibers known as *tow* come loose from the long strands, or *line*. (Thus the term *tow-headed* tends to imply short and unkempt, as well as blond, hair.) These are spun separately, producing lower grades of linen thread.

Of all these processes, only breaking, scutching, and hackling make use of special tools, and these are precisely the ones found in the Swiss lake dwellings. Emil Vogt (1937, 47 fig. 72; also Wyss 1969, 134 fig. 15) gathers together pictures of two sorts of hackles and a brake from various Swiss sites (Fig. 1.2).

The results of all this work are the long,

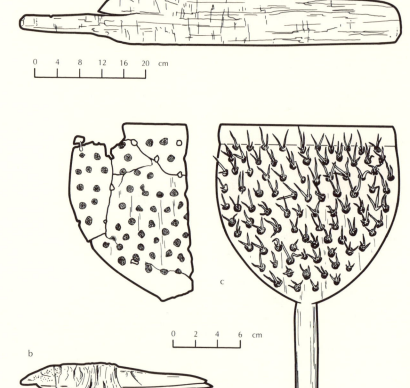

a

0 4 8 12 16 20 cm

c

b

0 2 4 6 cm

1.2 Swiss Neolithic flax-working implements: (a) wooden flax brake (Robenhausen); (b) flax hackles made from rib bones (Lüscherz); (c) reconstruction of hackling board of wood and thorns, and original fragment (Lattrigen). (After E. Vogt 1937, fig. 72; courtesy of Swiss National Museum)

slightly wavy hanks or *stricks* (from which the better thread is made) and the more tangled tufts of short tow. The long strands are actually made up of a number of short (2–4 cm) fibers that still cohere end to end. It is this aggregation which gives linen its uncommon strength among vegetable fibers, which makes it easy to work from this stage on, and which accounts for the fact that linen textiles become softer and more pleasant to the touch the more they are used—or, as Pliny put it, after describing how linen in his day was beaten in the strick, beaten in the

thread, and beaten again after weaving, *semper iniuria melius* ('ever the better for rough handling'; Pliny, *Nat. Hist.* 19.3.18). The individual filaments themselves are quite smooth, producing a lustrous, smooth, even slippery thread and fabric; thus the cloth feels smooth, cool, and non-irritating next to the skin. Since many of the filaments in the final thread still cohere by their natural bonding, linen tends to shed soil easily, dry quickly (although it is quite absorbent), and give off very little lint (Hess 1958, 299).

Linen bleaches nicely, provided one does

not use so much chemical that the individual fibers are loosened from each other, weakening the thread. The traditional method of bleaching by laying the linen out wet on the grass avoids this problem (Hess 1958, 298–99). There the gentle supply of ozone from the greenery does the job bit by bit. On the other hand, linen is notoriously difficult to dye well, even in this modern age of wonder chemistry. The problem is caused by the fiber's hardness, which keeps the dye from penetrating well into the fiber where it won't wash or rub off (Horsfall and Lawrie 1949, 144).

When one looks over this list of properties of linen, one can readily understand the ancient Egyptians' linen industry. They doubtless appreciated the cool, non-irritating feel and quick wash-and-wear properties in a hot climate, and the ability to shed dirt in a land so dusty. They generally wore it white until the New Kingdom, and employed it, in various grades, for every textile use from veils to sails and from loincloths to mummy wrappings.

The abundance and high quality of linen textile remains from ancient Egypt have led most of the handbooks to assume that Egypt

was the original developer of linen manufacture. But the evidence presented here makes it clear that this cannot be. True, the Egyptians began experimenting with linen, along with other vegetable fibers, very early in their own cultural development—we saw that it occurs already in the Neolithic Faiyum—and they soon settled on domestic flax to be their main fiber for the next few thousand years, developing such a high level of skill in linen manufacture that their products won the admiration of the Classical world. But the plant variety itself must have come to Egypt from still earlier domestication sites farther east, ultimately from somewhere like Iraq; and, although these more northeasterly areas are not well-suited to the preservation of textiles, we know by now that Anatolia and Palestine were producing high-quality linen fabrics many centuries before the Faiyum experiments. Who else was, we cannot prove, but it is significant that the range of technique found in the Neolithic Swiss linen is unmatched in Egypt before the Late Bronze Age. We are justified, then, in recognizing a lively and inventive linen industry extending ever farther across the North Mediterranean in the Neolithic era.

Hemp

A second bast fiber of importance for textiles is hemp (Fig. 1.3), from the plant *Cannabis sativa*, better known these days as marijuana.[3] Hemp is a much taller plant than flax, growing up to 12 or even 15 feet high (flax grows 3 to 4 feet high); it also tends to produce rather coarser fibers than flax. Hence among people with a wide choice of

fibers, hemp has generally been used less for clothing and more for rope and sails, particularly since it is also relatively unaffected by the rigors of saltwater (Hess 1958, 312). The methods for obtaining the hemp fiber from the plant stalk are essentially those for getting linen from flax, and the fibers are not easy to distinguish from linen. Herodotus

[3] The word "hemp" is also used loosely to refer to almost any long vegetable fiber other than flax. In particular, "deccan hemp," also called "guinea hemp" or simply "hemp," is more properly distinguished as *kenaf*, and comes from the plant *Hibiscus cannabinus*, of the mallow family (Kirby 1963, 102). True hemp, *Cannabis*,

is of the mulberry family (ibid., 46). Midgley's unelaborated identification of Badarian and other early Egyptian fibers as "hemp" may well refer to kenaf, or *Hibiscus*, which grows in Africa and India, but almost certainly not to *Cannabis* (T. Midgley 1937, 145 etc.; cf. Lucas and Harris 1962, 149).

1.3   Hemp being grown for rope fiber, eastern Romania, 1979

(4.74) mentioned that problem already in the 5th century B.C., saying that one not used to telling hemp and linen apart would not even notice the difference. Even with the microscope it can be difficult to tell for sure. The lumen, or interior tube-like channel, tends to differ: for flax it is "narrow and generally sharply defined" as well as "circular, often a point" in cross-section, whereas for hemp it is "usually broad and frequently indistinct," with a cross-section "in the form of a strip, often forked or star-shaped" (Koch 1963, 40–41). The common, on-the-spot test for telling the two apart, however, is to see which way the fibers twist when wet (Searle, quoted by G. M. Crowfoot 1951, 7; Koch 1963, 74, 93). According to Koch's sources, when held with the free end toward the observer, "fibre bundles and yarns of flax (as well as of ramie and stinging nettle) show numerous rapid twists to the left (clockwise) on being wetted, and soon after that a few twists to the right, whereas jute (as well as broom) can be recognized by many rapid twists to the right followed by a few to the left. With hemp the direction of twist is indefinite, but the number of twists is always very low" (Koch 1963, 93). Searle (quoted by Crowfoot 1951, 7) and others report hemp as twisting to the right, but at any rate as quite different from flax.

There is also a chemical test for distinguishing flax from hemp—applying aniline sulfate, which turns only flax a pale yellow-green (R. Schultes, pers. comm. 1987). In archaeological cases where carbonization or other ravages of time have rendered the fibers too brittle to retain either their ability to twist or their color, however, there may sometimes be technical doubt as to which fiber is involved. Geographical considerations are then called in.

The European evidence seems to point considerably to the north of Mediterranean latitudes for the source of hemp. Although late Greek and Roman writers know of hemp in Gaul, Italy, Greece, and Anatolia (Forbes 1956, 59–60; Hammond 1845, 388–89), Herodotus mentions its use among the Thracians in such a way as to imply that it was not yet produced in Greece in the mid-5th century B.C. (4.74). Hemp seeds, however, have been found in Neolithic European sites— Jane Renfrew (1973, 163) lists the earliest seeds as coming from a site in Germany of the Bandkeramik culture, a phase now dated by calibrated radiocarbon to 5500–4500 B.C. (J. Mallory, pers. comm. 1979); other, later Neolithic finds come from Switzerland, Lower Austria, and Romania. Kordysh reports (1951, 112, ref. Hamčenko 1926) that "imprints of hemp seeds were found in the clay layer of floors" of a house of the Tripolye culture in the Ukraine, now dated to about 5300–3500 B.C. Since these finds were of seeds, we have no proof that the plant was used for its fibers, only that it was known. In fact, Hamčenko lists the hemp seeds with wheat, barley, and millet seeds under "kitchen remains" (Hamčenko 1926, 38). We do know that the Tripolyans had cloth, for we find it impressed on the bottoms of their pots (see Chapter 4); but we have no way of telling the fiber used. A late Neolithic site at Adaouste, in Southern France, however, is said to have produced some fibers of both linen and hemp, caught in a bone implement. Furthermore, it was claimed that the hemp was dyed blue, some of the linen red, and some left white (Cotte and Cotte 1916, 764). If true, this suggests that hemp as well as linen was being used for fiber, not just for food.

Often botanists can help locate the area in which a domestic plant originated, by charting the probable lines of genetic descent of the known varieties against their geographical distribution. *Cannabis* has proved to be so adept at rapid and radical changes in response to new environments, however, that botanists have had a hard time agreeing on the genetic relationships, and consequently have set its origin variously over much of Asia (Schultes 1970, 16, 26–27). They have in turn resorted to archaeological, historical, and ethnobotanical evidence for help in untangling the problem (ibid., 17).

Archaeologically, the earliest known candidates for hempen cloth occur in the form of impressions on East Asian Neolithic pots: both from sites of the Yang-Shao culture in northern China (Andersson 1923, 26; Li 1974b, 438–39; Li 1983, 31), and from the 5th-millennium site of Ka Ruo, Chang-du county, Tibet Autonomous Region (Tong

En-Zheng, public lecture, January 15, 1981). Although it is not possible to prove directly that the fiber that made these impressions was hemp, the circumstantial evidence is strong for northern China. The fibers are too coarse to have been silk; no other fiber-producing source is known to have existed in northern China until the much later introduction of ramie and cotton from the south (Ho 1975, 81; cf. Kuhn 1987, 30); and fair quantities of what is probably hemp pollen have been found at Pan-p'o, one of the sites with these early textile impressions (Li 1974b, 439). The era in question is currently dated to the late 5th and early 4th millennia (Li 1974b, 439). The coarse textile impressions continue in the Late Neolithic cultures, until around the end of the 3rd millennium we are finally blessed with actual pieces of cloth more directly identifiable as hemp (Kuhn 1987, 23). We might also add that Chinese legend places the domestication of hemp back into the Neolithic period (Schultes 1970, 14).

The early Tibetan find is also interesting in that the botanists themselves now incline specifically toward central or south-central Asia as the native habitat for hemp (R. Schultes, pers. comm. 1987). Clearly hemp had already spread far and wide by early Neolithic times: to Europe, Tibet, and China. Had it travelled somehow with the Palaeolithic net-makers (see Chapter 2)?

In the Occident, the next solid evidence for hemp after the Neolithic seeds does not come until the Iron Age, and then we find a lot of it. We know from two sources that the plant was used for its narcotic effect by the steppe nomads in the first millennium B.C.: Herodotus gives a rather garbled account of Scythians inhaling the narcotic smoke of hemp pods (4.73–75); and equipment similar to what he describes has been found in the 5th century B.C. kurgan burials at Pazyryk, in the Altai Mountains, complete with little containers full of the plant (Rudenko 1970, 285; only seeds are mentioned, but they contain no narcotic: presumably drug-bearing parts of the plant had been there too but did not survive). In the same excavation were found shirts woven of hemp, called *kendyr* by the locals (ibid., 83; see Appendix to Chapter 1). It is interesting that even recently hemp still grew as a weed "around the camps of the nomads in the Altai where the soil had been enriched by the cattle during the winter" (J. G. Hawkes 1969, 19, ref. Sinskaja). Hemp is well known among farmers as needing quantities of fertilizer (cf. Schultes 1970, 19).

Just a little earlier, in the 8th century B.C. levels of Gordion, in Turkey, we have pieces of fabric that have been identified as hemp (Bellinger 1962, 8, 13, 32; but not positively verifiable by Ellis, 1981). Since the Phrygians who built Gordion seem to have come south into Anatolia from the steppe area shortly before the 8th century, during the many migrations at the beginning of the Iron Age, and since Herodotus connects hempen textiles with the Thracians, who lived to the north of Greece, and the narcotic with the Scythians, who lived north of the Black Sea, the presumptive evidence is strong that the textile use of hemp as well as the plant itself came into the Mediterranean countries from the northeast, and seemingly not before the beginning of the Iron Age.[4] The tremendous surge of Greek trade and industry in the 5th and 4th centuries B.C. must have done much to spread the use of the plant in Greece and Italy. Despite Herodotus's treatment of hempen fabrics as a foreign curiosity, a cloth

of this material has actually turned up in a 5th-century B.C. context at Trakhones, in Attica (Zisis 1955, 590). The theory that the piece (or at least the yarn) was imported and was still something of a novelty, however, is supported by the fact that the accompanying cloth proved to be of cotton, from a plant that we know, from both botanical and literary evidence, had not yet reached Greece (ibid., 590–92). Apparently some ancient merchant or collector had made a hobby of acquiring exotic textiles!

If we pull together all the evidence, then, it becomes clear that the plant itself, *Cannabis sativa*, grew and was known in the Neolithic period all across the northern latitudes, from Europe (Germany, Switzerland, Austria, Romania, the Ukraine) to East Asia (Tibet and China), but that although the plant appears in East Asia already in the 5th millennium, textile use of *Cannabis sativa* does not surface for certain in the West until relatively late, namely the Iron Age. At that time the use of this plant for cloth spreads from Thrace and the Black Sea to Greece. It is conceivable that the idea of spinning the fibers of the otherwise familiar hemp plant spread to or among the nomads from the Far East and came westward with them. In the same Pazyryk mounds that housed the narcotic equipment and hemp shirts were found pieces of Chinese silk embroidered with Chinese designs (see Chapter 7), showing contact with the east. But it is more likely that people in the steppe zone and central Europe had long been using hemp the same way as flax for textiles (and for food), and that we just haven't found the clinching evidence: we have almost no well-analyzed fibers from

[4] One could make the case from Herodotus's text that even the plant was unknown in Greece proper. Upon first mentioning hemp, Herodotus takes pains to mention that it is like flax except much larger, and that cloth can be made from it—as though he did not expect his audience to know either of these things. (And Herodo-

tus himself clearly does not understand the narcotic properties.) He even introduces the topic noun, κάννα-βις, with the verb ἔστι, "there is, there exists," usually reserved for the introduction of a word or topic that the speaker assumes to be unknown to the hearer.

the steppelands before the first millennium B.C., and when in doubt we have simply *assumed* all bast fibers to be flax. It may well be that, without cultivation, people merely grabbed whatever was ready to hand, whether flax, hemp, nettle, or tree bast. I strongly suspect, however, that what catapulted hemp to sudden fame and fortune as a cultigen and caused it to spread rapidly westwards in the first millennium B.C. was the spread of the habit of pot-smoking from somewhere in south-central Asia, where the drug-bearing variety of the plant originally occurred. The linguistic evidence strongly supports this theory, both as to time and direction of spread and as to cause (see Appendix to Chapter 1 for a full and rather surprising account of the language-based deductions).

Until we obtain more evidence, this is about as far as we can go. As we await the happy circumstance of finding actual textiles, however, we may be able to glean further information from indirect sources. Studies of the pollen profiles taken from a lake bed in England have shown a sudden appearance and rapid increase of pollen from hemp, flax, and nettle and their characteristic weeds at about the time of the Anglo-Saxon invasions. These findings fit other evidence that cultivation of these plants for fiber was introduced into the island at that time (Godwin 1967). Although good pollen sequences require special conditions not found everywhere, it is to be hoped that a scattering of such profiles can eventually be obtained where conditions permit, to build up a broader picture of the origins and spread of the plants themselves.

Nettle and Other Bast Fibers

The third bast fiber that we should consider is nettle, from the common stinging nettle, *Urtica dioica*. Other members of the nettle family have been used for fiber too; *Urtica urens* and *Urtica parviflora* can be lumped with *Urtica dioica* for our purposes, whereas *Boehmeria nivea*, which gives ramie (also known as Eastern Nettle, or Chinagrass), is native to the Far East and a latecomer to the West, and will not concern us (see Hald 1942, 37; Kirby 1963, 148, 180). The fiber is obtained by various modified versions of the process used for flax and hemp (Hald 1942), or by boiling with ashes, i.e., lye (Kirby 1963, 180). Nettle, which was still used into this century in northern, central, and eastern Europe (Hald 1942, 33–34), makes its earliest recorded entry onto the ar-

chaeological scene in Scandinavia in the later Bronze Age—early first millennium B.C.—at Voldtofte, Denmark.[5]

The case is highly instructive. A tomb opened in the mid-19th century yielded "some inconsiderable fragments of a fine white material" that was immediately assumed and later claimed, upon careful inspection, to be pure flax (Hald 1942, 40). It was not until Margrethe Hald, of the National Museum in Copenhagen, was collecting materials for her comprehensive treatise on "The Nettle as a Culture Plant" (1942), however, that the fragments from Voldtofte, among others, were put to closer scrutiny: the fibers from the samples—including the exact pieces inspected earlier—proved all to be of nettle (ibid., 40). Reporting in 1972 yet

[5] Apparently the awareness that wonderfully soft shirts had been made out of something so unlikely as stinging, prickly nettle, by inhabitants of another land or time, gave rise to the European fairytale motif that nettle shirts were magical ones—obviously made by magic and, by extension, endowing the wearer with magical powers (cf. Hald 1942, 34).

another example of a nettle-fiber textile that had been assumed by archaeologists to be flax, namely the "linen" fabrics of the great Oseberg Ship find, Agnes Geijer ruefully remarks that "the conclusion can be drawn that old determinations of bast fibres are not to be taken for granted" (Geijer [1972] 1979, 276 n. 9). Unfortunately, we would do well to keep that warning in mind with many of the fabrics used as data in the current discussion, especially where the pieces of the puzzle do not all seem to fit.

Yet other bast fibers have been used for making thread from very early times, probably well back into the Upper Palaeolithic period. Some carefully made string found in the Palaeolithic strata of the famous painted caves at Lascaux, in southern France, was definitely of vegetable fiber, most probably bast, although the extreme degree of humification made final proof impossible (Glory 1959, 149–50). Inhabitants of northern Europe during the next cultural stage, the Mesolithic, were using bast fibers for netting, especially basts from tree bark. The net remains from Korpilahti, in Finland, appeared to be of willow bast (Maglemosian era: J.G.D. Clark 1952, 227); while those from Šventoji in Lithuania are of linden bast (from the Narva culture: Rimantienė 1979, 27). Nor did this wide use of miscellaneous plant fibers stop soon: Egyptians of the Late Neolithic and Bronze Age seem to have used any and every plant fiber ready to hand, especially for cords, strings, and ropes. Lucas lists reed, grass, papyrus, and palm fiber, in addition to flax and esparto (Lucas and Harris 1962, 134–35). Even today, the peasants of these areas still collect fibers from the various indigenous wild plants when necessary or convenient.

WOOL

Another major class of fiber that concerns us is that of wool and related animal growths. Wool fibers differ markedly from bast fibers first in that they have scaly rather than smooth surfaces. It is these minute scales which in large part give wool its ability to felt: during the combined application of damp heat and kneading pressure, the scales of neighboring fibers become thoroughly caught in each other and thus cohere in a dense mass without benefit of glue or any other foreign substance. Wool fibers from modern domestic sheep also differ from bast in being kinky, in a random way, rather than relatively straight with a tendency to twist in one direction. This kinkiness accounts for the well-known insulating properties of wool, as opposed to linen and the other vegetable fibers. Spun or felted, the mass of wool contains myriad little air-pockets between the kinks, pockets that maintain their temperature very well. The kinks also, like the scales during felting, tend to catch on each other, and on everything else—such as burrs, twigs, or the hairs on the skin of the wearer. This "catchiness" allows wool to be spun in two quite different ways: the fibers can be combed to lie parallel, as the fibers in bast threads are; or the fibers can be carded to lie fluffily in all directions. The first method produces a hard, strong yarn called *worsted*; the second produces a soft, spongy, elastic yarn called *woolen* (like our typical modern knitting yarn), which depends as much on the kinks as on the spin to hold it together.

Not only the kinkiness but also the natural stretchiness of the wool fibers account for the remarkable elasticity of yarns made of wool. Herein lies another difference from bast. According to one report, the ultimate fibers of bast "can be stretched only one twenty-fifth of their natural length before they break, while sheep's wool will stretch from one fourth to one half before it gives way" (Hammond 1845, 390; cf. Backer 1972, 46; and see below). Human hair does the same (try it!). This extreme stretchiness of wool and its yarns produces several technical problems in weaving it.

The length and thickness of the fibers in a sheep's fleece vary enormously according to breed, season, and climate. With respect to textiles, however, we can say that the thickest fibers ever found on sheep, the *kemps* (Fig. 1.4), which range from about 100 to 250 microns (μ: one-thousandth of a millimeter)

| Wool | Hair | Kemp |

1.4 Diagrams of the structures of wool, hair, and kemp, as seen highly magnified

in diameter, are so stiff, bristly and brittle as to be unspinnable by themselves. The fibers that are next in thickness, called *hairs*, which range from about 50 to 100μ in diameter, can be spun more easily, especially when mixed with finer wool. But both hairs and kemps give the wool a harsh, coarse, even bristly feel, as the ends tend to stick out stiffly everywhere. Still thinner is the wool itself: it is classed as "medium" from 30 or 35 to about 60μ in diameter, and as "fine" if under

30μ—sometimes as fine as 6μ (Ryder 1969a, 497, 517–20; 1964b, 558).[6] One reason the kemps are all but unspinnable by themselves is that they also tend to be rather short in proportion to their thickness, running around 4 to 7 centimeters long, whereas modern long-staple wool can be several times that long. (By comparison, cotton and the ultimate fibers of flax, although short like kemps, lie in the thickness range of fine wool.) The other reason is that, unlike wool and hair, kemps break easily under either tension or torsion—fatal flaws when it comes to spinning (cf. Hundt 1959, 90).

Sheep's wool ranges in color from black and dark brown, through the reddish and buff or grey colors typical of wild sheep, to white. The naturally pigmented wools do not take artificial dyes well (Ryder 1969a, 495). On the other hand, white wool takes and keeps even primitive dyes more easily than almost any other fiber, having natural substances in it that act as mordants or fixatives (see Chapter 10).

The wool is obtained nowadays by shearing or cutting it from the sheep. But as Pliny said, in the first century A.D., "Not everywhere are sheep shorn: in some places the plucking of wool continues" (Pliny, *Nat. Hist.* 8.73.191). The method that he considers old, namely pulling the wool out during the molt, seems in fact to have been the chief early way of obtaining the wool (see Chapter 12). The raw wool is generally washed in cold water—sometimes even before being sheared from the animal!—to remove the worst of the dirt and lanolin grease. Then it must be combed to remove the bits of twigs,

---

[6] Kemps and hairs also differ from fine wool in having a medulla, or central channel (Ryder 1964b, 559; 1969a, 520). This medulla disappears in the medium wool range (Ryder 1965, 176), as classified above.

Note that other systems of classification for wool are also in use: e.g., Heyn, publishing in New York rather than in Britain, breaks the terms down as follows: coarse

wool 42–33μ, medium wool 33–23μ, and fine wool 23–17μ (Heyn 1954, 130). Another way of approaching the problem, more useful in some circumstances, is by mean diameters: thus Ryder (pers. comm. 1984) pegs the mean for fine wool around 20μ, for medium wool around 40μ, and for kemp/hair at 90$^+\mu$. Samples will tend to cluster around these means.

grass, and other debris caught in it, and to separate and untangle the fibers. The wool is then either combed straight for spinning worsted, or fluffed up by means of cards or a bow for so-called woolen yarn or for felt.

To most of us, wool means sheep and sheep means wool. We fall into a trap, however, if we apply the equation to early times, for primitive wild sheep were (and are) considerably more kempy than woolly (Reed 1960, 137; Bökönyi 1974, 159). So archaeologically we must ascertain the area and time not only for the original domestication of sheep, but also for the development of usably woolly sheep. Furthermore, varieties of goats produce usable, even if mostly rather coarse, wool or hair. (Cashmere goats, on the contrary, yield very fine fibers.)

Two knotty problems clutter the literature on the early domestication of sheep. One is that the bones of these sheep are almost identical to those of their cousins, the goats, which were domesticated about as early; only a few parts are idiosyncratic to each, and those few are not necessarily present among the osteological remains found (Reed 1960, 129–30; S. Payne, pers. comm. 1984). Such designations as "sheep/goats" in the reports therefore have often led the unwary to unwarranted conclusions; one must always read the fine print. The other problem is that the family tree of *Ovis* is none too clear. The American bighorn, *Ovis canadensis*, is certainly a separate species and had nothing to do with the domesticants; but the wild sheep of the eastern hemisphere are classed by various analysts into anywhere from one to four or more species, with consequently more or

fewer subspecies. (Reed 1960, 134–35, summarizes the positions of Lydekker and others to date; Zeuner 1963, 153–54 has yet another opinion; see also Ryder 1983, 20–22.) The amount of contribution to the domestic gene pool of each of the various species or subspecies is likewise disputed (Lydekker 1912, 2, 41; Reed 1960, 135; Zeuner 1963, 153–62; and Bökönyi 1974, 156–59, to name a few). Recent work with chromosomes, however, suggests that the Mouflon is the most likely (sub)species to have contributed most to the domestic sheep, and blood composition points specifically to the Mouflon of northwest Iran (Ryder 1983, 20–21).

On the whole, however, we can say that sheep of some sort or sorts appear to have come under the control of human beings very early in the era of incipient domestication. Even if we discard the evidence from Belt Cave, Zawi Chemi Shanidar, and Jarmo as not entirely conclusive that the sheep—undoubtedly present, and in increasing numbers—were actually domestic (Bökönyi 1974, 163–65; Reed 1960, 135), the combined evidence for wild and/or domestic sheep from these and other sites, such as Ali Kosh, Tepe Sarab, Çayönü Tepesi, and Argissa-Magula (Thessaly), points to domestication by or before 7000 B.C., and probably considerably before, even in the 9th millennium (Reed 1960, 135–36; Protsch and Berger 1973, 236–39; Çambel and Braidwood 1970, 56; and Ryder 1983, 51–54, but see also 22). If it is true, as zoologists now generally believe from the available evidence, that there were no wild sheep in Europe in the late Palaeolithic and earliest Neolithic,[7]

[7] The argument is that the wild sheep of Sardinia and Corsica are too far from the mainland to have gotten there on their own, and therefore that Neolithic people must have brought them—as domestic animals, some of whom escaped and became wild again. The fact that they look just like their wild relatives must then be interpreted as meaning that the domestic sheep of the Neolithic population still looked like wild sheep (Ryder, pers. comm. 1984)—a most interesting conclusion! Other sheep that through breeding had diverged significantly from the wild stock before becoming feral—such as the "Bronze Age" Soay and "Iron Age" Kilda sheep—have retained their bred-in characteristics to a recognizable degree, rather than reverting to the original wild phenotype the way feral pigs do.

then the Thessalian sheep of 7200 B.C. must have been imported by conscious human effort: that is, they were domestic and had to come from someplace where people had domesticated them still earlier (Protsch and Berger 1973, 238). All the signs currently point to some area in southwest Asia for that center of domestication.

We now come to the curiously convoluted problem of when people began to use wool independently of the hide on which it grew, and in particular used it for spinning, weaving, and felting. Some hold that wool was probably used early, almost as soon as the sheep were domesticated (e.g., Zeuner 1963, 162), others that it was not used until relatively late: in the Chalcolithic, when our first indisputable evidence appears, or at best at the end of the Neolithic (Bökönyi 1974, 159). The divergence of opinion seems to stem from not one but three differences of interpretation.

The first issue is that of woolliness. For example, Charles Reed states (1960, 137):

It is sometimes naively assumed by prehistorians and other non-zoologists that sheep were domesticated for their wool. Actually, wild goats and wild sheep [Fig. 1.5] have similar hairy coats with woolly underfur, the degree of woolliness depending upon species and/or subspecies and upon the season. A macroscopic examination of wild *Ovis* and wild *Capra* preserved at the Chicago Museum of Natural History would not indicate any greater degree of woolliness in the sheep. . . . [Thus,] to a prehistoric people just entering into a pattern of animal domestication, goats offered as good a hide (and one probably as warm) as did sheep.

Reed goes on to point out that "no prehistoric people could have foreseen any possible changes in the predominantly hairy coats of the animals (either goats or sheep) which were being domesticated," and concludes that if sheep "were domesticated for something, it would have been for factors familiar to early hunter-cultivators, that is, meat and hides. Not until some time after domestication could there have occurred the idea of other uses (e.g. milk), and only after the natural and random appearance in the sheep of an increased woolliness could that character have been recognized and selected for" (ibid.; see Fig. 1.6). Zeuner, on the other

1.5 *Ovis orientalis*: wild Persian Red Sheep (female), chief progenitor of domestic sheep. Note the coarse coat with much kemp and little wool

1.6 Fleece from a modern sheep bred for wool (*left*) compared with the kempy coat of *Ovis orientalis* (*right*: female above, male below)

hand, while not specifically denying that the original act of domestication occurred for a return other than wool, stresses the ease and quickness with which he feels this new use for sheep would have been discovered:

The presence of wool . . . is a matter of degree. . . . In the wild sheep of snowy winter climates . . . it is present in abundance, and there is no need to assume that the discovery of the use of wool was due to a special act of human intelligence. The winter coat is shed in patches, sometimes of large size. The writer has himself plucked such patches. They consist mainly of matted wool, with a small amount of hair. No early sheepbreeder could have failed to notice the useful qualities of this material. If he was already familiar with the art of twisting vegetable fibers into threads, he would have quite naturally proceeded

[8] To satisfy myself on this subject I went to the trouble of obtaining a sample of what grows on the back of a specimen of *Ovis orientalis*, the chief wild ancestor of modern sheep (see Figs. 1.5–6). And I can report that the winter coat of the kempier type of wild sheep is virtually unspinnable. The kemp fibers, which are a few centimeters long, lack the elasticity of wool and simply break into smaller and smaller fragments, while the true wool is so short and fine (on my samples, 1 cm or less in length, and 5μ in diameter) that it is insufficient to act as a binder. The reason that kemp and wool (or hair) differ so radically in their behavior under tension and

to spinning wool. . . . On the other hand, if he was not acquainted with that art, the making of felt would have suggested itself. (Zeuner 1963, 162)

Among the biologists, then, it comes down to a matter of opinion as to whether the first animal-keepers happened upon the woollier or the hairier (technically, kempier) varieties of sheep.[8] So what other kinds of evidence can we bring to bear? A single representation of a woolly sheep, in the form of a clay figurine, from Tepe Sarab in eastern Iran (Bökönyi 1974, 159 and fig. 44), attests at least that woolly sheep were known and available by 5000 B.C. It says nothing specific as to the use of the wool, of course, but Zeuner is probably not far wrong in guessing that when good wool *was* present, it was soon used. On the other hand, it is not until the 4th millennium and later that representations of woolly sheep suddenly begin to appear in some quantity (Hilzheimer 1941, 34–35, 38–39; Bökönyi 1974, 159, 171), followed by records of "sheep-shearing," or rather sheep-plucking (Bökönyi 1974, 169; Waetzoldt 1972, 4–20). Cuneiform tablets of the Archaic period from Uruk list six of the 29 recorded flocks of sheep as specifically "wool sheep": *udu-síg*, etc. (Green 1980, 4). A millennium later, Neo-Sumerian records mention four different types of sheep from which wool was regularly obtained: the *udu-gukkal*, apparently a woolly, fat-tailed sheep that gave a small amount—⅔ kilo—but a high quality of

torsion lies in the nature of their construction. The outer casing of scales (see Fig. 1.4) is very tough and elastic, whereas the interior tube, or medulla, has no strength. Since the relative proportion of medulla to casing is very high in kemp, such fibers have little strength. In wool (or hair), on the contrary, a large percentage of the fiber is made of the tough material, so the fiber can take enormous punishment and still bounce back.

My thanks to Dr. Gerald Esra and Dr. Gary Kuehn of the Los Angeles County Zoo for helping me obtain samples from the flanks of their male and female *Ovis orientalis*.

fleece; the *udu-gukkal-igi-nim-ma* or "high-land fat-tail," which gave the very best fleece; the *udu-kur-ra* or "mountain" sheep, with a much poorer grade of fleece; and the most frequent type, the *udu-uli-gi*, which gave a larger amount—over a kilo—of apparently very coarse wool (Waetzoldt 1972, 4–6, 17–20, 45–48).

The evidence from actual remains of thread and textiles is the second issue on which the interpretations depend. The earliest actual textiles found to date are those from Naḥal Ḥemar, in the 7th millennium, and those from Çatal Hüyük, around 6000 B.C. The textiles from Naḥal Ḥemar are largely of flax, with occasional evidence for other basts and human hair (Bar-Yosef 1985, 4; T. Schick, pers. comm. 1985), and the samples from Çatal Hüyük that Ryder analyzed proved definitively to be of bast fiber, namely flax. On the other hand, at the end of his article Ryder alludes to one piece of evidence given by Helbaek that at least some (other) textiles from Çatal Hüyük contained wool (Ryder 1965, 176). That evidence is a photomicrograph of a few fibers, the silhouettes of which give indication of a scaly surface (Helbaek 1963, 43)—scaly surfaces, as we have said, being present only on woolly-type animal fibers, not on bast fibers. The fibers need not have been specifically sheep's wool, of course: the excavator himself suggests "wool or mohair" (Mellaart 1967, 219). Until well into the 4th millennium, the other remains of thread and cloth either are in the form of impressions on clay, such as those at Jarmo (Braidwood and Howe 1960, 46), so that determination of the fiber type is not possible, or else are definitely bast fiber,

1.7   Middle Kingdom Egyptian hieroglyphic painting of hairy sheep, typical of the sort raised in ancient Egypt. From Beni Hasan, ca. 2000 B.C. (Griffith 1896, pl. 3.35)

such as the fabrics from Egypt and Switzerland.[9] Then, in the 4th millennium, wool and fleece turn up at several pre-dynastic sites in Egypt, earliest at el-Omari in Lower Egypt (Greiss 1955, 228–29; Reed 1960, 136; see Fig. 1.7 for the typical sheep of dynastic Egypt). Meanwhile, representations of woolly sheep become more numerous in the roughly contemporary Warka phase in Mesopotamia, and about 3000 B.C. a Proto-Elamite figurine was laid to rest in a cloth made of animal fiber (Hansen 1970, 7, 24)—presumably sheep or goat's wool. From then on, and in an ever wider area of the Near East and Europe, the identifiable textile remains frequently turn out to be woolen.

The third issue concerns the composition, with respect to age and sex, of the sheep populations represented by the bones found at Neolithic sites, and what this profile im-

[9] Ryder's own experience with analysis, in fact, has convinced him that "Neolithic textiles usually turn out to be flax" (Ryder 1983, 47), and that cloth that proves to be of wool and is claimed as Neolithic turns out to have been misdated—e.g., is actually Bronze Age. He has worked with a wide array of samples from Europe and some from the Near East, but almost nothing is available from the eastern end of this area. He also concedes, however, that our lack of Neolithic woolen cloth just might be the result of the hazards of preservation (ibid., 737).

plies about the uses for which the animals were intended. The topic is a very interesting one, and potentially very informative. So much groundwork still needs to be done, however, that we can as yet only lay out the problem and catch a glimpse or two, from the available evidence, of where this path may lead.

Although we still don't have a flawless base against which to assess age/sex distribution,[10] we can readily see the general directions of the deviations that interest us. For sheep, the primary uses in the past have been for meat (and incidentally, at the same time, for hides), for milk, and for wool. These uses are not entirely compatible since one must kill the animal for its meat and hide, but keep it alive for continuing supplies of milk and wool. The optimal point at which to slaughter for meat is when the creature has just achieved full size: the caretaking energy and the fodder required are at a minimum for a maximum return on the amount of meat (not to mention tenderness). Since the male is generally larger than the female, it will give somewhat more meat, but the advantage is not great. A large proportion of the sheep in a flock kept only for meat, then, should be killed off within a couple of years or so, with a much smaller number—mostly ewes—kept for breeding purposes (cf. Payne 1973, 281–84, with additional complicating factors). If the crop is to be milk, however, the male is useless—except for the few needed to service the ewes so that they lamb and begin to produce milk each season. Hence a milk

flock consists very largely of adult ewes, with enough rams kept for breeding. (Enough ewe lambs must be kept to replace the ewes grown too elderly; but most males can be eliminated at a young age, to save care and fodder.) For wool, the situation is different still. The best and most copious wool is grown by castrated males, the second best fleeces by the ewes, and the least by intact rams (Killen 1964, 5; Waetzoldt 1972, 17; the same distribution is reported in the New World for llamas [Cranstone 1969, 254]).[11] Wool flocks, then, have generally contained a preponderance of wethers (castrated male sheep), with a fair number of adult ewes for both wool and breeding, and just enough rams to maintain the flock (Killen 1964, 2–6). In fact, unless there were a shortage of pasture, all sheep of both sexes could grow to full adulthood, males mostly being neutered rather than killed. (For modern ethnographic and ancient examples, and for detailed charts of various flock types, see Payne 1973.)

The net results of the interaction of these economic considerations with sex and age are shown in Table 1.1. The most interesting thing about the picture it gives is that each use leaves its imprint on the flock, in the profile of ages and sexes. Of course, in actual practice a flock may be used for more than one purpose. The chart shows that at least some combinations are even convenient. Easiest are meat and milk (ewes live, for their milk, but most males die young, for their meat), or milk and wool (all grow old for their wool, most males being castrated and

---

[10] Among animals killed by hunting, the age/sex distribution depends in part upon the method of hunting (cf. Bökönyi 1969, 222). And the "normal" age distribution of a wild flock (if that can be adequately determined: cf. Chaplin 1969, 236, fig. 2) is also not satisfactory for us, since human protection can enable an unnaturally large proportion of the young to attain adulthood. What we need, to assess the full effects of human use on the composition of a domestic flock, is a sex/age population curve for a hypothetical flock that has been reared under full domestic protection but not used for

any particular purpose.

[11] Fleece-growing is interrupted by physical trauma such as sickness, giving birth, or castration. Thus the first fleece of a ewe is better than the first fleece of a wether (castrated male), because the wether has just gone through trauma, while the still-maiden ewe has not. Similarly, if a ewe is not shorn until after lambing in the spring, the wool will break during carding and spinning, at the point where it was growing when she gave birth.

TABLE 1.1
Sheep's Typical Age at Death/Slaughter,
According to Use of Sheep

	Age Pattern		
Use	Ewe	Ram	Wether
Meat	Some yearlings; some old (for breeding)	Mostly yearlings; a few old (for breeding)	(None)
Milk	Old	Mostly yearlings; a few old (for breeding)	(None)
Wool	Old	A few old (for breeding)	Old

the ewes being milked as well as shorn). But the only efficient way to combine meat and wool is to eat tough mutton. And then one may as well wash it down with milk. In short, if wool (which is what we are after here) is an important consideration in the flock management, theoretically it should show up in the composition—and culling—of the flock with respect to sex and age, whether it is the sole purpose for keeping the sheep or has been combined with obtaining meat, milk, or both.

At many archaeological sites, the animal bones have merely been identified as to species, if that, and then discarded. The feasibility of determining slaughter patterns, however, has been amply demonstrated (even as early as 1931: see D.M.S. Watson

1931). For example, a number of Early and Middle Neolithic sites show a similar skewing in age distribution, a skewing noted by their excavators as evidence for domestication of the sheep populations involved.[12] Already in 1963, Zeuner could see a pattern for the "pottery Neolithic" era, namely, "immature sheep predominate. This is taken to mean that young animals were killed for food, whilst mature females were kept for breeding and possibly milking" (Zeuner 1963, 171). Unfortunately, it is not clear when or where the shift back to a lower percentage of yearlings and higher percentage of adults takes place. But surprise caused by the age distribution in these Neolithic sites is some sort of evidence that the later sites, which are much more numerous and constitute the "expected," are different. Exploration of the subject would be useful to us, because it would help pin down when and where wool came to be of major economic importance.

Still more diagnostic of wool flocks, and still less well explored, is the determination of the presence of wethers. There is no point in keeping a fully adult, castrated male sheep for either milk or meat. So if wethers are present, especially in considerable numbers, we have virtual proof that the primary purpose of the flock was wool. Theoretically, at least, it is possible to detect the presence of wethers by looking at the skeletal remains, by at least three different methods.[13] And castrates have been noted. There were clearly three types of horn cores—male, fe-

[12] E.g., Zawi Chemi Shanidar, NE Iraq, 9th mil. B.C.: 54% yearlings among the sheep/goats, 98% of 1.5 years or younger (Perkins 1964b, 1566); Jarmo, NE Iraq, 7th mil.: "proportion of sheep-goat bones was very high, . . . almost all . . . yearlings" (Braidwood 1952, 64); Franchthi Cave, SE Greece, ca. 6000 B.C.: "increase in the number of immature animals killed" after introduction of sheep and goats (T. W. Jacobsen 1969, 8); Nea Nikomedeia, NE Greece, 6th mil.: 47% of sheep/goat bones immature (Rodden 1962, 272).

[13] The bones of the neutered male tend to be consis-

tently smaller and lighter than those of the intact male; so if a single breed is present it is sometimes possible to distinguish rams from wethers (Charles Schwartz, pers. comm. 1980; cf. D.M.S. Watson 1931, 199–200). It has also been shown recently that epiphysial fusion—a stage in the bone growth of animals—occurs much later in castrates than in fertile sheep (Hatting 1983, 120 and fig. 4). And castration can radically affect the growth of the horns if it is performed early enough (ibid.; Ryder 1969b, 45).

male, and castrate—among the remains of cattle at Skara Brae, a 2nd-millennium village in the Orkney Islands of northern Scotland (D.M.S. Watson 1931, 198–200; J.G.D. Clark 1952, 126). Unfortunately for our purposes, not enough of the relevant sheep bones remained to determine the status of the sheep (Watson 1931, 202–3).

And that, in fact, is the practical limitation almost everywhere: insufficient preservation. Since the evidence for age is typically determined from one group of bones, that for sex from another, and that for castration from certain relationships between the first two groups, we need to know which are the bones not from "sheep" but from *individual* sheep. But we do not have anything close to complete skeletons: we are looking at the disjointed and haphazard remains of cooking pots and dinner plates. So we are seldom in a position to make inferences that depend on relating several different parts of one skeleton. The same problem pertains to determining kill patterns in general, where one needs to know how many *individuals* one is working with. Then there is the fact that smaller bones and the bones from smaller (e.g., younger) animals are more likely to have disintegrated over the millennia, again skewing the picture. As research continues, however, it may become possible to tell more about age and sex (or loss of sex) from individual bones. It is thus important for excavators to salvage their osteological material (including the small pieces!) as they dig, and to save it for future reference and re-analysis, as methods of recovering information from them improve.

As for the specific practice of running wethers and ewes in wool flocks, from the late 4th millennium on we can infer it from the structure of Mesopotamian sheep accounts (e.g., Green 1980, 11; Waetzoldt 1972, 18, 61; Cross 1937, 24), and in Europe

of the late 2nd millennium B.C. from Mycenaean Greek accounts (Killen 1964).

If we now peer through the haze of all the things that need to be researched and ask again when people began to use wool independently of the hide it grew on, we see that the existing evidence from these various sources, although incomplete, is not contradictory. It is possible that sheep with evident and usable wool were known to at least some people early in the Neolithic, and that these people used their wool, even perhaps for spinning and weaving; but we have as yet no direct and indisputable evidence for that use. Evolution into a new niche—in this case a domestic environment—tends to occur quickly at first; and human protection in particular destabilizes the natural selection process "that led to the optimum wild type, and . . . causes . . . accumulation of many mutations normally suppressed or eliminated" (Ryder 1983, 32). It is also evident, however, that many sheep—Bökönyi thinks most (1974, 159)—were used primarily for other purposes, largely meat, until rather late in the Neolithic period. Only in the 4th and 3rd millennia do we begin to see much evidence, and then we see quite a bit, for woolly breeds of sheep, for woolen textiles, and for flocks managed for wool production (this last including the economic records, a new form of evidence). Bökönyi sums up his assessment by claiming that "in the Neolithic period woolly sheep were in all likelihood quite rare and appeared in great masses only in the Copper Age. However, by the end of that period and in the Bronze Age they became widespread also in Europe. . . . Of course, side by side with woolly sheep great numbers of hairy ones continued to live on. The sheepskin found in one of the Pazyryk kurgans of the 5th century B.C. had belonged to a hairy sheep, which was still close to a wild sheep" (Bökönyi 1974, 159).

The persistence of hairy sheep underscores the probability that the evolution of modern white, woolly fleece types was a slow and genetically complex process (Reed 1960, 137–38 n. 4). Michael Ryder has examined wool and skin samples from many parts of the ancient Near East and Europe in his attempts to document the steps in this evolution (see Ryder 1969a; also 1964b, 1972; Ryder and Hedges 1973). Predominant whiteness evidently developed before woolliness (Ryder 1969a, 500; Bökönyi 1974, 159–60). Whiteness seems to be genetically simpler than woolliness; also, whiteness is common among the relatively primitive, "hairy" domestic sheep, occurring for example in the hairy sheepskin from Pazyryk (Bökönyi 1974, 160). Wild sheep have large areas of color—buff to brown to reddish or greyish—on their backs and shoulders; only their undersides and occasional other patches are white, never the whole trunk (Bökönyi 1974, 156–57, 159–60). The general whiteness that evolved had a considerable effect on the use of the wool for textiles, partly because, as we have said, naturally pigmented wools do not dye well. On the other hand, sheep that are all brown or all black, or have dark face and feet, are also products of domestication (Zeuner 1963, 168–70), and their wool can be used to contrast with white wool without the tedious process of dyeing. Pliny, for example, recounts that the Romans searched far and wide for the best natural colors: black from Spain, reddish from "Asia" (Asia Minor) and southern Spain, and tawny from southeast Italy (Pliny, *Nat. Hist.* 8.73.191). In Neo-Sumerian times, natural reddish fleeces were very highly valued, and yellowish wool mentioned occasionally, but black wool was set aside as of lowest value (Waetzoldt 1972, 50–51).

The main event in the evolution of woolliness itself, according to Ryder (1969a, 496), was "a development of the wool at the expense of the kemp." That is, the wool fibers became more numerous, while the heavy kemps became finer hairs or disappeared. Furthermore, the characteristic of molting gradually disappeared with the kemps, a development related to the mode of collecting the wool (ibid., 501). In early times sheep were generally plucked at the time of molting (Ryder 1968, 77; Barber 1975, 296–97; Ryder 1983, 49; and see Chapter 12), a process that gave an extremely fine product, since the hairs and kemps molt a bit later than the wool fibers (Ryder 1969a, 500). Whether the invention of efficient shears with the advent of iron (which is springy: Forbes 1956, 7) prompted herdsmen to select against molting is unclear. But Mesopotamian records show that clipping was the regular mode of obtaining goat hair and an occasional mode of obtaining sheep's wool, from Old Akkadian times (late 3rd millennium) on down (Cross 1937, 25–28, 31, 47; *Chicago Assyrian Dictionary* 1956–, B.97–99 *baqamu* "pluck" and G.59–60 *gazazu* "shear"—the latter is an anachronistic translation for all but the latest texts). So both methods of fleece collection, plucking and cutting, were already known in the Bronze Age.[14] The cut product, however, with its harsher "feel" as a result of the hairs now being included, undoubtedly served as further impetus to develop still finer fleeces. Ryder has found, in fact, that some Bronze Age Scandinavian wool textiles show the fiber distribution expected from plucked wool,

[14] The earliest shears we have are two knives joined by a single U-shaped spring: compare examples from La Tène, France, and from Roman Egypt (Vouga 1923, 69 and pl. 22; Petrie 1917, pl. 58–59) with closely similar ones from Parthian Iran (Egami, Fukai, and Masuda 1966, 22 and pl. 39). Forbes states (1956, 8, without reference) that classical authors placed the invention of shears in Semitic territory.

whereas other examples from the Bronze and Iron Ages show the distribution expected on the sheep itself, that is, from cut wool (Ryder 1969a, 498–502). Furthermore, the early European sheep generally seem to be of the hairy type, like the modern Soay (ibid., 499, 501), whereas by the 2nd century A.D. in Palestine, breeds appeared that included not only medium-wooled but even occasional fine-wooled sheep (Ryder 1964b). From there it was a matter of further development and diffusion of breeds, the story of which has recently been compiled in great detail by Michael Ryder (1983).

OTHER HAIR FIBERS

As a postscript one might add that the hairy coats and/or woolly undercoats of other ruminants have not been ignored by spinners and weavers, those of goats (Pendlebury et al. 1951, 246; Green 1980, 14; Cross 1937, 31; cf. Exodus 26:7) and camels (Ripinsky 1983, 27; Lucas and Harris 1962, 135) being among the more important. These are generally plucked and spun much like sheep's wool, as are the fibers from certain dogs, such as the Samoyed. The spinning of rabbit hair and musk ox (S. Payne, pers. comm. 1984) is reported too. But sheep are unique in the degree of woolliness attained through breeding.

Hair of unusual length has been used, too, especially that from the human head and from horses' manes and tails. Human hair was apparently used as fiber material in a few objects at Naḥal Ḥemar, the 7th-millennium site in the Judaean desert (T. Schick, pers. comm. 1985). And an early example of horsehair came to light in a peat bog at Armoy, Co. Antrim (in N. Ireland). The elaborately woven object—perhaps a belt, but that is not clear—had been used along with a woolen cloth to wrap several metal artifacts datable to the early or mid-first millennium B.C. (Henshall 1950, 134–35). Both warp and weft are described as unspun single hairs of black horsehair woven into a displaced herringbone twill pattern and finished off with fringe and tassels (Fig. 7.6) for what Henshall describes as "an extremely fine and delicate piece of work" (ibid., 138). Finally, from Balabish, an Upper Egyptian site of the Second Intermediate period (early 2nd millennium B.C.), came a small bag described as plaited from the hair of an elephant or a giraffe (Wainwright 1920, 12, 46, 71).

SILK

At least three other fibers achieved some economic importance in the ancient Mediterranean world at some time, but evidently not at such times or places as to fall within the central scope of this book. I will therefore mention them only briefly.

Silk and cotton seem to have been relative latecomers into the Mediterranean, both arriving during early Classical Greek times. Silk we associate with China, although varieties of silkworms grow wild in other parts of the world, including Europe (Leggett 1949, 56). The problem for the weaver is that wild silk, having been broken by the departing moth, is too short and slippery to spin easily. The technological key was the discovery that the cocoon of what developed into the domestic Oriental species, *Bombyx mori*, could be unwound as a whole, producing unbroken threads of as much as a thousand meters, if the larva inside were killed with heat before it partially dissolved and broke the silk on its way out of the cocoon (Geijer [1972] 1979, 4–5; Hess 1958, 226–28, 232). Mythology credits this important discovery to a mid-3rd millennium princess, Si Ling-chi, wife of the pre–Shang Dynasty Emperor Huang Ti (who is himself the major culture-hero of Chinese legend) (Chang 1977, 215–16); and the tradition finds its most picturesque version in the story that a cocoon, falling out of a tree as the princess was taking her leisure in the garden, landed in her cup of tea; whereupon she saw that the hot water was dissolving the hardened gum (the sericin), making it possible for her to unwind the thread unbroken. However that may be, it has been determined that the silk only of *Bombyx*—both the domestic *Bombyx mori* and its wild progenitor, *Bombyx mandarina* Moore, which also grows in China—is of a form strong enough to withstand human usage intact, since it alone is more or less round in cross-section. According to Sylwan (1949, 16), "the thread of all other silkworms is flat and it becomes tangled more easily than the round one," and furthermore, the twin threads exuded simultaneously by these worms, as they harden in the air, "are usually so firmly combined that they do not separate, which happens more easily with the flat silk threads." Thus on two counts, ease of breaking and ease of tangling, the silk from all other species is apparently far less amenable to the kind of treatment that has made Chinese cultivated silk so special.

Our earliest direct evidence for ancient awareness of the silkworm comes in the form of an "artificially cut cocoon" of *Bombyx mori* discovered in the Yang-Shao Neolithic layers of Hsi-yin-ts'un, Shansi Province (Cheng 1960, 241; Li 1977, 58, ref. Li 1930). Then nothing until the Bronze Age, when we see

many casts in the oxidized surfaces of Shang Dynasty bronze pieces of what must have been truly elegant silks: not just plain silk, but pattern-woven fabrics[15] and embroideries, where it is clear that the silk thread is *reeled* (barely twisted from groups of very long fibers) rather than spun (heavily twisted from short fibers) (Sylwan 1937, 120; Sylwan 1949, 15, 19). Incontestably there was already a long tradition behind these Yin-Shang fabrics. For millennia, however, the Chinese aristocracy jealously guarded the secrets of producing domestic silk—the penalty for exporting silkworms or mulberry seeds was death—so that silk products alone were finding their way westward.

One means of westward movement, possibly the main one in the mid-1st millennium B.C. when we obtain our first clear evidence, was in the baggage of Central Asiatic nomads, whom the ancient Chinese frequently bribed with large quantities of woven silk to refrain from destroying Chinese cities (Ssu-ma Ch'ien, *Shih Chi* 110; B. Watson 1961, 166, 170 etc.; Baity 1942, 76; Barber, 1983). Indeed Chinese silk, handsomely embroidered in Chinese designs, came to light in the 5th century B.C. kurgan burials at Pazyryk, in the Altai Mountains (Rudenko 1970, 174–78). Centuries earlier, at Sapalli-tepa in Uzbekistan, silk described as "natural"—i.e., wild?—was laid into graves dated to 1500–1200 B.C. (Kohl 1981, xxi; Askarov 1973, 133–34).

But it has also recently been shown (Hundt 1969) that true silk had made its way to Greece and Western Europe by the mid-first millennium B.C., although before this direct evidence, scholars had debated whether apparent references in Greek literature to silk meant some other fabric alto-

---

[15] Described by Sylwan (1937) as twills, but redescribed by Geijer ([1972] 1979, 110–11) as "a woven pattern of lozenges . . . , in other words, a self-patterned tabby produced by picking up certain warp ends on rods."

gether, or true silk rewoven from imported oriental silks, or wild silk spun from local, native species (Richter 1929; Forbes 1956, 51–54; cf. Weber 1969–70), or even imported textiles spun and woven of the wild silk already well known in India (Hundt 1969, 64). Chemical tests on the scant remains of threads woven and embroidered into a typically local woolen chemise from Hohmichele, in Germany, show that the fiber had to have been domestic Chinese silk, not wild silk (Hundt 1969, 63). The undisturbed tomb in which it was found dates to the late Hallstatt period, about the mid 6th-century B.C. Preliminary inspection of the cloth in another unplundered Hallstatt tomb, at Hochdorf near Stuttgart, suggests that silk may have been used here too (Biel 1980, 438; Wild 1984, 17). By the late 5th century B.C., silk may have made its way a bit farther still to the northwest, since it is reported, though without confirmation, in a tomb at Altrier in Luxembourg (Wild 1984, 17).

What is more, textile remains from a grave firmly dated to the last quarter of the 5th century B.C., in the Athenian Kerameikos cemetery, also proved to be of true silk (Hundt 1969, 66): not just one piece, either, but at least six separate articles! (It is interesting, historically, that the grave is thought to belong to some member of the family of Alcibiades, the wealthy, upper-class, eccentric, and far-travelling roué.) The details of manufacture (ibid., 66–70) suggest that at least some of the pieces were rewoven in Europe—tablet-woven borders, for example, being typical of that region (see Chapters 4, 6, and 7)—although occasional characteristics, such as the virtually non-twisted weft on some cloths, point back to China.

It is possible and even probable, given the references in Greek literature, that local wild silks also came to be used around this time—Leggett (1949, 56) suggests the *Pachypasa* species—perhaps as a cheaper native substitute once the Greek appetite for this soft, filmy fabric had been whetted by a few imports of true silk. Of this we are sure, however: that not until Byzantine times did sericulture with domesticated *Bombyx mori* become an established western industry, based, it seems, on eggs of the Chinese silkworm brought west by a whole series of clandestine smugglings.

COTTON

Cotton, too, was first cultivated outside the Mediterranean area, in this case in India. What we generally know as "cotton" comes from the fibers attached to the seeds of certain plants, in particular those of the genus *Gossypium*, of the mallow family, although other such seed fibers are sometimes loosely included in the term. Directly identifiable fibers of *Gossypium* as well as numerous textile impressions have been found at Mohenjo Daro and Harappa (Allchin 1969, 325). John Marshall, the excavator of Mohenjo Daro, reports that the remaining fibers from a cloth used to wrap a silver vase came "from a plant closely related to *Gossypium arboreum*," not from a wild species, a fact that he says "disposes finally of the idea that the fine Indian cotton known to Babylonians as *sindhu* and to the Greeks as *sindōn* was a product of the cotton-tree and not a true cotton" (Marshall [1931] 1973, 33).[16] Although he dates the find to about 3000 B.C. (ibid., 194), current chronology would put it well into the 3rd millennium. Farther south in the Indian con-

---

[16] For a thoroughgoing analysis of the linguistics of cotton worldwide, see Johnson and Decker 1980.

tinent, thread dated to the second half of the 2nd millennium B.C. has been found that was made of cotton mixed with silk (Allchin 1969, 326), presumably one of the local wild silks.

The substance seems not to have reached the northern shores of the Mediterranean until early Classical times, coming perhaps chiefly by way of Egypt, which had obtained it from India a little earlier, although Sennacherib too, around 700 B.C., boasts of "trees bearing wool" in his royal Assyrian botanical gardens (Oppenheim 1967, 245; *Chicago Assyrian Dictionary* 1956–, I.217 *isu*: d). Herodotus describes a corselet worked with cotton and gold that was sent to Athena as an offering by the pharaoh Amasis in the 6th century B.C. (3.47), and mentions that this fiber is grown in India on trees (3.106). He appears to consider it as much a novelty for textiles as hemp or silk. One example of cotton fabric, however, has actually turned up in a 5th-century archaeological context: at Trakhones, in Attica (Zisis 1955, 590–91). Aware that a kind of native cotton now grows on Samos and other Aegean islands, the investigator of this cloth checked the possibility that the ancient cotton might be local. He found that the wild sort is so fine, however, that what thread could be made from it is too weak and fine to be used for anything other than embroidery onto a stronger base fabric. Furthermore, he could find no evidence for *Gossypium* itself having grown in Greece; and since the fibers of the cloth were evidently specifically *Gossypium*, he concluded that the material must indeed have been imported (ibid., 592).

The technology of cotton also differs considerably from that of wool and bast fibers. The hairs are so short and delicate as to require a special method of spinning, namely with a small, light spindle fully supported so as not to put weight on the half-formed thread and break it. Cool and absorbent like the bast fibers, but without their sheen, cotton dyes easily, unlike bast. The people of India seem to have begun early to dye it (Allchin 1969, 325), and this may have been one of its great attractions to the white-garbed Egyptians. From Egypt and Arabia it seems then to have passed to the North Mediterranean in the mid-first millennium.

ESPARTO

The third miscellaneous fiber of archaeological interest to us is esparto grass. Botanically this includes two different plants of the grass family, *Stipa tenacissima* (also known by the Arabic name *halfa* or its French equivalent *alfa*) and *Lygeum spartum* (*false alfa*), which grow in dry, sandy areas of southern Spain and northern Africa (Kirby 1963, 423). (The term "halfa" adds confusion to the picture, because it too is used for more than one plant, e.g., *Desmostachya bipinnata* [Lucas and Harris 1962, 134].) The Egyptians experimented freely with the fibers of these and other fibrous plants (including palm) in the 4th millennium B.C., although mostly for rope and other cordage, or for mats and baskets (Lucas and Harris 1962, 134–35). Late in the 2nd millenium B.C., a type of esparto was evidently still used for the smaller baskets among Tutankhamon's effects (Crowfoot 1954, 422–23).

In late Neolithic and Bronze Age Spain, however, where there was little choice in the fibers available, esparto grass was used for a wide range of products. Thick deposits of bat guano seem to have been responsible for the preservation of a remarkable find in the Cueva de los Murciélagos, in Andalucia. Here were found baskets, sandals, bags, caps, and even full tunics and a necklace, all of esparto; some objects were plaited, others woven, still others twined in a variety of techniques (de Góngora y Martinez 1868, 31, 34–35, pl. I, II). Unfortunately, as the author of the account bitterly complains (ibid., 36–37), the discoverers of the more than sixty burials in the cave thoroughly destroyed the site in their quest for marketable minerals, so that stratigraphy and many other details were hopelessly lost. Experts have come to date the group to the end of the local Neolithic (Melida 1929, 32), that is, late in the 3rd millennium B.C. (Baroja 1957, 28).

Evidence suggests that the industry was the same in prehistoric, Roman, and relatively modern times. The leaves are pulled, so as to leave intact the tuft-like plant, which may live half a century (Kirby 1963, 424). Pliny reports (*Nat. Hist.* 19.7.26–31) that in his time (as later) the leaves were then dried and retted much like flax, although in seawater. Rope of this fiber was evidently widely in demand for ship rigging, and the locals, he says, used it for many commodities, of which he gives a list strikingly similar to the inventory of the Cueva de los Murciélagos, including clothing. Esparto is used to this day for cordage and paper, but is still plucked from the wild stands: it has never been really domesticated (Kirby 1963, 424–25). For this reason it is undoubtedly safe to assume that it was essentially unused outside its native regions of southern Spain and northern Africa before the export trade of Classical times.

FROM the archaeological portions of the foregoing summaries, one can compile rough maps of the areas in which the various fibers were used for textiles at various times (Fig. 1.8). In some ways, the most informative period to display on such a map is the 3rd millennium, because it shows the strong areas of local development of fibers just before the

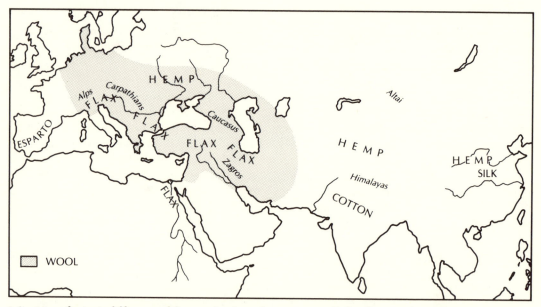

1.8   Map of principal fibers used for weaving in prehistoric times (3rd millennium). Areas for vegetable fibers are labeled; wool territory is shaded

upheavals and major realignments of trade associated with the Bronze Age quests for metals. From a map thus compiled from much widespread data, one can then read back the status of smaller areas that may themselves be poor in data.

We see, for example, that both flax and wool were as abundantly available in the Bronze Age Aegean as the inhabitants cared to make them, although textile evidence there is scant. The 8000 and more spindle whorls found at Bronze Age Troy can't have been there for nothing; nor were the spindle whorls that are so common at Neolithic Aegean sites made in the absence of fibers to spin. Throughout the Neolithic, flax had been present in Greece and widely used for textiles in Central Europe (cf. Bronze Age botanical evidence at Lerna: Hopf 1961, 241–43; 1962, 1, 4); and domestic sheep, too, had been raised in the Aegean since early Neolithic, the specifically woolly varieties being available at least from the beginning of the Bronze Age (cf. Fig. 1.9). Silk, cotton, and esparto, although used elsewhere in quantity at that time, were surely not available here, and hemp and nettle probably not either. Nonetheless, the Bronze Age inhabitants of the Aegean, like everyone else in southern Europe and the Near East, clearly had behind them a long and rich tradition of obtaining textile fibers.

1.9   Minoan bowl containing clay models of a shepherd and his flock of sheep. From Palaikastro, Crete; early 2nd millennium B.C. (Iraklion Museum no. 2903; Bosanquet and Dawkins 1923, pl. 7)

THE ARCHAEOLINGUISTICS
OF HEMP

Once the archaeology of hemp is understood from the material collected in Chapter 1, much of the linguistics untangles itself rather nicely, and adds new details in turn to the archaeological picture. People all across the middle latitudes of Europe and Asia—and that would include the early Indo-Europeans (IE's)—knew and were using hemp since 5000 B.C. So when IE groups started borrowing a new word four millennia later, it had to have been for a new use: drugs. The old northern varieties of hemp did not contain the narcotic THC; and the 2nd millennium was probably the first time that enough people were travelling *back and forth* between Iran (where it grew) and eastern Europe that they could spread a *habit*, along with its source, the THC-bearing hemp. And the early 1st-millennium B.C. is just when we begin to find evidence for pot-smoking in the new zone.

The spread of the word is seen most easily by looking at the sequence backwards. The Finns, at the northwest corner of the continent, borrowed their words for hemp from their IE neighbors to the south: Finn. *kaneppi*, Eston. *kanep*, borrowed from Baltic (Vasmer [1950–58] 1964–73, 2.312), and later, Finn. *hamppu* from North Germanic (Kluge 1975, 288). The Balts, however, had borrowed their own form (giving Lith. *kanãpės*, Latv. *kaṇepe*, O.Prus. *knapios*) from

their southern neighbors, the Slavs, who must have been living rather near to where we first pick hemp up in the European archaeological record. All of these forms, including Slavic (Rus. *konopljá*, Bulg. *konop*, Cz. *konopĕ*, etc.), show a **p*.

Latin, in the southwest, however, borrowed its form(s) *cannabis* (Vulgar Latin **can(n)abum*, **canaba*) from Greek. We saw that the Greeks, in turn, acquired their κάν-ναβις (*kannabis*) from northeastern neighbor(s)—Thracians? Scythians?—around the 5th century B.C. In Germanic, all the words (OE *hænep*, ON *hampr*, Gm. *der Hanf*) go back to **hanap-*, which by Grimm's Law would come from a form **kanab-*. But Grimm's consonant shift occurred, as other loans tell us, before the chief Romano-Germanic contact; nor would Roman hemp, a very minor rope industry at best, seem to have constituted a prized early commodity in a land full of flax, wool—and hemp (although Scythian narcotic might have!). So a Roman source (as Vasmer would have it: [1950–58] 1964–73, 2.312) is very unlikely. That leaves the hypothesis that the Germanic peoples learned a new kind of hemp, and a word for it with a **b* in it, from the same source as the Greeks (perhaps through someone living in between—but not the Slavs, who have the **p* form). (Armenian *kanap'* and Albanian *kanëp* [Kluge 1975, 288] don't help much.)

Schematically we have:

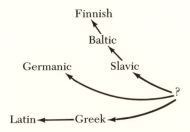

The direction of movement and the dating are clear and consistent; and the loans seem to be coming from forms of the shape *kan(n)aB-* (where *B* stands for some kind of labial stop). As for ending, there is so much variation that each language seems to be concocting its own—possibly to ease the strange phonological shape, if the original language had *no* ending.

The next question is who is at the center of the fan, ca. 1000 B.C. And from whom did the IE groups borrow their word, which already had developed into two forms (with *p* and *b*)?

Our first documented users of this drug, the Scythians, spoke Iranian dialects; and Indo-Iranian is interesting in having not one but two words for hemp. One is represented by Sanskrit *śaṇá-* 'kind of hemp' (*ś-* from a velar stop perceived as palatal, followed either by *a*, or by *e* which then merged with *a*: *k̂ana-*, *k̂ene-*); the other by Skt. *bhaṅgá-* (coming to us as modern Anglo-Indian *bang*) 'narcotic hemp, hashish; hallucinogen'—on the face of it unrelated to *kan(n)aB-*. But note that the word for narcotic hemp is merely a reversal of the other, with labial first and velar last. This must have to do with the fact, well documented in ethnographic data (see P. Barber 1988), that two of the most common ways of gaining access to the spirit world are by taking hallucinogenic drugs (soma, peyote, jimson, hashish, etc.) and by doing things in reverse (since re-flections and shadows were thought to be the images of spirits, people worldwide have concluded that the spirit world is reversed from ours). The documented backwards activities include linguistic ones (e.g., the Black Mass is a mass said backwards), and this is almost certainly another example: here an "efficacious" or "descriptive" reversal, to help out or simply describe the drug that takes one to the awesome world of the spirits—a previously unnoted way of deforming language. (See also Flattery and Schwartz 1988, 123-28 for a long linguistic discussion coming from the drug side.)

Seeing, then, that all these IE words came out of the same hopper, we can turn to the next major family to the east, Uralo-Altaic. No common Uralic word is known; but Cheremis preserves a word *keṅe, kiṅe* 'hemp' that looks remarkably like the labial-less Sanskrit form (Liddell and Scott 1968, 874, who add Ziryene *piš*). The only common Finno-Ugric word for such a plant (Vogul *polna* 'hemp', etc.: Collinder 1977, 121) seems to be equally usable for any fiber plant—hemp, nettle, or flax—and is embedded in a vocabulary layer that shows almost no technological advancement beyond the Mesolithic: hunting, gathering, food-storage; spinning, sewing, and net-making; and also reindeer herding(?) and milking (ibid., 94, 138), but no terms for agriculture, domestic animals and their breeding (including 'wool/ram/wether': ibid., 144), or metals, all of which appear as loans in the next layer of borrowing.

Western Altaic seems to perpetuate the same root with a different, non-labial suffix: Chuvash *kantăr*, Old Tk. *käntir*, and *kendir* in modern Turkic languages from Tuva to Istanbul; while the labial is seen again in Karakalpak *kenep* and Tk. *kenevir* (Tk. *benk* 'narcotic hemp' was borrowed from Persian).

Eastern Altaic is easiest to assess in tabular form:

Evenki	*onokto*	Manchu	*olo, x̯unta*
Negidal	*xontaxa*	Mongol	*oloson,*
			olasun
Orochi	*onokto*	Khalkha	*ol(son)*
Nanai	*onokto, x̯ontax̯a*	Buriat	*ulhan,*
			ylteneg
Ulchi	*onokto, x̯untax̯a*		

Each form outside of the Manchu *olo* seems to have a suffix of some sort; and the variant *xon-, xun-*, minus its suffix, begins to look suspiciously like a version of our **ken-, *kan-* word. Could it be that such a morpheme spread over much of Asia *with the hemp-plant* and its use for fiber and/or food in the late Palaeolithic and/or early Neolithic? In that case it was an enlarged version of this very word, local to Iran and perhaps northern India, that spread with the drug-bearing variety early in the Iron Age.

Still farther east, Chinese 麻 *má* 'hemp' (Old Chinese **mrar*) would seem to be outside the linguistic conspiracy (as is Tibetan, which borrowed its words late from Indic). But the Chinese evidence also proves a knowledge of the narcotic properties of *Cannabis* at least from the 1st millennium B.C., when the character, which pictures plants under a roof (i.e., hung up to dry, for fiber), first appears in the surviving records; for it is used already with a *secondary* meaning of "numbness" or "senseless" (Li 1974a, 297–98; Li 1983, 32). (Such a strong drug, however, suggests that the Chinese pharmacists had now obtained from far to the southwest not THC-bearing *Cannabis sativa* but *Cannabis indica*, so strong it knocks you out cold—wonderful for Chinese surgeons but useless for talking to spirits—and quite devoid of usable fiber [R. Schultes, pers. comm. 1987].)

In sum it is quite clear that the fiber use developed in the north and rather early, but the drug use started to the south and spread much later. These conclusions are multiply supported by the botany, archaeology, and linguistics. Further corroboration of the late date of the second spread comes from Neo-Assyrian cuneiform texts, where a word *qunnabu* (*qunnapu, qunubu, qunbu*) begins to turn up, for a source of oil, fiber and medicine, in the second quarter of the 1st millennium B.C. (Scheil 1921, 97; Meissner 1932–33; Oppenheim 1967, 245 n. 45; *Chicago Assyrian Dictionary* 1956–, Q.306 *qunnabu*). (Frisk [1960–72, 779 *kannabis*] and others wish to add a "Sumerian" [sic] plant-word *kunibu* to the heap of cognates; but the compilers of the *Chicago Assyrian Dictionary* [1956–, K.539 *kunipḫu = kunibu, kunipu*] feel that the internal textual evidence places this plant in the onion/garlic family.)[1]

---

[1] My sincere thanks to Jerry Norman for supplying most of the Mongol-Manchu-Tungus data and for helping with the Chinese forms.

CHAPTER 2

SPINNING

Natural fibers, once obtained, must be made into thread in order to be used for weaving; and they or the finished products may also be bleached, dyed, felted, and fulled. We have, then, not one but half a dozen textile crafts to consider, all of which began sometime in antiquity and had become full-fledged, separate industries by Roman times, as we know both from the descriptions by Pliny the Elder and from the remains of shops at Pompeii. To come to understand the craft traditions inherited by these later weavers, we must again explore the earlier and geographically wider archaeological evidence for each. As with the fibers, we will be plagued with the question of what may, might, and can't show up in the archaeological remains, and our conclusions will take the form of a range of probabilities, anchored by certainties wherever conclusive data exist.

TWISTED THREAD

Thread or cordage of some sort almost certainly came first among the textile arts. In the Upper Palaeolithic, especially in the Gravettian and Magdalenian cultures, we have a variety of clues that cordage was known: projectile points and other implements come to have shanks that require binding onto the shaft (Clark 1952, 226; Cole 1970, 47), and needles appear, some with eyes that are quite fine (Clark and Piggott 1965, 74, 99, 146; Forbes 1956, 151, 175). The Gravettians also liked ornaments composed of perforated stone, shells, teeth, fish vertebrae and such, strung into necklaces and bracelets (Clark and Piggott 1965, 78–79; Coles and Higgs 1969, 298; Clark 1952, 227). In one cave burial, in the Grotte des Enfants in southern France, four neat rows of pierced shells were found across the skull of a young man, while the old woman interred with him wore bracelets made of double strings of the same kind of shell, *Nassa neritea* (Verneau 1906, 29–30 and pl. 2). To have held such an exact position in parallel rows on the man's head, the shells must either have been sewn onto a cap or headband, or else have been strung onto a hairnet. Quantities of shell and tooth beads were found in many of the other Gravettian burials in the area, in positions suggesting bracelets, necklaces, headgear, and even decorated clothing (ibid., 29–36, and 27 fig. 3; Clark and Piggott 1965, 78).

None of this tells us what the people were using to make their string, or how they made it—only that humans had already learned to use cordage in a number of ways, and that some of the thread was quite fine. It could have been made of gut, sinew, or other stringy body parts. Indeed, the modern Lapps are reported to make very fine thread out of twisted strands of sinew (Forbes 1956, 175). To discover the origins of the textile crafts, however, we would want to know when humans discovered the principle that fine, breakable, and even short fibers could be formed into very strong, long, and supple threads by being twisted together.

We now have at least two pieces of evidence that this important principle of twisting for strength dates to the Palaeolithic. In 1953, the Abbé Glory was investigating floor deposits in a steep corridor of the famed Lascaux caves in southern France, when a lump of clay and calcite that he picked up from the cutting one night broke open in his hand to reveal the cast of a long piece of Palaeolithic cord. Painstaking analysis showed that the cord, of which we have about 30 cm (now in five pieces), had been neatly twisted in the S direction (see below) from three Z-plied strands of vegetable fiber, to a thickness of 6 to 8 mm (Glory 1959, 137–46 and figs. 1–6). The undisturbed layer to which it belongs seems to date to no later than 15,000 B.C. (Arlette Leroi-Gourhan 1982, 110 with photo). Unfortunately, the process of humification was so advanced in the specimen that it was not possible to determine the exact source of the fibers; but they seemed most probably to have been some sort of bast (Glory 1959, 149–50).

Some 5000 years earlier, however, we have a clear representation of twisted string on one of the well-known Palaeolithic "Venus" figures. At least two of the Venuses found so far are shown wearing a sort of garment known as a "string skirt," which consists of a belt band from which numerous strings hang down to form a skirt or apron. Bronze Age examples of such skirts have actually been dug up in Denmark (see Chapters 6, 11). The Venus from Lespugue, in the Pyrenees, wears hers only in the back (Fig. 2.1); but on each string the carver has clearly

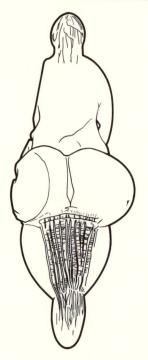

2.1 Palaeolithic "Venus" figure, wearing a skirt of twisted string. From Lespugue, France; ca. 20,000 B.C. (Courtesy of Musée de l'Homme, Paris)

shown with little incisions the twists of the cords (cf. Hochberg 1979, 10), and has shown as well the bottom end of each twisted string fraying out into a mass of loose fibers (not possible for, e.g., a twisted piece of gut or sinew). The Venus figures from both eastern and western Europe seem to fall in the period from late Gravettian through Solutrean (André Leroi-Gourhan 1968, 90–96). With their evidence for string skirts and hairnets, these figures seem to carry on the tradition of string use we saw in the Gravettian graves. We should therefore be correct in assuming that twisted fiber string has been known since the Gravettian period, before 20,000 B.C.; and we can prove for a fact that it was known by 15,000 B.C.

The question of what materials were first used for twisted fiber thread has been the source of an old controversy. Based on their practical experience of the various fibers, modern handspinners have felt compelled to assume that wool was the first fiber mankind would have spun into thread. We know that the exploitation of silk and cotton was fairly late (4th millennium—compared with the 7th or 8th millennium at least, for some other fibers), leaving animal wool or hair and bast fibers as the prime candidates. To obtain bast fibers from plant stems or leaves, one must go through the long, complicated, and laborious process of retting, hackling, etc. before one can form them into thread; whereas wool can be pulled from the back of a woolly beast and spun immediately, with no further processing than perhaps straightening out a few tangles with the fingers. Furthermore, the draft-spinning of flax or hemp is itself not particularly easy, compared to the spinning of wool. And, on top of all this, wool tends to roll up into long strings on the flanks of a molting sheep or goat (Ryder 1964a, 293; and Ryder 1983, 736, both with photographs), as if to say to the world, "Here I am: ready-made string." The availability of fibers hidden within a plant stem is by no means so immediately obvious.

The archaeologists, on the other hand, keep pointing out that whenever early thread or string is discovered, of which the fiber can be accurately determined, it turns out to be bast—usually flax. We have mentioned the Çatal Hüyük and Naḥal Ḥemar fabrics from before 6000 B.C., the long line of Egyptian textiles beginning around 4500, and the Swiss Neolithic cloth from the 4th and early 3rd millennia. To the early end of this list we can add the Palaeolithic plant-fiber rope, probably bast, from Lascaux; and some Mesolithic (Maglemosian) fragments of nets, found at Korpilahti in Finland. The strings for the Mesolithic netting were twisted into a "two-threaded cord, almost certainly of willow bast" (J.G.D. Clark 1952, 227; Kujala 1947–48), and probably date to the late 8th millennium B.C. (Rimantienė 1979, 27). Clark (1952) and Rimantienė (1979) list several other finds of early bast-fiber nets from the far north: from Lake Ladoga, from northeastern Estonia, and from Lithuania, all dating from the 4th millennium or earlier, and generally made of linden bast (see also Indreko 1948, 324–28 and fig. 79 no. 6—from Siivertsi; Äyräpää 1950, 6–7 and fig. 4f—from Antrea/Korpilahti; Rimantienė 1979, 26–28, 75–78 and figs. 19–20, 59–62—from Šventoji).

The solution to the craftsmen's objections concerning the practical difficulties of using bast—especially flax—before wool for the spinning of thread seems to lie in an important detail in the process of spinning. To understand this detail, we must understand the craft as a whole. This understanding, in turn, will help us comprehend the evolution of the tools for spinning, which form a major class of our archaeological evidence for the craft.

Spinning, Drafting, and Splicing

Spinning, technically speaking, involves both twisting and drawing out (or *drafting*) the fibers of the raw material into a thread. Since spinning is no longer the daily household task that it used to be, we now think of the word *spin* as meaning simply "to twirl," but originally the root had much more to do with the notion of drawing out or stretching from one place to another (as in English *span*, or the phrase *spin a tale*). The two aspects, the twisting and the drawing or drafting, can be achieved in various ways.

Thread can be spun with no tools at all, simply by using the fingers to draw out and twist the fibers, perhaps on the thigh or leg as a handy working surface. The method has two disadvantages, however. The twisting process is tediously slow, since each movement of the fingers gives only a few twists to the strands. Moreover, there is a serious problem of keeping the finished part of the yarn from tangling, untwisting, or performing any of an amazing variety of nasty feats the moment you let go of any of it to make more; and let go you must when the yarn reaches arm's length. The thread has to stay constantly under tension until the twist has been permanently set, for example by wetting or plying.[1]

Spindle Types and Spinning

The standard solution, world over, has been some sort of spindle, exactly because it helps with both problems at once. Twirling a spindle with thread attached is much faster than twisting the thread itself; and the spindle can also act as a neat packaging device for the finished thread, wound up under tension. In fact—to view the question from the other side—any package of completed thread *must* either twirl with the newly forming thread, or else be detached so as not to interfere with the spinning process (cf. Fannin 1970, 9; A. F. Barker 1936, 104). If the package is then not merely allowed but forced to turn in order to help twist the newly forming yarn, it becomes the dual-purpose implement known as the spindle.

A stick or a rock will do. Montell (1941, 114) describes camel drivers in Inner Mongolia using a rock as a suspended spinning device to make a length of string needed on the spot, and yanking the raw material as needed from the back of a shedding camel

(see ibid., pl. I.3). Spinning-sticks were used in Scandinavia until this century (Hochberg 1980, 24). And Crowfoot (1931, 10–14) tells how spinners in the Sudan used simple sticks, sometimes with a hook on the end, which they turned in the hand with a rapid motion "as indescribable as the movement of the hand of a skilled milker" (ibid., 10). Such spinning-sticks may well be depicted on an early 3rd-millennium vase from Tell Agrab in Mesopotamia (Fig. 2.2; see also Amiet 1961, 104). In these drawings, the otherwise pecu-

2.2   Restored design, showing three spinners(?), on an Early Dynastic vase from Tell Agrab in Mesopotamia; early 3rd millennium. (After Delougaz 1952, pl. 12)

liar angles at which the arms, fingers, round ball (of unspun fluff?), and straight line (stick? thread?) are held correspond well to the attitude of a spinner, but seem quite strange for someone holding a heavy, inert object like a mirror or hitting on a noise-maker. (Also, the plants to the left may be generic, but they look remarkably like flax.)

To achieve control over the fineness and evenness of the yarn, one must draw and twist the fibers simultaneously and with some speed. But the spindle absorbs enough

[1] Threads are often *plied* (from French *plier*, "to bend, double over"), forming a heavier yarn. If you take a few fibers, twist them thoroughly, and then let go, you discover that they instantly either untwist or roll up in a tangle. The simplest way to prevent both these undesirable occurrences is to catch the thread in the middle, bending one end back (still under tension) until it touches the other end, and then let go of the middle. The thread will twist quickly but briefly in the opposite direction from that in which it was spun, forming a doubled thread. But then you can safely let go of it; it will neither untwist nor tangle. (It is possible by other methods to ply the thread in either direction, and with more than two strands.)

of the work of twisting to free one hand for this constant drafting, as well as for speeding the twist and prolonging the time of continuous twisting.

Sticks are perhaps easier to wind onto, but hanging rocks make better flywheels and are thus much faster (if more awkward) for the spinning itself. Crowfoot notes (1931, 11) how much faster the Sudanese women could spin with their plain sticks when there was more yarn on them to give momentum. So a still more efficient tool comes of combining the stick and the stone—the shaft and the flywheel (cf. Hochberg 1980, 25). In practice, of course, the shaft can be made of wood, bone, ivory, or metal, and the little flywheel (or *spindle whorl*) can be made of any of those materials or of something heavier, like stone or clay. The whorl can be fastened near the bottom of the shaft, so the spindle can be set spinning by a flick of the thumb and fingers, like a top (a *low-whorl spindle*); or it can be placed near the upper end, in which case the spindle is set spinning by being rolled up or down the leg with one open hand (a *high-whorl spindle*). In either case, the spindle may be supported as it twirls, its end resting on the ground or in a cup; or the spindle may spin free, hanging from the thread wound up on it (a *drop-spindle*), the weight of the spindle aiding further in drafting the fibers (Fig. 2.3). Sometimes, as in parts of the Middle East even today, the spindle is set on the ground and twirled with the toes (Weir 1970, cover).

Speed is not the only factor involved, however, in the evolution or choice of a spindle. Cotton fibers are so short, slippery, and fine that they tend to draw out too fast with the weight of even a light drop-spindle. A very light supported spindle weighing an ounce or less is the most frequently used tool. Using such equipment, the hand-spinners of India were able to stretch a single pound of cotton into well over 200 miles of thread, a feat not

2.3   Modern Greek peasant woman winding up newly made thread while spinning with a low-whorl drop-spindle. Her distaff is stuck into her belt to free her hands for manipulating the fibers and the spindle. (Drawing by M. Stone after photos by author)

possible on the best of modern machinery (Hochberg 1980, 18; Forbes 1956, 156). Tunisian weavers, on the other hand, spin their weft thread on low-whorl spindles but their warp thread on high-whorl spindles, because warp thread takes all the strain and friction of the weaving process and so must be especially strong, even, and tightly spun. The hard twist imparted by the long roll down the thigh seems to give a superior product for this special purpose (cf. Crowfoot 1931, 31).

Another consideration is length. Crowfoot reports (1931, 13–14) that Trans-Jordanian women who knew several quite different methods of spinning preferred to use the *hand-held spindle* (a stick with or without whorl, turned within the hand; Fig. 2.4) for their short clippings of goat hair, but the suspended or the supported spindle for their sheep's wool, which was significantly longer. Indeed, when Mrs. Crowfoot asked some Sudanese women to spin some long "pure bred" sheep's wool with their hand-held spindles (they knew no other method), "the

2.4 Bedouin woman spinning with a hand-held spindle, from a pile of fibers on ground in front of her. (Pencil sketch by F. Goodall, ca. 1858; courtesy of Trustees of the British Museum)

women complained that the wool was too long and that it was almost impossible for them to spin it" (ibid., 13). With a longer-staple wool, one tends to need both hands free to draw out the fibers, but with fibers such as these women had, it was found more efficient to manage and support the spindle with the right hand "while the left hand just flicks up the short tufts of hair into the growing thread" (ibid., 14). Crowfoot quotes an onlooker describing the magical effect of watching an amorphous cloud of fluff on the ground materialize into an ever-growing thread under the flicking fingers and stretching arm, as though something were being created out of nothing (ibid., 11).

The various known methods of producing thread have been classified by Crowfoot (1931, 8) according to how she believes they must have developed structurally, one from another. In the most primitive of these methods, done with no spindle of any sort, the processes of obtaining length and twist

are quite separate steps. But simpler still is the situation in which the fibers as they come from nature are considered long enough to do the job for which the string is being made, and only twist need be applied. Silk, with its natural filaments hundreds of meters long, obviously needed no drafting once the trick of unwinding the cocoon was discovered. All it needed was just enough twist to make the several component strands stay together. For each of the purposes for which we see string being used in the Palaeolithic, however, a meter or so of string would probably have been enough. Bast fibers of this length are not hard to obtain.

Another Way of Making Thread

In this light, it is productive to investigate the technique of thread-making in the one ancient land in which we have lots of solid evidence, namely Egypt. Twisted thread is known from actual samples to have existed in Egypt at least as early as the 5th millennium in the Neolithic settlements of the Faiyum (Caton-Thompson and Gardner 1934, 90). But late in the 3rd millennium, in the tombs of the Middle Kingdom, we find a rich series of representations of the craft: as wall paintings, for example, in the 12th-Dynasty tombs of Baqt (Fig. 2.5), Khety (Fig. 2.10, 13.1), and Khnumhotep (Fig. 2.40, and Newberry 1893, pl. 29) at Beni Hasan, and of Djehutihetep at el-Bersheh (Fig. 3.8); and as a model from an 11th-Dynasty tomb at Thebes (see Fig. 3.6; Winlock 1920, 22 and fig. 13; Roth and Crowfoot 1921; Winlock 1955, 88–89 and pl. 24–27). One of the clearest representations is in the late 11th-Dynasty tomb of Daga, at Thebes (Fig. 2.6).[2]

---

[2] Cf. Crowfoot 1931, 14–32; Müller-Karpe 1974, vol. 3, pt. 3, 138, 142, 148, 120. Other representations include a wooden model from Geniemhet's tomb at Saqqara, ca. 2200 B.C., now in the Ny Carlsberg Glyptotek, Copenhagen; and paintings in Theban Tomb 104 (Crowfoot 1931, 14–16 and fig. 4) at Thebes, from the 18th Dynasty. Lucas and Harris (1962, 140) list yet others. (Khnumhotep = Khnemhotep = Chnemhotep; Djehutihetep = Tehuti-hetep; etc.)

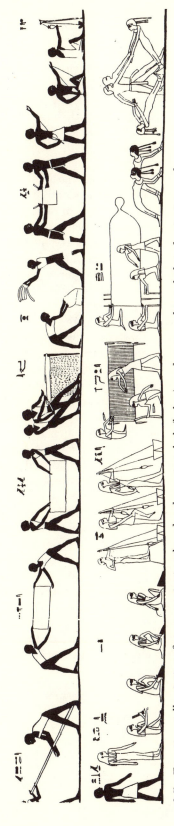

2.5 Egyptian wall painting of women spinning thread and weaving cloth (below), and men washing cloth and spinning cord (above). Middle Kingdom tomb of Baqt at Beni Hasan (no. 15). (Newberry 1894, pl. 4)

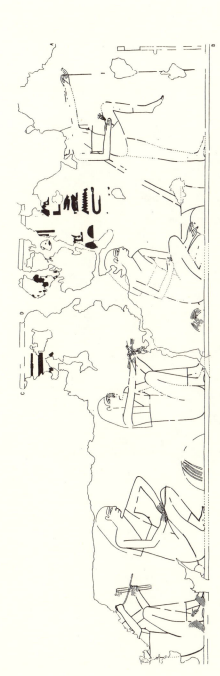

2.6 Women working flax, from a wall of the Middle Kingdom tomb of Daga at Thebes (no. 103); 12th Dynasty. The 1st and 3rd women appear to be removing the woody parts and separating the fibers of the flax stalks; the 2nd and 4th women are splicing the fibers into long continuous threads, which they roll or pile behind themselves; the 5th woman is using spindles to add twist to the already-formed threads she is pulling from a bowl. (Davies 1913, pl. 37; courtesy of the Committee of the Egypt Exploration Society)

At the start of the sequences we typically see women preparing the flax fibers—apparently "mangling" the individual retted stalks between two sticks, as a sort of scutching process to break the fibers loose from the woody part; and using the fingers to comb apart(?) the fine strands, which are then hand-spliced end-to-end a few at a time. The result is wound into a huge ball or coil (Davies 1913, 34–35; Crowfoot 1931, 9, 16, 22).

2.7 Eighteenth Dynasty Egyptian spindle. The thread groove beyond the whorl at the short end proves that it is here displayed and photographed upside down. (British Museum no. 4677; photo courtesy of Trustees of the British Museum)

The balls, placed in pots for tension and probably for wetting,[3] are then twisted into a tighter, stronger thread by women and occasionally men, who use high-whorl spindles, sometimes grasped but usually dropped (Roth and Crowfoot 1921, 98). Many complete examples of these spindles have been found (Fig. 2.7). The drop-spindle is set twirling by a roll with the right hand along the thigh (the knee evidently is lifted for each roll), and then let go. In some paintings the spinners stand on platforms so that the spindle can drop farther and hence twist a longer thread before it is stopped for the wind-up. Sometimes the spinners are shown working from two or more balls at once. Where they have only one spindle, one might assume they are plying the thread (but see below). In other cases they are shown working two spindles at once, a trick possible only for someone very skillful who is also spinning very carefully prepared fibers. The fact that the flax has been pre-formed (without a spindle) into a coherent thread by the women preparing the balls—often two such preparers are shown for each spindle-operator—in itself accounts for the possibility of such a feat (Davies 1913, 34; Crowfoot 1931, 23).

The difficulty that many modern scholars have had in understanding the Egyptian method of thread-making stems from the fact that we ourselves—peasants, handcrafters, industrial machines, and all—do it so differently. By our method, the carefully fluffed-up fibers are paid out a few at a time into the newly forming thread, so that their ends overlap everywhere, and cohesion is caused by the twisting together. This is *draft-spin-*

---

[3] See below, under "Bowls and Baskets." Flax is normally spun wet, because it is much less brittle and therefore handles much better in that condition. On a Classical Greek red-figure vase from Orvieto, a spinner is shown with the thread in her mouth (Blümner 1877,

pl. 6), much as Crowfoot describes women spinning flax "through the mouth" in modern Egypt (Crowfoot 1931, 33), although, with so short a distaff, the Greek girl may be biting snarls out of wool yarn.

ning. "Das Geheimnis der Spinnerei," the secret of spinning (by this method), according to an aged German farm-mistress around the turn of this century, is entirely in the preparation of the flax rove from which one spins; and when this is done properly "das Garn [läuft] in der gewünschten Stärke ganz von selbst heraus" (the yarn runs out in the desired thickness quite of its own accord; Orth 1922, 66). This "magic" is possible only because the fibers are slipping past each other, so that the ends of the individual fibers all come at different places—there are no splice points. The method seems already to have been prevalent north of the Mediterranean in the Neolithic period; at any rate I have not been able to find any evidence that the early northern textile yarns were *not* drafted continuously.[4] It is also the way peasants all over Europe have traditionally spun in our era.

The Egyptians, on the contrary, were not paying out the fibers continuously, but were splicing together the ends of pre-formed "strings"—fiber bundles two or three feet long, stripped from the flax stalks—so that the ends of the ultimate fibers overlapped in bunches and only at considerable intervals (Fig. 2.8). These splices have often been noted by examiners—although not always recognized for what they were. Louisa Bellinger, whose experience comes from trying to clean and restore ancient textiles, explains the process from the point of view of its product. A strong linen sheet, she says (1959b, 1; 1962, 7), is typically made of thread in which three fine strands of flax

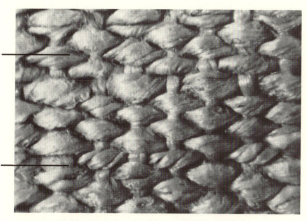

2.8 Magnified photo of splices in typical dynastic Egyptian linen

have been twisted together. Each strand consisted of lengths of fiber whose ends were overlapped by a few centimeters, and which then were twisted at the splice just enough that it would hold temporarily (Fig. 2.9). Then three of these long single strands were twisted together, in such a way that the rather evenly-spaced splice points in one strand would come at different places in the final thread than the splices of each of the other strands.[5] Wherever "two straight pieces of flax were spun with a twisted splice in the third roving the resulting length of yarn looks as though it were plied, for the splice keeps to itself and is slightly separated

2.9 Schematic representation of a linen splice (black and white threads), with another strand running parallel (grey)

order that the splices would always come at the same interval, and hence never fall at the same point as another splice. I have not had usable Egyptian materials readily available to me to test this interesting idea. Nor will it be easy to test, since on only her second try Hochberg was able to produce for me a flax splice so tidy as to be all but invisible. How invisible were the splices of skilled Egyptians?

from the other strands. Each length of yarn in which there is no splice looks, at a casual glance, like a single yarn spun from a single roving" (Bellinger 1959b, 1). Such a configuration is so unusual to European spinners that it evidently gave rise to the earlier "assumption that the weft was put in as separate short pieces, [because] some of these early [pre-Old Kingdom] cloths were said to have a certain number of wefts per inch 'doubled,' a few perhaps 'trebled,' and the remainder 'single' yarns" (T. Midgley 1928, 64). (Midgley himself showed the analysis to be untenable by noting the passage of the weft continuously through the selvedges, since he was able to examine larger scraps than had previously been available.)

But we must now also reconsider the usual interpretation of the girls shown with spindles. First, they are not "spinning" in our sense—that is, draft-spinning. The thread, which we see them pulling as such from a bowl (Fig. 2.10), has already been formed by

2.10   Spinner with two spindles and four threads; from a wall-painting in the Middle Kingdom tomb of Khety at Beni Hasan (no. 17). (Roth and Crowfoot 1921, cover; courtesy of the Department of Egyptology, University College London)

splicing. They are merely adding twist. Nor are they making the thread finer and evener, as a European who is re-spinning does (and as Roth would have it: Roth and Crowfoot 1921, 98): they *cannot*, because the fibers, having been spliced rather than continuously drafted, will not slip past each other. In some pictures we see girls pulling two or three threads per spindle (e.g., at Beni Hasan, Fig. 2.10: Roth and Crowfoot 1921, 101n, and cover drawing). Apparently they are in the process of "plying" from singles the heavier threads that Bellinger observed. She notes (Bellinger 1959b, 1) that although the heavy cloths used triple yarns, in finer fabrics she found two strands twisted together, and for the sheerest fabrics, only one strand. The fact that in some pictures we are *shown* spinners pulling only one thread per spindle may be a simplification on the part of the artist, but it may also show a practice of adding a strengthening twist to the fine "single" yarns, which are composed nonetheless of sizable bundles of ultimate bast fibers (on the order of 50 to 100, in the one sample I could pick apart to count).

This strange "relic" of hand-splicing the flax before twisting it with the spindle invites us to look at the fact that the entire conception of Egyptian thread-making is different from the European one. That is, a strand of flax is conceived as being already a thread, just as a strand of silk is. If it is not long enough, splice on a second piece; if it is not strong enough, twist it with another. And to strengthen the joins, stagger the splices so they fall beside the unspliced sections of the other component. The entire process would seem to be far more primitive than the continuous draft. The earliest known piece of Egyptian linen, from a 5th-millennium deposit in the Faiyum (Caton-Thompson and Gardner 1934, 46 and pl. 28.3; now in the Petrie Museum, London: UC 2943), shows the splicing very clearly (see Fig. 5.1).

On the other hand, wool—at least the very short-staple wool available in those days—cannot be made into thread by end-to-end splicing, because it is much too short. Since the Egyptians seem not to have used wool very much, in comparison with their copious use of flax,[6] there was evidently no cogent reason for them to change spinning methods during the entire period down to Roman times. The splicing method would seem then to have survived in Egypt for just that special purpose of dealing with flax fibers, which make noticeable and usable lengths of string each by themselves. As Crowfoot observed about spinning methods over 50 years ago in Egypt and the Sudan, "the new does not always slay the old, and some most primitive method may survive for some special use, surrounded by the methods of superior culture" (Crowfoot 1931, 7).

The antiquity—or ease of invention—of the Egyptian method is further implied by the fact that bast fibers are known all over the world for their usefulness in making lengths of twisted rope and string, whether or not true spinning is known. And where draft-spinning is not used, additional length is obtained by some sort of splicing. The Ainu of northern Japan, for example, who did not know spinning, were found to weave their clothes out of thread produced by tying the ends of long, very fine strips of elm bark together with tiny knots, and winding up the thread thus formed into large balls (Roth [1918] 1977, 9–10), much as the Egyptian women did in their first step.[7] I have also watched a Maori woman make both halves of a "plied" string at once, by overlapping and rolling a hank of fibers onto one component thread, then a second hank similarly onto the other component, and then twisting the two threads, thus made, deftly together along most of their length, reserving just enough of their ends free to splice in the next hanks.

[6] Wool, but not demonstrably textile use thereof, occurs here and there at Gerzean sites (Greiss 1955, 228–29; Reed 1960, 136); and sheep—hairy ones—are often shown in dynastic reliefs (Fig. 1.7). But woolen textiles are conspicuously absent from the huge mass of Egyptian artifacts, except in two places. One is 12th-Dynasty Kahun, where the excavators discovered "a handful of weaver's waste . . . mainly made up of blue worsted ends, and blue wool with some red and some green ends" and "a lump of red dyed wool, not yet spun" (Petrie, Griffith, and Newberry 1890, 28). The other place is Amarna, whence Pendlebury reports a sack made in "carpet weaving" technique from goat hair and containing a "mass of goat's wool" plus five large balls of spun wool and "a square woollen garment firmly woven 1.70 metres by 1.40" (Pendlebury et al. 1951, 246, also 109 and pl. 111.2–5). Although amazed at the unusually good state of preservation, Pendlebury protests that the sack was found a meter deep, in undisturbed surroundings, "wedged between two cornbins," and hence was not a late intrusion (ibid., 246). Ryder inspected some other(?) yarn at the Agricultural Museum in Cairo, "from the temple stores of Akhenaten," and reported it as S-spun from "hairy medium wool" that had been cut, not plucked, from the sheep (Ryder 1972). A further(?) scrap of woven wool from Amarna is deposited in the British Museum (no. 55137); and recently yet more wool has apparently turned up at Amarna (not yet published). Egyptologists have sometimes pooh-poohed Herodotus's statements (2.37, 81) that the Egyptians considered wool unclean for wearing in sacred contexts. But there must be some reason why we find so little of it, when so much delicate linen survived. I find it striking that our dynastic evidence for wool is restricted to habitation sites, and to the two places heaviest in evidence for contact with people of the north Mediterranean: Amarna, and the Kahun/Gurob area of the Faiyum. I suspect that for the most part wool was indeed being used in Egypt for secular purposes only—especially for cheap cloth, and as a cheap way of introducing attractive, permanent colors into cloth (extremely difficult and therefore expensive to do with linen). I also suspect that we are seeing the tail end of this tradition (begun in the 18th Dynasty?—see Chapter 5) in the early Coptic fabrics for daily use that have small tapestry figures in colored wools on plain white linen ground. One may point out that colored wool found in pharaonic Egypt correlates strongly with the presence of foreigners, and that such techniques may very well have been introduced to the Egyptians by these selfsame foreigners in the 2nd millennium.

[7] I was long puzzled as to how the Egyptian splices could hold without being knotted. Eventually I learned that flax has the peculiar property that when wet with saliva it partially disintegrates into a gluey substance (see below). Saliva is thus preferable to plain water in working with flax (B. Hochberg, pers. comm. 1980). Possibly the Egyptians induced their splices to stick together without knots by using saliva; the splicers do not appear to have bowls of water.

The woman was thereby able to lengthen her string by about 8 inches (the length of her fibers) each time, which exactly suited her purpose, since she was in the process of lashing down a huge sail; and by making the cord as she went, she saved herself the trouble of drawing a great length of string through each hole. In short, far from suffering from lack of technology, the "splice" method in this case was a clever adaptation to a particular need.

All of this analysis, then, suggests that the method of spinning by continuous draft, which is the only method usable on wool because of its shortness, was invented in wool country—although perhaps by people who already knew the usefulness of thread from having used bast-fiber string. At any rate, once invented, the continuous-draft method could be extended to flax (and could even oust the conceptually more primitive method that was usable only for bast), since there is nothing *preventing* flax from being spun that way except the shortness of one's arm. Since bast fibers tend to be several feet long, one needs to add a *distaff*, that is, a long rod to hold the fibers while they are being drafted, in order to be able to pull them out to their full length for spinning. Added proof that the Egyptians must have used a splicing method for their flax lies in the fact that nowhere in their pictures or equipment do we find any evidence whatever for a distaff—indispensable for the drafting of long flax—until they learned it from the Romans (Crowfoot 1931, 29).

That the Egyptian method of making thread differs from that of the wool-users to the east of them is also directly attested in ancient literary sources. In the Bible, the usual word applied to the spinning of wool by Hebrew women is *tavah* (טָ ו ה) 'spin.' But precisely in Exodus, when the Hebrews have just left Egypt after their long sojourn, they are repeatedly directed to produce for the new tabernacle fine linen described with the verb *shazar* (שָ ז ר) 'twist, twine, ply' (cf. Bellinger 1965, 26; the verb also can refer to glueing: cf. note 7 above). The colored woolens for the tabernacle are still referred to in these same passages as *tavah* (Exodus 26–28, 35–38). The timing accords well with the appearance of certain typically Egyptian spinning implements in the Palestinian archaeological record, mainly in the middle of the Late Bronze Age (see below).

By this point in the argument there is no longer any technical reason to feel, contrary to the archaeological evidence, that wool must have been used for thread before bast. Although it may have taken a long time to discover and perfect the process of retting, plants with strong, fibrous stems have always been readily available, and we are reckoning with a time span of thousands of years during the Upper Palaeolithic era for experimentation in this sphere. Furthermore, the difficulties of turning bast into thread by the continuous-draft process need not have been encountered, since our discussion suggests that the more primitive method of splicing could easily have been used. On the other hand, an abundance of wool separate from the hide on which it grew cannot readily be expected before the domestication of animals—that is, when the chief contact with animals ceased to be with slaughtered ones only. That would be in the early Neolithic period; and for really woolly sheep the wait was apparently rather longer.

Such a theory suggests that the technique of continuous-draft spinning may have spread precisely in association with wool: most likely either with the spread of domestic sheep and goats, or later with the spread of specifically woolly breeds of sheep. It also suggests that the more sophisticated process, namely draft-spinning, may have crept into territories where the method of splicing and twisting flax was already known and used, and may then have either coexisted with or replaced the old method. Let us now review the other ancient evidence for spinning, with all these possibilities in mind.

THE EVIDENCE FOR SPINDLES AND WHORLS

It has been suggested that the technique of separating the individual bast fibers by retting, so that they are suitable for thread, came initially from observing this separation in the bottoms of half-rotted baskets or mats, originally plaited with solid strips. This would imply that matting or basket-making preceded thread-making. In some of the oldest Neolithic strata we find evidence for mats and baskets: actual pieces at Naḥal Ḥemar ca. 6500 (Bar-Yosef 1985, plates) and at Ali Kosh and Çatal Hüyük (Singh 1974, 183, 185); and impressions at Jarmo (ca. 7000 B.C.) and Hassuna (L. S. Braidwood et al. 1974, 128, 131) and at Nea Nikomedeia (Rodden 1964, 605). But the earliest direct evidence for woven thread is just as old as that for mats and baskets: namely around 7000 B.C. at Jarmo (impressions: Braidwood and Howe 1960, 46); around 6000 B.C. at Çatal Hüyük in Turkey (actual cloth: Burnham 1965, 170); in the 6th millennium at Shimshara in Iraq (Mortensen 1970, 123–24); and in the earliest levels of Tepe Yahyā in southwestern Iran (Adovasio 1975–77, 228). Furthermore, we now know that twisted fiber string is millennia older than any of these.

What may be new here is the quantity and efficiency of manufacture. Early in the aceramic and early ceramic Neolithic, objects begin to turn up that look remarkably like spindle whorls.[8] A number of these sites

have also given other evidence of textile activities, such as bone needles and loom weights. Unfortunately, it is often difficult to be sure whether any given round object with a hole in it is an actual spindle whorl, or is instead a bead or weight. Only very rarely is the spindle shaft—usually a slim, readily perishable stick of wood—preserved in the hole of the whorl. When such an object *is* found, similar whorls at sites of the same culture can probably safely be assumed to be specifically for spindles. As for the remainder, we must consider a number of functional features.

Theory of Whorls

The smallest spindle whorls on record are those which were used in parts of the Middle East during Islamic times, as small as 8 mm in diameter and under a gram in weight (Liu 1978, 90–91). Presumably they were used for very fine cotton, which is not of concern to us here. But most spindle whorls outside of cotton territory are very much larger than that, a fact that helps greatly in distinguishing them from beads. Liu's study has shown that most round beads, the world over, are less than about 2 cm in diameter, for practical reasons. So a round, centrally pierced object significantly larger than 2 cm across is far more likely to be a whorl than a bead; and the burden of proof would fall to those wish-

[8] Some of the Neolithic sites that have produced possible or probable examples are: in Anatolia—Çatal Hüyük (in the middle levels, of unbaked clay: Mellaart 1962, 56), Suberde (30 clay specimens, some from sherds) and Hacılar (Late Neolithic level VI; Singh 1974, 102, 81, 72; Mellaart 1961, 46); in Iraq—Jarmo (3 stone ones), Shimshara (3 slate and one clay), Hassuna (numerous), Dabaghiyah, Yarim Tepe, Nineveh (Hassuna phase; numerous and of varied design), and Ras al 'Amiya (Singh 1974, 119–20, 126, 132, 134, 138, 140–41, 159); and in Greece—Nea Nikomedeia (Rodden 1964, 605), Sitagroi (E. Elster, pers. comm. 1985), Sesklo, and Dimini (Wace and Thompson 1912, 85).

ing to assign so large an object to the category of bead rather than whorl.

The hole in a whorl must be big enough to accommodate a suitable shaft, of course. In his wide ethnographic survey of spindle whorls, Liu found that the very smallest holes were 3 to 4 mm, while most ran 7 to 8 mm, occasionally larger (ibid., 97). Although bead perforations run from less than 1 mm to 12 mm or more (see ibid.), one would need excellent reason to assign an object to the category of whorl rather than bead if its hole fell outside the range of 3 to 10 mm in diameter. A straight or slightly tapered bore is ideal for a spindle whorl, although other types are known to have been used. We can eliminate any "whorl" whose hole is badly off center, because it will spin with a counterproductive amount of wobble. On the other hand, a doubly splayed hole is not out of the question, if well centered, since with some padding it can still be jammed onto the shaft. Liu states (ibid.) that unspun fibers, wax, or resin are sometimes used to wedge the spindle whorl tightly onto the spindle.

As to the maximum size of a whorl, weight is a better indicator than diameter: the recorded upper limit is 140 to 150 grams (something over 5 oz.; cf. Liu 1978, 90). On the other hand, loom weights (see Chapter 3) are seldom as small or as light as the largest whorls, and need not be pierced centrally (although in a few cultures they were). Indeed, a much-disregarded fact about spindle whorls is that they must fall within a certain range of weights in order to do a particular job. Tension is critical in spinning, and more sensitive the shorter the fiber. With a long-staple wool, it can be very helpful to have a heavy spindle, perhaps 4 to 5 ounces (100–150 g; cf. Hochberg 1980, 21); and for spin-ning a heavy thread of full-length flax or for plying wool yarns, the spindle might be heavier still. On the other hand, a heavy spindle is worse than useless for spinning short fibers like short wool, flax tow, or cotton. It pulls the fibers out so fast to their ends that the thread constantly breaks, if it can be spun at all. So for short fibers a light spindle is absolutely necessary. Ryder reports, for example, that modern peasants of Afghanistan use whorls of about 8 grams (less than 1/3 oz.) for short, fine wool, and a medium-light whorl of about 33 grams (a bit over an ounce) for "long staple medium-heavy wool" (Ryder 1968, 81). It should be added that, within the limits set by the fiber, the spinner will tend to prefer a lighter spindle to make fine thread and a heavier spindle to make heavy thread. A 33-gram whorl used with long wool thus suggests a fine thread. Supported spindles, too, tend to be light, since one of the principal reasons for using them is to avoid breaking the thread with the weight of the spindle: spinners in India traditionally use supported spindles of an ounce or less.

It is just this measurement of weight, ironically, that excavators have generally failed to publish. We are told the sizes, shapes, and materials, but seldom the weight so important to the spinner. It is possible that a comprehensive survey of the weights of spindle whorls from all over the ancient Near East and Europe could indicate to us noticeable regions where different types of thread and/or fiber were used. In the New World, for example, it is known that "different sized whorls are used for spinning cotton and maguey fiber, [and] the diameters and weights fall into distinctly separated peaks, not in a continuum of dimensions" (Liu 1978, 91).[9]

[9] A sampling of Egyptian whorls with spindles attached shows that although their weights tended to fall in the neighborhood of 1–2 oz., they ranged from ½–4 oz. (16–107 g). (My thanks to the curators of the British Museum and Helen Whitehouse at the Ashmolean for providing me with the data for these statistics.) Such a

The one way in which shape, as opposed to weight, can affect the spinning process is by the diameter of the whorl. Hochberg (1980, 40) chooses the analogy of a twirling iceskater: the slimmer she makes herself by pulling her arms in, the faster she turns. Just so with whorls. A broad whorl gives a long, slow spin, whereas a whorl of the same weight with a small diameter spins very fast, and for a short time. If the culture gives the spinner a choice of whorl, the whorl of smaller diameter will be selected to produce a tightly spun thread with many twists per unit of length, and the whorl of larger diameter will be used to make looser thread, with fewer twists.

Another telltale feature of spindles that is culturally if not always functionally indicative is the placement of the whorl on the shaft: at the top (high-whorl), at the bottom (low-whorl), or very occasionally in the middle. European peasants since Classical times at least have used low-whorl spindles. Indeed, this tradition is so ingrained in us that we can scarcely imagine otherwise. Yet as Crowfoot put it (1931, 30), "Herodotus might have added to those manners and customs of the Ancient Egyptians which exactly contradicted the common practice of mankind the fact that they dropped their spindles whorl uppermost instead of whorl downwards." Ancient Egyptian paintings of spindles in use invariably show the whorl at the top of the shaft; the very clear hieroglyph of a spindle, in the sign-groups for spinning, shows it there too (Crowfoot 1931, 30; see Fig. 2.11). Spindles often are given a groove or hook at

2.11 Egyptian hieroglyphics for "spin" showing a high-whorl spindle. (After Budge 1920, 563; and Gardiner 1957, 520)

the top end of the shaft in which to catch the thread while the spindle is twirling. Fully preserved spindles from Egypt generally have such a groove, and it is at the same end as the whorl. And Grace Crowfoot found that those who habitually used a spindle with its whorl uppermost were equally unready to believe the opposite possible. Said one of her Egyptian informants, "Everybody spins with the whorl above. Is it not called *ras el maghzal* (head of the spindle)? How then can it be below?" (ibid., 34).

Because our modern European tradition is so strongly low-whorl, all of Europe, and the Near East too, has been tacitly assumed to have been low-whorl territory since textile arts began. Indeed, museum exhibits generally "restore" their spindles with whorl at the bottom (see Fig. 2.7). But how far back can we prove that the spindles were that way even in Europe? And what about the rest of the ancient world?

For proof of what ancient spindles looked like and how they were used we need either clear representations or complete spindles with differentiable ends. We have the ancient Egyptian paintings, models, and artifacts already described, all of which show high whorls; and we have a number of Ar-

wide range is not unexpected, given that the Egyptians were twisting already-made thread rather than drafting, using one strand (for veil weight), two strands (for sheeting), or three strands (for canvas) (Bellinger 1959b, 1). For short wool, such as early domestic sheep must have had, we would expect a clustering toward the lower end of the scale—perhaps ½–2 oz. (or 15–60 g). We must keep an eye out, of course, for the possibility that some

communities might be using both fibers, and even both methods; and also for the fact that heavy whorls are also sometimes used for plying or doubling single wool-yarns. In short, the weights of the whorls from a single stratum or site may be too ambiguous to help much; but over a wide area and long time span we may be able to infer quite a bit about fibers and methods—if we can accrue the data.

chaic and Classical Greek representations showing girls using low-whorl spindles (never high ones); so we know that Greece at least belonged to the low-whorl drop-spindle tradition by the early first millennium B.C. But what about the other areas, and earlier eras?

North Mediterranean

North of the Mediterranean, representations of spinning are so rare before the Iron Age that we are exclusively dependent on evidence from the spindles themselves. Lone spindle whorls (or possible spindle whorls), as we have said, are plentiful enough. We have just catalogued the earliest Neolithic whorls of the Near East. In the Aegean the available sequence begins in the 7th millennium with a few flat, round, perforated stones, and then some lightweight perforated potsherds that have been rounded off at the edges, followed presently by fair quantities of stone, sherd, and baked-clay whorls in the Neolithic levels of Thessaly, Crete, etc.[10] Early Bronze Age Troy witnesses a veritable explosion of baked-clay whorls: Schliemann is said to have found about 8000 (Crowfoot 1954, 435), and after the Cincinnati expedition Blegen estimated 8000 to 10,000 whorls all told in Troy II alone (Blegen 1963, 88).[11] But it is not until this profusion at Troy that the first spindle shafts occur; and even then only two are reported.

In a pottery box found by Schliemann in "Treasure M" of Level II or III (Early

Bronze Age—mid 3rd millennium), there appeared, among other things, the remains of a "verkohlten hölzernen Spindel mit einem aufgewickelten leinenen oder wollenen Faden" (a carbonized wooden spindle with its linen or woolen thread wound on it: Dörpfeld 1902, 340; although Schliemann 1880a, 360–61 does not mention the spindle). A later expedition (1894) recovered another spindle in Level II, this time of bone and still stuck into its clay whorl, thereby demonstrating, as Dörpfeld said (1902, 390), that the multitude of "whorls" found at Troy, or at least some of them, really were used as spinning tools. Unfortunately, neither Schliemann nor Dörpfeld thought to describe further or to illustrate either the spindles or the thread, only the whorls. Hence we have no idea whether it was even possible to know which end the whorl was on, let alone where it was. (Cloth and also a full bobbin that Schliemann mistakenly calls a distaff [see below] might have contributed further textile information under modern analytic scrutiny: Schliemann 1880a, 361, 327.)

To the west a few spindles have survived among the whorls in the pile-dwellings of Switzerland and northern Italy. The alkaline lake-bed silts are excellent for preserving plant material such as wood and fibers. Spindle whorls themselves are rather rare in the oldest pile-dwellings (Cortaillod and Michelsberg cultures), as they are throughout the more northern European cultures in the Neolithic period, but stone whorls become rather common in the Horgen phase, and

---

[10] Light weight perforated potsherds rounded off at the edges occur early at Nea Nikomedeia (Rodden 1962, 285) and at Knossos (J. D. Evans 1964, 157, 164, 172, 182, 188). Stone, sherd, and baked-clay whorls occur in the Neolithic levels of Sesklo, Dimini, Tsangli, Tsani, and other Thessalian sites (Wace and Thompson 1912, 85, 125, 149, etc.); on the Cycladic islet of Saliagos by 4000 B.C. (Evans and Renfrew 1968, 70); at Sitagroi throughout middle and late Neolithic (E. Elster, pers.

comm. 1985); at Knossos in the later Neolithic layers (J. D. Evans 1964, 188, 192); etc.

[11] Obviously the industry was a major one. Note, however, that one spinner will often own and use several spindles—either for different purposes, or to avoid excessive rewinding. In Peru, for example, a single weaver's kit was found to contain 68 cotton-spindles (Liu 1978, 98). So 8000 whorls may or may not mean 8000 women spinning. See Chapter 14.

clay ones by the very end of the Swiss Neolithic. Very few of the whorls still have anything of their spindle shafts left: (1) from Meilen Rohrenhaab comes a Neolithic whorl made of a slice of antler still with two pieces of wooden shaft, but no "head" (Fig. 2.12); (2) Staub (1864, 49) illustrates a clay whorl evidently impaled by its original wooden spindle (Fig. 2.13), but he gives no specific provenance or date, and the spindle is pointed at both ends—that is, has no demonstrable "head"; (3) Gross (1883, 100) mentions the existence of several relatively complete spindles from Swiss lake-dwellings without further references or illustrations ("plusieurs . . . encore passés dans le tige de bois composant le fuseau"); (4) E. Vogt (1937, 48 fig. 73) illustrates a spindle shaft with linen thread still wound on it, but both ends, including the whorl, are broken away; (5)

Thurstan (1954, 2) mentions a complete spindle from Locray, without reference or illustration. In none of these cases can we deduce the placement of the whorl, high or low; so the frequent reconstructions of Swiss spindles with the whorl at the bottom, as in Vogt's classic work (1937, 47 fig. 72.8) and in some of the museum displays, would seem to be guesswork.[12]

In fact, we do no better in western Europe throughout the Bronze Age, although in the Terremare settlements of northern Italy we find at least one decorated whorl with a bit of shaft still in the hole (Fig. 2.14)—enough to prove that these fancy little discs, some of which look remarkably like the famous Trojan ones, were at least sometimes used as spindle whorls rather than as huge beads. Our first representation of spinning does not turn up until the Iron Age, with a 7th century B.C. Hallstatt vase from Sopron (Ödenburg) on the Austro-Hungarian border (Fig. 2.15; first published by R. Hoernes 1891, [75–76] and pl. 10). This handsome vase, recently re-restored and newly displayed at the Naturhistorisches Museum in Vienna, shows one woman weaving and another woman spinning with a drop-spindle. But the spindle is so crudely drawn that again it may be a matter of prejudice to see it as low-whorl.

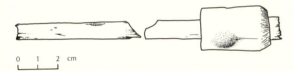

2.12   Late Neolithic spindle of wood with an antler whorl (current weight of whole: 15 g), from Meilen Rohrenhaab, Switzerland; ca. 3000 B.C. (Courtesy of the Swiss National Museum)

2.13   Late Neolithic spindle of wood with a clay whorl, from Switzerland. (After Staub 1864, pl. 4.7)

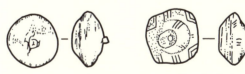

2.14   Two typical Terremare spindle whorls (top and side views), one with a bit of the spindle shaft remaining. Northern Italy, Bronze Age. (After Gastaldi 1865, 45 fig. 25)

[12] My own guess as to how I would try to use the first two spindles listed above is the same: low-whorl. But recall from Fig. 2.7 the strong European prejudice that tempts our museums to display all high-whorl spindles upside down—i.e., whorl at the bottom—despite the presence of very clear thread grooves! And compare the spindle from Marlik in Iran, discussed below (Fig. 2.22).

2.15 Urn from Sopron (Ödenburg) in western Hungary, showing women spinning and weaving. Hallstatt period, early 1st millennium B.C. For complete design, see Fig. 13.3. (Photo courtesy of Naturhistorisches Museum, Vienna)

Near East

In the Middle East, too, we fare no better with proof of the type of spindle used during most of the Neolithic; but in the late 4th millennium we begin to see some rays of light—and some surprises. A Protoliterate cylinder seal from Choga Mish in Khuzistan (in Iran), about 3300 B.C., shows a woman spinning while her companion churns butter (Fig. 2.16; Delougaz and Kantor 1972, 30). The spinner sits on a low stool or platform, with her legs tucked up, and with a tall, high-whorl spindle in one hand. The other hand controls the thread running to the top of the spindle; but it also seems to contain another object. It would be nice to know if the object were a distaff, but unfortunately the seal is damaged just there. Another seal from the period (purchased: Fig. 2.17) shows three women busy at textile chores. Two hold up what are apparently high-whorl spindles (or distaffs?) in one hand. The woman on the far

right holds her other hand out and away in a pose characteristic of spinning not with a drop-spindle but with a hand-held spindle (of the high-whorl sort). Grace Crowfoot both illustrates and describes Bedouin women spinning by this method (see Fig. 2.3), the "peculiar value" of which, she says, lay "in its command over short stapled wool" (Crowfoot 1931, 13, and pl. 11), probably the only kind of wool available in the 4th millennium. The middle woman may be spinning likewise, or perhaps is using her other hand to guide thread from her spindle onto a warping frame (if that is indeed what is in front of her), the other end of which is tended by a third lady.

From the 3rd millennium we have some delightful mosaic pieces at Mari (on the Middle Euphrates) of women variously occupied, one of whom holds a spindle in high-whorl fashion (Fig. 2.18; Parrot 1962, 163–68). She is not actually spinning, since she grasps the spindle with both hands. Unfortunately, her

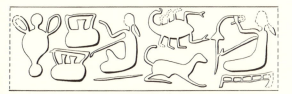

2.16 Seal from Choga Mish, in Khuzistan (east of Mesopotamia), showing a spinner seated on a platform at right; 4th millennium. (Delougaz and Kantor 1972, 32 pl. X.a; courtesy of the Oriental Institute of the University of Chicago; drawing by H. J. Kantor)

2.17 Seal from the Newell collection (NCBS 31), showing spinning and warping. (After von der Osten 1934, pl. 4.31; Amiet 1961, pl. 19.319; Buchanan 1981, fig. 153; courtesy of Yale Babylonian Collection; drawing by M. Stone)

seated companion is damaged just enough that we can't tell for certain if the two of them are reeling the thread off into a skein; but that seems likely. The next figure to the right, who seems occupied in the same task (and wears the same unusual hairdo), is clearer: she holds her hands in the canonical position for skeining.

About the same time we find some actual spindles. In the "A" cemetery at Kish, dated to the end of the Early Dynastic III period (roughly the third quarter of the 3rd millennium), Mackay found at least two copper spindles, with a hook at the short end just beyond the whorl (Fig. 2.19; Mackay 1925, 168, pl. 40.3.3 and pl. 58.1, no. 2454). The shaft is 28.5 cm long and 3 mm thick, while the thin, cupped copper disc is 4.1 cm in diameter. With it were found "two curious

rods," each about 20 cm long and "surmounted by a flat nail-like head" (see Fig. 2.19). The excavator suggested that these might be distaffs (ibid., 168), an explanation that I was inclined not to believe until I happened upon a remarkably similar pair of objects, also from Early Dynastic III, in a recent excavation report for Abu Salabikh: a copper spindle (now 20.3 cm long) and a companion copper rod (23.8 cm long) with a small nail-like head at one end (Postgate and Moon 1982, 131, 134, pl. V.c). If this explanation is correct, we have here our earliest evidence for the distaff.

Still farther to the east, at Hissar in northern Iran, the excavators found a handsome copper spindle (Fig. 2.20), about 6 inches long, that was "definitely associated with Hissar IIB objects in the well-equipped

2.18 Part of a mosaic panel from Mari, showing a spinner (center) skeining off onto the hands of a woman seated left. Another similar group begins at the right. Early 2nd millennium B.C. (After Parrot 1962, pl. 11)

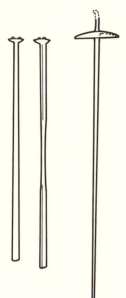

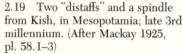

2.19 Two "distaffs" and a spindle from Kish, in Mesopotamia; late 3rd millennium. (After Mackay 1925, pl. 58.1–3)

2.20 Copper spindle with two whorls, from Hissar II, in N. Iran; 3rd millennium. Note the groove for hitching S-twisted thread (see Fig. 2.33). (After E. F. Schmidt 1937, pl. 29, no. H2171; courtesy of the University Museum, University of Pennsylvania)

grave of a woman" (E. F. Schmidt 1937, 120). This dates it to just before the middle of the 3rd millennium. Schmidt comments further (ibid.) that "two whorls are attached to the slender, tapering stem. . . . Although these whorls when found were attached to the stem by oxide, subsequent cleaning determined that they were originally loose." That, however, does not mean they were not spindle whorls, for whorls are frequently jammed onto the spindle with a little padding of loose fibers in the hole to get a tight fit; and putting two onto one spindle is also not that uncommon (see below). In the photograph, the whorls are presumably shown in the position they were in before cleaning, and it is interesting to note that there seems to be a long, spiral trace of a thread groove just beyond them on the short end. That is, it seems that here too we have a high-whorl spindle, although the original illustration, as usual, is then upside down.

Apparently nothing has survived from the turbulent millennium that followed; but

somewhere around the 9th century B.C. comes a handsome carved relief from Susa of a lady once again sitting on a low stool with her feet tucked up, and holding a full spindle with whorl uppermost (Fig. 2.21; Porada 1965, 68 fig. 43). To match it archaeologically we have, perhaps a century or two earlier, a

2.21 Neo-Elamite relief of a lady spinning, from Susa; early 1st millennium B.C. (Courtesy of Musée du Louvre: Sb 2834)

2.22 Metal spindle from Marlik in N. Iran, turned right side up; early 1st millennium B.C. Note the groove for hitching S-twisted thread (see Fig. 2.33). (After Negahban 1964, fig. 43)

slim bronze spindle from Marlik, a site in a valley west of Teheran (Fig. 2.22). There is no doubt whatever that the spindle is high-whorl: there is a clear thread groove on the short tip just beyond the whorl—it is visible in the photograph and the excavator mentions it. But a high-whorl spindle is so foreign to the Persians today that the spindle has been both photographed and described upside down. The shaft is 26 cm long, and the entire spindle weighs about 50 grams (Negahban 1964, 44).

The last bit of eastern evidence is a late Hittite relief, from the collection at Maraş in eastern Anatolia, dated to about 800 B.C. (Fig. 2.23). It shows a seated woman who holds in her left hand a full spindle (apparently whorl uppermost), from the top of which a thread stretches to her right hand and then runs down into a box at her feet.

Once again it is not clear what she is trying to do in such a position: perhaps plying—or perhaps the sculptor has taken some liberties.

All in all, the evidence from Mesopotamia and Iran comes in as unanimous for the high-whorl spindle, all the way down into the Iron Age—just the opposite of what people have assumed. Moreover, we have no representations of the spindle being dropped in either the European or the Egyptian fashion. On the contrary, in one early case it seems to be turned in the hand.

Anatolia

In Anatolia we have seen that our knowledge of whorls begins at Çatal Hüyük, along with the fine-threaded textiles found there. Whorl-type objects, as usual without shafts preserved, appear at sites throughout Anatolia across the next few millennia.[13] As in the Aegean area, the stone and potsherd whorls are typically found in the Neolithic

2.23 Neo-Hittite relief from Maraş, showing a seated lady with spindle. (After Bossert 1942, pl. 814)

---

[13] For example, at Hacılar in the Late Neolithic Level VI (Mellaart 1961, 46); at Mersin in the Late Neolithic, along with woven cloth, in levels 25–26, and abundantly thereafter (Garstang 1953, 32–33, 43, 52, 81, 108, 134–

35, 156–59, 215); at Beycesultan in the Chalcolithic and Bronze Ages (Lloyd and Mellaart 1962, 268–69, 274–77, figs. F.2, F.5, F.6). See Chapter 14 and Appendix C for more.

strata, whereas in the Bronze Age the whorls are generally of specially formed and baked clay. Where sherds have been re-used as whorls in this later period, there is usually some other indication of poverty at the site.

But the surprise comes from the Royal Graves at Alaca Höyük—elaborate, ritualistic, gold-filled graves of men and women from the same "Treasure Horizon" as Troy II and the Ur Royal Cemetery, in the mid-3rd millennium. In a general description of the contents of the tombs, the excavators tell us that the skeletons are laid on their sides with the knees drawn up: "ses armes sont posées à ses côtés si c'est un homme, des objets de toilette et de luxe si c'est une femme" (if it is a man, his weapons are placed beside him, if it is a woman, articles of toiletry and of luxury; Koşay 1951, 154). We are told further that religious emblems are placed near the face, animal statues in the middle of the tomb, and domestic utensils made of gold and silver, as well as other objects, all around the corpse (ibid.). Tomb L (ibid., 168–69) contained no weapons, but an assortment of typically female jewelry and domestic utensils in precious metals. Among the gifts laid in front of the torso near the hands were a silver spoon with a golden handle, and an unidentified object, L8 (Fig. 2.24), consisting of a silver disc impaled by a silver shaft with a carefully shaped gold or electrum head (ibid., 168–69, and pl. 197 fig. 1 left [French caption wrong]). The object would appear by its shape, size, and detailing to be a spindle, an interpretation strengthened by its position near the hands—and apparently those of a woman at that—along with other domestic utensils translated into precious metals. One is inevitably reminded of another, much later Bronze Age princess who was said to have been given gold and silver spinning gear as a present by a high-born lady-friend (*Odyssey* 4.130–35).

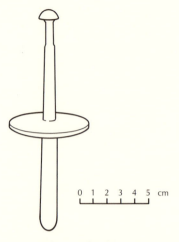

2.24 Silver and gold or electrum spindle from Tomb L at Alaca Höyük, in central Turkey. Early Bronze Age: mid-3rd millennium. (After Koşay 1951, pl. 197 fig. 1)

If this is indeed a spindle, it is rather different from what we might have expected. In particular, it has its whorl neither at the top nor at the bottom, but almost dead in the middle of the shaft. Such an arrangement does not make the instrument unusable—in fact, it would tend to make the spindle twirl more stably. But the placement means that the spindle cannot be set whirling by rolling it along the thigh the way the Egyptians handled their high-whorl spindles, nor can it be turned in the palm of the hand, as the Mesopotamian ones may have been. So it is presumably to be classed with the low-whorl types, which are flicked with the fingers (or even the toes). The head is quite different in shape from the slim, grooved heads of ancient Egyptian spindles, or the hooked top found at Kish, but is just as convenient for hitching the thread around while spinning. Heads of a similar shape are often encountered among modern hand-spindles. Then too, the shaft is rather thicker and the disc rather thinner than our numerous clay spindle whorls would have us expect. The overall shape of the spindle (except for the placement of the whorl) looks very much like that of certain modern spindles composed entirely of wood. The wealth of excellently carved wooden implements that happened to be preserved in Early Neolithic Çatal Hüyük should serve as a reminder that these people may indeed have used spindles and other tools made entirely of wood; and a different medium could lead to a somewhat different design. That is, we may be seeing a wooden type translated into precious metals. (See, e.g., Bazin and Bromberger 1982, 67–68 and fig. 43 for a wide variety of current Near Eastern spindles, including middle-whorl.)

Recently some more examples of these "middle-whorl" spindles have been dug up in Anatolia, from Early Bronze Age contexts. Two were discovered in a tomb at Horoztepe, one of cast bronze, the other of sheet electrum with a gold-covered head (Fig. 2.25; Özgüç and Akok 1958, pl. VIII 1–3). They are about the same size as the Alaca example, 14 and 16 cm tall respectively (ibid.,

45, 51). Two others from Merzifon are displayed in the Hittite Museum in Ankara (see T. Özgüç 1978, 89–90). One has much the same shape as the Alaca spindle, but has lost its head; it was about 15 cm long. The other is longer (about 20 cm) and slimmer, the shaft square in cross-section and the head a large, spherical knob. The disc is thin and slightly cupped toward the head, and the bottom end of the shaft is gently rounded. Thus it is similar to the nearly contemporary spindles from Mesopotamia and Iran, except that the head is at the opposite end (and note that the cup now faces the head). The appearance of this spindle makes it likely that yet another spindle had in fact been found at Alaca, in Tomb H. It can be seen in the excavation photograph (Fig. 2.26). The object might have been a dress pin; but whereas the "other" pins have pointed ends, this one can be seen in the Hittite Museum to have a flat end, most unsuitable for sticking through fabric.

Finally, the excavations at Karataş yielded

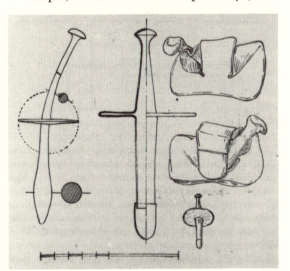

2.25 Early Bronze Age metal spindles from Horoztepe, in Turkey. (Özgüç and Akok 1958, figs. 25–26)

2.26 Contents of royal Tomb H. Alaca Höyük, with a spindle in precious metal at bottom right. (Koşay 1951, pl. 124)

a slim silver spindle, 14.6 cm long, with a small biconical metal whorl on it about two-thirds of the way from one of the two pointed ends (Fig. 2.27). The excavator remarks that "a perforated disc lay nearby . . . [which] fits neatly against the truncated biconical whorl" on the shaft, so that the whole may have formed some sort of complex spindle (Mellink 1969, 323). Spinners do indeed sometimes put a second whorl onto a spindle (cf. Liu 1978, 98; and see above), for example when shifting from spinning to plying. But to find a shaft with two so differently shaped whorls shows us again how little we know.

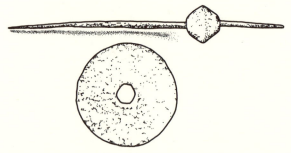

2.27   Bronze spindle with two whorls, from Karataş, in southwest Turkey; Early Bronze Age. (After Mellink 1969, pl. 74 fig. 23; courtesy of *American Journal of Archaeology*)

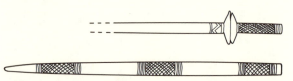

2.28   Probable spindles of ivory from Megiddo, in northern Israel. Late Bronze Age; mid-2nd millennium B.C. (After Guy 1938, fig. 175.6, pl. 84.1, 95.50)

Unusual Spindles

The procession of clay whorls so monotonous to excavators is broken again in the Late Bronze Age, this time by a flurry of handsome little bone and ivory spindles, which seem to have become the rage in the

Levant at that time, and which found their way as pretty trinkets even into Mycenaean pockets. The tomb excavations at Megiddo have produced a number of these. The excavator remarks that "an entirely new conception [in spindles] seems to begin in LB II, the period of most of the whorls and spindles found in the tombs" (Guy 1938, 170). The most interesting specimen consists of a shaft in two parts, each elegantly decorated with incised lines, and a whorl consisting of two domes set with the flat faces together (Fig. 2.28, top). A metal pin through the two halves of the whorl had been fitted into holes in the ends of the two pieces of shaft, joining the whole together (ibid., 170). Quite a number of other similar pieces were found, both shafts and whorls (ibid., 171 fig. 175, pl. 84.2–16, pl. 95.41–9), although "whether all so-called whorls were similarly mounted is of course not known" (ibid., 170–72). At least one shaft, of the same shape and incised with the same sort of pattern, appears to be complete without any whorl at all (Fig. 2.28, bottom). Similar artifacts continue at Megiddo well down into the Early Iron Age (ibid., 170–72).

Such pieces have also been found at other sites. At Hama, in Syria, the excavators found quite a few bone spindle-shafts, mostly between 21 and 25 cm long, and with them whorls, all decorated in the same way as those at Megiddo (Riis 1948, 171–74, and figs. 21, 209.A–B, 214, 217). And a spate of these ivory and bone whorls and shafts turned up at Enkomi, on Cyprus, from the end of Late Bronze II and Late Bronze III (Aaström 1972, 609–10; C.F.A. Schaeffer 1952, 194–95, 185, 215, and figs. 75, 82). Ivory scarcely occurs at Enkomi until Late Bronze IIb–c, according to Aaström, and when it does "the source of the ivory was probably Syria" (Aaström 1972, 608). He notes that the various specimens of carved shafts may have been used for different purposes, some for pins and others for spindles; and also that they have parallels in 18th–19th Dynasty Egypt, made of wood and of bone (ibid., 610; Petrie 1927, 24 and pl. 19). It is interesting that these parallels are precisely from Gurob and surroundings, an area showing a remarkable number of connections with Syria and the Aegean (see below; also A. P. Thomas 1981, pl. 18 nos. 421–26). Wooden and ivory pins and sticks, with very similar incised designs, can be traced back to predynastic times in Egypt (cf. Petrie 1920, pl. 8), where they are almost certainly *not* spindles, since spindles were traditionally of a quite different shape and size there. We are thus confronted with a situation in which ivory from Syria was being combined with a traditional design in wood from Egypt to produce a type of spindle apparently new to both areas, late in the Late Bronze Age. As for the whorls, some of those at Enkomi are larger, flatter, and more ornate than those from Megiddo; but as a group they have parallels from a variety of Syro-Palestinian sites (see Aaström 1972, 609, and nn. 4–11; also Iron Age Beth Shan: James 1966, 342–43 fig. 114.1).

In one peculiar case, a bronze disc was found still attached to such an ivory shaft by a gold-headed rivet (C.F.A. Schaeffer 1952, 194–95, fig. 75 [no. 335] and fig. 82[4]). Since this rivet clearly forms one end of the object, and there is no room to hitch a thread on it, the other end must have been the top, if this object is indeed a spindle: that is, it would have to be a low-whorl spindle. It might, however, be a distaff of the sort we saw from Kish and Abu Salabikh a millennium earlier.

A charming variation from Vounous in Cyprus occurs in the form of a painted clay im-

2.29 Late Bronze Age clay spindle from Vounous, Cyprus, ornamented to imitate the popular but expensive ivory ones. (After E. Stewart and J. Stewart 1950, pl.100.d)

itation of just the sort of spindle we have in ivory from Megiddo (Fig. 2.29; Crowfoot 1954, 433 fig. 273J; E. Stewart and J. Stewart 1950, 99 no. 6).

At least two and perhaps four more of these ivory spindles have been found at a 12th-century Mycenaean site: Peratí in Attica (Iakovides 1969, 54, 56, 72–73, 76, 95, 96 fig. 117, pl. 15.Δ211–12, pl. 23.Δ108, Δ112). Of the two nearly complete examples, one is so short at 13 cm (Δ211: ibid., 56; see Fig. 2.30) that it could hardly have been rolled down the thigh or turned in the hand, and must therefore have been a low-whorl drop-spindle. The other example (Δ108) is longer and plainer.[14]

We have two other strange pieces of evidence. First, two spindles decorated in the same way as the Late Bronze ivory ones, with ribs and incised chevrons, but made of bronze, have been found in a mid-first millennium B.C. cemetery at Deve Hüyük near Carchemish (Fig. 2.31). Both have thin bronze discs as whorls—one dead in the middle, like the early Anatolian ones, so that we would have to class it as low-whorl; and the other towards one end, but with both ends grooved. We seem here to have a mating of the two traditions just discussed, the Anatolian middle-to-low-whorl type and the Middle Eastern high-whorl type. Not unexpectedly, the union occurs approximately at the boundary between the two territories.

Second, we have noted that the Egyptian spindles, both in the numerous representa-

---

[14] Yet another, undecorated bone "spindle" with no whorl but an incised head was found at Phylakopí on Melos (Atkinson et al. 1904, 192 and pl. 40.9).

2.30   Imported ivory spindle found at Peratí, in Attica, Greece; Late Bronze Age. The end at lower left w probably the top. (National Museum Athens)

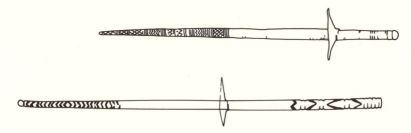

2.31   Bronze spindles from Iron Ag Deve Hüyük, in eastern Turkey; mid-1st millennium. (After Moorey 1980, figs. 16.399–400)

tions and in the many actual artifacts, had the whorl at the top, along with a groove for hitching the thread. There is one exception. At the New Kingdom site of Gurob in the Faiyum, a spindle turned up with a thread groove (necessarily the top) at one end, and a limestone whorl of about 150 g (5¼ oz.) most of the way toward the other end (Fig. 2.32; weight courtesy of the University Museum of Archaeology and Anthropology, Cambridge). It is definitely a low-whorl spindle. And a complete anomaly in Egypt. Gurob, however, is probably best known for the fact that it was found to be full of foreign objects—from the Levant, from Cyprus, and particularly from the Aegean. The site is not in good shape, but Petrie, the first excavator, was able to deduce that a temple had been founded at Gurob by Thutmose III in the mid-18th Dynasty (Petrie 1891, 16), with something of a settlement growing up around it. The Aegean foreigners are particularly in evidence at Gurob during the reigns of the Atenist pharaohs of the late 18th Dynasty, while the temple was apparently suffering considerable vicissitudes of fortune. Then, shortly thereafter, the temple was pulled down to the very ground, the blocks being carted off in all directions to be reused, probably by Rameses II of the 19th

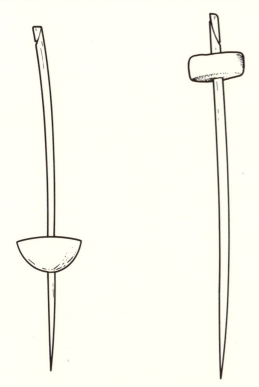

2.32 Spindle from Grave 11 at Gurob, in the Faiyum (*left*), and a typical Middle Kingdom Egyptian spindle (*right*) for comparison. Note the opposite slant of the thread groove, as well as the opposite position of the whorl. (*L.*: after Brunton and Engelbach 1927, pl. 13.8, courtesy of Department of Egyptology, University College London; *R.*: after British Museum no. 50980, courtesy of Trustees of the British Museum)

Dynasty. The town became a ghost town, and another small settlement sprang up nearby instead. But as late as the 20th Dynasty, occasional Aegean-related artifacts were still being placed in tombs in the nearby cemeteries (Petrie 1891, 21–24).

Very little was found with the spindle in Grave 11 to help determine its pedigree. The body was that of a female (Brunton and Engelbach 1927, pl. 14), and the other artifacts consisted of "fragments of red slippers, a top, and some netting" (ibid., 18), but no

pottery. On the face of it, the grave seems unidentifiable. But among all the artifacts of the hundreds of graves here, the only other top and the only other such limestone whorl in the cemetery are in graves with Aegean-related pottery (Graves 217 and 600 respectively: ibid., pl. 25 and 26). No other red slippers and no other such netting were found. Thus there is some implication that Grave 11 and its spindle belong to a specifically Aegean-related burial. Clearly the spindle is of foreign design, although of local materials: presumably it was made locally for a foreign resident. Hence the strongest hypothesis is that the form is Aegean, and that the Bronze Age Aegean people—unlike the Egyptians—were using the same sort of low-whorl spindle that their European descendents for the next three millennia have used. Very satisfying. But there is another detail that makes this conclusion even stronger.

Direction of Spin

One reason why the question of high- and low-whorl spindles is interesting is that it has been suggested that the type of spindle parallels the type of fiber used. We have already seen that we are dealing with at least two different spinning traditions around the Mediterranean, one in the south suited to flax exclusively, and the other to the north and east suited to both wool and flax. Now we see the distribution of high- and low-whorl spindles starting to fall into somewhat different geographic areas: Egypt and the Middle East with one sort, Anatolia and apparently Europe with another sort. There is yet another aspect of the craft of spinning that divides geographically: the direction in which the thread is spun, whether to the left or to the right—"S" or "Z" (see Fig. 2.33).

An *S-spun* thread (I prefer this terminology to "left" and "right" because the latter

2.33 "S" and "Z" directions of twisting threads. The names match the slope of the center of each letter

terms have been used in exactly opposite senses by different people) is one in which the fibers of the thread lie at a slant similar to that in the middle of the letter "S" when you hold the thread vertically in front of you (i.e., they have a negative slope). In a Z-*spun* thread, the fibers slope the other way, like the center part of the letter "Z."

Now, Egyptian linens as they have come down to us from dynastic Egypt are invariably S-spun, whereas the threads in the textiles of the other areas around, especially Europe and India, are typically Z-spun, starting with the textiles from around 6000 B.C. at Çatal Hüyük (Burnham 1965, 170). So we can see that the whorl on the Gurob spindle just discussed has *not* accidentally been stuck upside down onto the wrong end of the shaft, because the thread groove itself is cut backwards, from the Egyptian point of view. It is built for hitching Z-spun thread. And that points the spindle once again back to Europe.

Much ink has been consumed over the reasons for this difference of spin.[15] Louisa Bellinger, with her background in the conservation of textiles, has championed the position that the root of the difference is to be sought in the fibers themselves (see esp. Bellinger 1962, 6–10; and Bellinger 1965). It will be remembered from Chapter 1 that flax fi-

bers, when dampened, curl naturally to the left (S), whereas cotton and hemp tend to twist the other way. While attempting to wash old textiles in the laboratory, Bellinger found that the yarns spun in the same direction as the natural twist of the vegetable fiber would hang together during washing, whereas those spun in a contrary fashion tended to fall apart (Bellinger 1950, 1). She concluded that the ancient Egyptians had noted the same phenomenon and had for this reason come round to spinning their flax—their chief fiber for millennia—always in the S direction, whereas the Indians for similar reasons had come to spin their cotton in the Z direction, and other people had followed suit accordingly (ibid.).

Such an explanation does not, however, account for why the nations that used mostly wool should have spun them so insistently in the Z direction. After all, wool has only a vectorless crimp, not a twist, and so can be spun equally satisfactorily in either direction. Why, then, don't we find it spun half the time one way, half the time the other? (In actuality, we do see a series of woolens in northern Europe, for a time, in which part of the yarn is spun one way and part the other; but these were consciously constructed that way for very special effects, discussed in Chapter 6.) Bellinger suggested that the Z-spinners of wool must have learned to spin from people who were used to spinning cotton (Bellinger 1959b, 2; Bellinger 1962, 10). But that is unlikely on two counts. First, as we have seen, the earliest evidence for the use of cotton in the Old World dates from the late 4th millennium, whereas the wool industry was underway in the Near East well before then. Second, Ryder claims that the "first cotton fibres had no twist," that "the

[15] Increased archaeological evidence shows that the division is not so clear cut as earlier writers have thought: see below. But since the subject is passed off glibly as both clear and settled in so many works on early textiles, it seems useful to deal with it from scratch, to clarify the issues and possible conclusions.

twist of cotton fibres arose as a mutation in a cultivated form" (Ryder 1968, 78)—that is, only after people were long accustomed to using it. It is true that hemp and nettle are Z fibers; but their use started far to the north of wool territory. It is *flax* that has the same initial territory as wool, and flax has a natural S-twist.

So what force was powering the tradition? Studies in human "handedness" suggest that, as far back as diagnostic evidence is available, approximately 90 percent of the population has always been right-handed, the remainder being divided between left-handers and ambidextrous types (Coren and Porac 1977).[16] It seems more reasonable, then, that the answer lies mostly in the way a right-hander handles a spindle (Ryder 1968; Hoffmann and Burnham 1973, 53–54; Barber 1975, 299–301). It will be remembered that the Egyptians used a high-whorl spindle that was shown being rolled along (almost certainly down) the thigh with the right hand. Rolling a spindle down the thigh cannot produce anything but an S-twist. European and Indian spinners, however, traditionally start their low-whorl spindles whirling with a quick flick of the thumb and fingers, as one would start a top. Hand a top to right-handers and they invariably start it to the right: a fiber attached to the top would come out with a Z-twist every time. As for left-handers, they probably just conformed. Neither motion is particularly difficult to master with the non-dominant hand; nor is it inordinately hard to learn to flick to the right with the left hand—or to the left with the right hand, a trick needed by every spinner in order to ply the yarn. It just isn't the natural, automatic way to do it. As a strongly

left-handed person, I can vouch for the fact that, unless the task is really too difficult, left-handers tend to switch to match the right-handers at the first sign of a hassle over handedness; and such hassles immediately arise whenever one is being taught a traditional activity that involves directionality, whether it is spinning, tying knots, using sign language, or even formal dining. Also, archaeologists have found occasional anomalies in the domain of Z-spun wool: these may be from the few ornery left-handers.

What we seem to be seeing, then, is that the low-whorl spinners of Europe draft-spun their fibers on their finger-twirled spindles, automatically giving it a Z-spin, while the thigh-rolling spinners of Egypt twisted their linen on their long-shafted, high-whorl spindles, thereby giving it an S-spin. (Since the hand-held spindle can be handled variously, since some high-whorl spindles can be started with a finger-twirl, and since the Mesopotamian evidence for both thread and spindles is scanty and unclear, we cannot say yet what the Mesopotamians were doing.) It may also be, of course, that the Egyptian tradition of S-spinning, although chiefly a function of method, gained added strength to flout the surrounding sea of Z-spinners, from empirical evidence that their linens came out stronger or their yarn more manageable when made the old way. The Egyptians were certainly closely observant of their environment.

That they had at least experimented with—or learned first—another way of doing things in early times is shown by a single piece of spliced but Z-twisted, S-plied linen from the Faiyum (see Fig. 5.1; Caton-Thompson and Gardner 1934, 46 and pl.

---

[16] Coren and Porac's evidence fell chiefly within the last 5000 years; but 39 usable cases were found between ca. 15,000–3000 B.C., 90% of which also indicated right-handedness. The exact overall percentage was 92.6. No greater deviation was found by breaking down the sample geographically than by breaking it down chronologically.

28.3; Petrie Museum, University College, London, UC 2943). It is the earliest piece of linen we have from Egypt, dating to the 5th millennium (perhaps even to 5000 B.C., if we take the calibrated radiocarbon dates into account), and it shows other signs of being in the early, experimental stages of the craft by the fact that the two component strands were twisted sufficiently hard before being twisted together that the thread looks plied throughout.

It is not true, however, as much of the current literature implies, that one finds nothing but Z-spun thread outside of Egypt. Although the threads in the Neolithic textiles from Naḥal Ḥemar and the Swiss sites are Z-spun (and S-plied), some of the Swiss fishnets and balls of linen string were made of Z-plied, presumably S-spun, yarns (E. Vogt 1937, 48–49), and likewise the Naḥal Ḥemar

strings and cords used for nets, knotting, etc. are S-spun, Z-plied (T. Schick, pers. comm. 1985). The Chalcolithic textile threads preserved at Alishar, in Turkey, are S-spun (Fogelberg and Kendall 1937, 334). Far to the west, the scraps of fine linen cloth clinging to the Early Bronze Age bronzes from El Argar, in southeastern Spain, also seem to be S-spun.[17] Tiny fragments of fine cloth, also apparently linen, from Middle Bronze Age layers at Terqa, in Syria, are S-spun too.[18]

Are these latter pieces also evidence of an old linen-working tradition pre-dating the advent of woolly sheep and draft-spinning? Or did many different users of linen rediscover the principle that Bellinger enunciated, and figure out how to use the locally available spindle in such a way as to give the flax its stabilizing S-twist?

OTHER ACCOUTREMENTS

After the Bronze Age, the art of spinning seems to remain constant for a while: any further changes and refinements over the next two millennia were evidently fairly small, local, and unimportant to the general development of textiles. Certainly the spindles represented on Classical Greek vases are of the standard low-whorl drop-spindle type still in use among Greek peasants today. The introduction of cotton in Classical times presumably brought with it the technique of the supported spindle, if cotton was locally manufactured at all. Plato, in describing the universe as a sort of cosmic spindle, has this spindle turn on the lap of Necessity (στρέφεσθαι δὲ αὐτὸν ἐν τοῖς τῆς Ἀνάγκης γόνασιν, *Republic* 10.617b), which may indicate

familiarity with the supported spindle; but it might also represent poetic inaccuracy.

Hooks

Plato also mentions a hook at the top of his cosmic spindle so matter-of-factly (ibid., 10.616c) that it must have been a normal feature of his day; and in fact such hooks are visible in some paintings from a century earlier (e.g., plaque no. 2202 from the Athenian acropolis: Graef and Langlotz 1925, v.1.4 pl. 93). Five such hooks, made of bronze, with caps to go over the end of a rod, have been found in the Dictaean Cave on Crete (Fig. 2.34 a–b; Hogarth 1899–1900, 111–12). Unfortunately, we do not have good dates for

[17] Many thanks to Andrew Sherratt for searching out and allowing me to inspect the pieces in the Ashmolean Museum.

[18] Many thanks to the excavator, Giorgio Buccellati, for allowing me to inspect this material.

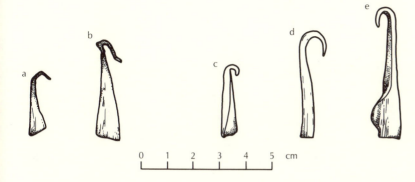

2.34   (a–b) Bronze hooks from the Dictaean cave, Crete, possibly for spindles (after Hogarth 1899–1900, 112 fig. 46); (c–e) bronze spindle hooks from Olynthus, Classical era (after D. M. Robinson 1941, pl. 119 nos. 1884, 1891, 1886; courtesy of Johns Hopkins University Press)

these artifacts: they could belong to either the Bronze or Iron Age. Classical examples were found at Olynthus (Fig. 2.34 c–e; D. M. Robinson 1941, 374–77, with further bibliography).

Distaffs

Although fashions in spindle shapes have come and gone, the only real innovation since the Bronze Age has been the spinning wheel, which reached Europe from China in medieval times (Kuhn 1979–80, 15–16). But it has not been widely adopted, for example, by Greek peasants even now, when hand-spinning is dying out altogether. One reason the wheel has not been popular in Greece is that one of the most convenient times there for spinning is while travelling about—from one village to the next, or while tending the flocks. This habit of spinning while walking, or riding a donkey, seems to be fairly old in the north Mediterranean. Herodotus (5.12) tells of King Darius's amazement at the (admittedly contrived) diligence of a Paeonian woman who spun flax as she walked to and from the river with her water pitcher on her head and a horse to be watered tethered to her arm. Herodotus also comments that such multiple activity was unknown to the Persians and to the inhabitants of "Asia" (Asia Minor); but he does not seem to find it

strange himself. Today it is observable here and there in various parts of the Near East (cf. Crowfoot 1931, 37), as well as throughout the Balkans (see Fig. 0.1).

The accoutrement that makes such spinning convenient is the distaff, a rod or board onto which prepared fibers are fastened to serve as a source of supply during spinning. Such a tool, which can be held in one hand or stuck into the belt or into a special back-strap, is readily portable. Since the distaff need be no more than a stick, perhaps conveniently forked, it does not generally turn up as an identifiable artifact in archaeological excavations until Classical times, although we saw some possible examples in Mesopotamia in the mid-3rd millennium. As for representations of spinning, Classical Greek art often shows distaffs. A long one appears in the hand of a spinner on an Archaic stele from Priniás in Crete (Fig. 2.35) and short ones in the hands of women on some of the vases (Fig. 2.36; see also Daremberg and Saglio 1877–1919, vol. 2, pt. 2, 1425–26 figs. 3381–82). A distaff also seems to be intended in the upper hand of the spinner on the 7th-century Hallstatt vase from Sopron (see Figs. 2.15, 13.3). Some of the Classical Greek and Etruscan distaffs are so fancy (often in bronze) that there would seem to be a considerable tradition behind them already. (The British Museum exhibit of them is

2.35   One of the earliest known representations of a distaff, which the girl holds with her spindle, on an Archaic stele from Priniás, Crete. (Pernier 1910, pl. 4.9)

2.36   Greek girl spinning with her thread in her mouth—either to bite out defects (if wool) or to wet the fiber (if linen). The basket and the shortness of the distaff suggest wool. Center of vase found at Orvieto; early 5th century B.C. (Blümner 1877, pl. 6)

quite extensive; see also Hencken 1968, fig. 27e.) As we have said, however, there is no sign of a distaff in the ancient Egyptian scenes and nothing provable among the artifacts there before Roman times (Crowfoot 1931, 29, 37). The "distaff" mentioned by Schliemann (1880a, 327) is a misidentified bobbin: it is wound lengthwise, and with spun thread, not raw fibers.

Bowls and Baskets

When not walking about, spinners usually keep their fibers in a bowl or basket, to keep them clean and tidy; this custom too goes back to early times. We see the Classical Greek ladies with their tall, slim wool-baskets on the vases, and hear from Homer that Helen has an elegant silver one on wheels for her expensive purple wool (*Od.* 4.125–35). Homer calls Helen's basket a *talaros* (τάλαρος), from a root meaning "to weigh" and

having to do with measuring wool out by weight for a project (see Chapter 12).

The Egyptian spinners, on their side, are usually shown drawing threads out of bowls to add twist. As Crowfoot points out, however, when one is pulling yarn from a ball rather than fibers from a soft rove or rolag (see below), something must be done to keep the ball from jumping about and out of the pot, and to provide tension—something is needed to pull against (Crowfoot 1931, 27). A lid with a hole would do, but it has also been suggested that certain bowls found with handle-like loops inside must have served this purpose too. Crowfoot picks up the suggestion from Peet and Woolley (1923, 61) that stone bowls of this sort found at Amarna may well have been used as "spinning bowls," but she complains at the lack of "clinching evidence" for their use (Crowfoot 1931, 27).

More recently, Trude Dothan (1963) analyzed a rather extensive series of such bowls from Palestine (as well as many more from Egypt), and pointed out some clinching evidence. The Palestinian bowls are mostly of clay, which is much softer than stone, and the undersides of the loops (as well as spots opposite them on the rim, on some examples) have been worn down in characteristic grooves—grooves that would be hard to explain in such strange places except by threads constantly rubbing past as they were pulled from a ball inside the bowl. The Palestinian bowls occur mostly in Late Bronze

and Early Iron Age contexts (Fig. 2.37; ibid., 97–99; Dothan 1982a, 762–63), exactly when influence from Egypt is strongest in the archaeological and historical record; whereas the Egyptian series begins already in the 12th Dynasty, many centuries earlier. One must thus conclude, with Dothan, that the "spinners" of Palestine got the idea for their bowls from Egypt, along with the peculiar Egyptian method of adding twist to the flax after splicing it into thread.[19]

It is interesting in this regard that the arrival of this type of "spinning bowl" in Pal-

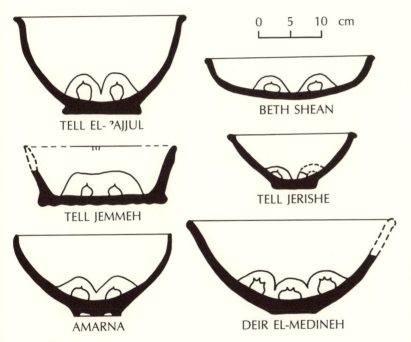

0 5 10 cm

TELL EL- ʾAJJUL

BETH SHEAN

TELL JEMMEH

TELL JERISHE

AMARNA

DEIR EL-MEDINEH

2.37 Clay bowls with internal loops, from Egypt and Palestine; Late Bronze Age. Note grooves worn inside the loops, from thread being pulled through. (After Dothan 1963, figs. 1, 3)

[19] A Chalcolithic rim sherd with a hole and thread grooves found in the "Cave of the Treasure" in the Judaean desert has been interpreted by the excavator as part of a "spinning bowl" of rather different design (Bar-Adon 1971, 192–93). The many slim grooves do suggest that thread was being pulled out of the bowl over the rim (not through the hole)—although a stick through a facing pair of such holes (and we have no proof that a second hole existed), as he suggests, would only keep the ball in the bowl while it was very large. However that may be, if his surmise is even roughly correct, we

must reckon with a very much longer development period for these bowls than our Egyptian evidence warns us about (see below). It also suggests that the technology of splicing as opposed to spinning flax had a much longer and broader history than our pitiful remains can tell us.

Bowls with internal loop-handles have also been found in Mesopotamia, particularly in the Early Dynastic period (cf. Strommenger 1970, 66 and 69 fig. 24); but they seem to be specifically kitchen utensils rather than textile tools.

estine in the middle of the Late Bronze Age accords well with what we now know of the date of the exodus of the Hebrews from Egypt after their long sojourn there. It is precisely then, as we have seen, that the linen is repeatedly referred to in the Bible with the special word *shazar* 'twine, twist; glue' (Ex. 26–28, 35–38; see above). Certainly these bowls are specifically suited to the art of twisting bast in the Egyptian fashion, and not well suited to the use of wool. There is nothing actually preventing its use with a ball of previously spun wool, except possibly the tendency for a woolen ball to jam into the loop; but even in that case it could be used only for the process of plying (or possibly of respinning), not for spinning itself. The bundles of combed wool, called *roves* or *rolags*, from which one spins that fiber are far too fluffy to treat this way; see for example the fluffy rolags in the hands and baskets of the Classical Greek wool-workers on a handsome lekythos in the Metropolitan Museum (Fig. 2.38). In short, this type of bowl would have to be either a "plying" bowl, for wool or for flax, or else a "twisting" bowl, for adding twist to spliced flax in the Egyptian fashion. The term "spinning bowl" is thus rather inappropriate. But before we decide just what to call such vessels (the term "twining," for example, has already

been pre-empted as a technical weaving term), we need to consider some other data.

There is yet another reason to associate such bowls specifically with the production of linen rather than wool or any other fiber not of the bast family. Bast fibers are a great deal easier to control and manipulate when wet. Thus people have tended to choose damp places such as cellars for spinning flax, which changes from being brittle, ornery, and full of slivers for the fingers to being limp and docile, in the face of water. European flax wheels are often distinguishable by a little dish for water built right onto the distaff, so the spinner could constantly wet her fingers as she drafted the flax. On the other hand, some linen-workers prefer saliva to plain water; and we have mentioned that the enzymes in saliva convert a little of the plant cellulose into a gluey substance that helps hold the fibers more permanently in place. Hungarian flax-spinners, I am told, traditionally sucked on plum pits while spinning, to induce a copious supply of saliva for their work. A little water in the bottom of the looped bowls of the Egyptians would provide the ideal conditions for working with the linen yarns.

Any doubts I had as to whether the Egyptian looped bowls were for dampening as well as for tension were removed recently by

2.38   Scenes of spinning and weaving on an Attic Greek lekythos, ca. 560 B.C. See Fig. 3.13 for the vase itself. (The Metropolitan Museum of Art; Fletcher Fund, 1931: no. 31.11.10)

the discovery that just such a bowl—loop, water, and all—was independently invented in Japan for working with another thirsty bast fiber, of the nettle family (*Boehmeria nipponivea*: M. Tsuboi, pers. comm. 1985; see Fig. 2.39). In a brief article on the village manufacture of fine nettle cloth, Mieko Tsuboi (1984) describes a number of neatly parallel details that are worth quoting. After retting, the nettle is "peeled" into strips, and the women "constantly wet the tip in their mouth before fastening the fibers together. When they put it onto the spinning wheel, when they weave—each time, they wet the yarn. Moreover, in order to keep it from getting dry, the weaving room is always built facing north." Describing a visit to a traditional workshop in Niigata Prefecture, run by a woman in her eighties, the author says that the nettle, thus spliced together into a long yarn and piled or coiled in a tub, "was pulled out from the nettle tub, then it was hung on a pole called 'hanging ring,' from which the yarn was led through the bowl, which [the woman] called 'that which makes (something) go through water,' and finally it goes to the spinning wheel." The bowl is described thus: "In the bottom of a shallow bowl . . . is attached a 'handle' in the shape of the Greek letter Ω. If you put a yarn through this 'handle' and fill the bowl with water, the yarn naturally comes through water. . . . Depending on the thickness of the yarn, [the woman] used wetting vessels of two different sizes, one 6–7 cm in diameter, and the other about 10 cm in diameter" (ibid.).[20]

In sum, in Japan the nettle fiber is stripped off the retted stalk, spliced by tying

2.39   Modern Japanese fiber-wetting bowl. (After Tsuboi 1984)

or twisting the strips together, coiled up as a long yarn, drawn through a looped bowl filled with water in order to wet it, and then given added twist. The parallel to what we see in the Egyptian wall paintings could not be much more exact. The Egyptians apparently stripped the flax fibers off the retted stalk, spliced them by overlapping with a twist, and either wound up the resulting yarn into a ball or coiled it on the floor (see Fig. 2.40). Before adding twist with a spindle, the women ran the end of the yarn through a looped bowl—the whole ball was put into the bowl if the yarn was in ball form, otherwise only the end was run through and the coil remained on the floor. For a ball, one could make a case that the bowl was primarily for tension and containment (as well as being convenient for wetting); but for the coil on the floor the primary use had to have been to force the thread through water. I propose, therefore, to call these objects "fiber-wetting bowls."

More and more vestiges of this practice have turned up in Crete, in Bronze Age contexts. At the Early Minoan site of Myrtos in

---

[20] Mieko Tsuboi informs me (pers. comm. 1985) that thread for warp is spliced by tying the two strands together, then twisting the two short ends over to one side; whereas the weft is made by merely twisting the two ends together (facing the same way) and then—as with the warp thread—bending the two intertwisted

ends over to one side and twisting them into the main thread.

My thanks to Nobuko Kajitani for bringing this article to my attention, and to Paul Sato for making me a complete translation.

2.40   A Middle Kingdom Egyptian textile shop, from the tomb of Khnumhotep at Beni Hasan (no. 3).
The woman kneeling center right is splicing flax into thread, which she coils in front of her, while the girl
standing at right is adding twist, with two spindles, to two threads she pulls from two wetting bowls on
floor. Two other women weave, while an overseer looks on. 12th Dynasty; early 2nd millennium B.C.
(Photography courtesy of the Metropolitan Museum of Art; Rogers Fund, 1933: no. 33.8.16)

southern Crete, Peter Warren found a wide, flattish bowl with an internal "handle" (Fig. 2.41), and a fragment of another such bowl (Warren 1972, 153, 207, 209). He seems to have been the first to recognize that the Cretan bowls had something to do with thread-making, although others had been found earlier (ibid., 209). Bowls with internal loop-handles have been found in Middle Bronze Age contexts in a tomb at Drakones (Fig. 2.42; cf. Warren 1972, 209); at Phaistos (Iraklion Museum no. 5847); at Palaikastro

(Bosanquet and Dawkins 1923, pl. VIc); and in a house at Kommos (M. Shaw, pers. comm. 1983); and at least two have been found at Arkhanes (Lempese 1970, 269 and pl. 378δ). Of these, the Early Minoan bowl and at least four of the Middle Minoan examples have a small area of wear under the loop, as if from thread: not always very visible, but quite palpable to the finger, and easily differentiable by feel from shallow chips in the same pottery.[21]

The Palestinian bowls were rather obvi-

---

[21] I have not been able to see the bowl from Palaikastro. On the other hand, one of the bowls from Arkhanes, no. 19260, has no such worn spot. Perhaps it was new when destruction occurred? The second example that I

was allowed to inspect from Arkhanes, no. 131075, is considerably smaller than the others—being a mere 12 cm in diameter, more like a cup; yet it has a very palpable groove. Was it for finer thread, like the smaller

2.41 Looped bowl, probably for wetting linen thread, from an Early Bronze II village at Myrtos, Crete; late 3rd millennium. Note the wear inside the loop. (Photo courtesy of P. Warren)

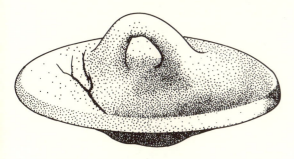

2.42 Looped bowl, from Drakones, Crete; Middle Bronze Age. Note wear under loop. (After Xanthoudides 1924, pl. 42 no. 5033)

ously a borrowing from Egypt. But what about the Minoan examples, if, as the worn spots suggest, they were also for thread-making? According to Dothan, the earliest Egyptian specimens yet known date to the 12th Dynasty (Dothan 1963, 101), which is generally taken to correspond roughly with Middle Minoan I; and the earliest representation of the use of such a bowl is from the 11th Dynasty, a model from the tomb of Meketre

(see Fig. 3.6). We know that there was indeed contact between Crete and Egypt at that time, both from Egyptian objects in Crete, and from the notable quantity of Middle Minoan pottery, especially Kamares ware, found in the 12th-Dynasty deposits at Kahun and other sites (Petrie 1891, 9–11 and pl. I; Kemp and Merrillees 1980). So the several Middle Minoan bowls would seem to cause no problem as an Egyptian idea that

Japanese examples? (At 12 cm, it is already a bit bigger than the smaller of the Japanese types mentioned; but the larger Minoan bowls correspond in size to the Egyptian and Palestinian examples.)

The bowl from Phaistos is puzzling for a different reason. The potter reamed a small hole through the bottom (for what purpose?), and in doing so kicked up a little roll of clay inside that is so rough that a ball of linen thread rolling around in the bowl as proposed would

constantly get caught on it. Unless the hole were made to anchor some additional fitting that covered this spot, the bowl would not hold water, and it would be quite unusable even just for tension without the protuberance somehow being covered.

My thanks to Maria C. Shaw for making the Kommos material known to me, and to the Iraklion and Agios Nikolaos museums for letting me inspect the other bowls.

wandered to Crete. But Myrtos is an Early Minoan II site, and corresponds rather to the height of the Egyptian Old Kingdom, Dynasties IV–VI. Our one representation of "spinning" from the Old Kingdom, a 6th-Dynasty relief of a man making string (Fig. 2.43), does not show such a bowl. Instead, the man is holding his ball of string on the floor under his leg.

2.43   Man spinning string; fragment of a 6th Dynasty Egyptian relief. (Firth and Gunn 1926, 36)

So we are left with four possibilities: (1) the Cretans and the Egyptians evolved flax-wetting bowls independently (but the evidence seems too close in time and place for such a coincidence); or (2) the idea came from early Egypt to Crete (but we have not yet tripped over the Old Kingdom Egyptian examples—although it seems unlikely that they exist in view of the failure of an explicit relief to show the bowl); or (3) the Cretans thought up the flax-wetting bowl and gave it to Egypt (perhaps rendered unlikely by the relative quantities of such bowls found in the two areas); or (4) the Minoan bowls are not for wetting flax (despite the similarities and the worn spots). We will have to await more data to make a secure choice.

But the most interesting implication, in any of these cases but the last, is that the

Cretans knew the process of splicing flax and adding the twist afterwards, and they knew it already in the Early Bronze Age. We know that making thread (and weaving) was already an old tradition in the Aegean by then; but we aren't absolutely certain how or what the people spun. If they spun wool at all in the Early Bronze Age, and that seems highly likely (indeed, Warren reports many sheep bones at Myrtos: 1972, 27; Jarman 1972), they had to know how to spin by continuous drafting, a method that can also work well for flax, given the distaff.

The possibilities we are left with are as follows. We know that Egypt had been using some form of the splice-and-twine method since pre-dynastic times, since we have the actual linen. So clearly Egypt did not borrow the basic method in the Bronze Age from the Aegean. On the other hand, the Aegean must therefore have had this method either as an old Neolithic skill that was still conserved for use with flax (continuous draft being still confined largely to wool), or as a borrowing from Egypt that replaced a different way of dealing with flax. If the former is true, then the Cretan populace must have invented the flax-wetting bowl on their own, or borrowed it readily because it fit a need. But if it was a borrowing that replaced a different method, there must have been some special cause for adopting the technique of splicing and twisting from Egypt. Such reasons might include a migration of enough people (including women!) from Egypt to Crete that the art survived in the households because of the sheer numbers of people involved (as in the Palestinian adoption of the bowls with the advent of Egyptian garrison-colonies and/or immigrants such as those involved in the exodus; see above, and Chapter 14); or at any rate the introduction of the technique (again almost certainly by women, since they were the only ones plying the textile crafts in

Egypt at that time; see Chapter 13) into such a milieu that it was retained because it produced much finer, more luxurious linen than the local method did. Either explanation also readily accounts for the disappearance of this method and accessory in Crete, and its permanence in Egypt: Crete moved over to major wool production by the Late Bronze Age, if not sooner (the Linear B tablets show it; but we can't yet read Linear A), whereas Egypt clung to its archaic but excellent linen manufacture until Roman times.

Winders

Yet another peculiar pottery object from Late Bronze Age Crete is a type of vessel that the excavators of Knossos dubbed "Ariadne's clew-box" (Fig. 2.44; Evans 1928, pt. 1, 308–9 and fig. 179). In its basic shape the object is a truncated cone, open at the bottom and closed over at the top except for a long narrow slit. The cone also has two little legs projecting from the side at the small end, as though to provide at least two working positions: one with the cone standing upright on its flat, open end, with the slit at the top; and the other lying on its side, stabilized by resting on the two legs as well as on the rim at the open end. In this second position the handle that projects from one side of the cone is on top and the slit is at one end. (The object can even stand steadily on its "closed" end.) A stick passed through the two small holes opposite each other on the sides of the cone would lie horizontally in any of these three positions. Evans suggests that such a "rod across the interior was for winding or unwinding a skein of wool, which would have been drawn in or out through the slot and over the projecting 'tongue' "—a little shelf of pottery that runs parallel to the slit all the way across the end of the vessel (ibid., 309). In this case the "clew-box" could have served

2.44 Late Minoan pottery vessel of uncertain use, possibly for winding bobbins; found in the "House of the Sacrificed Oxen" at Knossos, Crete, and dubbed "Ariadne's clew-box" by Sir Arthur Evans (1928, fig. 179). (Courtesy of Iraklion Museum: no. 7742)

the purpose of a tension bowl; but the function of the tongue is not immediately clear, and the slot is very rough along its inner edges so that thread or yarn would catch on it easily. These peculiar objects, of which evidence for several was found, may of course have had nothing to do with textiles at all.

Knee Guards

Other accoutrements to spinning occasionally appear. In classical Athens we find an object called *epinētron* (ἐπίνητρον, from *epi* 'upon,' an old root *nē- having to do with thread, and -tron, a nominalizing suffix often used for tools) or possibly *onos* (ὄνος, literally "donkey"). It is a sort of knee guard, made of baked pottery, with the main working surface roughened slightly by an incised scale pattern (Fig. 2.45). It lay on the lap as one sat, extending from knee to hip, and saved having to roll up one's skirt to find a suitable working surface on which to form the combed wool into long, soft, fluffy rolls

2.45   Knee guard or *epinētron*, used by Greek women as a surface on which to prepare roves of wool for spinning. Attic; 6th–5th century B.C. (The Metropolitan Museum of Art; Rogers Fund, 1910: no. 10.210.13)

for spinning (Xanthoudides 1910). In the vase paintings, most of the women doing this chore are using their bare legs, but a few are using the *epinētron*. Although most of the surviving examples come from 6th- and 5th-century Attica, at least three *epinētra* are of late Mycenaean manufacture and come from Rhodes (Xanthoudides 1910, 333–34 and figs. 6–7).

IN THIS brief history of early spinning, we have seen a theme that we will encounter constantly in the history of textiles, namely a powerful conservatism. One does it this way because one's ancestors did it this way and it works. In fact, remarkably little has changed during fifteen to twenty thousand years of making thread. Once the principle of strengthening fibers through twist was discovered in the Palaeolithic era, the major innovations were few: (1) the invention of the spindle and its flywheel (in a small variety of forms) to make the process more efficient; (2) the invention of drafting to make the lengthening process continuous rather than modular; and (3) the invention of a few secondary aids (e.g., distaff, wetting bowl, *epinētron*) to ease the work.

The small differences of spinning method in the part of the ancient world under consideration, meanwhile, seem to fall generally into two or three areas: (1) Egypt (spindle high-whorl, thigh-rolled, dropped; thread chiefly S-spun linen); (2) Europe and Anatolia (spindle low-whorl, finger-flicked, dropped; thread chiefly Z-spun wool and linen spun both ways); and (3) the Middle East (spindle high-whorl, perhaps hand-held; thread—?).

It was the invention of the spinning wheel in the Middle Ages out of (apparently) oriental prototypes that finally opened a new and different era of spinning, for those who accepted it. But the older methods continue here and there to this day, carefully conserved for some special reason.

CHAPTER 3

LOOMS AND WEAVING

We have said that weaving, in the narrow, technical sense, involves two operationally different sets of elements: a pre-arranged and more or less fixed set, the *warp*, and a second set, the *weft* (or *woof*), interlaced into the first set. Weaving differs from plaiting and basketry partly in the differentiation of a weft from a warp, partly in the fixed nature of the warp, and partly in the extreme length and flexibility of the typical weft. It is noteworthy that thread or yarn, the basic material for weaving, must first be manufactured, and by a not entirely obvious process. Thus it has generally been assumed that the simple over-under-over-under plaiting technique was first invented in the medium of matting or basketry, where the material comes straight from nature unaltered (and any given strand serves as both warp and weft indeterminately), and was used only later to form a second art, that of weaving, once the principles of the twisted thread had been hit upon (cf. Ryder 1968, 74). We are now in a position to improve on the details of this theory.

As we have seen, twisted cord appears to date back to the Upper Palaeolithic period, much earlier than the oldest evidence for matting or basketry. So the discovery of how to twist fibers was not, presumably, the impetus for the differentiation of weaving from plaiting. Indeed, the earliest direct archaeo-logical evidence for true weaving is exactly as old as the earliest direct evidence for mats and baskets in the Old World: both occur in the 7th millennium at Jarmo (Braidwood and Howe 1960, 46) and Çatal Hüyük (Mellaart 1963a); and other roughly contemporary sites have produced alternatively textiles or mats or baskets, according to the vagaries of preservation and discovery (see Chapters 2, 4).

On the other hand, various kinds of birds and primates can be observed to plait the elements of their nests, some roughly, some carefully. So it seems likely that humans too, with so many models around, would have long known or frequently rediscovered the principle of interlacing, if only for building temporary shelters of wattle or reeds. Why, then, do we have no evidence for mats or baskets or textiles until suddenly in the early Neolithic?

The problem may, of course, be one of preservation rather than existence. The farther back we go, the less likely it is that fibrous materials would survive; and from times before the use of clay became common (in the Neolithic), we don't find impressions on clay. On the other hand, what may have been new in the Neolithic was a rapid development of this rough principle of interlacing into the careful crafting of many small, portable objects—mats, bags, cloth, etc.[1] And in the Old World, at least, the differentiation of

[1] Recent ethnographic studies suggest that as nomadic hunter-gatherers settle down today and become crop-raisers, and no longer need to carry anything and everything they choose to own, they radically shift their time/

weaving from plaiting seems to go back at least to this point. Certainly as far back as we can reconstruct linguistically in the west (not so far as pre-ceramic Neolithic), the processes were already known by separate names: for example, the Proto-Indo-European (PIE) root for "weave" (seen in Eng. *weave, weft, woof, web*; Greek ὑφαίνειν; Sanskrit *ubhnáti*) is distinct from the PIE root for "plait" (Latin *plecto*; Greek πλέκειν, πλοκαμίς; Old Church Slavic *plet-*; English *flax*, and also *plait* by way of Latin and Old French).

If we look carefully at what differentiates weaving from matting and basketry, however, we must still conclude that, within that short time span in which all these arts rather suddenly appeared, weaving must have come second, if only barely so. Mats and baskets are made from fairly short, stiff materials that have body of their own. But the extreme flexibility of string, which is what makes cloth so useful in its own peculiar ways, makes the process of interlacing terribly difficult without some artificial way of holding part of the string in one place. That is, one needs some sort of brace or frame—a special tool—to provide some tension, as a temporary substitute for the stiffness not inherent in the materials. And that brace is what we call a *loom*. It must have been the invention of a means or tool to provide tension, then, that made true weaving possible; and it is the addition of that tool that makes weaving logically secondary to matting and basketry. Interestingly, the words for this device in Indo-European languages tend merely to be general words for "tool" in origin (e.g., Eng. *loom*) or for "stand, frame" (e.g., Gk. ἱστός or Ru. *stanók*, both from the verbal root *stā-* 'stand'), with or without the specifica-

tion that the stand is for weaving (e.g., Ru. *tkátskij stanók*; Gm. *Webstuhl*).

Looms can be very simple or very complicated, but they all fulfill at least the function of holding taut one set of threads (the warp). In the simplest form, one end of the warp is tied to the weaver's waist and the other to a convenient tree or post. The weaver can then adjust the tension easily by leaning back to various degrees. Such a strategy is used to this day by handweavers making belts and bands of various sorts, because it is so simple and so portable. But tying the end of the warp in a bunch to one spot places severe limits on the width of the cloth that you can conveniently weave. The warp must be allowed to spread out, as the weft is introduced, to the full width of the cloth; and three or four inches (perhaps ten centimeters) is about as wide as you can spread the warp tied to a single point without serious tension problems because of the angle of the threads.

The solution, of course, must be to tie up the warp at more points—points on a line at right angles to the stretched warp. One way of achieving this is to fasten the warp threads to a stiff rod, doing so individually or in bunches at suitable intervals. The rod thus attached to one end of the warp can be hitched, as before, to the weaver, and the rod at the far end—the *warp beam*—to a tree or post, or even to the weaver's own feet, as in Han Dynasty China. We have now gained in width from a few inches or centimeters to half a yard or meter: for that seems to be the effective maximum for such looms the world over. But the toll in heaviness, instability, and awkwardness (especially for inserting the weft bobbin) becomes too great after that. To solve these problems we must abandon the

energy values toward stockpiling and possession (Leakey 1981, 99–105, 226–29). These changes make it worthwhile to invest more time making things—i.e., to de-

velop various crafts. So perhaps the apparent explosion of crafts at the beginning of the Neolithic is not merely an illusion born of how we retrieve artifacts.

backstrap loom, as it is often called, and hitch both ends of the warp to something other than the weaver: something potentially bigger, stronger, and more stable.

Note that up to this point nothing in our loom will survive as an artifact recognizable alone for what it is. All we have used are random trees or posts, perhaps a strap around the waist, and perhaps a couple of straight sticks. Unless we find a representation of weavers weaving, as in the tiny bronze figures from China in Figure 3.1, or the sticks

3.1 Bronze figurine of a woman weaving on a backstrap loom with tension controlled by the toes. Yunnan, China; early Han Dynasty (late 1st millennium B.C.). (After no. 176 of the travelling Exhibition of Archaeological Finds from the People's Republic of China)

warped up with a half-finished piece of weaving on them, as are sometimes found in Inca tombs in high, dry parts of the Andes, we have no way of knowing that such a loom was in use, except perhaps by surmise from the types of textiles we find. So far we have no known representations of looms or weaving before the Late Neolithic period, and no certain examples at all of ancient backstrap looms or other looms specifically designed for making bands, belts, and other such nar-

row strips of cloth—although we have narrow textiles quite early, both at Çatal Hüyük, where carefully woven tapes bound up the packages of bones under the flooring (Helbaek 1963, 39–41), and also in the Neolithic Swiss pile-dwellings (Vogt 1937, 58–62).

One widespread solution for stabilizing the beams or rods holding the warp—we shall explore the alternatives one by one—is to peg their ends firmly to the ground. The resulting loom, known as the *horizontal ground-loom*, is exactly what we find in the earliest representations of weaving that we have from Egypt and Mesopotamia (see below). The ground-loom ostensibly solves the problem of making the cloth as large as is needed, since one can stake it out to any size. If the cloth is wider than the weaver can reach, however, she (or he) must continually stand up, walk around to the other side of the loom, and squat down again, with every row (or pick) of the weft—or else have a helper. And if the warp is too long for the weaver to reach from the end of the loom, it may become necessary to sit down right on the finished cloth itself (as is still done, for example, by Bedouins [Roth (1918) 1977, 45 fig. 89] and by Turkish women [Acar 1975, 4]); or else, unless the cloth is also too wide, again retain a helper so as to reach it from both sides. The ancient Egyptians frequently wove very wide sheets of linen—widths of 2.8 m (9 ft.; Picard-Schmitter 1967, 25) have been reported—and they adopted the method of always having at least two women working the loom, one on each side.

Part of the problem here is that the loom uses the earth to provide its solidity. By constructing a rigid, free-standing frame, however, one can not only achieve some measure of portability, but also set the frame at any angle desired. A more or less vertical position has the distinct advantage that the weaver can walk back and forth in front of the loom while working, and so get by without a helper even if the cloth is very wide. We find one version of this solution in prehistoric Europe. There, the beam against which the cloth builds up—called the *cloth beam*—was fastened at the top of the frame with the free warp hanging down, and weights were hung at the bottom ends of the warp threads to provide the necessary tension. Because of its mode of tensioning, it is known as the *warp-weighted loom*. The second basic type of vertical loom has a beam at the bottom as well as at the top. Appearing in the archaeological record rather later than the other two loom-types, it proved to be the most adaptable loom, and spawned a number of sub-varieties. I will refer to the generic type simply as the *vertical two-beam loom*.

Another major problem confronting the weaver, besides tension for the warp, is how to introduce the weft into the warp to form the cloth. The crudest, conceptually simplest way of putting in weft is to "darn" it in, by running the leading end under the first thread, over the second, under the third, and so forth, one thread at a time, back and forth across the warp, a process tedious in the extreme. The next step is to discover that

a rod can be stuck into the warp in such a way that every second thread passes over the rod while the threads in between pass under. By pulling the whole rod and its burden up or forward (depending on whether the loom is horizontal or vertical)—or even pressing the rod and what is behind it down or away—the threads can be separated by one motion into a passageway, or *shed* as weavers call it (from a root meaning "divide"; cf. Gm. *scheiden*), through which the weft can be passed all at once: a quick way of putting in one whole row of weft. (Such a bar is known as a *shed bar*, and forms the *natural shed*.) The return row, however, would still have to be darned in, because if you simply try to put in a second bar with the other set of threads on top, the two bars interfere with each other in the making of the opposite sheds. Somehow the device to produce the second shed (or *countershed*) has to be made discontinuous, so as not to negate the work of the first shed bar.

The principal solution to this difficult problem, which may have taken considerable time to resolve, is to provide the warps in the second group with individual holders, or *heddles* (from the same root as *heave*, cf. Gm. *heben* 'to lift'), which in turn are at-

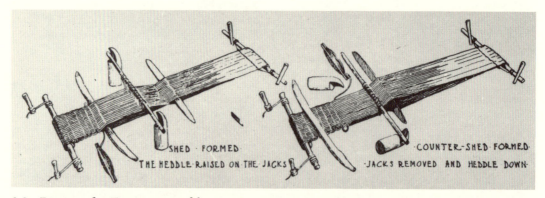

3.2   Diagram of an Egyptian ground-loom in use, as reconstructed by E. Winlock (1922, fig. 2). It is not, however, strictly necessary to remove the heddle jacks (which support the heddle bar) to form the countershed. (Courtesy of Department of Egyptology, University College London)

tached to a bar running above or in front of the warp. When the *heddle bar* (as it is called) is raised, it pulls only the threads caught by the heddles and does not interfere with those threads controlled by the shed bar (see Fig. 3.2). Ancient heddles, like some

THE GROUND-LOOM

Our earliest depiction of a ground-loom is on a dish found in the grave of a woman at Badari, dating to the early 4th millennium B.C., or Late Neolithic (Fig. 3.3; Brunton and Caton-Thompson 1928, pl. 38). We can see the four corner-pegs holding the two beams at either end, with the warp running between them. A little bit of woven cloth appears at one end, and three bars are painted across the middle—presumably shed, heddle, and beater bars (see below).[2]

All of the Middle Kingdom models and paintings of textile workers, and those New Kingdom scenes which show women weaving (as opposed to men), also show the horizontal ground-loom, although an Egyptian convention of perspective requiring all functional parts to be shown may make that appear untrue at first glance (see p. 44 and note 2 above for a list of these representations). In the Mesopotamian cultural area, too, the

modern ones, seem generally to have been fashioned out of string (see below).

With these details in mind, let us take up the archaeological evidence for the development of each type of loom, beginning with the ground-loom.

3.3   Neolithic Egyptian dish showing a ground-loom (below). From Badari; early 4th millennium. (Photo courtesy of Petrie Museum, University College London: UC 9547)

only certain representation, from Susa in the 4th millennium (Fig. 3.4; for photograph see Amiet 1966, pl. 43), depicts this same form of loom. Late 3rd-millennium accounts in cuneiform that mention replacement parts for

[2] There has been some debate as to whether either or neither of the two objects depicted on this bowl is in fact a loom. The main reason for rejecting the one as representing a ground-loom seems to be the difficulty of interpreting the other scene. Thus Vandier (1952, 285–86), who thinks the two human figures are building "a palisade," molds his interpretation of the other object to fit the first; he identifies it as part of a hunting scene, complaining that the proposed shed, heddle, and beater bars are not close enough to the "cloth" for the object to be a loom. Baumgartel (1947, 1.30), at the other extreme of enthusiasm, takes the one object as a ground-loom and then finds a commensurate explanation for the other, calling it a vertical loom (which, since it has no lower beam, would have to be a warp-weighted loom). Although it does not look like the typical warp-weighted loom used for woolen textiles, and although we have ev-

ery other reason to believe the early Egyptians knew nothing of such a loom (see below), it might be a primitive, stone-weighted mat-loom of the sort still used in Syria and Iran (Barrois 1939, 464–65, especially fig. 180; P. J. Watson 1979, 190). Crowfoot, with her usual restraint, merely describes the human figures as "hanging strands over a pole" (1954, 432), an interpretation that makes no complicated claims but works well with her interpretation of the other object as a ground-loom, much as I have described it. One might add that the painter seems even to have depicted the fringe-like weft loops that Egyptian weavers (and they alone) typically made at the left edge of the fabric (compare, for example, the loom shown in the tomb of Khnumhotep, Fig. 3.5). This idiosyncratic detail adds a great deal of weight to the loom interpretation.

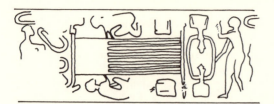

3.4   Early cylinder seal designs from Susa, 4th millennium (drawings courtesy of Dominique Collon). *Left*: ground-loom (center) with a weaver crouching on either side, and someone warping (right). Loom and warp viewed as if from above (GS 673; Le Breton 1957, 106 fig. 20 no. 20; Amiet 1961, pl. 16.275). *Right*: at left, warping frame viewed from side; cf. Fig. 2.17 (GS 674; Amiet 1961, pl. 16.273)

looms imply this loom type also (Waetzoldt 1972, 130–36). So we are fairly safe in saying that looms of this design were being used in the area from Egypt to Iran in the Neolithic and Bronze Ages.

The depictions from Egypt are sufficiently detailed that we can learn a great deal from them about how this loom functioned and what its component parts looked like. We see, in general, that two women helped each other in managing the loom, dividing up the tasks of changing the shed, entering the weft, and beating it home. Where the detail is sufficient to distinguish them, we observe at least three rods besides the warp beam and cloth beam: a long, heavy beater closest to the finished cloth, and two shorter, lighter rods farther away, which the women are sometimes shown manipulating. Roth has shown, in his extended discussion of the mural in the tomb of Khnumhotep at Beni Hasan (Roth [1913] 1951, 6–15), that these rods served in effect as heddle and shed bars (Fig. 3.5). In addition, on some of the little wooden funerary models (which are not complete), there are supports (called *heddle jacks*) next to the loom at the place where these rods ought to be (e.g., on the wooden model from the tomb of Meketre, Fig. 3.6: Winlock 1955, pl. 25–27; cf. C. R. Clark 1944, 27), supports on which the heddle bar rested while it was raised, to free the hands for putting in the weft. Sometimes one or

3.5   Egyptian ground-loom depicted in the Middle Kingdom tomb of Khnumhotep, at Beni Hasan (see Fig. 2.40 for entire scene); 12th Dynasty. The loom represented is in fact horizontal, although Egyptian conventions of drawing make it appear vertical to us at first glance. (Drawing by Norman de Garis Davies: Roth [1913] 1951, fig. 6; courtesy of Calderdale Museums Service: Bankfield Museum, Halifax)

two more rods are depicted still farther up the warp away from the cloth. In such a position, they must be *laze rods*, the function of which is merely to stabilize and space the warp. On Khnumhotep's loom we see a twined spacing cord fulfilling this function.

Few Egyptian representations show how the weft was kept. Picard-Schmitter (1967, 24) thinks that the vague shape in the hand of the left weaver in the mural from the tomb of Khnumhotep (Fig. 3.5) is some sort of

3.6 Egyptian funerary model of female textile workers, from the Middle Kingdom tomb of Meketre; 11th Dynasty. Splicers sit along the wall at left, spinners stand in front of them. Two looms are pegged out on the ground, and two women are warping on wall pegs at right. (Egyptian Museum, Cairo. Photography by Egyptian Expedition, the Metropolitan Museum of Art)

"shuttle" or bobbin.[3] One hand of the left weaver in the mural in the tomb of Daga (Fig. 3.9) seems to hold a smallish stick that could be a weft bobbin. Davies, who drew copies with great care, says this is definitely not the beater (Roth [1913] 1951, 9). The cloths themselves, however, show that often the weft was regularly only two rows long, in which case a bobbin was hardly necessary (de Jonghe 1985, 10, 19, etc.).

The *beater* is generally shown as a wide, flat bar long enough to reach all the way across the warp and stick out at both ends, one end being shaped into a convenient handle. Thus—ideally—a whole row of weft

could be beaten into its place next to the previous row at one blow. The bar must have been quite heavy for average widths of cloth (4 or 5 feet), and would have taken considerable strength and elbow room to wield. For truly huge cloths—we have mentioned one 9 feet wide—smaller beaters must have been used and inserted at several points across the warp.

Despite the fact that all the parts of the ground-loom are made of wood and thus are highly perishable, the southern climate is so hot and dry that a few remains of looms have survived in Egypt and Palestine. The caves of Naḥal Mishmar, in the Judaean desert,

---

[3] The true *shuttle* (the word is from the same root as Eng. *shoot*) is a smooth container, usually boat-shaped (cf. Gm. *Schiffchen*, Fr. *navette*, both meaning "shuttle" but literally "little boat"), with a bobbin inside, that is so streamlined that it can be literally thrown or shot through the opened shed from one side of the loom to the other—a tremendous time-saver. The shuttle seems to have come to the Mediterranean world relatively late (certainly by the tenth century A.D., but not much earlier: cf. Kostrzewski [1947] 1949, 266 fig. 140; Broudy 1979, 141 fig. 8.4), perhaps with the horizontal treadle

loom from the Orient. It is *a priori* unlikely that a thrown shuttle was used on the ancient Egyptian ground-loom in any case, because it requires an extremely wide opening of the shed—wider than the ancient Egyptian technology probably allowed, given that they used a shed bar rather than a second set of heddles. The true shuttle shown by Petrie (1917, pl. 66 no. 127) among his Egyptian artifacts was purchased, not excavated (see D. L. Carroll 1985, 169 n. 8), and the equally anachronistic reed is also unstratified (Roth [1913] 1951, 22).

contained deposits from both the Chalcolithic (4th millennium) and Roman eras, including many textiles and textile-related tools. A number of wooden sticks were singled out by the excavators as constituting most of the parts of a loom (Bar-Adon [1971] 1980, 180–81). I find it difficult to believe that all the parts functioned as assigned: in particular, a curved heddle bar (ibid., 179) would be exceedingly difficult, probably impossible, to manage; and the two "shed" bars in the reconstruction sketch (ibid., 182) would hopelessly interfere with each other. But it seems reasonable to believe that we have two examples of notched beams to which the warp could be tied, and one or more grooved sticks for manipulating the sheds.

The "warp beams" in this loom (no. 61–42/2 + 61–56/2, and no. 61–79/1 + 61–19/5: ibid., 181) are interesting in that one is half again as long and as thick as the other (note that the dimensions in the excavator's descriptions seem to have been switched), running 54.5 and 35.5 cm in length. They may have belonged to different looms; or it may be, as the strange "perspective" in the weaving scene in the tomb of Khnumhotep suggests (Fig. 3.5), that in fact the warp beam was sometimes longer than the cloth beam. (Spreading the warp in this way may have been a considerable help in keeping the warp straight without a modern reed.) The difference portrayed in Khnumhotep's drawing, if Davies's careful rendition of the mural is accurate in this dimension, is about 5 to 4 for the beams and 4 to 3 for the spreading of the warp. The beams at Naḥal Mishmar differ rather more (3 to 2), and are both quite short compared to dynastic Egyptian looms, as estimated by the widths of surviving cloth. Such a narrow loom certainly would not require two weavers—an indication of self-reliance not incommensurate with the early

date. Indeed, perhaps this loom was still being used backstrap-style!

The grooved sticks at Naḥal Mishmar—especially the relatively straight ones—bring us to another problem, that of how the warp was manipulated during weaving. A number of long, grooved sticks have been found in Bronze Age Egyptian houses (e.g., Gurob: Petrie 1917, pl. 66 nos. 133–36; A. P. Thomas 1981, pl. 45 no. 98, pl. 5 no. 99; Amarna: Peet and Woolley 1923, pl. 20.3 top and left). Some, like the Naḥal Mishmar examples, have friction grooves, that is, grooves that seem to have been produced accidentally by the friction of threads running over them again and again. Others have had deep grooves or slots purposefully carved into them at regular intervals. On Gurob specimen 98, the slots occur every 6 to 8 mm on one side, whereas the opposite side of the stick is plain and sliced flat (Thomas 1981, 39).

Now, we know from representations that the Egyptian women worked with three major rods: a shed bar, a heddle bar, and a beater. From the practical craft of weaving we know that the beater *must* be flat and smooth to do its job, so as to slide inside the warp without snagging or opening the shed unduly. (Roth illustrates an ideal example from 12th-Dynasty Kahun: [1913] 1951, 21 fig. 21.) The shed bar *can* be round, but is most efficient if wide and flat: that way it can be turned up on edge to form a nice open shed, and can lie flat and unobtrusive in the shed when the countershed is open (cf. Roth [1913] 1951, 21 fig. 20). The heddle bar lies outside the warp, so its cross-section is not critical, and it need not slide in the warp. Therefore the only possible use on a loom for a stick with deep slots (which won't slide) is as a heddle bar, and the only uses that could cause the shallow friction grooves are those of shed bar and beater. The flat underside of the slotted bars would allow them to rest stably on top of the warp with the slots always uppermost. We seem to see just such a heddle bar on the Meketre model (Fig. 3.6).[4] Our specimens *could* be merely for spacing the warp, but then they would have no need of the "handles" they have at the end.

Heddle bars as such need not have handles: you can hold the bar up by hand from the center—if you can reach it, and if you have extra hands. The wily Egyptians, however, had a much more clever solution. By the time of the Middle Kingdom, at least, they had developed remarkably efficient jacks (Fig. 3.7; also Petrie, Griffith, and Newberry 1890, pl. 9 no. 12) to support the heddle bar, which therefore had to stick out beyond the warp at each end. From the pictures, artifacts, and personal experimenta-

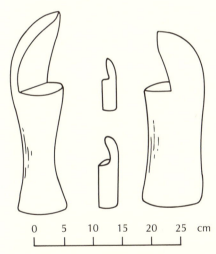

0   5   10   15   20   25   cm

3.7 Egyptian heddle jacks from Kahun (Middle Kingdom), now in the Petrie Museum, London. (After Roth and Crowfoot 1921, 100 fig. 4; courtesy of Department of Egyptology, University College London)

---

[4] It is not clear to me how the heddles would be arranged on such a bar—whether several heddles would be bunched into each slot, or whether every *n*th heddle

tion, Winlock reconstructs a rather noisy scene:

The heddle-rod is . . . raised by hand, first at one end and then at the other, and the jacks inserted. . . . The spoon-shaped top is expressly contrived to slip under the end of the rod when it lies close to the floor; the rod end then slides into the notch; a quick jerk is given, and the jack sits upright, firmly held on its broad base by the tension of the warp threads. To lower the heddle-rod a smart blow on either jack brings down the whole affair. (Winlock 1922, 72)

A number of these jacks have been found, some of which are slim and "designed to be pulled or knocked out by hand; but the stouter ones . . . show deep battering on the sides and marked rounding on the bottom, from long use in looms where the tension of the warp was so great that heavy blows were necessary to tip the jacks over on the earthen floors. This indeed seems to have been the usual thing, for in all three Beni Hasan pictures [Fig. 2.5; 2.40, 3.5; 13.1], and in the Mehenkwetre' [Meketre] model [Fig. 3.6], the assistant weaver (the one who wields the beater-in) holds a stone in her hand to knock her jack down" (ibid.).

Winlock seems to envision knocking the heddle bar down at each change of shed. An alternative interpretation draws from modern Near Eastern custom in the use of the ground-loom (see, e.g., Starr 1939, pl. 30B). Here the ends of the heddle bar are placed on sizable stones or inverted pots on either side of the loom, where they remain propped more or less permanently. In other words, the state of affairs "at rest" has the countershed (the one produced by the heddles) standing open. The other shed is produced as needed exclusively by manipulating the shed bar—standing it on edge or laying it

---

would be made shorter and put into a slot to control the spacing at regular intervals.

flat. It is only when the weaving has progressed so far that the heddle rod is too close to make a good opening in the warp that the entire set-up, support blocks, heddle bar, and all, is taken down, shoved farther along the unused warp, and set up again. Such a procedure would involve much less energy (not to say noise) during the course of the weaving. But the shape of the Egyptian jacks would still facilitate knocking them out and moving them when the time came. It is likely that the large, square blocks depicted opposite the free warp on either side of the loom on the Susa seal (Fig. 3.4) are crude heddle jacks, although no bars of any sort are shown.

Although the very smallest details—like heddles—in ancient representations of looms are very difficult to interpret, it is interesting that already in the very earliest picture of a loom, the ground-loom on the Badarian bowl (Fig. 3.3; early 4th millennium), there are three parallel lines across the middle of the warp. These are most easily interpreted as shed and heddle bars, the third bar being either for beating the weft home or possibly for maintaining the spacing of the warp (a laze rod). There is nothing to prove any particular reading; we can only go on probabilities. It should be pointed out, however, that the denials that these rods *could* be for shedding were first written at a time when it was thought that weaving must have been invented for the world in Egypt, at about the time this vase was painted, and hence that it was too early for such sophistication. But now that the finds at Çatal Hüyük and Jarmo have pushed weaving history back another two or three thousand years, this view hardly

seems cogent. Moreover, the several grooved sticks from Naḥal Mishmar as well as other finds from Europe support the idea that the principle of the heddle was well known over a wide area by the 4th millennium. And cuneiform records from the 3rd millennium imply knowledge of the heddle in Mesopotamia at that time.[5]

In Egypt, relatively few sites have been dug that would give direct evidence for looms, since one needs to search humble working/living areas rather than the tombs or temples preferred by excavation underwriters. We have looked at miscellaneous artifacts from Kahun and Gurob. For a more systematic layout, the workmen's village at Amarna would seem ideal, and there is certainly much evidence of local spinning and weaving—but no provable looms. The excavators repeatedly suggest that the frequent pairs of stone blocks, socketed to receive the two ends of a heavy beam, formed the bases of looms, although of the vertical type (see below; Peet and Woolley 1923, 60–61, etc.). But if one inspects the seven houses in which those sockets occur (12 East St.; 3, 7, 8, and 9 Main St.; 10 and 12 Long Wall St.), one finds very little supporting evidence, and considerable counter-evidence, for such an interpretation. In particular, the socket stones in 8 and 9 Main St. are clearly associated, as the excavators say, with a large hole through the front wall of each of these houses, a hole that opens directly onto a covered trough under the street outside (ibid., 68, 79–80). (A third such trough runs from the neighboring house, 7 Main St., apparently also opposite a hole in the front wall; see plan, ibid., pl. 16. A pair of sockets was

---

[5] Waetzoldt (1972, 133–36) works through a number of references to loom parts in the Neo-Sumerian economic texts. The terms are very difficult to interpret; but in each case, as he remarks, it seems that the parts being issued to the various weavers never constitute an entire loom, but rather replacement parts or sometimes perhaps extra parts (e.g., extra heddle bars?) needed for the particular project. All of them have the determinative for "wood," and there is nothing to make them seem incommensurate with a horizontal ground-loom.

found in this house also, but in the central rather than in the front room; ibid., 78.) I know of no reason whatever for a loom to need an underground trench just outdoors from it; and the placement of a loom from wall to wall across these rooms, as indicated by the socket positions, would make weaving very difficult—one needs considerable elbow room at both sides to insert beaters, bobbins, etc.—and would totally cut off access to the back half of the room. Instead, in these houses the sockets seem more likely to have braced the bedding beam of some kind of heavy equipment producing run-off that could be directed out through the hole in the wall and into the trench outside—for example, a press of some sort. And there is no particularly higher porportion of ancillary weaving equipment in these houses than elsewhere in the village.

The occupants of the house at 3 Main St., on the other hand, are much more likely to have been running a weaving establishment. In the blank wall opposite this house were found a group of pegs for making warps (ibid., 69, 75), just as the women are shown doing in the model of a weaving workshop found in the tomb of Meketre (Fig. 3.6; Winlock 1955, pl. 26–27; see below). The street fill just here contained the remains of many spindles and/or spindle whorls (Peet and Woolley 1923, 69), which must have been used as the source of the warp thread, again just as in the Meketre model. We should therefore expect to find one or more looms in this vicinity; but even here clear evidence fails. In the front hall, indeed, the excavators found a pair of the socketed stones, this time set up 1.37 meters apart in the middle of the floor, along the long axis of the room (ibid., 75), a much more practical arrangement for a vertical loom than in the other houses. But there is nothing else in the room to associate these sockets in any way with weaving. If

this is not the loom, then where is it? For a ground-loom, we would like to see four stakes or pegs in the floor; but the best we have are three loose pegs shaped like eye-bolts, one from the front hall, one from just outside the door, and one from elsewhere in the street nearby (ibid., 75–76, 69). (The loom pegs in the models and drawings, however, are always simple rather than eyed.) These might have fallen from the flat roof above, where much activity always went on. At 10 Main St., where at least fifteen spindles were found, two wooden weaving swords (a short type of beater) turned up in the staircase area (ibid., 80–81)—again suggesting that the textile activity was upstairs. But we have no proof of anything. On the other hand, if weaving normally was carried out on the roof, then we have a good reason why we *don't* have clear remains of looms in situ.

The question of how the warp was constructed for this type of loom is of import to the weaver; and we find some helpful evidence for it among the monuments that have been discussed. In the blank wall opposite 3 Main St. at Amarna, as we mentioned, the excavators found pegs set for measuring out a warp, much as we see in the model from the tomb of Meketre (Fig. 3.6). In the latter the women are running thread from their spindles around the pegs in the wall, just as many handweavers do today. A painting in the 12th-Dynasty tomb of Djehutihetep (Fig. 3.8) shows us some other warping tricks. Here we see a woman pulling thread simultaneously from twelve balls of yarn, presumably so that she can measure out a dozen warp threads at once, thus saving much labor. The same painting shows some women removing a finished warp from the pegs to the loom, where they have spread it and fastened it to (looped it around?) a cloth beam but have not yet set up the warp beam.

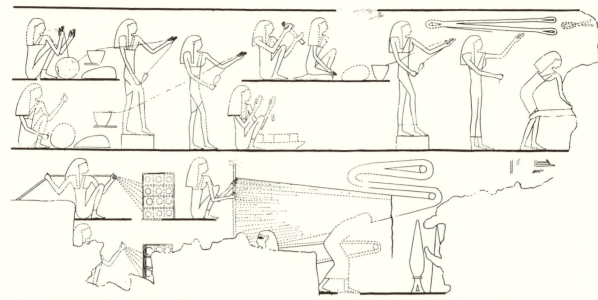

3.8 Textile manufacture depicted in the Middle Kingdom Egyptian tomb of Djehutihetep at el-Bersheh. Note women warping on pegs on the wall, top right, and removing warp to loom, bottom center. 12th Dynasty; early 2nd millennium B.C. (Newberry n.d., pl. 26)

The Middle Kingdom tomb of Daga, on the other hand, shows the warp being stretched between two pairs of straight poles that have been set upright in stands (Fig. 3.9); while the New Kingdom tomb of Neferronpet depicts a similar arrangement except that the poles are set so as to form a V shape (Davies 1948, pl. 35). Gardiner (1957, 520) shows a hieroglyph (Fig. 3.10a) that looks much like the latter, which he interprets as "warp stretched between two uprights."[6] This sort of technique is (apparently) shown at least twice more on our Mesopotamian cylinder seals: once on the seal with spinners, of unknown provenance (see Fig. 2.17), and once on the seal with weavers from Susa (see Fig. 3.4). Both seals were carved in the 4th millennium. Warping onto long, straight poles suggests another possible detail of the craft: that one pole at each end of the frame

is in fact a beam of the loom, destined to be removed from the stand and pegged out on the ground with the warp already on it. The warp would then have been of the continuous variety, and could be treated either as circular or as already divided into the primary shed. The seal from Susa seems to show lozenge-shaped end posts, however, rather than straight beams; so the warp here would have to be transferred, as in the scene from the tomb of Djehutihetep (Fig. 3.8).

Miscellaneous textile equipment turns up in the excavations, too, all over the territory of the ground-loom. Hayes, for example, suggests that the implements in the Metropolitan Museum of Art that match the hieroglyph for "netting bobbin" (see Fig. 3.10b–c)—a shaft about 8 inches long with a crescent at either end to hold the thread—may also have been used as "shuttles" (Hayes

[6] My thanks to Richard Ellis for pointing this hieroglyph out to me.

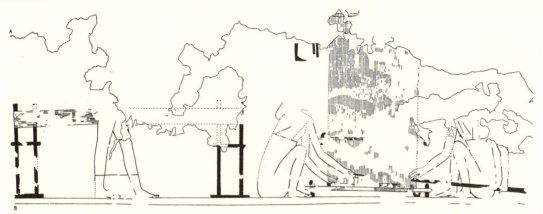

3.9   Warping (left) and weaving (right) in the Middle Kingdom tomb of Daga at Thebes (no. 103). (Davies 1913, pl. 37; courtesy of the Committee of the Egypt Exploration Society)

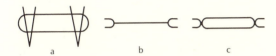

a   b   c

3.10   Egyptian hieroglyphs, depicting (a) "warp stretched between two uprights"; (b) "netting needle; reel"; and (c) "netting needle filled with twine." (After Gardiner 1957, 520, 525; Hayes 1953, 292)

1959, 69). He mentions that "thread seems also to have been wound on little reels, or bobbins, of which we [the Metropolitan Museum] possess fourteen examples carved of wood or limestone or modeled in pottery, clay, and faience" (Hayes 1959, 411). These specimens date to the New Kingdom.

In summary, we can say that the two-beam ground-loom seems to have been used in the Middle East and Egypt from the Neolithic—

perhaps the beginning of the Neolithic—to the present day. It also seems to have possessed both shed and heddle bars from at least the 4th millennium on. We see the loom reach Egypt in the middle of the Neolithic, apparently spreading ever southwards, towards India and the Sudan, in succeeding ages. Triangulation therefore suggests that it originated in the northern part of the Fertile Crescent.

THE WARP-WEIGHTED LOOM

North of the Mediterranean, representations of weaving show a quite different type of large loom. We see it first depicted in the Late Bronze Age, on the great rock at Naquane, in the Camonica Valley in northern Italy, among a group of carvings dated to about the 14th century B.C. (Fig. 3.11; Anati 1960a, 60–62; Anati [1960] 1961, 138–42); and also perhaps in certain ideograms found in the Cretan Linear Script A, from around

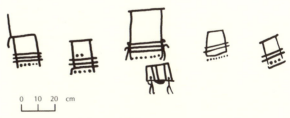

0   10   20   cm

3.11   Some of the probable representations of warp-weighted looms carved on the Great Rock at Naquane, in northern Italy; mid-2nd millennium B.C. (nos. 225, 165, 102, 103, 128, 182; after Anati 1960a, fig. 5)

3.12   Cretan Linear Script A sign apparently representing a warp-weighted loom, on a clay sealing from Hagia Triada, mid-2nd millennium B.C. (Iraklion Museum no. 73; cf. Brice 1961, Table 1: L70, 75, 75')

1500 B.C. (Fig. 3.12). Representations are more copious in the Iron Age: first on the Hallstatt urn from Sopron, Hungary (see Figs. 2.15, 13.3), and then on an Etruscan bronze pendant (see Fig. 12.2) and on various black- and red-figure vases from early Classical Greece (Fig. 3.13).[7] This loom stood more or less upright (usually at a slight angle); had its warp hung from a single top beam, the cloth beam; and used weights instead of a beam at the bottom to pull the warp taut. The weights were usually of clay or stone, and were attached by cords to bunched groups of warp threads. The weaving started at the top, and the rows of weft had to be packed upwards, against gravity.

Although the pictorial representations of this loom may be relatively late, of all the looms this one type has some fairly indestructible parts, namely the weights; and these the archaeologists have found in Europe in great abundance, and from very early periods. The problem is that weights can be used for many purposes; so we have the same sort of difficulty here that we had with

3.13   Women weaving on a warp-weighted loom. Greek lekythos, ca. 560 B.C. (For the rest of the scene, see Fig. 2.38.) (The Metropolitan Museum of Art; Fletcher Fund, 1931: no. 31.11.10)

[7] To the list of Greek representations of the warp-weighted loom given by Marta Hoffmann ([1964] 1974, 297–98, 386), which includes four Boiotian skyphoi, the Metropolitan and Chiusi vases (Figs. 3.13 and 3.26), an Attic hydria, the Corinthian aryballos (Fig. 3.24), and the Pisticci krater (Fig. 3.28), I can add: (1) two fragments of painted clay pinakes from the Persian dump heap on the Akropolis: no. 2531a and c (Graef and Lang-

lotz 1925, pl. 104), one showing the cloth, warp, and beater(?), the other the warp and weights; (2) a black-figure sherd from the Black Sea colony of Olbia (on display in the Historical Museum, Kiev), showing cloth and warps; (3) sherds of a black-figure vase from Corinth (Williams and Fisher 1973, 13 and pl. 8.13A) showing two women tending a weighted warp; (4) a Thessalian relief (Fig. 3.25).

the spindle whorls, of demonstrating that the objects were indeed used in textile production rather than for some other purpose.

The most direct proof that a set of weights belonged to a loom comes when the loom happened to be set up for use at the time it was destroyed, so that the weights are found lying in distinctive rows, having dropped a few inches to the ground when the warp threads from which they had hung were destroyed by fire or decay. Such was the case at Troy, in Level IIg (Early Bronze Age, mid-3rd millennium), where on the floor of Room 206, "between [two] post-holes and the wall, lay three or four rows of clay loom weights just as they had fallen" (Blegen 1963, 72; see Fig. 3.14), surrounded by charred fill through which were scattered nearly two hundred tiny gold beads (ibid., 73). The fire that so suddenly overwhelmed the palace and its inhabitants caught this loom for us while it was set up. Unfortunately, the whole affair seems to have burned so hot that no remains of the cloth were found.

Similarly at Aphrodisias in southwestern Turkey, on the eastern fringes of the Aegean world, loom weights were found where they had fallen directly from a loom during the sudden and complete destruction of "Complex II," an assemblage within Early Bronze II–III. The loom weights, of which there appear to have been about a dozen, were lying in a swath across the pavement, just beyond the end(?) of a wall, with their pierced ends all pointing north (Fig. 3.15; Kadish 1971, 136), as though the whole loom had fallen over in the same direction in which the walls fell.

But these two looms from the Early Bronze Age, from the mid- to late 3rd millennium, are by no means the beginning of the line. The earliest examples of warp-weighted looms yet postulated have been found in Hungary, at sites belonging to the Körös culture (the northern version of the Starčevo and proto-Sesklo cultures), now calibrated to the 6th or even late 7th millennium B.C.—that is, early Neolithic. In one of the houses at Tiszajenő, the excavators found two post holes for shaped posts—itself an un-

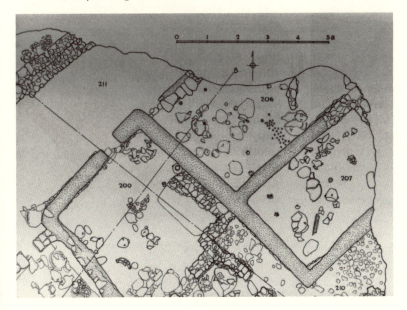

3.14 Troy, Level IIg, with remains of a loom extending out from the southeast wall of Room 206. Remains include fallen loom weights and a pair of post holes for a tilted upright supporting a cloth beam. Early Bronze Age; mid-3rd millennium. (Blegen et al. 1950, fig. 461; courtesy of Princeton University Press)

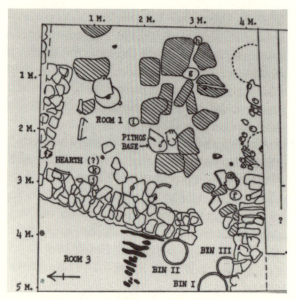

3.15 Plan of an Early Bronze II–III room at Aphrodisias, with fallen loom weights on the right along the south side of the excavation trench. Note that all the weights lie with their holes to the north-northeast. (Kadish 1971, fig. 11; courtesy of *American Journal of Archaeology*)

usual occurrence—and close by, although not quite between the posts, a heap of clay weights (Fig. 3.16; Selmeczi 1969, 18–19). Apparently only eight of these weights were found in retrievable condition, although there had been more (P. Raczky, pers. comm. 1984). Some of these are now displayed in Szolnok. They are small, perhaps 2 inches high, and are formed like truncated cones or pyramids. At Szolnok-Szanda, similar sets of weights turned up in two of the seven Early Neolithic houses dug. The excavators estimated these sets to contain upwards of 20 weights apiece (N. Kalicz and P. Raczky, pers. comm. 1984). A set of about 20 somewhat larger weights came to light on a house floor at Kisköre, also Early Neolithic (eleven of these along with excavation photos are on display in the National Museum in Budapest). About 30 more were found as a set at Dévaványa-Sártó. Apparently the warp-weighted loom was already fairly standard household equipment in Hungary in the 6th millennium.

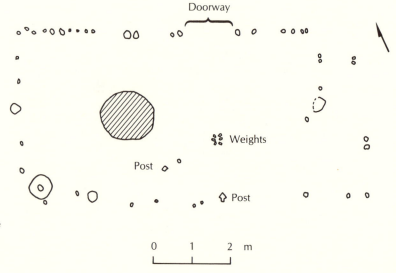

3.16 Plan of an Early Neolithic house at Tiszajenő, Hungary, with probable remains of an upright loom facing the doorway; ca. 5000 B.C. Note holes for shaped posts, and pile of weights. (After Selmeczi 1969, 18)

3.17 Neolithic weights from the Tisza valley in Hungary: left and bottom are for looms, upper right for a fishnet. (Damjanich János Museum, Szolnok)

Weights of this type continue in Hungary in fair quantity throughout the Neolithic (Fig. 3.17). By the Middle Neolithic, some of them are even decorated with inscription-like marks: half a dozen of these, from Su-koró (an early Vinča site), are on display in Székesfehérvár (cf. Gimbutas 1982, 87, 88 fig. 44). They are about 2 inches high. Other decorated weights from the Late Neolithic period were found at Herpály, south of De-brecen. In a Late Neolithic house at Aszód, Kalicz found a group of 32 roughly made weights that show thread wear in the holes, and the imprint of a heavy but well-made cloth on one (N. Kalicz, pers. comm. 1984). A few stray Late Neolithic weights of the small sort, from Dévaványa-Sártó and now in the Ashmolean Museum, run 4 to 6 oz. in weight, while some others of the larger sort,

from Battonya Parazstanya, run 9 to 14 oz. These weights would seem to be typical of the whole lot.[8]

The second area in which impressive numbers of early remains of warp-weighted looms occur is Late Neolithic Switzerland, where their discovery more than a century ago caused something of a sensation. As the modern lake waters receded meter by meter during terrific droughts in the 1850s and 1860s, the remains of ancient pile-dwellings began to appear all over the newly created mud-flats. Groups of large conical weights were found all through the excavated houses, along with abundant evidence of flax-working at every stage from raw flax through spun thread to finished cloth (see Chapter 4). One of the first demonstrable looms turned up in a "lake village" dug by Jakob Messikommer, and consisted of two shaped posts set half a meter apart with a dozen weights lying between them (quoted without reference by Heierli 1887, 426; cf. Kimakowitz-Winnicki 1910, 1). Others have been excavated since, some rather recently at lakeshore sites in the city of Zurich. For example, a rough line of half-a-dozen large clay weights was found on a house floor at the Färberstrasse site in the Utoquai area (Fig. 3.18). Another set of half-a-dozen came from excavations at the Rentenanstalt site (Pfyn or perhaps Horgen culture; that is, Late Neolithic). They run from about 500 g to nearly 1000 g in weight, and show evidence of heavy wear around the string holes.[9]

Such differences in weight within a set seem bizarre and unnatural to us in our modern, machine-regulated world. But research shows that great variation is not fatal to weaving on the warp-weighted loom, although it does not make life easier. While in-

[8] My thanks to Andrew Sherratt for helping me find these and many other useful artifacts in the Ashmolean Museum.

[9] My thanks to René Wyss for enabling me to work with the collection and photo files of the Schweizerisches Landesmuseum in Zurich in 1982.

3.18 Neolithic loom weights among other artifacts on a house floor at Utoquai-Färberstrasse, Zurich, Switzerland. (Photo courtesy of Swiss National Museum, Zurich)

vestigating modern Scandinavian use of this loom type, Marta Hoffmann found that the women simply tied proportionately more warp threads to the heavier weights, and fewer to the lighter ones (Hoffmann [1964] 1974, 42). In one case, the weights being hung onto a single loom at one time weighed anywhere from 1¼ to 4½ kilos! (They were made of shaped field stones, and were heavy expressly for weaving heavy woolen bedspreads.) The scene is worth quoting in detail for the light it sheds on the practical use of this loom:

The stones varied in weight and size from five to eighteen marks (250 gm). An old steelyard was brought in, and every stone weighed. . . . There had to be two stones of approximately equal weight to maintain a balance between the front threads and the back threads [of the natural shed]. Two people helped each other, and sometimes three: one weighed the stones, the second tied the weights to the front threads, and the third to the back threads. One double end was tied to each stone for every mark of the weight. There

was a cord through the hole in each loom weight, and it was to this that the threads were fastened. It was sometimes necessary to tie two loom weights to one group of warp threads in order to balance one heavy weight on the other half of the shed. (Hoffmann [1964] 1974, 42)

On another farm, Hoffmann saw the weights tied first to the entire back half of the shed, then to the front half (ibid., 65–66, 68 fig. 28). The weights here were smaller and all about the same size, 400 g apiece, except that the last weight tied to each end of the shed was much heavier, about 850 g (ibid., 65). This feature was clearly part of an attempt to strengthen the side selvedges, which get a lot of wear. A similar distribution of different-sized weights is vaguely recognizable here and there in the archaeological material (e.g., Troy, Hradčany); but unfortunately the published reports mostly have not given us adequate details to see just what the ancient weavers were up to.

The Swiss weights are noteworthy in being

large, clumsy, and few to a set—in a word, crude—in comparison with those from Neolithic Hungary. But they are equally ubiquitous. Already in 1866 Keller remarks that Messikommer was finding "at least half-a-dozen of these clay cones" in each room at Robenhausen, and that throughout the Swiss pile-dwellings "the almost universal prevalence of clay weights for weaving" suggested that "most, if not all, of [the huts] were furnished with a loom" (Keller [1866] 1878, 514, 9). Messikommer later (1913, 71) reports the Robenhausen loom weights as occurring typically in groups of 10 to 12, with remains of threads still in the holes. And for all the crudeness of the weights, the cloth produced was sophisticated and elegant (see Chapter 4).

Clearly, weaving with the warp-weighted loom was a central cultural activity in Hungary from the Early to the Late Neolithic (and, incidentally, all the way down to medieval times), as well as in Switzerland from the Late Neolithic on. Presumably the technology was spreading westward up the Danube Corridor. But when and how it spread around and between those two fixed points is not at all clear.

In Romania, numerous Neolithic weights have come to light, although it is not so clearly demonstrable that these weights belonged to looms. For example, the Late Neolithic site of Căsioarele furnished several

hundred clay "weights" without any evidence that would tie any of them directly to textiles (Dumitrescu 1965, 224–25).[10] Net sinkers, thatch weights, and spit supports are all equally tenable hypotheses for at least some of them.[11] Farther west at Salcuţa, excavation of a platform in House 4 next to a kiln or oven brought to light a heap of 28 clay "weights" of various sizes and shapes along with a female figurine (Berciu 1961, 179–82). Of these, 5 were conical, 6 truncated pyramids, 1 box-shaped with two pierced ears at the top; and 16 could be described either as crescent-shaped with a hole near each tip, or as two pierced cone-weights that had been broadly joined in the middle (ibid., 240–46 and figs. 74–80). Unfortunately, there does not seem to be any evidence specifically linking these weights with weaving—and nothing preventing such a link. (Crescentic weights are well known in northern Italy in the Late Neolithic and in Anatolia in the Bronze Age, but their connections with the warp-weighted loom are disputed.) Given the clear presence of the warp-weighted loom in nearby Hungary, however, and the similarity in shape (truncated pyramids) of most of the weights, we are probably not far wrong in assuming that at least some of the weights were used for weaving. But we are left without details.

The situation in Bulgaria is no clearer. Surveys of the Bulgarian Neolithic in gen-

[10] Unfortunately, R. K. Evans's report (1974, 110) that "ten loom-weights were found in two parallel rows of five each" at Căsioarele seems to be the result of a mistranslation of Dumitrescu 1965, 224, which states that piles of "weights" were frequently found next to the kilns or ovens, along with strange clay objects (brush handles?) that had on their bases "about ten holes placed in two parallel rows of five each."

[11] Weights for holding down roof thatching, and particularly pairs of supports for holding a spit over the fire, or the two ends of a spindle for unwinding, tend to be rather large, larger than most (but not all) loom weights. Spit supports generally have fire marks, and both they

and spindle supports must be able to stand up steadily. Fishnet weights (see Fig. 3.17), on the other hand, must be well fired (which many loom weights aren't) so as not to disintegrate in the water. Net sinkers are often small, like loom weights, but—as Jill Carington Smith points out (1975, 104)—unlike loom weights they are normally stored in the boat, not in the house. About the only reason for net sinkers to be in the settlement area would be if they had just come out of the kiln, or if the settlement were right along the water's edge. Thus, much of the time it is in fact possible to tell these various types of "weights" apart by size, context, firing, etc.

eral, by Gaul, and of Bulgarian Neolithic textile artifacts in particular, by Petkov, list a few Early and numerous Late Neolithic sites with clay weights that were probably, but not indisputably, for looms (Gaul 1948, 11, 45, 67, 88, 106; Petkov 1965, 46–48, and figs. 2, 4). I find it interesting that in addition to the usual truncated pyramids, some of the weights are very slim, flattened pyramids and even discs, somewhat like the later Minoan ones (see below), while others, from the Early Neolithic levels of Slatina (Fig. 3.19; Petkov 1959, 102 and fig. 103; Petkov 1965, 48), are shaped rather like dumbbells,

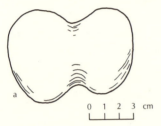

3.19   Dumbbell-shaped loom weight from Slatina, Bulgaria; Early Neolithic (after Petkov 1965, fig. 2∂)

and in this are reminiscent of the "waisted weights" of uncertain use from Macedonia and farther south (e.g., Servia: Heurtley 1939, 64, 138 fig. 6j–k, 243 pl. IV.6j–k; Saliagos: Evans and Renfrew 1968, 80 and pl. 51; *varia*: Carington Smith 1975, 139–41). In short, we might be seeing connections southward into the Aegean as well as northwestward into Hungary. But we know nothing further of the looms.

By the time the Cucuteni/Tripolye culture is well established in Romania and the Ukraine in the Late Neolithic (or Chalcolithic), clay weights of various descriptions are known as far east as Kiev. In her helpful summary of Tripolyan evidence for weaving

compiled from sources difficult to obtain outside the Ukraine, Kordysh describes the weights as follows:

There were round ones with narrow holes; round, rather flat ones with fairly large holes; cone-like shapes with holes in the narrow top part; pear-like shapes with a drilled narrow top part. The size of the weights varied from 5 to 10 centimeters in diameter. Such weights could be used both on fishing nets and on weaving looms. There were also some groups of weights which were obviously unsuited for the role of fishing weights because of their inadequate firing or unsuitable material. (Kordysh 1951, 107–8, with references)

Jugoslavian sites are beginning to produce evidence of Late Neolithic looms, besides just the clay weights. In particular, at Gomolava in Vojvodina (northeast Jugoslavia), 9 pierced clay weights were found scattered in a swath across the floor of a room in House 5/80.[12] The length of this swath is about 120 cm, which compares very favorably with known warp-weighted looms (see below). The fact that the weights are not in a narrow line could be explained by the fact that loom weights falling from their tie-up on the loom itself would fall several inches at least, and could easily roll. But the case for a loom here is hardly airtight. Several of the weights (e.g., nos. 1141–43) are shaped like a squashed sphere pierced through the short axis, somewhat like the few found at Çatal Hüyük (Mellaart 1962, 56), at Middle Neolithic Franchthi Cave in southern Greece (Carington Smith 1975, 137), and at Selevac, not far from Gomolava (R. Tringham, pers. comm. 1982). It is worth bearing in mind at this point Raczky's warning that in Hungary, at least, the round "weights" (pierced or solid) are clearly for cooking, and only the elongated ones (pierced cones or pyramids) are for weaving (P. Raczky, pers. comm. 1984). Indeed, in House 3/80 at Gomolava, a

[12] My thanks to Bogdan Brukner for permission to see and work with the Gomolava plans and drawings at the site in 1982.

large number of clay balls, mostly solid but a few pierced, were scattered about behind the "stove" area (B. Brukner, pers. comm. 1982). Solid balls are quite unsuited to weaving, and these must therefore be construed as cooking stones.

The pierced balls in the row in House 5/80, however, are mixed (as they are at Selevac) with weights of a still flatter, donut shape that was popular for loom weights from Israel to Britain in the Iron Age (see below), and with at least one weight of the thick conical shape so typical of Neolithic Switzerland. So perhaps House 5/80 did contain a loom. Down the way in House 6/80, a set of 15 or more weights were found all in a clump, as though they were being stored together, as we find so often with loom sets (B. Brukner, pers. comm. 1983).

The most general pattern that one can draw out of all this scattered evidence from Central Europe is that clay weights that are probably loom weights begin to abound in the area southwards from Switzerland and Czechoslovakia in the northwest to Kiev in the northeast in the Late Neolithic (cf. Neustupný and Neustupný 1961, 48; Comşa 1954, 387–88). Relatively abundant evidence for the warp-weighted loom in the Early Neolithic is at the moment confined to the Tisza valley in Hungary. Whether that is telling us something important about the origin of this loom or is merely a product of the way sites have been dug remains to be seen (see Chapter 11).

To the south, in the Mediterranean areas, we find the same situation: lots of weights in Anatolia, Italy, and especially Greece that could be loom weights, but aggravatingly little evidence for what craft we should associate them with—weaving or anything else.

The earliest of this southern evidence comes from the ceramic levels of Çatal Hüyük, in Turkey, around the beginning of the 6th millennium. Mellaart found not only a few rough clay weights shaped "like an apple with a hole poked through" (J. Mellaart, pers. comm. 1981; cf. Mellaart 1962, 56), but also pieces of cloth, one of which shows a possible heading band, a feature typical of cloth made on the warp-weighted loom (Burnham 1965, 172, fig. 3, and pl. 33b; see Chapter 4). Since the only corner of Çatal Hüyük that has been dug is apparently not the one in which the numerous crafts were practiced, we can only hope that the archaeologists and authorities will soon find a way to continue the excavation of this critical site and will find us the looms, of whatever type(s) they may be. Much later in Anatolia, in the Chalcolithic period, the excavators at Alishar found "several 'nests' of pyramidal . . . weights"—including a group of 5, and another group of 9 lying on a special floor area of tamped earth (von der Osten 1937, 1.93 and figs. 44, 99). Certainly central and western Anatolia seem to be part of warp-weighted loom territory, at least from the 4th millennium on.

In an extensive survey of early Greek textile artifacts, Jill Carington Smith found only one possible loom weight for the Early Neolithic era—a truncated pyramid from Corinth, showing string wear around the hole (Carington Smith 1975, 123, 157; Davidson 1952, 147–48 and pl. 146c). For the Middle Neolithic, she lists possible weights at Sitagroi in the north (cylinders, pierced lengthwise, with string wear; cf. Neolithic Poland: Fig. 3.20; Kowalczyk 1956, 39), Tsani in central Greece (tall, oblong weights), and Franchthi Cave in the south (spheres; Carington Smith 1975, 136–37; Wace and Thompson 1912, 149). This last site produced within a small area a set of at least 5 ill-fired spheres that must have run a little over 100 grams apiece when complete (Carington Smith 1975, 137–38). The poor firing sug-

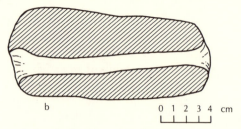

3.20   Cylindrical loom weight from Gródek Nadbużny, Poland; Late Neolithic. (After Kowalczyk 1956, pl. 2.18)

gests that they were neither fishnet weights nor cooking stones; the size and shape rule out spit supports; and their location in a cave-dwelling makes thatch weights unlikely. The hypothesis that they are loom weights thus wins, for the moment, by default.

For the Late Neolithic in Greece, Carington Smith concludes that the warp-weighted loom, "ever more prevalent in the north, almost seems to have gone out of use in the south" (ibid., 145). The one seeming exception is on the island of Crete, at Knossos, where evidence for spinning and weaving begins to proliferate toward the end of Middle Neolithic. In Stratum III (late Middle Neolithic to early Late Neolithic), J. D. Evans found two groups of poorly fired clay weights—doubly pierced rectangles—one in a set of 7 and the other in a set of 13, in addition to the usual miscellany (J. D. Evans 1964, 180, 234–35, and pl. 56 groups 2 and 1 respectively). The relatively intact specimens of the latter group range from 350 to 635 g, whereas the examples for the former group are smaller (and more damaged), probably running around 200 to 300 g when first made, to judge from the current weights and amounts missing.[13] Toward the very end of the Late Neolithic, however, Carington Smith reports tall, heavy weights—oblong, pyramidal, or conical, with a hole near the

top—beginning to spread in northernmost Greece (Carington Smith 1975, 154–56). Some of these, such as the four-pound weight at Olynthus (Mylonas 1929, 80, n. 6, and pl. 88–89), may well have been spit supports (cf. Wace and Thompson 1912, 43, 53); but they may also be relatives of the crude, heavy loom weights found in Switzerland and Jugoslavia to the north.

Italy seems to form the southwestern corner of the warp-weighted loom area: all the evidence from Neolithic Spain suggests that no large loom was known there until the Bronze Age. But we begin to find "heavy conical and cylindrical loom weights" already in the Square-Mouthed Pottery Culture of northern Italy (Barfield 1971, 48), roughly in the 5th millennium. Although this culture is replaced in the Late Neolithic by the quite different Lagozza Culture (connected with Switzerland and the Rhone Valley), the conical weights continue, but are joined by quantities of weights shaped like crescents with a hole at each tip (Fig. 3.21; Barfield

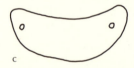

3.21   Crescentic weight, presumably for a loom, from Lagozza, in northern Italy; Late Neolithic. (After Barfield 1971, fig. 23)

1971, 50–51). Unfortunately I can discover no more exact evidence for looms, or anything tying the crescent weights to textiles. I can only add that this is strong warp-weighted loom territory later, so that we are probably not far off in assuming that loom's presence at this time.

From our southern evidence we can add to our overall picture of the warp-weighted

[13] My thanks to H. Catling and J. A. MacGillivray for enabling me to study the Knossos textile artifacts in 1984.

loom a strong suspicion that it reached southern Greece and northern Italy in the Middle Neolithic—let us say roughly the 5th millennium. That is clearly earlier than its arrival in Switzerland, but rather later than its appearance along the Tisza in Hungary. Çatal Hüyük is the only site, in fact, that rivals the Tisza area in earliness—if our interpretation of the possible heading band and few clay balls is correct. As always, we must await more information; but in the meanwhile we have some useful hypotheses that we can work on backing up or knocking down.

By the Bronze Age, and in the Iron Age, weights of this sort are so common all over Europe and Anatolia that to rehearse all the evidence would be tedium itself. Therefore I have summarized in Appendix A all the significant groups of loom weights that I have encountered in my research, and will discuss only a few instructive cases, problems, and conclusions.

There are three situations in particular that may determine the archaeological disposition of loom weights on a site. The first and most informative case occurs when the set of weights was actually in use on a loom when destroyed, so that the weights dropped in a row or rows corresponding to the loom itself. Besides the Early Bronze looms at Troy and Aphrodisias discussed above (Figs. 3.14 and 3.15), we can cite a 2nd-millennium loom of the Unĕtice Culture in Moravia, at Hradčany, where a group of more than 80 weights lay in a row several deep along a wall (Fig. 3.22; cf. Hoffmann [1964] 1974, 388 n. 30). Most of the weights are donut-shaped, about 9 cm in diameter and 3 cm thick, badly fired and with considerable signs of thread wear in the holes (Červinka 1946, 141 figs. 2–10); but at each end of the row was a "club-shaped" weight (kuželovitém: conical?—cf. Červinka 1946, 141 no. 1, shown at left in Fig. 3.22), presumably used

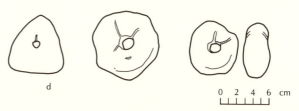

3.22 Conical and donut-shaped loom weights from Hradčany, Czechoslovakia; Bronze Age, Unĕtice Culture. (After Červinka 1946, 141 nos. 1, 6, 9)

in constructing the selvedge. In the Iron Age such finds become more and more common: an early Iron Age loom at Gordion, Turkey, discussed below; 14 large weights fallen in 2 rows 60 cm long, in an early La Tène house near Niemitz, in Niederlausitz (northeast Germany: Jentsch 1886, 584); two looms from Italy, at Monte Loffa and Sottosengia, north of Verona, in the late first millennium B.C. (Barfield 1971, 141); and a rather considerable series from Britain and Scandinavia from the 1st millennium A.D., including those at Sorte Muld, Bornholm, Denmark, and Grimstone End, Suffolk, England, for which Hoffmann shows clear photographs of the neat lines of weights (Hoffmann [1964] 1974, 312–14, figs. 131–32). In addition, recent excavations in Israel have been uncovering copious evidence for warp-weighted looms destroyed during use in that area in the Iron Age (see Chapter 14).

That we do not have more actual remains of looms for the Bronze Age, a period so richly attested through careful excavation, is explained by the second and third possible cases. There are a number of instances like those at Kato Zakro, in eastern Crete, where objects assumed to be loom weights were found in quite a number of localities, but virtually always in stratigraphic contexts that made it clear that they had fallen from the upper floors (Platon 1971, 57, 191, 281, etc.). In addition, the ethnographic evidence suggests that warp-weighted looms were generally dismantled by their owners and stored away when not actually in use (Hoffmann [1964] 1974, 31 etc.). Hesiod, too, suggests as much for his era in his admonition τῇ δ'ἱστὸν στήσαιτο γυνὴ (on such [a day] a woman should stand/set up her loom; *Works and Days* 779). So it should not be surprising if we seldom find a loom that happened to be destroyed while set up; we should rather expect to find the weights stored away in a set most of the time.

The clearest possible example of such storage occurs at Akrotiri on Thera, where a jar was found that contained a number of typically Aegean discoid loom weights, with many more discs scattered around in the fill just beyond its mouth, everything having fallen into the basement from above when the floor collapsed during the catastrophic eruptions that encapsulated the whole site soon after 1500 B.C. (Marinatos 1967a, 136–37 and pl. 115; Luce 1969, pl. 48–49; Galanopoulos and Bacon 1969, pl. 17). All told, more than 160 weights were recovered from this house (to judge from Marinatos 1968b, pl. 116α: the excavator does not think to give us this helpful information), of which perhaps 30 were either inside or just beyond the mouth of the one jar, to judge from the photographs. Impressions of a wooden beam 8 cm thick were found close by, which Marinatos at first suggested might have been part of the loom itself, although he later changed his mind (Marinatos 1967a, 137; Marinatos 1968a, 24; but then Marinatos 1969a, 18).

So we have three basic cases: working looms destroyed in situ, looms fallen from above, and looms in storage—and it may be hard to tell if things fallen from above been in use or in storage. There are many situations where we can't be sure which case we are dealing with, and of course there are the uninformative cases of miscellaneous stray weights from dump heaps and rubbish.

There are also the occasional precious situations in which the relation of the weaving to other factors can be recovered: e.g., the interplay between storage and work areas at Gordion, the Phrygian capital in Central Anatolia.

As the fiery destruction meted out by the Kimmerians overtook the citadel of Gordion early in the 7th century B.C., a group of 21 weights fell to a house floor in a row 1.59 meters long (de Vries 1980b, 39). The loom had been set up in the anteroom of the women's working quarters TB7. This porch contained over 150 loom weights and 90 spindle whorls, while in the main room of TB7 more than 450 more loom weights and 46 spindle whorls were available to hand, along with rows of grinders for milling grain (ibid.). Workhouse CC3 contained another 500 loom weights (and over 175 spindle whorls), some with string still in the holes; and in the rear storeroom of Megaron 4 were found another 75 weights (ibid., 39, 37). But all of these numbers are dwarfed by the contents of the royal storage-houses TB 1 and 2, which together produced more than 1100 of these donut-shaped loom weights "with some 464 heaped up together in a single great pile" (ibid., 38–39; see R. S. Young 1962, 165 for shape). At a site so rich we begin to see the movement between storage, set-up areas, and actual weaving, as well as the vast quantities of weights used where the industry was an important one.

Nearly 2300 loom weights within 100 yards of each other! At 21 weights per loom we can calculate that King Midas of Gordion could have kept over a hundred women busy weaving for him, which makes him more than twice as rich as Homer's fabulous King Alkinoos, who had fifty (*Od.* 7.103–6). No wonder the Greeks viewed Midas as synonymous with gold!

When we have an actual loom in situ, if we

study the excavation plans and other details we can often glean considerably more than just the fact of its existence. When the weights fall in a row, and particularly when the ends of the rows are delimited by post holes or walls, we can estimate fairly accurately the width of the loom, and hence the maximum width of the cloth that could be woven on it. The posts of the Early Neolithic Hungarian loom at Tiszajenő were 185 cm apart (Selmeczi 1969, 19); those of the Late Neolithic Swiss loom were 40 to 50 cm apart (Heierli 1887, 426); the Troy II posts lay 110 cm from the wall, posts and wall delimiting the ends of the row of weights (Blegen et al. 1950, 350); at Aphrodisias, to extrapolate from the plan (Kadish 1971, fig. 11), the row of weights extended 130 to 140 cm; at Late Neolithic Gomolava the row was 120 cm long; at Iron Age Niemitz it was 60 cm long; and the Gordion loom was 159 cm in working width. These figures tally well enough with the warp-weighted looms still in use in this century in Scandinavia: in Marta Hoffmann's register, the cloth beams run from 165 to 240 cm, the usable width (between the uprights) ranging from 135 to 180 cm (Hoffmann [1964] 1974, 24ff., 57ff.). Only the Swiss and German looms fall far outside the range, being much narrower, but there is nothing intrinsic in the design or use of warp-weighted looms to make that particular difference a serious one. One can always choose to weave a cloth narrower than the widest possible.

There is, on the other hand, no consistency among the few archaeological remains in the placement of such looms in the houses. The Trojan loom is at right angles to the wall; the Aphrodisias loom on the same line as the wall, seemingly as an extension of it; and the Tiszajenő loom at a slight diagonal. Interestingly, however, this third loom

is directly opposite the doorway where, as the excavators point out, there would be the most light to work by (Selmeczi 1969, 19). At Gomolava, the row of weights goes diagonally across part of the middle of the room, and the loom at Hradčany ran right along beside the wall.

The evidence for the much-debated degree of uprightness of warp-weighted looms also does not come in with overwhelming unanimity. It is hard to see how the Tiszajenő loom could be anything but strictly vertical, considering how close one post is to the house wall, not to mention the peculiar angle of the loom from the wall. The Aphrodisias and Gomolava remains give no particular indication for either vertical or slanted, and one cannot glean enough evidence about Hradčany. The fact that the row of Trojan loom weights is quite wide, however, and ends with not one but two posts set on a line at right angles to the row of weights, suggests strongly a main "upright" braced at something of an angle by a second post supporting it from behind (cf. Hoffmann [1964] 1974, 311).[14] Such a position would match that commonly used in Scandinavia in this century (Hoffmann [1964] 1974), one with the distinct advantage that it uses gravity along with a shed bar at the bottom to separate the threads into a natural division or shed. Perhaps the early Neolithic loom at Tiszajenő was so early that the principle of the mechanical separation of shed had not been discovered yet. Certainly there would be no reason whatever to tip a loom with no bottom bar—that is, a loom with only warp weights at the bottom—until the principle of the shed bar had been discovered (see below).

The number and heaviness of weights used on these looms is also of considerable

---

[14] The other end of the cloth beam presumably was stuck into a niche in the wall.

interest. Of course, as ethnographic and practical evidence shows, one does not need so many weights to make a narrow piece of fabric as to weave a piece the full width of the loom. So the number of weights used on a single loom can vary from one occasion to the next. Furthermore, one needs heavier weights for heavy, dense fabrics, and lighter ones for finer or looser fabrics. To avoid tedium, this material too is summarized in Appendix A. Unfortunately, too often the excavators fail to give us the number of weights found in a group, and they almost invariably fail to give us the weights(!) of the loom weights. Until we obtain a better collection of data, it is not possible to draw many of the interesting potential deductions, such as variations in composition and design of looms and especially of producible textiles, by area, culture, and date.

One can say, however, that the archaeological data again roughly fit the ethnographic evidence. Hoffmann's survey of Scandinavian warp-weighted looms shows a range of 13 to 59 weights per loom, with most looms having a number falling between 20 and 30 (Hoffmann [1964] 1974, 24ff., 57ff.). The archaeological table in Appendix A shows a far wider range, from 4 to 800. But 4 was taken as an arbitrary lower cut-off point for what might be deemed a "set," given the high probability that part of any set would have gotten separated or destroyed in the intervening millennia; and all the cases over a hundred are clearly storage groups, and almost certainly represent either several looms or spare parts. If we stick to looms that had been set up at destruction, however, we typically find sets of 6 to about 30, with occasional numbers that are much higher: e.g., 44 at Troy, 80 at Hradčany. A possible reason for those higher numbers will be discussed presently. One might add that "few" and "heavy" tend to go together, as do "many" and "light." Such tendencies make perfect sense in terms of trying to weave on the loom.

One of the more puzzling questions has to do with how the weights were attached. To begin with, one has to assume that the ancients, like the modern users of the loom, tied the bunch of warp ends not to the weight itself but to an intermediary—e.g., a ring or loop of cord run through the hole(s) in the weight. For one thing, the holes are generally much too small to stuff a bundle of warp through. The donut-shaped weights are an exception; but they often show string marks of a sort that suggest a permanently attached "intermediary" cord too (e.g., at Hradčany).

The fact that all the Aphrodisias weights were pointing the same direction, however, shows that they had also been attached to each other by some sort of chain or bar, rather than hanging entirely freely. This deduction in turn brings up the question of why many of the Minoan disc-shaped weights are grooved at the top, while others, even from the same set, are not (e.g., at Myrtos and Kythera; see Fig. 3.23). The

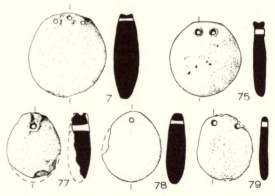

3.23 Small, disc-shaped clay loom weights from a Minoan village at Myrtos, southern Crete; Early Bronze Age; mid- to late 3rd millennium B.C. (Warren 1972, 243 fig. 96)

groove seems ideally suited for snuggling against a slim rod. Were the Minoan weights held in order, as they hung from the warp, by being lashed to a rod? The front row of weights that hangs over the shed bar need never budge as the weaving proceeds; but the others swing and clank with the moving of the heddle bar (Jill Carington Smith complains bitterly of the noise created by her model loom: 1975, 93). If several heddle bars were in use, the swinging and clanking might well get out of hand. (See Haynes 1975 for a firsthand assessment of the problems of weaving twill on a warp-weighted loom.) It would be interesting to know, for example from well-stratified groups like the Theran weights, the proportions of grooved and grooveless weights per deposit. Half and half—for plain weave? Three-quarters grooved—for twill, with the weights hanging from each of the three heddle bars organized by lashing to a rod? One-quarter grooved— for twill, but with the grooved weights lashed to the shed bar and the other three rows merely chained with a spacer-string? Do the proportions differ from house to house or era to era? In short, could we see from this detail when people were weaving different products?[15] Perhaps the crescent-shaped weights were an attempt to deal with the problems of movement.

So far, we have dealt almost exclusively with the evidence afforded by the loom weights. But there are a number of other interesting problems that we can attack other ways. For example, we have evidence for various ingenious solutions to the weaver's problem of how to increase the size of the cloth.

A ground-loom, as we have seen, can be staked out to be as large as the cloth to be woven, if the weaver is willing to climb

around on top of the cloth while weaving. But with other forms of loom, the distance that the weaver can reach to work limits the size of the loom, and hence also of the cloth, unless some way around this problem can be found. The trivial solution is to extend the weaver's reach. Now, for a warp-weighted loom, to manage width the weaver can walk back and forth in front of the loom, as did Calypso, who lived alone on an island (*Od.* 5.61–62). We also have charming evidence that sometimes two or more women helped each other, not only from the representations (e.g., the Metropolitan vase, Figs. 2.38, 3.13), but also from a detail frequently found in the large woolen cloths from the Danish bogs. In analyzing the weaves of these pieces, Broholm and Hald discovered that the wefts crossed in such a way that several women, with several bobbins, must have been working the shed at the same time, each passing her current bobbin along to her neighbor every time the shed was changed (See Fig. 6.6). Modern Scandinavian women who still use the loom often work in pairs also. After all, it is much more entertaining.

To gain length on such a loom, however, is a much more difficult proposition. Current users of the warp-weighted loom in Scandinavia stand on a bench during the early part of the weaving, to obtain a little extra height (Hoffmann [1964] 1974, 43 and figs. 13–14). That is the prosaic solution. On a tiny oil flask from Corinth, however, which shows what is apparently the famous weaving contest between Arachne and Athena, the artist represents the women as wearing platform clogs on their feet (Fig. 3.24; Weinberg and Weinberg 1956, pl. 33)—little self-portable benches, as it were. Still greater heights were achieved by the Etruscan lady depicted on a bronze pendant from the 6th century

---

[15] Where *all* the weights in a single set are grooved (if ever), we can also consider the possibility of a short rod

being lashed to the top of the weights, around which to wind extra lengths of warp.

BROWN
RED

3.24   Small vase (aryballos) from Corinth, Greece, showing weavers wearing platform clogs, ca. 600 B.C. It probably depicts the weaving contest between Arachne and Athena. (Drawing by M. Welker, in Weinberg and Weinberg 1956, fig. 1)

B.C., who seems to have hung her loom beam from the top of a balcony, where she sits weaving while a friend hands up to her a basket of prepared yarns (see Fig. 12.2; Govi 1971, pl. 53–54). On the other hand, the Hallstatt weavers seem to have thought downwards rather than upwards, digging trenches for the weights to hang down into. Such a trench seems to be indicated on the Sopron urn, where the weights hang far down into the next register (see Figs. 2.15, 13.3). Trenches for such loom weights were actually found in two Hallstatt weaving huts on Goldberg bei Nördlingen (E. Vogt 1937, 112, and figs. 152–54).

A practical solution that can be combined with these is to roll or wrap somehow, to hold some of the materials temporarily out of the way. At the bottom, where there is no beam, the extra warp can be rolled up or looped, and tied securely, as on a backstrap loom. One could even wind it around the loom weights themselves (cf. Hoffmann [1964] 1974, 65–66 and 72 fig. 32). At the top of the warp-weighted loom, where there is a beam, the finished cloth can simply be wound around the beam, if there is some way of loosening, turning, and re-fixing the beam while the weaving is in progress. How

early such devices may have been invented is unclear to us, since the actual artifacts, being wooden, do not survive. But a rollable cloth beam seems to be represented in various of the Classical Greek depictions of the warp-weighted loom (e.g., the Metropolitan vase, Figs. 2.38, 3.13).

One might well wonder why the weavers went to such extremes to gain extra height on their loom if they had the roller beam. The problem is, however, that with a loom of human height, nearly every time the weaver rolled a finished portion of cloth onto the roller beam, she would also have to wrestle with moving the weights down the warp—a tedious task at best, and terribly time-consuming with 20 weights to move, let alone 50 or 80. With the added height, one could weave and roll more times for each time that the weights would have to be moved.

Another question of concern to the weaver is how to keep adequate supplies of weft at hand. The weft may be maneuvered simply from the loose end of the thread, of course, if it is short. But it is usually more efficient to wind a considerable length into a loose "butterfly," or a ball, or a skein with a tightly wrapped tip—ideal for shoving between warp threads—as the Scandinavian women do (Hoffmann [1964] 1974, 43, 66–67, and figs. 16, 19). Or one can wind a length onto a stick and use the end of the stick to help part the warp. The stick may even be the shaft of the spindle on which thread was originally spun (see Chapter 14).

Clay objects suggested to be spools, bobbins, reels, or "shuttles" occur in Bronze Age Aegean sites. Pieces molded into the shape of our modern thread spools, both with and without perforations, have been found with some frequency.[16] Goldman suggests that two bone objects from Eutresis may have had the function of shuttles; one (Early Helladic) has three holes in one end, the other (Late Helladic) is crescent-shaped (Goldman 1931, 212–13, 215, and figs. 283.6, 284.17). And in the Neolithic levels at Knossos—specifically Early Neolithic II through Late Neolithic—J. D. Evans found a total of nine small clay bars with vaguely crescentic ends, which he classified with the numerous other remains of textile industry as "shuttles" (J. D. Evans 1964, 233–35 and figs. 56.1–9).[17] There is no proof that any of these implements were actually used for thread or weaving; on the other hand, all the sites involved gave other evidence of textile work, sometimes even in abundance.

Aside from bone, the material we would most expect thread to be wound around is

wood, which of course seldom survives. Schliemann, however, with his usual luck, found a piece of wood "11 in. long, around which is wound lengthwise a large quantity of woollen thread, as black as coal, evidently from being charred." He found it in the heavily burned layers of the "royal mansion" of Troy II; one of his staff experts, Dr. Moss, told him that the wood "was the stem of a very young tree" (Schliemann 1880a, 327).[18]

This yarn was wound lengthwise; but in our next indisputable evidence for weft storage—in the Archaic and Classical Greek representations—we invariably find the weft yarn wound around sticks the other way, as it would be wound, for example, on a spindle shaft. In fact, the Greek lexicographer Hesychius describes πηνίον (pēnion), a word that we know from much earlier sources to mean some sort of bobbin or spool, as ἄτρακτος εἰς ὃ εἰλεῖται ἡ κρόκη (a spindle on which the weft is wrapped). We see this three times on the Metropolitan lekythos (see Fig. 2.38), again on the Ashmolean skyphos (Hoffmann [1964] 1974, 299 fig. 125), and yet again on a Classical relief found in Thessaly (Fig. 3.25; Robert 1900, 333). On the skyphos from Chiusi (Fig. 3.26), although Penelope has stopped weaving and has sat down in dejection, we see what appear to be six such sticks with fat balls of yarn

---

[16] For example, such "spools" were found at Nea Nikomedeia (Early Neolithic, unperforated: Rodden 1962, 285 fig. 11.SF7), Thermi (Early Bronze, unperforated; Middle or Late Bronze, perforated lengthwise: Lamb 1936, 164, 204, pl. 23.31–26 and pl. 24.32–2), Eutresis (Early or Middle Bronze, perforated lengthwise: Goldman 1931, 193, and fig. 266.2), Phylakopí (Late Bronze, unperforated, 20 in all: Atkinson et al. 1904, 213), and Vardaroftsa (Iron Age, perforated lengthwise: Heurtley and Hutchinson 1925–26, 36 fig. 21.17–18).

[17] When I handled these objects in the Stratigraphic Museum at Knossos, my instincts as a longtime weaver and stitcher cried out against attempting to use them for anything to do with textiles, least of all as bobbins. They are awkwardly heavy, breakable, and much too fat to hold thread efficiently. I then requested, in a neutral way, the opinion of a specialist in much later textiles who happened to be nearby, Jane Cocking, and her re-

action was much the same as mine had been.

Again note that the true shuttle had not yet been invented (see note 3 above), and that the true shuttle requires the weaver to have both hands free—one to throw and the other to catch. Such was clearly not the case with the Classical Greek warp-weighted loom, at least, since one hand was needed to hold the heddle bar forward (see below).

[18] Schliemann persists in calling the object a distaff, which it cannot be. A distaff is a stick or holder from which the as-yet unspun fibers are drawn for spinning; but these fibers were present in the form of spun thread, he says. Nor would it work as a supplier in the re-spinning of already spun thread, because with the thread wound end for end the rod could not be twirled so as to pay the thread out rapidly for the re-spinning; it would have to be wound the other way (cf. Forbes 1956, 168).

3.25   Classical Greek relief showing Penelope (right) weaving with a raised bobbin, while her nurse washes the disguised Odysseus's feet; from Thessaly. (After Robert 1900, pl. 14)

3.26   Greek vase found at Chiusi, Italy, showing Penelope in front of her warp-weighted loom; early 5th century B.C. Note the roller beam, and the depiction of tapestry on the cloth. (Furtwängler 1932, pl. 142; by permission fee)

wound around them stuck into the top of the loom, much as the women on the Metropolitan vase have stuck their extra bobbins into convenient spots on the uprights.[19] The placement shown on the Chiusi skyphos,

which depicts an elegant, presumably multicolored tapestry in progress, is much like what weavers of multicolored pile rugs and tapestries in the Near East do today to keep the many colors ready to hand: namely, tuck

[19] Agnes Geijer published an interesting article pointing out that there are no loom weights visible in the photographs of the Chiusi vase (Fig. 3.26), and hence that the loom must not be the usual warp-weighted loom

but some other kind (Geijer 1977). I asked a competent art historian living in Italy to inspect the vase carefully in person for me. This was her reply: "The loom weights and perpendicular warp ends are just as they are shown

them all around the edges of the loom (compare, for example, Iten-Maritz 1975, 26 photo).

In our final evidence for weft storage, the Hallstatt urn from Sopron (Figs. 2.15, 13.3) shows what appears to be a simple ball of weft, with no stick. Clearly traditions varied.

Another major question for exploration concerns the use and form of heddles on the warp-weighted loom. Heddles controlled from a single bar generally seem to be made of thread or string, fashioned into loops for the warp threads to go through. Thus, among users of warp-weighted looms in Scandinavia, Hoffmann found that the heddles were made afresh with one long string each time the loom was warped (Hoffmann [1964] 1974, 42–43, 66, and figs. 12, 30). That is, the heddles were formed right around each warp thread after the warp was already on the loom, and unraveled when the piece of cloth was finished. The job can be done by a simple loose spiral wrap around the heddle bar; or by laying a loop alternately to either side of the bar (cf. Roth [1918] 1977, 2 fig. 1A); or by some fancier stitch, such as the buttonhole stitch used by a Lappish woman (Hoffmann [1964] 1974, 66). Alternatively, a set of permanent heddles can be made that are re-used each time. In that case, the warp ends must be threaded through the heddle loops during the process of putting the warp

onto the loom. Hoffmann mentions (ibid., 62, 72–73) that the only people she found using permanent heddles on their warp-weighted looms were a few nomadic Lapps, who took only the cloth beam and the heddle bar (heddles and all) along with them on their wanderings, making new uprights and gathering fieldstones for weights when they needed to weave.[20] The use of permanent heddles seemed to be a carryover from the use of the horizontal loom, which was more common in that area. But in all these cases, nothing was used but a plain stick and a string.

With no recognizable heddle bars available, and no representations of the warp-weighted loom until very late, we have to turn to other types of evidence for the beginning of mechanical shedding in the northern zone. An impression of textile from the Late Neolithic site of Kephala, on the Cycladic island of Keos (or Kea), shows what is evidently a weaving error of a type virtually never committed by a weaver darning in the weft, but very easily and commonly made by someone using mechanical shedding devices: two threads in one shed for a considerable distance (Carington Smith 1977, 115—with a detailed explanation of how such errors occur).[21] Carington Smith points out that to manufacture such fine textiles as those impressed on her sherds *without* mechanized

---

in the drawing (after Furtwängler et al., 1932). They are not visible in the photo because they have been drawn with a pin, probably incised after the vase was fired. Looking at the vase straight on through the glass of the display case they are quite invisible. To see them we had to press our noses to the glass and look down diagonally. The weights however are quite visible, especially between the feet of Telemachos. The main difference between the Furtwängler drawing and the vase is that in the drawing the warp weights are shown white, whereas on the vase they are black and opaque" (A. M. Valeri, pers. comm., August 16, 1984). Shortly thereafter Brunilde Ridgway kindly pointed out to me a note being published by Louise Clark (1984) to the same

effect.

[20] A warning that we may not be able to recognize the presence of even the warp-weighted loom in some areas and periods!

[21] The only other possible explanation is at least as radical in terms of how far ahead the textile arts were: that the second thread in the shed was purposely laid in as a pattern thread, presumably in another color. For a patterned textile to be used as an old rag for making pottery would then imply that such things were rather common. The fact that the two threads in the shed are so similar, however, suggests they came from the same ball of yarn and hence represent a mistake, not a pattern.

shedding would be "remarkably tedious" (ibid.); and furthermore that the other Late Neolithic textiles that have been found—in Egypt, in the Aegean, in Switzerland—are of comparable or even greater fineness (ibid., 117; see Chapter 4). We have seen that Egypt even has representational evidence of mechanical shedding in the Neolithic period.

In the Early Bronze Age we find yet another type of evidence pointing strongly toward mechanical shedding, and a sophisticated variety at that: the remains of the loom at Troy, level II. As we have already seen, the double support and the fact that the weights fell into not one but two or three rows demonstrate that this loom was tipped for shedding, had a shed bar, and had possibly even several heddle bars. Multiple heddle bars make it possible also to mechanize the weaving of patterns such as twill and rosepath (see Chapter 7); and mechanization of pattern weaving is the only reason for having multiple heddle bars. (Even the simplest monochrome twill has a more interesting "pattern" to it than plain weave.) We will see presently that the extant fabrics support the hypothesis that mechanized pattern weaving began in Europe during the Bronze Age.

With such a long history of mechanical shedding, it seems strange that classicists have been so reluctant to believe that the warp-weighted looms of Classical Greece could have had heddle bars. Unfortunately, we must assume that the looms we are shown on Greek vases work a little differently from the chief working model we have for the warp-weighted loom, namely the Scandinavian. It is worth some effort to sort out the differences (Fig. 3.27).

The Scandinavian looms fix the shed bar rather low on the loom. The heddle bar, which is so heavy that it is "not possible for one person to lift it by grasping it at the center" (Hoffmann [1964] 1974, 44), is supported in either "open" or "closed" position by strong wooden forks sticking out about in the middle of the loom uprights. In the Greek representations, however, there is no bar towards the bottom, but a very heavy bar about in the middle that is supported by the uprights (in the Metropolitan vase [Figs. 2.38, 3.13] it appears to be lashed to them). This has to be the shed bar, despite its height: first because the simplest laws of mechanics dictate that the shed bar must lie on the far side of the heddle bar from the cloth being woven, so as not to interfere with the countershed, and second because the one known side view of a Greek loom—on a 5th-century Greek vase found at Pisticci, in Italy (Fig. 3.28)—shows that this bar is indeed performing the function of separating ("shedding") the warp. This vase also shows something above the shed bar deflecting the path of the remaining warp threads: in short, the expected heddle bar, however clumsily drawn.

What is noteworthy in the representations, however, is that this upper bar has no visible means of support, a state of affairs that would be impossible for the heavy Scandinavian heddle bar. There are no signs of anything perpendicular to the uprights, in the side view or elsewhere, and sometimes the upper bar is even shown as too short to reach the uprights. A little experimentation shows, on the other hand, that it is quite feasible to use slim rods for the string heddles, as long as one doesn't require that the whole countershed be opened all the way across at the same time. It is also more feasible to use slim rods with the small terracotta weights used in antiquity than with the great heavy fieldstones used by the Scandinavian farm women, who prefer this loom expressly for making heavy bedspreads. The light rods, bound as they are by the heddles to the warp, held from falling forward by the pres-

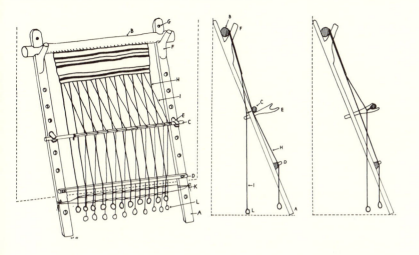

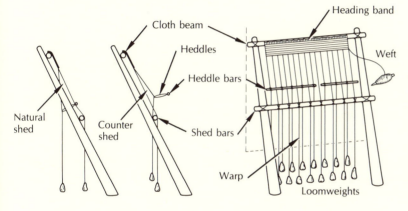

Cloth beam

Heddles

Heddle bars

Natural shed

Counter shed

Shed bars

Heading band

Weft

Warp

Loomweights

3.27　Comparative diagrams of the versions of the warp-weighted loom as used in Scandinavia in this century (above; Hoffmann [1964] 1974, fig. 2) and as used in Classical Greece (below; inked by M. Stone). Note the higher shed bar and flimsier heddle bar(s) in the ancient version.

3.28　Side view of a warp-weighted loom, on an early 5th-century Greek vase found at Pisticci, Italy. Note the deflection of the warp by both shed and heddle bars. (Quagliati 1904, 199 fig. 4)

sure of the weighted threads behind, and held from sliding all the way down by the fixed shed bar (which itself is normally bound to every thread in the front half of the warp by a continuous spacer cord, as is so clearly shown by the row of X's on the shed bar on the Metropolitan vase, Figs. 2.38, 3.13)—these light rods cling nicely to the front of the warp just above the shed rod without any need of support, just as they are shown on the vases. To open part of the countershed, you simply take hold of the rod and pull it forward, holding it with one hand while inserting the weft with the other. So Homer describes the action in a simile for closeness (*Il.* 23.760–63): "as near as a heddle rod (κανών) is to the chest of a woman, [a rod] which she pulls well with her hands while drawing the bobbin out through the warp, and she holds it close to her chest." The fact that one hand is occupied with holding a heddle rod while the other puts in the weft makes this design less convenient than that of the Scandinavian version, of course; but then it is also 2500 years earlier than the latter. And holding part of the countershed open with one hand is by no means uncommon among the looms of the world (e.g., Roth [1918] 1977, 28–29 figs. 49 and 51A; Broudy 1979, 53–55). I have seen it myself in the Greek islands, where each successive heddle rod was only a few inches long.

We have yet one more clue about heddles: the weft bobbin. Roth ([1918] 1977, 4–6) points out that, on a loom with a poor mechanical shedding device, the shed does not open wide enough to admit a weft spool of any thickness, and weavers with such looms tend to wrap their weft lengthwise, for flatness. The same is even more true of darning in the weft, where the entire spool has to be passed back and forth between all the neighboring warp threads. Consider now the bobbins we are shown. Even if we discount the Boiotian skyphoi as by nature grotesquely

exaggerated, still the other representations show the weft bobbin as quite large and fat—even in the sedate, carefully proportioned Thessalian relief (Fig. 3.22). So large a bobbin could hardly have been used comfortably if the loom had no mechanical countershed, that is, no heddles. Note too that, with a true heddle rod in the position suggested, the current bobbin of weft can be laid on the little shelf formed within the shed by the heddle strings, while the weft is beaten home or while the weaver momentarily attends to something else. And thus we find it in the paintings (e.g. Fig. 3.13), "floating" in the warp just above the upper rod without pushing aside the warp threads. If there were no heddles, there would be nothing for it to rest on.

All in all, it seems difficult not to conclude that some sort of mechanical shedding was known all over the east Mediterranean from at least the beginning of the Late Neolithic. Starting with the Keos weaving fault (and the Badarian dish) in the 4th millennium, we receive a steady trickle of evidence down through the Bronze Age and into the Iron Age, even, presently, in the far-flung parts of Europe, such as the heddle-produced weaving error in a Late Bronze Age cloth from Armoy, in Ireland (early 1st millennium B.C.; Henshall 1950, 144–45), and the representation of four clear shed and heddle bars on the Hallstatt urn from Sopron (see Fig. 13.3). The device was far too useful, nay critical, to be casually lost in the time gaps between our pieces of direct evidence; nor could the bright, progressive Greeks have been ignorant of a basic contraption that had been in use all around for three thousand years or more.

We have at least one bit of evidence, moreover, that by 700 B.C. people had even come up with the notion of extra heddle bars set up specifically for patterns—in some sense the predecessor of the drawloom. This evidence is a mechanically repeated error in the pattern of one of the Gordion textiles (Fig. 7.8; Ellis 1981, 300–301), discussed at length in Chapter 7.

In summary, then, we can say that the warp-weighted loom seems to have been used in central Europe and perhaps Anatolia from the early (pottery) Neolithic onwards. We see it expanding into southern Greece and northern Italy in the Middle Neolithic, reaching Switzerland in the Late Neolithic, and Scandinavia and Britain in the Bronze Age—a generally northwestward movement. In the various upheavals of the 2nd millennium B.C. we also see it carried suddenly southeastward into Palestine. It continued to be used in central Europe until at least late medieval times, and in rural Scandinavia up to the present.

And the center of the expanding circle—the ultimate point of origin? One is so accustomed to *lux ex oriente* that Anatolia seems the logical and conservative choice; but the claim of Hungary and the Old Europeans is much too strong to shove aside, not only because of the copious early evidence, but because the Danube seems to be the radiating center of elaborations and sophistications in the cloths as well. The principles of shed and heddle seem to have been known from well back in the Neolithic in the northern zone, and multiple (pattern) shedding from at least the Early Bronze Age, long before this technique reached the Middle East.

The Vertical Two-Beam Loom

Besides the warp-weighted loom and the horizontal ground-loom, we have evidence for a third major type of large loom, one that stretched its warp between two beams, like the ground-loom, but stood more or less vertically, like the warp-weighted loom. Our earliest representations occur in Egypt in the New Kingdom, where a type of vertical loom seems to have been introduced about that time from elsewhere, presumably from Palestine or Syria. It is always shown with the weavers, usually male, seated directly in front of it, as in the tomb of Thutnofer at Thebes (Fig. 3.29), some looms having one weaver, others two (Roth [1913] 1951, fig. 9), as opposed to the old indigenous ground-loom, which is invariably shown worked by a minimum of two women (never men), who squat at either side. The end of the warp to be used last is attached to a warp beam near the top, and the end with the finished cloth is tied to a cloth beam at the bottom of the loom. Thus the weaver is weaving from bottom to top, and packing the weft threads in with a downward motion, exactly the opposite of the warp-weighted loom. Badly preserved though they are, the few representations of this loom nonetheless show us two bars in positions appropriate for shed and heddle rods, and what seem to be two laze rods (spacers) higher up—e.g., in the Theban tombs of Thutnofer, Neferhotep, and the "overseer of the weavers," Neferronpet (Fig. 3.30).[22]

It is hard to see how these New Kingdom Egyptian looms could have been worked al-

[22] All of these are reproduced and discussed at length by Roth [1913] 1951, 14–18 and figs. 9, 13, 14, 16, q.v. Since then, further reproductions have been published, but they do not entirely supersede Roth's. Chronologically by tomb owner (see Gardiner and Weigall 1913 for the Theban tomb numbers), they are:

Thutnofer—Tomb 104, time of Amenhotep II to Thutmose IV (Davies 1929; Badawy 1968, 16 fig. 1);

Neferhotep—Tomb 50, time of Akhenaton, Ay, and Horemheb (Davies 1933, 38 and pl. 49, 60);
Neferronpet—Tomb 133, time of Rameses II (Davies 1948, 49–51 and pl. 35).
(The tomb of Daga, no. 103, does not show a vertical loom, as Davies [1933, 38] thinks, but a horizontal one according to Egyptian rules of drawing.)

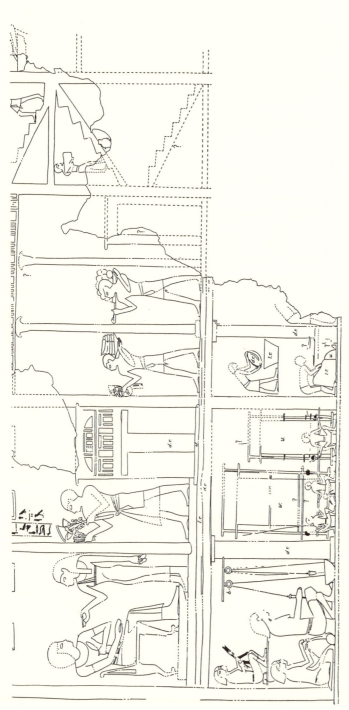

3.29 Weavers and spinners working in the basement(?) of a townhouse of the 18th-Dynasty nobleman Thutnofer, at Thebes. This is the earliest known Egyptian representation of vertical two-beam looms. From a wall painting in Thutnofer's tomb (no. 104) at Thebes, reign of Amenhotep II or Thutmose IV; late 15th century B.C. (Davies 1929, fig. 1; courtesy of the Metropolitan Museum of Art)

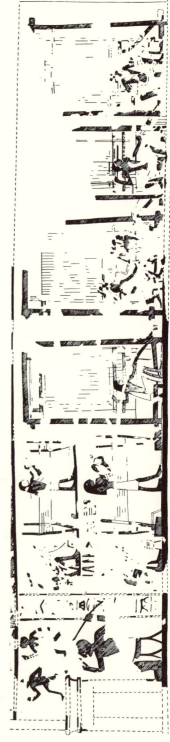

3.30 Weaving workshop showing four vertical two-beam looms (right), two warping frames (left of center), and a doorman chasing away children (far left). Tomb of Neferronpet (no. 133) at Thebes; reign of Rameses II, 13th century B.C. (Davies 1948, pl. 35; courtesy of the Committee of the Egypt Exploration Society)

ways by seated weavers, as shown, without some device to keep bringing the working area into reach. The drawings do not show clearly what that device is, and roller beams are one possibility. Or perhaps, as Schaefer suggests (1938, 548), the cloth beam rolled and the warp beam was simply raised and lowered as needed. In the clearest Egyptian drawings, the warp beam appears separate from (and below) the beam that stabilizes the top of the frame. Another way of storing the extra warp on a vertical two-beam loom is to string it over the warp beam and then across the room, where it can be fastened somehow so as not to lose its tension. For example, the warp can be passed over a second beam, bunched together, and weighted down with a third beam or with one or more large weights. The weights can move up freely to let down warp as the finished cloth is rolled onto the cloth beam. (Note that in all other constructional features this loom differs radically from the loom traditionally called the "warp-weighted loom"). All of these solutions are used today by craftsmen in the Near East (Broudy 1979, 109–11 figs. 6.10–12; Crowfoot 1941). Mace (1922) suggests that the numerous "loom weights" found toward the end of the Bronze Age at Lisht, in Egypt, belonged to this type of loom rather than to the northern type of warp-weighted loom; yet inspection of them in the Metropolitan Museum shows that they are not big enough—at least not to do the job the way it is done today. Furthermore, Egyptian artists were so particular about showing all the major working elements of an object, even if doing so destroyed all natural perspective, that it is hard to believe that they simply omitted such a large device as a weight system in the drawings.

Yet another remedy is to bring the warp around full circle behind the working face of the loom and back up to where it started. This strategem allows one to store twice as much warp as the loom is high; or still more if the warp is passed around yet a third beam at some distance behind the loom (Geijer [1972] 1979, 29 fig. 2.8). The weaver has only to keep sliding the warp around the circle, so that the section where the weaving is being done is always within easy reach. Sometimes, as we saw with the ground-loom, the warp threads themselves are passed around and around the two (or three) beams, forming right on the loom what could literally be called a "spiral warp" (ibid., 28). But although this looks like a quick and easy way of making a warp, the problem of adjusting the tension of each warp thread so that it is equal to that of the others is probably harder with this method of warping than with any other.[23]

Alternatively—and here the archaeological finds have a surprise in store for us—the ball of warp can be passed first one way around the two beams of the loom, then around a rod that marks the end of the warp, then back the other way around the loom; around the same rod again, and so forth, forming a tubular warp (fig. 3.31). In this case, when the work of weaving has progressed all the way from one end of the warp to the other—that is, from one side of the rod all the way around to the other—the weaver has two interesting choices for finishing: either to stop just short of the end of the warp, thereby producing a rectangular cloth with four selvedges (when the rod is pulled out); or to insert the last threads in such a way as to weave the two ends of the warp together, replacing the rod and making the complete

---

[23] Cf. Hald 1950, 453. Anywhere that warp threads are looser than their neighbors, the weft will tend to bow outwards; conversely, anywhere that warp threads are too tight, the weft will tend to pack in too tightly to keep a straight line across the fabric. Equal tension is thus very important in making the final product neat and even.

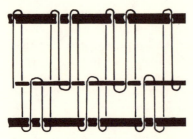

3.31 Diagram showing construction of a tubular warp, as found on a few textiles from Denmark in the Bronze Age, late 2nd millennium B.C. (Munksgaard 1974a, fig. 13; courtesy of National Museum, Copenhagen)

cloth into a tube. (A spiral warp, of course, will *always* produce a tubular cloth, unless the warps are cut. These are two ways of making a "coat of no seams.")

As a matter of fact, several pieces of cloth

BAND LOOMS

I stated at the beginning of the chapter that the same caveat holds specifically for band looms. We have no clear representations from the entire ancient world of any loom suited to weaving narrow bands; and yet from 6000 B.C. onwards we have direct evidence, in the form of surviving bands, that people were weaving them (e.g., at Çatal Hüyük, Naḥal Mishmar, etc.: see Chapter 4). Furthermore, since at least the Late Neolithic, it has been customary to form, organize, and secure the warp for a warp-weighted loom by weaving a heading band, the weft of which is the future warp of the big loom (Hoffmann [1964] 1974, 63–67, 151–83, etc.; Vogt 1937, 49–51 etc.; see Chapter 4). This band must have been made on a special band loom, separate from the warp-weighted loom, because of the problems of measuring out the warp-to-be.

Although the band-loom portion of it is totally unclear, we do in fact seem to have one representation of a warping device for the

woven as tubes from alternating warps have been found in Denmark, dating from the early Iron Age, or mid-1st millennium B.C. (Hald 1950, 430–37 and fig. 172; Munksgaard 1974a, 32; Broudy 1979, 50 and fig. 3.17). Obviously from its construction, such a cloth had to have been woven on a two-beam loom, not on a warp-weighted loom. Yet we have no representational or other artifactual evidence for anything but the warp-weighted loom anywhere in Europe for the preceding five millennia and for several more centuries to come—in fact, until the two-beam vertical loom is introduced into Rome from the East Mediterranean. It should serve as a lesson to us not to feel sure that a given culture did not have one of the completely perishable types of looms just because we have no remains or representations of it.

warp-weighted loom—on the "weaving" side of the Etruscan bronze pendant from Bologna (Fig. 3.32, 12.2; Govi 1971, pl. 53–54). There, in an obvious textile scene, we see a stand in the center with lines going out to a series of pegs on a second stand at the right: just what we might expect, if the stand in the

3.32 Scene from an Etruscan pendant of bronze, showing two women producing a warp. One sits at a (damaged) band-loom structure with a bobbin or pin-beater in one hand, pulling the heddles(?) towards her. The other is probably pulling out a new loop of warp to put onto the pegs of the stand behind her (see Fig. 12.2 for the whole scene); ca. 600 B.C. (After Govi 1971, pl. 53–54)

center is the (unfortunately) end-on view of the band loom, with the future warps measured and pegged out to one side. But the angle chosen robs us of every chance to learn the details of the band loom.

If and when the band weaving was done backstrap-style, of course, there would be nothing to survive except perhaps the heddle mechanism. With the types of heddling devices we have discussed, after the heddle bar has been pulled up or forward to let the weft pass through the countershed, the only force present to return the threads to their original shed is the tension on them. Such an arrangement is not terribly satisfactory, especially with woolen warp, which tends to catch and not slide through. Sometimes, therefore—and both modern floor looms and older band looms are generally built this way—the heddles are strung between two parallel bars, one in front of (or above) the warp and the other behind (or below) it, often joined at the side to form a rigid, rectangular frame. Then the weaver can pull to form one shed, and push to form the other. The heddles within these frames theoretically may be of string (as with so many West African band looms), or of wood, reed, wire, bone, horn, or some other stiff material, with an eye in the middle: the so-called *rigid heddle* so often seen in craft shops today. The contemporary Lappish women observed by Marta Hoffmann used a rigid heddle for weaving the heading bands for their warp-weighted looms (Hoffmann [1964] 1974, 64–65, 82–83, 104–9 and figs. 48–51).

Rigid heddles with their frames are so distinctive in form, and their materials are so relatively resilient, that one might hope they would turn up in the archaeological record if they had existed. But so far no such object has been found anywhere in the prehistoric world, even where wood is preserved.

On the other hand, it is interesting in this regard that some of the closing borders of the

Swiss fabrics preserve a detail that suggests certain of the features of the vanished band loom: namely the fact that every second warp thread was held taut during the weaving, while those in between took up all the slack necessary to accommodate climbing over and under the weft (see Figs. 4.13–14). Clearly it was possible to make half the warp on the band loom tight and keep it fixed, while using the other half alone to change the sheds both ways and adjusting its tension at will. The rigid heddle is one way of achieving this effect, if the warp passing through the heddle frame is left looser than the rest. But it could also be achieved by a band loom of the sort shown by LaBaume (1955, fig. 60; also Broudy 1979, fig. 2.12), used by the Lapps for weaving heading bands, in which the two halves of the border's warp are each independently weighted by a stone (instead of being tied to the same peg, as Hoffmann observed in modern times: [1964] 1974, 64, 82–83), and the shed is controlled by a small bar anchoring string heddles that catch only half the warp. If the weight attached to the heddled (moving) half is rather lighter than the weight attached to the other, stationary half (or if the stationary half is tied to the band loom itself and only the heddled half is weighted), half the warp will end up doing all the work (as it were) of binding in the weft, just as we see it in these closing borders; and by putting equal weights on the two halves one can produce the even weave that we more normally find.

For these borders, then, we are led in all probability to another sort of "warp-weighted loom"—a small band loom with one or two warp weights on it, in which the weights might be of different sizes to give different effects, or else half the warp could be tied directly to the loom instead of to a weight.

This deduction throws some interesting light, in turn, on our interpretation of the large warp-weighted loom. For we know from certain details of the cloths that the ornamental side borders (as opposed to heading and closing borders) must have been woven not on a small band loom but on the full-sized warp-weighted loom. Each pass of the weft in the main cloth clearly also went through the sheds of the border warp, but the border sheds were demonstrably controlled independently both of the main shed and of each other (E. Vogt 1937, 52 and fig. 83). What we must have had, then, was a set-up in which a special group of weights—which could be of different heaviness from the main set or even from each other—was

attached to the warp strings of each border when ornamental side borders were desired.

We find hints of confirmation of these hypotheses among the groups of weights that have been found in situ—although for lack of a framework to make it seem important, some of the crucial information has been lost. At Troy, for example, the weights in the row left by the destroyed loom were not all of the same size and weight. Apparently 24 large and 18 small weights were recovered, while a few others disintegrated (Blegen et al. 1950, 350). But unfortunately we are not told which size was where in the lineup.

TABLET-WEAVING

There is a second, quite different solution besides the heddle to the problem of mechanically dividing the shed on a band loom, one that has considerable antiquity. By this method, each warp thread is fed through a hole in one corner of a card or tablet that has at least two (but possibly several more) perforated corners (Fig. 3.33). Neighboring warps go through holes in the same or neighboring tablets, in such a way that all the tablets end up in a pack or deck, with the flat faces all held vertically. Rotating the pack forces the various warp threads up or down,

forming different sheds automatically. Because of its simplicity and portability (it is usually used backstrap fashion), the system is ideal for weaving narrow bands, but is limited in width by the number of cards one can conveniently manage as a deck with one's hands. What makes this card-weaving or tablet-weaving so very popular is that numerous patterns can be made with so little equipment: all you need is more than two holes per card, giving the equivalent of multiple heddle bars. Typically the card is square, with a total of four holes, and is fashioned from a thin sheet of bone, wood, or other stiff material.

There has been a great flurry in the literature as to who did and didn't know tablet-weaving in the ancient world, ever since van Gennep and Jéquier came out in 1916 with their treatise claiming tablet-weaving for the Egyptians on the basis of the sorts of border designs depicted on the monuments and on an attempted reconstruction of the girdle of Rameses III, now in Liverpool (Fig. 3.34). Even before that, others had made a similar claim for the Babylonians, also based on the

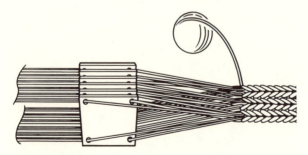

3.33 Tablet-weaving or card-weaving: a deck of pierced cards or tablets is used to create the sheds. Here the cards have four holes each

designs shown on the pictorial monuments (Lehmann-Filhes, cited in Götze 1908, 482).

The obvious ways of demonstrating the existence of card-weaving would seem to be through ancient pictorial representations or through finds of the tablets. But neither of these has been forthcoming in Egypt; and in Mesopotamia the best we have is a group of about 40 square ivory tablets from late 3rd-millennium Susa, only some of which have the necessary holes in them, and some of which seem awkwardly small for this purpose (they run 1.5 to 3.5 cm on a side: Mecquenem 1905, 121). The next cards that I know of are from the La Tène period, that is, late 1st millennium B.C.: some 4-hole cards found at Deibjerg in Denmark (Hald 1950, 453), and some small, pierced, boxwood cards from Grave 200 at Cigarralejo in eastern Spain (Hundt 1968, 192–93 and fig. 5). Then we have a deck from Coptic Egypt (Staudigel 1975, 77 and pl. 4), while the majority of finds come from the Viking age in Scandinavia: at Björkö (van Reesema 1926, 14), at Birka, at Lund, and on the Oseberg ship, where they are even threaded up with a warp (Götze 1908, 488 fig. 5; Hald 1950, 453; Schuette 1956, 5; Munksgaard 1974a, 43 fig. 22).

But we are not restricted to the evidence of the cards themselves, because tablet-weaving, unlike most other forms of weaving, can leave its own unmistakable mark on the finished product. If the deck of cards is merely flopped back and forth to make the sheds, and only a single weft is inserted, the cloth looks like any other. But if the cards are rotated a full revolution in the same direction, the warp threads are forced to twist around each other in a unique way. And if cards with more than two holes are used (necessary for patterns), they can be manipulated in such a way as to produce two sheds simultaneously on a regular basis, sheds that

can be used for a second weft and that can also lead to types of repeated errors that would never happen any other way.

Apparently none of the fabrics found in Egypt show this corded effect, since the main textiles that have been claimed as tablet-woven have been examined for the effect and found wanting: e.g., the Rameses girdle and some bands possibly of the 22nd Dynasty in the Graf collection (Crowfoot and Roth 1923; Riefstahl 1944, 28; the latter apparently no longer in existence). But quite a few of the textiles preserved in northern and western Europe over the last three millennia do show the distinctive cording produced only by tablets. The earliest of these include a 6th century B.C. find in a Hallstatt tomb at Hohmichele (requiring probably 14 cards: Hundt 1962, 208); another Hallstatt textile that is less easy to date (requiring 7 cards: Hundt 1960, 145–47 and fig. 9); a woven border requiring at least 35 cards, from a Hallstatt chieftain's grave at Apremont, in eastern France (Hundt 1970, 67); and two borders needing up to 33 cards, from the same Early La Tène grave at Cigarralejo that contained the weaving tablets (Hundt 1968, 189–93). During the main La Tène period, from which we have many more fabrics, these card-woven borders turn up more and more frequently, until in the early centuries A.D. we find such *tours de force* as the great mantle from Thorsberg, where the tablet-weaving, done in blue and white wool along all four edges, would have required decks of 178 tablets (Schlabow 1976, 64). (For other, later pieces, see Schlabow 1976 and Hoffmann [1964] 1974, 168–76). Many more border strips, all the way back to the Swiss Neolithic textiles, *could* have been woven with cards, but do not have the twisting that proves it.

Because of the lack of cording, and in an attempt to find a simpler solution for the known facts, Crowfoot and Roth (1923) undertook to demonstrate that all the Egyptian patterns can be produced equally well by other, more conventional modes of weaving; and van Reesema even went so far as to show in detail, pattern by pattern, that some of the belt designs "reconstructed" by van Gennep and Jéquier with cards were grossly inaccurate copies and could not be made more accurate by that method, but could be produced down to the last detail by yet another method of making cloth, generally known by its Scandinavian name "sprang" (see below; van Reesema 1926, 26–50).

Nonetheless, duplicating the front of the Rameses girdle (Fig. 3.34), even approximately, was difficult, and many others tried it as the controversy raged (see Staudigel 1975). Part of the problem was that the strips with the repeated *ankh* sign and with the zigzag required manipulation of 5 threads, whereas the simple dots and stripes between them required groups of 4 threads. And none of the attempts succeeded in duplicating and elucidating the nature of the faults on the back. Finally Otfried Staudigel undertook to analyze mathematically what was necessary to produce each little part of the repeating

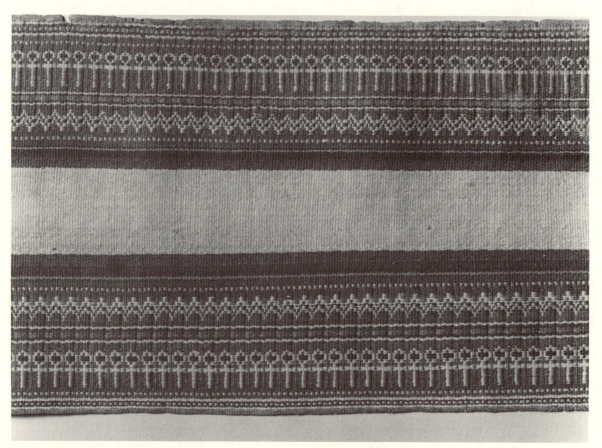

3.34   Girdle of Rameses III (ca. 1200 B.C.), a long, tapering sash tablet-woven from alternating decks of 4-holed and 5-holed cards. (Courtesy of Liverpool Museum, Merseyside County Museums)

pattern, and demonstrated that it was not only possible but necessary to use cards—some with 4 holes and others with 5—in order to come up naturally with the particular errors of the girdle, which show only on the back and occur only in neighboring 5-thread patterns but not in the 4-thread portions between (ibid.).

This piece is so complicated, with its four alternating decks of 4-hole and 5-hole cards, that we must accord the Egyptians not only tablet-weaving but a very long tradition of it from somewhere. It presumably came into Egypt with the other foreign textile techniques in the New Kingdom (see Chapters 5, 15), but the craft itself would seem to be much older.

We have one more piece of evidence to consider, however, in relation to the early phases of tablet-weaving. I was startled, in flipping through a publication of early 3rd-millennium artifacts from the northeast Caucasus, to see a cast of a "textile" that showed very clearly the cording associated with tablet-weaving. Among the large hammer-headed pins typical of the kurgan burials around Nalchik (Kabardinski Park) were some that had been decorated by impressing twisted cords onto the inside of the clay molds from which the bronze pins were then cast (see Degen 1941, 271–73, figs. 34–39), much as twisted cords were used to decorate the famous Corded Ware pottery. Most of

3.35 Bronze pin (two views) cast from a mold decorated with impressions of what appear to be card-woven textiles. From Nalchik, in the northern Caucasus; early 3rd millennium. (Degen 1941, pl. 16.1)

the impressions show single and double rows of cording; but one pin (Fig. 3.35) has row upon row of cording with alternating twists so perfectly matched that they could only have composed a single integrated fabric.[24] It

[24] I know of very few other possibilities that might have produced this effect. One is a technique known to American children as spool knitting. A few pegs or nails (typically four) are pounded into the end of a hollow wooden tube, the yarn is looped around the pegs, and with each successive row the old loop is pulled up and over both peg and fresh loop, and dropped into the center. A plump, round cord, which looks like purled knitting, thus grows downward through the hollow tube. The technique is a simple one, closely related to both crocheting and knitting—but we have no evidence for those techniques, either, for several more millennia, far later than for tablet-weaving. A cord produced by spool knitting, however, should show the loops neighboring each other sideways on a slight slant, which our speci-

men does not.

Chain stitch, which has a similar look, is used a millennium later as an embroidery stitch on a tunic of probably Syrian workmanship in Tutankhamon's tomb (Crowfoot and Davies 1941, 126; and see Chapter 5). It is barely conceivable that a closely chain-stitched cloth was rolled up to form this impression.

Finally, more than two millennia later, in Poland, elaborate gold chains were being made that look rather like this (Bukowski 1977, pl. 32.2, 32.4). But that is late in the Iron Age, whereas we are talking about the very dawn of the age of metalworking. Were the goldsmiths already so accomplished?

Whichever solution we choose, we are pushing a high form of some craft back thousands of years.

seems possible, then, that the technique of card-weaving was already known this early in the Caucasus, where it was shared (which direction?) with Mesopotamia and eventually Egypt, and from which it spread westward with the Corded Ware culture into central Europe, whence comes our first evidence of tablet-weaving in Europe some two millennia later.[25] We will need more pieces of this puzzle, however, before we can say just who invented this technique, or where, or when.

SPRANG

Sprang is "plaiting with stretched threads," as van Reesema calls it (van Reesema 1926, 5), and is closely related to the string game known to every American child as "cat's cradle." Threads are stretched between two parallel beams, much like a warp on a two-beam loom, but the fabric is made by twisting neighboring threads around each other (as in cat's cradle) and not by introducing a weft. The twists are pushed symmetrically to both ends and held by a rod until the next twist can be put in to secure it. The work progresses in this fashion until the two groups of twists meet in the middle, where a cord is darned in (or some other special step taken) to keep everything from unravelling. The resulting fabric—not a true "textile," in the narrow sense, but a cloth-like object nonetheless—is very elastic in nature, unlike most woven cloth, and seems to have been much used for hairnets, stockings, and sleeves, which had to go around great lumps like hair buns or awkward corners like knees and elbows. Its place has now largely been taken by the still-later technique of knitting (the earliest certain examples of which are from the mid-3rd century A.D., from Dura Europus in Syria, according to Forbes 1956, 179). But the craft of sprang was still being pursued in this century in Galicia and in Scandinavia (van Reesema 1926, 5, 20–21).

Most of the surviving objects in this technique are quite late, by our standards. An object in the nature of a sleeve or stocking, done in sprang with a tablet-woven border, turned up in the Tegle find (Norway, 3rd to 5th century A.D.; Hoffmann [1964] 1974, 169 fig. 81); other pieces come from Roman Vindonissa, in Switzerland (Munksgaard 1974a, 47), from the La Tène Grave 200 at Cigarralejo (Hundt 1968, 198–200), from Iron Age Denmark (Store Arden: Hald 1950, 23 fig. 15; Munksgaard 1974a, fig. 136), from a Classical tomb at Kertch (Granger-Taylor, in Jenkins and Williams 1985, 417–18), from late Egyptian tombs said—shakily—to be of the 22nd Dynasty (Riegl 1889, 51 and pl. 8; van Reesema 1926, 5; apparently no longer extant), as well as quite a few from Roman and Coptic Egypt (e.g., that on display in the museum of the Oriental Institute in Chicago; see also van Reesema 1920; Winlock 1942, 116; Jenkins and Williams 1985, pl. 45.9–10). From earlier periods, however, excavations of Danish bog burials have produced elegant sprang caps or hairnets of the Early Bronze Age from Skrydstrup and Borum Eshøj (Fig. 3.36; Munksgaard 1974a, 45–47 and fig. 24,

[25] Note that we have essentially no remains of textiles themselves from central Europe during precisely those two millennia. The Swiss lake material is Neolithic; the next major group is associated with Hallstatt remains, that is, early Iron Age—although I suspect that the "Hallstatt-type" fabrics go well back into the 2nd millennium, since we see very similar cloth represented on Late Minoan I–II paintings (see Chapters 7, 15). Some Hallstatt and many La Tène textiles have tablet-woven borders. So who are we to say that tablet-weaving had not existed in Europe during that gap?

3.36 Bronze Age hairnet done in sprang (twisted thread) technique, from Borum Eshøj, Denmark; late 2nd millennium B.C. (Photo courtesy of National Museum, Copenhagen)

53–55; see Chapter 6). Earliest of all, impressions of fabric evidently made by the sprang process were found on Neolithic potsherds from north Germany (Schlabow 1970). We thus have direct evidence that sprang has been around in Europe since the Neolithic period, apparently spreading southwards across the Mediterranean only at the start of the Iron Age.

But we also have other kinds of evidence. Elizabeth van Reesema and Jan Six, two of the pioneers in working out the technique, noticed that the hairnets depicted on Classical ladies, e.g., on a south Italian plate, looked suspiciously like sprang (van Reesema 1926, 6 and fig. 1). And others have pointed out that the objects dubbed "tapestry frames" (e.g., by Roth [1913] 1951, 31) or "embroidery frames" (e.g., by Jehasse and Jehasse 1973, 469, 508, and see pl. 49, 51, and 47) on 5th-century Greek vases were almost certainly sprang frames instead, since the fancy work is shown growing symmetrically at both ends, as is necessary for sprang but not done in tapestry (Six 1919; Hald 1950, 254–55 and figs. 255–56; L. Clark 1983, with pl. 14–16; Jenkins and Williams 1985, with extensive illustration pl. 44–46), whereas the straight, vertical lines in the middle show an as-yet unworked section of warp, a feature that is hard to explain if the frame is for embroidery. The frames show much the same features, including size, as the typical sprang frames found still in use (see Hald 1950, 254 fig. 254; van Reesema 1926, 8 fig. 5). Just when and how the technique reached Greece from the north would be useful to know. Was it with the explosion of textile techniques rippling outwards from the Hallstatt culture at the start of the Iron Age? Obviously the technique was invented long before the time of the Hallstatt folk, but they may have been the ones to pass it around.[26]

CONCLUSIONS

If we now review the evidence for the various major tensioning devices, that is, basic looms, we find the following. The only indication we have for the existence of the simple band loom is the fact that we have narrow textiles, even as far back as ca. 6000 B.C. at Çatal Hüyük. Although no accompanying remains of looms or representations of looms on which one could produce such bands have survived, the logical, if unprovable, explanation is that they were being made on the simplest of all weaving devices, the backstrap band loom. When we begin to get evidence for the nature of the larger looms, we find that they are already of a somewhat sophisticated technology, and are already of two quite different types. In Egypt, from the mid-5th millennium on, we find increasingly copious evidence for the two-beam ground-loom; our one representation of a loom from Mesopotamia is also of a ground-loom; and the Early Neolithic and Chalcolithic evidence from the Judaean desert points in the same direction. On the other hand, in the lands north of the Mediterranean we have much direct evidence for the one-beam, vertical, warp-weighted loom.

Now, it is possible that the ground-loom existed farther north also: to the northeast, in the steppes (where, however, large cloths to this day are by preference made by felting), and to the northwest, where it might conceivably have co-existed with the warp-weighted loom, the two looms having been specialized for different purposes. Yet the warp-weighted loom is so different in its concept that it is hard to believe that it was not independently invented, by people who originally knew nothing of the two-beam ground-loom, although they almost certainly already knew the principle of weaving under tension, as with a backstrap loom, for example (see Chapter 11).

It is particularly striking in this context that in the Middle Bronze Age the evidence for warp weights begins to extend southeastward into Syria and Palestine from Anatolia (see Chapter 14), which, to the best of our knowledge, had been the northwest edge of horizontal, two-beam, ground-loom terri-

---

[26] Is it possible that sprang was already known to the Aegean people of the Late Bronze Age? I am thinking of the stretchy-looking headbands worn by some of the girls picking saffron, on the frescoes from Xeste 3 at Thera (Marinatos 1976, pl. A–K); but these could also be ribbons.

tory; and immediately thereafter we find evidence of the adoption in Egypt of a new, more efficient loom, the vertical two-beam loom—evidently as a result of new contact with Palestine and Syria (cf. Hayes 1959, 4). From this evidence one might extrapolate that the Levant, and most likely specifically Syria, which was already famous far and wide for its textiles by 2300 B.C. (especially Ebla: Waetzoldt 1972, 144–45; Matthiae 1980, 60, 179–81), was the site of a fruitful amalgamation of the convenient verticality of the warp-weighted loom with the two-beam tensioning system of the ground-loom. The fact that the weaver wove toward him/herself on the new upright loom, as on the ground-loom but not as on the warp-weighted loom, also suggests that the genius who invented this new loom was merely transferring the notion of verticality to a basic notion of weaving derived from the standard ground-loom. Such a hypothesis, at any rate, is inherently simpler than assuming the reverse (it presumes one major change rather than two), and it appears also to be consonant with the geographical hints.

Certainly this new, vertical, two-beam loom, on which one wove with a downward motion while sitting, rather than upward while standing, spread all over the ancient Near East, where it is used to this day in making Persian-style carpets and tapestries. The warp-weighted loom, on the other hand, continued to be used in the lands north of the Mediterranean until the turn of the era, when the Romans began to adopt the vertical, two-beam loom, presumably from their subjects in the Near East, and to spread its use northwestward across the European parts of their empire. Even then, warp-weighted looms continued to be used in parts of Europe into medieval times (Broudy 1979, 138 and fig. 8.3), and in the far north into this century (Hoffmann [1964] 1974). The horizontal treadle loom, which is the sort we are most accustomed to seeing today, was a very late development from our point of view (cf. Carroll 1985).

As for the development of shedding devices, anthropological studies as well as logic suggest that where mechanical shedding is unknown, twining and other such techniques will be either on a par with or preferred to true weaving (cf. Broudy 1979, 78–80). After all, without heddle bars to open either entire shed at once—or at least a shed bar to open one of the two sheds at a swipe—it will take just as long to darn in the weft with a true weave as with a twining technique (see Chapter 4). In the esparto fabrics of Neolithic Spain and in the early linen fabrics of Çatal Hüyük (see Chapter 4), as well as in the older cloths found in the New World, we see precisely this distribution, with a high percentage of twined fabrics versus woven ones. Later, in each area, the statistics change and we find the woven goods ousting the twined ones altogether. The presence of a strong weaving industry, then, in itself becomes evidence for the advent of mechanical shedding.

We have looked in detail at the form and development of the looms, and will do so again in Chapter 11. But it is time to turn our attention to the skills that people developed on these looms: that is, to the development of plain and pattern weaves, and to other, minor modes of decoration of the textiles.

CHAPTER 4

THE TEXTILE WEAVES
(1) THE BEGINNINGS

What types of weaves the ancients attempted is a question we must in general consider quite independently of what sorts of looms they had, for virtually any weaving pattern can be produced on any loom that is big enough for it—if the weaver wishes to take the requisite time and trouble. It is quite true that certain looms tend to lead the weaver into one technique or another, as being easier on that loom. But only the tablet deck and the tubular-warped loom, as we have seen, sometimes—and only sometimes—leave small, idiosyncratic details behind that could not have been produced any other way. For weaves, then, there is only one sure source of data: the fabrics themselves or their impressions. Since we do not have a great deal of this sort of evidence, we must again be content to try to put together a picture of the broad trends: what might be considered expectable or unusual for a given time and place.

I say we do not have a great deal of evidence: that is relative. We have many thousands of fragments and impressions of textiles that have survived from early periods; but most of them are the size of a thumbnail or smaller—a minuscule inheritance from so proliferous an industry—and so they tell us next to nothing individually (which is one reason they have been so relentlessly ignored by the archaeologists who dig them up). It is only when we have the rare and precious groups of well-preserved textiles, such as those from Egypt, the Swiss lakes, or the Danish bogs, that we can understand readily what we are looking at. Within the context of these finds, however, the other, tiny scraps begin to make sense. My strategy, therefore, will be to take up the material by periods and areas (those which the data have shown me to be structurally relevant), first looking at the key finds to get some idea of context, and then laying the tiny pieces of the puzzle in around the big ones. In order to avoid excessive backtracking, I shall consider at the same time other integral forms of patterned decoration, such as sewing.

THE EARLIEST REMAINS

Right from the beginning of our evidence we discover that weavers were already aware of more than one possible way to bind threads together (Fig. 4.1). At Jarmo, the very earliest site from which proof of textiles has been forthcoming, one of the two preserved impressions on clay seems to show just what we might expect a priori, namely

a   b   c

4.1 Diagrams of the simplest weaves: (a) plain weave; (b) basket weave; and (c) triple basket weave

plain weave,[1] with single warp and weft;[2] but the other shows something else: plain weave with double warp and weft, a so-called *basket weave* (Fig. 4.2; Adovasio 1975–77, 224; Adovasio 1983, 425). These impressions are dated to the early 7th millennium.

In fact, when our first major evidence appears—the various pieces of actual cloth from Naḥal Ḥemar in the Judaean desert (ca. 6500 B.C.) and Çatal Hüyük on the Anatolian plateau (ca. 6000 B.C.)—we see an astonishing variety of bindings for the threads. I will treat the younger group first, since it is both

larger and fully published, and will explain briefly some technical problems that will concern us throughout these next few chapters.

The Çatal Hüyük fabrics, like the Jarmo impressions, already show variation even within the basic plain weave. Some cloths were "coarse," some "fine," and some had coarse thread one way and fine the other way (that is, warp differed from weft, but we can't be sure which is which; Helbaek 1963, 41). Some were fairly broad—how broad cannot be said, since they were too brittle from carbonization to unfold—and others were woven as narrow tapes, of 7 to 15 mm in width (Fig. 4.3; Burnham 1965, 171–72). More interesting: whereas some of the tapes, like the broader pieces of cloth, had roughly the same number of threads in either direction (*balanced* plain weave: Fig. 4.4a), one kind of tape had more than four times as many warp as weft threads per unit distance (Burnham 1965, 170, 172). In such a construction the warp threads are so densely packed that they hide the weft altogether—a so-called *warp-faced* plain weave—and give an entirely different visual effect from a weave in which both elements are visible (Fig. 4.4b).

4.2 Earliest direct proof of weaving yet known: impressions of textiles from Jarmo, in northeastern Iraq, ca. 7000 B.C. Left: plain weave; right: basket weave. (Adovasio 1983, figs. 169.9–10; photos courtesy of the Oriental Institute of the University of Chicago)

[1] Or *tabby*: a simple alternation of over one thread, under the next, for both warp and weft. Weaving terms in this book conform as much as possible with the definitions given by Irene Emery (1966). One notable exception is the term *faced*. The archaeologist, unlike the weavers who write the terminology books, seldom can tell warp from weft because the scraps are so small.

Hence we need a generic term *faced* for "warp-faced or weft-faced" (see Fig. 4.4).

[2] This impression shows the single threads at just enough of a deviation from right angles to each other, however, that there might even be some question of oblique plaiting rather than true weaving with distinct warp and weft.

4.3   Narrow tapes in warp-faced weave, from Çatal Hüyük, an Early Neolithic town site in south central Turkey; ca. 6000 B.C. (Photo courtesy of J. Mellaart)

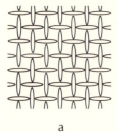 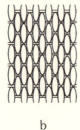 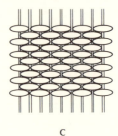

a   b   c

4.4   Varieties of plain weave created by different densities of warp and weft: (a) balanced plain weave; (b) warp-faced plain weave (warp covers weft); (c) weft-faced plain weave (weft covers warp). Since often one cannot tell which is warp and which is weft in ancient textile scraps, the term *faced weave* is used in this book to cover (b) and (c) where the difference is not ascertainable

Fabrics also occurred with two other, quite different types of interlacing, which some consider to be "weaving" and others do not. One is *weft-wrapping* (Fig. 4.5, left), in which the weft has been wrapped once around each successive warp thread (instead of merely going either over it or under it). The other is *weft-twining with paired weft* (Fig. 4.5, right), in which two weft threads run along together in such a way that one goes over and the other under a given warp; then they take a half-turn around each other before going (respectively) under and over the next warp (Fig. 4.6; Burnham 1965, 171). The rows of weft are spaced so far apart along the warp that the result in both cases is a net-like fabric.

The easiest way to treat the side edges, or *selvedges,* is either to turn the weft back into

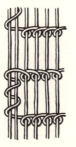 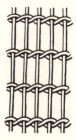

4.5   Diagrams of twining techniques used at Çatal Hüyük; ca. 6000 B.C. Left: weft-wrapping; right: weft-twining with paired weft. (Burnham 1965, figs. 1–2)

the next row around the outermost warp thread, or else to leave its end sticking out as a fringe and take up a new thread for the next row of weft. In the Çatal Hüyük textiles, Burnham states he was unable to find any certain examples of selvedges on the larger

4.6 Enlargement of weft-twined fabric from Çatal Hüyük; ca. 6000 B.C. (Photo courtesy of J. Mellaart)

pieces in plain weave, but both kinds of tapes showed a simple turn at each side. The edge of one of the twined fabrics, on the other hand, was formed by wrapping the weft a couple of times around the last *two* warps (Burnham 1965, 171–72 and fig. 1), thereby strengthening the edge against the extra wear that it would receive (see Fig. 4.5, left). (Selvedges nowadays are almost invariably reinforced somehow.)

The other two edges of the cloth, where the weaving begins and ends on the warp, entail quite different problems from those encountered on the sides. In most types of weaving, loose ends of warp will be left sticking out from the tail of the cloth. They can be left that way permanently, or tied off in some fashion to prevent the last weft from raveling out. Burnham suggests that a "confused layer of disordered threads" at one place in a bundle of Çatal Hüyük fabric may have been "the remains of a natural warp fringe" of this sort (Burnham 1965, 171). Another way to handle the end is to trim off the loose threads, then turn the edge back and sew it: that is, to hem it as one might hem

any cut edge. Burnham in fact describes two cases of "a plain rolled hem . . . sewn in coarse running stitch" (ibid., 172), although we do not know where on the fabric the hems occurred. The other place where sewing was visible seems to have been a mend, with the "join formed by overcasting two edges" (ibid.).

At two other places Burnham recognized what seem to have been *starting* or *heading bands* (ibid., 171, 172). Whereas on a two-beam loom the warp tends to be tied directly onto the beams at either end (or sometimes wrapped right around one or both beams), on a warp-weighted loom the warp is generally looped over or through a cord, or woven into a strip (with the future warp hanging out one side of the strip like a fringe many feet long), and the cord or strip in turn is fastened to the upper beam of the loom with the warp hanging down (see Hoffmann [1964] 1974, 41, 64–67, 151–83 etc., and many illustrations, for a detailed account of starting borders). Thus the starting edge is a closed one, and often is quite different from any of the other three edges of the cloth.

In this case, according to Burnham's diagram (Fig. 4.7), the warp loops are first caught by a pair of twined cords, then passed either over or under a set of three (perhaps four) wefts before the plain weave of the regular cloth is begun. The crudest form of heading cord found by Marta Hoffmann in

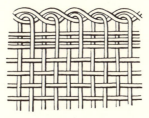

4.7 Diagram of the structure of the edge—possibly the heading band—of a textile from Çatal Hüyük; ca. 6000 B.C. (Burnham 1965, fig. 3)

her modern fieldwork was made by fastening the ends of a heavy cord to the top corners of the loom and simply hanging over it the pre-measured warp, which was then spread out and lashed down (Hoffmann [1964] 1974, 41 and fig. 8). The heading band from Çatal Hüyük, however, if that's what it is, is considerably more sophisticated, in that the twining around each warp thread shows that the cord and the warp were made at the same time, as a unit, with the twined cord serving as spacer and organizer. The tripled weft that comes next could have been put in either then or later, but it probably acted mainly to reinforce the edge. It would not have done much to keep the warp threads from pulling through when the weights were attached—if indeed we are correct in assuming a warp-weighted loom from the probable header[3]—so presumably the weights had to be tied onto both ends of a given thread at once. Hoffmann describes the users of the simple heading cord as doing just that: one person tied the front threads while another tied the back ones to balanced pairs of stones sorted out for them by a third person (Hoffmann [1964] 1974, 42). (Those who used the more solidly woven type of starting band theoretically could tie weights on in any order they pleased, although by tradition it was generally done in some orderly way, a way that differed slightly from one community to the next. This sort of problem will account for the variety among heading bands in the chapters that follow.)

THE finds from Naḥal Ḥemar are similar in certain details to the Çatal Hüyük textiles, and remarkably different in others. To begin with, the techniques used to make the cloth-like objects of early date have all proved to be other than true plain weave.[4] The predominant technique, in fact, is weft-twining (which also occurs at Çatal Hüyük), carried out in various grades of fineness (Fig. 4.8). In addition, a number of pieces are made in knotted or twisted *netting* techniques, including a very handsome and sophisticated net "bag" with a polished stone bead sewn onto its collar.

As at Çatal Hüyük, the predominant fiber seems to be flax. And certainly these people were very familiar with its preparation into thread, string, and cord. But a large number of the artifacts made from fiber string and cord at Naḥal Ḥemar were not textiles. Much of this string had been wrapped closely around core objects, densely plastered with bitumen or asphalt from the desert valley, and removed from the cores to form solid containers. In fact, it seems that the inhabitants of nearby areas were at-

---

[3] Such a construction is unlikely as a side-selvedge, so it probably *is* the beginning of the cloth in any case. As for other evidence for the loom, these levels at Çatal Hüyük are so early that they are virtually pre-ceramic, so clay weights are not to be expected. But Burnham comments (1965, 173) that "two carefully worked stones of unknown use . . . would have served the purpose admirably." And Mellaart reports finding a few crudely pierced blobs of clay of an appropriate size (see Chapter 3). It is to be hoped that some day excavation of this archaeologically rich and important site will be resumed and extended from what seems to be chiefly a shrine district into the zone of common dwellings and work areas. Then we might find real loom evidence.

[4] This material has not yet received its full publication. The two main publications that have come out are

Bar-Yosef 1985 (with excellent—unnumbered—photographs of the finds, many of them in color), and Schick 1986. Unfortunately, the radiocarbon dating was not yet completed at the time of these publications, and it has now been determined that the few bits of plain-woven cloth, which came from the disturbed top layers, are much more recent (T. Schick, pers. comm. 1987). Most of the details mentioned here are derived from personal communication with Tamar Schick (based in part on analysis by Carmela Shimony), who is currently engaged in the full technical analysis of the perishable remains from this important early site. This footnote will therefore serve as reference for all that follows. My warmest thanks to Tamar Schick for her generosity in sharing this material with me.

4.8   Weft-twined linen cloth from a dry cave at Naḥal Ḥemar, in Israel; Early Neolithic, ca. 6500 B.C. (Israel Museum; photo courtesy of the Israel Department of Antiquities and Museums)

tracted to this particular desert valley precisely to collect asphalt (*hemar*), which wells up here and there in natural tar-seeps (Bar-Yosef 1985, 3). They used this gooey substance for many purposes, as the artifacts from the cave show, not just for the caulking of various types of vessels (ibid., 4 etc.).

As a matter of fact, natural tars have been recognized at other early Neolithic sites where plant remains are less well preserved: for example at Ali Kosh (mid-7th to mid-6th millennium), where the excavators found "many bits of matting . . . preserved because they had been coated with asphalt, perhaps accidentally" (Hole and Flannery 1962, 125). It is likely now that these are not accidental, but are the remains of a caulking industry

similar to that at Naḥal Ḥemar, where the base structure to be caulked was built up somehow out of plant fibers. It suggests once again an early and thorough familiarity with plant fibers in an extensive area of the Near East; and it shows that the people across this area were busy sharing technological ideas about fibers, containers, and so on.

If the Naḥal Ḥemar finds are reasonably representative of Palestine in the mid-7th millennium, we can begin to make some sense out of the relationships among the earliest textiles, cordage, mats, etc., that we now have in the Near East. For in at least two ways the Naḥal Ḥemar assemblage appears to give us an intermediate stage of development: in showing weft-twining before true weaving, and in showing the use of worked fibers for caulked containers before the invention of pottery.

There are four sites or areas that concern us in particular, and they form a sort of broad square. Jarmo, to the northeast, shows true textiles close to 7000 B.C., in a very early pre-ceramic phase of the Neolithic, and Tell Shimshara nearby has given us a plain-weave textile impression from the 6th millennium (Mortensen 1970, 123 and 124 fig. 113). Çatal Hüyük, to the northwest, shows full-fledged textiles by 6000 B.C., in early Neolithic levels that already teeter on the brink of having pottery as a major commodity. Naḥal Ḥemar, to the southwest, is still thoroughly pre-ceramic at about 6500 B.C., and does not yet know true weaving, but has a lively fiber industry that includes weft-twined and netted cloths and bags as well as mats, baskets, and caulked-twine receptacles. Ali Kosh, to the southeast, shows at least a knowledge of caulking mats or baskets around 6000 B.C.

There is quite a bit of shared technology along the sides of this square. Thus we see true weaving shared in the north and caulked fibers shared in the south at remarkably early dates. Furthermore, in the southwest corner we see strong similarities between the culture of Naḥal Ḥemar and the famous Pre-Pottery Neolithic B culture of Jericho, where textiles have not been so lucky as to survive, and some of these similarities stretch on up through the old Natufian territory into the central Anatolian plateau, to Çatal Hüyük, where in addition to the weft-twining we find very similar polished bone belt-hooks (not to mention the selective treatment of skulls, etc.; compare Mellaart 1963b, pl. 27c–d and Mellaart 1967, pl. 101 with Bar-Yosef 1985).

It seems, then, that fiber crafts were busily developing throughout the Early Neolithic in this entire area, but that true weaving was a northern phenomenon, spreading south only after twining, netting, matting, and basketry were known there. Such a vector is confirmed by the fact that our first evidence of weaving in Egypt appears, looking a bit clumsy, only in the 5th millennium (see Chapter 5), and likewise our first evidence from Iran comes in the 5th millennium, from Tepe Yahyā (Adovasio 1975–77, 228). This picture, however, can be expected to change as we find more sites.

ONCE weaving was well started, the quest for easy ways of varying the texture began (or perhaps continued). An early textile impression was found at Mersin, in southern Turkey, under the bones of a Neolithic burial of the pre-Hassuna phase (Garstang 1953, 33), therefore perhaps mid-6th millennium. Unfortunately the imprint, although quite clear at the moment the overlying bones were removed, was no hardier than a "curious sort of film" on the earth and soon disintegrated; but the excavators were quite definite that "the strands in this pattern were seen to be arranged by threes with a total of nine strands to the centimetre (22 to the inch)" (ibid.). A diagram in the original field notebook shows clearly that we have here not a twill but three successive threads in the same shed—i.e., a triple basket weave, a simple variant of plain weave (see Fig. 4.1c).[5]

By the late 4th millennium, with the plain art of weaving spread far and wide, we find still clearer evidence for patterned decoration in the cloth. The early levels of Susa, the great capital of the eastern neighbors of the Mesopotamians, disgorged a copper axehead that had preserved in the life-killing oxides of its surface the clear outlines of a

[5] Mersin fieldnotes of D. B. Driffield for 1946–47, pp. 73–74 (February 12, 1947). My thanks to H. M. Bell, Seton Lloyd, O. R. Gurney, and the library of the Institute of Archaeology in London for helping me track down this information.

4.9 Remains of texture-striped cloth preserved on a copper axe-head. Susa; 4th millennium. (Lacaisne 1912, pl. 43)

cloth—a cloth that had evidently been put around the axe, ironically, to protect and preserve the costly metal (Fig. 4.9). (Such an oxide cast is known as a *pseudomorph*.) The original analyst described the remains in terms of two plain-weave cloths, one fine, the other coarser (Lacaisne 1912, 163). But it is clear from the photograph that one set of fine threads—let us call them "warp" for convenience here, although we cannot prove which set is actually the warp and which the weft—passes directly into the coarser part as the same continuous "warp." This "warp" remains fine throughout; all that changes is the heaviness of the "weft." Moreover, there is a deliberate pattern to the changes. After a long stretch of cloth with equally fine warp and weft, we come to a stripe made of 10 very thick "weft" rows, followed by 6 more of the fine "weft," then another 10(?) rows of the thick, and finally another expanse of the fine, at least 14 rows, until we lose everything at the top edge of the axe. Fossilized on top of the large piece lie two smaller scraps of cloth, one of which shows a sequence of fine and thick rows that tallies with the stripes just described, and the other of which preserves 8 or 9 rows of the thick "weft."

This example shows clearly that 4th-millennium weavers in the Middle East had already figured out the principle of the stripe, which only requires putting some warp or weft that contrasts in quality and/or color into the same old weave. Whether the weavers were in fact using color too is an interesting question, although obviously not one we can provably answer from this specimen. Linen is difficult to dye well (see Chapter 10), and this piece with its open, totally unmatted appearance was most probably linen (cf. Lacaisne 1912, 163). Perhaps that is why the weaver resorted to such drastically different sizes of "weft" for the stripes—so they would show up in an all-white fabric.

NEOLITHIC EUROPE

Moving to Europe, we find that the earliest direct remains of the fiber crafts come from the Mesolithic as well as the Neolithic periods there—the Mesolithic of northern Europe being contemporary with the opening stages of the Neolithic farther south. We have already mentioned that Mesolithic nets of spun bast fiber have been found in Finland and Lithuania (Chapters 1, 2), and that impressions of sprang in an unidentifiable fiber have turned up on Neolithic potsherds from northern Germany (Chapter 3; Schlabow 1970). Of true weaving, however, we have essentially nothing preserved until the late 4th millennium. That does not mean that the Europeans had not been weaving before that: we have seen the rather considerable remains of looms that begin in the mid-6th millennium (Chapter 3), we have a very occasional textile-impressed potsherd (e.g., from the Vinča-Pločnik level I at Supska: Garašanin and Garašanin 1979, pl. 2.4), and later we will inspect some of the copious early representations of fabrics (Chapter 13). But our first major group of fabrics from Europe is the linen textiles from the Swiss Neolithic pile-dwellings, belonging, it seems, to the Cortaillod, Pfyn, and Horgen cultures—that is, to the centuries on either side of 3000 B.C. They have been published with great care and in great detail by Emil Vogt (1937);

so we will start there, to gain a solid grounding in what the Europeans were doing.

The basic weave in the Swiss cloths is balanced plain weave, in various grades and widths (Fig. 4.10). The two really striking features, however, are the pattern weaves and the great variety of borders. Heading bands occur in several examples and varieties, but seem always to be of the most sophisticated type: a tightly woven strip about a dozen threads wide, through which the warp had been pulled in long loops, i.e., doubled (Fig. 4.11). We thus have a pattern of over two, under two, in one direction, but only over one, under one, in the other direction, giving a slightly ribbed effect. Some of Hoffmann's Scandinavian informants used what seem to be virtually identical techniques (Hoffmann [1964] 1974, 64–66), although they divided the shed differently afterwards (cf. ibid., 154–62). And in the Swiss group we are definitely justified in assuming a warp-weighted loom, because we have the loom weights in distinctive configurations to prove its presence (see Chapter 3).

4.10   Late Neolithic linen Cloth 11, from Robenhausen, Switzerland, in balanced plain weave with supplemental-weft stripes; ca. 3000 B.C. (Photo courtesy of the Swiss National Museum)

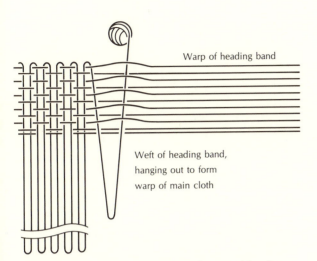

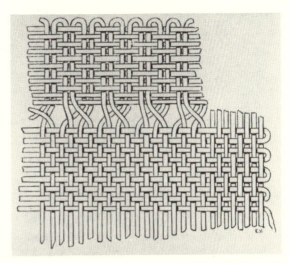

4.11   Diagram of the construction of a typical heading band and warp, for the warp-weighted loom. See also Fig. 15.14

4.12   Diagram of the construction of the selvedge and heading band of linen Cloth 1, from Robenhausen, Switzerland; ca. 3000 B.C. (E. Vogt 1937, fig. 82)

Selvedges frequently show reinforcement (e.g., Vogt 1937, 54 fig. 88); but what is a bit surprising is that some of these borders demonstrably do not coincide with the sheds of the fabrics they border. In Cloth 1,[6] the weft at the edge always goes through the same shed twice in succession, forming a slightly ribbed border, whereas in the main part of the cloth it changes shed with every pass (Fig. 4.12). The border sheds were thus being controlled independently of the main sheds. Moreover, in Cloth 2, Vogt tells us, the two selvedges suddenly cease to match each other partway down the fabric, and hence were independent not only of the main shed but of each other. We thus get a

picture of a loom with a main shedding system supplemented at either side by two very narrow, independent systems for the borders. Bizarre though it seems, we will encounter this picture again.

But all of this is child's play compared ·to the ingenuity expended by the pile-dwellers on closing borders. The simplest border, as in Cloth 4, involves binding the warp ends into little bunches with a separate, heavy thread in a figure-eight loop, to form a fringe. In another case, Cloth 5 (Fig. 4.13), after binding off the warp threads in pairs with an extra twined thread, the weaver set up a new warp of two dozen threads, longer than the fabric was wide (we presume) and at

[6] For the reader's convenience, the textiles referred to in the following discussion can be found in Vogt's 1937 publication as follows (from Robenhausen, unless otherwise mentioned):
Cloth 1: 49–51 and figs. 80–82;
Cloth 2: 51–52 and fig. 83;
Cloth 3: 52 and figs. 84–86;
Cloth 4: 52–55 and figs. 87–88;
Cloth 5: 55–57 and figs. 90–92 (from Schaffis am Bie-

lersee);
Cloth 6: 58–61 and figs. 94–95;
Cloth 7: 61–62 and figs. 97–99;
Cloth 9: 63–66 and figs. 102–4 (from Lüscherz am Bie-
    lersee);
Cloth 10: 66–68 and figs. 105–7;
Cloth 11: 74–76 and figs. 108–9;
cloth from Irgenhausen: 76–90 and figs. 112–50;
cloth from Murten: 36–37 and figs. 62–64.

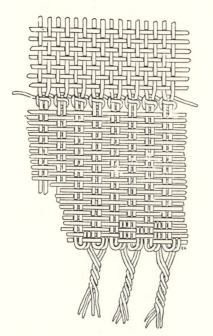

4.13   Diagram of the closing border
of linen Cloth 5, from Schaffis,
Switzerland. The warp ends of the
main cloth (above) have been used in
pairs as weft for a band-warp set up
at right angles to the original warp; ca.
3000 B.C. (E. Vogt 1937, fig. 92)

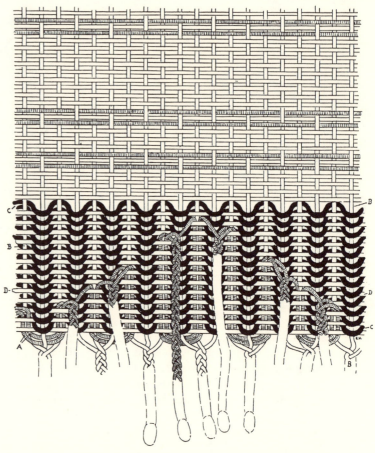

4.14   Diagram of striped cloth and elaborate closing border: linen
Cloth 9, from Lüscherz, Switzerland; ca. 3000 B.C. (E. Vogt 1937,
fig. 104)

right angles to the original warp, and proceeded to weave a closing border using each
pair of warp ends from the main fabric as the
weft for one row or "pick" of the border, running the ends back into the next shed a few
threads to secure them as they came out the
far side—and then, just for good measure,
twisting the ends into a fringe.

It is quite possible, as Vogt suggests (1937,
57), that the extra "warp" of this border was
of a different color, or even several colors—
it is no longer possible to tell, either by eye
(everything is now stained dark) or by chem-

istry. But color must surely have been used
in the most elaborate border of all, on Cloth
9 (Fig. 4.14). Here the alternate threads in
the closing border, those parallel to the main
weft, have been woven in more loosely than
their mates, creating a strongly ribbed appearance as they dive over and under the
same warp ends; and additional pairs of
threads have been worked in from the "bottom" in the original warp direction in those
rows where the warps are visible, climbing
higher and higher, then lower and lower in
successive rows to form a pattern of trian-

gles. (As in the previous example, the border must have been woven with the threads parallel to the main weft functioning as the warp, and the original warp threads and these supplemental ones as the weft.) Both the supplementary threads and the original warp ends have then been braided in threes into a fringe. Most of the elegance of this design would have been lost without colors to set off the parts.

Yet another closing border, on Cloth 10 (Fig. 4.15), although not so flashy as that on Cloth 9, is even more ingenious in its means of preventing unraveling. Like the other two cloths, it must have been made sideways to the original direction of weaving, and like Cloth 9 every second thread (parallel to the original weft, but warp as the band was being woven) is looser than its neighbors, producing a strongly ribbed effect. Also as before, the original warp ends are paired for use as the weft of the border. But this time, as they come out the far side, the ends are doubled back and used as weft in the next shed as well, so that they finally emerge on the back side of the cloth at the point where the main fabric and the border meet. It would be hard to devise a tail end to a fabric that would be more secure against unraveling.

In the borders alone, then, we have seen weft used double, giving a mild ribbing; weft used double in conjunction with an alternation of tight and loose warp, giving a very strongly ribbed effect; and supplementary weft laid into the sheds in restricted areas in such a way as to produce a pattern of triangles. The technique for producing pronounced ribbing was also used for warp-faced plain-weave bands or tapes, woven independently of a larger cloth—e.g., Cloth 6. And some of these are made as the binders of elaborate fringed tapes, as in Cloth 7, perhaps again multicolored, perhaps to be sewn onto unfringeable edges of a larger cloth.

4.15　Late Neolithic linen Cloth 10, from Robenhausen, Switzerland; ca. 3000 B.C. (Photo courtesy of Swiss National Museum)

The technique of using supplemental wefts, however, blossoms into greater variety in decorating the main fabrics. Also, the idea that one thread can skip or *float* over two or more threads in the opposite system, instead of being bound in by every second warp or weft thread, is developed far beyond the regular passing of warp threads over and under pairs of weft threads in the borders. Remarkably often we encounter stripes formed by allowing the weft to float over three warp threads before ducking under one (e.g., Cloths 3, 9, and 11: Figs. 4.16, 4.14, 4.10). Sometimes these pattern threads are woven in between the normal plain-weave wefts (the so-called *ground wefts*), but in Cloth 3 the middle thread in each three-thread stripe lies on top of the ground weft, so that it cannot be seen from the other side—the beginnings of a second layer, or *double-faced* technique (Fig. 4.16). Thus the stripe looks wide and solid on the obverse, but on the reverse like a pair of thin dotted lines (Post et al. 1925, 44 fig. 27b). In still other cases, the supplementary weft is twined into the warp—as, for example, in

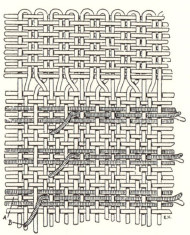

4.16 Photograph and constructional diagram of the heading band and supplementary weft stripes on linen Cloth 3, from Robenhausen, Switzerland; ca. 3000 B.C. (E. Vogt 1937, fig. 86; photo courtesy of Swiss National Museum)

4.17 Remains of a Late Neolithic linen cloth heavily decorated in a sort of "brocade" done with supplementary weft, from Irgenhausen, Switzerland; ca. 3000 B.C. (Photo courtesy of Swiss National Museum)

the second pattern on the fancy piece from Irgenhausen, where the pattern weft floats over 10, then back under 2 warp threads, before progressing over 10 more warp threads (including the two it just went under; Vogt 1937, 81–84 and figs. 124, 128).

But the pile-dwellers also knew that one could add a supplementary weft without having to take it all the way from one side of the cloth to the other like the ground weft: that

is, extra thread could be zigzagged back and forth over a small area to make discontinuous fields of color instead of a continuous stripe. Having discovered this principle, they let their imaginations run. One result was the famous "brocade" from Irgenhausen (Figs. 4.17–19), which displays a variety of floats, twines, and supplemental wefts carried diagonally across the surface, forming what Vogt breaks down as six distinct weaving pat-

4.18 Irgenhausen "brocade" reconstructed in a modern reweaving. Warp runs vertically. (Photo courtesy of Swiss National Museum)

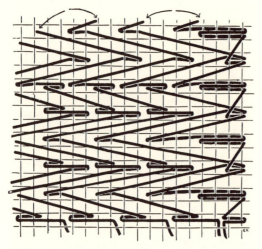

4.19 Diagram of some of the supplementary weft techniques found on the Irgenhausen "brocade." (E. Vogt 1937, fig. 138)

terns laid out in elegant stripes, checkerboards, and triangles. Again, such refined subtleties as checkers within checkers would have been lost without some use of color.

The Neolithic Swiss weavers had other techniques as well for elaborating their textiles. A small scrap from Murten is composed of a strip of knotted netting joining two woven sections of cloth (Fig. 4.20). The netting,

4.20 Neolithic linen fragment composed of two woven sections (top and bottom) joined with knotted netting. The lower piece is ornamented with beads and woven stripes (the weft probably runs downwards). From Murten, Switzerland; ca. 3000 B.C. (Photo courtesy of Swiss National Museum)

which would add considerable elasticity to the textile, is knotted directly onto the outermost edges of both woven parts, which in turn have been ornamented in two ways. Beads made of small seeds occur in patches of unknown shape (the scrap is too small to tell), on either side of a triplet of stripes. Presumably of one or more contrasting colors when made, the stripes had been woven in, whereas the seeds had been sewn on with a thread that runs regularly over two and under one thread of the base cloth, occasionally piercing the latter (and therefore definitely sewn on with a needle). Like the Irgenhausen "brocade," this beaded cloth from Murten must have been quite handsome and intricately patterned.

Indeed, one of the most striking things about the Swiss remains is that almost every one of these pieces teaches us something new—shows us some new trick that these prehistoric weavers were using to embellish their fabrics. We have seen a rather sophisticated variety of weaves beyond plain weave: chiefly ribbed bands and borders, sometimes with fringes, as well as the imaginative use of supplemental wefts, both continuous (for stripes) and discontinuous (for localized patterns). These latter were generally floated over the surface of the plain weave of the ground cloth, bound in either by simply being passed under a ground warp at intervals or by being laced or twined into the warps somehow. This lacing or twining may originally have sprung out of the sort of netting technique that was used together with weaving in one fragment—and there are many other examples of twining, netting, and even pile among the nets and basketry found in the lake dwellings (see Vogt 1937, 1–41). There is even a piece that has a regular network of threads laced diagonally in both directions through the plain-woven cloth at intervals of two warp and two weft threads (ibid., 40 and figs. 70–71). And to all of this we must add the use of color, and also patterned beadwork, even though the beads themselves are of the most primitive sort, namely little hollow seeds with the ends cut off. With so many techniques crammed into so few pieces, we have to wonder what else we will find the Swiss weavers knew, as more evidence is unearthed.

SO MUCH for the Swiss linens, which are by far the most extensive group of textiles to come down to us in Europe prior to the 2nd millennium B.C. But we have a few other pieces. Linens generally similar to the Swiss ones have been dug up recently in the neighboring areas of southeastern France, also from pile-dwellings. In northern Europe, on the other hand, we have both woven and twisted fabrics attested, some of them possibly of wool, from the area around Magdeburg, Hannover, and Kassel.

Impressions of several sorts of cloth have been found on numerous potsherds of the Middle to Late Neolithic period (Funnel Beaker/Globular Amphora and local Wartberg cultures) from excavations at Pevestorf, near Hannover, and at Rietzmeck, *Kreis* Rosslau, as well as from the collection in the museum at Fritzlar (Schlabow 1970). In some cases no structure is determinable; but 69 of the sherds had impressions of cloth made from twisted threads, apparently in the sprang technique, while 13 sherds showed woven cloth with a fat yarn running in one direction and a very thin thread the other way (ibid., 419–21 and pl. 169–71). Sprang is a technique that we pick up next in Denmark, in the Bronze Age, and is probably to be connected with northern net-making. All these impressions appeared to the analyst to be of bast rather than wool fibers (ibid., 419).

The earliest actual pieces of cloth that have survived in the north however, seem to be those found in some late Neolithic passage graves in the foothills of the Harz Mountains, south of Magdeburg: at Kreienkopp, near Ditfurt, *Kreis* Quedlinburg; and at Spitzes Hoch, near Latdorf, *Kreis* Bernburg. These textiles owe their preservation to the fact that tremendously hot fires had been built outside the closed-up burial chambers—which in at least one case contained a large number of inhumations of men, women, and children—so that everything inside was carbonized rather than burnt up. In the rectangular tomb at Kreienkopp, the numerous tiny shreds of cloth lay among the bones, along with remains of matting and ornaments made of the pierced teeth of wild animals (Schlabow 1959, 115). But in the great round ossuary at Spitzes Hoch—which also contained skeletal remains, ornaments of pierced animal teeth, and pottery—apparently the oak rafters themselves had been swathed in cloth, some of it quite ornate (ibid., 101–2).

Karl Schlabow, who analyzed and published the textiles, was constantly astounded at the fineness of the fibers in these Neolithic pieces, in comparison with the coarse, kempy wool found in the succeeding era—although the suggestion that these people were plucking rather than shearing their sheep goes a long way towards explaining the difference (ibid., 113, 115; cf. Chapters 1, 12). Even more remarkable to him was the skill and long experience that would have been required to spin wool into such extremely fine, regular threads (ibid., 115–16). An entirely different explanation is also possible: that the cloth was not made of wool but of linen (Schlabow cites no evidence for his assignment of fiber, and Michael Ryder repeatedly disavows any proof of woolen textiles in Europe before the Bronze Age: e.g., Ryder 1983, 47).

On the basis of technical details, the fragments from Spitzes Hoch could be divided into four types and those from Kreienkopp into two, representing a total of perhaps six different cloths. All the fabrics were in more or less balanced plain weave. In several cases, what Schlabow took to be starting borders were preserved, suggesting the use of a warp-weighted loom. These particular borders were done in a warp-faced plain weave (Schlabow 1959, 107–8, 111, 117, and fig. 4A; 1976, figs. 17, 18, 20): that is, the border was evidently produced off the large loom by a band-weaving technique, with the future warp as a weft completely hidden in the shed by the temporary warp, much as in the Neolithic Swiss examples (although there the weave was the more usual half-basket). The one recognizable ending border showed the warp ends grouped and braided (Schlabow 1959, 116–17 and fig. 4C).

Several tricks had been used to vary the plain weave in the cloth, however. Stripes or bands were formed either by packing the weft so closely for several rows that it completely covered the warp, or by using a much thicker weft for one or more passes (ibid., 110 and fig. 2; 1976, fig. 19). Whether these texture stripes were also enhanced by color we will probably never know, since everything was so thoroughly carbonized. Other pattern devices clearly were used also. Unfortunately, the 19th-century discoverers of the Spitzes Hoch ossuary separated out the most interesting and elaborate bits of cloth, and it is precisely that group which has been lost; only some sketches remain (Fig. 4.21; Schlabow 1959, 111–13).

It is thus no longer possible to do more than guess at the fanciest techniques. On the basis of the drawings, however, it seems that faced weaves were present (scraps 9, 12, 14, and perhaps 8), and that decorative patterns were applied either by embroidery or—more likely, given what we know of other European textiles—by lacing in the pattern threads at the time of weaving, as in the Swiss fabrics (scraps 3, 4, 5, and 13). One particularly tantalizing little fragment (scrap 6) shows a checkerboard design, but reveals nothing about its mode of manufacture. It may have been produced by colored stripes of warp and weft (for this simple technique see, for example, Windeknecht and Windeknecht 1981, esp. 24 top right), but presumably everything was charred black; or it may be a supplementary weft pattern, like the checkerboard on the Irgenhausen "brocade" (discussed above); or it may even have been a "shadow-stripe" plaid, caused by alternating bands of Z-spun and S-spun thread. We will see this technique often in the Hallstatt wools of a much later date, and occasionally in the Early Bronze Age Danish fabrics (see Chapter 6).

Although some of the fancier techniques differ—for example, the precise method of making starting bands is not the same—much of this north-central German material looks rather like the bulk of the Swiss Neolithic textiles in degree and type of sophistication. Most of the patterns applied seem rather similar, and may well be in the same technique. On the other hand, those which differ—the faced weaves and the possible shadow plaid—seem more natural to the use of wool; and both these types as well as the sprang foreshadow what we see developing in the north in the Bronze Age. It is possible that, if we had wool preserved in Switzerland, the overall resemblances between the two groups might seem closer. (And it is conceivable that the Swiss pile-dwellers too were working in wool: Messikommer [1913, 71] reported one find of linen with holes that suggested missing woolen threads.) But as things stand, these northern German textiles look very much like a combination of the northern net-making skills and the long Neo-

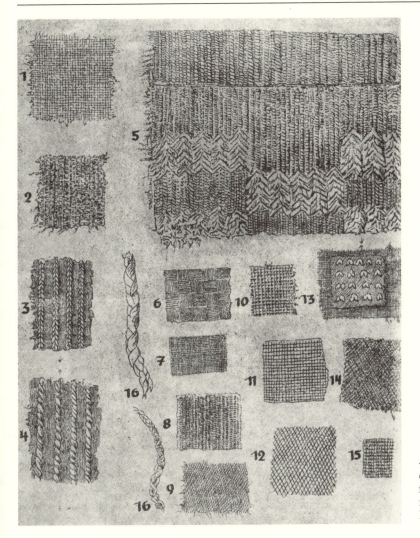

4.21   Drawings, made at the time of discovery, of now-lost patterned fragments of cloth from Spitzes Hoch, in north-central Germany; Late Neolithic. (Schlabow 1959, 112 fig. 3)

lithic development of weaving in Central Europe.

Indeed, the chartable spread of loom weights (Chapter 3) suggests that weaving, or at least weaving on the large warp-weighted loom, spread slowly north and west across Europe in the Neolithic and Bronze Ages. This vector is corroborated by what we see of the cloth itself. For while the Neolithic inhabitants of Switzerland and Germany were making all those large and handsomely ornamented textiles, the people of Scandinavia and of the extreme west of Europe were apparently still ignorant of large mechanized looms, if not of weaving itself. The single scrap of cloth reported for Neolithic Denmark, from Øksenbjerg, has turned out to be modern cotton, not ancient linen, clinging to a piece of steam-tube, not a piece of cow horn (Munksgaard 1979); and we shall see presently that the numerous Bronze Age cloths from Denmark look as though the craft had just arrived.

Far to the southwest, in Late Neolithic Spain (probably late 3rd millennium), we find a distribution of techniques rather similar to that at Naḥal Ḥemar, executed entirely in the local esparto grass. Mineral hunters in the mid-19th century had ransacked the more than sixty burials in an Andalusian cave, the Cueva de los Murciélagos, before a local historian was able to salvage what artifacts they did not destroy outright. These included a few scraps of the plain-weave tunics in which the bodies had still been entirely clothed, along with remnants of their caps, belts, sandals, pouches, bags, baskets, and even a necklace, done in techniques that included weft-twining with paired weft (almost identical to the Çatal Hüyük example, Figs. 4.5–6), and various sophisticated plaiting and coiled basketry techniques (de Góngora y Martínez 1868, 30–35 and pl. 1–2). In the Bronze Age, plain weave of a fine and regular variety had taken over in Spain from the twining techniques (see Chapter 6), and we can deduce that the mechanized loom, i.e., the heddle, had finally arrived.

If the large warp-weighted loom and its pattern techniques were spreading outwards from a center in southeast Europe, as all the evidence indicates, then what must the tex-

tiles of that ancient center have looked like? What elegant and ornate patterns in how many colors must have graced the textiles of Hungary and the lower Danube, during the height of the Cucuteni/Tripolye and related cultures, when a poor and remote backwater like Neolithic Switzerland was creating textiles like the Irgenhausen brocade? So far we have not been fortunate enough to find these treasures: the Danube basin is not conducive to the preservation of such materials. For example, a survey by Petkov (1965) of prehistoric weaving and mat remains in western Bulgaria turned up only a few sherds with textile impressions, all in plain weave, along with several times as many sherds with impressions of twined and twill-woven mats. The latter are more natural pedestals to choose for making or drying a pot on, while those textiles that *were* used were almost certainly old rags—hardly sufficient to show us what the top weavers of Old Europe were capable of. In Jugoslavia exactly the same situation holds, for example at the Late Neolithic site of Gomolava in the northeast, where the few textile impressions were all in a coarse plain weave.[7] On the other hand, the lavish decoration on the pottery and the indications of ornate clothing on the figurines (see Chapter 13) both suggest that many of the textiles were exceedingly beautiful. We can only mourn our loss.

[7] My thanks to Bogdan Brukner and Ruth Tringham for allowing me to study the Gomolava finds. It might still be worthwhile to do a survey of cloth impressions and pseudomorphs (metallic oxide casts) throughout Central and Eastern Europe, especially by going through the museum collections. Certainly a good deal of material of this sort exists there. For example, Paster-

nak mentions half-a-dozen sites in the Ukraine with cloth-impressed sherds (Pasternak 1963, 534–35 and fig. 364); Brjusov illustrates several from the northwest U.S.S.R. (Brjusov 1951, 24–26 and fig. 6.2–5); and apparently such sherds are extremely common at Neolithic and Eneolithic sites in the Caucasus (see Chapter 6).

CHAPTER 5

THE TEXTILE WEAVES
(2) EGYPT

If we now turn to the south, to the wealth of cloth preserved in the dry heat of Egypt, we find, as we did with looms and spinning, a somewhat different tradition. It is here, of course, that we have the largest single corpus of cloth in the ancient world, spanning several millennia in a nearly continuous, if rather one-sided, coverage.

EARLY TECHNIQUES

The earliest attestation of weaving in Egypt seems to be the swatch of coarse linen found in a Neolithic—probably early 5th millennium—deposit in the Faiyum (Fig. 5.1; Caton-Thompson and Gardner 1934, 46 and pl. 28.3). To one accustomed to the incredibly fine and even linens of pharaonic Egypt, the cloth is startlingly crude. The binding is plain weave, but rather loose and sloppy, and the thread is coarse. What is more, it is Z-spun and S-plied, unlike everything else from Egypt, as though the strong later tradition had not yet been settled upon. It does, however, have the expected splices (see Chapter 2). One has to suspect from this mixture of details that one is looking at the very beginnings of the art in Egypt, or at least in the Faiyum, and that the technology of textiles had only fairly recently spread southwest from Palestine.

Half-a-dozen traces of cloth were also found in the nearly contemporary "Tasian" or early Badarian levels at Mostagedda, far to the south in middle Egypt, but were too fugitive for closer analysis (Brunton 1937, 27,

30). Scraps from the later Badarian levels were a bit easier to salvage. The weave was invariably plain, but came in a variety of grades: "somewhat open weave," "regular close weave," "very poor irregular weave," "coarse regular weave," in yarns running from "thick, soft" to "very hard-twisted" to "coarse" (T. Midgley 1937, 61–62). According to the excavator, the cloth along the thigh of one body appeared to have a fringe (Brunton 1937, 34, 47–48), which seemingly did not survive long enough for an analysis of the means of manufacture. At the type-site of Badari, too, the cloth was all in plain weave with plain selvedges, although the warp threads were packed more closely near the edge—probably as a result of the natural tendency of the weft to draw them inwards (T. Midgley 1928, 64–65).

The most memorable find of pre-dynastic cloth, however, occurred at el-Gebelein, in central Egypt, where the material lay folded up beside a mummified body in an otherwise unidentified tomb (Scamuzzi 1965, pl. 1–5 and foreword). Although the linen itself is all

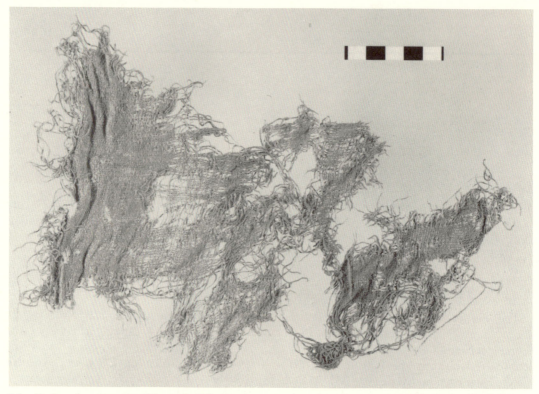

5.1 Earliest known piece of linen cloth from Egypt. The thread is spliced, but Z-spun and very coarse. Faiyum, 5th millennium B.C. (Courtesy of Petrie Museum, University College London: UC 2943)

of an unremarkable plain weave, the pieces had been painted in red, black, and white with scenes of boating, hunting, fishing, and funeral rites—clearly an early antecedent of the great funerary murals of dynastic Egypt. One fragment of fringe—apparently warp fringe—also survives (ibid., pl. 5). Despite the extremely poor documentation left by the original excavator, Giulio Farina, in 1930, these important cloth paintings can be fairly securely dated by style to the first half of the 4th millennium.

The rather simple textile repertoire of plain weave, plain selvedge, and simple fringe seems to continue with gradual refinement but without apparent innovation until dynastic times, and even then the changes

are not startling. Among the linens from the 1st Dynasty "mastaba" tombs at Tarkhan was a piece that had been given a lacy texture by weaving only six weft per inch, against a warp count of 72 per inch (W. W. Midgley 1915, 50 and pl. 58.5). The side edge of another cloth had been made by giving each weft a turn or two around the last warp and leaving the end to stick out as a fringe (ibid., 49).

Fringe seems often to have been used on garments as a decoration, by arranging the cloth so that the fringe occurred along the seam down one side. We have just mentioned a Badarian mummy with traces of a fringe in precisely this position; and from among the funerary linen that ancient tomb robbers had evidently heaved out of a 1st Dynasty "mastaba" (no. 2050) at Tarkhan, straight into the preserving embrace of the hot, dry desert sands, comes a nearly complete tunic with such a fringe (Fig. 5.2). According to two conservators, who recently resurrected this shirt from "a tumbled heap of dirty linen" in labelled storage somewhere at the Petrie Museum of Egyptian Archaeology in London, the fringe consisted of "extended weft threads turned back to make a decorative finish" where the cloth was "joined selvage-to-selvage down one side" (Landi and Hall 1979, 141, 143 and fig. 11). A warp fringe also occurred along the length of the tapered and elaborately pleated

5.2   Pleated and fringed Egyptian shirt of fine spliced linen, from the 1st Dynasty: currently the oldest complete ancient garment we have. Tarkhan; ca. 3000 B.C. (Courtesy of Petrie Museum, University College London: UC 28614B')

sleeves—even the pleats had miraculously survived the millennia—and another weft fringe edged one side of the long, straight neck opening (ibid., 143–44 and figs. 1–2). The seams and hemmed edges were sewn with whipping stitches (ibid., 144). At least three other pleated but nearly decayed garments, presumably much like this one, were found laid as gifts on top of shrouded bodies in the smaller graves nearby at Kafr Ammar, graves from the 3rd to 5th Dynasties (Petrie and Mackay 1915, 18–19: graves 516, 535). In at least two other cases the shrouds themselves were fringed, one of the fringes having been woven separately and sewn on (Petrie and Mackay 1915, 9). Other such garments turn up in increasing numbers from the 5th Dynasty on (e.g., Riefstahl 1944, 8 fig. 7; Landi and Hall 1979, 142; Hall 1981a; Hall and Pedrini 1984). This same sort of elaborate pleating, incidentally, is recognizable on a number of the sculptured monuments of the Old Kingdom, for example on the double-pleated kilt of King Sahure, of the early 5th Dynasty, in his funeral temple at Abusir (see, e.g., Aldred 1965, 127 pl. 133).

Another interesting trait of these Early Dynastic fabrics is that not infrequently we find the warp or weft somehow multiplied. In some cases it appears that the yarn used had been made by twisting together two already twisted strands (W. W. Midgley 1915, 49; and compare T. Midgley 1928, 65); but in other cases two quite separate threads seem to have been laid beside each other into the same row—sometimes two warp (e.g., specimen nos. 6, 10) and sometimes two weft (e.g., specimen no. 9: W. W. Midgley 1915, 49 and pl. 52.9–12). The examples just cited were from the 1st Dynasty tombs at Tarkhan; but similar phenomena occurred in the 3rd–4th Dynasty mummy cloths from Meydum

(W. W. Midgley 1911, 37) and the 4th–5th Dynasty linens from Kafr Ammar (W. W. Midgley 1915, 51 and pl. 53.7 and 53.9). It is possible that some of these pairs indicate errors—getting two warp into one heddle, or forgetting to change the shed before putting in the new row of weft; or that they indicate accidents—breaking a warp or heddle midway through the weaving, for example. Indeed, the pairing seems from Midgley's description to be sporadic in all cases.

On the other hand, it seems hard to believe that weavers who were so deft that they could manage 200 warp per inch,[1] as in the 1st Dynasty sample no. 9 (W. W. Midgley 1915, 50), would have missed so many heddles and forgotten to change so many sheds. It is possible that one or both of the threads in the pairs was of a contrasting color that has since faded, and that what we have here was originally a pinstriped decoration; or that the pairing itself was intended to break the monotonous white expanse with texture stripes. Midgley, however, had to work from a series of samples, evidently rather small, that had been "made up in mounted sets and distributed in cases to many museums" by the redoubtable head of the expedition, Sir W. M. Flinders Petrie (Petrie, in W. W. Midgley 1915, 48)—a largesse that precluded the possibility of seeing any bigger decorative scheme. The 1st Dynasty pleated tunic, however, is largely complete, and sports on its shirttails a quite noticeable grey pinstripe running vertically every so often. The conservators state that the stripe is caused by a "darker yarn used in the warp" and also mention "a slubbed [i.e., irregularly thickening] yarn which gave an irregular grey stripe in the warp which could have been used deliberately for the decorative effect" (Landi and Hall 1979, 143). Of the weave

---

[1] For comparison, a fine percale sheet or pillowcase today runs around 100 threads per inch.

structure we are told that it was plain weave, with "two [warp] running as one in places" (ibid.), a result that can occur accidentally whenever a warp breaks unnoticed.

Whether or not any of these particular pieces was purposely striped, however, we have evidence, possibly from the 3rd millennium, for colored stripes in two cloths said to come from the pyramid of the late–5th Dynasty pharaoh Unas, at Saqqara (now Museum of Fine Arts, Boston, TL 2869.1). One of these "has four blue stripes along the selvage, the outermost being the widest," while the other "has, at what may have been either selvage or warp-end, two pink and two blue stripes and a blue fringe" (Riefstahl 1944, 49 n. 4). The thread count is very fine, running about 40 warp by 20–25 weft per centimeter for the former, and 45–50 warp by 10 weft per centimeter for the latter. Although the warp predominates heavily, it does not actually hide the weft, except near the very edge of the second piece.

Occasional fine stripes, generally at or near one edge, are reported in Egyptian linens from the 18th Dynasty on, with only one 11th Dynasty example in between, that I know of (with "a border of blue lines," from Deir el-Bahari: Naville, Hall, and Ayrton 1907, 44). In fact, the pattern of the first piece described (that from the pyramid of Unas, with a wide stripe at the edge and a few narrower stripes within) as well as its dark blue color, make me wonder seriously whether this cloth should not be dated instead to the 19th Dynasty or later, where it has much company with the same configuration of stripes and the same deep color. The pale powder blue and baby pink of the other piece, and the softer, finer look of the thread, suggest that this might indeed be an early textile; and yet, having cast doubt upon

the one, I cannot make a strong case for the other, both having been collected under rather less than scientific conditions in the 19th century. One might also add that the fringe was formed by sewing a bundle of blue threads onto a slightly rolled edge, rather than being woven in. I know of no exact parallel for this at any period.[2]

Whatever may be the case for colored stripes, our next evidence for new techniques comes from the very beginning of the Middle Kingdom, from a burial associated with the first pharaoh of the 11th Dynasty, Mentuhotep II. The technique of *weft-looping* (in which the weft is looped up above the surface every little ways) occurs in several pieces of linen, including one of the many towels drafted to help wrap up and give decent collective burial to sixty of the pharaoh's soldiers, evidently all slain together in one of the many bloody battles and raids whereby Mentuhotep finally managed to reunite Egypt. In this particular piece, the weft of every eighth row is doubled and raised in a small loop every 6 mm along the row, with the loops in successive rows being staggered (Winlock 1945, 32, 31 fig. 3, and pl. 20B). The result, as Hayes remarks (1953, 244), gives "an over-all dotted pattern like that of our modern dotted Swiss." The excavator mentions that two other weft-looped towels were found in "a near-by Eleventh Dynasty tomb" there at Deir el-Bahari (no. 813; Winlock 1945, 32). One of these, now in the Egyptian Museum in Cairo, not only has looping but has its loops raised in such a way as to form handsome patterns of zigzags and stripes of different widths (Fig. 5.3; Riefstahl 1944, 17 and 16 fig. 19; Winlock 1942, 206 and pl. 37). In some of these cases the loops are large enough to resemble modern chenille, and are so regular in size that the

---

[2] My thanks to the staff of the Boston Museum of Fine Arts for allowing me to inspect these and many other pieces in their collection, on more than one occasion, and for making their acquisition information available.

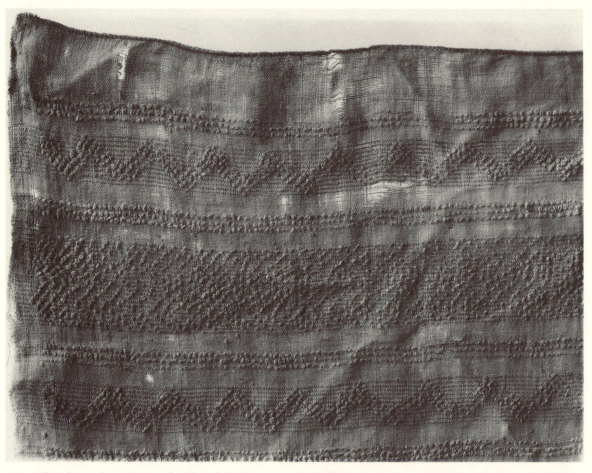

5.3   White linen sheet patterned with weft-looping, from the 11th Dynasty. Deir el-Bahari; ca. 2000 B.C. (Egyptian Museum, Cairo. Photography by Egyptian Expedition, the Metropolitan Museum of Art)

weaver would seem to have passed the weft over a rod or other template, which was removed when the row was finished. On the other hand, a number of the sheets from the tomb of the estate manager Wah, also of the 11th Dynasty, show individual long loops very occasionally across the sheet, as though their only function were to allow air in between the layers (N. Kajitani, pers. comm. 1984).

Weft-looping continues as a not-uncom-

mon technique in Egypt until the Iron Age. At least two handsome specimens of it occur, for instance, among the copious linens from the mid–18th Dynasty tomb of Kha (Schiaparelli 1927, figs. 113, 116). Here the loops are both so long and so closely spaced, in a large square across the center of the cloth, that they produce a shaggy texture like pile; and one tends to think that the purpose of this looping was warmth—a winter wrap or coverlet. Another such shaggy cloth, without site or date mentioned, is pictured by Wreszinski (1914–39, pl. 39b.3) from a collection in Cairo.

On one of the linens from the Middle Kingdom tomb of Wah, we find a tiny example of a radically different technique, in which the warp threads have been twisted past each other to form a small patch of *gauze* weave (Fig. 5.4). The patch is so small that it does not form part of a decorative scheme— one must hunt to find it—so presumably it functioned as some sort of weaver's mark (see below). In making it, the entire rhythm of the weaving process would have to have stopped while each twist was put in, one at a time, by hand. Other such bits of gauze weave occur from time to time among the 18th Dynasty linens of Ramose and Hatnufer, the parents of Hatshepsut's minister Senmut (e.g., on Metropolitan Museum nos. 36.3.92 and .115: N. Kajitani, pers. comm. 1984). Occasionally, instead, a tiny patch will have supplementary weft twined or looped about a few warp threads, but again so subtly that the spot is not easy to find (e.g., Metropolitan Museum nos. 36.3.118, .136).[3]

Another technique which may not be brand new, but for which we find our first copious evidence in the 11th Dynasty, is inlaid fringing. Sometimes, as we have seen in much earlier material, a fringe is made simply by letting ends of the weft (or warp) stick out beyond the edge instead of binding them somehow (cf. de Jonghe 1985). In other cases the weft seems merely to have been brought out in a wide loop to one side before being returned to the next shed (cf. Landi and Hall 1979, 143). It is possible that both of these weft-fringe types represent in origin a practical expedient, which happened to be deco-

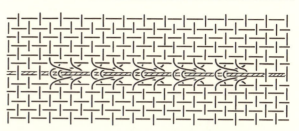

5.4 Diagram of a tiny patch of gauze weave, found as "weaver's mark" among linens from the Middle Kingdom burial of Wah; 11th Dynasty. (The Metropolitan Museum of Art, no. 20.3.249)

rative, against the constant tendency of the weft to pull the fabric in at the sides—that is, a way of ensuring that the cloth wouldn't keep getting narrower. Whatever the reason, in some of the paintings of weaving, such as that in the tomb of Khnumhotep at Beni Hasan (see Fig. 2.40; Roth [1913] 1951, 3–10 and fig. 6), we see a row of loops accumulating at the left edge of the cloth, just as we seem to have them—again on the left edge— way back in the Badarian representation of a ground-loom (Fig. 3.3). It is interesting in this regard that the sheets that survived whole in the soldiers' tomb also typically show one regular selvedge and a fringe on the opposite edge, while the warp ends are fringed at one end and hemmed at the other (Hayes 1953, 260).

IN some of the Middle Kingdom linens, including in general the soldiers' sheets, this side fringe is formed or amplified along the selvedge by laying an additional bundle of thread into the shed at the edge of the cloth for a short space, then bending it back in a U-shape and laying the next portion of the bundle into another shed, so that both ends stick out for the fringe (Fig. 5.5). The weav-

[3] My thanks to the Metropolitan Museum of Art in New York, which possesses the linens of Wah, the Slain Soldiers, and Ramose and Hatnufer; and my thanks most particularly to Nobuko Kajitani for allowing me to

profit by all the work she had already done, and for helping me find the most interesting pieces within this vast quantity of linen.

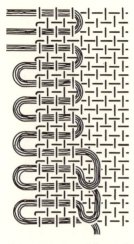

5.5 Diagram of three closely related types of Egyptian "inlaid" fringe, done with supplementary weft. The top version can be produced by inlaying separate U-shaped bundles, or by cutting the continuous S-form shown in the middle. At the bottom, the interior loop has been enlarged to form an extra row of fringe

ers in fact seem often to have laid the bundles into the sheds in a running S-shape, rather than in a series of Us, and then cut the loops open later or left them closed, as they pleased, to form the fringe. So, for example, in otherwise unlabelled 11th Dynasty cloths in the Egyptian Museum in Cairo; so too on some of the Slain Soldiers' linens (e.g., Winlock 1945, pl. 15.6, where a second fringe has been sewn on as well). Some of the ornamental bands adorning the clothes from Tutankhamon's tomb (18th Dynasty) are also edged this way, with a very regular row of tiny uncut loops (cf. Pfister 1937, 216 and fig. 4). Sometimes, too, the supplementary thread is allowed to hang out in a long loop at *both* turns of the inlaid S-shape, so as to form twice as thick a fringe, half of it set in from the edge by a centimeter or so. Most of the fringes from the Tomb of the Slain Soldiers were made this way (Winlock 1945, pl. 14.3, 18.28, etc.). The techniques were

probably related conceptually to the production of the loops on the 11th Dynasty towels, so that the bundle of threads was passed around a rod that served as a template to keep the fringe length even. By the 21st Dynasty the variations are considerable (see Henneburg 1932; de Jonghe 1985).

But perhaps the most interesting aspect of these fringes is that many of them involve the weaving technique of laying a supplemental thread into the regular shed for ornamental purposes—called *inlay*. If indeed the paired wefts (and warps too) in the Old Kingdom textiles were part of an intentional and originally visible decoration, then the technique of inlay was not new in the Middle Kingdom. But its possibilities were now explored. In particular, one begins to find cases in which a heavy supplementary thread was laid into the shed along with the ground weft for a ways, then suddenly given a right-angle turn so as to become supplemental warp (Fig. 5.6). Strange as it seems to modern weavers who are constrained by a reed to leave the warp alone, this technique continued to be used in that part of the world on down through the New Kingdom (e.g., Riefstahl 1944, 26 and 29 fig. 37; Crowfoot 1933) to at least the end of the 1st millennium B.C. (Crowfoot 1951, 8–12 and figs. 1–3; Pilar 1968, 102 and figs. 5–6—but note that these latter are poorly dated).

Some of the Middle Kingdom linen also contains examples of a small woven design or

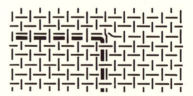

5.6 Extra weft laid into the shed, then turned to become warp, a weaving trick found on Egyptian linen from the Middle Kingdom to Roman times

5.7 Weaver's mark inlaid with stained thread, on a linen sheet from the mummy of Wah. (Photo courtesy of the Metropolitan Museum of Art; Rogers Fund, 1920: no. 40.3.51)

group of hieroglyphs, representing the logo, as it were, of the weaver (Fig. 5.7; Hayes 1953, 260). These emblems were made by laying a single supplementary thread into the sheds of the weaving, as it progressed, in the outline of the shape desired. Generally the inlaid thread is heavier than the ground warp and weft; in the linens from the tomb of Wah it has also sometimes been stained dark, with tannin or carbon (N. Kajitani, pers. comm. 1984), but that is unusual. The technique of making these glyphs seems simple enough, but note that a thread laid in during the process of weaving can only move forward and/ or sideways, where the warp and weft are not yet interlocked: it cannot turn back into what has already been woven together. Hence the shape to be outlined with a laid-in weft must be carefully planned in advance to avoid the need for such turns. In this respect, designs are much more difficult to produce by inlay in the weaving than by embroidery, where the needle can take the thread freely anywhere across the finished cloth.

The habit of inlaying weavers' marks, usu-ally in white on the white linen, continues on through the New Kingdom. We find it, for example, on sheets from the 18th Dynasty tombs of Maherpra, Kha, and Tutankhamon (Daressy 1902, 58 and pl. 12, no. 24099; Schiaparelli 1927, fig. 71 bottom right; Riefstahl 1944, 27; Barber 1982, 443), ranging from early 15th to mid-14th century B.C. Again among the copious linens of Ramose and Hatnufer, from the time of Hatshepsut, we find numerous examples of heavy weft laid into part of a shed, run down across one or two sheds, brought back along the next shed, and so forth, in such a way as to form long "hairpin" designs within the cloth (all in white on white!) or even, as in no. 36.3.95, a long snaky trail across the fabric.[4]

But it is only in the 18th Dynasty that we begin to see evidence for a more extended use of the decorative potential of inlay. Among the wonderful array of clothing crumpled and crushed into chests by the ancient Egyptians who tidied up Tutankhamon's tomb after an aborted robbery, was a tunic decorated in a new way that is nonetheless the logical extension of the accumulated

[4] Again, my thanks to N. Kajitani and the Metropolitan Museum.

5.8   Tunic decorated with blue and brown woven stripes and inlaid hieroglyphs. Tomb of Tutankhamon; mid-14th century B.C. (Courtesy of Egyptian Museum, Cairo)

bands at spacious intervals also contain the inlaid glyphs. And as a final festive touch, the warp ends have been fashioned into a long fringe.

What we see as the demonstrably inherited tradition of patterned weaving in existence before the New Kingdom, then, consists of the following: first, the simple stripe, which requires only a change of color or texture in the yarn, not a change of weave; second, the technique of laying a supplementary weft—and even a warp—into the weaving as it progresses, but laying it in to form pinstripes or an outline rather than to fill in a large, solid area; and third, looping. We have found sewing used very little, its chief functions being for hemming raw edges, sewing seams, and mending (cf. Landi and Hall 1979, 144, and Hayes 1953, 260).

How, then, if this is all we have examples of, are we to interpret a fair number of representations of colored patterns on garments before the New Kingdom? This question has been addressed by a number of authors, most notably by Elizabeth Riefstahl in her excellent and comprehensive survey of those "patterned textiles in Pharaonic Egypt" known in 1944 (Riefstahl 1944, 11–17). One of the main sources of these patterns seems to be a very fashionable bead netting worn over the linen kilt or dress (ibid., 11–12 and figs. 10–12).

Such bead nets have been found: for example a bead dress was discovered in a 5th Dynasty context at Qau (Hall 1981b, 37–39 and pl. 1). Remains of others were found around the bodies in burials of the late Middle Kingdom or Second Intermediate period at the outpost of Kerma, in the Sudan just south of the Third Cataract of the Nile (Reisner 1923, 103–4, 300, 303, and pl. 63.1). In some cases at Kerma the beads covered a ba-

techniques we have been looking at (Fig. 5.8). The bulk of the cloth is a natural linen color, but vertically along the selvedges and horizontally at various intervals are slim stripes alternating blue and brown, with uncolored spaces between. Moreover, around the perimeter runs a band that contains two alternating hieroglyphs, which were produced with a laid-in thread. Within the vertical bands the glyphs are further set off by a short laid-in weft that has the effect of marking off a little box for each sign. Horizontal

sic girdle of cloth, which in turn served as anchor for a long beaded fringe or a beaded network of blue and white or black and white that hung down free over the tunic or kilt. In one instance the beads were strung so closely that they formed a coherent skirt all by themselves (ibid., 303). The excavator describes most of the beads, except for those found in disturbed fill, as lying around the waist, pelvis, or leg areas, in the dozen or more burials in which these beads were found (ibid., 103–4). One particularly interesting grave, K421:x, contained something like 3800 ball-beads and a "large lot" of small blue ring-beads, some of which had been sewn to cloth or woven into it (ibid., 103, 300). The very heavy weft carrying the beads was seen to alternate row for row with a much lighter weft, but was worked in some undescribed way that made the beads come up in lozenge patterns (ibid., 300 and pl. 63.1). In most of the other graves, beads still attached directly to cloth were sewn on (ibid., 103–4). That such beading continues in the New Kingdom is amply attested by beaded garments in the tomb of Tutankhamon (Carter and Mace 1923, 167–69 and pl. 34; Riefstahl 1944, 39 and fig. 45).

The other interesting kind of cloth at Kerma was found always under the bodies, where these were undisturbed, and was described as a sort of napped rug, or *pile weave*. Warp and weft are both paired, i.e., form a basket weave, while bunches of extra material are "folded in the middle and passed around every four threads (i.e. two doubled threads) of the warp, so that the ends hang down" (Reisner 1923, 301 and pl. 63.2–3). Several rows of plain paired weft intervene between the pile rows. Although the pile in most of the rugs is of the same fiber as the warp and weft (presumably linen), in two separate cases the pile is made of the long feather-barbs stripped off of ostrich feathers (ibid., 300–301). This finding lends credence to the theory that the other colored decoration shown on Middle Kingdom garments, the so-called feather pattern, may have been just that in origin (Riefstahl 1944, 12–13). As an ethnographic parallel one may point to the Polynesians, who twined both threads and feathers into the weft of their blanket-like cloaks (see Burt 1977, 2–3 for Maori examples of each), the most famous, of course, being the gorgeous red and yellow feathered capes of the Hawaiian nobility (see, e.g., P. H. Buck 1964, 218–26). By the New Kingdom, the "feather pattern" too seems to have been transmuted into surface beads or platelets, or to have become at times entirely symbolic—that is, not corresponding any longer to an actual garment (Riefstahl 1944, 36–37 and fig. 41).

With the added techniques of beading—whether sewn on or strung on the weft or netted—and of the simplest sort of piling, both of which may have entered Egypt from the south, we are ready to move on to that abrupt proliferation of textile techniques at the start of the New Kingdom.[5] And we may

[5] Linen pile also appears to occur among the coverlets from the tomb of Kha (Schiaparelli 1927, fig. 105, and perhaps fig. 113); but since no details of the weaves are given for any of the fabrics, it is difficult to be certain. These may be further examples of weft-looping. Another shaggy cloth, from the tomb of Madjar at Thebes (no. 1370, time of Hatshepsut and Thutmose III) and now in the Louvre, is described as having "supplementary weft yarns looped or knotted to produce a pile on one side . . . [and] a design of triangles and bands on the other face" (L. Smith 1982, 183: no. 210).

One last oddity: a net formed of macramé knotting, and ending in a hanging border of four-petaled flowers, is in the Boston Museum of Fine Arts—but unfortunately it is of uncertain ("probably New Kingdom") date (ibid.: no. 209).

There is one very early representation of clothing that still puzzles me: the jubilee cloak carved on a small ivory figurine from Abydos, of an unknown early pharaoh, ca. 3000 B.C. (see, e.g., Aldred 1965, 62 pl. 52; or Riefstahl 1944, fig. 1). It has an all-over pattern of concentric lozenges that I am at a loss to explain from either pleating

note, as others have, that these changes appear to coincide with the advent of the two-beam vertical loom in Egypt. Whether the new techniques are coming from the same source as the new tool, however, is a question we should try to answer on independent evidence.

THE LATER (18TH DYNASTY) TECHNIQUES

Up to this point in Egypt the warp and weft that form the basic cloth—the ground warp and weft—have been more or less balanced. That is, although the warp may predominate somewhat over the weft in some pieces, we have no recorded instance of one set of elements entirely hiding the other set: the so-called warp-faced and weft-faced weaves (see Fig. 4.4). But now we find both.

The earliest example we have happens to be a handsome warp-faced band sewn onto the horsecloth of Senmut (Fig. 5.9; Lansing and Hayes 1937, fig. 15; Riefstahl 1944, 20 and fig. 26), powerful Chief Steward of the first female pharaoh, Hatshepsut, and the possessor in his two tombs of at least two other novelties: the carefully swathed body of a horse—that important animal introduced into Egypt from the northeast only a century or two earlier—with its saddle-cloth tied on upside down (Lansing and Hayes 1937, 10 and figs. 14–15); and a variety of running spiral decorations of northern inspiration on the ceilings and on trial sketches in the debris (Hayes 1959, 110–11; see Chapter 15). The pattern in the long, narrow, warp-faced strips, which have been sewn onto the horse-cloth in a large square formation with the usual whipping stitch, is formed by warp threads of red, yellow, and brown that have been brought to the surface as needed for the design (often called *warp pick-up*),

whereas the unneeded ones float on the back or between the faces. The weft, of course, cannot be seen.

This is a technique very common among handweavers today for making belts and ribbons, and it seems to have been adopted with gusto by the ancient Egyptian weavers, for we find it developed with great ingenuity from the 18th Dynasty on. In particular, there are many handsome examples among the textiles in Tutankhamon's tomb, where elaborate bands, sometimes only a centimeter wide, with exceedingly fine warp and sometimes extra(?) weft showing as a delicate fringe at the sides, are used to trim the king's garments (see Crowfoot and Davies 1941, 117–25 for details of the technique; Pfister 1937 for catalogue and photographs). A remarkably large warp-faced piece, 46 by 96.5 cm, was found by Howard Carter in an unknown 18th Dynasty Theban tomb (it is now in the Victoria and Albert Museum: T251/1921). It has a warp-faced design of running lozenges, described in 1937 as being done in blue, red-brown, and brown (Pfister 1937, 209, 218, and fig. 5), but in 1922 as blue, red, and yellow (*Burlington Fine Arts Club: Catalogue . . .* 1922, 54). The famous tapering "girdle of Rameses III" in Liverpool (see Fig. 3.34), too, is done in a *double-faced* warp-faced weave, that is, with the warp handled in such a way as to form two sepa-

---

or what we know of contemporary linen weaving in Egypt. It might represent beading, or even(?) leather plaiting: compare, for example, the much later piece constructed of fine strips of green leather in a diamond twill pattern, found in the tomb of the 18th Dynasty

princess Aahmesi, in the Valley of the Queens at Thebes (Schiaparelli 1923, 14 and 17 fig. 12). R. Ellis suggests to me that the little ivory may also have been misdated (pers. comm. 1986); it looks Amarnan.

5.9   Detail of warp-faced band sewn onto a linen horsecloth, from a horse mummy in the 18th Dynasty tomb of Senmut at Thebes; early 15th century B.C. (Egyptian Museum, Cairo. Photography by Egyptian Expedition, the Metropolitan Museum of Art)

rate faces to the cloth at once, some of the warp being hidden inside when not wanted for the patterns visible on either face. It has recently been shown that this handsome sash, with its polychrome pattern of *ankh* signs, zigzags, and dotted stripes, must have been woven with the aid of alternating decks of 4-and 5-holed tablets to form the double faces (Staudigel 1975; see Chapter 3).

OUR next examples of a new mode of weaving have weft-faced designs and come in a group from the tomb of Thutmose IV (Carter and Newberry 1904, 143–44 and pl. 1, 28: no. 46526–29), who died some 70 years after Hatshepsut. Here at last we have the earliest attestation yet known of *tapestry*, a plain-weave technique in which wefts of different colors are woven back and forth to fill in just those areas where the particular colors are needed for the design, and packed down so that the warp doesn't show through and spoil the solidity of the color field. In none of these early pieces, however, have the weavers quite abandoned the idea of the white ground, so long a mainstay of Egyptian textiles. In three of the fragments (nos. 46526–28) we see tapestry-woven hieroglyphs in brilliant polychrome floating in a sea of balanced white plain weave. What is presumably the earliest cloth of the group (nos. 46527–28) has part of a cartouche of Thutmose III, grandfather of the owner of the tomb and energetic founder of Egypt's Asiatic empire (see Color Plate 1).

In considering the origin of this technique,

which differs so radically in its conception from what we have seen in Egypt before, it is perhaps relevant to note that one of Thutmose III's greatest triumphs was the sacking of Megiddo (Biblical Armageddon) in Palestine, from which we are told he brought home great quantities of clothing, among other things (Breasted 1906, 188); and in the annals of this same pharaoh we read of Syrian captives serving as artisans at the temple of Amon (Lutz 1923, 58)—quite possibly weavers among them. We have already seen in Chapter 3 that the vertical two-beam loom, historically associated with tapestry, also entered Egypt about this time, and also apparently from Syria or Palestine.

Another of the scraps found in the tomb of Thutmose IV (no. 46526) carries, between a lotus border and a scattered field of lotus flowers, a tapestry-woven cartouche of his father Amenhotep II, who was son and successor to Thutmose III. The colors used on these pieces included red, blue, yellow, green, brown, and black (if the discoloration over three-and-a-half millennia has not deceived us). It is interesting to note in passing the heirloom status of these textiles—a status that implies great expense and specialness (see Chapter 15).

The variety of minor techniques used by the weavers of these pieces to solve problems inherent in tapestry is noteworthy: in particular, the question of how to negotiate the border between two adjacent color fields when it runs parallel to the warp. The natural thing to do when you come to the end of where you want a color is just to turn the weft back into a new row, going around the last warp in the field. If the neighboring fields adjoin on a slant, there is no problem; but if they run parallel to the warp for a considerable distance, with one color of weft always running around one warp and the other always going around the one next to it, a slit

will begin to form that causes ever greater problems in the cohesion of the fabric the longer it gets. (This type is called *slit tapestry*; see Color Plate 1, top.) An alternative is to let first one weft, then the other pass around the same warp, a solution that stabilizes the fabric by avoiding the slit, but causes the border between the two fields to show up as a small zigzag, rather than a cleanly straight line (see Color Plate 1, left). Thus *dovetailed tapestry*, as this method is called, has aesthetic drawbacks. The weavers of these early 18th Dynasty pieces tried out everything. In no. 46527 from the tomb of Thutmose IV, the dovetailing is done with such a fine thread that from a distance the zigzag becomes invisible, and in other places the warp and weft are loosened and pushed around, out of the normal right angles, as if to avoid the problem of slits at all costs. Its companion, no. 46528, which may well be from the same cloth although the hieroglyphs run across the warp instead of up it, allows a few slits closed up at very short intervals in addition to the dovetailed edges and deformed weft. And along the lotus border of no. 46526, where a tapestry-woven dividing line parallel to the border would have opened up a slit the length of the fabric, the maker resorted to sewing in a dark line with whipping stitches.

The fourth piece found in this same tomb (Color Plate 1, right) is equally notable, for quite different reasons. Again the basic fabric, the ground, is white linen in roughly balanced plain weave, this time divided into bands by double rows of very thick weft in the normal sheds. According to the excavators, these threads were pink (Carter and Newberry 1904, 144 no. 46529), although by now they are virtually white from exposure to the sunlight in the Cairo museum. Some of the bands are ornamented further with rosettes "composed of a pale green centre with six pale pink petals, except in the thirteenth row, where pink rosettes alternate with green petaled rosettes with pink centres" (ibid.). Each petal and each center consists of a small rectangular or roundish patch of heavier thread, which had evidently been put in not by embroidery, as the excavators suggest (ibid., 144; and from them, Riefstahl 1944, 20), but by a weaving method closely akin to tapestry. The colored pattern weft has been woven onto the warp with a tightly packed, weft-faced plain weave, as in tapestry; but this weft supplements the white ground weft (which seems to continue its course inside the petals) instead of replacing the ground weft locally as in tapestry (Barber 1982, 442–43 and fig. 1). Technically, then, the procedure is one of "discontinuous supplementary weft patterning"—just like our old friend, outline inlay, which we traced back at least to the start of the Middle Kingdom; only here, instead of outlining, we have a solid space filled in with color as in tapestry. Popularly known as "brocading," this would seem to be a hybrid, transitional technique within the history of Egyptian textiles.

"Transitional" because we don't find it here again. Tapestry takes over, and slit tapestry at that: no more little zigzags from dovetailing. In the tomb of Kha, a high official laid to rest about at the end of the reign of Thutmose IV's successor, Amenhotep III, huge piles of neatly folded household linens were found; and among them were two largish wraps or blankets in a combination of tapestry and weft-looping technique, plus a tunic with a polychrome warp-faced(?) edging (Schiaparelli 1927, 93, 129–30 and figs. 69, 114–16; Riefstahl 1944, 21–22). We see from these that already the top officials had acquired luxury garments in the new techniques. Presumably the fragments of tapestry from "various tombs" of the Valley of the Kings published by Daressy (1902, 302–3,

nos. 24987–8) come from roughly this era also. The smaller, no. 24988, contains a row of red, white, and blue rosettes and triangles (leaves?) on a white ground. The other (no. 24987), however, is of a more ambitious pattern but cheaper make; for, whereas the red and black colors were *woven* into this rendition of the elaborate and traditional Nine Bows and Captives design, the blues and greens were merely *painted* onto plain ground. One has the impression that now tapestry is becoming well known, so that some people are "keeping up with the Joneses" by finding a cheaper means to look suitably ostentatious.

Kha's tapestries as well as these various fragments are still in the form of scattered polychrome figures on a white ground; but by the time of Tutankhamon, who followed Amenhotep III's son Akhenaton, the Egyptian weavers had taken the last step in tapestry and now colored the ground as freely as the figures. Tapestry objects occur in profusion in Tutankhamon's tomb, including tunics, belts, and even gloves (Pfister 1937; Riefstahl 1944, 25–26); and they occur all the way down into Roman times, when the Copts become famous all over the Mediterranean for their classicized tapestry cloths. Indeed, the 18th Dynasty seems, in textiles as in so many ways, to include a time of broadening and experimentation, followed by a gradual narrowing again into a few new ruts destined to last another eon.

Perhaps the most startling of these experiments in fabric decoration is in the embroidery on a gala tunic of Tutankhamon (Fig. 5.10; Carter and Burton 1929, 197; Carter 1933, 124–25; Pfister 1937, 212–13; Crowfoot and Davies 1941). As we have seen, sewing has counted for very little so far, having been used where needed for seams, hems, and mends, but for decoration almost not at all. All the earlier fabrics published here and

5.10 Linen tunic belonging to Tutankhamon, embroidered on the chest with his name (at the center of the *ankh* cross), and decorated with warp-faced bands and embroidered hem-panels that have been sewn on. (The two sleeves are above.) Mid-14th century B.C. (Egyptian Museum, Cairo; Crowfoot and Davies 1941, pl. 14; courtesy of the Committee of the Egypt Exploration Society)

there as embroidered have turned out to have their designs basically woven (with a supplementary weft: Barber 1982); and among the fabrics from Tutankhamon's tomb, stitchery is used merely to close up long slits and eke out a bit of the woven design here and there (exactly as in Coptic weaving!) with the long-attested whipping stitch—except in the case of this tunic, and three fragments.

The tunic, which is almost fully preserved although stained very dark, has a long row of large, squarish panels all around the bottom and an embellished area just below the neck opening, both of which are embroidered in chain stitch and running stitch (Crowfoot and

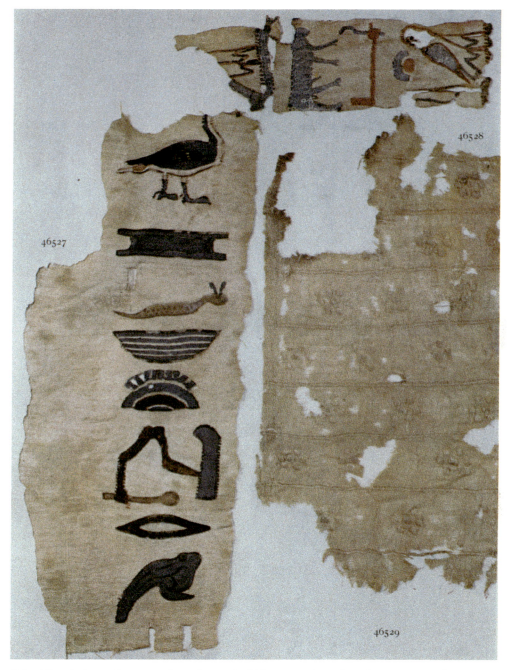

Color Plate 1. Linen fragments from the tomb of Thutmose IV; early 15th century B.C. (see Chapter 5). (Cairo; Carter and Newberry 1904, pl. 28)

Top and Left: Tapestry-woven fragments, with part of the name of Thutmose IV's grandfather, Thutmose III. Vertical edges of color fields are mostly dovetailed; but note the slit-tapestry edge along the back of the bull hieroglyph in the top fragment

Right: Linen decorated with inwoven pink and green rosettes and stripes

Color Plate 2. Fresco figure of a woman dancing(?) in a garden; Hagia Triada, Crete; mid-2nd millennium B.C. (Late Minoan I). Note the ornate textile patterns, including interlocked quatrefoils on the skirt, and edgings of snail-shell spirals (see Chapter 15). (Halbherr 1903, pl. 10)

Color Plate 3. Egyptian ceiling patterns (18th Dynasty) probably copied from contemporary Aegean weavings (see Chapter 15; color drawing by M. Stone)

Top Left: Quatrefoil interlock pattern decorating the soffit of a doorway in the tomb of Amenemhet (Thebes no. 82); early 15th century B.C. (After Nina Davies and A. Gardiner 1915, pl. 32D; courtesy of the Committee of the Egypt Exploration Society)

Right: "Wrought-iron fence" motif and two meander-based patterns from the ceiling of the tomb of Hatshepsut's herald Antef (Th 155); early 15th century B.C. (After Säve-Söderbergh 1957, pl. 19)

Bottom Left: Ceiling pattern from the tomb of Menkheperraseneb (Th 86); mid-15th century B.C. Note the unusually skinny lines and shifting border-pattern. (After Davies and Davies 1933, pl. 30B; courtesy of the Committee of the Egypt Exploration Society)

Color Plate 4. Woolen cloths from the frozen tombs at Pazyryk in the Altai Mountains; mid-1st millennium B.C. (see Chapter 7). (Hermitage Museum, Leningrad)

Left: Woolen *shabrak* (saddle cloth) pieced together from tapestry apparently woven in Iran (Pazyryk Kurgan 5)

Right: Polychrome spirals woven in slit-tapestry technique, sewn to strips of plain red woolen twill; from a large wall-cover (Pazyryk Kurgan 2)

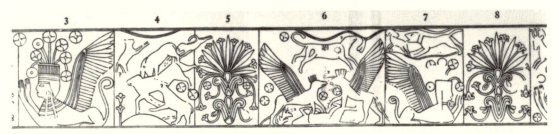

5.11   Detail of embroidered hem-panels from Tutankhamon's tunic, with a schematic drawing, below, of the same six front panels shown above. (Crowfoot and Davies 1941, pl. 20.3–8; courtesy of the Committee of the Egypt Exploration Society)

Davies 1941, 126), and edged like the rest of the tunic in a lavish array of patterned, warp-faced bands. The subjects depicted in embroidery include typically Egyptian designs such as the royal uraeus and a cartouche with the throne name of Tutankhamon, both in the center front of the tunic. Yet down below (Fig. 5.11) they also include some typically Syrian designs such as palmettes and female sphinxes, and other subjects of still wider origin (but almost certainly channeled through Syria, as their style shows), such as the "predator biting prey" motif, winged griffins, and beasts in a flying gallop (Crowfoot and Davies 1941, 126–30). Iconographically, then, the piece looks distinctly Syrian, except for the pharaoh's name and royal insignia. Add to this the fact that the technique

too seems foreign—namely embroidery, and in stitches unknown to us from Egypt either before or after. Furthermore, the embroidery has been done on separate little panels that have been sewn onto the tunic and don't make it quite all the way around the garment (ibid., 126–27).

What can we make of all this? Clearly the tunic was made specifically for Tutankhamon: his name is part of the design. But it is worth noting that the name and the *ankh*, or propitious "life" sign, that forms the collar are up near the face, in the iconographically most important locations, while the Syrian-looking panels are all down around the hemline: a far less important space for cultural messages, or for the most valued artists' work. (One is reminded of a similar distribution in much of the Amarna art, where the front of an object will carry standard Egyptian designs while the back will teem with Syrian- and Aegean-looking motifs; or one might think of the portraits of recent Europe, in which the master painted the face and hands while the apprentices filled in the less important areas.) Clearly, too, these embroidered panels were made separately—they were sewn on afterwards, and don't quite fit the space—and therefore all the more certainly were done by Syrian handicrafters (cf. Crowfoot and Davies 1941, 127). Here we may recall again Thutmose III's captive Syrian craft workers only a century earlier, and point out that this part of the world had become even closer after Thutmose IV took the unprecedented step of marrying a Mitanni princess (who brought with her several hundred handmaidens!). Then, too, Tutankhamon lived a rather short life of 18 or 19 years, and the portion of it after which he changed his name from Tutankhaten and before he was buried is only half of that; the tunic must have been made within that short period. There was not much time to send him suitable gifts from abroad. All of these facts add up to the conclusion that the tunic must have been made *in* Egypt, by a combined effort of Syrian and Egyptian artisans.

There is, then, no question that Syrian textile technology was intimately influencing that of Egypt; and the art of embroidery appears to be one of the techniques specifically associable with Syria.

Three other small pieces from Tutankhamon's tomb also contain interesting stitchery (see Pfister 1937, 214–17 and pl. 53a, 54e). One has, embroidered on it in chain stitch, a row of Maltese crosses—a pattern that I do not know of elsewhere in Egyptian art, but that does occur on Syrian pottery of the period. Again the evidence points to Syria. A second is decorated with an elaborate Egyptian *nekhbet* vulture, done partly in chain stitch and partly by sewing onto the surface bits of cloth rolled up into tiny sausages, the whole design being highlighted with small, round platelets of gold fastened to the fabric. The third fragment, very small, also has little bundles of cloth sewn on, but in longer rolls that snake across the surface to make an unknown design; and it, too, shows the remains of gold studs. I know of no parallels or other examples, at any time or place in the ancient world, of this technique of applying little sausage-rolls of cloth to form a design. Once again we are faced with our own ignorance in a most tantalizing way.

From here on, Egyptian textile workers seem to have settled again into a mold. Alternative techniques with which we have seen them experimenting are evidently abandoned in favor of staying with slit tapestry, warp-faced bands, the now-ancient inlaid fringes and stripes, and the ever more lavish beadwork, which has expanded to include studs or sequins of metal, and small platelets of faience or metal (cf. robes of Tutankhamon: Carter and Mace 1923, 167–71, and pl. 34, 37, 38). We find this same repertoire scatteringly attested, after the uniquely lavish and well-preserved textiles of Tutankhamon, all the way into the Greco-Roman era.

CHAPTER 6

THE TEXTILE WEAVES
(3) THE BRONZE AGE

Now that we have a modest picture of how textiles developed in the area where they are best preserved, even though that area is a rather static backwater for pattern weaving until the middle of the 2nd millennium, we can return to the remainder of early Near Eastern and Mediterranean textiles with better hope of making sense of them. We will be severely disappointed by the extreme scarcity of material in these other areas, until we reach the late 2nd or even early 1st millennium B.C. In most cases it is impossible to form a coherent picture across time within a given area, because we catch only glimpses here and there of some technique that existed, with little or no internal indication of where it came from or when it arrived. Having something of a framework of textile development from other areas and periods, however, will give us much more secure in-terpretations of the meager evidence than would otherwise be possible.

I will start in the east and work my way toward the northwest. The coverage will deal with rather later periods in the west than in the east, partly because of the differing times at which historical texts become our major source of evidence. In effect, in Europe I will bring the development of textiles all the way to the first major literate period in Europe, the Classical era—say 500 B.C., for round numbers; whereas in the ancient Semitic territory—Mesopotamia and the Levant—I will in general cover the textile remains only into the 2nd millennium, at which point the cuneiform texts become so copious (and the textile fragments remain so exceedingly scarce, small, and uninformative) that the subject needs treatment primarily from the historical records.[1]

---

[1] This is not so neat and tidy a division as it may sound: of all Europe, only small parts of Greece and Italy were literate in 500 or even 400 B.C.; and at 1500 or 1200 B.C. we know essentially nothing about Palestine, for example, from local documents. (In fact, I have pursued various aspects of the textile industry in Palestine down to about 900 B.C., for several reasons.) But one has to draw a line somewhere, and in general my guideline for this first half of the book has been to stop at the point where the ancient texts must be consulted in great detail. The chief exceptions are (1) Egypt, which, because of the accidents of preservation, *must* be our anchor for the Bronze Age elsewhere; and (2) northern Europe, where I have finally cut things off somewhat arbitrarily around 500 B.C., knowing that most of the later "prehistoric" material there has already been well published. Another important factor, of course, is what happened to be available to me of the scholarly material—both because of where I live and because of what languages I can and cannot cope with.

MESOPOTAMIA

Unfortunately, cloth very seldom survives in the Mesopotamian climate. We left the Mesopotamian area with the discovery of striped cloth at Susa in the 4th millennium, and our next trace of textile appears in the corroded exterior of a silver figurine of a bull-creature, dated stylistically to the Proto-Elamite period, ca. 3000 B.C. (Hansen 1970, 7). The cloth is constructed in a faced plain weave, running 22–30 threads per centimeter one way versus 10 the other, from an S-ply, Z-spun yarn apparently made out of some animal fiber like wool (ibid., 24 and figs. 17, 25). A number of other metal figurines from 3rd-millennium foundation deposits at various Mesopotamian sites—e.g., Nippur and Lagash—also still show the remains of the cloths in which they were wrapped (Haines 1956, 266; Hansen 1970, 14 and n. 25); but they do not add anything to what we already know, since they are in plain weave.

Our next landmark, then, is the remains of textiles from the middle of the 3rd millennium that were found by Sir Leonard Woolley in the Royal Tombs at Ur. Although few fragments were found, their natures are tantalizingly diverse. Most were in plain weave, but some bits, preserved here and there in the Great Death Pit, of a "thick but closely woven fabric" seem to have been dyed a brilliant red (Woolley 1934, 239). Around the legs and feet of the body in PG/357 lay "a great quantity of cloth," which was "all reduced to fine powder but did, so long as it was undisturbed, preserve the texture of the original sufficiently for three varieties of material to be distinguished." One was a coarse plain weave; another, with a ground of loose plain weave, sported on one side "long threads forming either a very deep pile or else 'tassels' like those on the skirts of the figures represented on the monuments" (ibid., 238). It would be interesting to know how these threads were attached: whether they were loops of the running weft, as in the looped towels from 11th Dynasty Egyptian tombs half-a-millennium later, or supplementary threads tucked around the warp like the linen and feather-barb pile fabrics from Kerma.

The third and most intriguing type of weave appeared in a "finely woven cloth with a diagonal rib" (ibid., 238). From the description, one would think that this must be some sort of diagonal twill. Yet our chief evidence for twill comes from Hallstatt sites in central Europe over a millennium and a half later, where it suddenly becomes the most popular weave—although one instance of twill has been reported from a Chalcolithic burial in Anatolia, at Alishar, and another from the early 3rd millennium in the Caucasus (see below). The illusion of diagonal ribbing, however, can also be given by packing the warp or weft together so closely in a plain-weave fabric that the other set of elements is hidden, causing the eye to follow the slope opposite to that of the fibers in the thread (some of the Bronze Age Danish fabrics, as we will see, rely on this illusion for decorative effect). What seems more likely, then, is that the inhabitants of Ur, who were probably no less acquainted with warp-faced and/or weft-faced plain weaves than their Elamite neighbors, were producing the *appearance* of diagonal ribs by this simple means. Here the lack of any sort of diagram or photograph of the finds, even in the excavation daybooks, really hurts. For these few finds are about all we have, at the moment, to give us direct evidence of the nature of millennia of ancient Mesopotamian cloth. We know, in fact, far more from the texts and artistic representations (see Barrelet 1977; and see Chapter 7).

THE LEVANT

Moving westward we pick up a somewhat fuller sequence in Palestine, starting with poorly preserved fabrics in plain weave from the Chalcolithic levels (4th millennium) at Jericho and Teleilat Ghassul (E. Crowfoot 1960, 519), and a few Upper Chalcolithic impressions of plain-weave textiles on potsherds from Lachish (one of which has two threads in one shed; Tufnell 1958, 72 and pl. 13.90, 13.93–94).

A more various group of Chalcolithic textiles was found among the considerable hoard of objects in the Cave of the Treasure at Naḥal Mishmar. According to the excavator, 37 pieces of linen and 8 of woolen cloth were found that could be assigned directly to the Chalcolithic period (Bar-Adon 1971, 159).[2] Of these, one scrap of linen was in basket weave (ibid., 170 no. 146 = no. 62-28), everything else in plain weave. One narrow woolen tape or cord, however, which was only three warp strings wide (but five threads, since each selvedge has two threads), had its weft packed down so as to hide the warp completely (ibid., 159 no. 130 = no. 61-22/8-h). Two others seem to have texture stripes. The analysts mention several slim stripes made with four heavy threads in no. 61-29/7-a (Zindorf, Horowitz, and Blum 1971, 249; Bar-Adon 1971, 168 no. 142—running vertically), and similar stripes can be seen in the photograph of no. 61-204 (Bar-Adon 1971, 167 no. 138—running horizontally). Several of the linen pieces show selvedges, with the weft merely turning back around the last warp (or doubled warp, for strength) into the next shed, and sometimes

pulling the last few warp closer together as it is wont to do on any hand-loom (e.g., ibid., 168 no. 141 = no. 61-72/4-a).

There are also examples of stitching. Here the analysts distinguished two types of stitch, a "hem stitch" and a "binding stitch" (Zindorf et al. 1971, 249). Both appear to resemble the whipping stitch we have seen so often in Egypt (see Bar-Adon 1971, 169 no. 144 = no. 61-22/8-a for the "hem stitch," and 168 no. 139 = no. 62-61-b for the "binding stitch"), and they are used for the same purposes—sewing seams and hems, and binding off raw edges or even selvedges.

The linens are all natural color, but the woolen fragments are reported to be in four colors: red, green, black, and tan or yellow (Bar-Adon 1971, 159 no. 128 = no. 61-22/8-d; Zindorf et al. 1971, 249), the last two perhaps natural.

What we see, then, is not so very different from what we saw in Mesopotamia: plain weave, sometimes packed to hide one set of threads (i.e., faced), plus texture stripes and experimentation with solid color in the wools. There is also a fair amount of sewing.

Slightly more complicated are the textiles from the Middle Bronze Age tombs at Jericho. Here the body of the fabric was always plain weave, but every selvedge was a "decorative reinforced" selvedge in *half-basket weave*—the lone weft going over and under pairs of warp (E. Crowfoot 1960, 519 and 520 fig. 226.1).[3] Sewing has progressed a bit beyond the whipping stitch, still used for seams, to include a running stitch used to make a drawstring along the selvedge edge

---

[2] Note that the textiles were divided into three groups: those clearly from the early (Chalcolithic) layers, those clearly from the late (Roman) layers, and an "intermediate" group that might be either early or late. (I have referred in this section to the original Hebrew edition of Bar-Adon, because the textile photos are much

clearer in it.)

[3] This kind of edge weave we will see heavily associated with the European warp-weighted loom. And in Chapter 14 we will see that the warp-weighted loom was abruptly imported into Palestine precisely in the Middle Bronze Age.

of some garments (ibid., 520 and fig. 226.3), and what Elisabeth Crowfoot calls "a form of twined embroidery," in which two threads have been sewn in together to form a long, narrow line, twisting around each other as they go (ibid., 520 and fig. 226.2).[4]

And finally, at the very end of the 2nd millennium, at the start of the Iron Age, we find a few impressions of textiles on the bottoms of "Negev Ware" pots. One of these, from Tel Masos, shows traces of a handsome double-knotted fringe at the edge of a strongly faced (warp-faced?) cloth in plain weave, probably of wool (Sheffer 1976, 84–86, fig. 2, pl. 2.3 and 4.3). From about the same time there are "impressions and/or traces" of a balanced plain-weave fabric "on a plaster wall surface of the Philistine temple" at Tell Qasileh, showing the colors red, white, and blue (ibid., 85 and n. 7). Other scraps of textiles are known from Palestine, including Egyptian-style linens in the Late Bronze Age (e.g., at Deir el-Balas: Dothan 1979, figs. 154–55; plus more recent finds there: T. Dothan, pers. comm. 1983); but as far as I know they add nothing to the list of weaves and other decorative devices until late in the 1st millennium B.C.

In Syria, to the north, remarkably little in the way of textile remains has been discovered, or at least salvaged and reported, from any pre–Iron Age period whatsoever. This is

doubly a pity, as the texts from Ebla show that Syria was the center of manufacture and export of the most expensive and sought-after textiles of the 3rd millennium, which found their way to such far-flung places as Ur and Kish in Mesopotamia, and Megiddo in Palestine (Matthiae 1980, 179–81). As a result of the paucity of actual textiles, we can only guess at their nature from other sorts of evidence.

We have one small find nearby, however. During recent excavations at Terqa, on the west bank of the Euphrates, the excavators found some small scraps of cloth in a burial of ca. 1600 B.C. They are all in plain weave, but some are hard packed into a faced weave, whereas others are woven very loosely with a fine thread that gives them an almost lacy look.[5] The fine, faced scraps suggest (but so far do not prove) that the Syrians may already have begun to make tapestry— a weft-faced technique that later seems to spread to Egypt from this area, as we have seen, and that would account quite well for the high cost and great attractiveness of the Eblaite textiles. But to *prove* the presence of tapestry we need a scrap or impression, however small, that shows a bit of slit or dovetailed turnaround between fields. Let us hope that future excavators in Syria will be on the lookout for such evidence.

ANATOLIA, THE CAUCASUS, AND THE AEGEAN

Although Anatolia is generally reckoned as part of the Near East, with respect to early textiles it has at least as much in common with Europe as with Syria and Mesopotamia.

In particular, we have already seen that the "European" warp-weighted loom was used in western and southern Anatolia. The Bronze Age Anatolian textile remains, too,

---

[4] From the regularity of the diagram, however, it would appear possible that the "embroidery" threads once again may have been laid in during weaving (in this case being twined around each other at the same time) as we so often found was the case in Egypt for reported "embroidery." On the other hand, if they are truly em-

broidered, we may cite as a parallel the rather later twisting stitch on several Early Bronze II pieces from Denmark (see below).

[5] My warm thanks to Giorgio Buccellati for letting me analyze the unpublished fragments from Terqa and mention them here.

6.1 Some of the fragments of a 2/2 twill cloth from burial L4.e.x14 at Alishar, Turkey; late 4th millennium. (Photo courtesy of the Oriental Institute of the University of Chicago)

will be seen to have a number of close connections with the west, as well as a few very intriguing ones with the northeast. As in so many other eras and aspects of culture, Anatolia seems to have been functioning as the crossroads where different traditions met; and I will take it as the pivot of the following discussion.

Anatolia has produced several interesting textiles that are later than the magnificent find at Çatal Hüyük and the filmy traces of triple basket weave at Mersin.[6] In the Chalcolithic levels at Alishar, late in the 4th millennium, fragments of textile were found

clinging to a jawbone and to some animal skin in the box burial of a child (Fig. 6.1; von der Osten 1937, I.44, 51, and 50 fig. 60; Fogelberg and Kendall 1937, 334–35). The cloth was originally said to exhibit a 2/1 twill weave (see Chapter 7), warp and weft going "over one thread and under two" (Fogelberg and Kendall 1937, 334). After careful analysis of the photographs, I am quite convinced that the cloth is indeed twill, but of the more expectable 2/2 variety (over 2, under 2).[7] "Expectable" I say, because 2/2 twill (see Fig. 7.1) requires 4 sheds, which is easy to do on the looms for which we have evidence

[6] There are also a number of remains in plain weave, just to reassure us that everyone was busy weaving. Those which have come to my attention include "the ghost of a tabby-weave textile" impressed on an Early Bronze floor at Aphrodisias (Kadish 1969, 56), and remains of a plain-weave cloth on the surface of a bronze blade from Tekeköy, also Early Bronze (Kökten, Özgüç, and Özgüç 1945, 373–74 and pl. 65 (= IV).7; T. Özgüç 1948, fig. 85).

[7] The problem is that the threads do not lie at right angles—presumably because they have been skewed by pressure. But I can follow many of them, especially on

the largest piece, over 2 and under 2 in both directions for a considerable distance; and nowhere do I find a patch that convinces me of "over one and under two." I have also shown the photos to several highly skilled analysts of more modern textiles, and they came independently to the same conclusion. One other possible interpretation, because of the oblique angle, is that the cloth has been plaited rather than woven on a loom. But it is still 2/2 twill in structure. My thanks to the Oriental Institute in Chicago for providing me with very clear enlargements of the original photographs to work with.

in Anatolia (just divide each half in half again); whereas 2/1 twill requires 3 equal sheds—a much less obvious step from a 2-shed loom, especially one that depends upon balanced sets of weights. On the other hand, the presence of twill here is a surprise, in that it represents our first example of a mechanizable pattern weave. For twill patterns can be set up ahead of time entirely on the loom, and do not need the time-consuming "hand tending" that primitive float weaves and tapestry require. It is also a surprise in that, with one exception, we will not see any more examples of twill weave in cloth for another 2000 years, until it suddenly deluges us in central Europe with the Hallstatt culture (see Chapter 7 for a full discussion of twill technique). The one exception is far to the northeast.

In about the 4th millennium we begin to pick up textile evidence from another major area—the Caucasus, by which term I mean to include Georgia to the south and the Kuban and Terek watersheds to the north of the Caucasian mountains. But for all the size of the area, we will be looking at frustratingly little data—not because there are no remains but rather because the information is so formidably difficult to obtain. Nonetheless, the few gleanings are so tantalizingly rich that it is worth our while to investigate them.[8]

In a quick summary at the beginning of a primarily ethnographic article on "Peasant Methods of Preparation of Cloth at Kakheti" (in the Georgian S.S.R.), the Georgian scholar Ts. Karaulašvili informs us that impressions of cloth on clay begin in the "Eneolithic" in that area, followed by actual remains of cloth in the Early Bronze Age (to which is appended a list of no less than seven sites and an "et cetera": Karaulašvili 1979,

32). By "Eneolithic" and "Early Bronze" we are apparently to understand roughly the 4th and 3rd millennia B.C., respectively. Kuftin (1950a, pl. 74–77) actually illustrates a number of textile-impressed sherds of the Eneolithic from Ochamchira, on the Abghaz coast of the Black Sea, to the west. They all appear to be in plain weave, although of various textures. Solovjev (1950, fig. 13) shows five others from unspecified sites in the same area. One piece is a faced weave, with very fine threads covering much thicker ones. Karaulašvili, on the other hand, illustrates three artifacts from the Early Bronze Age (Karaulašvili 1979, pl. III.1–2, captions p. 179). Two are potsherds with impressions in what appears to be plain weave, one considerably finer than the other. The third, however, is an actual piece of woolen cloth, from the site of Martkopi, done in a very clear 2/2 diagonal twill!

So we have a 4th–millennium example of twill from central Anatolia, and a 3rd-millennium piece from Georgia, but do not encounter this important type again until the start of the first millennium, in Hallstattian Austria. Part of our problem, of course, is that we have essentially no textiles preserved in Eastern and Central Europe during that long gap, so we cannot trace *anything*. But it is worth reminding the reader that in Chapter 3 we investigated a bronze pin from the northeastern Caucasus, dated to the first quarter of the 3rd millennium, that was cast from a mold decorated with impressions of what seemed to be tablet-woven textiles; and there too the next European evidence for the technique was among the Hallstatt cloths.

But there are more surprises. From the mid- or late 3rd millennium we have a much more extensive single find at Tsarskaja, from

---

[8] My thanks to Elena Balashova, Harold Wayland, George Mchedlishvili, and Julie Christensen for their valiant but still fruitless efforts to put me directly in contact with the Georgian scholars who apparently are actively working on the ancient textile remains in that area.

6.2 Black-and-yellow plaid cloth from a kurgan at Tsarskaja (now Novosvobodnaja) on the Fars River just north of the Caucasus; 3rd millennium. (Veselovskij 1898, 37 fig. 56)

one of the many kurgans of that date in the Kuban area, the northwest watershed of the Caucasus. This particular tribal chief had been laid to rest in a large wrap of black fur, under which he wore two garments: an undergarment of linen-like fabric "brightly decorated with purple color and covered with red threads in the likeness of tassels" (*v" vidě kistej*), and an overgarment of fluffy (or downy: *pukhovaja*) yellow cloth ornamented with narrow black stripes forming a close-set and regular plaid (Fig. 6.2; Veselovskij 1898, 37).

The parallels to what we have later are striking. White vegetable-fiber shirts or chemises, worn next to the skin and embroidered chiefly with red, have been the standard garment among the Slavs for both men and women right up to this century (cf. Barber 1975, 309 and figs. 3–5); and, as we will see in Chapter 7, just such shirts have also

been found in the 1st millennium B.C. kurgans at Pazyryk.[9] As for the plaid, this is our earliest surviving example of that simple but effective technique of ornamentation. Is it accident that our next examples come to us— and by the dozens—from the Hallstatt culture again?

There is one more Bronze Age find of great interest in the northeastern zone, although it is still farther afield, in the steppes of the lower Volga. Here another wealthy chieftain was laid to rest in a rather unusual tomb now known as Kurgan 9 at Tri Brata (Sinitsyn 1948, 150–53 and figs. 16–17). The deceased was laid in the bottom of a pit (Fig. 6.3), his knees up, his head propped against the wall, and his remains well sprinkled with red pigment. Around his bones the excavators found some bronze objects, wooden and pottery dishes, and the skeletons of two large snakes. (According to Gimbutas [1956, 78–

[9] Using the notion from linguistics of comparative reconstruction of structure points, and using data from the folk costumes of the daughter cultures, I reconstructed years ago an undergarment of just this sort for the late proto-Indo-European inhabitants of the southwestern steppes (Barber 1975). It was only later that I learned of the Pazyryk shirts, which are not often mentioned in the general literature, and only much later that I came upon Veselovskij's publication. Both of these finds appear to me to vindicate the new application of the comparative method to the reconstruction of costume. See Chapter 8, and note 11 below.

79] the bronzes have their nearest parallels among the Early Bronze Age objects in the North Caucasus; so apparently this burial too is from the 3rd millennium.) In the collapsed fill of the pit and around its top edge were found most of the parts of a wheeled cart or chariot, one heavy wheel having been placed at each of the four corners. The pit had been roofed by placing poles across the top, covering these in turn with mats and rugs, and then piling stones and a mound above that. To our good fortune, a large rug had stretched out far beyond the southwest corner, where it left its imprint—and the im-

6.3 Impression of a patterned rug (lower right) beside the burial pit in Kurgan 9 at Tri Brata, near Elista, west of the Lower Volga; 3rd millennium. (Sinitsyn 1948, 152 fig. 16)

print of its decoration!—in the clay (Fig. 6.3, lower right).

The pattern consists of a lozenge with broad bands radiating from the long sides, and what looks like a border design of a zig-zag between stripes. (If that *is* in fact the border of the rug, however, the rug stretched away from, not over onto, the roof of the pit.) The imprinted swatch measured approximately 1.30 by 1.20 m, if the drawing was accurately scaled. Although we are given no further details (except that fragments were taken to two local museums), one might hazard the guess that the textile technique most likely to leave an *imprint* of its design beneath it would be tapestry. In pile knotting, the other chief candidate for such a figured rug, the knots tend to be all the same size regardless of color; whereas in tapestry each color of thread backtracks at the edge of the color field, leaving quite palpable discontinuities between the color zones of the design.

The closest parallel for this find takes us back to Anatolia, although to even hazier data. In 1959 a report was published of a "clandestine excavation" of several tombs that had taken place during wartime many years before, near the village of Dorak in northwest Turkey (Mellaart 1959, 754). Many unfortunate emotions not in the best interests of science were stirred up, and neither the objects nor the original photographs have ever surfaced. Some have cast doubt on the authenticity of the finds, or of the report. If, however, we take the whole thing at face value, then we can say the following. Among the finds, on the floor of one of the tombs, was a rug estimated to be a little over 2½ by 5½ feet, and woven in red, yellow, blue, and black, with geometric patterns composed of intricately arranged lozenges in the main field, and lozenges within stripes along the end borders (ibid., pl. II and fig. 13). It was said to be woven of wool, in *kilim* technique, i.e., tapestry. The artifacts as a group place the date roughly in the middle of the 3rd millennium, while one Egyptian object in particular would date this tomb to just past the middle of that millennium. Although this rug seemed unique and even anachronistic when first reported, our evidence for fancy rug-weaving at such an early date northeast of the Mediterranean is closing in around it. A design that is not so very different, done several centuries later with inlaid frit, has been found at Mari on the Euphrates and has been flagged as a typical carpet pattern (Dalley 1984, 53 fig. 24).[10]

Of totally different character is the next elaborate textile, found at Acemhöyük in strata from the days of the Assyrian trade colonies in central Anatolia, around 1800 B.C. Fragments of the cloth, which was said to resemble white linen, were scattered about on the floor of a palace room that also contained pieces of ivory and gaming boards—that is, wealthy surroundings. All over one side of the cloth, tiny light and dark blue faience beads had been sewn on in a geometric design with gold thread (N. Özgüç 1966, 47 and pl. 22). In the lumps on display in the Museum of Anatolian Civilizations in Ankara, one can still make out a pattern of stacked chevrons and part of a swastika or meander. Cloth ornamented with tiny faience ring-

beads sewn in geometric patterns is highly reminiscent of the nearly contemporary fabrics of that sort from Kerma, in southern Egypt, although these latter are not sewn with gold thread. Citing the quantities of textiles, some very expensive, which the Assyrians recorded that they were importing into Anatolia at this time, the excavator gives her opinion that this cloth too "must have belonged to an expensive fabric among the imported textile wares" (ibid., 47). And it may indeed have been imported into Anatolia.

On the other hand, this discovery of beaded fabrics of a luxurious nature right within Turkey should give us occasion to stop and rethink a curious find at Troy, in the Early Bronze Age strata, half-a-millennium before.

We know from the configuration of the loom weights that the loom in Room 206 of Troy IIg had been set up and was in use on the day when the city was burnt to the ground (see Chapter 3; Fig. 3.14). But all through the fill around the loom were quantities of tiny gold beads, many "so diminutive that they could only be recovered by sifting and panning the earth" and in such "disorder" that they afforded to the excavators "no clue to the form of the ornament to which they had presumably belonged" (Blegen et al. 1950, 350). Their solution was to suggest that perhaps the woman who was weaving at

---

[10] Although we do not have actual samples of pile carpets until the mid-1st millennium B.C. (see Chapter 7), this frit design looks as though it could have been copied off a pile carpet quite as well as off a *kilim*. The time and place of origin of pile carpets has been discussed for years by carpet enthusiasts, but various recent discoveries lead me to expect to see traces of 3rd-millennium pile rugs turning up in Soviet Turkmenia or northern Iran. Khlopin (1982) has recently recognized special pile-cutting blades in a series of peculiar bronze knives from women's graves in the Sumbar valley, east of the Caspian. In addition, he mentions similar curved blades (also with the outer, not inner, edge sharpened) from Hissar IIIв and Shah-Tepe II (ibid., 116), levels that

Thomas cross-dates to the late 3rd millennium (H. L. Thomas 1967, chart II:5b).

Khlopin uses the old "short" chronology and places the Sumbar graves a millennium later, while agreeing that all three sets of knives must be contemporary. Khlopin's low date, however, also leaves stranded in time the fact that the pottery of the Namazga III–IV cultures in Turkmenia shows many designs that we consider typical of recent pile carpets of that area (Pinner 1982b). These pots, being of the 4th to 3rd millennium, fit right into the scheme of early pile carpets and their traditions by Thomas's dating frame (which was set up according to quite different evidence).

the loom rushed out when the terrible disaster struck, "abandoning her bracelet or necklace which may have caught in the fabric she was weaving, or which she may have taken off and hung up while performing her task" (ibid., 351). Perhaps—less romantically but more intriguingly for the history of textiles—she was weaving a cloth with beads strung right on the weft, as we saw at Kerma, or was sewing them onto the finished web as it hung there conveniently stretched out on the loom before being cut down. Only here the beads themselves are of gold, the metal for which Troy II is so famous, rather than of Egyptian faience: truly a royal fabric, and one that would merit the epithet which Homer gives to the royal cloth of a later Troy: ἀστὴρ δ'ὣς ἀπέλαμψε (and it gleamed like a star; *Il.* 6.295).

Such an interpretation is strengthened by yet other evidence. Elsewhere in the late levels of Troy II, in the same terracotta box as held the remains of a wooden spindle with its thread (see Chapter 2), Schliemann had found some carbonized remnants of apparently linen cloth together with some small beads, all of which he postulated as representing the remains of "a dress ornamented with beads of glass paste" (Schliemann 1880a, 361). Schliemann was assuming that the box, which is less than 3 inches high and 4 inches in diameter (ibid., 360 no. 266–67), was part of the remains of a funeral pyre stashed in a larger urn, complete with the ashes of the body, offerings, and personal possessions (ibid., 360–61). But later investigators denied that possibility, finding no trace of bones or grain, only the spindle and its thread, sherds of a small vase, the charred remains of linen cloth, and 11 ring-beads on bits of thread: 6 of faience and 5 of gold (Götze 1902, 340; H. Schmidt 1902a, 244). The cloth with its(?) beads must therefore have been small, rather than the remains of

a whole dress. The recurrent association of tiny beads and cloth is interesting, however. Little biconical beads of green and yellow faience were found elsewhere in Schliemann's excavations (Götze 1902, 339 and 385 fig. 358), likewise other tiny beads of gold and of electrum (Schliemann, diary, Sat., March 3/15, 1873 [= vol. 14, p. 87]).

To pursue beadwork for a moment more: rather later than either the Troy II or Acemhöyük finds, but still within the Bronze Age, comes a much more extensive discovery in a Late Bronze Age chamber tomb at Dendra, near Mycenae in the Peloponnese. Here Persson found a spread of what he estimated to be about 40,000 small beads of faience, running from .3 to 1.5 cm in diameter, and forming—where still stuck together in the more solid lumps of earth—"a zigzag pattern with the colours in the following order: yellow, brown, black, blue, and white" (Persson 1931, 106 no. 51 and pl. 34.4). "They undoubtedly," he concludes, "adorned a beaded garment of the same kind as that found in Tut-ankh-amen's tomb" (ibid.). The "750 flat beads of blue and white glass paste . . . found close to the sword hilt" (ibid., 106 no. 50) in one of the graves may have adorned a sword-belt, though whether the belt was of cloth or leather we cannot say.

The presence of faience beads in some of these finds suggests an influence from Egypt. And yet sewing all manner of beads, sequins, and platelets onto garments seems to have been a favorite thing to do in prehistoric Europe as far back as the Palaeolithic. In Chapter 2 we mentioned the rows of shell beads sewn or strung onto some sort of cap, in the Gravettian Grotte des Enfants (Verneau 1906, pl. 2); and we have just seen in Chapter 4 that the Neolithic lake-dwellers of Switzerland were practicing beadwork in seeds—most of this before faience had even been invented, and all of it before faience reached Europe in the 3rd millennium. So it is hard to maintain that Egypt provided anything more than a flashier material.

There is another aspect of this vogue that bears mentioning: namely the "sequins" or platelets that formed such a spectacular part of the earlier Mycenaean burial dress. In excavating the Shaft Graves, Schliemann found large quantities of gold ornaments, or gold foil over carved wood, that had clearly been sewn and/or pasted to the outer garments of the deceased (Schliemann 1880b, 165–84 etc.). Many of them are round, with various handsome repoussé designs on them, especially circles and spirals; whereas others—also detailed in repoussé—have been cut out in the form of women, lions, stags, birds, butterflies, octopuses, griffins, sphinxes, bulls' heads, leaves, flowers, and even shrines. A few are strips that must have encircled the sleeve at the wrist—in fact, by careful analysis of the positions in which the

platelets were found, one can deduce quite a bit about the shape of the clothing (Barber 1975, 316). The sheer wealth and variety of these golden ornaments dazzle any visitor to the National Museum in Athens today. The use of these platelets has a long and interesting history within the archaeology of eastern Europe.[11]

Meanwhile, the evidence for the actual cloth graced by these beads and platelets is as insufficient and barren of information as it could possibly be. The fact that the Aegean people, like the Anatolians, knew how to weave and were doing so is steadily attested, from the Middle Neolithic on, but the scraps are so tiny as to give us virtually no further information. The climate of Greece, unfortunately, like that of most of the lands along the east and north coasts of the Mediterranean, is simply not conducive to the preservation of textiles. Almost every shred of evidence that has survived prior to the Iron Age

[11] The use of platelets appears to begin in the Neolithic, along the north shore of the Black Sea and eastwards, where they turn up, for example, in astonishing abundance on burial clothing at the site of Marijupil' (= Mariupol; Makarenko 1933; 1934), carved from shiny laminae of boar's tusk, mostly in the natural shape of the tusk, but some in the shapes of animals. (For other sites see Gimbutas 1956, 53–55.) As time goes on and the use of metal becomes more common, they are partially replaced by even shinier metal platelets, or carved wood covered with metal foil. For example, gold "sequins" of various shapes have been found at Late Neolithic Varna, on the Bulgarian Black Sea coast (Gimbutas 1977, 46–48), while magnificent gold platelets—68 of lions, 19 of bulls, and 38 plain rings—graced the fabrics buried in an Early Bronze Age kurgan at Maikop, in Georgia, of the early 3rd millennium (*Otchët Imperatorskoj Arkheologicheskoj Kommissii* 1897, 3–4 and figs. 1–4; see Tallgren 1934, 33 fig. 27 for possible reconstruction as a canopy). From these northern lands they spread west and south with the expanding Kurgan culture.

At some point the tradition of ornamenting clothing with these platelets split into two uses: (1) for ostentatious decoration and display of wealth, and (2) for deflecting weapons, i.e., as armor. Both these uses are reflected in the Shaft Graves as well as other Mycenaean tombs, the first by the many hundreds of elaborate gold platelets on the women's and occasionally the men's clothing, and the second by the boar's tusk laminae on

the helmets (Homer's famous "boar's-tusk helmet"—*Iliad* 10.261–65) as well as by derivative faience and gold-covered platelets sewn closely together to form armored tunics and helmets (Schliemann 1880b, 165–84 etc.; Persson 1931, 16, 36, 64–65, 104–5 and figs. 41–44 and 80, etc.; J. Borchardt 1972, 18–37 and pl. 1–4; cf. Linear B descriptions—see Chapter 15). Both types of platelets continued to be used back in their homeland by the Scythians in the next millennium: the armor plates were translated into metals such as bronze (on display in the Historical Museum, Kiev), and gold platelets continued on the women's clothing (on display by the thousands in the Hermitage, Leningrad; compare *From the Lands of the Scythians* 1975, pl. 9 and 27, the latter showing a 4th century B.C. Scythian burial of a princess startlingly like the burials of the Shaft Grave princesses). Apparently the women of central Europe, and especially of the Hallstatt culture, were fond of these metal platelets too, because in addition to the examples that have come down to us, we see them depicted on the Hallstatt women's clothing (e.g., on the Sopron urn, Figs. 2.15, 13.3). Even today they persist, translated into convenient coins, covering the folk costumes of women from the Mordvins of central Russia to the Croatians and Macedonians of the Balkans. The use of ornamental platelets on clothing thus has a continuous documentable history for some 6000 years in East Europe. (See Chapter 11 for other long-lived traditions.)

consists of either an impression on pottery or a metallic oxide cast or pseudomorph on a metal artifact, usually on the blade of a sword or dagger.[12] In none of these cases—setting a pot out to dry on a rag, incorporating scraps into the body of the pot for strength, wrapping an object for burial in the ground, or making a sheath—would the ancients have been likely to use their fanciest textiles, which would probably have been reserved for clothing and hangings. The only apparent exception is the discovery under a skeleton in the unplundered *tholos* at Routsi, near Pylos, of a "hauchdünne Schicht tiefblauer

Farbe mit Spuren von Rot an den Rändern" (breath-thin layer of dark blue color with traces of red at the edges; Marinatos 1967b, A16). The excavator interprets this colored material variously in his writings as the remains of a cloak or dress (ibid.) or "a rush mat or perhaps a thick blanket" (Marinatos 1957, 540). Since it was not clear even to the discoverer that the object was cloth, however, we had best set it, too, aside as inconclusive, although not at all beyond what we would expect of the capabilities of Late Bronze Age weavers anywhere in the eastern half of the Mediterranean.

ITALY, FRANCE, AND SPAIN

Weaving techniques appear to spread gradually and continuously west and north through Europe in the Bronze Age. We see the loom weights moving, and also the remains of the cloth itself, although the latter are few and far between.

From the Terremare district of northern Italy we have a few textile remains apparently

dating from the 3rd and early 2nd millennia. The fine, regular, plain-weave linen is decorated in one case with tiny seeds sewn on like beads in some design that is no longer recognizable (Battaglia 1943, 51–52 and pl. 20, esp. 20.2a), much as in the earlier fragment from the Swiss lake-dwelling at Murten (see Chapter 4).

---

[12] From oldest to most recent, for the Aegean area and Cyprus: plain-weave impression on a Middle Neolithic potsherd at Sitagroi (C. Renfrew 1972, 351); plain-weave impressions on Late Neolithic potsherds at Keos, one with a weaving error suggesting heddles (Carington Smith 1977, 115–18 and pl. 90); linen scrap on a dagger blade from a tomb on the Cycladic island of Amorgos, Early Bronze Age (Zisis 1955, 587 n. 2; Carington Smith 1977, 116); casts on Early and Middle Bronze Age daggers from several Cypriote sites, always in plain weave and evidently of flax wherever such details are determinable (e.g., at Vounous: Dikaios 1940, 57 and pl. 42c; see Aaström 1964, 111–12 and fig. 1, and Aaström 1957, 243, for several other, relatively informationless finds); tiny flecks galore, both of garments or shrouds and of what were evidently linen sheaths or wrappers around bronze blades and vessels, found in both grave circles at Mycenae, always plain weave when anything at all could be determined (Circle A: Schliemann 1880b, 155, 283; Snodgrass 1967, 16; Aakerström 1978, 52; Circle B: Papademetrios 1951, 203; Mylonas 1973, 22 etc.; and others that I have seen in storage at the National Museum, Athens); bits of cloth on a blade in a tomb at Zafer Papoura, near Knossos (Evans 1935, 4.866 and fig. 852; determined by personal observation to be entirely in a

rather open plain weave, resembling linen); plain-weave impression on clay from the "post-LM II" layer of the Unexplored Mansion at Knossos (Popham 1984, pl. 222.5); and Late Bronze Age scraps of which we know nothing whatever, one from an Argive tholos at Kazarma (Protonotariou-Deilaki 1969, 4–5) and another at Idalion, Cyprus (Aaström 1964, 112). Pieces of cloth in which the fibers themselves had been preserved were found in Early Bronze Age Troy (heavily carbonized, probably flax: Schliemann 1880a, 361; H. Schmidt 1902a, 244); at Paleoskoutella, Cyprus, from the Middle Bronze Age (plain weave, probably flax: Aaström 1964, 112 and fig. 1; but described as "two-ply technique"—basket weave?—in Aaström 1957, 162); and Late Bronze Age pieces in plain weave, one from inside the bowl of a lamp in chamber tomb 2 at Dendra ("large," we are told, but with no further details!—Persson 1931, 77, 94), and the other from inside the Granary at Mycenae ("small piece of carbonised canvas," perhaps a grain bag: Wace 1921–23, 55).

To all this we can add, sadly, that Schliemann repeatedly mentions having found "black ashes" around the bodies in the Shaft Graves, these "ashes" now being "recognized as the decayed remains of shrouds" (Hägg and Sieurin 1982, 179) or funeral clothing.

6.4 End of a 6-foot-long linen cloth, showing a woven pattern, from Lago di Ledro, northern Italy. Early Bronze Age; 3rd millennium. (Perini 1967–69, 226–27 figs. 2–3; courtesy of Museo Tridentino di Scienze Naturali)

In another remarkable case, excavators of the pile-dwellings at Ledro found a rolled-up bundle that proved to be a narrow linen cloth more than 6 feet long (2.027 m), the two ends of which had been woven with a pattern of concentric and touching lozenges

[13] The pattern is not embroidered, as Barfield states (1971, 74). My thanks, however, to Professor Barfield for

(Fig. 6.4; Perini 1967–69, 225–27 and fig. 1). The diagonal lines were formed by floating successive warp threads over a few (3? 5?) weft, while letting the pattern climb up a row or two of weft and sideways one warp each time.[13] The principle is much the same as in twill, but not yet generalized. The main ground of the fabric is in plain weave. From these meagre remains, one has the impression that the complex float techniques of the Neolithic Swiss fabrics were continuing.

In southeastern France, too, we find occasional bits of cloth preserved in lake sites that appear to continue the same textile tradition as the Neolithic Swiss cultures. The earliest is a scrap of plain-weave cloth from the end of the Neolithic period, found at Charavines near Grenoble, followed at other sites by just enough Bronze Age pieces that we know the local people were indeed weaving (Masurel 1984a, 47, 52; most of the French textile material is apparently in the process of analysis and publication).

We get one other tantalizing glimpse. Peroni mentions an unpublished find, apparently also from Ledro, which "sembra attestare l'uso di tessuti 'stampati' mediante l'impresione di sostanze forse resinose" (appears to attest the use of textiles "printed" by means of the impression of apparently resinous substances; Peroni 1971, 100). If the stamps found in many places in central Europe from the Neolithic period were in fact being used for textiles, as well as or instead of for people's skins (see Chapter 13), this technique may not have been particularly new. It would be interesting to know what kinds of designs were used, and whether the resin acted as dye or as reserve (see Chapter 10). As further evidence for the claim that polychrome fabrics were known to the Bronze Age inhabitants of northern Italy,

helping me track down the original reports to clarify this point.

Peroni reproduces a jaunty depiction of a checkered and fringed textile drawn on the rocks at Borno (ibid., fig. 31).

Spain, meanwhile, makes a clear step forward in its textile crafts; for the Neolithic pieces in esparto grass were generally twined, less often woven, and suggested that the local people did not yet know the loom with heddle, whereas the Bronze Age pieces are woven, and beautifully so. They are always in plain weave, generally with a fine thread in handsomely even rows; and they are apparently all in linen or other vegetable fibers.[14]

DENMARK

In northern Europe we are blessed with one more major series of textiles, of a rather different nature from what we have seen before, and we do well to tackle it next since it helps us make sense of the more fragmentary remains round about. I refer to the group centering in Denmark in the mid- to late 2nd millennium B.C.

Whereas in Switzerland and its environs it was the alkaline waters of the airless, muddy lake bottoms that saved the linens and destroyed the animal substances, in the far north it was usually the acid groundwater, wherever it was trapped to the exclusion of air, that did the preserving. And that environment kept the wool, hair, skin, and leather intact, while destroying most of the bone and vegetable matter. This effect of the acid is most noticeable in the human remains, where the hair and facial features, and even the brain with its convolutions, are sometimes startlingly well preserved with scarcely a bone left (cf. Glob [1970] 1974, 27, 58–59). But we also find textiles where both animal and vegetable fibers had clearly been used, yet only one set survived. Thus, for example, in an Early Bronze Age piece from Unterteutschenthal, just east of the Harz Mountains in north-central Germany, we see a set of well-preserved woolen threads felted into a just barely cohesive mass, all lying par-

allel and carrying the clear impression of an entirely missing "weft" (warp?; Schlabow 1959, 118–19 and pl. 17; contrast Schlabow 1976, 33 and figs. 3–5). Similarly we sometimes find woolen fabrics with clear signs of stitching or lacing, but no threads left in the holes. We know enough, in short, to realize that in studying the surviving woolen fabrics we are only getting part of the picture of northern textile technology.

We have no evidence of any sort for weaving in Denmark or farther north before the beginning of the Scandinavian Bronze Age (ca. 1800 B.C.). At that point we finally find a small fragment of woolen cloth in plain weave adhering to the unornamented side of a bronze spearhead from an Early Bronze I mound at Stubdrup, in northern Jutland (Broholm 1938, 81; J.G.D. Clark 1952, 234). One might think that we are merely short of evidence for the earlier periods; and of course we are always short of textile evidence. But the cloth in the relatively large sample that we have from Early Bronze II (perhaps 1700–1300 B.C.) shows such crudeness in certain details, and is so unlike the earlier north German and Swiss fabrics, that either the particular loom or the entire technique of weaving must have been relatively new to the Bronze Age inhabitants of Scandinavia.

---

[14] For a growing catalog of the Spanish remains, see Castro-Curel 1983–84. My thanks to Zaida Castro-Curel for keeping me well informed of the progress of her work in pulling together the Spanish textile material, most of which has never been published. My thanks also to Andrew Sherratt and the Ashmolean Museum, Oxford, for helping me inspect the textiles clinging to their Argaric bronzes.

Needlework, on the other hand, was not new. We are confronted with elegant and highly skillful "embroidery" on incongruously coarse and faulty cloth. But then netting, which is usually done with a needle of some sort, had been a forte of the northerners since the Mesolithic at least, and presumably the sewing of skins and furs into clothing had been a necessity of life of equal antiquity in these latitudes. It still is practiced with great skill today among the Lapps.

Most of these Bronze Age Danish finds of cloth come from a dozen or so burials of what must have been upper-class men and women, laid to rest fully clothed in coffins hollowed out of huge oak logs. In the primary burials, the log had been propped all around by stones on the level ground, then heaped over with a gigantic mound of earth, a memorial visible for miles around. Later, secondary burials in oak coffins were let into some of these mounds or barrows—possibly members of the same family (see Glob [1970] 1974 for a comprehensive account). The groundwater in these mounds, full of humic acid, then "tanned" the remains much as a tanner tans hides with tannic acid. Indeed, the excavators of the Danish barrows typically found that they were nearing their goal when suddenly a great quantity of water would come rushing out of the mound into their trenches (ibid., 23, 67, 75, etc.).

The woven pieces in which the Mound People were dressed, and which were laid over and under them for their comfort in the next world, are remarkably uniform in the picture they give of local textile arts. All are made from the rather kempy wool of the primitive Faroe sheep (Broholm and Hald 1939, 39 fig. 16), ranging in color from light

to dark brown, now darkened still more by the murky groundwater in which they steeped so long. Only one piece seems originally to have been white: a shawl with handsome fringes at both ends, from a man's grave at Trindhøj (Broholm and Hald 1935, 240). The body of the fabric is invariably plain weave, in a rather coarse yarn, and throughout the cloths are irregularities and errors (e.g., ibid., 281 fig. 65). In particular, the weavers seem not to have understood—or at least not to have been able to control—the tension of the warp and its relation to obtaining a straight line of weft, for they were constantly having to fill areas with extra weft in order to make things come out even.[15] This problem is particularly noticeable in the great capes from Muldbjerg and Borum Eshøj (høj means "mound"), where big wedge-shaped areas have repeatedly been

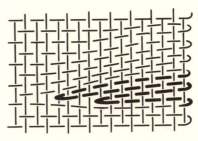

6.5   Use of regular weft to fill in a bowed line of weft that develops in the weaving when the warp tension is uneven; known as a "weaving wedge," from the shape of the fill. (Direction of weaving is down)

filled in from the edge, giving rise to the textile analysts' nickname "weaving wedges" (vævekile; Fig. 6.5); and sometimes it was even necessary to fill in lens-shaped pockets—double wedges—in the middle of the

[15] A tight warp forces the weft to pack tightly, and a loose warp won't *allow* the weft to pack tightly. When neighboring groups of warp threads are under different tension, it is impossible for the weaver to make the weft lie straight. After ten or twenty rows, there may be several inches of discrepancy. The frequency of these

wedges in the northern fabrics makes me wonder whether the weavers were using a two-beam loom with some sort of continuous warp that was impossible to adjust. Hans-Jürgen Hundt has also suggested to me that at least some of these wedges may have been intended to shape the garments somewhat (pers. comm. 1984).

cloth (ibid., 216, 222 fig. 5.2, 254–56, and figs. 39, 41; Hald 1946, 80–81; Hald 1950, 155 figs. 146–47).

Not all of the irregularities are strictly errors or incompetencies, however. Most of the large pieces show numerous places where the weft from one shed switches into the next shed in mid-row, and the weft from the second shed crosses it as it switches into the first shed (Fig. 6.6). Now, a weft can't be put into a shed that has already been closed. The logical explanation, therefore, is that two people were weaving at once—just as they are shown on the Metropolitan lekythos (Fig. 3.13)—and were passing the shuttles to each other and changing the shed whenever they met in the middle somewhere (Hald 1950, 426–27). Such an arrangement would be a handy way of dealing with the rather considerable width of the loom in question, as well as being much more neighborly than working alone. Indeed, the investigators demonstrate that on at least some pieces three and even four shuttles were going at once (as in Fig. 6.6; Broholm and Hald 1935, 242 fig. 31, 307–8 and fig. 89)—a veritable working-bee.

It may be, of course, that the weaver considered it a waste of time to worry about all these irregularities (a most un-Egyptian attitude!), because they all got covered up anyway before the garment was done. In order to make the woolen clothing as nearly wind-proof and waterproof as possible—advan-tages that skins and furs have over textiles—the cloth was put through some sort of fulling or felting process before being cut, so as to mat the fibers together into an impermeable sheet (see Chapter 9). Exactly the same is done to this day by peasants all over central and northern Europe, the most famous example being the grey and green Loden coats of Bavaria and Austria.

Another characteristic of many of these cloths is that the warp and weft yarns had been spun in opposite directions. In fact, in nearly three-fourths of these fabrics, the warp is S-spun and the weft Z-spun. In two cases we apparently have the reverse (a blouse from Egtved and footcloths from Skrydstrup: Broholm and Hald 1935, 284; Broholm and Hald 1939, 57–59). In the remainder both sets are S-spun.

Difference of spinning direction was also exploited to provide decoration, for otherwise identical S- and Z-spun threads laid side by side will catch the light differently. A woolen belt found on the woman at Borum Eshøj (Fig. 6.7), woven in warp-faced plain weave, appears to have three diagonally ribbed stripes, the two running along the selvedges being slightly darker and zigging one way, and the one running along the middle being a bit lighter and zagging the other way (Broholm and Hald 1935, 278 and fig. 63). Much ink was expended on how this effect was produced, tablet-weaving being the favorite guess, until Karl Schlabow pointed out

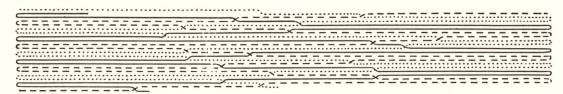

6.6 Diagram of the passage of weft, in a blanket from Trindhøj, Denmark, showing by the crossings that 3 weft bobbins were being used at once by 3 weavers working simultaneously; late 2nd millennium B.C. (Broholm and Hald 1935, 242 fig. 31; courtesy of National Museum, Copenhagen)

6.7 Woolen belt from Borum
Eshøj, Denmark, with the end
fringed in the manner of a string skirt
(see Fig. 6.9); late 2nd millennium
B.C. (Photo courtesy of National
Museum, Copenhagen)

that the belt was in plain weave and the zig-zag a clever optical illusion (Schlabow 1937, 45–47 and figs. 66–68). The impression of diagonal ribbing, as we have said, can be produced simply by packing one set of elements so closely together that the other set can't be seen—and the eye will follow the slope opposite to that of the fibers in the thread (Fig. 6.8). Thus, in a warp-faced weave where the warp is S-spun, so the fibers appear to have negative slope, the eye will travel up toward the right, that is, along a positive slope; and if the warp is Z-spun (positive slope), the eye will seem to see a diagonal moving up to the left (negative slope). The warp of the belt, Schlabow shows, was cleverly put together of 10 or 12 S-spun threads on either side, with 16 Z-spun threads in the middle. That alone

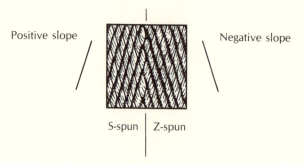

Positive slope

Negative slope

S-spun | Z-spun

6.8   Manner of producing the apparent zigzag in the Borum Eshøj belt, by alternating groups of S-and Z-spun threads (known as "shadow striping"). The belt is warp-faced plain weave.

would have produced the illusion, but the effect was heightened by selecting slightly paler wool for the middle threads. This technique of "shadow striping" by changing merely the spin of the thread became a favorite in Scandinavia and other parts of western Europe in the 1st millennium B.C. (e.g., the Haastrup and Hallstatt finds: Munksgaard 1974a, 37–38 and fig. 17; Munksgaard 1974b; Hundt 1959).

Many of the pieces retain what are assumed to be starting borders (although some could be closing borders, especially if the loom had two beams instead of warp weights). A few were produced by a plaiting technique in which the closed loop representing the end of a pair of (future) warp threads was run through the border as warp and then turned and interlaced back through the border as weft (see Fig. 6.10, right; Broholm and Hald 1935, 248 fig. 36, 249 fig. 37.3, 271 fig. 53). (Schlabow [1937, 33–34 and fig. 45] conceives the process in a different order, but the result is the same.) The corners where starting band and selvedges meet give the distinct impression of having been negotiated ad hoc, that is, any way the weaver could manage (Broholm and Hald 1935, 270 and 271 fig. 53.1–2). On the other

hand, starting borders in the half-basket weave traditional for the warp-weighted loom have been found in virtually every one of the mound burials that preserve textiles (ibid., 249 fig. 37.1 and references throughout; Broholm and Hald 1939, 50 fig. 31). They are like some of the Neolithic Swiss heading bands, except that the threads are not crossed as they come out of the border into the main body of the cloth, a detail that suggests merely that the steps taken to shed and weight the warp were slightly different. At Trindhøj, the form was embellished slightly by bringing the closed loops of the edge out an extra distance for a fringe, to balance the warp fringe at the other end (Broholm and Hald 1935, 240–42 and fig. 30.1). Did these loops once encircle the cloth beam?

Closely related to this method of weaving starting borders is that used to make the famous—or infamous—string skirt found on the body of a girl at Egtved (Fig. 6.9; Broholm and Hald 1935, 285–87 and figs. 70–71). The garment consists of a warp-faced band, the weft of which passes around a heavy cord at one selvedge and through the shed, then hangs out (or down) on the other side for a considerable distance to form the skirt, just the way the threads of an incipient warp for a warp-weighted loom would hang down from the starting band (see Chapter 3). These weft threads in the skirt go through the shed in groups of roughly half-a-dozen, giving the waistband (or rather, hipband— she wore it quite low) a strongly ribbed appearance. They are then twisted in pairs, and then in pairs again, to form heavy cords. The heavy cords in turn have been caught together in order again, almost at the bottom, by a twined spacing-cord, and the very ends rolled into little ornamental loops.

Historians in the 1920s and 1930s considered it scandalous that their ancestresses

6.9 String skirt from Egtved, Denmark, of wool woven at the waistband and knotted at the bottom; late 2nd millennium B.C. (Photo courtesy of National Museum, Copenhagen)

could have gone about in a costume that left so little to the imagination (Glob [1970] 1974, 63–64), but the find is not unique. Several little bronze statuettes are known from slightly later in the Scandinavian Bronze Age that show girls wearing such corded miniskirts (Fig. 11.3; Munksgaard 1974a, 77 fig. 50), and other, less well-preserved fragments of actual skirts have been found. The scraps from Hagendrup, for example, show a very narrow waistband in which the threads of the skirt fringe are secured by only three pairs of warp threads after they pass over the heavy cord at the top (Thomsen 1935, 192–94 and

fig. 22). The resemblance of these string skirts—especially if one imagines them before the final step of twining the strings at the bottom took place—to the prepared warp of a warp-weighted loom is striking. Also associated with the Hagendrup skirt were small tubes made by curling little rectangular sheets of copper around the twined strings, some still clinging to the strings and others having lost their purchase over the millennia (ibid.; Munksgaard 1974a, 76 fig. 49). Such tubes have been found in various other mound burials: for instance, in a neat row across the upper leg area in the oak coffin at Ølby (Glob [1970] 1974, 48, 44 fig. 15). I will discuss further aspects of the pan-European string skirts in Chapter 11.

Returning, meanwhile, to our Bronze Age Danish burials, we find three types of selvedges: the simple sort in which there is no change of weave but the warp threads are pressed closer together (e.g., at Muldbjerg, Trindhøj, Egtved, Borum Eshøj, and Skrydstrup: Broholm and Hald 1935, 242 fig. 30.5 and references throughout); another simple sort in which heavy bunches of thread lie where the two outermost warp would be expected (e.g., at Muldbjerg, Trindhøj, and Borum Eshøj; ibid., 222 fig. 5.1 and references throughout); and a selvedge in the form of a plain-weave tube (Fig. 6.10, left) a conceptually complex type akin to the elaborate, separately woven side borders we saw among the Swiss Neolithic fabrics, and a specific technique more common in the next millennium. Since the tubular selvedge occurs only once, on a piece of unknown use from Lille Dragshøj, one might think it had been imported from the south; and yet the cloth has the typically northern S-spun warp and Z-spun weft with a slightly higher warp than weft count (ibid., 248 and 249 fig. 37.2).

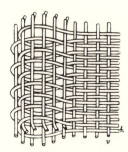
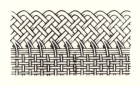

6.10 Diagrams of a tubular side-selvedge (left) and a plaited heading band (right), as found on Danish Bronze Age fabrics; late 2nd millennium B.C. (Broholm and Hald 1935, fig. 37.2–3; courtesy of National Museum, Copenhagen)

Again we are reminded of the great gaps that undoubtedly exist in our knowledge.

The real elaboration on these garments, however, takes place, as we have said, in the sewing. Not always in the seams: these are sometimes quite crude, as with the fat whipping stitches taken to sew up a huge rectangle into the Borum Eshøj woman's tubular skirt (ibid., 270–72). But the many layers of the thick, hemispherical caps found at Muldbjerg and Trindhøj have been sewn through with 15 or 16 neat rows of stitching (ibid., 218, 232–36), and the tunic from Muldbjerg was pieced together from 9 odd-shaped scraps, the edges of which were "carefully stitched together and overcast" with a buttonhole stitch (Glob [1970] 1974, 80; Broholm and Hald 1935, 222 fig. 5.4). The elegant cap from Muldbjerg, too, is edged with buttonhole stitch (Broholm and Hald 1935, 218, 221 fig. 4), as are the cut neck holes of the blouses on the women at Egtved and Borum Eshøj (ibid., 284, 273–74, and fig. 57).

But the high point in what we know of these people's needlework is seen on the woman's blouse from Skrydstrup (Fig. 6.11). The work on the neck hole began with a row of buttonhole stitches to overcast the edge; but then another row of buttonhole stitching was added using the first row as anchor, and so on for nearly a dozen rows out beyond the edge of the fabric—in effect, a netting technique, and one that we know was then being used all over the north for netting (Broholm and Hald 1939, 54–56 and figs. 38–39). Finally, a further triplet of threads was overcast into each row of buttonhole stitch in such a way that the 3 threads twined around each other as they went (ibid.). (Similar stitchwork, although not so many rows deep, occurs on the hemispherical cap from Trindhøj [Broholm and Hald 1935, 232–36 and fig. 20].) Large patches on each sleeve of the

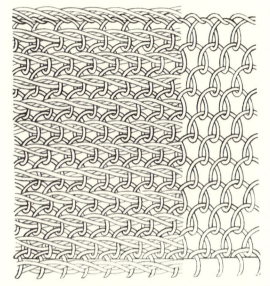

6.11   Diagram of netted "embroidery" built out from the edge of a woman's woolen blouse from Skrydstrup, Denmark; late 2nd millennium B.C. (Broholm and Hald 1939, fig. 39; courtesy of National Museum, Copenhagen)

blouse were also embroidered: three rows of the twining stitch just described were used to outline the areas, and the center filled in by row upon row of running loops (ibid., 53–54 and figs. 35–37)—a sort of variation on the buttonhole stitch requiring two stitches per loop rather than one.

At least one other textile art is represented in highly developed form among the Danish finds, and it too points away from the large looms: namely, sprang. So far at least two pieces have been found from the Early Bronze II period, both of them quite elaborate. One, from a man's grave at Skrydstrup, is a cap showing both interlinking and interlacing techniques (Hald 1950, 260 and fig. 259; see P. Collingwood 1974 for terms). The other, a woman's hairnet from Borum Eshøj (Fig. 3.36), has an intricate and lacy pattern composed from three different types of twists

or interlinks, finished off with a chained center (Hald 1950, 259–60 and fig. 253). It is a charmingly attractive piece even now. We have seen that the sprang technique, which is more closely akin to netting than to weaving, is attested in northern Europe already in the Neolithic, so the high degree of development should occasion no surprise.

All in all, one cannot escape the strong impression that these northerners possessed well-developed skills in various "thread crafts," which they were now transferring to a new medium, woven textiles. The elaborate piecing of small scraps into large garments suggests habitual work with skins that come in inconvenient shapes and sizes—whether or not we accept the interesting argument that the very pattern of the blouses is a carryover from the typical shape of a pelt (Hald 1950, 468–73; Nielsen 1971). Even the casual visitor to the National Museum in Copenhagen notices the resemblance to fur of the thousands of little threads sewn to the outside of the hemispherical caps from Muldbjerg and Trindhøj. As we have seen, too, the fancy embroidery seems to point to an origin in netting, as does the sprang. And the crudeness and lack of know-how demonstrated in many details of the weaving would seem to clinch the matter. On the other hand, the cleverness and tidiness shown in the weaving of belts suggests that perhaps band-weaving had been known for some time and that what was new was a form of loom that allowed the weaving of large cloths. Certainly some of them were now very large: the skirt on the woman from Borum Eshøj, which has three closed edges, was woven (a little unevenly) to a width of 110–30 cm selvedge to selvedge, and to a length of at least 341 cm (Broholm and Hald 1935, 270, 272)—over eleven feet; and the great capes are nearly as big.

GERMANY, HOLLAND, AND BRITAIN

Scattered examples of Bronze Age textiles have been found in Europe outside Denmark. Two of the earliest pieces, one from the Harz foothills and the other from farther to the northwest, near Hannover, show an interesting combination of wool with some sort of vegetable fiber, now destroyed. We have already described one plain-woven piece from the Early Bronze Age burial mound at Unterteutschenthal, which had well-preserved woolen threads running one direction and little but the impression left of the linen(?) threads running the other direction (Schlabow 1959, 118–19 and pl. 17; Schlabow 1976, 26 and figs. 1–3). The yarns were S-spun, and the rather kempy wool had been felted after weaving, whether by long use or by design (as Schlabow believes: 1959, 118). An accompanying piece of cloth is made entirely of wool of a better grade, S-spun and Z-plied in both warp and weft, and here the binding is a faced plain weave (Schlabow 1959, 119–20).

The scrap from Wiepenkathen, near Hannover, was found wrapped around the tang of a flint dagger as a cushion on which to seat the wooden handle of the dagger more firmly (Cassau 1935, 205). Although the dagger with its handle and its leather holster was found quite alone in a peat cutting (ibid., 199–200), it can be dated by the style of the blade to the transition between the Neolithic and Early Bronze Ages (J.G.D. Clark 1952, 234). The remains showed that the cloth had been in plain weave with wool running one way and vegetable fiber the other way; but only the Z-spun woolen threads, full of heavy kemp, had survived the acids of the peat bog (Cassau 1935, 205). Walter von Stokar, in his report to the chief investigator of the find, treats the wool as weft and the vanished vegetable fiber as warp (ibid.), but gives no indication of how he could decide which system was which.

Slightly later we have a few nondescript woolen scraps in plain weave from Schwarza, in South Thuringia (Schlabow 1958), and a more interesting pair of textiles from Roswinkel, in North Holland, that are notable for having been dyed red (Schlabow 1974, 208). Found in a bog with a bronze axe, a horn comb, a string of amber beads, and a strip of leather, the red cloths were dated by pollen analysis to the local Middle Bronze Age, 1300–1000 B.C. (Schlabow 1974, 193). One piece is a texture-striped, red woolen belt in the usual warp-faced plain weave. Its stripes were obtained by alternating three groups of 8 Z-spun threads with four groups of 6 threads that were both Z-spun and Z-plied, for a total of 48 warp threads (ibid., 207–8).[16] The other fabric is a portion of knotless netting of unknown use, but the trouble taken to dye the wool red suggests that it was an article of apparel. The yarn was S-spun and Z-plied (ibid., 208).

A number of Bronze Age textiles have been found in the British Isles. Audrey Hen-

---

[16] Note that $6 \times 4 = 24$ and $8 \times 3 = 24$. The number 24 and its divisors seem to be fraught with significance among the later, Germanic, inhabitants of the area (e.g., the 24 and 32 magic runes, in subdivided sets of 8); so I can't help wondering each time I see these numbers whether some of the magical superstitions had already been attached to them at this early date. It is not uncommon, among cultures of the world, that textiles when "properly" made are believed to take on magical and especially protective or prospering functions (see Chapters 13, 16). Many a European legend tells of magic girdles of one sort and another: how was the "magic" to be woven in? Putting magical symbols on it is one obvious way; but why not also by such means as number magic? (See Chapter 16 for some other ways.) Of course, as Freud is reported to have said, "Sometimes a cigar is only a cigar." I have no proof of this hunch—I merely offer the suggestion as something for those interested in the history and development of early Germanic number magic to keep an eye on.

shall lists 10 for the Early Bronze Age and 23 for the Late Bronze in her comprehensive catalog of all datable prehistoric British fabrics known as of 1950 (Henshall 1950, 158–59, q.v. for full bibliography). In the Early Bronze Age the weave, where known (7 of the 10 textiles), was always plain weave. In only two cases was the fiber identifiable, one being wool, the other some sort of vegetable fiber. Five of the pieces were from inhumations—two in hollow logs like the contemporary Danish burials—whereas the other five were found wrapped around dagger or axe blades. The blade wrappers as a group were of finer cloth than the body wrappers from the graves; on the other hand, the grave cloths tended to be quite large—one was estimated as at least 3 feet by 5 feet. The placement of fabric and other related remains in the graves was also highly reminiscent of the Danish finds: large cloaks covering (clothing?) the entire body, foot-wrappers, shoes, buttons, and even bits of string around a female skull, reminding one of the Danish women's hairnets (ibid., 131–33).

The similarities of British to continental textiles continue in the Late Bronze Age, but I will delay discussion of them until later. For we have now taken our survey of the north down to about 1000 B.C.; and the succeeding period, which constitutes the Late Bronze Age in northern Europe and the incipient Iron Age, or Hallstatt era, in central Europe, presents radical changes in what we know of the textile technology. We would do best to enter this new world by way of its largest remaining corpus of cloth.

CHAPTER 7

THE TEXTILE WEAVES
(4) THE IRON AGE

Early in the 1st millennium B.C., the textile artifacts begin to bear witness to a veritable explosion of textile techniques in Europe, apparently evolving quite independently of what was going on within the Near East or Egypt. The major—and earliest—group of remains that bear witness to this proliferation of techniques comes from the Hallstatt sites; so to them we will turn first.

HALLSTATT, NORTH, AND SOUTH

The Hallstatt culture at this time extended through much of Austria and Switzerland, and into eastern France, southern Germany, and Hungary. In the succeeding period, a further developed form, the La Tène culture, spread rapidly across Europe to Spain and Britain. Since we know from written records that the La Tène people were Celts, at least some of the Hallstatt folk were undoubtedly Celtic also. And it is indicative of the long-lasting nature of textile arts that the two most remarkable characteristics of the Hallstatt textiles are twill and plaid—both strongly associated by us today with the surviving Celts in Britain, in the form of Scottish tartans and tweeds (alias twills).

The cloths that we will be looking at come largely from two sites, the salt mines at Hallstatt and those at nearby Hallein (*hall-* is a word-stem for "salt"), high in the mountains above Salzburg ("salt city"). During the Late Bronze and Early Iron Ages, a group of apparently Indo-European miners, who must have come into the area looking for metal ores, dug shafts deep into the mountains to mine the vast salt deposits as rock salt. They lit their way with torches made of wooden splints, dropping all manner of burnt-up splint stubs, broken tools, and used-up rags in the mine shafts. Eventually they learned to flush out the salt as brine, as we do today, rather than laboriously breaking up the rock with picks and hauling it out of the mountain in backpacks. The old shafts gradually filled in, as the salt mass repeatedly recrystalized in local areas. As the modern tunnels are built, the workers occasionally come upon pockets of the ancient debris in the crystal mass, pockets that they call *Heidengebirge*, or "heathen rock." Over the last few centuries, more than a hundred pieces of ancient cloth have been salvaged this way (many more were discarded), dating loosely from before 1000 to perhaps as late as 400 B.C. Thus the textiles from the site of Hallstatt itself are sometimes rather older than the classic Hallstatt culture; yet they are all of the same type. So I shall treat them in a lump,

referring to them all as Hallstatt textiles—
not only those from Hallstatt and Hallein,
but also the few relics of the same type from
other sites of the Hallstatt culture.

Most of these cloths are *twills*. The simplest twill weave involves passing the weft alternately over two and under two warp (2/2
twill)—it was this pairing or "two-ing" that
gave the names *twill, twilling*, and likewise
tweed, tweedling, from the same root as *two,
twice*, and *twin*. But twill differs from half-
basket weave in that the pairing in each row
of weft is offset one warp thread from that in
the previous row, so that it forms a diagonal
instead of perpendicular rib (Fig. 7.1). Once
this diagonal patterning has been discovered, it is easy to go on and reverse the slope
of the diagonal at intervals to produce a zigzag: just change the direction of the offset.
This zigzag can be arranged either during the
setting-up of the warp (*pointed* twill) or when

the weft is inserted (*herringbone* twill). Once
both of those possibilities have been discovered, the next logical step is to zigzag both at
the same time to form perfect or imperfect
lozenges (*lozenge* or *diamond* twill and its
many variants).

Futhermore, all of these 2/2 patterns can
easily be mechanized, by the simple ruse of
dividing each half of the warp in half again,
and doubling the number of shedding mech-
anisms. On a two-beam loom such as we typically use nowadays, that means a total of
four heddle bars instead of two—hence the
alternative name for these patterns, *four-
shaft* (where plain weave would be called
two-shaft: cf. Danish *firskaft* and *toskaft* respectively). On a warp-weighted loom, because one set of threads rests on an immovable shed bar, only three heddle bars are
needed.

Mechanized patterning means a tremen-

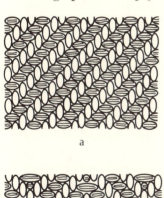
a

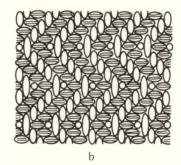
b

d

c

7.1   Some basic types of twill weave:
(a) 2/2 diagonal twill; (b) herringbone
twill; (c) pointed twill; (d) diamond
twill

7.2 Woolen twills from the salt mines at Hallstatt, Austria. No. 74 (right) is olive-green with brown plaid stripes. Early 1st millennium B.C. (Photo courtesy of Naturhistorisches Museum, Vienna)

dous economy in time and labor to achieve a fancy fabric. The Hallstatt weavers went crazy with this clever idea: of approximately 117 pieces of cloth that have been dated to the Hallstatt culture and also fully described,[1] some 75 (about two-thirds) are in twill weave. Of these, at least 10 are in a twill more complicated than plain diagonal (Fig. 7.2)—herringbone (5), pointed (4), and lozenge (1) twills. But many of the "pieces" are such small scraps, running 10, 5, or even 2 centimeters in one or both directions, that

we cannot exclude the possibility that the percentage of fancy twills ran far higher. Indeed, at least one fragment switches from basket weave to twill in mid-course (Hundt 1967, 46–47 no. 64), so it is possible that some or all of the other four specimens of basket weave did the same. However that may be, of the remaining third that today show no twill, more than half have been elaborated in some other way: we find basket weave, half-basket weave, and faced weaves (whether warp-faced or weft-faced we cannot

[1] I say approximately, because it appears that sometimes more than one scrap belongs to the same fabric. Where it seems reasonably certain that this is so, I have counted them as one. On the other hand, where an obviously different fabric has been sewn to a numbered

piece, I have counted them as two. The principal sources are: Hundt 1959; 1960; 1961; 1962; 1967; 1969; 1974; and Klose 1926. Hundt 1970 also provides a succinct overview.

say), characteristically twisted card-weaving, and two examples of float weaves ("brocades"). Of the 33 with nothing fancy in their binding system, we nonetheless find 6 woven with color stripes, 4 with shadow stripes (from alternating the spin or ply of the yarn), 2 with shadow plaids, and 2 with embroidery. That leaves only 19 (or 21 if we discount those with non-woven embellishments) for which we have no direct evidence of pattern—less than one-fifth.

Nor have we any reason to believe that the sample is unfairly skewed. In most other cultures, we find our textiles chiefly in upper-class burials, where we might expect to find only the best cloth. But most of these textiles come from the bottom of the salt mines, where they had been abandoned in shreds after every last bit of usefulness had been wrung out of them. They were by that time mere rags, torn and threadbare, wrapped, for example, around the haft of an axe to cushion the blows (see Fig. 7.4; Kyrle 1918,

57 n. 66; Klose 1926, 346). And some of the few recognizable remains of clothing—in twill, with ornamental stitching—have lice in them! (See e.g., Hundt 1960, 141 no. 34.) Where we have high-class grave goods, we find technique piled on technique in a dazzling display: the aristocratic lady of Grave 6 at Hohmichele was laid to rest in a fine woolen chemise (Fig. 7.3) woven in lightly ribbed half-basket with silk stripes, silk and wool embroidery, and a fancy tablet-woven border, while other parts of her apparel were in dyed and undyed twills (Hundt 1962, 204–9; Hundt 1969, 59–63).

The only "skewing" comes from the fact that almost everywhere else textiles are preserved by carbonization or oxidation, either of which totally destroys the color, whereas the textiles in the salt mines have been preserved through dryness (like those in Egypt), since the salt removes every bit of moisture and also kills the microorganisms that might eat organic material. So we are in a better

7.3   Reconstruction of designs on the bottom of a woman's garment, done in silk on wool; from Hallstatt tomb VI at Hohmichele, in southwest Germany; 6th century B.C. (Hundt 1969, color plate)

position to know about the use of color here than elsewhere. Colors included the white through beige to brown of the natural wools—those were the easiest to obtain, of course. But many of the woolen yarns were dyed copper-red, blue, or olive-green, while yellow, black, and other shades of red and green also occur. The white of bast fibers also served sometimes for contrast, as in one Z-spun linen piece embroidered in blue and copper-colored wools (no. 18: Hundt 1961, 19 and pl. 7.2–3).

Wool was in fact the main fiber used by the Hallstatt folk, but they by no means restricted themselves to it. Approximately six pieces of cloth are in some sort of bast fiber, probably flax (Hundt 1960, 129–30, nos. 26, 27; Hundt 1961, 18–19, nos. 15–19). Two of these are in twill weave (nos. 26, 27), proving that twill was not confined to wool; and a third was embroidered with blue and copper-red wools (no. 18), colors typical of the wool-on-wool embroideries. At least once, white bast thread was sewn onto dark wool cloth (Hundt 1960, 138–39, no. 33). And then we have the one example of silk, at Hohmichele, in which the silk was both woven into the garment and embroidered onto it. The embroidery on the wool and silk piece is done with overcast and stem stitches (Hundt 1969, 62 and 61 fig. 1), which together with simple running stitch are the most common forms of ornamental sewing in the Hallstatt repertoire.

We have mentioned the great variety of techniques within the non-twill fabrics, but these Hallstatt weavers also did not hesitate to stack up techniques on a single cloth. The Hohmichele chemise is certainly elaborate, with its ribbing, stripes, and embroidery, and is remarkable for its use of the luxury fiber, silk. But even the miserable rag

wrapped around the axe haft (Fig. 7.4) had green, brown, and yellow stripes along its edge and a warp-float design of changing checker patterns in green and brown on a yellow ground! Since the green and the brown yarns were respectively rather thinner and thicker than the yellowish ground yarn, there was considerable play of texture patterns as well. Twills were often combined with shadow stripes (9 examples), color stripes (1), shadow plaids (5), and color plaids (9). Moreover, the weavers seem to have had a particular love for combining plaids or stripes with zigzags: every example of pointed twill and every example but one of herringbone shows this feature, where the exception is such a narrow fragment—only 2.5 cm wide (Hundt 1960, 130–32, no. 29)—that it doesn't mean much. The breakdown into types is interesting:

2 in herringbone with color plaid that is *not* in phase with the twill (no. 30, 65);

2 in pointed twill with color plaid that is *not* in phase with the twill (no. 56, 74);

1 in herringbone with color stripe in weft that is *not* in phase with the twill (no. 30 patch);

1 in herringbone with shadow stripe in weft that *is* in phase with the twill (no. 13);

1 in pointed twill with shadow stripe in warp that *is* in phase with the twill (no. 50);

1 in pointed twill with shadow plaid, warp of which *is* in phase with the twill (no. 69).[2]

Apparently, although the sample is small, color designs were conceived as functioning independently of the weave, whereas designs formed by changing the spin of the yarn were conceived as integrally related to the twill.

This difference seems random at first glance, but it may be hiding an important clue to the development of twill. In describing a plain-weave patch sewn onto a piece of

---

[2] No. 13: Hundt 1959, 76–77 and pl. 19. No. 30 and patch: Hundt 1960, 132–33 and pl. 18–19. Nos. 50, 56, 65, 69, 74: Hundt 1967, 40–52 and respectively pl. 7, 12, 21.1, 24.1, and 26.

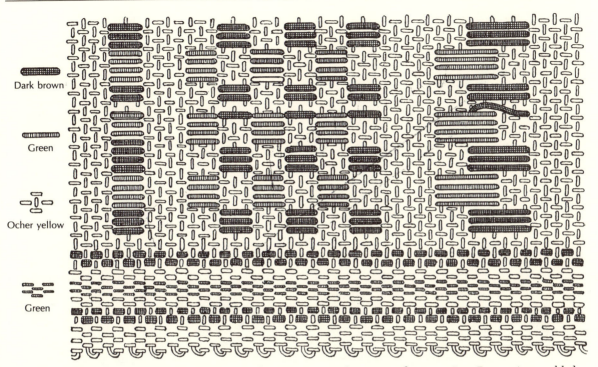

Dark brown

Green

Ocher yellow

Green

7.4   Scrap of polychrome woolen cloth with stripes and float-weave designs, used to seat a Late Bronze Age axe blade, found in the salt-works at Hallein, Austria; ca. 1000 B.C. Warp runs horizontally. (After Klose 1926, 347 fig. 1)

twill, Hundt makes the interesting observation that the alternation in groups of 8 between S-spin and Z-spin in a hard, shiny yarn gives the *impression* of herringbone twill (Hundt 1967, 47–48, no. 64). And shadow stripes, as we have seen, were already in use in the previous millennium in Scandinavia, in a textile industry probably learned from the south. It is possible that the familiarity with diagonal and zigzag effects from shadow striping fed directly into the elaboration of the diagonals and zigzags of twill, once the technique of twill had been learned.

Although borders apparently did not take up quite the time and attention accorded them in Neolithic Switzerland, yet like those early examples (and unlike, for instance, Egyptian borders) they are frequently formed with a different weave from the main cloth—usually a ribbed half-basket weave, sometimes a double-woven tubular side-selvedge (e.g., Hundt 1960, 134–35 and fig. 4, no. 31; and Hundt 1967, 47, no. 64 patch), and sometimes a "corded" card-woven border (Hundt 1969, 59; and see Chapter 3). (Bands, unlike large pieces, seem invariably to have simple side-selvedges; and simple selvedges, where found, are generally on pieces that were demonstrably woven as bands—although the fragmentary state of the evidence prevents us from proving every case.) In some instances the cloth was given a fancy border after weaving, with a tablet-woven band sewn onto a hemmed edge (Hundt 1960, 145, no. 43; Hundt 1962, 201 and pl. 28; both diagonal twills). This tendency to "frame" a large cloth with distinguishable borders is a trait, interestingly enough, that we find in Central Europe not only in the preceding Neolithic Swiss fabrics but also in the succeeding La Tène and later periods of the Iron Age (see Chapter 3), the most famous example being the great Thorsberg mantle so lavishly reconstructed by Karl Schlabow (1965), but well backed up by the garments from Hunteburg, Vehnemoor, Vaalermoor, etc. (Schlabow 1976). The predilection for borders almost certainly is related to the use of the warp-weighted loom, which requires a special border at the start and makes elaborate strengthening of the side edges easy.

One can deduce a good deal more about the Hallstatt textiles, however, than just these surface descriptions and statistics. In particular one can learn much about both the textiles and the weaving practices by attempting to reproduce some of the extant pieces (with or without a warp-weighted loom). It soon became apparent to me, for example, when I was weaving a replica of no. 74 (Hundt 1967, 52), that one could indeed tell which was the warp and which the weft, even though no selvedge has survived—and that I had them backwards. (Hundt identifies them the same way I eventually did, without saying how he reached his conclusions.) Weaving 7 narrow stripes of 4 threads each was a nuisance for all the juggling of bobbins; and warping stripes that never had the same number of threads as each other was also a tremendous bother. It eventually occurred to me that, given the way the warp is typically made for a warp-weighted loom, by pulling a loop of thread—i.e., two future warp threads at once—through the header (see Chapter 3), little warp stripes of 4 threads would be the easiest and most convenient possible: you pulled two loops through the header, which gave one thread for each of the four warp divisions. Easy for

the warper, and virtually foolproof for the weaver. Furthermore, the restlessly uneven thread counts in the other direction (19, 20, 18) suddenly became perfectly clear: the weaver was not counting, but judging the width of the bands by eye alone.

When did all the far-reaching innovations in fancy weaving—twills, plaids, etc.—begin? The evidence is difficult to assess because the fabrics from Hallstatt and Hallein, although beautifully preserved by the salt, generally occur in virtually undatable contexts. The fact that one particularly complicated piece (the one with a float design on plain-woven color plaid: Fig. 7.4) found its last use as a rag cushioning a local Late Bronze Age axe haft suggests that plaids were already in the repertoire and that the preference for fancy cloth was alive and thriving at the beginning of the 1st millennium.

Moreover, a large cloak of checkered twill (Fig. 7.5) found far to the north, at Gerumsberg in southwestern Sweden, has been ascribed to an equally early date. Unfortunately this mantle—clearly identifiable as such by the folds worn into it—had apparently been laid into a cutting in the peat all by itself, so that no datable artifacts lay with it (Post, Walterstorff, and Lindqvist 1925, 46). But an analysis of the peat itself, and a comparison with the peat surrounding a datable ring found in another nearby bog, seemed to show that the mantle had been put into the moor significantly before the ring; and the ring was stylistically datable to the beginning of the Scandinavian Late Bronze Age (Late Bronze IV: ibid., 58, 68), that is, the first centuries of the 1st millennium B.C. That the mantle was no earlier than the Bronze Age was determined in the minds of the investigators because it was scarred by a number of slits (in pairs corresponding to the way in which the mantle had been worn doubled), which they felt had to

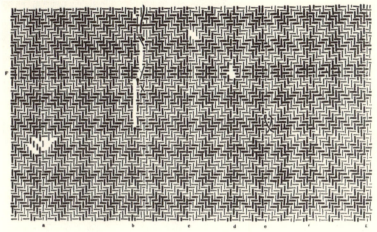

7.5 Twill pattern of the woolen mantle from Gerumsberg, Sweden. Note the row of offset lozenges ("goose-eye twill") toward the top. Late 2nd millennium B.C.? (Post et al. 1925, 28 fig. 6; courtesy of the Royal Academy of Letters, History, and Antiquities, Stockholm)

have been made by a sharp metal instrument such as a dagger (one might wonder about the fate of the owner!—ibid., 35 fig. 15, 37 figs. 17d, 63–5), and hence within the metal age (ibid., 68). Its date was thus bracketed by circumstance between about 1800 and 1000 B.C., and presumably it fell near the end of this period.

Now, that would not be particularly surprising in terms of textile history, were it not for two details. First, the mantle is not in simple diagonal twill, but in pointed twill with 8 scattered rows of goose-eye (ibid., 60). That is, it is already well along in the development of twill, not at its beginning. Second, the cloak is full of the same sorts of jury-rigged "weaving wedges" that we saw in the Early Bronze Danish mantles and skirts, which seemed to stem from a lack of skill in controlling the warp tension on the large looms required for such enormous textiles (ibid., 61–62 and pl. 2). The bulk of Scandinavian Bronze Age fabrics, as we have seen, are in plain weave, embellished chiefly by shadow stripes and by sewing (although occasional pieces have modest color striping). The only other piece of twill yet known from Bronze Age Scandinavia, a scrap of diagonal

twill combined with shadow plaid, comes from a Late Bronze VI find at Haastrup, in Denmark (Munksgaard 1974a, 37 fig. 17; Munksgaard 1974b)—several centuries later and roughly contemporary with the height of the Hallstatt culture.

Thus the presence of twill at all in the Gerumsberg mantle, let alone its complexity, should make us stop and think. What is such a piece doing so far north at so early a date? The coupling of the twill with not just stripes but plaid, and the idiosyncrasy of the changes in the slope of the twill at seemingly random intervals, all point toward the Hallstatt area. On the other hand, the crudeness of the weaving, in sharp contrast with the long tradition of care and skill in weaving that we have seen in Central European cloth, suggests a northern manufacture. Furthermore, the changes of slope, although not at even intervals (see Fig. 7.5), do occur in some sort of coordination with the color stripes, landing alternately on the first thread of a light stripe and the third thread of a dark stripe. In the Hallstatt fabrics that we have, by contrast, the pattern of colors uniformly fails to correspond to the pattern in the weave. Might this be the sort of difference introduced by a craftsman copying models from another tradition without knowing the "lore" of how to make them?

There are several conceivable solutions. It may be that the Gerumsberg mantle has been misdated; if it is in fact considerably later, then there is no difficulty with Hallstatt twills as models. Or perhaps we have been too conservative in our dating of the salt-mine fabrics: perhaps some of them are older by a few centuries than we have estimated. In that case, whoever invented twill had done so a very great deal earlier, for such complexities to have developed. It may be, however, that the source of the Gerumsberg weaving technology came not from Hallstatt but from the Caucasus (via who knows what intermediaries), where we have found both narrow plaids of this sort and twills back in the 3rd millennium. That raises the question of what relationship Hallstatt itself might have had to the Caucasus; and that we cannot answer within the scope of this book. We have given all the available textile evidence.

Italy

"Bordered cloths [*praetextae*]," says Pliny, "find their origin among the Etruscans" (*Nat. Hist.* 8.74.195). And so they may have, from the point of view of the Romans. But we have seen that fancy borders on textiles were a favored feature among the Hallstatt and La Tène weavers, and all the way back to the Neolithic pile-dwellers in Switzerland. In fact, just as in the Bronze Age, so too in the Iron Age northern Italy shared many of its textile traits with Central Europe. Very few actual pieces of cloth have come down to us: Italy is as unfavorable a place for their preservation as Greece. But we have enough that, together with the Etruscan representations of their own costumes, we can see where Etruria fits in.

A Late Villanovan tomb at Sasso di Furbara produced scraps of cloth showing a pile made by cutting loops formed in the weft, and other fragments of a 2/2 pointed or herringbone twill with shadow stripes in phase with the zigzags of the twill (Masurel 1984b, 53–54). This peculiar combination, which, as Masurel says, prevents the eye from favoring one half of the pattern over the other, is a trick that we have encountered several times already among the twills from the salt mines (see above). One might well ask whether the inhabitants of Italy had imported this second cloth from the other side of the Alps. But the statues and other local artistic representations show such a wealth of plaids, diagonals, chevrons, diamonds, and fancy borders (see Bonfante 1975) that we must discard that theory from sheer numbers. Surely the Etruscans didn't clothe their whole population in imported Hallstatt cloth. The much simpler hypothesis is that they made it themselves, by the same techniques as the Hallstatt weavers.

Linens, too, have been found: a rather coarse swatch used to line the inside of a bronze shoulder-piece, from the Warrior's Tomb at Tarquinia (8th–7th century B.C.), and the pseudomorph of much finer cloth, possibly from a woman's dress, on a bronze bowl from Veii (6th–5th century B.C.; D. L. Carroll 1973). The latter had been woven into a strongly faced fabric from single Z-spun yarns (ibid.). Whether the famous Zagreb mummy-wrapping, which bears the longest Etruscan inscription we have, was made of Egyptian or European linen does not seem to be known—although it could probably be determined.

Fancier objects existed, too. Remains of cloth "of purple linen, mixed with bits of gold," were found clinging to the shoulder of an early Etruscan funeral urn in a chamber tomb at Poggio della Sala—but when a textile researcher went to try to determine just how the gold had been attached, she was unable because "the flood of 1965 in Florence [had] reduced them all to an unrecognizable mass" (Bonfante 1975, 11, 106 n. 3).

Still more amazing, however, is a complete funeral outfit that turned up recently in a tomb at Decima, near Rome. A remarkably wealthy lady had been laid to rest wearing a gold hairnet, clothes of unknown structure pinned with bronze fibulae (themselves decorated with gold, silver, and amber), and a skirt or shawl, stretching from her waist to her feet, made from silver and decorated with amber ornaments and faience beads ranging from blue to white (Bedini 1976, 288; Bonfante 1985, 325). Unfortunately the organic fibers of the basic cloths seem to have been destroyed by time, and even the silver was largely pulverized; so we have no details on technique. All we can salvage is an awareness of the spectacular nature of the decoration sometimes lavished on cloth and clothing by the Etruscans.

Britain

To the Hallstatt tradition of weaving we can now add the Late Bronze Age pieces from Britain, which despite the label of "Bronze" cultural stage are contemporary with the early part of the Iron Age in southern Europe. Some of their techniques are closely associated with weaving developments during this period in that area.

Where determinable, the pieces from Britain are most often plain weave, and of wool. Two of these, which come from a habitation site at Island MacHugh, in County Tyrone in northern Ireland, are said to give the appearance of "repp" or ribbing (O. Davies 1950, 36), an effect often produced either by pulling half the warp tighter than the other half or by packing the weft tightly into

a weft-faced weave. But a third sample from the same site proved to be woven in 2/1 twill, the earliest known example of that weave from the islands (Henshall 1950, 137; Davies 1950, 36).

Not far away at Armoy, in County Antrim, local peat-cutters in 1904 cut into a cache of objects wrapped in a large woolen cloth with an ornate horsehair sash laid over the bundle (Coffey 1907, 119). The large cloth had been sewn together out of two plain-woven pieces, each about 18 inches wide; and one of these still has three original closed edges (ibid., 121–22 and fig. 1; Henshall 1950, 144)—which therefore must represent two side-selvedges plus a starting band of the sort required on a warp-weighted loom. Apparently all three edges are done in half-basket weave (Coffey 1907, 122 fig. 2), thereby matching the tradition of edge-making that we have traced in Neolithic and Bronze Age Switzerland, Germany, and Denmark.

The other textile is long and narrow, woven in displaced herringbone twill from naturally black horsehair, and elaborately fringed at both ends (Fig. 7.6; ibid., 122–24; Henshall 1950, 138). The fringe is described by Coffey (1907, 123–24) as "formed of bunches of horsehair, closely wound round for a short distance, then separated into lesser bunches also wound, which are again separated into branches, wound as before, . . . and terminating in neatly made pellets." (For more of the technical details, see Henshall 1950, 138.) The little "pellets" on the ends, together with the chevron pattern in the weaving and an intervening horizontal band, make the Armoy belt seem very similar in its visual impression to the rather earlier sash from Borum Eshøj. The objects found with the belt and cloth restrict the dating of the cache to between 750 and 600 B.C. (Henshall 1950, 134–35).

1

2

3

7.6 Remains of a black horsehair sash, done in twill with elaborate fringes, from a bog at Armoy, County Antrim, in northern Ireland. Late Bronze Age; early 1st millennium B.C. (Coffey 1907, pl. 12)

GREECE, ANATOLIA, AND THE STEPPES

For our final group of textiles, we shall look at the remains of what was being produced in Greece, Anatolia, and the steppelands at the same time that the Hallstatt cloths were being made. As it happens, this rather unlikely-sounding combination will allow us to pick up nearly everything else currently available that would shed direct light on the beginning of the Classical era; and, as we shall see, the influences range so far and so freely that it is hard to treat the textiles of one area separately from those of another. I shall therefore proceed roughly chronologically within the whole territory at once.

Almost nothing has survived in this area from the period immediately after the upheavals of 1200 B.C. that ended the Bronze Age and started the Iron Age. The earliest cloth remains that I know of are several recent finds made at Lefkandi, on the island of Euboia, where small scraps of cloth adhering to metal were found in various graves dating to roughly 1000 B.C. They were all in plain weave, some balanced and some so heavily faced that they have the appearance of ribbing (Popham, Sackett, and Themelis 1979–80, 227–29 and pl. 237.a–b). A much fancier tomb, however, which appeared to be the center of a hero cult, yielded the earliest find to date in Greece of relatively complete clothing. Carefully folded up into a bronze amphora was a tunic or "robe of ankle length, made of two sheets of linen sewn up the sides. The borders and bottom half are plain, but the upper part is of a shaggy weave" (Popham, Touloupa, and Sackett 1982, 173 and pl. 25), produced apparently by weft-looping. Completing the outfit were decorated woven bands (ibid.), one done with supplementary warp floats, in a pattern of zigzags that become chevrons and diamonds, and another bit decorated with embroidered meander hooks.[3] We see from these few pieces that ornamental cloth had not died out.

Some three centuries later, the Phrygians living in their capital at Gordion, in west-central Anatolia, built a tomb for one of their kings that was so immense that many of the textiles and other perishable objects heaped

within it survived to modern times. The dead king was apparently lowered into the partially built tomb on an open bier covered with layers of blankets, along with many gifts of carved wooden furniture and bronze implements, after which the roof was built over the chamber and covered with a thick layer of stones, and the entire structure buried beneath what may be the largest grave mound ever raised. Two other tumuli proved to contain textile remains, as did buildings in the city itself, which was burned by the Kimmerians in a violent attack about 690 B.C. In addition to blankets, there were wall hangings, bags, clothing, pads, and tapes for tying up bundles and for edging garments.

There were plain-weave cloths of linen, wool, and possibly hemp and mohair—some large and sturdy, others woven as narrow bands (Bellinger 1962, 13–15). Some of the fabrics have heading bands in half-basket weave, of the type we associate with the warp-weighted loom (ibid., 13–14; Ellis 1981, 298–300 and pl. 99.B–C). Selvedges, where preserved, were plain; and some edges had been folded or rolled in various ways, and hemmed with either straight or overcast stitches (Ellis 1981, 297–98).

Heavy coverlets of wool were apparently formed by felting over a loosely woven base, where the warps of the base cloth were spun the opposite direction from the weft (Bellinger 1962, 13) as in the Bronze Age Danish woolens. In other cases the felters seem not even to have bothered to weave the threads first, but simply laid them on top of each other crossways (Ellis 1981, 297).

Many of the textiles are quite fancy, as one might expect for royalty. Simple colored stripes were not uncommon, and may have

---

[3] My thanks to Evi Touloupa for allowing me to inspect this find in the laboratory of the National Museum; and my thanks to Peter Kalligas for permission to publish this description. For excavation photos in color, see Papagianni 1981.

There are other remains of textiles from Greece; they

simply show no patterning. Possibly the largest piece is a 5th-century linen cloth from Eleusis, 2.2 by .5 m (Mylonas 1953, 81 and fig. 9). One of the finest is a linen cloth from a copper vessel in a Late Geometric grave at Eretria, showing a count of 18 by 22 threads per cm (Bloesch and Mühletaler 1967, 130).

been crossed sometimes to form checks (ibid., 302, 304); looped material was made by looping the weft after every warp thread at 10-row intervals (Bellinger 1962, 15); and some bits from the city mound show examples of soumak, or weft-wrapping (Ellis 1981, 296). Tantalizing fragments done in slit tapestry were also found in the city (Bellinger 1962, 14–15; Ellis 1981, 305, 310).

7.7 *Left*: lozenge and warp-stripe patterns; *right*: meander pattern; from among numerous textile scraps from Gordion, Turkey, a Phrygian city destroyed about 690 B.C. (Ellis 1981, pl. 101 C–D; courtesy of the University Museum, University of Pennsylvania)

Perhaps the most interesting textiles from Gordion, however, are the narrow warp-faced bands woven in handsome patterns with *complementary warps* of purplish-red wool and yellowish-white vegetable fiber (Fig. 7.7; Ellis 1981, 305–8 and pl. 101.A–E). Here the pattern is formed by letting the unwanted color of warp float on one side of the fabric while the other color is used on the other face to form the pattern and bind the weft. (Some of the bands from Egypt in the 18th to 20th Dynasties were constructed along similar lines, although entirely in linen: see Chapter 5.) The preserved patterns include quadruple lozenges, meanders, and double barred stripes—that is, a double strip running parallel to the warp, each strip having bars of alternating colors. One of the most interesting constructional details that Richard Ellis noticed is that there exists what is clearly a mistake at one spot in the lozenge pattern (Fig. 7.8), and the mistake is repeated as the pattern is repeated down the warp—a circumstance that suggests strongly that "the pattern threads were controlled by individual groups of string heddles for each part of the pattern" (Ellis 1981, 301, 305).

The Phrygians were famed in antiquity for their embroidery, but of this we possess not a shred. Pliny even ascribed the invention of embroidery to them (*Nat. Hist.* 8.74.196), a statement that we now know to be untrue, although it may well record the source from which the Greco-Roman world learned some important or evolved form of the art.

The Lydians, too, on the west coast of Anatolia, were famous in Classical times for their textiles, especially polychrome carpets (see Greenewalt and Majewski 1980, 134–38 for a full discussion). From that region also came the famous tale of Arachne, who suffered the fate of being turned into a spider doomed to weave eternally, because she had the audacity to boast that she could weave fancier cloths than even the goddess of weaving,

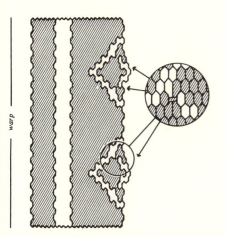

warp

7.8   Analysis of the lozenge pattern shown in Fig. 7.7. *Left*: diagram of the repeated error in the complementary-warp design, which suggests that pattern heddles were being used. *Right*: probable completion of pattern. (Ellis 1981, fig. 147; courtesy of the University Museum, University of Pennsylvania)

Athena (see Fig. 3.24). But still less has been recovered here than in Phrygia, namely a few tiny if remarkably informative fragments from a plundered burial in tumulus B 63.2, datable to "anywhere from the seventh to the beginning of the fifth century B.C." (ibid., 138). On the outer faces of two iron plates used to reinforce the upper corners of the coffin were found the remains of several layers of cloth, evidently once laid over the coffin, that included: (1) a piece of "fuzzy" (woolen?) weft-faced cloth in plain weave with a portion of selvedge; (2) "evidence of embroidery" as well as of "threads indicating sewing of parts together"; (3) some fringe, apparently of warp and possibly knotted; and (4) a tiny section of a "quite complicated" patterned float weave, where "some threads float over as many as seven" threads of the opposite system (ibid., 139–40 and figs. 8–10).

None of these scraps seems heavy enough to have been from the famed rugs; but in his delightful study of secondary evidence for Lydian textiles, Greenewalt points out the similarity between a typically Lydian form of rosette and the rosettes on a pile carpet of the same era found at Pazyryk, far away in the Altai Mountains (ibid., 133–34 and figs. 1, 3). These Pazyryk cloths, although so very

distant from everything else we have looked at, are so spectacular and so informative that we must take a brief look at them.

Pazyryk

High in the alpine valleys of the Altai, not far north of the point where the modern countries of Mongolia, China, and the Soviet Union meet, Russian archaeologists found and excavated a group of half-a-dozen large and several smaller kurgans. Built by mounted herdsmen over a period of about 50 years in the late 5th and/or early 4th century B.C., these kurgans were robbed in antiquity—but not, to our good fortune, completely.

We have seen large groups of textiles preserved by dry desert heat, by waterlogging, and by salt, but this group at Pazyryk was preserved by freezing. When the robbers dug into the tombs from the top, they discovered that the contents were already partially solidified in frozen groundwater, especially in the second mound. They took what they could wrestle and chop loose, especially of the gold, but left behind quantities of textiles, leatherwork, and other perishable objects, many of which were buried outside the chamber walls, amid the bodies of the riding horses interred with their owners. As the seasons came and went, more water poured in through the holes left by the robbers, gradually filling up each tomb and the area around it with layered ice. When the archaeologists came, they found that pick and shovel were of no use. The ice was hard as rock, and very thick; and they wanted to remove the remaining objects intact. In the end they excavated the tomb chambers with buckets of hot water, slogging about in the mud at the bottoms of the pits. But the results were worth the trouble.

The majority of the cloth objects were not woven at all, but made of brightly colored fiber-felt: coats, headgear, stockings, saddle blankets, saddle covers, floor covers, and great pictorial wall hangings (see Chapter 9). The woven objects, too, impress one immediately with their colorfulness. Among the simplest are the white shirts, of plain-weave hempen cloth, sewn together with thread of twisted sinew and then decorated over the seam lines and around the openings with stitching and applied braid, both done in red wool (Rudenko 1970,[4] 83–85, 199–200, 202 and pl. 63, 67).

Stitching, as a matter of fact, figures very heavily in the Pazyryk finds, for the most common forms of ornamentation were felt and leather cutouts, in contrasting colors, stitched over objects of cloth, felt, leather, fur, etc. Beads and even pyrite crystals were applied as well, in elaborate patterns (ibid., 95, 96–97 figs. 38–39, and pl. 64), in addition to numerous metal platelets and gold-covered wooden buttons, much like those we have already seen in the Mycenaean Shaft Graves. I can find no evidence that anything other than a plain running stitch was ever used (except on the Chinese piece described below); but in a number of cases the stitches were employed for embroidering simple figures (rosettes, and twill-like chevrons and lozenges), while some of the belts were trimmed along the edge with rows of stitches done in sinew thread wrapped with fine strips of tinfoil (ibid., 98–99 and pl. 67A, F)—our first example of metallic embroidery.

Plain-woven woolen cloth occurred also, both balanced and faced, but generally dyed bright red; and woolen 2/2 twill was common, also usually red but at least once dyed green, and at least once densely packed into a completely weft-faced cloth (ibid., 203–4). In two of the kurgans were found pieces of brown woolen cloth woven with rows of weft-looping between multiple rows of plain weave (just as we saw it in Egypt). The long loops had been left as such in some examples, but cut open in others to form a shaggy pile (ibid., 204 and pl. 134C).

The most spectacular piece of pile, however, is the great woolen carpet with Lydian-style rosettes (Fig. 7.9; ibid., 64, 298–304

---

[4] Rudenko's monumental book on the Pazyryk kurgans originally came out in 1953, in Russian. The English translation, which appeared in 1970, includes subsequent revisions made by the author himself, plus helpful additional notes, catalog, and index provided by the translator. The English edition is thus both easier to use and more up-to-date. On the other hand, while some of the plates are clearer in the English edition, I find others to be clearer, and the colors a little truer, in the Russian. But for efficiency of printing the translator also regrouped and renumbered the many plates and diagrams, so it is not easy to move from one version to the other. I have finally chosen to make my references exclusively to the English edition, but recommend to the serious student of these finds that leafing through the Russian edition is still worthwhile.

The technical descriptions of textiles are sometimes very hard to follow in both languages. I have done my best to interpret the descriptions of certain pieces from having seen them on a visit to the Hermitage in 1979 (before I expected to be discussing these particular cloths in detail in my book). I wish to thank the curator of the Altaic textiles, Lidia Barkova, for her extreme helpfulness in showing me as many of these treasures as possible, and for her patience in explaining things to me in Russian.

7.9   Knotted pile rug from the frozen Kurgan 5 at Pazyryk, in the Altai mountains; mid-1st millennium B.C. (Rudenko 1953, pl. CXV [1970, pl. 174])

and pl. 174–76). Done predominantly in a dark rust-red, with concentric, rectangular friezes of figures around a grid of rosettes, the rug gives a modern visitor to the Hermitage Museum the eerie feeling that nothing has changed in 2500 years, so well does it match the impression of the Persian rugs to be found all about us today. Nor is this rug substantially different in construction. Three

or so rows of plain weave alternate with a row of knotted woolen yarn that hangs out to form the pile, the knots having been tied in at a density of 3600 per square decimeter. The knot used is the *symmetrical knot* (also called the Turkish or Ghiördes knot), which twines fully around each of two adjacent warp threads (Fig. 7.10a). Lest it be thought, however, that this knot is therefore the ear-

7.10 Diagram of the principal knots used in pile carpets: (a) symmetrical, Turkish, or Ghiördes knot; (b) asymmetrical, Persian, or Sehna knot (can open in either direction)

liest, Rudenko adds that fragments of another pile carpet were found in a 6th century B.C. kurgan at nearby Bash-Adar, knotted in *asymmetrical knots* (which go all the way around one warp and halfway around the other; also called Persian or Sehna knots: Fig. 7.10b) at a density of 7000 knots per square decimeter.[5] The pile in the Pazyryk carpet, which showed signs of considerable wear, had been sheared until it was a mere 2 mm thick. Rudenko cites a number of parallels with Achaemenid Persian art in the details of the deer, horses and their riders, griffins, and other motifs that appear on the carpet, finally concluding that the rug must have been made by Iranians of some sort—whether Persian, Parthian, or Median—in the 5th century B.C. He does not appear to have searched farther west than Assyria; but regardless of the conclusion one comes to as to who made this carpet, it is clear that both textile motifs and actual rugs were travelling thousands of miles.

Another of the Pazyryk textiles also points

to Iran. This is a *shabrak*—an ornamental horsecloth that hangs down from under the saddle—that was found on one of the horses buried in Kurgan 5 (Color Plate 4, left; ibid., 168, 205–6, 296–98 and pl. 177). Over the usual felt base had been sewn a cover made of cut-up pieces of woolen, weft-faced, tapestry-woven cloth, apparently in dovetail technique. The predominant color in each of the three designs (which probably came from the same original cloth) is cherry-red, with details in white, tan, and blue-black. The most distinctive composition is a repeated square motif showing pairs of women with toothed crowns and long veils approaching a censer on a tall altar. Again Rudenko draws numerous parallels with Neo-Assyrian and Persian art, as he does for the precise form of the lions that parade along another section of the tapestry.

In Kurgan 2, strips of woolen cloth done in slit tapestry were sewn to either side of the standard red twill (Color Plate 4, right; Rudenko 1970, 204–5 and pl. 157 A–B; Rudenko 1968, 70 fig. 57). The polychrome design consists of hundreds of small spiral hooks in offset rows, with the five colors and the direction of the hooks arranged to lead the eye in a zigzag or herringbone pattern. We have no exact parallel for this motif, but clearly it is also utterly at home in the textile medium. Unfortunately we have almost no textiles from anywhere else during this era to compare it with. Spiral hooks, of course, are

[5] This works out to about 234 knots per square inch. A coarse modern hand-tied carpet might have 50 to 100 knots per square inch, a very fine silk carpet maybe as many as 800. (Many pile carpets, of course, are now woven without knots on a machine. They have no knots because no one has ever figured out how to make a machine tie the knots efficiently.) Note that the asymmetrical knot is a little more compact than the symmetrical knot (Fig. 7.10), so finer counts are easier to obtain.

A scrap of another pile fabric was found in the 7th–6th century B.C. level at Karmir-Blur in Armenia, along with a garment with a small amount of tapestry decora-

tion done in wool and bast on a wool warp (Verkhovskaja 1955). Unfortunately, we are given no information as to how the woolen pile was introduced. Similarly, the charred remains of both pile and weft-faced textiles in some sort of animal fiber were recovered farther south at Hasanlu, from the late 9th century B.C. (Dyson 1964, 21). The pile in one case was looped, and "sometimes . . . as much as three centimeters long" (ibid.); so it is apparently not of the sort we are discussing. Another textile in this group was red, and still others were of bast (ibid., 21–22).

a longtime favorite of the Aegean world, but by this time the motif had spread around Anatolia and Syria. We have also seen that slit tapestry seems to have entered Egypt in the early to mid-2nd millennium from Syria; but by this time it had surely spread elsewhere. From his eastern perspective, too, Rudenko associates slit tapestry with the west, specifically Asia Minor: from our data, that seems quite reasonable, though not certain. And there is one last clue. Although the kurgan robbers seem generally to have ignored the textiles—they probably stank—in this case, Rudenko says (1970, 204), "the cloth evidently caught the attention of the looters, who left the red cloth but carefully tore off the polychrome, of which only relatively small tatters remained." That is, this particular cloth was remarkable to them, and hence almost certainly an import from far away. (It must be remembered that almost all the other imported cloths discussed here were found on the bodies of the horses buried in the fill outside the tomb chambers, and thus were never seen by the robbers.) The best we can suggest is that the textile came from far to the west, from Syria or Anatolia or some other area around the Black Sea.

The last group of Pazyryk cloths that concern us here, however, came from nearly as far in the opposite direction: silks from China (ibid., 174, 206, 305–6, 175–78 figs. 89–92, and pl. 134A–B, 178). There are three of them. One, from Kurgan 3, is a simple pouch in plain weave. The second, from the same mound, is a small swatch of double-faced 3/1 twill with a complex geometric pattern. According to Rudenko, one face was formed with a grey weft, the other with a green weft; and each color of weft was bound into the shed at every fourth warp (a base weave that must have given a rather satiny look) in such a way that the second color did not normally show on a given face. The pattern was then formed by bringing each color to the opposite face—patterning with complementary weft.

The third silk, which served as the ornamental cover of a *shabrak* from Kurgan 5, is in plain weave again, but elaborately decorated with chain-stitch embroidery of pheasants or phoenixes amid typically Chinese shrubbery. Clearly the piece was both woven and embroidered in China for Chinese clientele—possibly "for a princess at the time of her marriage," as Rudenko would like to think because of the symbolic motif (ibid., 305–6)—and it was made to serve as the cover for a native Altaic felt *shabrak* only rather later. With or without a princess attached, again the textiles had to have travelled thousands of miles.

Western Silks

Indeed, textiles sometimes travelled even farther; for it will be remembered that we have already encountered Chinese silk woven and embroidered into the chemise of the Late Hallstatt noblewoman at Hohmichele in southwestern Germany, from the 6th century B.C. (see Fig. 7.3). Let us look at that find again. The chemise is woven in a weft-faced half-basket weave that takes the warp threads in pairs out of a tablet-woven starting border (Hundt 1969, 61 fig. 1). Parallel to this starting band, the weaver had put in several narrow stripes made of a now badly decomposed fiber; and a largish design of meanders, diamonds, swastikas, etc. had been embroidered with the same strange fiber onto the area beyond. This fiber, after much analysis, turned out to be the partly degummed silk of domestic Chinese *Bombyx mori* (ibid., 63–64).

The cloth otherwise seems like a fairly typical Hallstatt woolen fabric, so the most reasonable conclusion is that the silk had been woven and embroidered into it right there in the middle of Europe. One can imagine that an original silk cloth exported from China had become so ragged and frayed that it was no longer good for much by the time it got so far west; but that the colors of the silk threads were still so radiantly bright (silk dyes well and washes nicely) that a special garment like our chemise could still be decorated handsomely by unraveling the silk and respinning it into the small amounts of thread required here. We know that much later, in Roman times, unraveling and reweaving Chinese silk for western tastes became a big industry.

This is not the only early find of silk in the west. Preliminary reports of another well-preserved Hallstatt tomb from Germany, at Hochdorf near Stuttgart, suggest that among the relatively well-preserved textiles there may be more silk embroidery (Biel 1980, 438). This tomb is also dated to the late 6th century (Biel 1981, 18).

Furthermore, a veritable treasure-trove of half-a-dozen pure silk objects has been recovered from a late 5th century tomb in the Kerameikos in Athens (Hundt 1969, 66–70). These purple and white silks, which apparently belonged to a member of Alcibiades' family, must have been handsome and exceedingly expensive luxuries. Three are in plain weave, and apparently had originally been plain white (although one is now green from the bronze funerary urn, and another, of particularly filmy texture, is stained brown). Another plain-weave piece (no. 5) had little rows of holes from no-longer-reconstructable embroidery that seems to have included small purple squares. There were also remains of a three-ply cord (no. 6).

The most complex piece (no. 3), however, was a heavy white cloth with purple stripes and a tablet-woven border, presumably a starting band, very similar to that on the Hohmichele chemise. Now, tablet-weaving is something that we have seen mainly among the Hallstatt fabrics—on the Hohmichele find and also on at least one piece from the salt mines (no. 43: Hundt 1960, 145–47 and fig. 9). And by the next era, the La Tène culture, these West European card-woven borders had become so fancy that some of them required 30 or 40 on up to 178 tablets for construction (Hundt 1968, 190–91 and fig. 4; Schlabow 1976, 64–67). The technique suggests, then, that this piece of silk had been woven somewhere in Europe: perhaps in central Europe, where our other specimens come from; but if in Greece, then the Classical Greeks and the Hallstatt people shared many of their weaving techniques as well as their looms.

Which way were the influences going? Hundt raises the question of whether garments such as the Hohmichele chemise may have been imported from Greece by the Hallstatt nobility as conspicuous prestige items, just as they imported Greek vessels (Hundt 1969, 71). The apparent centering of the 1st-millennium "textile explosion" in Hallstatt territory, however, would suggest movement of this particular commodity in the other direction, perhaps in payment for the vases and their contents. On the other hand, we have so much more cloth preserved from the Hallstatt area than we do from Greece that our sheer ignorance may be tricking us.[6]

---

[6] Yet we know that the Romans, a few centuries later, were importing large quantities of cloth into Rome from Gaul, together with names for the many novel types. See Wild 1966, with further references.

There is another problem, too. The tablet-woven border on the silk is generally taken as a sign of a starting border and hence of a warp-weighted loom. But Ramona Duncan (pers. comm. 1983) has thoughtfully pointed out to me that, since silk is exceedingly slippery, it is difficult to imagine weaving silk at all on a loom in which the shed opens downwards, let alone producing a fine and even weave on it—or having the stamina to weave

However that may be, we are still faced with the fact that by this time textiles as well as ideas were travelling far and wide. In addition to the silk, we have mentioned in our discussion of fibers that plain hempen cloth, presumably from Thrace or the Black Sea, was imported into Attica in the 5th century, along with plain cotton cloth from either Egypt or India (both found at Trakhones: Zisis 1955, 590–92). The hempen cloth is particularly interesting in this context, because in pointing us northward again, it gives us a glimmering of how the silk might have reached Greece and Germany. Given that silk was travelling from China to the Altai, and that the Altaic tribes were obtaining textiles from great distances to the west and south as well, it seems most reasonable to think that the silk continued west across the Ukrainian steppes to the Black Sea. At that point it could reach Athens directly, via the ships of the Greek colonists along the north shore of the Black Sea; and it could also find its way up the Danube, from the river's mouth in the Black Sea all the way to its headwaters in southwestern Germany.[7]

---

so fine a cloth on a loom at which one has to stand and to beat upwards! I do not know what the solution may be, although I can think up several scenarios. In any case it would seem to be one more little bit of evidence that the ancients knew and used more loom types than we currently think they did.

[7] This is the only explanation that I can find that accounts for the distribution of these early finds of silk. Given the northern locations of them all (see Chapter 1)—Germany and Luxembourg, Greece, and the Altai—it seems far more likely that the European examples were coming precisely by way of the Altai than by the more southerly route through Sinkiang and Syria, the later Silk Road. So far we have no evidence of traffic across the Tarim basin at this early date: the trade caravans carrying Chinese goods appear to begin penetrating this difficult area only at the end of the 2nd century B.C., as chronicled in the *Shih Chi* of Ssu-ma Ch'ien.

Those bringing the silk west along this more northerly route must then have been not "merchants" but "consumers"—users of the silk who, just like the mounted horsemen of the Altai, were pleased to wear the shiny, bright-colored stuff on objects of conspicuous consumption and who were evidently happy enough to pass the commodity on, either as a guest-gift or in exchange for something else that struck their fancy (Barber 1983).

That the Chinese were busy feeding quantities of elegant silks into the far end of the pipeline is clear. We know from the pseudomorphs of silk cloth on Shang bronzes that the Chinese had been weaving patterned silks, as well as sewing silks into color mosaics, already in the 2nd millennium B.C. (Sylwan 1937). Then we learn from Ssu-ma Ch'ien, the Grand Historian of the late 1st millennium, that during the time since the Shang era the Chinese had been more and more pressed by the troublesome nomads on their northwest borders, the Hsiung-nu. Building the Great Wall was only a partial solution to the frequent raids and pillaging; and the Chinese emperors also began sending vast quantities of food, gold, and especially silks to the Hsiung-nu periodically as "gifts"—or rather bribes—to keep the peace (*Shih Chi* 110: B. Watson 1961, 166, 170, etc.). The silk pieces from Pazyryk may well have left China as part of such a bribe.

That objects could move so far without benefit of our sort of merchants is also clear. The obvious mechanism is the common custom among these pastoral peoples of giving prestige gifts to honored visitors and to valiant compatriots, and also of giving massive bride-prices and dowries. Odysseus and his family still lived in such a world, where Telemachus could go calling on family friends in order to strengthen bonds and collect a little wealth with which, eventually, to keep his own band of retainers. For Odysseus, on the other hand, who is coming upon total strangers, it is largely a matter of "trick or treat." Those he encounters have a choice of either wining and dining him and heaping him with gifts—or seeing him raid them of as much movable property as he can. Either way they stand to be out a fair amount of clothing, livestock, expensive metal goods, and possibly women. (The Vikings had the same code, both of behavior and of what was considered valuable; and both groups differed from the central Asian herdsmen chiefly only in using ships instead of horses for locomotion.) Note that clothing is one of the prime objects of giving and of plundering—a fact that is frequently reflected in the vocabulary of clothing, as in English *robe*, ultimately from the same source as *rob* (cf. Lane 1931, 9).

The final point is that the prestige of such a "movable" object went up enormously the more one could say about it. Thus the boar's tusk helmet mentioned in the tenth book of the *Iliad* is given a pedigree of no fewer than five previous owners, which Homer catalogues at great length, despite the fact that his hero is in a terrible rush just then. Storytelling was one of the few great pastimes in those days, and anything that carried wonderful tales with it must have been particularly desirable. What stories of far-off lands might the Altai chieftain have been able to tell concerning the pedigree of his silken saddle blanket?

The Greek Colonies

Knowledge of techniques was travelling too. With so little data to go on it is hard to say, for example, who invented metallic embroidery. But the one other noteworthy textile that we have from Greece from this era is a small swatch of Z-spun linen embroidered with metallic thread, which was found nestled inside a bronze urn at Koropi, in Attica (Beckwith 1954). The pattern consists of a diaper with a tiny lion inside each lozenge, each lion "walking with tail lifted in the air and one of the forepaws raised, as it were, in salutation" (ibid., 114.1). The metal thread seems to have consisted of gold and silver wrapped around a fiber core, although very little of it is left. Such metallic embroidery, when it surfaces again much later, is generally connected with the east (Dura Europus, Palmyra, etc.), so we are probably wise to look to the east for some of the technology, at least, behind the Koropi embroidery.

The vast extent of this mid-1st millennium intercourse between the Mediterranean world and the northern steppes is borne out once again by the last group of textiles that we shall look at: those from the north shores of the Black Sea, where the Classical Greeks had thriving colonies from the 7th century B.C. on. Here the local Scythian horse-riders of Indo-Iranian affinities, and the equally far-travelling Greek seafarers, passed back and forth enormous numbers of ideas and commodities. In fact, many of the Greeks seem to have been buried in kurgans like the Scyths, while many of the Scyths took Greek objects with them to the next world.

Among the numerous groups of mounds on the Taman' peninsula opposite Kertch (the ancient Greek colony Pantikapaion) is a cluster called the Seven Brothers (Sem' Brat'ev), which proved to be exceptionally rich in textile remains. Kurgan 4, dated to

the mid-5th century, contained two pieces: a coarse, undecorated linen cloth inside a bronze lamp (for a wick?), and a plain-woven cloth of wool that had been painted or resist-dyed in tan, dark red, and black, with "waves, meanders, squares, dotted rosettes, braids, and checkers" (Gertsiger 1973, 72–73, 88–89: nos. 2 and 1). We have seldom encountered this technique of textile decoration among the many hundreds of pieces we have investigated in these chapters. So it is particularly interesting that Herodotus, in describing the many strange customs that he saw during his sojourn in the northern colonies, specifically mentions that the inhabitants of the Caucasus Mountains, not far to the southeast of here, *painted* their clothing with colorfast designs of animals, etc. (1.203; see Chapter 10).

And that is not the only example of this technique. In Kurgan 6, draped over a wooden sarcophagus, lay the tattered remains of an enormous woolen cloth sewn together from eleven long strips and "painted" with frieze after frieze of figures from Greek mythology (Figs. 7.11, 16.15; Stephani 1878–79, 121–24, 131–32, and pl. 1, 4; Gertsiger [1972] 1975; Gertsiger 1973, 73–78, 89, and figs. 1–7: no. 3). The personages include Athena, Nike, Jocasta, Phaidra, Eulimene, Hippomedon, Iolaos, and Mopsos, plus many others whose names are mostly destroyed. If the technique alone weren't enough to show that the piece was locally made—Gertsiger describes it more accurately as equivalent to a "hot batik" process (Gertsiger [1972] 1975, 51)—the form of four-wheeled wagon depicted is specifically of the type found from the Black Sea to the Altai (ibid., 53). This tomb is dated to the early 4th century B.C.

And there was more. Inside the same wooden sarcophagus in Kurgan 6, across the legs of the deceased, were found pieces of

7.11 Reconstruction of part of a resist-painted cloth, used as a sarcophagus cover, from Kurgan 6 of the Seven Brothers, near Kertch in the Crimea (see Fig. 16.15); early 4th century B.C. (Gertsiger [1972] 1975, pl. 24)

beautiful and delicate woolen tapestry that must have formed part of the funeral clothing (Fig. 7.12). The design consists of polychrome ducks scattered about on a cherry-red ground, with stags' heads along the border, and the figures were executed in yel-lowish-white and green with details in blue-black (Stephani 1878–79, 133–34); Gertsiger 1973, 78–80, 89, and figs. 8–9: no. 4).

Across the straits in the Pavlovskij kurgan, a few miles south of Kertch, the excavators found pieces of cloth in a similar color

7.12 Woolen fragments from the body in Kurgan 6, Seven Brothers, Taman', east of Kertch. *Upper right*: ducks woven in tapestry technique on a cherry-red ground. *Lower right-center*: tapestry-woven stag heads (upside-down) on the same red ground. *Left*: geometric designs. (Stephani 1878–79, pl. 5)

scheme among the bones of a woman in a wooden sarcophagus there. It too was apparently the stuff of which the dead person's clothing had been made, but in this case the technique is embroidery. The fine, purplish-red wool is elaborately stitched with yellowish-white, black, and green in the form of palmettes and other leaves with spiral tendrils, and one tantalizing fragment shows a horse and rider above a line of running-spiral waves (Fig. 7.13; also Gertsiger 1973, 80–81, 90, and fig. 10: no. 5). Accompanying arti-

facts date the tomb to the mid-4th century B.C. (Gertsiger 1973, 90).[8]

There are other, later textiles from these great kurgan fields, some as late as the period of the Roman Empire (see Gertsiger 1973); but we will not follow them. It is clear that we are into an unprecedented era of rapid diffusion of textiles, and consequently of the invention and diffusion of new textile techniques, and I will leave the sequel to others.

---

[8] My warm thanks to Dora Gertsiger for enabling me to see all of the Scytho-Greek fabrics at the Hermitage in 1979.

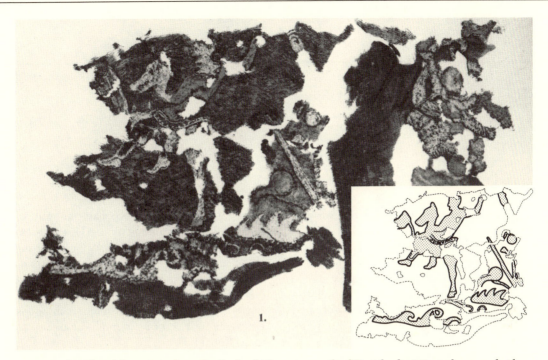

7.13   Embroidered fragments from the Pavlovskij kurgan, south of Kertch, depicting a horse and rider above a line of waves. (Inset is marked to show design.) Early 4th century B.C. (Stephani 1878–79, pl. 3; inset by M. Stone)

CHAPTER 8

THE TEXTILE WEAVES
(5) AN OVERALL VIEW

As we survey our evidence for the various types of basic weaves thus collected from a wide geographical and temporal expanse, we can begin to see some patterns emerging. There are still great gaps and many questions; but it seems worthwhile to pull together even now some sort of coherent, hypothetical model of development—if only to provide an organized basis for future research in ancient textiles. Such hypotheses can show us how either to prove or to refute interesting sections of the theory with new evidence, and can guide us both to the areas within this territory and to the archaeological levels from which the crucial evidence should come.

Broadly speaking, the material on weaves seems to separate into four developmental groups in the Late Neolithic and Early Bronze Ages. These four then begin to influence each other.

Right from the start, at Jarmo, we saw both plain weave and basket weave, although the latter is conceptually the same as plain weave, but with both warp and weft running in pairs. We also find weft-twining extremely early—at both Naḥal Ḥemar and Çatal Hüyük—and it continues over a very wide area for many millennia. These techniques are eventually held in common by everyone in the areas with which we are concerned. Simple color stripes were also almost certainly

used rather early, but we have no way of documenting this among our earliest textiles, all of which owe their preservation to means that render them uniform in color (carbonization, oxidation of metals, etc.). In the Late Neolithic/Chalcolithic/Early Bronze period, however, we find different techniques emerging in different geographical areas (see map, Fig. 11.1).

In Europe we find a versatile repertoire: warp-faced bands or borders in plain weave; warp-faced borders in half-basket weave (the warp, which is single, runs over and under pairs of weft—an asymmetrical binding system for the first time); weft-faced stripes and "shadow" patterns in plain-weave cloth; and an astonishing variety of supplemental-weft techniques based on floating the pattern threads above the ground weave. In Egypt, on the other hand, we find a modest and subtle set of elaborations: the use of supplemental weft for inlaid fringes, pinstripes, and hieroglyphs (but never floating, as in Europe, always bound into every shed); and the looping of an otherwise plain-weave weft to lie on the surface, sometimes for a purely utilitarian purpose but sometimes in an ornamental pattern. We apparently have a third tradition developing to the east, in Mesopotamia and Syria/Palestine: faced weaves, stripes, possibly pile, and the mysterious "diagonal ribbing"—possibly twill but more likely a strongly faced plain weave. (Pile technique also occurs at Kerma, in the Sudan, during the Second Intermediate period.) In the Caucasus yet a fourth tradition seems to be developing—if we can extrapolate safely from the available evidence—with twills, plaids, and possibly tablet-weaving and tapestry.

It is undoubtedly no accident that the difference between loom traditions correlates with the division between the European set of weaves on the one hand (from the home of the warp-weighted loom) and the Egyptian and Middle Eastern traditions on the other (in two-beam ground-loom territory). Although some differences in the weaves that these craftspeople pursued may be happenstance, others are surely attributable to the loom design. Just try, for example, pulling a pile knot up tight on a warp string that isn't fixed immobile at the other end. Contrarily, there is no inherent reason on a two-beam loom to develop the independently woven border that is necessary to warp up a warp-weighted loom sturdily.

It is also no coincidence that the division, while it lasts, between the Egyptian tradition and the other three falls along the boundary of who was and wasn't using wool. Everyone had linen, but for Egypt it was in effect the only major fiber, whereas for the other groups wool became more and more important until it largely eclipsed linen. And part of the reason wool became the fiber of choice was surely color: white wool is infinitely easier to dye than linen, and bright colors are attractive to the human eye.

The picture we get from all these points of view, then, is that there were four major zones of textile development in the Late Neolithic and Bronze Ages in the part of the world with which we are concerned here (see Fig. 11.1). One is Egypt; another includes Mesopotamia and Syria as well as Palestine (when this last area is not under the strong domination of pharaonic Egypt); the third region combines most of Europe other than the extreme east with the central and western parts of Turkey; and the fourth is the irritatingly mysterious but creative zone starting in the southern Caucasus and extending north and east across the steppes.

THE fact that our scattered and fragmentary evidence for weaves matches in a general way the major outlines of what we have learned from looms and fibers strengthens all three models. Clearly the warp-weighted loom led to a variety of developments in Europe rather early; clearly, too, the isolated linen tradition in Egypt, combined with the peculiarities of the ground-loom, led to a conservative and specialized set of weaving techniques there. What is not so clear is what was going on in the east, in the other two zones. Somehow we would like to account for the development of the three great and famous techniques: tapestry, knotted pile rugs, and twill. But how?

Almost certainly all three were developed by wool-users. Tapestry depends upon color for its existence, and knotted rugs seem invariably to use color, even if looser forms of pile do not always. Even without dyeing, wool comes in many natural shades, and white wool is easy to dye; whereas bast fibers come only in very pale gold to silvery-white colors and are hard to dye. Twill, on the other hand, is not dependent upon wool, but rather is a natural solution to weaving wool for clothing in a cold climate. As Bellinger puts it (1961, 1), "when wool warp ends were set close together like Egyptian linen, they wore thin if a wool weft which went over one and under the next was beaten in firmly enough to make a dense fabric." One solution is to space heavy warp threads rather widely and pack a finer weft down very tightly—exactly the weft-faced weave used in tapestry. The other solution is to keep the fine, close warp, but with each new row of weft to pair the warp threads in rotation, so each thread gets half as much wear—less than half, since you can work with a looser warp this way. And the mates nestle closely together to form a very dense fabric. If one uses the simplest possible rotation, 1-2, 2-3, 3-4, 4-1, one produces standard 2/2 twill. But the order of pairing is also easy to vary, to obtain a handsome pattern for almost no additional effort.

It certainly seems to be the Hallstatt people who spread the twill technique far and wide in the west during the Iron Age. But in light of the evidence reviewed in Chapter 6, the standard hypothesis that they also *invented* twill becomes untenable. Not only did twill occur in Turkey (Alishar) in the 4th millenium and in Georgia (Martkopi) in the 3rd, but there appeared to be so many other textile connections between the Caucasus and Hallstatt that we can't just dismiss it all as a fluke. Furthermore, twill had demonstrably spread east of the Caucasus, too, in the early first millenium—hardly attributable to the Hallstatt weavers! (Quite a few impressions on clay of plain and herringbone twills have been found at various sites in the Ferghana valley, considerably east of the Caspian, dating from at least the 11th to 4th centuries B.C. and later: Korobkova 1962.) If we are not willing to appeal to two or three independent inventions of twill-weaving (twill-binding was, after all, widely used for mats), then it seems we must look to the highlands of central and eastern Anatolia, in the 4th millennium at least, for the origins of twill cloth.

Our earliest actual samples of tapestry and knotted pile carpet, as we have said, come respectively from Egypt in the mid-2nd millennium and the steppes in the mid-1st. The Egyptian tapestries, although locally made, were being treated as heirlooms by Pharaoh himself; and the circumstances as a whole suggest that they were connected with the sudden appearance of the two-beam vertical loom and that both technique and loom were coming to Egypt from Syria (see Chapter 5). The knotted pile rugs, on the other hand, were found in the kurgans of semi-nomadic horsemen who had collected magnificent textiles made in China, Iran, and Anatolia, the knotted pieces showing generally Near Eastern motifs (see Chapter 7).

An informative document from Assyria, dated to the reign of Tukulti-Ninurta I in the late 13th century B.C., describes two multicolored textiles that were received by the palace. The one, covered with designs of people, animals, towns, fortifications, etc., was the work of a "weaver," while the other, decorated with pictures of plants and animals, and bordered with rosettes and a fringe, was the work of a "knotter" (Barrelet 1977, 56–62). Thus it seems quite likely that both tapestry and fancy knotted rugs were alive and well in Assyria at that time. Furthermore, Marie-Thérèse Barrelet points out that the term used here for what is obviously a tapestry, namely *mardûtu* or *mardatu*, was being used already at Mari in the Old Babylonian period, some 600 years earlier, and at Ugarit and Nuzi in the Middle Babylonian era—that is, particularly in the northern periphery of Mesopotamia—while the term that she translates as *noueur* or "knotter," which is specifically associated with making special textiles, appears in the late Old Babylonian period, becoming frequent soon thereafter (ibid., 57, 59–60, with references). All of this suggests that knotted pile rugs had been made in the Near East for at least a millennium before we see our first example, while the pile-cutting knives of Turkmenia (see Chapter 6 n. 10) add yet another millennium to their invention. It also suggests that we were not far off in looking for the origins of tapestry in Syria or even farther to the north. Within this context, our three hazy indications of tapestry rugs from the 3rd millennium—the report from Dorak in northwest Turkey, the rug impression from the steppes of the lower Volga, and the huge fame and expensiveness of the textiles from Ebla in Syria—come to appear quite reasonable.

In Chapter 3, on the basis of what we know directly about looms, I hypothesized that the invention of the vertical two-beam loom might have taken place in the middle of the 3rd millennium in Syria, which seems at that time to have been on the border between the horizontal and vertical (warp-weighted) loom areas. We know nothing whatever of the prehistoric looms of the Caucasus. It is possible that the vertical loom was actually invented there—possibly from the same models and for the same reasons as I suggested for Syria—and spread southwards into Syria with these new techniques. If so, and if the Hallstatt connection is strong enough by now to lean on, we may have still further evidence for this hypothesis in the representation on an urn from Rabensburg, Austria (Fig. 8.1), rather similar to the famous one from Sopron (Fig. 2.15), showing a

8.1 Part of a design from the shoulder of a funerary urn of the Hallstatt era, from Rabensburg in Lower Austria, showing a woman, a square frame thought to be a two-beam loom with checkered cloth, and perhaps a warping stand. (After Franz 1927, 97 fig. 1; and Rosenfeld 1958, fig. 58)

woman and square frames with checkered patterns in them—suggested by Rosenfeld (1958, 235) to be two-beam looms with plaid cloth on them.

By the late 2nd millennium B.C., in the east and south, the three older, separate territories were merging, passing around freely their techniques and design of equipment. In the northwestern, that is, European area, this same era witnessed instead the sprouting of a new offshoot in Scandinavia, the parents of which seem to be the weaving traditions of central Europe and the netting and needlework traditions of the old Mesolithic north. This was followed presently by the "explosion" of textile techniques radiating from Hallstatt. But the separateness of Europe was short-lived. As communication, movement of people, and the populations themselves continued to grow, both actual cloth and ideas for its manufacture moved still farther and in ever greater quantities. Clearly by the early centuries of the Iron Age, where this survey stops, we are into an unprecedented era of rapid diffusion and invention of textile materials and techniques.

Despite the constant innovations, however, and despite all the comings and goings of new cultural groups, we see a tenacious continuity in some of these textile traditions that is truly remarkable. In central Europe, for example, the warp-weighted loom starts early and ends late. We pick it up in Hungary before 5000 B.C., again in Switzerland about 3000 B.C., then among the Hallstatt folk of the 1st millennium B.C. in Austria and Hungary, and we still find it hanging on in an Austrian manuscript drawing from the 13th century A.D. (Broudy 1979, 138–39, fig. 8.3), well after the advent of the treadle loom. In the weaves, too, we find certain features that begin early and end late: for instance, the elaborate treatment of borders as quite separate from the main cloths of which they are physically a part. We pick this trait up with our first Neolithic Swiss linens and our first Neolithic German pieces; we pick it up again among the Hallstatt era textiles, see it elaborated magnificently in the Iron Age cultures with the Thorsberg mantle and others, and find it alive and well in the cloth of women's headgear in Germany and Holland in the 15th century A.D. (E. Maeder, pers. comm. 1985). Another example, if our extrapolation is correct, may be found in the twills and plaids of the Hallstatt folk, which seem now to have a 5000-year history at least. And we have pushed the origins of the Near Eastern carpets, so prized today, far back into the Bronze Age and beyond. *Plus ça change, plus c'est la même chose.*

CHAPTER 9

FELT AND FELTING

In ancient times, the chief alternative to weaving, in making large, floppy coverings out of fiber, was felting. Felting is the process of matting wool or hair together into a stable fabric by a combination of pressure, warmth, and dampness. Heat and moisture cause the tiny scales on the surface of the hairs to stick out; and prolonged kneading when they are in this condition makes them catch on each other until they are inextricably interlocked. It is that inextricableness that makes felt a solid fabric without benefit of weaving or knotting.

Until this millennium, felt-making was apparently restricted to Europe and Asia (Laufer 1930, 1), with the center of the art undeniably falling among the nomadic tribes in the Asian interior, who depended upon felt (and still do) for tents, clothing, and covers of every kind (cf. Russian *vójlok* 'felt,' borrowed in Old Russian times from Turkic *ojlyk* 'covering' [Vasmer (1950–58) 1964–73, 1.335; Laufer 1930, 18]). To the east (China) and the south (India and the Middle East) and the west (Europe), felting has taken the position of a minor art beside weaving.

In other parts of the world, a not-unsimilar process was performed on plant fibers, Polynesian tapa cloth being the most famous. Again we see the application of warm moisture and a mashing of the fibers. But here it is a matter of breaking down just the right amount of cellulose into a gluey substance by

fermentation, then beating the remaining fibers to spread them into a thin sheet while the gluey substance keeps the fibers from coming loose altogether. The resulting product, when dried, forms a thin, fairly supple sheet that strikes us as being somewhere between cloth and modern paper in texture. In the Old World, a similar process was used in ancient Egypt to prepare paper out of papyrus stalks; and the fermentation step is like the retting process used to prepare flax and hemp for spinning (where, however, the slime is purposely washed away in order to free the fibers completely).

But only animal hairs will felt, because these are the only natural fibers with a scaly surface. The bonding in felt is mechanical, not chemical as in tapa cloth and paper. For this reason felt is extremely tough, and is not damaged by subsequent wetting. Because of the tiny air pockets formed between the matted hairs, felt is also an excellent insulator.

Such a craft requires large supplies of wool; so Laufer (1930, 1–2) must be right in suggesting that large domestic herds would have been necessary for the development of a felt industry, although perhaps not necessary for the actual invention of the craft. He also notes, however, that having wool-bearing flocks is clearly not a sufficient condition for the invention of felt, since the principle of felting was never discovered in the New World.

Felts are divided into two types: fiber felts, which are made directly from loose fibers; and woven felts, in which the fibers are spun and woven first and the resulting cloth is then subjected to a felting process.[1] In many cases it is difficult to tell which sort of felt a given piece represents, without a lot of poking and prying into the inner layers. We find both types of felt within our purview, with fiber felt attested well before woven felt.

The hand methods of felting are also only slightly different in the two cases. To make fiber felt, the folk of Asia and India lay out their cleaned wool on a mat in layers corresponding in area and shape to what is desired for the finished piece. Warm water or whey is sprinkled on,[2] and the mat is rolled and re-rolled, kneaded, beaten, stamped on, dragged about, and otherwise subjected to as much friction and pressure as possible over the course of many hours, until the fibers are thoroughly interlocked (Laufer 1930, 3 and passim; Meister 1936, 56). When the felt has become fairly cohesive, colored wool (or scraps of colored felt) can be laid on in patterns, and the whole rolled up and pounded some more until indissolubly bonded (Laufer 1930, 3 and passim; Meister 1936, 56–57). Woven material, since it already forms a cohesive sheet, does not need to be rolled up in a mat for felting; it only needs to be kneaded, stomped, and pounded in wet and preferably warm conditions until the surface is matted to the degree desired.

This last process has often been a part of the "finishing" of cloth after it comes off the loom, along with washing, bleaching, raising nap, trimming the surface, and so forth. It generally goes under the name of *fulling*—a term borrowed into English from Latin. (We have excellent information on all these processes in Roman times, from Pliny and from the fullers' shops dug up in Pompeii [Forbes 1956, 85–95; Moeller 1970; Moeller 1976, 19 etc.].) *Walke* 'fulling,' an older Germanic term still found in German, seems originally to have referred specifically to the procedure of pommeling, heaving about, and trampling the cloth or mat full of wool: the cognate Anglo-Saxon *wealcan* meant "to roll or toss about," and descended into later English as *walk*, "to go from place to place; to journey, wander" (*Oxford Universal Dictionary* 1955, 2379), and only recently "to go by foot." In rural Scotland, to this day, a "wa(u)lking song" is a song not for hiking but for trampling the newly woven tartan cloth, soaking wet, on a corrugated board so as to make it waterproof and windproof—i.e., for felting it (W. H. Murray 1973, 195). Similarly, felted woven wools are still worn by peasants throughout Central Europe and the Balkans, especially in inclement weather, Loden coats being the only type present in Western fashion. Indeed, the very word *mantle* in English seems to have come, by a number of bounces via Latin, from a Gallic word for "cloak" that literally meant "trodden on" (Wild 1966).

There are two contenders for the title of the earliest evidence that we have for felt or felting. At Çatal Hüyük, early in the 6th millennium, Mellaart alludes to "the identification of felt among the textiles from graves in Level VI" (Mellaart 1966, 180), with no further technical details. Mary Burkett (1977, 113 n. 13) adds the information that "there was no sign of pattern, but [the find] proved to be animal hair, pressed together." She backs up the probability of such early pres-

---

[1] In fact, Swedish peasants make thick winter caps from yet a third type of felt: knitted felt. Traditionally they knit a cap fully twice the size needed, and then felt it and shrink it down to half the size—and double the thickness (S. Deny, pers. comm. 1985).

[2] Whey apparently has just the opposite effect from the modern hairdresser's creme rinse, which makes the scales lie down so the hair is silky and not prone to tangle. The whey seems instead to promote the tangles needed for good felting. Yak whey for example, is used in modern Tibet to promote felting (G. Yablonsky, pers. comm. 1983).

ence of felt by analyzing two of the Çatal Hü-yük wall paintings in terms of their similarity to modern objects of decorated felt from the Near East (ibid., 113–15). There is some re-semblance—just as there is some resem-blance between other wall paintings from this site and modern Turkish kilims (see Mel-laart 1963a, 197). On the other hand, the overall picture of ancient textile and fiber de-velopment that we have been building up suggests that neither kilims nor felt are likely to have developed for two or three more mil-lennia. (Remember that sheep were still pre-dominantly kempy rather than woolly, and brown rather than white; and that it is ex-tremely difficult to dye either flax or brown wool to obtain the contrastive colors neces-sary for either kilims or felt objects of the sort suggested.) It seems best to withhold judgement for the moment concerning the find of pressed animal hair from Çatal Hü-yük: it may be just that. Animal hair has long been used for simple padding.

The first well-documented specimen of felt comes from the site of Beycesultan in the heart of Anatolia: what was apparently a felt rug on the floor of an Early Bronze II sanc-tuary (Lloyd and Mellaart 1962, 40–45 and figs. 13–16). It was not the only floor cover-ing in the shrine. In a portion of the room in front of the "altar" lay the remains of woven rush matting, while in a strip behind the "al-tar" and leading through the doorway to the next room lay a "thick deposit" of felt, partly burnt by the fire that destroyed the building.

We then have no further examples until early in the next millennium, when we see not fiber felt but felted woolen textiles, from a number of sources in Central and Northern Europe. In the case of isolated pieces it is difficult sometimes to be sure that the felting was intentional, rather than a function of wear (belts in particular can become felted from the damp pressure of an active body). In other cases, comparison to unfelted com-

panion pieces strongly suggests that the felt-ing was carried out on purpose.

The earliest European piece showing felt-ing is the scrap with woolen weft and missing warp of bast that cushioned the handle of the dagger from the Wiepenkathen peat bog (Cassau 1935, 205; see Chapter 6). It has been dated by the style of the blade to the transition from Neolithic to Early Bronze (J.G.D. Clark 1952, 234), and it is not en-tirely clear whether the cloth had been felted on purpose. Soon after, in the Early Bronze Age, comes the coarse scrap of faced weave from a grave mound at Unterteutschenthal. Again one set of threads was wool—pur-posely felted by fulling, Schlabow believes—and the other set, undoubtedly bast, is now gone (Schlabow 1959, 118–19). Whether the second fragment from the same source, a piece that has wool for both warp and weft, is also felted is not stated directly by the an-alyst; he merely says that "in der Webart ähnelt dieser Fund dem ersteren sehr" (in the manner of weaving this find greatly re-sembles the first; ibid., 119).

In the next era, however, the felting of the woven wools becomes so intense that Schla-bow often finds the weaves difficult to ana-lyze, and assigns the felting to intentional fulling (Schlabow 1958, 29). The scraps from the Schwarza grave mounds ranged from glossy and totally unfelted, through lightly felted, to heavily felted from prolonged fric-tion (ibid., 29–31). Much of the woolen clothing from the roughly contemporary Danish mound graves was also fulled: the capes were usually heavily felted, as were some of the skirts, blouses, tunics, shawls, belts, and footcloths (Broholm and Hald 1935, passim)—presumably to protect the wearer from the copious northern wind, rain, and snow. But the felting seems to have had another important (though perhaps orig-inally secondary) function: with the wool matted so thoroughly that the weave could not come undone, it was possible to cut the great capes into semicircular form without having to bind or hem the edges; and the strangely shaped leftover pieces, too, could be and were used for other garments without wasteful loss (cf. Nielsen 1971). One might even be tempted to think that the Bronze Age Danish tailors' notable disregard for the rectangularity of woven cloth (the designs of blouses and caps show it too) stemmed from a prior familiarity with felt only, were it not for the fact that pelts and hides permit the same freedom. As we have seen (Chapter 6), these people were not very good at weaving and hid a multitude of sins under the felted surface.

The practice of giving cloth a more or less felted finish continues in the Hallstatt era, although it is not a particularly frequent feature: Hundt flags four pieces as thoroughly fulled (Hundt 1959, 71 no. 2, 75 no. 11; Hundt 1960, 145–46 nos. 42 and 44), and two more as probably intentionally fulled (Hundt 1961, 13 no. 7; Hundt 1962, 209 and pl. 40.2—this piece is heavily felted but only on one side). One other piece showed heavy felting along one edge, but the matting here was clearly the result of wear along the neck opening of a vest (Hundt 1960, 141 no. 34.3), and not of an intentional process. One reason why the Hallstatt weavers did not use a felted finish so often as the mound-grave people of the preceding era did may well have been that the Hallstatt people were weaving predominantly patterned fabrics, and the felting would of course muddy the pattern. Furthermore, it was not so necessary to felt a twill in order to weatherproof it since the nature of the weave allows the

threads to lie closer together to begin with. On the other hand, none of these considerations entirely discouraged the Hallstatters from fulling their twills: two of the four definitely fulled pieces that we have were simple twills, along with two in plain weave; and much farther north, in Sweden, the Gerumsberg mantle (Fig. 7.5) for all its fancy plaid twill was so heavily felted in places that the analyst had a hard time seeing the weave (Post, Walterstorff, and Lindqvist 1925, 61).

For fiber felt, I know of only one more little example within the Bronze Age. Among the artifacts in a Late Bronze Age grave mound at Behringen in northern Germany was a tubular fitting (one of several such, perhaps part of a bridle) with some remains of felt inside (von Stokar 1938, 98, 105; Forbes 1956, 91).[3]

The flood of examples of fiber felts begins around 700 B.C., with the rich trove of textiles from Gordion, the central Anatolian capital of the Phrygians, who had recently arrived from the steppes. Inside the largest tumulus (kurgan) the excavators found the unplundered and remarkably well-preserved contents of a burial chamber made of great logs, in such condition that it was possible to reconstruct roughly how matters had stood when the tomb was closed. The dead man— a rich and powerful Phrygian prince, one supposes—had been laid out on a large wooden bed or bier that was covered with thick layers of cloth; and apparently, though this point is not entirely clear from the reports, quite a number of blankets made of various fibers and in various techniques had been laid on top of each other as a sort of mattress above the planks (themselves slung

[3] I keep wondering whether some of the *ikria* or deck-shelters shown on the Minoan ships in the Maritime Fresco from Thera were made of felt. Maria Shaw, in her interesting articles on the subject (1980; 1982) shows how these must have been constructed out of panels of cloth and/or leather, and shows that some of the designs on them correspond to Minoan cloth designs or to the

Minoan conventions for depicting leather. But other designs fit neither category. Might they be felt—painted or otherwise decorated in their own way? Felt, like leather, would certainly form an ideal windbreak, especially when one requirement was that it could be rolled out of the way on occasion.

from iron crossbars resting on four thick corner posts), forming the basic platform for the bed (R. S. Young 1958, 150). In places it was still possible to discern as many as twenty layers (ibid.), small pieces of which were analyzed. For the most part, the layers were fiber felt, interspersed occasionally with loosely woven wool (Bellinger 1962, 12–13). Because everything was in a thick lump, Bellinger suggested that the Phrygians had used the loosely woven woolen blanket as a ground upon which to form the felt: that is, they had laid out directly onto the woven piece the flocks of wool to be felted, building up many layers, which were eventually "rolled together into a single thick fabric" (ibid., 13). But she also describes various layers as being of different colors, perhaps even patterned, a fine piece of labor that would have been entirely pointless had everything

9.1 Felt *shabrak* decorated with felt cutouts. From Kurgan 5, Pazyryk; mid-1st millennium B.C. (Rudenko 1953, pl. CI [1970, pl. 160])

then been felted into a single cohesive mass. It seems more reasonable to suppose that the bed had been made by laying down one fancy blanket after another, some perhaps pure felt, others perhaps woven, and still others perhaps indeed of felt formed around a woven cloth as a basis; and that the whole had become stuck together as it lay for nearly three millennia with the dampness and pressure from the body. But whatever the exact interpretation, it is clear that here we have an abundant and even lavish use of felt for bedding.

Richard Ellis, who reexamined the Gordion textiles later, states that felt was found in the other two large tumuli, too, in places "suggesting use as a pad, mat, or tablecloth" and possibly "hangings or clothing as well." Furthermore, "several samples were found together with layers of woven cloth and leather," and in the case of at least one stool, "purplish felt adhered to the seat" (Ellis 1981, 309). Still more fragments of felt came from an elaborately furnished room in the city mound (de Vries 1980b, 35).

The group of felts from Phrygian Gordion is followed by a truly spectacular series found frozen in the 5th-century B.C. grave mounds at Pazyryk, in the Altai Mountains. Much more numerous than the woven goods, the felt artifacts included clothing such as caps, shawls, and booties or stockings, as well as rugs, horse blankets, saddles, elaborate mask-like headgear for the horses, ornamental "stuffed animals" (e.g., swans), and a half-meter-high tent for catching the narcotic smoke of hemp (marijuana; Rudenko 1970, 35, 285; Artamonov 1965, 106–8 and sketches). The most common means of decorating involved cutting out intricately shaped pieces of felt (or occasionally leather) and appliquéing them to felt or cloth of another color. This handsome technique, which is used profusely on both the clothing and the horse trappings (Fig. 9.1) and magnificently carried out on one of the huge rugs (Rudenko 1970, esp. pl. 147; Artamonov 1965, 100, 105, and cover; Trippett 1974, 132–33), persists to this day among the steppeland nomads (Trippett 1974, see coverings on p. 146) and among such settled descendents as the Hungarians. In practice, this sewing lends not only beauty but extra strength to the felt. Stitching in a straight line makes felt easy to tear, whereas sewing in spirals or zigzags strengthens it (Meister 1936, 57). Hence the typical Central Asian designs.[4]

We know from numerous literary references and descriptions that the Classical Greeks knew and used felt, particularly for such things as hats and caps, where weatherproofing and non-rectilinear, molded forms were needed. The earliest reference seems to be a passage in the *Iliad* (10.260–71) in which Odysseus, while preparing for a midnight spying mission, borrows a helmet from his friend Meriones. Although Odysseus himself is in such a hurry that he hasn't time to fetch his own helmet, Homer takes the time to give us a long pedigree of former owners, and four full lines concerning its construction. It is the now-famous "boar's-tusk helmet": made principally of leather, with straps firmly stretched inside, and row upon row of boars' teeth fastened to the out-

side (good armor plating, and verified by the archaeology; see Chapter 6 n. 11, and also J. Borchardt 1972, 28–29); and finally μέσση δ'ἐνὶ πῖλος ἀρήσει (in the middle felt was fastened; *Il.* 10.265). Presumably the felt formed the innermost layer, serving the double purpose of cushioning the skull against the blows of blunt weapons and helping to stop sharp ones (felt armor has long been used against arrows).[5]

That we do not have examples of felt from Mesopotamia may be an accident of archaeology, thanks to adverse conditions for preservation. Steinkeller (1980) has made a good case for its existence in at least a crude form in the Ur III period and later, by identifying plausible Sumerian words for felted or felt-like goat-hair bed-pads ($šag_4$-TAG), for felt pieces used to top tables and chairs and to line sheaths, boxes, wagons, and footwear (*túg-du$_8$-a*), and for the craftsmen who made these felts from supplies of goat's hair and low-grade wool (*túg-du$_8$*). As the clincher, Steinkeller points out that "the meaning 'felt' of *túg-du$_8$-a* is also supported by the enormous size (18 × 5 m) of the *túg-du$_8$-a* listed in [one of the texts], which makes it very unlikely that this fabric could have been woven" (ibid., 100).

These references to felt continue into the Old Babylonian period at least (ibid., 81).[6]

---

[4] As stated above, Mellaart (1966, 180) and Burkett (1977, 113–15) remark on the similarity of some of the wall-painting motifs at Çatal Hüyük to designs used today in traditional felt appliqué. I, too, had been struck by the similarity of the Hacılar-style pottery motifs (and some at Sesklo and Dimini) to typical felt cutouts used in Pazyryk and right on down to the present in Central Asia and in Hungary. But I have also been equally struck by the similarity of the Hacılar designs to the Hopi pottery I grew up seeing; and in the New World there is no possibility of the influence of felt—although there may very well be influence from other crafts involving *flat cutouts*. (The Pazyryk burials are full of appliqué leather cutouts, too; and the Hopi jewelers today laminate negative cutouts of silver.) So I have to conclude that such designs can occur quite independently

of each other and of the exigencies of feltwork; and therefore I must reject on a second ground the arguments for feltwork at Çatal Hüyük.

[5] Compare, for example, a Celtic-type shield made of layered wood carefully covered with felt, found in a 2nd century B.C. grave in the Faiyum (Kimmig 1940). Such a Celtic tradition of use may have reached far back into the Bronze Age.

[6] Not everything translated as "fulling" corresponds, however, to what we are discussing here. Thorkild Jacobsen (1970, esp. 226) discusses "fullers" who turn out to be processing linen in the same way as wool. They must therefore be cleaning, sizing, etc., but not primarily *felting*, since linen doesn't felt. Compare Waetzoldt (1972, 153ff.), who prefers the translation "finisher" for *aslag*.

Much later, the Medes and Persians were known for their felt headgear.

In Egypt the few remains of wool we have before Roman times, most notably those from Amarna, are not felted; nor are the scraps from Palestine—and in fact, felt is not mentioned anywhere in the Old Testament (Olschki 1949, 37). Apparently this area was outside the felt-making zone entirely.

What conclusions are we to draw from all of these data? First, we have no hard evidence for felt or felting before the 3rd millennium. When we do have it, we find it in Anatolia in the "Treasure Horizon" of the Early Bronze Age,[7] and then associated with the burial-mound builders of the 2nd millennium in Germany, Holland, and Scandinavia, wherever we find remains of their cloth. In the early 1st millennium, too, we find it among the Hallstatt descendents of the central European people, as well as in the giant royal tumuli of the Phrygians (who had recently entered Anatolia from the north), and in the kurgans or burial mounds of the Altai Mountains.

In the archaeological record, then, pure felt—fiber felt—seems to be associated chiefly either with the recent arrival of people from the steppelands and/or with use where woven cloth won't lend its shape easily to the job (especially for headgear). The exceptions to this rule are the late Sumerians, who seem to have employed felt mainly for such relatively simple uses as pads and liners, and who may have either invented felting for themselves or learned of it from their trade contacts far to the north, with whom they were demonstrably sharing the technology of working precious metals.

[7] It is often suggested that the gold-using cultures of Anatolia in the 3rd millennium represent an early wave of (Indo-European?) peoples coming in from the steppes. The "royal burials" on at least one other site of this culture, Alaca Höyük, have been specifically compared with varieties of kurgan burial. Either we must

Felted finishes on woven cloth, on the other hand, seem to be associated either with the recent arrival of grave-mound builders or with the need to weatherproof garments against inclement weather (the farther north, the more necessary).

In both cases, the use of felting seems to have been moving south and west, in our territory, with people and technologies emanating originally from the steppes—just as it seems to have reached the Chinese from the Central Asian nomads harassing them on their western and northern frontiers (Laufer 1930, 3–4). Where these felt-users come to mingle with people whom we know to have been weaving (but not felting), we seem to see two typical reflexes: a transfer of the weatherproofing qualities of felt to the woven woolen fabrics, in the form of heavy fulling, where the weather is raw enough to make that useful; and a retention of the process of fiber felting for articles where a woven base is a nuisance—especially in the making of hats, caps, and liners.

It seems, then, that our archaeological evidence merely substantiates the hypothesis made some fifty years ago by Berthold Laufer, in his "Early History of Felt" (1930, 2), that "we are compelled to attribute the invention of felt . . . to the Asiatic nomads." Most of his data were ethnographic and literary rather than archaeological; and he was particularly impressed by the fact that these nomads use and have used felt for practically everything, not just rugs, clothes, and horse trappings but dishes, baggage, and housing too. The ultimate argument for him was: "Eliminate felt from Chinese, Greek, and Roman civilizations, and they would still re-

take the felt at Beycesultan as an independent discovery, or else we must conclude that the evidence of felt corroborates the suggestion that some sort of steppeland influx or influence had reached Anatolia already in the 3rd millennium.

main what they are, not being in the least affected by this minus. Eliminate the same element from the life of the nomadic populations, and they would cease to exist, they would never have come into existence" (ibid., 2). To this we can add that the invention may have come relatively late within the vast time span we have been considering for the development of spinning and weaving: perhaps not in the Neolithic at all, but early in the Bronze Age. For this deduction we have the backing of the linguistic evidence: there is no common word for felt among the Indo-Europeans, although they have common words for weaving and for bronze (see Chapter 12). We can also surmise a significant correspondence between the use of felt for large coverings and the paucity of large looms in the steppeland area. Perhaps the nomadic herdsmen invented the former because they did not possess—or care to haul around—the latter.

CHAPTER 10

DYES

The craft of coloring textiles is easily dealt with in the most general terms: dyeing began at a very early date and developed with an increasing array of colors, techniques, and color sources. But what can be definitely proved in detail about ancient dyes is very little, and what can be fairly directly inferred is not much greater. Most of what has been written on the subject, and that is a good deal, concerns possibility. Copious botanical, zoological, geological, and chemical studies have shown that potential sources of pigments and dyestuffs existed in profusion throughout the ancient world (see especially Brunello 1968, 3–118; S. Robinson 1969, 20–27). In particular, colored earths like ochre and famous dye plants like madder, woad, and weld occurred naturally over wide areas, just waiting, as it were, to be used. We even have proof sometimes that they were collected by the ancients—as when we find heaps of ochre or of murex shells, or frescoes of people picking recognizable plants like the saffron crocus. But to prove that these materials were used specifically to color textiles is another matter entirely. Minerals are much more often used as pigments for painting walls, etc., than for either dyeing or painting cloth, while plants and animals like saffron and murex can also be used simply as food. If we analyze the surviving textiles we are not much better off, since the ravages of time and certain indeterminacies of chemistry often make it impossible to demonstrate exactly what dye was used, or even whether any was employed. Nonetheless there are some things we can say with certainty.

SURVEY OF THE ARTIFACTS

Let us begin with the textile artifacts themselves. Our earliest direct inference of the use of colored thread comes from the same site as some of our earliest preserved textiles, Çatal Hüyük. In general the cloth found there was so heavily carbonized that it was impossible to tell whether it had been dyed (a typical predicament). But Mellaart also found a group of beads with traces of red inside the string holes (Mellaart 1967, 219). Since there was no other source of red within the interment, the simplest conclusion to be drawn is that the now-missing string that held the beads together had itself been colored red. Furthermore, in at least two cases the cloth that wrapped bundles of bones was found to be heavily impregnated with red ochre—although whether the ochre had been applied originally to the bones or to the cloth was unclear (Helbaek 1963, 41, 43).

Our earliest demonstrable or inferable uses of color for textiles after Çatal Hüyük are rather later, starting in the 4th millennium. We shall take them area by area.

LEVANT. A scrap of red woolen cloth (perhaps also green, if not intrusive) was found in the Chalcolithic (early 4th millennium?) layers of the Cave of the Treasure at Naḥal Mishmar, in Israel (Bar-Adon 1971, 159, no. 128). When we again find textile evidence, in the 2nd millennium, we find embroidery that strongly suggests the use of color—at Jericho in the Middle Bronze Age (E. Crowfoot 1960, 520 and fig. 226.2)—and traces of a blue, white, and red fabric in a Philistine temple at Tell Qasileh, early Iron Age (Sheffer 1976, 85 and n. 7).

EGYPT. The sporadic red or brown linen mummy wrappings begin with one from the 1st Dynasty (brown, Tarkhan: W. W. Midgley 1915, 50) and another from the late 3rd or early 4th Dynasty (red, Meydum: W. W. Midgley 1911, 38 no. Fa). A variety of later examples also exist (e.g., Hayes 1959, 13; Riefstahl 1944, 49 n. 4; Pfister 1937, 209). Red and blue fringes and pinstripes were sometimes woven into the borders of white linens and have been found occasionally throughout dynastic Egypt, beginning perhaps as early as the pharaoh Unas of the 5th Dynasty (Riefstahl 1944, 49 n. 4; but see Chapter 5 for date). Later examples of striping are on display in the British Museum, the Metropolitan Museum, and the Egyptian Museum, Cairo; others are described by Henneburg (1932, 7–16). Bright yellow linen mummy cloths of the 12th Dynasty have also been unearthed (Huebner 1909). From Kahun, likewise in the 12th Dynasty, we have "a handful of weaver's waste . . . mainly made up of blue worsted ends, and blue wool, with some red and some green ends" and "a lump of red dyed wool, not yet spun" (Petrie, Griffith, and Newberry 1890, 28; but see Chapter 15 for source). Royal Egyptian linens suddenly blossom into polychromy—

red, yellow, blue, green, brown, black—in the 18th Dynasty, just before the middle of the 2nd millennium, from the time of Hatshepsut on.

WEST EUROPE. Late Neolithic textile fibers dyed red with kermes, others dyed blue, as well as kermes itself, were discovered in a cave site at Adaouste in southern France (Cotte and Cotte 1916, 764; Cotte and Cotte 1918, 92). Some of the late Neolithic, 4th and 3rd millennium, cloth from Switzerland and Germany had been worked in patterns too elaborate to have been visible (and therefore presumably not worthwhile to make) without color: for example, the Irgenhausen "brocade" linen (Figs. 4.17–19), Robenhausen linen pieces nos. 3 and 9 (Figs. 4.16, 4.14), and several scraps from Spitzes Hoch (see Fig. 4.21). Von Stokar is claimed to have detected the presence of red, blue, lavender, and yellow on Neolithic cloths (see Brunello 1968, 12). These cloths are followed in the local Middle Bronze Age (late 2nd millennium) by two red woolen pieces—a fancy belt and a net—from Roswinkel, Holland (Schlabow 1974, 193, 207–8). Slightly later still we find the wealth of Hallstatt-type fabrics of the Late Bronze and Early Iron Age, done in both wool and linen and showing dyes of greens, reds, blues, browns, black, and possibly yellow (see Chapter 7). Purple cloth (linen?) occurred in an early Etruscan tomb (Levi 1935, 94; Bonfante 1975, 11).

MESOPOTAMIA AND ENVIRONS. Traces of thick cloth of "a bright ochrous red colour" were found in several places in the Royal Death Pit of Ur, mid-3rd millennium (Woolley 1934, 239). "Remnants of some red coloring" were discovered at Hasanlu in northwestern Iran, from the late 9th century B.C. (Dyson 1964, 21).

EAST EUROPE. Traces of red and purple ornamentation were found on a white linen(?) undergarment, and black stripes and plaid on a yellowish overgarment, of the occupant of a Bronze Age kurgan at Tsarskaja in the Kuban area, southeast of the Ukraine (mid- to late 3rd millennium; Veselovskij 1898, 37).

NORTHEAST MEDITERRANEAN. Traces of a red and blue blanket or mat were found under the body in a Mycenaean tomb at Routsi (Marinatos 1967b, A16); red-and-white patterned textiles were found at Gordion in Turkey, ca. 700 B.C. (Ellis 1981).

Red, especially if we take that term in a broad sense to include "browns" and "oranges," has clearly been a popular textile dye-color right from the beginning. Something in the "ruddy" range of red to brown is the first attested color in each of the major geographical areas treated here. Blue seems to be the next color to establish itself widely, with yellow soon after. Green apparently came later, generally (if not always) having been the result of combining something with yellow (Lucas and Harris 1962, 152).[1] Real polychromy in the fabrics—the showing of several different colors on one piece of cloth—seems from the direct evidence to have developed gradually in the 3rd and 2nd millennia.

DYE PROCESSES

The most primitive way of dyeing is to throw the entire piece of finished cloth into the dye pot (cf. S. Robinson 1969, 20). Bicolored and polychrome patterned weaves, on the other hand, require a progression to dyeing the fibers either raw or as hanks of spun yarn. Our first evidence for this practice, other than the isolated red string at Çatal Hüyük, comes in the 4th to 3rd millennia with the fancy Swiss and German pieces and with the Egyptian colored fringes and pinstripes possibly from the 5th Dynasty. Color embroidery, too, requires separately dyed thread; and indeed, given that we have no evidence for embroidery until long after we know thread is being dyed separately, we might even speculate that embroidery followed (at an as-yet undetermined distance) in the wake of a general acceptance of dyeing fibers in the hank or skein.

There are other ways to produce patterned cloth without dyeing the yarn, however. One of these is *resist-dyeing*, in which the entire cloth is dunked in the dye bath after parts of it have been treated to resist absorbing the dye: e.g., by tying up sections of it very tightly—*tie-dyeing*—or by treating areas with wax or other protective chemicals. The form of this latter process known as *batik* is usually considered to have originated in southeast Asia and India, rather than in the area of our study, and at a still undetermined ancient time. But something similar may have made its way to or been invented in Egypt by Roman times, for Pliny describes how the Egyptians—those chemical wizards of the ancient world—would sometimes put different colorless chemicals onto a plain cloth, then drop it into a dye vat, from which it miraculously emerged with several differ-

[1] Some of this observed sequence may be attributable to the effects of time. Certain reds and blues are extremely durable, despite adverse conditions, whereas other dyes (and colors) are not. Elisabeth Munksgaard (pers. comm. 1979) has pointed out to me that this is the principal reason why the national flags of the older (pre-synthetic-dye) nations are made up of blue, red, and/or white.

ent colors on it (Pliny, *Nat. Hist.* 35.42.150; Forbes 1956, 133). The presence of several different colors, however, suggests strongly that in addition to or instead of a resistive substance like wax, which leaves the material unchanged, the Egyptians were applying various mordants (dye fixatives: see below), which would combine differently with the unnamed dye to give different colors. As far as I know, we have no surviving specimens of cloth from Egypt that had been colored by this technique until the 2nd and 5th centuries A.D. (Kendrick 1920, 15; S. Robinson 1969, 14).

Furthermore, cloth decorated with figures of people, animals, and plants in black, red, and buff, apparently produced by painting the images on in a two-stage resist-dyeing process, has been found in a 4th century B.C. tomb near Kertch in the Crimea (see Figs. 7.11, 16.15; Stephani 1878–79, 120–30 and atlas pl. 4; Gertsiger [1972] 1975, 51 and color pl. 21). Herodotus, half-a-century earlier, describes the inhabitants of the nearby Caucasus Mountains as drawing animal figures all over their clothes with a paint or dye obtained by mashing the leaves of certain local wild plants into a paste that they mixed with water, the designs being completely colorfast throughout the life of the garment (Hdt. 1.203).[2] Since his account is clearly secondhand, we are free to speculate on the exact technique behind his verb *engraphein*,

but the proximity in time and space of the only surviving ancient textiles that could fit such a description suggests that Herodotus's 5th-century Caucasians and our 4th-century Crimeans shared a dyeing technology that was quite different from what we know from the rest of Europe and the Near East.

One can, of course, also add colored designs to a finished cloth by applying color simply to the surface. One way is by painting: we find this, for example, in the handsome group of pre-dynastic cloths from el-Gebelein, in Egypt, which have scenes painted in red, black, and white on the buff linen (Scamuzzi 1965, pl. 1–5 and foreword). Another way is by printing—this is how most modern figured fabrics are made. It has sometimes been suggested that the little clay stamps (*pintadera*) found all over Neolithic Europe could have been used equally well for printing cloth or for decorating human skin.[3] From the Lago di Ledro excavations Peroni reports some remains of textiles that had been printed in some way with a resinous substance (Peroni 1971, 100). He does not say, however, what sort of design had been used, nor have we any way of knowing whether the "resinous subtance" had been used as dye or as resist medium. Nonetheless it is intriguing to have even this much direct evidence for printing cloth in early Europe.

---

[2] The exact passage is: ἐν τοῖσι καὶ δένδρεα φύλλα τοιῆσδε ἰδέης παρεχόμενα εἶναι λέγεται, τὰ τρίβοντάς τε καὶ παραμίσγοντας ὕδωρ ζῷα ἑωυτοῖσι ἐς τὴν ἐσθῆτα ἐγγράφειν· τὰ δὲ ζῷα οὐκ ἐκπλύνεσθαι, ἀλλὰ συγκαταγηράσκειν τῷ ἄλλῳ εἰρίῳ κατὰ περ ἐνυφανθέντα ἀρχήν.

[3] We have evidence of people decorating their skins in Europe. Note, for example, the colored figures on the cheeks of Bronze Age Aegean faces: e.g., the large white limestone face from Mycenae (Marinatos and Hirmer 1960, pl. XLI–XLII), the idol from Mycenae (Warren 1975, 131 right), and perhaps even the Keftiu emissaries to Egypt (Vercoutter 1956, pl. VI–VIII).

There are also places in central Europe that preserve

a tradition of reserve-printing small designs on cloth, which is then dyed so the design comes out white on a colored ground. I have seen this in Hungary and Austria; and Vydra (1954) describes the art in detail as practiced in Slovakia, where he traces it back to Roman and Celtic times (ibid., 9–11). I have also seen the same sorts of little stamps used with dark paint to decorate the whitewashed interior and sheltered porch walls of village houses in Hungary and northern Jugoslavia. And a Croatian friend has described to me seeing village women with small designs painted on their chests, under their clothes, for fertility and protection (K. Marinković, pers. comm. 1986). See Chapter 13.

Some Dyes

Of all the surviving early specimens of color on cloth, only a few have been tested for the source of the dye, and virtually no testing has been done since the development of the most reliable and least destructive techniques known today: thin-layer chromatography and infrared spectroscopy (cf. Saltzman, Keay, and Christensen 1963). The field desperately needs some systematic work done in this quarter; and much of the "evidence" reported below from the literature should be thoroughly reviewed in the chemistry lab. Note, in particular, the abundance of unnamed "tests" and of outright guesses. It seems worthwhile nonetheless to pull together what has been done, if only so that those who redo it in the future have the best framework currently available from which to start, and can see where some of the most interesting questions lie.

One of the most thorough reports on testing ancient dyes is that on the fifty or more yellow mummy wrappings from the 12th-Dynasty Tomb of the Two Brothers. Most of these were apparently dyed with safflower (*Carthamus tinctorius*), which grows "abundantly" in Egypt but produces a highly fugitive yellow dye—one that will wash out immediately and also is destroyed by light (Huebner 1909, 225). The cloths were so evenly and heavily colored, however, that the analyst could only conclude that the linens had been "specially dyed . . . immediately before they were used as bandages" (ibid). Two pieces, on the other hand, were of a "richer and a more solid yellow" than any of the others (ibid., 223) and proved to be colorfast (ibid., 225). These turned out to have been colored with iron buff, evidently developed with some form of calcium salt (the author calls it generically "calcium hydrate"), all of which processing "will probably have been much more costly than . . .

the fugitive yellow of the Safflower" (ibid., 226).

Other Egyptian finds have been analyzed, but without the methods being made public and therefore assessable. One of the reds used on cloth in Tutankhamon's tomb was identified as coming from madder (Pfister 1937, 209)—another common dye plant (bot. *Rubia tinctorum*) and one of the most frequent later sources of cheap red dye. Henna (*Lawsonia* sp.) and safflower have been tentatively identified as the origins of the reddish hues on some 21st-Dynasty mummy cloths (ibid., 210).

The blue of late Egyptian fabrics seems always to be from the extremely colorfast indigo dye, although just which of the several plants that contain it were actually used is still debated (Lucas and Harris 1962, 151–52; Crowfoot and Davies 1941, 116 n. 2), since chemistry can't tell us that (see below). The same source is apparently responsible for earlier Egyptian blues (cf. Pfister 1937, 208, 211). The blue of the Philistine cloth is described as possibly indigo (Sheffer 1976, 85 n. 7), but no evidence is given for the determination. Presumably the shade of blue merely matched the peculiar shade of the indigos, so well known today from their use in dyeing blue jeans. In Europe, the Cottes (1916, 1918) claim to have found indigo blue—presumed to come from woad—on some of the bast fibers from Neolithic Adaouste, as well as kermes red on other fibers, along with actual remains of kermes insects (see below for kermes). Von Stokar, too (1938, 60), claims to have found the indigo blue chemical, which he assumes to be from woad, on unspecified early European fabrics.

Finally, the typical olive-green of the Hallstatt fabrics was produced using iron in some way. Hundt finds it most likely that the method was similar to that of an old, traditional Swedish recipe for this color, made by first heating the wool in a brew of heather (genus *Erica*) or dyer's broom (genus *Genista*), which leaves it yellow, and then simply steeping it again in a hot iron kettle to turn it just this shade of green (Hundt 1959, 85). Another expert who studied one of these pieces felt that the textile was not purposely dyed, but had picked up its color secondarily somewhere from copper and iron (W. Specht 1959, 100). The uniformity of color throughout the piece, however, and the fact that it is so nearly the same color as a number of other Hallstatt textiles (Hundt 1959, 84) make purposeful dyeing seem more probable.

These are the few textiles and fibers that we have for which dye identifications have been claimed. But another place we can look for purposeful dyeing is in the remains of the dyeing materials.

The purple-bearing mollusc is archaeologically unique in that, like the warp-weighted loom among weaving devices, it alone among dye sources can leave a quite distinctive and relatively durable memento behind, namely its shell; and the evidence lies not just in the presence of shells of the various purple-bearing species—all sea snails from the genera *Purpura, Murex, Thais*, and *Nucella*—but in those shells smashed open in a way necessary in some species to get at the tiny dye sac efficiently, a crushing that is quite unnecessary and indeed counterproductive if one is merely going to eat the shellfish.[4] Who first developed purple-dyeing is still unclear, although current information suggests that the front-runners were the Minoans of East Crete and the West Semites along the coast of the Levant. Whoever did it, however, was intimately acquainted with the creatures of the sea, for the dye substance as it comes out of the mollusc is not purple but yellowish-white (the so-called leuco-base), and becomes purple only after it has been oxidized somehow.

The earliest proof of a Minoan purple industry comes from a bank of strategically crushed murex shells found with Middle Minoan II Kamares ware on the small island of Kouphonisi, south of East Crete, and more of these shells at the contemporary site of Palaikastro, on the east coast of Crete (Bosanquet 1902–3, 276–77; Bosanquet 1904, 321), and at Knossos in Middle Minoan III (Reese 1980, 81–82). Quantities of shells of *Murex brandaris* along with a few of *Murex truncu-*

---

[4] Although a fairly sizable quantity of crushed shell needs to be present for us to feel certain that a dye industry was present, it is not true that there was no dye industry without these masses. In Central America, to this day, the peasant women go down to the seashore with their skeins of yarn, at low tide during the proper seasons, where they search out the local purple-snails, press them against the yarn in such a way as to get the dye onto it, and then throw the snails back into the sea for next time. Nobuko Kajitani, textile conservation expert at the Metropolitan Museum of Art, has described to me accompanying the women on such an outing, and has shown me the skein that she dyed on that occasion. The dye, of course, is still in the leuco-form (see below) and therefore is colorless as it is being applied; so it is impossible to dye the yarn evenly this way, one dab at a time. As the hunt continues, however, the sun and the saltwater gradually cause the dye to oxidize right there on the skein to a handsome if uneven purple.

Apparently the Mediterranean purple-snails either do not carry their dye so near the shell opening, or are not so easily induced to squirt it out; for the literature insists

that these shells must be crushed. But there is nothing to prevent one from crushing the shells a few at a time, just enough to dye a skein or two, for small-scale use. Jensen (1963, 104) tells the following anecdote: "On a spring afternoon at Sidon some years ago, our attention was drawn to some children at play on the shore. They were dyeing rags with a mash of murex sea-snails. The youngsters mixed the snail extract with lemon juice and produced . . . colors reminiscent of the splendor of the defunct Caesars."

At the early Neolithic site of Khirokitia, on Cyprus, shells of *Murex trunculus* were found; but the excavators were sure that they were not yet being used for a dye industry because there was "no sign of breakage of the shells for this purpose" (Dikaios 1953, 439). That site is certainly very early. On the other hand, it seems unwise to exclude the crushed and scattered Minoan shells at, for example, Thera and Knossos (see below) just because they do not occur in huge middens. They cannot constitute proof, of course, but they may be telling us something about dyes nonetheless.

lus and *Purpura haematostoma* were found in Middle Minoan III and later levels on Kythera (Coldstream and Huxley 1973, 36–37). And the large amount of crushed murex shell "used secondarily to strengthen earthen floors" at the site of Akrotiri, on Thera, around 1500 B.C., suggested to the excavator that purple-dyeing was done there too (Doumas 1983, 117).

Not much later, in the 15th to 13th centuries B.C., gigantic heaps of crushed murex shells were piling up on the shore of the port of ancient Ugarit, at Minet el Beida, on the north coast of Syria (C.F.A. Schaeffer 1951, 188–89 and fig. 1). Not only the shells survived here. Part of a kettle still stained with purple was found beside one of these heaps, as were remains, near the shell banks, of workshops for the dyers (ibid., 188); and the contemporary texts from the city of Ugarit give evidence of considerable commerce in purple wool and purple cloth (Thureau-Danguin 1934; Schaeffer 1951, 190–92). One can deduce incidentally from these texts that the wool was at least sometimes dyed before being woven, an important prerequisite to pattern weaving, as we have said. Even the Egyptians got into the act, leaving us several New Kingdom recipes for purple in the Papyrus Holmiensis (Bruin 1967, 296). Albright states that the Canaanites of Palestine were already dyeing their cloth with murex in the Middle Bronze Age (roughly the first half of the 2nd millennium), although he does not give the source of his evidence (Albright 1960, 96). Later mounds and pits full of shells are being discovered all the time—re-

cently, for example, at the port of Akko, in Israel, where "thick deposits . . . continue from the thirteenth through the twelfth centuries B.C." (Raban 1983, 61), and at Phoenician Sarepta (Pritchard 1978, 126–27). The shell mounds are said to be visible at Sidon and Tyre "and in fact, intermittently along the coast from Acre to Latakia" (Jensen 1963, 106).

The purple industry continued to flourish on the coast of the Levant throughout the 1st millennium, making its purveyors rich and famous throughout the Biblical and Classical worlds on account of Tyrian purple and Phoenician red. But each animal yields only a single drop of the dye, and even that only when freshly caught. In their quest for new sources of the molluscs, among other commodities, the Phoenicians eventually set up colonies all around the Mediterranean and out on the Atlantic shores of Spain and Africa, leaving a trail of shell heaps behind them (S. Robinson 1969, 24; see Reese 1980, 82–83 for a pan-Mediterranean list of sites). By that time, the Cretan industry had dropped completely into the background, perhaps from over-fishing, although a 4th-century inscription concerning a "tithe of purple" from Leuke suggests that the indigenous folk of Kouphonisi (classical Leuke) were still producing a little of the precious commodity (Bosanquet 1902–3, 276); and Herodotus (4.151.2) mentions a *porphyreús*—a worker or fisher of purple—living at Itanos, also at the extreme east end of Crete, a few generations before the Persian Wars of 490–480 B.C.

SOME COLORS

From the texts we know with certainty, or near certainty, that particular dyes were known and used as such by some of the early literate societies. We are also frequently told of colored cloth without mention of the par-

ticular dyestuff, although it is usually hard to determine just what modern shade of color is meant. We have already mentioned the "purples" of the Ugaritic texts, and they provide a good case in point, for the various species of mussels together with variation in habitat and in dyeing procedures can yield final colors ranging across various reds, purples, and blues (and even—although not in the east Mediterranean—to black and yellow-green: Forbes 1956, 117–18, 120). Furthermore, the geological identification of one of the minerals mentioned as an early dye source for "royal purple" clothing, in the Hittite/Ugaritic correspondence, shows that dark red was within the range of acceptability to the king (Quiring 1945–47, 99). Sea-purple and something else in the range of red-purple-blue are also mentioned repeatedly in the Old Testament (e.g., Exodus 25.4 etc.; 2 Chronicles 2.7 etc.; see Eakle 1950 for a survey of texts), as well as at least once in an Assyrian "chemist's" manual (Campbell Thompson 1934, 781–84). Considerably earlier, the Nuzi tablets mention quantities of dyes for the cloth coverings for couches and chairs: *takiltu* (blue-purple?), *kinaḫḫu* (red-purple?), *tabarru* (dark purple?) and *šuratḫa* (unknown; Starr 1939, 536–37; Oppenheim 1967, 242 n. 20). Egyptian texts, on the other hand, repeatedly mention red linen (*insw, insy*) and dyers of red cloth in conjunction with funerary and religious rites (Gardiner 1947, 64–66; Ward 1971, 49; Erman 1955, 100, under *inšj*), although we possess only occasional pieces. One of the terms in the linen lists, *idmy*, seems to have started out meaning a particular kind of cloth variously colored red, green, brown, etc., but later, in the New Kingdom, came to mean a specifically red cloth (W. S. Smith 1935, 138–40). Let us look, then, at the chief colors one by one.

RED. As we have already seen, red was one of the most popular colors from very earliest times, found among the first surviving examples of dyed textiles or fibers in every area: Mesopotamia, the Levant, Egypt, Anatolia, the Caucasus, and the various parts of Europe. Much of this preference can surely be laid to our physiology, since we distinguish the electromagnetic waves at the "red" end of the spectrum most easily and infallibly (which is why we still use red for our most urgent signals). This ease in distinguishing reddish colors also undoubtedly explains why, across the world, languages that separate such stimuli any further than "light" versus "dark" invariably have a term centering on red even if they distinguish no other prismatic colors (Berlin and Kay 1969, 17–21, 25–28). But the love of red, which finds further linguistic expression in many cultures in a synonymy of "red" with "beautiful,"[5] must also have found support in the fact that there are abundant sources of red to brown dyes.

One of the most famous red dyes, because of its brilliance and colorfastness, is kermes. This dye comes from the unlaid eggs of a tiny insect the approximate size and shape of a ladybug: *Kermococcus vermilio*, of the family *Kermesidae*. As we have already said, direct evidence for this dye has been found quite early, in a Neolithic cave-burial at Adaouste, Bouches-du-Rhône (Cotte and Cotte 1916; 1918). Along with the red, blue, and white bast fibers was found a paste containing, among other things, the dried bodies of kermes insects, which still grow, although very sparsely, on the oaks of southern Europe and the Near East (Cotte and Cotte 1916, 764).[6]

---

[5] For example Russian *krásnyj* now means "red," but earlier meant "beautiful" (cf. Ru. *krasívyj* 'beautiful' or Czech *krasny* 'beautiful'). Thus what we call "Red Square" meant "Beautiful Square" when it was named.

[6] Max Saltzman warns (e.g., lecture, March 8, 1985) against the confusion in the literature between *Kermo-*

coccus vermilio, a source of dye, and *Coccus ilicis*, a related insect that carries no red dye whatsoever in its body (e.g., Forbes 1956, 103). A careful search of the oak stands of southern France turned up large quantities of *Coccus ilicis*, but only a half-dozen specimens of *Kermococcus vermilio*, according to Saltzman.

Late Sumerian, Akkadian, and Egyptian words have been suggested to refer to red dyes that may perhaps have been kermes (Forbes 1956, 103–4, 144–45 nn. 12–13) or one of its relatives; but the philology needs to be reassessed. Quite a number of other scale insects (members of the super-family *Coccoidea*) also yield red dyes; the most famous of these are cochineal, a New World scale insect that lives on cacti (see Baranyovits 1978); Polish grains, alias St. John's Blood, which live on the roots of certain northern European plants (Pfister and Bellinger 1945, 4; "Karmin" 1924, 411; Forbes 1956, 102); and the lac- (and shellac-) producing insects of India and southeast Asia (Forbes 1956, 106). Yet another variety has been used for millennia in a small area at the foot of Mount Ararat, where an insect producing carminic acid (like cochineal, and unlike kermes) grows in profusion on certain types of local grass (Kurdian 1941, 105–6).[7] We are told that Sargon II of Assyria took the trouble to carry off red cloth from Armenia during his campaign of 714 B.C. (Forbes 1956, 102; Dyson 1964, 21); it would probably have contained this dye.

But the simplest way of coloring cloth a reddish hue is to soak it or its yarn in iron-bearing—i.e., red-brown—mud. Such stains, as we all know from childhood play, can be quite permanent; and we also know how easy it is to discover the principle. If we put with this the love of both Palaeolithic and Neolithic people for red ochre—they often brought it from miles away, sometimes in astonishingly large quantities[8]—it seems likely that such would have been the first common pigment for cloth, although we have no actual proof (cf. Brunello 1968, 5–8, 20–21, esp. 8 n. 3 concerning a German peasant woman dyeing aprons with mud). Shades into the oranges, yellows, and browns can be obtained the same way depending on the exact color of the earth used. According to the Hittite/Ugaritic correspondence, wool was sometimes dyed a royal shade of "purple" (in this case, blood-red) by use of a soft but handsome mineral called the *ûqnu* stone, mined in Armenia and Persia and identified now by some as realgar, the "arsenic ruby" (Quiring 1945–47).[9]

Other common red dyes come from plants. Permanent red-brown to yellow-

---

[7] The distinction between translation and identification has caused Kurdian some difficulty. The description demonstrates that the insect involved is not the particular species to which the English word *kermes* has long been consistently applied; and the fact that the Armenian word for the Caucasian species is *kirmiz* does not mean, as Kurdian would have it (1941, 106 and n. 7), that the standard definition for the English word *kermes* is wrong. (Both *kirmiz* and *kermes*, like *carmine* and *crimson*, are descended via sound changes and borrowings from an Indo-Iranian root meaning "worm.") This is like saying that the English word *library* is wrongly defined as a place that lends books just because French *librairie* and Spanish *librería* mean a place that sells them. Forbes, on the other hand, may be jumping to conclusions in assigning the Armenian species to *Coccus cacti*, which he does only on the basis of the contained acid (Forbes 1956, 102). The carminic acid indeed proves that the insect is not kermes (which contains kermesic acid), but there are many other dye-bearing members of *Coccoidea* to consider.

[8] At the early Neolithic site of Marijupil' (Mariupol),

in the southern Ukraine, for example, enough ochre was brought to bury the dead in it entirely. A strip was laid down 1½ to 2 meters wide, which eventually reached some 27 meters in length and roughly a meter in depth. The local soil is black, and the bright red ochre had to be carried from 10 kilometers away (Makarenko 1934, 136).

[9] Realgar is a soft red compound of arsenic, AsS, which Quiring says was known to Pliny and other classical writers as *sandaraca* (Gk. σανδαράκη) and also as "dragon's blood" (Quiring 1945–47, 99). (For Pliny, see *Nat. Hist.* 33.38–39.115–17, 34.54–55.176–77.) Tiny amounts of arsenic can give one a particularly handsome complexion; but the continual wearing of garments impregnated with this highly toxic substance, which, like lead, builds up in the system, would make the wearer extremely sick within a month (J. Woodhouse, pers. comm. 1987). This information, together with the Hittite/Ugaritic textile use, suggests a whole new meaning to the Bronze Age myths of death from clothing dipped in dragon's blood.

brown hues are easily produced by soaking cloth in solutions of tannin, available from a wide range of leaves (e.g., blackberry) and barks (e.g., oak). But the really red plant dyes, always in great demand, include certain lichens (archil, orseille, litmus, etc.), madder (*Rubia tinctorum*), henna (*Lawsonia* sp.), alkanet (*Alkanna tinctoria*[10] or *Anchusa tinctoria*), and asafoetida (*Scorodorma foetidum*). Words for all of these have been at least tentatively identified in ancient Egyptian documents—at any rate, the words refer to different sorts of specifically red dyes (Loret 1930, 23–28; Forbes 1956, 103, 107–9, 144–45). In the Middle East today, henna and asafoetida are used more commonly to color the human body than its clothing. But henna was identified as the source of the staining on an Old Kingdom Egyptian statue (Forbes 1956, 109), so apparently its dye properties were at least appreciated already in the 3rd millennium. Henna may also have been responsible for the pink to orangey-brown dyes on some 21st Dynasty textiles (Pfister 1937, 210). For cloth, however, madder and the lichens seem to have been the most widely important red dyes. Lichen is apparently the crucial ingredient in an Assyrian recipe for red dye, to be fixed with alum as a mordant (Campbell Thompson 1934, 776–77), while madder was positively identified on linen from Tutankhamon's tomb (Pfister 1937, 209) and has been suggested as the colorant on still earlier cotton cloth found with a silver vase at Mohenjo Daro, in India, from the late 3rd millennium B.C. (Marshall [1931] 1973, 33, 585). Cuneiform words for madder have also been located (Stol 1983, 534–35). Seemingly indigenous to Asia Minor, Greece, and the Levant, the madder plant spread from there to Egypt and through the more central and western parts of Europe as a cultigen (Loret 1930, 31), but northern Europe was too cold for it (Brunello 1968, 15). Although the advent of synthetic dyes made it commercially obsolete, madder still grows wild in profusion around old ruins in these areas, especially on Crete, where it is known as ῥιζάρι (*rizari*) or "little root," from the fact that it is in the root that the dye is found.[11]

Safflower, or *Carthamus tinctoria*, which we have mentioned as the source of a highly fugitive yellow dye on some 12th Dynasty mummy bandages, is also the source of a colorfast red dye, obtained by a more complicated process of adding first alkali and then acid (Mell 1932b, 99). Words for this plant have been tentatively identified in Egyptian (Forbes 1956, 147 n. 77) and also in Linear B (Ventris and Chadwick 1973, 226). Since safflower is also commonly used for oil, however, the mere use of the plant does not prove its use for dye. But the distinction in Linear B of a "white" component and a "red" component, where the seeds are in fact white and the flowers (the source of both dyes) reddish (ibid.), does indeed suggest that the florets were being saved for dye. Furthermore, the etymological relation of Greek *knêkos* 'safflower' (κνῆκος, Lin. B *ka-na-ko*) to such other Indo-European words as

---

[10] The three words *henna*, *al-kanna*, and *al-kan-et* all contain reflexes of the Arabic word for henna, the latter two having in addition the Arabic prefix *al-* 'the.' See Loret 1930, 23–28, for a full discussion of alkanet in ancient Egypt.

[11] See Murray and Warren 1976 for discussion of a possible red dye plant in Linear B. If there is indeed a botanical connection between φοινικ- *phoinik-* 'red' and φοινικ- 'Phoenician,' one might expect it to come from madder, the only red dye substance known to the later Greeks that seems (on biological grounds) to have reached the Aegean as a cultigen from the southeast corner of the Mediterranean. (I disagree with Murray and Warren's analysis of safflower and red: see below.) Madder was also popular as a medicine (Forbes 1956, 104), a fact that might help account for the parttime textual association of *po-ni-ki-jo* with coriander, an edible condiment.

Greek *knēkós* (κνηκός) 'yellow,' Sanskrit *kāñ-caná-* 'golden,' and English *honey* strongly suggests that the simple but fugitive yellow dye was known to the Greeks before these Mycenaean documents were written. Otherwise there would be scant reason for naming by association with yellow, especially while describing the plant explicitly as "red."[12] Whether by late Mycenaean times the Greeks had also progressed to an understanding of the more complicated but stable red dye we cannot yet say.

YELLOW. As it happens, yellow dyes are about as numerous as red ones, and three of them are still well known today to any gourmet cook, from the irritatingly permanent stains they leave on hands, napkins, and tablecloths. These are saffron, turmeric, and pomegranate rind. Both the Minoans and the Therans left us 2nd-millennium frescoes depicting the gathering of saffron, the stamen of *Crocus sativus* (or the wild *Crocus cartwrightianus*: Douskos 1980, 143–44; Evans 1921, pl. 4; Marinatos 1976, 34–38, and pl. A-K, 59, 61), but we don't know for sure whether it was then used as dye or spice (but see Chapter 15). It was grown all around the Mediterranean, and was reportedly used as a dye by the Neo-Assyrians (Forbes 1956, 123).

Turmeric (*Curcuma longa*) and pomegranate rind (*Punica granatum*), it is claimed,

were used in ancient times for dyeing in Mesopotamia, the latter as early as 2000 B.C. (and by 1500 B.C. in Egypt, according to Forbes 1956, 123), and the former at least in Assyrian times—as we learn from a recipe for dye fixed with carbonate of soda as a mordant (Campbell Thompson 1934, 780). Onion skins also produce a handsome array of yellow to orange to brown dye-colors, the shade depending on the mordant and on the soil the onions were grown in.

As for weld (*Reseda luteola*), apparently there is no pre-Iron Age evidence for the use of this plant (Horsfall and Lawrie 1949, 3; Forbes 1956, 124), which later became such an important resource for dyers since, when lightly mordanted, it gave "the best and fastest of the yellow natural dyes" in Europe (Mell 1932e, 337). On the other hand, the suspiciously Indo-European shape and correspondence of the Latin and West Germanic words would imply that the plant itself had long been important enough to receive and retain a name.[13] Botanically, weld is thought to have originated in southeastern Europe, whence it could not have spread northwards except by careful cultivation, since the dyestuff occurs in the flowers, but the plant propagates exclusively by seed (ibid., 336).

BLUE. For blue, besides—undoubtedly but unprovably—any of a number of berries, the

---

[12] The appropriation of the "golden" root for *honey* was apparently a fairly recent linguistic affectation of the Germanic languages, because it is shared by all the North and West Germanic languages but not by Gothic, which retains the old Indo-European honey word, **melit-*, in its word *miliþ* 'honey' (Kluge 1975, 315–16 *Honig*).

Safflower probably would not have been encountered by the Greeks (or other Indo-Europeans) until they had drifted fairly far south, since the plant is thought by botanists to have grown natively only along the Mediterranean littorals and to the south and east of there (Knowles 1955, 274). Mell (1932b, 98n) states that

"seeds of the safflower plant have been found in Egyptian tombs from which were taken red cloths dyed with safflower," but I have not succeeded in finding the archaeological source for his statement, let alone the date of the artifacts.

[13] Latin *lūtum*, ME *welde*, *wold*, MLG *walde*, etc., suggest the same sort of initial reflex as in the root *lana/wool*, but require a final accent to explain Latin *t* against Germanic medial *d*: **wl̥t-ón*. The plant was traditionally used in Rome to dye women's clothes—especially those of the Vestal Virgins (Horsfall and Lawrie 1949, 3). This detail, too, suggests great antiquity. See Chapter 15.

principal dye in Europe, western Asia, and northern Africa was indigo dye. Considerable confusion has arisen in the literature, however, because, in addition to the plant indigo (*Indigofera tinctoria*), which gave the dye its name, fifty or so other plants also contain the chemical indican (Brunello 1968, 30–31), a substance that must be broken down into a water-soluble white (leuco-) compound for the dye bath, and then oxidized to give indigo blue. Although chemical analyses may determine that a particular colorant is "indigo," the dye did not necessarily—as people too often assume—come from the plant indigo. To determine the plant source, we are forced back onto botanical probabilities.

The indigo plant seems to have started out natively far to the southeast of the area of our study: the name itself is a reflection of the fact that the inhabitants of the Near East and Europe associated it with India (Forbes 1956, 112; Lucas and Harris 1962, 151). The chief indigo-bearing plant of Europe, however, is woad, *Isatis tinctoria*, famous as the dye with which the Britons smeared their

bodies (to the amazement of the conquering Romans) until they were the "color of Ethiopians" (Pliny, *Nat. Hist.* 22.2.2; cf. Caesar, *De Bello Gallico* 5.14).[14] The continental ancestors of the British Celts had long since been using woad for blue dye (or, less likely, some other indigo-bearing plant), since a blue, purportedly from woad, is found on some of the Hallstatt fabrics (Brunello 1968, 14). Earlier still, in the (Late?) Neolithic, bast fiber dyed blue with what the investigators assumed to be woad was found caught in an implement at the cave site of Adaouste in southern France (Cotte and Cotte 1918, 92), while woad seeds had reportedly been stored up by the inhabitants of one or more Neolithic sites (von Stokar 1938, 60: no details). Since the woad plant is thought on the basis of its morphology to be native to southeastern Europe (perhaps even to southeast Russia; Hurry 1930, 2–8), it had already travelled a long way, presumably as a cultigen in the hands of Neolithic farmers, for dye and/or medicine.[15] The fact that etymologically related versions of the name for the woad

---

[14] Pliny, *Nat. Hist.* 22.2.2: Simili(s) plantagini glastum in Gallia vocatur, Britannorum coniuges nurusque toto corpore oblitae quibusdam in sacris nudae incedunt, Aethiopum colorem imitantes.

Caesar, *De Bello Gallico*, 5.14: Omnes vero se Britanni vitro inficiunt, quod caeruleum efficit colorem, atque hoc horribiliore sunt in pugna adspectu.

Cf. Hurry 1930, 51–52, who quotes all the early references to woad. In particular, we are told, the Britons painted themselves blue-black on festive occasions, a practice that is quite possibly the real origin of the custom of blackening the faces of the English "Morris dancers," who perform a pageant cognate with certain pre-Christian dance rituals still hanging on in the central Balkans, the Pyrenees, Poland, and Scandinavia. Since the origin of the skin-blackening as well as of the rest of the pageant had been locally forgotten, it apparently led to a repeated popular folk etymology of "Morris" as "Moorish," i.e., black-face. But the custom was probably far older than European consciousness of the Moors.

The blackening of skin with woad, and hence the woad, may even have come into Britain with a pre-Celtic wave of invaders, who also came from the continent. In the process of showing that the "fifth estate" in

Ireland and Wales consisted originally or predominantly of the remnants of the pre-Celtic peoples, who are therefore outside the four Indo-European castes (kings, priests, warriors, and "yeomen"), the brothers Rees point out that this fifth group, treated as lowly scum, vassals, and demon-foes, includes all musicians (except for a few harpists and of course the singers of clan history), and not least a type of entertainer called the *crossáin*: "lewd, ribald rhymers or buffoons who went about in bands" and were described as "jet-black and hairy" and compared to "jet-black birds" (Rees and Rees 1961, 128). Such a pre-Celtic origin would accord better with the nature of the ritual dance cycles just mentioned. As is shown below, the demonstrable use of woad in continental western Europe long antedates the expansion of the Celts and even of the Indo-Europeans.

[15] Mell states that "a considerable amount of woad-indigo was found, in lumps and powder," in a "barrow at Sheen, near Harlington," the opening of which was witnessed and reported to him by Sir Thomas Wardle (Mell 1932c, 167). Beresford (1909, 2–3) states, moreover, that woad dyestuff was found "in two North Staffordshire barrows lately excavated, the one at Sheen and the other at Leek." These would seem to be referring to the same

plant occur in Greek, Latin, and Germanic[16] corroborates the idea that at least the western Indo-Europeans had learned of that plant by sometime early in the 1st millennium B.C.

In Egypt, starting perhaps in the late 5th Dynasty, we find cloth with stripes of a typical "indigo blue" color, although the precise plant or plants from which the dye came is still uncertain (Lucas and Harris 1962, 151–52, with many references; Brunello 1968, 45–46). The sources of the indigo dye reported from Palestine (Sheffer 1976, 85 n. 7) and the blue dyes mentioned in Egyptian texts (Forbes 1956, 111) are subject to the same questions. Cuneiform candidates for woad have also been put forward (Oppenheim 1967, 242–43). Woad, however, was doomed to take a back seat to the indigo plant wherever the latter was known (if only by importation), since the indigo plant contains ten times the concentration of indigo colorant as woad (Ponting 1976, 75).

MORDANTS

Certain dye sources, such as indigo and murex purple (which are chemically closely related: the latter is 6,6′ dibromindigo, differing from indigo only by the bromine), produce colorfast dyes all by themselves, although the processes of reduction by fermentation and later oxidation make the "vat-dye" procedure long, complicated, and far from obvious. Most of the vegetable dyes, however, require some sort of mordant to set permanently in any fiber. A *mordant* is a separate chemical that combines with the dye in such a way as to attach the coloring matter to the fiber with a lasting chemical bond (*mordant* means "biting in"), thereby making the color stand fast against light and washing. It would thus seem to be a crucial ingredient in most dyeing processes. Some mordants will also change the hue of certain dyes (different mordants on the same dye may darken, brighten, or drastically alter the color).

The dyes that benefit from this extra chemical for colorfastness may be classified as either acid (including most of the non-vat dyes we have mentioned) or basic (including the lichens). *Acid dyes* are "so named because they require acid solutions to control their union with the fiber," since they attach themselves "to basic sites on a protein fiber" (J. W. Rice 1963, 57). Called a *leveling agent*, this acid generally seems to have been obtained in ancient times either by adding vinegar (acetic acid), just as we do today when dyeing Easter eggs at home, or by putting the mashed dye plant in water and helping it to ferment somewhat before using it as a dye. The fermentation, which also pro-

---

excavations; but neither author states the dating of the finds, and I have been unable to track them down further. From the context of Beresford's discussion, however, they would seem to be somewhere from Celtic Iron Age to early Saxon—that is, late, from our point of view.

[16] Apparently borrowings from related sources, but, as with all these early textile loans, borrowed before the consonant shift: Greek ἰσάτις (isatis < *Ϝισάτις) 'woad,' Latin *vitrum* 'woad; blue; glass' (with semantic extension), Eng. *woad* < OE *wād* < PG *waizda- (cf. Gm.

Waid, Go. *wizdil-) (Kluge 1975, 833 *Waid*).

The semantic association in Europe of "blue" with "glass" seems to have begun because the glass and faience exported from the Near East and Egypt in the Bronze Age and early Iron Age, necessarily the first glass the European inhabitants ever saw, was almost invariably of a blue or bluish-green color (S. Kurinsky, pers. comm. 1986). The same semantic association is also to be found in the Celtic word *glas-*, for "blue, green," from which the ancestor of English *glass* was presumably borrowed quite early.

duces acetic acid, occurs very easily in these brews, "since very many of the naturally occurring dyestuffs are glucosides or a combination of glucose and acid colorants" (ibid., 58). The rarer *basic dyes*, on the other hand, contain "an amine group which will attach itself to an acid site on the protein molecule," and the leveling agents for these dyes, "if necessary, are either alkalis such as ammonia or sometimes neutral salts" (ibid., 58). The neutral electrolytes most often used in dyeing are common salt (NaCl) and Glauber's salt ($Na_2SO_4 \cdot 10H_2O$). Because the acid and basic dyes attach themselves to different parts of the fiber structure, "basic dyes may be accepted by the protein fiber after it has been dyed by an acid dye. This is called topping" (ibid., 58).

For most dyes, however, in addition to or instead of the dye and the leveler, one needs to add an appropriate mordant, either by treating the fibers with the mordant first (as in the passage quoted above from Pliny) to make them more receptive to the dye, or by putting the mordant right into the kettle with the dye—a process known as *stuffing*. Mordanting is particularly necessary with plant fibers.[17]

Mordants themselves are of two types, acid and basic, where basic mordants are used to bond acid dyes, and acid mordants to bond basic dyes. Acid mordants have generally been derived from tannin, readily available from oak balls or bark; occasionally they are vegetable oils (ibid., 59). Basic mordants, however, come from the salts of various metals, particularly aluminum, chromium, iron, copper, zinc, or tin. Among modern handdyers, the most popular mordants are "alum"

(any of various aluminum sulfates that occur naturally as minerals), stannous chloride, potassium dichromate, cupric sulfate, and ferrous sulfate. The use of different mordants with a given dye often produces different shades or colors: for example, iron mordants tend to make the color more somber, whereas tin and chrome mordants brighten it, and copper makes it greener.

Finally we should mention the use of *developers*—chemicals that are applied after the fiber is removed from the dye bath and that react in such a way as to alter or enhance the color, and then fix the dye again. Thus, for example, wool that has been dyed in madder with alum mordant turns a richer, deeper red when dunked in ammonia water as it comes out of the dye bath.

What we know for certain about ancient mordants and developers is even less than what we know about dyes. As we have seen, the ancients in some cases simply didn't worry about colorfastness: the mummy cloths dyed with safflower yellow would not have stood up to either water or light, so we have to assume that they were dyed that color immediately before being put where they would be subject to neither element, namely in a tomb (Huebner 1909, 225). One historian of dyes even remarks that some societies make a virtue out of fugitive dyes, dyeing the same garment different colors for different occasions (S. Robinson 1969, 21).

In other cases, however, we know that the dyes were permanently fixed—whether on purpose or by accident. The chemicals found by Huebner in his analysis of the colorfast yellow in two of his 12th Dynasty mummy linens indicated that the color came from

---

[17] Note that the dye-bonds have been described for protein—i.e., animal—fibers, such as wool. One reason that linen is so hard to dye is that, being made of plant cellulose rather than animal protein, it does not have either the acid or the basic "docking sites" that protein has for the dye to bond to. Furthermore, natural acids

associated with wool will make some dyes attach themselves to that fiber without any extra mordant; but linen has no such ally. One generally needs to soak vegetable fibers in tannic acid in order to get them to take either dyes or metallic mordants for dyes (Furry and Viemont 1935, 6).

iron buff together with a calcium compound probably used as a developer (Huebner 1909, 226: he suggests "calcium hydrate," i.e., hydrated or slaked lime, $Ca(OH)_2$). At Mohenjo Daro, in India, the presence of alum as a mordant in cotton fabrics of about 2000 B.C. has apparently been demonstrated (Hofenk-de Graaff 1972, 12, but with no explanation or reference). The largish amounts of aluminum and calcium in the colored linens from Tutankhamon's tomb that have been analyzed suggest the use of aluminum and calcium salts as mordants—although not enough was used to make the colors boilfast (Pfister 1937, 210–11). And the olive-green of some of the Hallstatt wools, a millennium later, seems to have been produced by turning a yellow vegetable dye green with iron as a mordant/developer (Hundt 1959, 85).

The fact that our earliest hints of mordants fall around the beginning of the millennium in which polychrome fabrics begin to appear in some numbers is probably no coincidence, although I am not convinced that the discovery of mordanting occurred at only one place in the area that we are considering. Given the textile data currently available and the known trade connections (or lack of them), I would be inclined to suspect that India, Mesopotamia, Egypt, and possibly the Levant shared one or two such discoveries, and that the European polychrome fabrics (if indeed they were colorfast) developed separately.[18] The only polychrome textile we possess from the southeastern group that is possibly earlier than the Mohenjo Daro mordant is the delicate blue, red, and white piece said to be from the pyramid of Unas, who is dated to about 2350 B.C. (see Chapter 5). Although the dyes have never been chemically ana-

lyzed, the blue has the peculiar shade typical of indigo—which does not specify what plant the dye came from but does imply that no mordant was needed. The source of the delicate pinky-red beside it is another question. It may not be colorfast, of course; but if it is (and if the piece is really so early), then the Egyptians either went a long way very early for a self-fixing red dye, or had already discovered mordants, or had learned of them from their neighbors (the Indus Valley folk?). At a later date, one would expect an extract of a local plant like madder, fixed with alum, for such a pink.

Again we must take heed that relatively little chemical analysis has been done of the dyes and mordants in ancient fabrics—partly because the only processes known until recently destroy good-sized samples, and partly because the earlier methods were very inexact, depending "mainly on the skill and experience of the analyst" (Abrahams and Edelstein 1964, 20). The recent development of much more exact identification, either from the infrared spectra of extracted chemicals (ibid., 19–25) or from thin-layer chromatography (Hofenk-de Graaff 1972), may help out in the future. The thin-layer chromatography method has the added advantage that it requires only a half-centimeter of thread, or even just a few fibers (ibid., 14).

Meanwhile, we have some other sources of direct and indirect evidence. Some of the storage jars regularly found in the 8th- to 7th-century dye-works at Tell Beit Mirsim in Palestine were discovered to contain hydrated lime (Albright 1941–43, 57), a useful mordant. Late though this period is, the presence of this chemical strengthens the

---

[18] Presumably in two groups: the West/Central European tradition, which includes the Swiss linen "brocades," is utterly different from the Caucasian tradition of "painting" designs with local vegetable dyes. The

Caucasus might have learned the notion of colorfast dyeing directly from the Levant; or even vice versa, if the former, rather primitive tradition is in fact much older than our scanty evidence proves.

case for lime having been purposely used as mordant or developer in the 12th and 18th Dynasty Egyptian fabrics just mentioned (Huebner 1909, 226; Pfister 1937, 210–11). Another jar, in a "dye-plant of a different type" at Tell Beit Mirsim, was filled with "light gray ashes," which the excavator felt sure were the remains of "decomposed potash" (Albright 1941–43, 59)—potash (potassium carbonate, K_2CO_3) being another chemical used in conjuction with dyeing, typically obtained by leaching wood ashes. Albright cites as a parallel the current Palestinian dyers' practice of putting slaked (i.e., hydrated) lime and potash into the dye vats which were presently to be filled with indigo (ibid., 60). Of course, potash is also used in making soap for cleaning cloth, etc., and the difference in the type of textile establishment might have been a difference between dyers and cleaners.

One of the most popular metals for mordanting in ancient times, as now, was aluminum, in the form of alum, where "alum" is a convenient term for any of a considerable variety of hydrated salts formed between aluminum, the sulfate radical, and some other metal or radical with a valence of one. (The most common types involve either potassium, sodium, or ammonium as this other ingredient: $KAl(SO_4)_2 \cdot 12H_2O$, $NaAl(SO_4)_2 \cdot 12H_2O$, or $NH_4Al(SO_4)_2 \cdot 12H_2O$.) In addition to the aluminum salts found in the Tutankhamon fabrics (Pfister 1937, 210–11) and in some 7th century B.C. textile remains from Karmir-Blur in Armenia (Verkhovskaja 1955, 67–68), we find a number of references to alum in ancient documents. The Assyrian "chemist's manual" mentions alum specifi-

cally as a mordant or developer for dyeing with some sort of lichen (Campbell Thompson 1934, 776–78; see also Stol 1983, 537 *gabû*), along with carbonate of soda as a developer for turmeric (Campbell Thompson 1934, 780), and iron plus tannin for murex (ibid., 781–84). In Egypt, according to Lucas and Harris (1962, 154), "there is textual evidence which may indicate the use of alum as a mordant with madder during the New Kingdom." We know that alum occurs and was mined there (ibid., 257–59), and some Neo-Babylonian tablets from Uruk record—along with dyes, wool, and other commodities—the importation of 233 minas of alum from Egypt (Oppenheim 1967, 237, 243). In Roman times, according to Pliny (*Nat. Hist.* 35.52.183–84), alum was obtained not only in Egypt but also in Cyprus.[19] Further, two Linear B texts from Pylos and one from Tiryns also seem to mention alum as a commodity (Ventris and Chadwick 1973, 174, 422; Godart, Killen, and Olivier 1979). The occurrence of the word *ku-pi-ri-jo* on one of these Pylos tablets suggests that we might even be dealing with alum imported from Cyprus (Godart, Killen, and Olivier 1979, 456 n. 25).

If mordants were indeed being sought in distant countries by the late 2nd millennium, we might also speculate as to whether those same Phoenicians who ventured the length of the Mediterranean for purple-bearing molluscs, and to Spain and perhaps even Britain for tin, might have been using a little of their precious tin to mordant their equally lucrative dyestuffs. Tin produces particularly bright and attractive colors.[20] And it is not always necessary to employ the toxic salts

[19] Natural alum minerals, which are formed by the evaporation of certain seawaters, include "common alum or kalinite (K, Al), soda alum or mendozite (Na, Al), ammonium alum or tschermigite (NH$_4$, Al), alum rock or alunite (Al, K), alunogen (Al)" (Bateman 1942, 783). Pliny lists further sources of alum as Spain, Armenia, Mace-

donia, Pontus, Africa, Sardinia, Melos, Lipara, and Strongylos (*Nat. Hist.* 35.52.183–84).

[20] One might also wonder about the Old Assyrian traders, who carried mixed loads of tin and textiles to Anatolia (Veenhof 1972).

used nowadays: in some cases, throwing scraps of the metal itself into the dye pot will have some mordanting effect. Some dyes will also dissolve the metal right out of the wall of the pot, as in the Swedish recipe for green mentioned by Hundt (1959, 85), which involved re-boiling yellow-dyed wool in an iron kettle. If the Hallstatt dyers were not using metal cauldrons, they had only to throw in a handful of nails, as I know from experience.

Certainly iron was known as a mordant quite early in the Iron Age, and not only at Halstatt. From the other end of the ancient world we have the above-mentioned Assyrian recipe using iron—although unfortunately this early chemist does not say how the iron is to be introduced into the brew. Did the Assyrians of the Middle East and the

Proto-Celts of Central Europe indeed discover iron mordant independently, or did the knowledge of this property spread from the Caucasus with the use of iron itself?

Another common chemical that would seem to have been used in the dyeing process at an early date is ammonia. The readiest source is urine; and we know that the later owners of textile-finishing shops in Pompeii used to put jars outside with signs entreating the passers-by to contribute then and there to the shop's supply (Moeller 1976, 20). Indeed, the revulsion with which dyers were viewed in much of the ancient world may have been as much from the stench of stale urine and ammonia as from the stink of fermenting the dyestuffs. In Roman times, at least, the urine was also used as a detergent.

DYE-WORKS

Perhaps because of the strong and unpleasant smells associated with most dyeing processes, and also because of the need for lots of water for rinsing and air for drying, ancient dye-works tended to be located on windy promontories or beaches, with a good water supply nearby. The earliest facility that has been tentatively identified as a dye-works is at Myrtos, on just such a windy hill in southern Crete, from the Early Bronze II period (Warren 1968; Warren 1972, 262–63). In order to assess its claim, however, let us first make a list of appliances and resources needed for the craft.

To begin with, of course, one needs the raw, natural materials from which the dye is to be made, and a supply of fibers, yarn, or textiles to be dyed. The latter may need to be cleaned of grease and dirt so that they will take the dye evenly, for which process tubs or channels, lots of water, and perhaps detergents and/or beaters are useful. Since most

of the plant and mineral materials, as well as some of the animal substances, must be mashed or ground up before they can be used as dyes, mordants, etc., mortars and pestles, grinders, and pounders are typical equipment of a dyer. Then one needs large pots for steeping the dyestuffs in water, either to dissolve or to ferment out the color principle. The same pot may later be used to immerse the fibers as well. If whole cloths are to be dyed rather than hanks of thread or fiber, these vessels may have to be quite large. And whatever the material to be dyed is, it must be kept swimming freely in the dye to avoid uneven coloring. Furthermore, since dyes take much better if they are kept hot, preferably simmering, during the dyeing process, some means of heating the pots is desirable—although not absolutely necessary, especially if colorfastness is not sought or understood. When the cloth or fiber is removed from the dye bath, some means is needed to extract (and preferably to salvage) the excess dye liquor, this step being more necessary the more expensive the dye. If the dye is cold, one can simply wring it out by hand, but if hot, some sort of sieve or funneled drainboard is helpful. (In many dyeing operations, two or more pots are kept going, one with fresh dye, others with nearly spent dye, so as to use the precious substance as efficiently as possible.) Next comes an enormous amount of rinsing, if the dye is colorfast; and finally, one needs lots of airy racks or platforms on which to dry the dyed materials—for some dyes in the sun, for others in the shade. Particularly large amounts of space are needed if whole cloth has been dyed, to spread it out.

It will be noted that much the same equipment is needed simply for washing clothes: water, tubs or channels, a way of heating the tubs (helpful but not necessary), and drying places. The few differences include the grinders for mashing the dyestuffs, and a means of salvaging the excess dye from the fibers or cloth. Traditionally, the mere washing of clothes has not required large industrial-type establishments, and certainly not several such arrangements in one small community. Furthermore, whereas wash or rinse water could be allowed to soak into the ground in the immediate area if not too plentiful, it is quite unlikely that foul-smelling dyestuffs would be disposed of in this way on a regular basis.

At Myrtos, according to the excavator, we find several installations of tubs and channels: in Rooms 8, 59, and 81 (Warren 1972, 26–27, 53–54, 75, with plans). Clearly a liquid was intended to drain out of the tubs and away, at some point in the operations—a loss

that, as Warren points out, is unsuitable for pressing grapes for wine. In Room 8, a burnt area adjoins the tub, although the tub itself was not over the fire, while in rooms next to 59 and 81 quantities of loom weights were found, from looms set up either in or above Rooms 58 and 73–74 respectively (ibid., 26–27, 52–54, 64–65, 75). Spindle whorls, quern stones, and/or stone weights[21] accompanied each of these groups of finds. In Room 83 nearby was found one of the peculiar bowls with the interior "handle" associated elsewhere with making linen thread (ibid., 153; see Chapter 2). Analysis of the few remains of bones on the site indicated a very high percentage of sheep/goat remains—specifically sheep where distinguishable, and generally adults rather than yearlings—all of which points, not surprisingly by this period, to wool production (Jarman 1972). Analysis of the fatty residues in the tub from Room 59 showed that these were of animal origin (Bowyer 1972), such as might have been left from "washing the wool and textiles being produced" nearby (Warren 1972, 54).

All in all, it is very clear that we have two and possibly three areas devoted to textile work within this one small settlement, two complete with spindle whorls, sets of loom weights, large tubs, grinders, and stone weights, and a third area (Room 8) with a similar tub, run-off channels, and a hearth. We can deduce that wool was available and being spun, and suspect that linen too was being spliced into thread. Natural dye plants abound in the area, as well as the kermes-bearing oak (Warren 1972, 262–63), while the murex beds exploited in the next era lay not far away—perhaps still untapped, since "so few [shells] were found in the settle-

---

[21] Pierced stone weights are characteristic of later dye-works, e.g., the Hellenistic complex on the hill above Corinth (Kardara 1961, 262), and the half-dozen 8th–7th century B.C. shops at Tell Beit Mirsim (Albright

1941–43, 57, 60). These excavators debate whether the stones were used for pressing out excess dye or for holding the dyed items down as they dried in the wind.

ment" (ibid., 263). Although we cannot prove that the Myrtos facilities were dye-works, no crucial resource is missing and the collocation of all the necessary elements constitutes strong circumstantial evidence.

It is interesting in this regard that large spouted tubs similar to those at Myrtos have been found at a number of other Cretan and Cycladic sites (ibid., 138; Carington Smith 1975, 60–62). At Bronze Age Phylakopí on Melos, a stone tank was found full of loom weights, pestles, and cups (Atkinson et al. 1904, 17). Elsewhere on the site, two stone "sinks" were found together, and yet again a masonry tank with a large outlet (ibid., 14, 53); but nothing seems particularly to have linked these latter with textiles. On the other hand, "stones pierced or grooved for suspension form a large and puzzling class" throughout the site (ibid., 200). Hogarth found a particularly elaborate set-up of connecting tubs, channels, etc., in a house at Kato Zakro (Block J, House I: Hogarth 1900–1901, 138, 140–41). There is nothing in the room itself (xvi) to connect the basins with textiles; but the storeroom across the hall contained, among other things, "about twenty pierced stones and several pierced clay weights" and a strange, multiply-pierced vessel "shaped like a six-inch gun shell" (ibid., 141). Could the pierced vessel have been used for draining dyed wool? In another nearby hall (xiii) more clay weights were found (ibid., 141–42), perhaps, as in so many other Minoan dwellings, from a loom set up in the upper story. Clearly textiles were manufactured somewhere in this house. On the other hand, Warren wisely points out that the great tubs could have served a variety of purposes as the seasons came around: wine-pressing in the fall, olive-pressing in the early winter, and wool-washing and dyeing in the spring (Warren 1972, 139).

Later installations elsewhere that are demonstrably dye-works are similarly endowed. The two best studied are the Hellenistic textile-production community on a windy hill above Corinth (Kardara 1961) and the 8th to 7th century B.C. town at Tell Beit Mirsim in Palestine (Albright 1941-43, 55–62). At both sites, the excavators found elaborate sets of vats, tanks, and channels, quantities of loom weights, an occasional container full of ash-like material, and "a large number of pierced stones" apparently used either for pressing or for weighting down the dyed materials (Kardara 1961, 262). At Tell Beit Mirsim, 6 or 7 such facilities were excavated (Fig. 10.1), distributed about the site in such a way that there may have been 30 or so in the entire little town, a town that must therefore have been devoted largely to weaving and dyeing textiles (Albright 1941–43, 55–56).

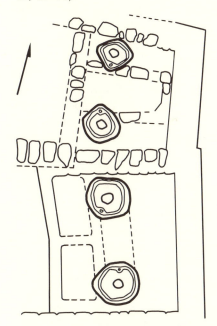

10.1   Dye-works installation of 4 large stone vats (see Fig. 10.2) at Tell Beit Mirsim in Israel; ca. 700 B.C. (After Albright 1941–43, pl. 11b)

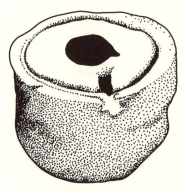

10.2   Dye vat from Tell Beit Mirsim, ca. 700 B.C. The flat top, channel, and small hole near the edge were for pressing out and salvaging excess dye from the wool as it was removed through the large central hole. (After Albright 1941–43, pl. 52–53; composite drawing by D. Keast and M. Stone)

The dye vats are particularly interesting (Fig. 10.2). Each consists of a large stone cylinder with a flat top, which has a smallish hole in the middle leading down into a "relatively small and roughly spherical basin, between 30 and 45 cm in diameter" (ibid., 56). Around the rim of the flat top "was chiseled a circular groove, obviously to catch the dye, which ran back into the vat through a connecting hole" that could be stopped up (and still was in several cases) by a small stone (ibid.). Kardara is undoubtedly right in suggesting that the top of the vat was designed wide and flat so as to provide a convenient surface on which to press the excess dye out of the yarn, just as it was lifted from the vat; the incised channel with its hole leading back into the pot would make a very efficient salvaging mechanism (Kardara 1961, 263). One wonders if the strange pottery vessel from her own site above Corinth, with a flattish upper compartment draining into a wide lower compartment (ibid., pl. 81 fig. 8), might have served the same purpose. Numerous cisterns, jars (some containing the aforementioned mordants), and basins sunk

into benches completed the usual equipment at Tell Beit Mirsim (Albright 1941–43, 55–62). Similar facilities have also been found at the Hellenistic site of Tell Mor, near Ashdod in Israel (Kardara 1961, 263), and in the 8th to 6th century B.C. levels at Beth Shemesh, Bethel, and Tell en-Nasbeh (Albright 1941–43, 61–62; compare Grant and Wright 1931–39, 5.75).

It is interesting that at Late Bronze Age Enkomi in Cyprus, pierced stones and querns or grinders, in addition to wells and pits, are frequently associated with groups of loom weights. Particularly noteworthy is the group from Level IIIb (12th century B.C.), Area III court Θ-I 22–24 east, which is composed of 9 loom weights, a spindle whorl, a pierced stone weight, and a grinder, all in the immediate vicinity of a well, a large slab (for working or drying?), and a post hole (for the loom?) (Dikaios 1969–71, 2.736–37 and plan III, pl. 256). Other, not unsimilar, but less diverse groups occur in the fill immediately above the house floors elsewhere in Area III, as though they had fallen from above, as in Aegean houses: one with 4 loom weights and a partly pierced stone disk in Room 32B, which also contains a well and a hearth (13th century B.C.); and another consisting of 5 loom weights and one fully and one partially pierced stone disk, in Rooms 25–26, with several querns plus a few hearths and tubs in neighboring rooms (12th century B.C.; ibid., 2.664–65 and plan III, pl. 251; 2.756–57 and plan III, pl. 276). There is not enough evidence to press the point, but again the collocation suggests that some dyeing was accompanying the weaving.

And it is far from surprising, by that period. Across the channel at the port of Ugarit, dyeing with murex purple had been a big industry for centuries. Unfortunately we don't know much about the actual factories as yet: we are only told that among the heaps of murex shells on the beach, near a workshop, was found a fragment of a large *marmite* (cooking-pot) stained with purple (Schaeffer 1951, 188). On the other hand, it may be that dyeing, although obviously practiced earlier, did not become an efficient, specialized industry for dyes other than purple (which required processing enormous amounts of raw material) until sometime in the 1st millennium B.C. Even Palestinian sites like Nir David (Tel ʿAmal) from the 10th century B.C. do not yet show vessels specially designed for dyeing, although dyeing appears to have been a major industry. Here the excavators found several workshops full of pots stained inside and out from prolonged contact with some sort of acid substance like dye (Levy and Edelstein 1972, 335). The presence of

textile manufacture was independently proved by a number of groups of loom weights from warp-weighted looms, along with an ivory spindle and a number of spindle whorls (ibid., 333–34). The workshops also had means to heat the pots (ibid., 335).

In fact, if we are right in our analysis, from other evidence, that polychrome weaving had begun in Syria by the middle of the 3rd millennium, and in central Europe even earlier, we should eventually be able to trace small dyeing facilities back to those eras, as we apparently have in Crete. One can hope that a better understanding of the grouping of artifacts needed for dyeing will help excavators recognize these remains when they encounter them.

PART II

DISCUSSIONS

In the first and largest section of this book I have presented the immediate data that we possess for early textiles—fibers, spindles, looms, dyes, and of course the remains of the cloth itself. In general I have limited my further remarks to the first level of deduction: pointing out patterns and relationships in this data and summarizing the results. But to me that is only the beginning of the study of ancient textiles. Textiles affected every part of life, from survival to ostentation, from art to economics, from language to religion; and some treatment of these matters is wanted to fill out the picture.

It is not possible, however, to treat every ramification of textile studies—especially across ten thousand years and five million square miles—in one book of reasonable size. So I have selected half-a-dozen topics, presented here, that give an idea of the possible range of subjects related to textiles, and to which I felt I could make a special contribution given my particular fields of knowledge. I hope that these discussions, in the course of providing a few answers to some intriguing questions, will by their example point the way for others into this rich world of study.

Each chapter is self-standing, in the sense that it can be taken out and read independently of the rest. Thus Chapter 15, "Minoans, Mycenaeans, and Keftiu," can be read all alone by the historian of Aegean or Egyp-

tian art, for what it contributes to those fields—but I hope it will also convince such people that they ought to look more deeply into the subject of textiles to truly understand what the artists and traders were doing. And Chapter 12, "Word Excavation," can be read out of context by the linguist or the Greek scholar, for what it contributes to Indo-European studies, to theory of reconstruction, or to Greek lexicography—but I hope that these scholars, too, will be convinced of the usefulness of wrestling with sizable chunks of archaeological and ethnographic knowledge to learn about their own fields.

The organization of these topics is not the usual "binary branching" one, but rather is like that of a waterfall: each leads into the next, raising new questions to be answered and providing new conclusions that can be built on, sometimes in the very next chapter. A few of the chapters provide a second and grander level of deduction and synthesis—such as Chapter 11, "Beginnings Revisited"—whereas others are more in the nature of interdisciplinary pilot studies. Foremost among the latter is Chapter 12, "Word Excavation," in which the massive power of linguistic reconstruction is harnessed in the service of archaeology—and proves to get as good as it gives. Such chapters are necessarily aimed at the specialist: to understand every last detail of such an essay requires a background in both Greek and linguistics. But any linguist or classicist reading these parts will recognize that they are still primarily *textile* studies, and belong in a book on ancient textiles rather than in a journal of linguistics or classics.

Furthermore, the gist of the argument and the general conclusions drawn in these "specialist" chapters are neither abstruse nor un-important to the general field. It is only that the artillery needed to win the battle of proof can become rather heavy at times. I have tried to explain myself clearly, if succinctly, every step of the way; and I hope that the ambitious "lay" reader, while skipping over some of the finer details, will find each chapter worth the effort.

CHAPTER 11

BEGINNINGS REVISITED

For a kind of artifact as perishable as textiles, we have just amassed and laid out an astonishingly large amount of basic data. But in a sense, we have only begun: now we can go ahead to combine these data with still other sources of information, to answer old questions of wider import and to raise new ones. Let us begin by looking again at the question of how and when—perhaps even why—spinning and weaving began in the territory we are considering.

If we take all the evidence together, we find ourselves with four major textile traditions in the Neolithic (Fig. 11.1; see Chapter 8), which, as a result of regional circumstances, had developed from common Palaeolithic inheritance and Early Neolithic diffusion of ideas and/or people.

The easiest of these four areas to chart is that of the warp-weighted loom, because of the higher probability that artifacts directly attributable to it will survive: namely, the weights and the heading bands. We pick up our first possible evidence for this loom in southern Anatolia around 6000 B.C., at Çatal Hüyük, and can trace it to the northwest over the succeeding millennia. By 5500, the loom is being used in the central Danube Valley and along the Tisza, where it blossoms into the loom of the "Old European" cul-

tures; and by the end of the 3rd millennium it is ensconced in Switzerland to the west and in southern Poland to the north. This loom type appears to follow essentially the same path across Europe as the early Neolithic cultures. The users of this loom seem to employ bast fibers right from the start, and eventually wool in quantity as well.[1] In the 2nd millennium, the warp-weighted loom apparently moves on up into Scandinavia, where it bumps into a Mesolithic-based tradition of netting and needlework.

The horizontal ground-loom, on the other hand, was apparently used throughout the territory to the southeast. The evidence for this deduction is mostly negative: lack of sets of loom weights, and lack of heading bands, in spite of ample evidence for largish textiles. In Egypt we have enough representations of looms to demonstrate the correctness of the conclusion there, from close to the time when the Egyptians learned the art of weaving in the Neolithic until post-dynastic times. And in Israel, the finds at Naḥal Mishmar suggest the use of ground-looms there at the end of the Neolithic. In the remainder of the Middle East we have only one representation of weaving—the Susa cylinder seal, from the 4th millennium (Fig. 3.4). But it shows us exactly what we expect anyhow: a

---

[1] I am ignoring for now the late and rather confined importation of the warp-weighted loom into Syria and Palestine. For that subject, see Chapter 14. For the other data on looms, see Chapter 3.

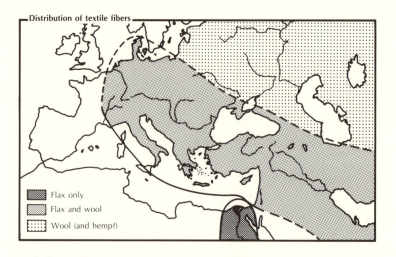

Distribution of textile fibers

Flax only
Flax and wool
Wool (and hemp?)

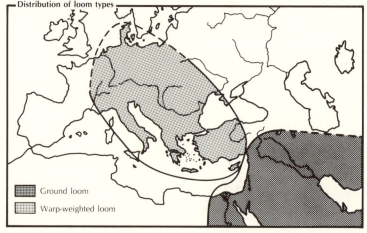

Distribution of loom types

Ground loom
Warp-weighted loom

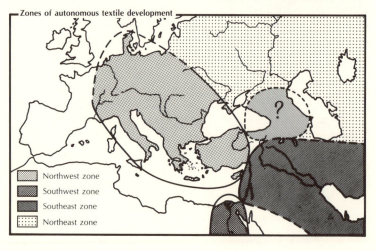

Zones of autonomous textile development

Northwest zone
Southwest zone
Southeast zone
Northeast zone

11.1   Map of the major prehistoric textile zones (bottom), seen by plotting loom type (center) against fiber type (top). This plotting also roughly matches the distribution of types of pattern weaves in four major zones, before trade muddies the picture in the 2nd millennium. (Dashed lines over land masses indicate an uncertain or expanding boundary)

horizontal ground-loom, in this case a large one worked by two people.[2]

When we come to look at other ingredients of the textile business, however, we find a sharp division within this great zone of the ground-loom. Egypt goes its own way, a nearly isolated tradition once it picks up the art of weaving around the start of the 5th millennium. It uses virtually only bast fibers, perpetuates its own idiosyncratic and archaic way of making thread, and develops its own techniques for pattern weaving (chiefly inlay), quite different from those of its neighbors. Mesopotamia, Syria, Palestine, Iran, and the Caucasus, on the other hand, seem to pick up (indeed, develop) the use of wool and methods of spinning it, in addition to using linen; and they begin to work on the faced weaves, a technique not shared by the Egyptian zone (and rare in the European zone) until learned from the east relatively late. (To the south of Iran there is yet another zone, of course: India, with its cotton fiber and hence its own ways of spinning. But that is outside our scope.) I see our ground-loom territory, therefore, as consisting of two quite distinct textile zones.

The fourth zone that concerns us somewhat is the northeastern one, spreading eastwards across the steppes from the area north of the Black Sea and the Caucasus.[3] How far it reaches in the early millennia we don't know; but starting from the late end and the nearest corner, and extrapolating into the darkness, we can say that this area is predominantly wool territory, with only specialized use of bast, particularly hemp. It is characterized in the 1st millennium, and indeed to this very day, by the copious use of felt (and furs) for covering, and by bandweaving where tensile strength is needed (see below).

The paucity of evidence for the weaving of large cloths in the steppes may be telling us something else. We saw in Chapter 9 that felt is used extensively to this day by nomadic pastoralists of the steppeland for most of the purposes for which we use woven cloth. It seems unlikely to me that such a tradition would have started—that is, that people would have been pushed by necessity into inventing a whole new way of making large, floppy coverings out of fiber—if large-sized weaving had already been a going concern among them. The first solid evidence of felt occurs at Beycesultan just after the middle of the 3rd millennium, among northern immigrants into Anatolia—which suggests that felt had already been invented up north rather earlier. But such a craft would also have to have gained its importance there after the introduction of woolly breeds of domestic sheep (5th or 4th millennium—see Chapter 1). Felt would thus seem to have been invented on the steppes in the interval between the introduction of woolly sheep and the peripheral introduction of large looms (or at least large cloth) into that area.

Note that large looms surround the northeast zone on three sides: the European warp-

---

[2] One other bit of evidence is afforded by Sanskrit vocabulary, in which the concept of "weft" is sometimes indicated by a pair of terms, *prave* and *apave*, where *ve-* (or *vā-*) is the root for "weave," while *pra-* means "toward" and *apa-* "away" (Rau 1970, 17). The simplest explanation for such a pair of terms is that the speakers used a ground-loom, specifically one operated by a single weaver who sat to one side of the warp, alternately pushing the weft spool away from herself and feeding it toward herself through the sheds. Vertical or backstrap looms position their weavers squarely in front of the warp, where there is no "toward" or "away" for the weft. In their trek through the entire length of the southeastern zone, the Indic women clearly encountered and picked up the horizontal ground-loom. I suspect they never encountered any other form of large loom (see Chapter 12).

[3] I am excluding the Caucasus itself from this survey since we know too little about it and its dynamics. It looks as though it may constitute a small but highly innovative fifth area.

weighted loom to the west, the ground-loom and the vertical two-beam loom to the south, and the various Chinese looms to the east. We find the looms themselves encroaching slightly from each of these directions; and we find imported woven luxury goods coming in from each direction. But the people in the heart of the steppeland never really seem to take up the weaving craft seriously. Where they make larger cloth at all, the uses are strongly limited: to carpets (unless these are all imports from the south), and to soft white bast-fiber shirts and chemises (more comfortable than felt next to the skin). We have seen in Chapter 9 that felt was found to be generally more in harmony with the lifestyle of the steppes, both for its inherent properties

(warmth, weatherproofing, and shapability) and its ease of manufacture.

Felt is not, however, good for cinching, strapping, and girding. Although leather does these jobs well, woven belts and bands have the advantage that one need not kill an animal to get the materials, while the work of spinning and weaving is easily balanced against the work of cleaning and curing or tanning. Felting and belt-weaving thus appear to form a felicitous combination for most purposes, leaving other types of weaving to fill in the little specialized niches.

So we have four major zones, delineated by the interaction of looms and fibers, and reflected by considerable differences in the textile techniques used by each area. Prior to

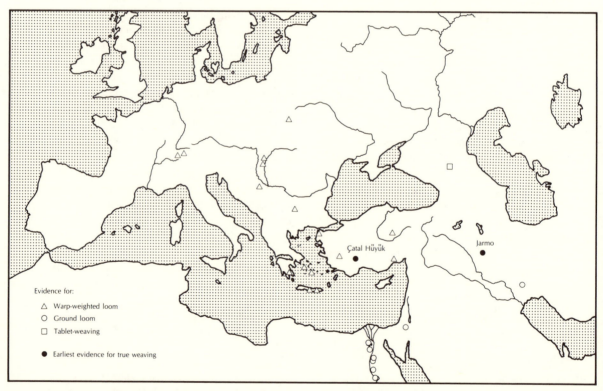

11.2   Distribution of the direct evidence for types of looms, prior to ca. 2000 B.C., and the location of the two earliest sites yet known with true weaving

2000 B.C. (after which extensive trade and warfare begin to mix things around rapidly), the situation was approximately as follows:

NORTHWEST ZONE:
warp-weighted
  loom
band-loom
bast and wool
supplemental-weft
  floats

NORTHEAST ZONE:
felt

band-loom
wool and a little bast
stitchery

SOUTHWEST ZONE:
ground-loom
bast and very little
  wool
supplemental-weft
  inlay

SOUTHEAST ZONE:
ground-loom
bast and wool

faced weaves, includ-
  ing tapestry

THE PRESENCE of more than one loom right from the start, in the Neolithic, seems to me to be a puzzle worth investigating. Leaving aside for the moment the band-loom, we have seen that the warp-weighted loom was clearly moving northwestward while the ground-loom was moving southeastward (Fig. 11.2; Egypt and India seem to have picked up both weaving and this loom rather later than their northern neighbors). These facts suggest that it is no accident that our first proof of weaving comes from the area of Jarmo, not very far from the borderline between the two zones and right in the middle of the area in which flax, sheep, and goats were first domesticated. But which loom was the original one, the loom to the southeast or the loom to the northwest?

I suspect, from a variety of evidence, that neither was. One reason is that the two looms are so differently conceived that I find it impossible to imagine either developing from the other. Verticality versus horizontalness, one versus two beams, working toward versus away from oneself—all suggest that the two types developed relatively independently of each other. On the other hand, the fact that they spring up at so nearly the same time in such close proximity makes it impossible to assume that the basic notion of weaving was invented separately. As we saw from our survey of loom construction, however, there is one type of loom that is simpler than either of these and from which each could be logically and directly derived: the backstrap band-loom.

It is not difficult to see the differences between the two larger looms as local solutions invented to solve, one by one, the problems of trying to make larger fabrics, when starting from a backstrap loom in particular. As you spread the end of the warp out on a bar tied to the weaver's belt—and this is the critical end—it gets too cumbersome to be tied to the weaver beyond a certain width. One could simply stop widening at that point: the inhabitants of East Asia seem to have done just that—which suggests that they too might have learned weaving from the same ultimate source and at the band-loom stage. Or one could fasten this cloth beam to some fixed object, rather than to the weaver. If you fix the cloth beam and its warp in a horizontal position, analogous to the position it has with a backstrap loom, then a logical next step is to spread the other end out on a similar bar, a warp beam, and fix that down too: the classic horizontal ground-loom. On the other hand, if you hang the cloth beam up in a tree or on a rafter, you can then use gravity to provide the necessary tension by weighting the other end of the warp with handy fieldstones, in as many little separate bunches as the width of the warp demands. Presto: the warp-weighted loom.

It has been suggested that the critical choice of vertical or horizontal, from which most of the rest follows, was a function of the weather. In the northern climates, rain was likely to fall at any and every time of the year, so that having one's weaving pegged out on the ground outdoors was chancy business; yet indoor space was at a premium. The only efficient way to enlarge the loom and have it indoors was to hang the warp from the rafters (or rather, from a beam that itself could hang from the rafters). Moving indoors was not so important in southern climes, the argument goes, and so the horizontal band-loom could grow as big as it pleased without causing insurmountable problems for anyone but a weaver trying to put in the weft single-handed. (To this day in parts of the Near East one can see warps pegged out dozens of yards in length, although seldom more than a few feet wide.)

It seems to me that if southern Turkey were the first home of the warp-weighted loom, the area has a dry enough climate that this consideration would not be critical there. But if the two loom types were invented through random choices and then began to compete, one might see here a good argument as to why the vertical loom won out in Europe.

At any rate, that is one theory. Another possible theory within the current framework of facts is that the warp-weighted loom was invented not in Turkey but in Central Europe, perhaps even considerably prior to 6000 B.C., and that it spread radially outward from there, its southeastward progress being stopped for a long time at about the Syrian border by encountering in that area the competition of the ground-loom. Such a theory could explain why ancient Anatolia is consistently part of the territory of the warp-weighted loom, and also why the very early loom weights and the evidence for weaving innovations are concentrated along the Danube and Tisza rivers.

However that may be, the fact remains that the band-loom, especially in backstrap form, is a natural and reasonable ancestor to the other two loom types, which are not suitable ancestors for each other.

AT THIS point it no longer seems irrelevant that from early times band-weaving is more widespread and often more sophisticated in the two northern zones than the weaving of larger cloths, whereas it does not seem to play much of a part in the south until quite late. At Çatal Hüyük, around 6000 B.C., we have not only large pieces of cloth but also carefully woven narrow tapes. The late Neolithic Swiss fabrics, as we have seen, have band-woven starting borders, astonishingly elaborate band-woven closing borders, and side-selvedges apparently made by hanging a band-weaving set-up onto each side of the loom. (This detail suggests that at least one form of the European band-loom was a miniature warp-weighted loom, with one weight on each half of the warp: see Chapter 3.) Just north of the Caucasus, we have possible evidence for tablet-woven bands already in the early 3rd millennium. And when weaving finally reaches Denmark in the 2nd millennium B.C., it is striking that the mound-building newcomers bury their dead in clothing that shows careful band-weaving and elegant stitchery, but remarkably sloppy, inept weaving of the major fabrics, as though this last technique, and only this last technique, were a brand new enterprise to these people.

It can hardly be coincidence, furthermore, that the only word for cloth or clothing that can be widely reconstructed for the Indo-European languages is the word for "belt" (as found in Greek ζώνη [zōnē], Lithuanian júosta, and Old Church Slavic pó-yasŭ, all meaning "(a) belt"; Greek ζωστός [zōstos], Lithuanian júostas, Avestan yāsta-, all meaning "belted"; Albanian ngjesh, meaning "I belt"), despite the fact that the textile crafts were sufficiently well known to the proto-Indo-Europeans that the difference between weaving (*webh-) and plaiting (*plek-) was carefully distinguished (see Chapter 12). Although argument from silence is hardly strong, the linguistic evidence tallies well in this way with the archaeological evidence. Note, among other things, that we never see the Indo-Europeans using any kind of large loom *other* than that of the various indigenes they move in with, a fact that suggests that they did not learn how to weave large textiles until after the main dispersion of the Indo-European tribes.[4]

We could also argue that belt-weaving was a logical place for Europeans, at least, to begin weaving, since the belt or hip-band had apparently been an integral part of northern dress (but not of most southern dress) since surprisingly early times.

One of the objects that the Bronze Age Scandinavians are particularly good at weaving is a peculiar garment for women known as a "string skirt" (Fig. 11.3). In their hands, this consists of a nicely woven hip-band with the weft pulled out in long loops at one side of the band of warp, so as to hang down and form the skirt (see Fig. 6.9). If the weaver had stopped at this stage, the skirt would look for all the world like the newly prepared warp for a warp-weighted loom, hanging from its heading band. The technique is essentially identical. But for the garment, the loops are shorter than for a normal warp,

hanging down only a foot or so, and the bottom ends are fastened together by a twined spacing cord, with little ornamental loops or metal sleeves below—in exactly the way that these people finish off the warp ends into a tassle on their more elegant belts (see Fig. 6.7). From internal evidence, then, it seems as though the making of these string skirts was based on old and familiar belt-weaving techniques, perhaps coupled with a newly learned technique of how to make warps for a warp-weighted loom.

We know of string skirts from other sources in the ancient world. They appear in clear representations on female statuettes from the "Old European" cultures (Fig. 11.4), most particularly from the Cucuteni/Tripolye and Vinča cultural areas, in roughly the 5th millennium (see Gimbutas 1982, map 3, pl. 13, 21, and fig. 8). More than a millennium earlier, the inhabitants of Çatal Hüyük produced some little tubes, cold-hammered out of native copper and attached to strings, which the excavator thought had been used on the string ends of a string skirt (Mellaart 1963a, 196), as in Denmark. But our first representations of string skirts are earlier still: they occur at least twice on the Upper Palaeolithic "Venus" figures. One we have already mentioned (see Chapter 2; Fig. 2.1),

---

[4] We may even have in this time sequence an important clue to the origin of the steppeland "chemise" or tunic, still with us today. It has been argued on linguistic grounds that this bast-fiber garment may ultimately have been Mesopotamian: Linear B *ki-to*, Gk. χιτών, (khitōn), and perhaps Latin *tunica* (<*ctunica?), and Hittite *kattanipu*-(?) may all go back to Akkadian *kitinnu*-'linen garment' (Hebr. *kuttoneth*), a word derived from Akk. *kitû*- 'linen, flax,' which itself may have been borrowed in the 3rd millennium from the Sumerian for linen/flax, GIŠ.GADA (Forbes 1956, 73 n. 284; Barber 1975, 317; *Chicago Assyrian Dictionary* 1956–, K.473–75 *kitû*). But taken alone, the linguistic evidence for timing is rather vague and confusing. All the Indo-European languages that contain these possibly related names are found in a geographical clump—as are the Indo-European cultures that attest the garment as an

old part of their tradition (Barber 1975, 307–13). So we are left wondering whether it was truly the proto-Indo-European community that borrowed the word and concept, or simply a group of linguistically related neighbors who did so. The archaeology now suggests the latter: that the bast-fiber chemise was borrowed from Mesopotamia in the mid- to late 3rd millennium, during the time when the spread of Caucasian metalworking techniques proves to us that there was extensive contact between the two areas. This would seem to be just after the primary breakup of the Indo-European tribes, but before the Greek, Italic, or Hittite speakers had moved very far from the area north of the Caucasus. As we have said, our first evidence so far of large textiles in that region comes precisely in the form of a white chemise, in the 3rd millennium B.C. (Veselovskij 1898, 37; see Chapter 6).

11.3   Bronze figurines of girls wearing string skirts. From Grevensvaenge, Denmark and Itzehoe, Schleswig; Late Bronze Age; early 1st millennium B.C. (Photos courtesy of National Museum, Copenhagen)

11.4   Neolithic clay statuette of a woman wearing a string skirt, from Šipintsi, in the Ukraine. (Naturhistorisches Museum, Vienna)

namely the Venus of Lespugue, with her half-skirt of twisted cords hanging low in the back. The other is a statuette recently discovered in the Soviet Union at Gagarino, on the upper Don, with a short string skirt riding just above the waist and hanging down only in front (Fig. 11.5; Tarasov 1965, 132–38, figs. 14–16). Both figures are thought to be Gravettian (about 20,000 B.C.). It seems, then, that the string skirt was part of the equipment known across the entire European continent in the Upper Palaeolithic. Where we find it later, it is not necessarily the case that one Neolithic or Bronze Age group learned it from contact with another,

but more likely that each was still using it as an archaic holdover from the Palaeolithic, keeping it for reasons that we will do well to investigate.

The string skirt is too skimpy and breezy to be of any real use in keeping warm. And I long marvelled at the fact that, wherever I found it, it also invariably failed to hide precisely those portions of the female anatomy that our modern European-style culture teaches women to hide at all costs. In fact, the garment seems more like an advertisement designed to call attention directly to the pubic area, either by framing it without covering it, as in the Palaeolithic examples,

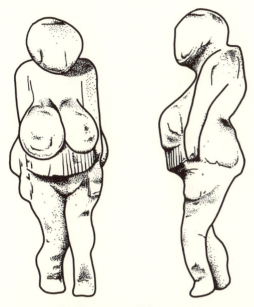

11.5 Palaeolithic "Venus" figure wearing a string skirt; from Gagarino, on the upper Don. (After Tarasov 1965, fig. 14)

or by making it the object of an intriguing game of peekaboo, as in the Neolithic and Bronze Age examples. I have mentioned the shock of the early Danish excavators at discovering how indecently their young ancestresses attired themselves (Chapter 6). So what could possibly be the function of a garment that served neither for warmth nor for modesty, a function so strong that the garment representing it remained in use for some 20,000 years?

I think the clue lies, in fact, in the region to which it draws the eye. It must have served as a non-linguistic statement of sexual capacity or availability on the part of the female wearer, a statement of nubile status, and probably a badge of rather considerable honor.[5] Such a hypothesis fits everything we

know about the occurrence of the string skirt in Europe from the Palaeolithic on. Our actual examples occur on young women, and our representations are on figurines of women clearly of childbearing age. It also suggests that we have more evidence for this culture-garment than the purely archaeological.

In a charming episode in Book 14 of the *Iliad*, Hera conspires to seduce Zeus so that the course of the Trojan War can be temporarily changed while he is too occupied to notice. In preparation, she carefully washes, dresses herself in an undetermined "immortal garment" (ἀμβρόσιον ἑανόν), and then "belted onto herself a girdle crafted with a hundred tassels" (ζώσατο δὲ ζώνην ἑκατὸν θυσάνοις ἀραρυῖαν; *Il.* 14.181). What could this be, given her mission, but the ancient string skirt advertising sexual readiness and availability? She then obtains a second girdle from Aphrodite, the goddess of sexual love. This object is described as a pierced (or "embroidered") strap or belt (κεστὸν ἱμάντα):

> . . . ἔνθα τέ οἱ θελκτήρια πάντα τέτυκτο·
> ἔνθ᾽ ἔνι μὲν φιλότης, ἐν δ᾽ ἵμερος, ἐν δ᾽ ὀαριστὺς
> πάρφασις, ἥ τ᾽ ἔκλεψε νόον πύκα περ φρονεόντων·
>
> (14.214–17)

"and there in it have been crafted all bewitchments—love, and sexual desire, and intimate persuasion, which has stolen away the mind of even those who think carefully."

Aphrodite takes off this persuasive girdle and hands it over to Hera saying:

> τοῦτον ἱμάντα τεῷ ἐγκάτθεο κόλπῳ.
>
> (14.219)

"Put this girdle on under the fold of your breast" (lit. "in under your breast-fold"—just

[5] Overt signs that a woman has reached marriageable status are not uncommon among the cultures of the world. For example, the famous "squash-blossom"

hairdo of the Hopi women announces exactly this status to all viewers.

where the Gagarino Venus wears her string skirt). And she adds that now she is quite sure Hera's designs "will not be unaccomplished" (14.220–21). Nor are they. When Hera, thus girded, finally approaches Zeus, claiming she is setting out on a distant errand, Zeus's reaction to her is everything Hera was aiming for and more. He cries out, "Hera, there is time later to rush off thither; but for now, come let us take pleasure lying down together in love. For never has the lust for any goddess or woman ever so conquered my spirit . . ." (14.313–16). And he hastily gathers a great golden cloud-curtain about them, as he begins to list all the women he has seduced in the past, claiming that he now wants her more than any of those.[6]

Homer apparently does not understand the constructional details of the girdle very well. Although his language is hedgingly ambiguous, he conveys a vague impression by his wording that the girdle may have had allegorical (or graphic) *pictures* of love, desire, and seductive talk woven into it, rather than itself being a *signal* that sexual advances were appropriate. Probably, like so many other Bronze Age artifacts that he reports, he had never seen one, at that late date. But he certainly knew what it was for, at least from a man's point of view: one can understand why it had "become legendary" among the men even as it became largely obsolete among the women.

The Scandinavian Bronze Age skirts and the Homeric remembrances seem to mark the end of the ancient evidence for the string skirt in Europe. But I have seen it still alive and well among the women of eastern Serbia (worn over a white chemise), the band decorated with female fertility symbols and the long fringes seductively swished during the

11.6 Girl from eastern Serbia dancing, wearing woolen front- and back-aprons that consist more of fringe than of apron. The design on the woven part is formed from "hooked lozenges," a female fertility symbol traceable in Europe back to the early Neolithic. (After Belgrade State Folk Ensemble)

dances. "Very old," they called it. Indeed! It has been around for over 20,000 years.

So important a culture-garment, based on both twisted fibers and belt bands, may well have served as catalyst for the invention of band-weaving during its first 10,000 years, and as a model for the invention of the warp-weighted loom during its next 5000.

AGAIN it is noteworthy that our earliest evidence for weaving, at Jarmo, is not very far from the border between the southern and northern zones, relatively speaking. Granted, we don't know exactly where that border is, because we have so little informa-

---

[6] My thanks to John Fischer for noticing and suggesting to me this connection as something to pursue.

tion about what was happening in textile production in the area from the Caucasus south to Jarmo. Apparently this area was not warp-weighted loom territory. At the farthest, the border for the ground-loom lay just north of the Caucasus, and it may have been much nearer to Jarmo in the Neolithic. In any case, a simple mapping shows that our earliest evidence for weaving is close to the juncture of not just two but three textile areas. And the smallest loom type, the band-loom, is the logical ancestor of each of the large looms.

To push the origins of weaving back any farther than our first proof, about 7000 B.C. at Jarmo, we must choose between the relative claims of two very thin sets of data. Jarmo, sitting in the piedmont zone east of the Tigris, is in the heart of the territory in which the plants and animals bearing the most important fibers were first domesticated: flax, sheep, and goats. This territory stretches to the south-southeast and to the west-northwest of Jarmo. The early availability of flax fibers and goathair, and later sheep's wool (when the sheep became woolly enough to provide its masters with usable wool), argues that the piedmont zone was the original home of weaving. On the other hand, if the band-loom was indeed the ancestral form of loom, and hence belts and bands were the first products, we might look rather to the pan-European tradition of wearing belts for the origin of the craft. And it is in the two northern zones, comprising the whole of Europe plus Anatolia, that we have found the band-loom so strong. We have

seen the arguments that bast fibers, collected from any of a number of wild plants, were being used in Europe in the Upper Palaeolithic for nets and for sewing, and apparently even for string skirts. We have no need to assume that domestication was necessary for the invention of weaving, when the objects produced were so small.

Could weaving, like thread-making, then, go back into the Palaeolithic? We could argue, against this, that it is surely no coincidence that our first direct proof of weaving comes within the area and at the time of the first domesticates. But we could also argue, on the other side, that the only reason we have that evidence preserved is because the perishable textiles happened to be impressed into clay, a newly exploited commodity. No fired clay, no evidence—not necessarily no textiles.

Did weaving, in fact, begin in Palaeolithic Europe? We could argue that weaving could have developed easily enough out of netting techniques, as a new way of binding long bast fibers together to make the "belts" so important to European culture. And finally we could argue that maybe, just maybe, the extensive use of weaving then sprang up precisely on the border between two quite different ways of doing things—where the European epipalaeolithic sphere met the sphere of the incipient Near Eastern Neolithic. Growth catalyzed by mixture has occurred many other times in many other places, and in many other fields of human endeavor.

CHAPTER 12

WORD EXCAVATION

Words survive better than cloth; and from time to time we have appealed to linguistic evidence here. But we very much need to improve the data base on which we stand, and also to reap the harvest of additional information on ancient textiles available from an organized study of the vocabulary. Of the four Indo-European languages attested within our time frame, only two have had their textile terminology explicated as a coherent technological unit: Sanskrit (Rau 1970) and Latin (by several authors, most notably Wild 1970a; 1967; and Moeller 1976, 10–28). Hittite terms are scarce and often indeterminable within the rare contexts in which they occur. But the same cannot be said of Greek, where, despite the copious texts and the explication of occasional terms by people who knew weaving, subtle mistranslations, misinterpretations, and missing terms abound. Now that we have a clearer picture of the form of weaving technology used by the Greeks, however, we are in a position both to improve our understanding of the base vocabulary and also to draw a number of further archaeological and technical inferences.

The most productive approach that I have found for dealing with ancient textile terms is to consider them in roughly the order in which the weaver needs them while going through the steps of making thread and cloth. This keeps us firmly connected to the exigencies of the craft. It also gives us some notion of the historical depth of the various processes.

As before, let us begin with the fibers. Wool was apparently the most common textile fiber in Mycenaean as well as in Classical Greece (to judge from the quantity of Linear B tablets dealing with wool); and we find a number of words for it. From the old Indo-European word that gives English *wool*, Latin *lāna*, Hittite *ḫulana*, etc., we have λῆνος (*lēnos*). The most common term is ἔριον (*erion*), Homeric εἶρος (*eiros*), Attic (pl.) ἐρεᾶ (*erea*), Myc. *we-we-e-a* (*werwe(h)e(h)a* 'woolen'; Ventris and Chadwick 1973, 591). Latin *vervēx* 'ram' suggests the word is common at least to the Indo-Europeans who ended up to the southwest. A somewhat less common word, μαλλός (*mallos*), has no accepted etymology, but its variant μάλλυκες (*mallukes*), listed by Hesychius as meaning τρίχες (*trikhes*) 'hairs,' looks suspiciously as though it should have something to do with the Linear B "monogram" for wool, MA + RU; and the whole group may well be from a local Aegean word (see below; cf. Ventris and Chadwick 1973, 52, 435; Killen 1962, 47–50; Greppin 1981, 73–74). Other words for fluff, fuzz, down, or hair are easily drafted to mean wool since wool was the chief such commodity. We will discuss more of these words presently.

To obtain the wool from the sheep (ὄις

[*ois*], another Indo-European word, or πρόβατα [*probata*]: see Puhvel 1983, 226), one goes through the process designated by πέκειν (*pekein*). This verb is given by Liddell and Scott[1] as "to comb, card; shear," but it is clear from this strange-sounding combination, and from what we have learned in Chapter 1, that the verb originally referred to the process of pulling the wool off of the molting sheep, as was done before shears were invented in the Iron Age. "Shear" thus has to have been a late, transferred meaning; and we learn the interesting information that the Greeks, at least, had recently been in the habit of removing the loose wool by combing it out.[2] The root itself is Indo-European, showing up in Latin as *pectere* 'to comb' and *pecten* 'a comb'—so the Italic people, too, must have gotten their wool by combing— and also in Lithuanian as *pèšti* 'pluck'— which suggests that the root in Indo-European antedates the progression from plucking to combing the wool out. The meaning "to card" is, however, suspect: we have no evidence until much later for carding wool (which makes the fibers lie fluffily in all directions, and produces a soft, weak yarn) as opposed to combing it (which makes all the fibers lie parallel, and produces the hard, sturdy yarn called *worsted* that we find in all our artifacts). We might redefine the verb *pekein*, then, as originally referring to the process by which one obtained wool from a molting sheep, a process that was at first one of plucking, it seems; then (for both Greek and Italic) refined to one of combing the wool out; and finally transmuted to one of shearing. Before this last transfer, the verb had also come to be applied to the combing of wool, whether on or off the sheep, and even to the combing of the hair on one's own head. That plucking rather than combing was the original Indo-European process is supported not only by the meaning of the Lithuanian cognate, but also by the fact that some other Indo-European languages chose different verb roots for this wool-gathering process, which themselves mean "pull," "pluck," or "yank": e.g., Slavic (Old Rus. etc.) *rŭvati* 'to tear or pull out' beside *runó* 'fleece' (from a widespread Indo-European "pull" verb), and Indic *lu-* 'obtain wool from a sheep' (Rau 1970, 14).

At least two other verbs occur in this semantic, and practical, area. One is τίλλειν (*tillein*), which hangs onto its sense of "pluck out [hair, fur, feathers, whatever]" and even generates a specialized derivative νακοτιλτεῖν (*nakotiltein*) 'pluck wool.' The other is κείρειν (*keirein*) 'cut, crop, shear,' an old Indo-European verb for cutting in general, cognate with English *shear, short, shirt,* etc., as well as with Hittite *karš-* 'shear,' Tocharian A *kärst-* 'cut', Sanskrit *kr̥ṇā́ti* 'he wounds,' and others.

The mass of fibers obtained by *pekein* is

---

[1] I have used the 1968 Jones edition so extensively in the research, for all spellings, accents, meanings, and references, that this footnote serves for all. Other reference works that I have consulted heavily include Vasmer [1950–58] 1964–73; Kluge 1975; Yonge and Drisler 1893; Lewis and Short 1958; Ventris and Chadwick 1973; and the *Random House English Dictionary* (1973). After most of the work was done, I also obtained access to Chantraine 1968–80 and Frisk 1960–72. For Semitic I have used the *Chicago Assyrian Dictionary* 1956–. Where the same information is found in several of these works I have not tried to sort out citations. Where an individual word is cited, as here, it can be found under that entry in the appropriate dictionary. Some of the Indo-European material I treated several years ago (Bar-

ber 1975), when I investigated clothing terms as well, but I did not have the benefit of so full an archaeological base as now.

I am also indebted to Benveniste (1954; [1966] 1971) and Matisoff (1978) for models and ideas of how to proceed with the semantic reconstruction of an interlocking set; and to Jaan Puhvel, Gordon Fairbanks, and Henry Hoenigswald for reading drafts of this chapter and giving me very helpful suggestions and references.

[2] Plucking and combing seem already to be distinguished, as ways of obtaining wool, in Mesopotamia late in the 3rd millennium among the Ur III texts (Hallo 1979, 4–7). It also seems that plucked wool was considered "a variety inferior to combed wool" (ibid., 5), even when it came from the same breed of sheep.

πόκος (*pokos*), meaning "fleece," then "wool" in general or "tuft of wool." Another word for this fluff is ἄωτος (*aōtos*), a term that, with its other meaning of "choicest of its kind," may reflect the fact that the wool plucked during the first cycle of molting was much finer, softer, and "choicer" than wool shorn off, kemps and all (see Chapter 1, and Barber 1975, 297). It is conceivable, even probable, that the *pe-ki-ti-ra₂* (*pektriai*) of the Linear B tablets were women who not only combed wool for spinning but also combed it off the sheep, that is, collected wool to begin with. In that case, the type of cloth labelled *pe-ko-to* (Ventris and Chadwick 1973, 315–16) may have been luxury cloth woven from fine, soft, kempless wool gathered this way—if in fact clipping was already becoming known as an alternative way of obtaining the wool.

Once acquired, as Lysistrata tells us (Aristophanes, *Lys.* 574–86), the fleece is then washed, cleaned of knots and burrs, and combed (ξαίνειν, *ksainein*) into a wool-basket (καλαθίσκος, *kalathiskos*, diminutive of κάλαθος, *kalathos*[3]). Because Aristophanes is using the passage to make a political point, it is hard to follow what happens next in real life; but (to take it backwards) Lysistrata will weave a cloak from the great τολύπη (*tolupē*—see below) 'ball of wool' that she makes after compacting the κάταγμα (*katagma*) of wool that she takes from the basket. It appears from this and other passages that *katagma*, *tolupē*, and ἠλάκατα (*ēlakata*; see below) are the chief lexical candidates for the roves or rolls of combed wool from which one spins (see Figs. 2.36, 2.38, 12.1).

Linen (λίνον, *linon*), which also has an Indo-European root, requires quite different processes to prepare it for spinning. After a brief preliminary drying, the stalk (στύπος, *stupos*) of flax has to be retted—the trickiest and most critical part of the process. We don't know for certain what term was used specifically for retting flax, but of the known verbs for rotting, σήπειν (*sēpein*) seems more likely than πύθειν (*puthein*), because the former frequently refers to objects rotting in water. In either case, the verbs have the sort of agentless sense of spontaneous happening that a worker in charge of retting might wish for.

After retting comes the lengthy, tiring, and noisy ordeal of beating loose the remaining woody bits of the plant while softening up the bast fibers. No verb for this process is identified in the dictionaries, but it is not hard to flush it out of hiding by looking at the surrounding terms. As the beating goes along, one needs to comb out the loosened bits and keep the fibers from getting too tangled. The short pieces of fiber that break off (as well as sometimes the longest, best fibers) are called *tow* in English: στύππη (*stuppē*), στυππεῖον (*stuppeion*), κέσκεον (*keskeon*) or κέσκιον (*keskion*) are listed for Greek. The last two words come from an Indo-European word for "comb" or "scratch," seen also in Slavic *česati*, Hittite *kiš(š)-* 'to comb,' Old Irish *cír* 'a comb,' and Sanskrit *kacchū-* 'itch,' not to mention one of the Greek verbs for combing fibers, ξαίνειν (*ksainein*; see also Puhvel 1976, 159–61). The *stup-* root, on the other hand, turns up in quite a number of compounds in Greek referring to those who prepare and/or sell the scutched flax fibers. From the same source we have two infrequently attested verbs: στυπάζει (*stupazei*),

---

[3] It is not clear where this word comes from. Jaan Puhvel (pers. comm. 1984) suggests it was derived from κλώθειν (*klōthein*) 'spin' in the same way that βάραθρον (*barathron*) 'cleft, pit' may have been derived from βιβρώσκειν (*bibrōskein*) 'eat, gnaw'; and elsewhere he suggests connection with Hittite *kaluti-* 'circle' (Puhvel 1977, 151). It may also be that both the Greek and the Hittite words are borrowed from a common source, rather than being Indo-European. See below.

which the ancient lexicographer Hesychius gives as meaning βροντᾷ, ψοφεῖ, ὠθεῖ (thunder, make noise, push/thrust), and ἀποστυπάζω (apostupazō), which Liddell and Scott define as "drive off with blows." Within the practical context we have set up, these seemingly disparate meanings merge easily in the noisy hitting and pounding associated with making stuppē, giving us a highly probable verb (ἀπο)στυπάζειν ([apo]stupazein) for the scutching process itself.

After all these various steps, and after being combed into neat roves for easy handling, both the flax and the wool are ready for spinning: νῆν (nēn), νήθειν (nēthein), or κλώθειν (klōthein). For tools we have chiefly the spindle: ἄτρακτος (atraktos), κλωστήρ (klōstēr), or νῆτρον (nētron), which consists, according to Plato's description (Republic 616c–617b) of a shaft (ἠλακάτη, ēlakatē) with a whorl (σφόνδυλος, sphondulos) at one end and, in Classical times, at least, a hook (ἄγκιστρον, aŋkistron) at the other. The most staunchly Indo-European of this cluster of words is the basic process-verb nēn,[4] with its derived tool-forming noun nētron and a host of other derivatives such as nēthein. The verb klōthein, on the other hand, although also the center of a whole set of derivatives, is of unknown etymology (see note 3 above). The most famous of its relatives is Κλωθώ (Klōthō), the Fate who spins the thread of men's destiny along with her sisters Lachesis (Allotment) and Atropos (Unturnable or Inflexible).

If it is Indo-European at all, the word atraktos is presumably an old derivative of the same "turn" root that we see in τρέπειν (trepein) 'turn' and Latin torquēre 'twist, turn.' Semantics excludes the negative prefix as the ancestor of the initial a-; it could be explained either as the "copulative" *sm̥- ('twist into one, twist together'?) or as a prothetic vowel.

Putting an aŋkistron or hook onto the end of the spindle seems, archaeologically, to be a Classical innovation, and linguistically the word seems to have been drafted from the realm of fishhooks. Putting a sphondulos or whorl onto the other end, however, is a far older custom throughout the Aegean, the Balkans, and the whole Near East, as we have seen. The word belongs to a nest of round objects: it refers also to vertebrae and column drums; the feminine noun σφονδύλη (sphondulē) refers to an insect, possibly kermes (which is very round), and to some plant from a family that has globular roots; and both may be related by different derivation to σφενδόνη (sphendonē) 'sling; slingstone,' a slingstone being just about the same size as the average Bronze Age spindle whorl, although more egg-shaped to suit its special purpose. It is, however, curious that there is no common Indo-European word for the spindle whorl, and that instead Greek and Latin (which uses fūsus) seem to have picked up a loan word for this little utilitarian object, taking it in common from some apparently southern European language that

---

[4] There are many, many Indo-European cognates of Greek nēn (including Eng. net, needle, and nettle), all having to do with thread, its making, or its primary uses. Some of them require a reconstruction *nē-, others a reconstruction with initial s (*snē-), and still others defy classification, since an initial s would have been lost regularly in this position. The s, ever a footloose phoneme in Indo-European, may have crept over to this root in some of the languages by semantic association with another basic root for sewing materials, *sneu(r)-

'stringy body-part, especially sinew': e.g., Iran. snavarə 'sinew'; Lith. snaujis- 'sinew'; Gm. Schnur 'string'; Gk. νεῦρον (neuron) 'sinew', νευρά (neura) 'string, bowstring'; Lat. nervus 'nerve' (which Puhvel points out to me [1984] parallels the development of Lat. alvus: Gk. αὐλός, aulos); Toch. B ṣñor 'sinew'; etc. Perhaps also, as Schwartz suggests (1980, 464–66), these two stems are ultimately related to each other, being different extensions of a common root for a twisting or winding motion. See Schwartz for various other possible cognates.

supplied both languages with a variety of cultural, floral, and faunal terms.[5]

When we come to the word ἠλακάτη (*ēlakatē*), however, we find that we have to rebuild the dictionaries written by people who understood nothing about spinning. With the exception of the passage cited from Plato, where a spindle is being described piece by piece, the occurrences of this word are generally translated as "distaff." And yet wherever there is any determining context whatever, the only reasonable interpretation is that *ēlakatē* refers to a spindle and not a distaff. When the servant brings Helen her equipment in the fourth book of the *Odyssey* (4.125–35), she brings two and only two objects: a silver wool-basket and a golden *ēlakatē* that had been given to Helen by a foreign princess. If Helen has before her only the wool-basket and a distaff, she cannot spin by any normal method; but if she has the basket and a spindle she is all set, especially for the typical Bronze Age method of spinning. Again, in Euripides' *Orestes* (1431–32), a slave describes how Helen "with her fingers twisted/wound [ἔλισσεν, *helissen*] the linen on the ἠλακάτᾳ [*ēlakatai*]" as she made her thread. No spinner would twist or wind flax onto a distaff. Linen fibers on a distaff must at all costs hang loose so they can be pulled off without binding and tangling. This can only be a spindle, with the thread being twisted and wound upon it. A late transference to the meaning "distaff" is possible, but not necessary. Two of the four transferred meanings listed by Liddell and Scott refer to the shape of the shaft ("one joint of a reed or cane" and "arrow"), but two refer also or instead to the ability of the object to turn ("the upper part of the mast, which was made to turn round" and "windlass"). Distaffs don't turn; spindles do by their very nature.

Two other related words exist in Greek. One is a neuter plural, ἠλάκατα (*ēlakata*), which refers to the wool ready to be spun and may therefore correspond to our term "roves" for the long, loosely compacted rolls of combed (or nowadays, carded) fibers. On Classical Greek vases showing several women working on their wool, we see just such fluffy roves being coiled up in the wool-baskets ready for spinning (e.g., on the Metropolitan vase, Fig. 2.38—compare the passage about Helen just discussed). The neuter plural form of the word suggests that it might be an old collective formation. The other related word shows that the root goes back at least to Mycenaean times, for in the Linear B tablets concerning women personnel, and again in the textile tablets, we find the uniquely female occupation *a-ra-ka-te-ja* (*ālakateiai*) 'spinners' (Ventris and Chadwick 1973, 533). One gets the impression, in fact, that *ēlakatē* and its relatives constituted the spinning terms of the earlier Greeks living in the Aegean, and that *atraktos* may have gained, or regained, ascendancy later. The *ēlakat-* stem may therefore have been borrowed from the local Aegean population along with much else in late Bronze Age culture. The only Indo-European cognate suggested so far is Lithuanian *lañktis* 'reel' (Wharton 1882, 55), which presents phonological problems, and more likely is directly from *leñkti* 'to bend, bow' (G. Fairbanks, pers. comm. 1984).

There is another term that is often translated as "spin," namely ταλασιουργεῖν (*ta-*

---

[5] Manu Leumann (1964, 118) lists σπόγγος (*spoŋgos*)/*fungus*, σφίδες (*sphides*)/*fidēs* 'harp–strings', and σφενδόνη (*sphendonē*)/*funda* as belonging to this group. One could also add σφάλλω (*sphallō*)/*fallo* 'to trip'. And one might suspect several (but not all) of the other Greek vocabulary words beginning with *sph-* of belonging to

lasiourgein), but the word seems to mean something rather more general, probably involving all the processes between shearing/plucking and weaving (illustrated anciently as a group in Fig. 12.1), and perhaps specifically—certainly generally—referring to wool. The translation chosen by some, "to work wool," thus seems more accurate; but we can make even more refinements. It is clearly derived from τἁλασἱα (*talasia*) 'woolworking,' and is presumably connected to τἁλαρος (*talaros*) 'wool-basket, work-basket,' an implement that figures prominently in all the wool-working scenes. Now, *talasia* occurs in Mycenaean Greek (*ta-ra-si-ja*), but with the much more general meaning "amount weighed out and issued for processing"—"used also of bronze and materials for manufacture of wheels" as well as of wool (Ventris and Chadwick 1973, 583). The entire group of words thus belongs to the τἁλα- (*tala-*) root for weighing things on a balance. We see this process of weighing the wool clearly portrayed on the Metropolitan vase (see Fig. 2.38); and Homer too gives us a touching vignette of the step in a simile for absolute even-handedness (cf. Puhvel 1983, 221):

. . . ὡς τε τἁλαντα γυνὴ χερνῆτις ἀληθής,
ἥ τε σταθμὸν ἔχουσα καὶ εἴριον ἀμφὶς ἀνέλκει,
ἰσἁζουσ᾽, ἵνα παισὶν ἀεικέα μισθὸν ἄρηται.

(*Iliad* 12.433–35)

(Thus a careful woman, a handspinner, having the weights and the wool, holds up the balances keeping them even on both sides, so as to earn a miserable wage for her children.)

Apparently the usual procedure in Mycenaean times was to weigh out the wool needed for a particular weaving project right at the start, and to allocate it for the next round of processing as a weighed unit. *Talasiourgein* is thus, at heart, the weighing out of a certain allotment of raw material—by

12.1 Τἁλασιουργεῖν (*talasiourgein*): preparing the wool (below) and spinning it (above). Etruscan bronze pendant; Bologna; ca. 600 B.C. (Govi 1971, pl. 52)

narrowing, of wool; and by extension, the processing of this mass of wool through spinning up to the next stage (weaving). Latin *pēnsum* 'a quantity of wool given to be spun or woven; an allotment of spinning or weaving' (Glare 1976, 1325) from *pendere* 'to hang, to weigh' seems to have developed very similarly (G. Fairbanks, pers. comm. 1984). Furthermore, the *talaros* would appear to have been (at least originally) not just any old wool-basket, but a separate container for one weighed-out allotment of wool.

Turning now to words for the product of spinning, we find as huge an array of terms for different sizes, shapes, purposes, and materials as in any other language: thread,

265

string, yarn, cord, twine, rope, etc. I shall ignore grades too fat and heavy for normal weaving (e.g., σειρά [*seira*], σχοινίς [*skhoinis*], ἱλλάς [*illas*], πεῖραρ [*peirar*], σπάρτον [*sparton*], πλεκτή [*plektē*], etc.), and weed out the group of words referring to strings or cord not spun from fibers but derived instead from a variety of long, tough, stringy parts of animals, such as νευρά (*neura*, cognate with Latin *nervus*, Iranian *snavarə*, etc.), which is a string made of νεῦρον (*neuron*) 'sinew'; and χορδή (*khordē*), a string of gut (cognate with Latin *haru*- 'entrails,' Lithuanian *žarnà* 'gut,' English *yarn*, German *Garn*). This leaves us with a few words whose etymologies we have already established: νῆμα (*nēma*), which is the most general, generic term for thread, κλωστήρ (*klōstēr*), and λίνον (*linon*) or λιναία (*linaia*, 'linen thread'); plus a few interesting words to be tracked down: ἁρπεδόνη (*harpedonē*), (σ)μήρινθος ([*s*]*mērinthos*), and μίτος (*mitos*).

The first of these, *harpedonē*, denotes line for a hunting snare, as well as for weaving; and its apparent connection with ἁρπάζειν (*harpazein*) 'to seize, grab' indicates that the hunting connection is the original one. In such a context one would expect the thread to be linen.

The second word, (*s*)*mērinthos*, is connected with a cluster of other words clearly having to do with thread, with winding, or with winding up thread and other long, thin things:

μήρινθος, -ου (fem.) (*mērinthos*) *μήρινς (*mērins*), acc. μήρινθα (*mērintha*) σμήρινθος (*smērinthos*)	'cord, line, string'
μηρινθίᾳ (*mērinthiai*)	(Hesychius: σπάρτῳ) 'with rope'
μήρισμα (*mērisma*) or μήρυσμα (*mērusma*)	(Hesychius: κάταγμα, ἢ σπάσμα ἐρίου) 'wool thread (rove?)' or 'piece of wool'

μήρυμα (*mēruma*) (once μήρυγμα [*mērugma*])	'strand, thread; skein, coil'
μηρύομαι (*mēruomai*) (Doric μᾱρύομαι [*māruomai*])	'roll up, wind up, wind around or through'
ἀναμηρύομαι (*anamēruomai*)	'wind up'
ἐπιμηρύομαι (*epimēruomai*)	'wind a layer on top'

The earliest attestations seem to be Odysseus rolling up a sail (*Od.* 12.170) and Hesiod using it as a poetic synonym for "weave":

στήμονι δ' ἐν παύρῳ πολλὴν κρόκα μηρύσασθαι.

(*Works and Days* 538)

(Entwine much weft into little warp.)

The noun forms in -*nth*- suggest strongly that the origin is to be sought in the local Bronze Age Aegean language from which so many loans with that formant came (cf. Glotz 1925, 386–87; Haley and Blegen 1928; Moreschini 1984; but contrast Čop 1956). The diversity of derivational form is easily understandable as locally varying attempts to adapt a foreign word to native declension classes. We also see the forms built alternatively with two vowels that neither Greek nor Indo-European put into alternation, *i* and *u*—although these vowels are remarkably common among the Aegean loan words. Pursuing for the moment the shape of this borrowed word-stem, we find: (1) initial *m*- or *sm*-; (2) a vowel occurring as *ē* in Attic but *ā* in Doric (so the *ā* would be the earlier form, later caught in a well-attested Attic sound change); (3) an apical continuant, *r*; (4) a vocoid that is sometimes *u* and sometimes *i* (possibly according to derivational rules of the lending language): **mār-u/i*-. It is perhaps accident that we again have a word that looks as though it could be the origin of the MA + RU ideogram of Linear B. If it is not an accident, however, we have some interesting consequences. It suggests that μαλλός (*mallos*) and μάλλυκες (*mallukes*; see above) came from the same source, but with a different rendition of some "foreign" apical continuant in the local language, and an interchange of quantity (between -*a*- and -*l*-) somewhere along the line.[6]

The third "thread" term, μίτος (*mitos*), is in need of semantic investigation. What do we know about it? We know that it denotes some kind of thread, because, for example, it is a ball of this material (ἀγαθὶς μίτου [*agathis mitou*]) that Ariadne hands to Theseus (according to a 6th century B.C. text). We know that it occurs on a loom: Homer describes a woman drawing a weft bobbin along it (παρὲκ μίτον [*parek miton*]—*Il.* 23.762). We also know that it occurs in some remarkably orderly form there, because it generates expressions for orderliness or ordering: κατὰ μίτον (*kata miton*) or κατάμιτον (*katamiton*) 'in due order.' Now, there are three types of thread on a warp-weighted loom, all of them orderly: the warp, the weft, and the heddles. Each of these involves, or can involve, a quite different sort of thread doing a different job. The warp—usually wool, but sometimes linen in ancient Greece—must be strong and hard-spun to take the constant beating-in of the weft. The weft, too, was usually wool and sometimes linen; and since it takes no strain, it need not be strong, but can be made soft, fluffy, and warm if so desired. Although we have no technical description of it, we know from the exigencies of the craft (and from all the ethnographic parallels) that the thread of the

heddles had to have been made of linen, so as to be strong enough not to break under the constant strain and smooth enough for each heddle loop to slip itself and its cargo past the surrounding warp threads (themselves usually of catchy wool) with every change of shed. Let us recall from Chapter 3 that traditionally the heddle loops of a warp-weighted loom are re-made around the warp in the desired order or pattern each time the weaving is set up, and unraveled again at the end of the project. The linen string is then wound up in a ball to be saved for the next time; it is a precious part of the loom equipment.

Of the three sets of orderly threads on the loom, the weft is the worst candidate, not least because *mitos* is contrasted with it in our earliest text. The warp is certainly orderly: it hangs on the loom in a neat, ever-visible row from the start to the finish of the weaving. The heddle string, however, has as its very function the ordering of the warp, and thus would seem to be an even more natural propagator for expressions of orderliness. There seems to be no passage in which "heddle" is not at least as good as "warp" for *mitos* (although there are places where simple "string" is as good as either). One could argue (weakly) that in the Homeric passage, since the heart of the simile is the heddle bar (κανών, *kanōn*), the heddles it bears are more likely to be focused on than the warp: ". . . the heddle bar, which she holds taut with her hands while drawing the weft past the

---

[6] It is well known that we find double reflexes of apical liquids elsewhere among Mediterranean borrowings: e.g., ἐρέβινθος (*erebinthos*) and λέβινθος (*lebinthos*) 'chickpea.' The clear singleness of the original phoneme here presumably fits in with the fact that the users of Linear B had to make do with one set of signs for both *r* and *l*, even though these were distinct phonemes in Mycenaean Greek. (A similar mismatch, with similar consequences, exists between Japanese and English, where the one Japanese retroflex lateral is heard by English-speakers as sometimes an /r/ and sometimes an /l/, and someone writing English words in the Katakana sylla-

bary has to use the single Japanese set of symbols for both English sounds.) Hence a connection among *mall-u/o-* 'wool, hair,' *mār-u/i-* 'thread; to wind,' and MA + RU 'wool' is not unthinkable, although far from proven.

Quite different problems are encountered if one assumes, on the other hand, that the word μέρμιθ- (*mermith-*) 'strap, chain' is also of the same family as μηρ- (*mēr-*; cf. Moreschini 1984, 69). If the original vowel is -*ē*- rather than -*ā*-, then the Doric form would have to be seen as a hypercorrection, and the connection with *mall-* becomes unlikely.

heddles." A handy ball of heddle string would suit Theseus's legendary purpose admirably: it would be long, fine, and strong—as warp thread also usually is.

Are there cognates to help us out? Apparently there is nothing in the other Indo-European languages; but in Greek we have some derivatives, all having to do with cloth or weaving. Among other words, the Romans equated μίτινοι (mitinoi) with Latin licinae, μιτίσασθαι (mitisasthai) with liciare, and τρίμιτος (trimitos) with trilicarius. The adjective licinus means "bent back on itself" (which is true of each and every loop of a string heddle but has no ready application to a warp thread); the base noun līcium apparently meant "girdle," "noose," or even "tether" (Puhvel 1983, 226); and the verbs in both languages presumably refer to making the respective objects. But trimitos (and trilicarius), which refers to some important type of cloth, would seem to be insoluble, unless we again look at the overall picture of textile technology.

In the known vocabulary for ancient Greek types of cloth, there is a gap that is very surprising to one acquainted with the history of the craft: we have no known word for twill, the darling of the Iron Age European weavers. Our own word twill, as we saw in Chapter 7, refers to the doubling ("two-ing") of

the threads, which is accomplished by the use of four heddle bars instead of two, on our horizontal treadle looms. The use of four heddle bars gives rise to the other type of name for twill, fourshaft. But the warp-weighted loom has a shed bar at the bottom and only one heddle bar, for making ordinary plain-woven cloth. To make normal 2/2 twill (or "fourshaft"), one needs therefore to add two more heddle bars, which makes a total of three. Why is it, then, that we find precisely this compound trimitos as the name for an important type of cloth—never *τετράμιτος (*tetramitos) or δίμιτος (dimitos)?[7] "Three-heddle," for a warp-weighted loom, is a precise description of the most popular cloth of that millennium in Europe.

We can use the same sort of argument from a gap for mitos itself. As we shall see, we have several clear and frequent words for "warp" in Greek, but no other possible candidate for "heddle." And yet it is unthinkable that a weaver should not have a term, and a relatively specialized one, for this crucial loom-part that she wrestles with at almost every moment of the weaving process.

Returning to our sequence of terms, we find ourselves armed with all sorts of thread, which can be wound up (τολυπεύειν [tolupeuein], ἑλίσσειν [helissein], πηνίζεσθαι [pēnizesthai]) in different ways—most

---

[7] The only attested occurrence of dimitos in Liddell and Scott is medieval, and refers to a felt hat—which has neither warp nor weft (but might have two loops on it?).

In much of this I would seem to disagree with Wild (1967), who takes mitos as "thread," and as "weft" in particular. It may be, however, that our differences stem from a semantic widening of the meaning of the word, such that, in the early period I concentrate on, it meant primarily "heddle thread" and then "thread," whereas by the late period that he concentrates on, it had gone on to mean "any thread used in weaving," even "weft." Certainly the technology had changed and enlarged tremendously by Roman times. We could perhaps settle Aeschylus's πολυμίτων πέπλων (polumitōn peplōn; Suppliants 432) amicably as referring to cloth made with more heddle bars than one—i.e., twill or a warp design,

rather than necessarily brocade. I agree with Wild that we know of no brocade from the Near East until rather late. But there are other fabrics that would fit the description as well or better. In particular, one of the pattern-woven cloths from Gordion, from around 690 B.C., indicates by its weaving error that multiple-heddle patterns were already being made at that time (see Chapter 7 and fig. 7.8), and right next door to the Greeks. (See also Wipszycka 1965, 112, for a discussion of later polymita.)

It is interesting that in both Latin and Greek, these paired word-stems are also associated with the name for some kind of woman's girdle or tie: licium and μίτρα (mitra). Licium is also used as the Latin equivalent of mitos itself. Does the connection come through the notion of tying a loop around a (vertical) entity?

generally into a τολύπη (tolupē), ἀγαθίς (agathis), or μήρυμα (mēruma). Tolupē and its verb have no certain etymology, although they are apparently connected somehow with Hittite tarupp- 'gather into one place; twist or wind together' (see Joseph 1982 for full discussion; both may well be borrowed from a common source—note the r/l problem again). That the end product is a ball is shown by the transference to (from?) some kind of gourd and some kind of cake. On the other hand, mēruma we have seen associated with the coils of a snake, and with a verb for rolling up a sail, so it may be either a ball or a skein. The rather uncommon word agathis is interesting chiefly for the fact that its phonological shape suggests a borrowing (from "the" Bronze Age Aegean language?—see below), but we haven't much clue to the shape of the end product, unless Hesychius's gloss to a sesame confection indicates that, like mēruma, a globular (or coiled?) form has led to a transfer to the world of pastry. The verb helissein is used repeatedly and specifically of winding hair, thread, etc. onto a spindle (περὶ ἄτρακτον [peri atrakton] in Herodotus 4.34, ἠλακάτᾳ [ēlakatai] in the Euripides passage already quoted), as well as of all sorts of other turnings and twistings. Finally, pēnizesthai is from πήνη (pēnē), a basic word for weft that we will discuss shortly. At least originally, the verb must have meant "to wind weft onto a weft spool."

We are now ready for the host of words relating to looms and weaving. To begin with, the Greeks, like the Indo-Europeans in general, distinguish between weaving (on a loom), ὑφαίνειν (huphainein) or ὑφᾶν (huphan), and plaiting, πλέκειν (plekein).[8] The Greek words in fact carry on the Indo-European roots for these two crafts (cf. Barber 1975, 301). The other words are either more

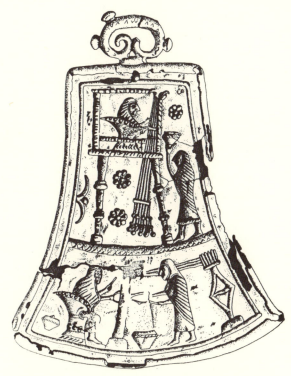

12.2 Ἱστουργεῖν (histourgein): making the cloth by warping (below) and weaving (above). Etruscan bronze pendant (reverse of Fig. 12.1); ca. 600 B.C. (Govi 1971, pl. 54)

general—ἱστουργεῖν (histourgein), literally "to work at the loom" (and like its mate, talasiourgein, referring to the whole set of associated activities, as illustrated anciently in Fig. 12.2)—or more specific—e.g., κρέκειν (krekein) and σπαθᾶν (spathan), both referring to different ways of beating up the weft, as we will see presently—or poetic, as in μηρύεσθαι (mēruesthai) 'to wind around or through.'

The loom itself is called ἱστός (histos), a word generally assumed to be from the Indo-European root meaning "stand" (although a present-type reduplication in a noun forma-

---

[8] Jenkins and Williams (1985, 413) come up with the interesting and likely suggestion that the verb plekein also referred to making sprang.

tion is unusual). That the term was in use among the Bronze Age Greeks is attested by the profession name *i-te-ja-o* (*histeiaon*) 'of the (fem.) weavers' and perhaps also *i-tę-wę* (*histeu-*) '(male) weaver' (Ventris and Chadwick 1973, 161, 506, 548). In favor of the "stand" root is the fact that other Indo-European languages, such as Russian, have made words for looms from this root, although probably independently. Also, the warp-weighted loom was generally dismantled when not in use (see Chapter 3), and so had to be set up—literally stood up—anew each time. Hesiod admonishes (*Works and Days* 779): τῇ δ'ἱστὸν στήσαιτο γυνή (then a woman should set/stand up her loom).

Grace Crowfoot (1936–37) has provided an excellent analysis of the Greek loom and its parts (see Fig. 12.3). Its uprights are ἱστό-ποδες (*histopodes*) or κελέοντες (*keleontes*), the latter apparently a borrowed word for "beam" or "wood" (cf. κελεός [*keleos*] 'wood-

pecker'; but compare Frisk 1960–72, 814–15). The crossbeam from which the warp is hung and on which the cloth is rolled seems to have been called the ἀντίον (*antion*); at least, we know that this name denoted some important part of a loom in Classical Greek, and the same word in Modern Greek refers to both the cloth beam and the warp beam of the two-beam loom (Crowfoot 1936–37, 46). *Antion* contains an Indo-European preposition meaning "opposite, in front of" (from a still older word for "face, front")—here presumably something opposite the weaver. On the warp-weighted loom, that does not help us much, since the entire loom stands before the weaver. The word may go all the way back to the warp tied to the bar immediately in front of the weaver in a backstrap loom, i.e., the cloth beam. (Of course, on the warp-weighted loom there is only one "beam," the cloth beam.)

The weights hung on the warp are called

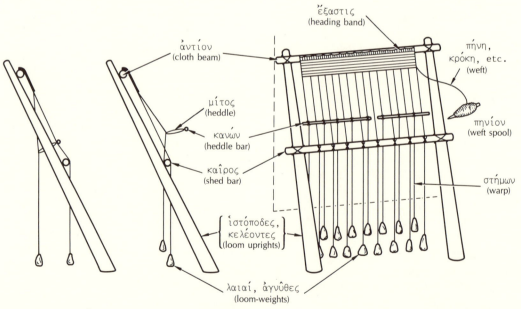

12.3   Diagram of ancient Greek type of warp-weighted loom, with parts labelled in Greek (cf. Fig. 3.27)

λαιαί (*laiai*), presumably related to λᾶας (*laas*) 'stone,' or are called ἀγνῦθες (*agnuthes*), another word with no Indo-European etymology and a suspiciously Aegean-sounding phonology.[9] Indeed, the two words may originally have referred respectively to the large, roughly conical or pyramidal weights of Danubian style, for which one could easily have substituted a stone (as the Scandinavians still do), and to the slim, discoid weights common in the Minoan world (see Chapters 3, 14). The Mycenaeans knew both types, as the archaeology shows.

The heddle bar was named κανών (*kanōn*), as we saw in Chapter 3. Crowfoot (1936–37, 46) adds the interesting semantic information that Syrian weavers to this day call the heddle bar a *kanūn*, a word that, in this form with final *n*, must have been a rather late loan from Greek. The Greek word itself, however, came ultimately from Semitic, apparently having been derived within Greek from κάννα (*kanna*) 'reed, cane,' which was borrowed at some point from some Semitic language. The base word is attested as *qanû* 'reed, cane' in cuneiform all the way back to the 3rd millennium. From this etymology we can wring the information that the slim little heddle bars that we see depicted in the Greek vases (see Chapter 3) were at some point being made of lengths of reed or cane—necessarily short ones, since long ones would be liable to snap under the tremendous weight as they were pulled forward.

The shed bar, as Crowfoot also points out (ibid.), is called καῖρος (*kairos*), and functions partly as a template to which the immovable half of the warp is bound (we can see the bindings on the Metropolitan vase, Figs. 2.38, 3.13) to keep it in its proper place and width as the warp threads of the other shed are pulled past. That is, it serves also to regulate the warp.

With our loom all assembled, we are now ready to begin work on the cloth. The first step is to make the warp, which for this loom involves making a heading band at the same time. We see this heading band, incidentally, represented repeatedly on the Parthenon and on other Classical sculptures as a narrow, corrugated band on the part of the fabric that is flung over the left arm (Fig. 12.4). The corduroy look comes, as we saw in earlier chapters (3, 4, and 7), from the fact that the weave here is half-basket, not plain weave. (For a Classical example that has actually survived, see the linen from Eleusis: Mylonas 1953, 82 fig. 9.) Although the dictionaries don't recognize it, there is an interesting cluster of words that seem to refer to just this heading band and its manufacture. As listed in Liddell and Scott, these words are:

ἄσμα (*asma*), δίασμα (*diasma*)	'warp'
διάσματα (*diasmata*)	(Hesychius: φάρεος ἀρχήν) 'beginning of the cloth'
ἄττομαι (*attomai*), or διάζομαι (*diazomai*)	'set the warp in the loom'
δίεζετο (*diezeto*) (alphabetized by Hesychius as διαζ-)	(Hesychius: διεσχίζετο) 'divided'
ἔξαστις (*exastis*)	'selvedge'

The only efficient way to make sense of these seemingly disparate meanings is to assume that the (*di*)*asma* refers specifically to the heading band with the long strings of warp hanging from it. From such a starting point, all the remaining explanations become elegantly simple. The verbs must refer either to the manufacture of the band cum warp or to the long process of binding the band onto the upper beam while dividing ("shedding") the

---

[9] Polysyllabic, with accented -*u*-, and "consonantal declension" stem ending in -*th*-.

12.4 Ἔξαστις (*exastis*): ribbed heading band visible on cloth over the left arm of each figure on the Parthenon frieze; 5th century B.C. (Courtesy of Trustees of the British Museum)

trailing warp threads and hanging the weights on in balanced pairs. This crucial division of the warp also accounts both for Hesychius's gloss "divided" and for the association of the relational morpheme διά (*dia*), with its base notion of cleaving through or sending in different directions. Once the cloth is completed, this same band remains

as the funny-looking edge resulting (ἐξ, *ex*) from all of this, the *exastis*—not originally side-selvedge (which may be παραίρημα [*parairēma*]), but the heading band we see distinguished in the sculptures (see Fig. 12.4). By this analysis the entire group of words receives a cohesive set of meanings.[10]

The threads of the warp that hang down

[10] These deductions suggest that the female textile profession *a-ze-ti-ri-ja* found in the Linear B tablets (Ventris and Chadwick 1973, 317, 536) might have to do with this nest of words, and therefore with making warps for the warp–weighted loom. The interpretation is bolstered by KN Ln1568, where *a-ze-ti-ri-ja* occurs on a textile tablet with an accounting of *o-nu-ke*, which are some sort of textile edgings (see ibid., 317; Killen 1979, 157–61; and Chapter 15 n.8). Killen (1968a, 641) refers to *a-ze-ti-ri-ja* and its companion on Ln 1568, *ne-ki-ri-de*, as "feminine trade-names with strong textile connexions," and interprets the entry to mean that this kind of worker, in such-and-such a workshop, has produced "one unit of *o-nu-ke*," made of wool. A warp with heading band?

Killen (1979) has also shown very convincingly from the internal evidence of the tablets, however, that the accounted cloth seems to come in from the weavers, and then be sent out again to workers who enhance it in var-

ious ways before sending it back. One of the major forms of enhancement is with *o-nu-ke*, or edgings, which may be either white or multicolored (see Chapter 15), and these seem to be applied, among other places, in the workshops of women denoted as *a-ze-ti-ri-ja*, which term Killen sees as being identical with the much more frequent *a-ke-ti-ri-ja* and as coming from ἀσκεῖν (*askein*) 'finish; decorate' (Killen 1979, 165–67). So we must also deal with the question (asked, e.g., by Killen 1972, 428–29; Ventris and Chadwick 1973, 158, 536; Killen 1979, 165 n. 23) as to whether *a-ze-ti-ri-ja* is simply a variant of *a-ke-ti-ra₂/a-ke-ti-ri-ja* or is a different word entirely.

Now, *attomai* and *[di]azomai* (which are the same in meaning) require a difference in voicing in the source form, but could come from either a dorsal or apical stop, plus a (frequent) derivational suffix in -*y*-: *attomai* < *$*aky$*- or *$*aty$*-, *azomai* < *$*agy$*- or *$*ady$*-. The associated nouns, however, both require apicals, although they could be either voiced or voiceless: -*astis* < *$*at/d$*-*tis* (or

are regularly called στήμων (stēmōn; from the same "stand" root that we mentioned with the word for the loom), less commonly ἤτριον (ētrion; Doric ἄτριον, ātrion). The latter form is not related in any normal phonological way to the root used for the heading band; but if both are loans from a common source, there may in fact be a connection. The weft, however, is designated by a number of words, such as πήνη (pēnē), κρόκη (krokē), ῥοδάνη (rhodanē), ἐφυφή (ephuphē). The last of these terms is built on the root for "weave," while rhodanē seems to be from a notion of moving in and out, to judge from the adjective ῥοδανός (rhodanos) 'flickering, wavering.' Neither of these is so common as the first two terms, however. Of them, pēnē has a series of derivatives and mates, such as πηνᾶσθαι (pēnasthai) or πηνίζεσθαι (pēnizesthai) 'to wind weft onto a bobbin,' πηνίον (pēnion) 'spool of weft,' πήνισμα (pēnisma) 'weft,' and πῆνος (pēnos) 'web.' It has etymological connections with Latin pannus 'cloth,' Gothic and Old English fana 'cloth,' and German Fahne 'flag.'

Krokē, on the other hand, hurls us into a large family of difficult terms. The heart of it all seems to be a verbal root κρεκ- (krek-), which has to do with hitting strings noisily with sharp instruments. From looking just at the Greek, one has trouble telling whether the meaning began with weaving or with playing a stringed instrument; but since all the cognates outside Greek have to do with weaving, we can assume weaving as the semantic base for Greek too: Old Norse hræll 'pin-beater,' English reel 'device for winding thread onto' (see below for the semantics), and perhaps Latvian krekls 'shirt' and Old English hrægel 'dress, garment.' Ignoring the meanings and derivatives having to do with making music or noise, in Greek we have a kind of cloth called κρεκάδια (krekadia), a term κροκύς (krokus) for the nap on the finished cloth, a word κέρκος (kerkos) meaning a handle or a beast's tail or other rod-like appendage, and κερκίς (kerkis), also some sort of peg or pin, specifically used for weaving. As Crowfoot (1936–37), Landercy (1933) and others have shown, the kerkis is undoubtedly a pin-beater. Among the Greeks the kerkis seems at least sometimes to have carried the weft on it (compare the English cognate reel 'device for winding thread onto'), thus functioning in the place of our shuttle, while the sharp tip was used to slip in between the warp threads and beat the weft into place, in this way functioning like our reed. These actions of hitting the weft home with a twang, and of running the tip of the pin-beater across the taut warp

---

*as-tis), and asma < *at/dsma (or *as-ma). If indeed the two Mycenaean words are equivalent, then the two Classical nouns cannot belong to the group, despite their semantics; but if the Classical nouns do, in fact, belong to the same word family as the verbs, then an original dorsal stop is not possible and a-ke-ti-ri-ja is out—at any rate by our known sound laws. It is conceivable that the two Mycenaean words are not equivalent: both forms occur at both Knossos and Pylos, so simple dialect variation is hard to appeal to. It is also conceivable that all of the words do belong together, but have been borrowed at least partly independently from a lender language whose sound laws we know nothing of. If a-ke- is from aske-, then we have to stand on our heads to get a-ze- from it by Greek laws.

Whatever the phonological solution to the Mycenaean

terms, we can at least say that the picture of textile manufacture that we have built up shows the reasonableness of having women who manufacture edgings that are applied to woven cloth also be makers of warps with heading bands. One might also recall the closing borders of some of the Neolithic Swiss fabrics described in Chapter 4, in which the cut warp ends were used as the weft for a fancy edging constructed, like the header, on a band loom. For any or all of these activities, the women would need supplies of yarn: large amounts for warps, much smaller amounts for borders to be sewn on, and less still for Swiss-style closing border (since the weft of these borders is provided by the warp ends of the cloth itself). As Killen points out (1979, 164), the accounts also show amounts of wool being allotted for the o-nu-ke and other "finishing" processes.

threads to free them from each other as the sheds are changed (cf. Plato, *Cratylus* 388–89; Landercy 1933), seem to be the situational center from which all else follows. That the *kerkis* indeed tapered to a point is corroborated by the transference of meaning to a wedge-shaped section of theater seats.

Along with the pair κερκίς (*kerkis*) 'pin-beater' and κρέκειν (*krekein*) 'hit weft home, weave' we have another pair: σπάθη (*spathē*) 'sword-beater' and σπαθᾶν (*spathan*) 'hit weft home, weave.' A *spathē* was actually any broad, flat blade, like a fighting sword, or in this case a flat wooden blade that was slipped into the shed after the weft to beat it home. Band weavers use a finger in exactly the same way. On the Metropolitan vase (Figs. 2.38, 3.13) we see yet a third type of beater, in the form of a long, thin rod. The generic term for a rod was ῥάβδος (*rhabdos*), and this word may have been used here, although I can find no direct evidence. It may also have served as a name for the distaff (for which we know no particular term, if my analyses above are correct); and Aristophanes uses it (*Lysistrata* 576) for rods used to beat the burrs out of raw wool—and the sins out of citizens.

When the web is finished, the weights are generally cut off the bottom of the warp, leaving a fringe of warp ends. On a modern loom, the cut warp ends left on the loom are known as *thrums*, in English, from the zero grade of the Indo-European root whence Latin *terminus*, etc. From the selfsame root we have a Greek textile word, τερμιόεις (*termioeis*), which the early poets use to describe some typical feature of tunics. To judge by the pictures, the cut warp ends were often left at the bottoms of the tunics in Mycenaean and archaic Classical times (Fig.

12.5 Τερμιόεις (*termioeis*): "thrummed" or warp-fringed. Mycenaean soldier wearing a fringed tunic, depicted on the Warrior Vase from Mycenae; ca. 1200 B.C. (National Museum, Athens). See Fig. 16.8 for the whole scene

12.5; Barber 1975, 311–13 and fig. 6). Perhaps that is what this adjective refers to.

Once it was woven, the Greek housewife often sent her woolen cloth to a fuller (κναφεύς, *knapheus*) for a nice finish. He would wash it (πλύνειν, *plunein*) with soaps (ῥύμμα, *rhumma*; or κιμωλία γῆ, *kimōlia gē* 'Kimolian earth') or ammonia as detergent, then compact it (νάσσειν, *nassein*; νάττειν, *nattein*), tease the surface (κνάπτειν, *knaptein*; ξαίνειν, *ksainein*) to raise the nap (κροκύς, *krokus*), and trim (κείρειν, *keirein*) the nap until it was even. We have dealt with *keirein*, *krokus*, and *ksainein*; we will consider *nassein* below. The κναφ- (*knaph-*) root, however, occurs in Linear B (*ka-na-pe-u*) and has several proposed cognates among European languages: English *nap*, OE *hnoppa* 'tuft,' *hnoppian* 'to pluck' (but Greek φ should correspond to Germanic *b, not *p), Welsh *cnaif* 'fleece,' Latv. *knàbt* 'pick, peck at.' Given the phonological problems,[11] we may be dealing with a loan word that came independently into several Indo-European branches. Is it relevant that the process of

[11] The Germanic/Greek correspondence may be soluble; but even within Greek there is the problem that this same morpheme sometimes turns up with γν- (*gn-*)

instead of κν- (*kn-*). (My thanks to H. Hoenigswald for pointing these details out to me [1985].)

fulling woolen cloth seems to be a Central European invention? (See Chapter 9.) In the 2nd millennium, of course, the Proto-Celts were still in central Europe along with the other groups.

After all these processes, the lady could sew her cloth (ῥάπτειν, *rhaptein*; κασσύειν, *kassuein*) or embroider it (κέντειν, *kentein*—literally "prick" it) with a needle (ῥαφίς, *rhaphis*; βελόνη, *belonē*) and colored thread. As elsewhere, we see two layers in the vocabulary. The unusual verb *kassuein* 'to stitch,' with its antique assimilation of prefix to root, preserves the old Indo-European "sewing" word (seen in English *sew*, Latin *suere*, etc.), as does ὑμήν (*humēn*) 'membrane' (one of those stringy body-parts that one used to sew with). And *belonē* 'needle,' related to βέλος (*belos*) 'dart,' is from another Indo-European root having to do with sharp, slim tools or missiles (cf. Lith. *gelonìs* 'needle'). But the ῥαφ- (*rhaph-*) root, which in Classical Greek is the only one productive of sewing terms, has no known etymology.[12]

At any of various stages along the way, one could dye the fibers: before or after spinning, and before or after weaving. The dye was called βαφή (*baphē*) or φάρμακον (*pharmakon*) and the process βάπτειν (*baptein*), ῥέζειν (*rhezein*), ἀνθίζειν (*anthizein*), and μιαίνειν (*miainein*). The last term is more properly "to stain," while the *baph-* root, which dominates the Classical dyeing terminology, has a more general sense of "to dunk." The verb that perpetuates the Indo-European terminology is the infrequently attested word *rhezein*, with its relatives ῥέγος (*rhegos*) or ῥῆγος (*rhēgos*) 'blanket, rug';[13] ῥεγεύς (*rhegeus*), ῥογεύς (*rhogeus*), ῥηγεύς (*rhēgeus*), or ῥεγιστής (*rhegistēs*) 'dyer'; and ῥέγμα (*rhegma*) 'something that has been dyed.' The members of this set are largely Doric, except for *rhegos*, which is common in Homer. Again the words produce an impression of layering in the vocabulary. The *rheg-* root, with its Indo-European ablaut grades, is cognate with Indic *rájyati* 'is dyed, is red' (causative *rajayati* 'dyes, colors red'), *rāga-* 'color, dye, red,' and *mahārajana* 'dye-plant: safflower' (Rau 1970, 27), whereas the root *baph-* is almost certainly a loan word.

Of the other words, *anthizein* is clearly from ἄνθος (*anthos*) 'flower,' and can also refer to either decorating or flavoring with flowers. From the wording of Liddell and Scott's definitions, it is clear that they have in mind the idea that *anthizein* colors something so that it is bright and colorful *like* flowers; and so it may be. But since flower heads produce so many of the natural dyes, I wonder if it wasn't originally a matter of coloring *with* flowers (cf. the use of the verb for flavoring wine with flowers). On the other hand, *pharmakon* means primarily "drug," or better yet, "any substance that will do something for you and that is made in small quantities out of natural resources, especially plants and minerals." In the Linear B tablets, the minor herbs, spices, remedies, and dyes are all lumped together in a way that seems odd to us, but evidently seemed quite natural to the Mycenaean storekeepers.[14] It is

---

[12] The root used to be assumed to be cognate with Lithuanian *veřpti* 'spin' (O. Schrader 1886, 175; etc.), but the Mycenaean form shows that it did not have an initial *w-* (cf. Winter 1958, 206). Sewing is not spinning; so the semantics were already strained. Rather than throw out the Mycenaean form as therefore not connected to the Classical form, I would point out that this root fits in quite nicely with a whole group of other loan words that relate to textiles, discussed below, and there-

fore is very unlikely to be Indo-European.

[13] I find it significant that the Indo-European "dye, color" root should turn up precisely in the name of an article, namely a rug or blanket, that was almost necessarily made of wool, which is by far the easiest fiber (other than silk) to dye.

[14] Although *pa-ma-ko* occurs in Linear B, the context does nothing to clarify the meaning.

this semantic lumping (from our point of view) that makes "dye" seem the appropriate translation for *pharmakon* in some contexts.

Mordants, too, as we saw, had been known since Mycenaean times at least. The verb is στύφειν (*stuphein*) 'to pull together, as with an astringent; to treat with a mordant, fix.' The connection in meanings comes from the fact that the chief astringents used were any of a variety of alums, known indiscriminately as στ(ρ)υπτηρία (*st[r]uptēria*; Mycenaean *tu-ru-pte-ri-ja*), which are also—as we saw in Chapter 10—the best mordants for general purposes.

The last set of words that we will look at is composed of two little groups having to do with felting. The principal verb of one group is νάσσειν (*nassein*; Attic νάττειν, *nattein*; root νακ-, *nak*-), which is used for piling up, pressing, squeezing, or stamping various types of substances. Related to this verb are nouns, an adjective, and another verb, all having to do with fleece: νάκος (*nakos*) 'fleece,' νακή (*nakē*) 'woolly or hairy skin,' τὰ νακτά (*ta nakta*) 'felt,' νακτός (*naktos*) 'close-pressed, solid,' νακοτιλτεῖν (*nakotiltein*) 'pluck wool.' Clearly the various meanings associated with *nak*- all follow logically from the actions involved in felting: piling up the fluffed-up wool on the mat, then pressing and squeezing it by whatever means available until the wool is thoroughly matted. One of the chief products of felting in ancient Greece, however, is named from another root entirely, and one with relatives in other Western Indo-European languages: πῖλος (*pilos*) 'felt hat; felt.' From this root comes a verb πιλεῖν (*pilein*) 'to make felt, compact wool into felt,' and a number of other derivatives: πίλημα (*pilēma*) 'felt; felt hat,' πίλησις

(*pilēsis*) 'compression of wool into felt; compression,' and so forth. Within Greek the base meaning seems to be that of compaction, with felt and in particular the making of felt hats being the chief applications. But the related Latin *pilus* 'hair' and *pilleus* 'felt cap' suggest a different starting point, namely the raw ingredient, while the Germanic group sticks entirely to the product, felt: English *felt*, German (and Old High German) *Filz*. Once again, one gets the impression of cultural layering from the double sets of vocabulary.[15]

ARCHAEOLINGUISTICALLY, the most striking and productive aspect of the Greek textile vocabulary is the large number of doublets or near-doublets, some terms being Indo-European and some not demonstrably so. One is reminded of the vast quantities of such doublets in English between inherited Germanic and borrowed French terms (*room—chamber; eat—dine; sheep—mutton; cow—beef*). From the archaeological evidence, a thick layer of borrowing is exactly what one would expect in Greek. It is important to take into account that the Indo-European tribe that we know of as the Greeks moved from the Indo-European "homeland" to Greece, perhaps in several stages, and that the evidence is strong that these Greeks were picking up local technology (and its terminology) along the way, as well as in the Aegean area where the tribe finally settled.

Linguists who specialize in Indo-European have, for good reasons, tended to start from the assumption that every word in the daughter languages (such as Greek) must have an Indo-European etymology unless proved otherwise. If we had not tried out

---

[15] The *nak*- root has no Indo-European etymology, and is probably borrowed. But whether the *pil*- root is truly Indo-European or not is not entirely clear to me, despite the related words in Latin, Germanic, and

Slavic. Again we see a clustering among late neighbors, suggesting the possibility of prehistoric borrowing from a common source.

such a hypothesis we would not have successfully overcome a large number of difficulties with Indo-European phonology. Now that we have such a tremendous body of both linguistic and archaeological data, however, it is time also to try out as an assumption the scenario that our textile data beg us to consider: that whole *groups* of words for a new type of technology may have been borrowed from one source, and may even have been borrowed from roughly the same source by several neighboring Indo-European daughter languages. That is, it may be that we are having so much trouble solving the phonological problems of correspondences in certain corners of the vocabulary because of common technological borrowing.

One linguistic signal of this sort of problem will be that the correspondences in vocabulary are only between close geographic neighbors (many of our Greek textile words showed known correspondences only in Hittite or Latin, or only in Latin and Germanic, or only in Germanic and Balto-Slavic). Another sign will be the frequency of quasi-correspondences—those which don't quite work (we have seen many of these). Yet a third linguistic signal will be double vocabulary: subtly different terminology coming from two different traditions (as with the famous English doublets for the animals, tended in the barnyard by Anglo-Saxon peasants, versus the meats therefrom, served on a silver platter to the Norman French overlord). But linguistics alone is not sufficient to untangle the puzzle. We need the larger patterns of context to differentiate between accidental lack (of cognates, or of enough data to work out a particularly tricky sound law) on our part and collusive borrowing on their part.

A compilation of the doublets in our Greek textile vocabulary is given in Table 12.1.[16]

Phonologically there are three things that strike me about this list. One is the group of words that have phonological shapes pointing (some strongly, some weakly) to the *-nth-* language of the south Aegean. That we should find them here is no surprise whatever; the only problem is to determine exactly which words belong in fact to this layer. The noun formations in *-nth-* or *-th-* are the most obvious; and evidence of the r/l confusion is indicative; the unanalyzable word bases tend to be long, by Indo-European standards (that is, two- or three-syllable stems before the Greek inflectional ending); and, as with most loans of any non-Indo-European origin coming into Greek, there is an un-Greekish favoring of a/u/i compared to e/o. With one exception, there is very little Greek derivation from this group, suggesting perhaps that the words are relatively recent and unassimilated. The exception is *mār-u/i-*, which we discussed above at length, and which seems to have been borrowed several times in several forms, sometimes with the noun-deriving morphology of the lender already attached (e.g., *-inth-*), and once as a verb stem (μηρυ- [*mēru-*]) from which a small number of other nouns were derived by purely Greek means.

The second notable phonological pattern is the set of single-syllable verb roots with a not-very-Greek vowel and a final aspirated stop: C(C)VCh- (where C = contoid, V = vocoid, h = aspiration). Three of these roots have generated a large number of derivatives. And to them we can add some other words of the same shape that do not have doublets, e.g., κναφ- (*knaph-*) 'fulling,' and στυφ- (*stuph-*) 'mordant,' both of which refer to technologies that we have seen developing outside the Indo-European homeland.

The third phonologically notable point is

---

[16] Here I am excluding terms that belong first and foremost to another industry, like "sheep," which belongs to stock-raising.

TABLE 12.1
Greek Double Vocabulary, Divided by Type of Etymology: Indo-European or
Non-Indo-European

Indo-European	Not Clearly Indo-European	Meaning
λῆνος (lēnos)	μαλλός/μάλλυκες (mallos/ mallukes), ἔριον (erion)(?)	'wool'
πεκ-/ποκ- (pek-/pok-)	τιλ- (til-)	'pluck wool'
νη- (nē-)	κλωθ- (klōth-)	'spin'
ἄτρακτος (atraktos)	ἠλακάτη (ēlakatē)	'spindle'
——	τολύπη (tolupē), ἀγαθίς (agathis)	'ball of yarn'
(νη- [nē-])	(κλωθ- [klōth-]), μήρινθος (mērinthos)	'thread'
——	μηρυ- (mēru-), ἑλικ- (helik-)	'wind thread'
ὑφ- (huph-)	ἀζ-/ἀττ-/ἀστ- (az-/att-/ast-)	'weave'
ἱστόποδες (histopodes)	κελέοντες (keleontes)	'uprights'
——	λαιαί (laiai), ἀγνῦθες (agnuthes)	'loom weights'
στήμων (stēmōn)	ἤτριον (ētrion)	'warp'
πήνη (pēnē), (ὑφ- [huph-])	ῥοδάνη (rhodanē)	'weft'
κρεκ- (krek-)	σπαθ- (spath-)	'beat weft in'
-συ-/ὑ- (-su-/hu-)	ῥαφ- (rhaph-)	'sew'
βελόνη (belonē)	(ῥαφ- [rhaph-])	'needle'
ῥεγ- (rheg-)	βαφ- (baph-)	'dye'
——	νακ- (nak-), πιλ- (pil-)(?)	'felt'

that there are patterns at all. That is, just as one can learn to spot fairly readily a French, Chinese, or Japanese loan in English on the basis of typical and rather distinctive phonological shape, so one might well be able to learn to spot different sources of borrowing within Greek on the basis of phonological shape or patterning. As long as we are flailing about in the sea of Greek vocabulary as a whole, that is not generally very easy for linguists to do. But when certain analysts moved into the shallow cove of place names, with a contextual anchor called geography,

the language of -nth- and -ss- began to sort itself out (Glotz 1925; Haley and Blegen 1928; etc.; see Chadwick 1972, 103–4 for still other layers); and a similarly greater clarity could be expected within the vocabulary of a single—and rather humble—craft like cloth-making, where a large number of borrowings may come from a fairly small number of sources. Here the anchor is archaeology.

In order to challenge archaeolinguists to discover where this hypothesis of non-random sets of borrowings in the vocabulary might lead us, in Table 12.2 let us rearrange

TABLE 12.2
Further Division of the Greek Double Vocabulary for
Textiles, by Etymology

| Indo-European | Not Clearly Indo-European | | |
	South Aegean?	C(C)VCh-language?	Unknown
lēnos	mall(u)-		erion
pek-			til-
nē-		klōth-	
atraktos			ēlakatē
	agathis		tolupē
(nē-)	mērinthos	(klōth-)	
	mēru-		helik-
huph-			az-/att-/ast-
histopodes			keleontes
	agnuthes		laiai
stēmōn			ētrion
pēnē			rhodanē
krek-		spath-	
-su-/hu-		rhaph-	
belonē		(rhaph-)	
rheg-		baph-	
			nak-, pil-

our list tentatively into four columns: one for clearly Indo-European words, one for the words possibly belonging to the *-nth-* language of the southern Aegean (the most recent layer), another for an unknown language postulated to have generated words of the C(C)VCh- shape (a somewhat older, more northern layer?), and yet another for the unassigned residue. I am quite aware that this division is not proved. I merely wish to point out some internal patterns, in case it becomes possible at a later date and with other evidence to build and refine (see below).

Meanwhile, the plot thickens when we look at what is *not* on the list, and compare the semantics. Table 12.3 shows the chief textile terms that do not involve semantic doublets. At first glance, the semantic distribution of the terms may seem random; but I think it is not. I see as interesting and highly significant the distribution in particular of the terms for looms and weaving. Let us rewrite them once more, pulling out just this set from both tables and grouping them according to a weaver's concerns, as in Table 12.4. What we see is that all the terminology necessary for band-weaving is old: "weave," "loom," "warp," "weft," "beat in with small pin-beater." And all the additional terms necessary for the warp-weighted loom have

TABLE 12.3
Non-Double Greek Textile Terms, Divided by Etymology

Indo-European		Not Clearly Indo-European	
λίνον (linon)	'linen'	στυπ- (stup-)	'stalk; scutch'
κεσ-/ξ- (kes-/ks-)	'comb, scratch'	σφόνδυλος (sphondulos)	'spindle whorl'
πλεκ- (plek-)	'plait'	μίτος (mitos)	'heddles(?)'
ἱστός (histos)	'loom'	καῖρος (kairos)	'shed bar'
ἀντίον (antion)	'cloth beam'	κανών (kanōn)	'heddle bar'
		στ(ρ)υπτηρία (st[r]uptēria)	'mordant'
		κναφ- (knaph-)	'fulling'

TABLE 12.4
Greek Weaving Terms, Divided by Etymology

Having Indo-European Etymology		Having No Clearly Indo-European Etymology	
huph-	'weave'	az-/att-	'weave header'
histos	'loom'(?)	laiai, agnuthes	'loom weights'
histopodes	'loom uprights' (lit. 'loom feet')	keleontes	'loom uprights'
		kairos	'shed bar'
antion	'cloth beam'	kanōn	'heddle bar'
		mitos	'heddles'
stēmōn	'warp; foundation'	ētrion	'warp'
pēnē	'weft'	rhodanē	'weft'
krek-	'beat weft in [with small implement]'	spath-	'beat weft in [with large implement]'

been added as loans—"weights," "uprights," "weaving the heading bands," and "beating in with a large sword-beater"—with the exception of *histopodes*, which is, however, a descriptive compound that could have been made up at any time. Likewise, *antion* could probably have been derived at any time: if it is old (as we saw the semantics weakly sug-

gest), it implies that the primitive Indo-European band loom at least sported a cloth beam; but both the concept and the word could have been added later.[17] Within the borrowed terms, one doublet occurs—for loom weights—and corresponds in its own layering to the two types of loom weights actually in use in the Aegean in the late Bronze

[17] Henry Hoenigswald kindly points out to me (pers. comm. 1985) that this formation could not, however, be very old within PIE, since it is accented on the second syllable

rather than the first syllable—i.e., was formed off the preposition rather than off the original noun.

Age: the heavy Danubian "blobs" and the slim Minoan disks (see Chapters 3, 14).

Furthermore, the terms for the mechanization of the weaving process are also without Indo-European etymologies: shed bar, heddle, and heddle bar, the last having been borrowed from a language family we can both name and document, Semitic. In fact, even outside of Greek I know of *no* reconstructable Indo-European terms for any of these three devices, which suggests strongly that the early Indo-European belt-weavers had to darn in the weft. If that is what was happening in the southern steppes in the Late Neolithic and Early Bronze Ages, no wonder the people up there invented felt for large coverings!

Surely this series of matches with the archaeological findings is too close for accident. We do not know the names of the peoples or languages that the Greeks encountered as they travelled south and/or west into Greece; but we know that there *were* people and languages along the way, and that some of the nearest people, especially those in the lower Danube valley, had been developing both the warp-weighted loom and elaborate textile techniques for millennia (unlike the people in the steppes). We also know that some incoming group in the Middle Bronze Age virtually wiped out the use of loom weights in peninsular Greece for a while (see Chap-

ter 14), but that by the Late Bronze Age everyone was using them again, in two overlapping varieties (the large "blobs" and the little discs).

Clearly some of the new textile vocabulary of the Greeks came from the people and language(s) of the southern Aegean. On the basis of semantics, I would suspect that at least some of the "unknown" and C(C)VCh-groups of loans were coming specifically from the central Balkans, from the region that developed the warp-weighted loom and its products so richly in the Neolithic and Bronze Age—from the region of the "Old Europeans." But whatever the precise origin of the languages, here among the textile terms of Greek we can see them casting some remarkably distinctive shadows. It would be interesting to see if a similarly thoroughgoing analysis of some other adopted craft, such as the art of building permanent houses,[18] would reveal similar shadows lying across the face of the Greek language. If we could begin to triangulate from several craft/language/archaeology constellations of loans, we might even be able to pinpoint more exactly the region in which one or another of these shadow-languages was spoken.

WE started out in this chapter to redefine the Greek lexicon pertaining to textiles,

---

[18] People have long remarked that the complex Minoan palace architecture must have appeared "labyrinthine" to the simple Mycenaean Greeks accustomed only to one- or two-room houses (not to say tents); and πλίνθος (*plinthos*) 'brick; column base' has received frequent notice as an architectural term borrowed into Greek from the infamous -*nth*- language. More recently, Marinatos suggested that the Minoan custom of building a window right next to the main door of the house, so obvious and ubiquitous in the new Theran excavations (where houses are regularly preserved to two and three stories), provides at last a reasonable and attractive explanation for the Greek word for "window," παραθυρίς (*parathuris*, Mod. Gk. παράθυρο, *parathuro*), literally "beside the door" (Marinatos 1972, 18). The term appears to be descriptive of what the Greeks saw in Mi-

noan architecture, and may even have been a loan translation. These examples demonstrate that it would be well worth the effort to conduct a systematic archaeolinguistic "excavation" of the strata of Greek architectural terms. Similar analyses of the Greek terms for weaponry, for ceramics, and for food should all produce new insights, especially when correlated with what has been done here.

For those who doubt this possibility, consider, for example, what could be deduced about fields of cultural indebtedness of English (and other European languages) to Arabic from the words beginning with *al-*: *algebra*, *alcohol*, *alchemy*, *alkali*, etc. There are non-Arabic *al-* words to weed out, of course; but a coherent and unmistakable shadow is there.

given what we now know about that ancient craft, and to see what else we could learn about the craft from the derivable histories of the words. In both endeavors our crop of new insights has been plentiful. The procedure clearly is worth repeating for the other well-attested language families (not to mention other crafts). But we have shown more than that. We have demonstrated in a new way the value—and relative ease—of semantic reconstruction when undertaken for a large, concrete, interlocked semantic field, where holes in the system ("scutching," "heddles," "twill") and sets of doublets or multiple "synonyms" (e.g., "loom weight," "thread") can work powerfully together when tied to a carefully reconstructed context—in this case the exigencies of the ancient craft. We have shown that languages, like habitation sites, can contain "excavatable" strata that turn out to correlate with tangible cultures. And we have demonstrated that as linguistics and archaeology pass their information back and forth and build on each other's findings, both fields stand to gain enormously from this process of word excavation.

CHAPTER 13

WOMEN'S WORK

As we sift through the evidence for ancient textiles, we will see that this industry has generally held a peculiar place in the economy, deriving its energy from an all but invisible source, for special reasons, and with unusual results for the archaeologist. Let us begin by considering the energy source.

Among the interesting results of redefining some of the ancient Greek textile vocabulary (in Chapter 12) is the fact that we now find ourselves with a cohesive set of terms showing the successive stages of Mycenaean textile production:

(1) a. *pe-ki-ti-ra₂* (*pektriai*): women whose profession is to "comb," that is, apparently, women who either get the wool from the sheep by combing it out during the first molt, or clean and comb the loose fiber so it is ready for spinning, or possibly both;
  b. *ri-ne-ja* (*lineiai*): female flax-workers (whose tasks included drying, retting, and scutching?);
(2) *ta-ra-si-ja* (*talasia*): the weighing out of the prepared raw commodity (here the loose fiber) into amounts suitable for individual purposes (e.g., specific bolts of cloth), for distribution to the individual craftspeople;
(3) *a-ra-ka-te-ja* (*ālakateiai*): women who spin thread, apparently from weighed allotments of fiber;
(4) a. see 5a;
  b. *i-te-ja(-o)* (*histeiai*): women who weave the cloth; we may also have the masculine form of "weaver" on PY Un 1322 where rations are given to workers who include one *i-te-we*, and on KN As 1516 where a man has the personal name *i-te-u* (*Histeus*?)—cf. KN Dd 1376,

where an actual shepherd is treated as though *named* Shepherd (*po-me* = *Poimēn*; Ventris and Chadwick 1973, 572);
(5) a. (and 4a?) *o-nu-ke-ja* (*onukheiai*): women who make borders (heading bands?—closing bands? [cf. the Swiss linens]—separately woven decorative edgings?); and *a-ze-ti-ri-ja* (*aze-triai*): women who weave edgings, and also perhaps construct the warp for a warp-weighted loom, by weaving the heading band on a band-loom warping-frame;
  b. *ka-na-pe-u* (*knapheus*): (male) fuller;
(6) *ra-pi-ti-ra₂* (*raptriai*): seamstresses; and *ra-pte(-re)* (*rapter[es]*), male sewers—but the men seem to be associated with stitching leather rather than cloth (Ventris and Chadwick 1973, 578).

These words, among them, account for enough steps to get the wool from the backs of the sheep to the backs of the human wearers; and in fact they inform us rather nicely of what those steps were in Mycenaean Greece, and of the fact that wool was not processed from start to finish by a single person but was moved from one specialist to another. Most striking of all is the fact, clear from the vocabulary, that most of these textile specialists were women.

When we add to this set of words the information deducible from the Linear B tablets, we can reconstruct quite a bit about the system of Mycenaean textile production. First the wool was collected: perhaps sometimes the shepherds themselves clipped the sheep whereas other times the women combed the wool out to obtain a particularly high-quality product. The tablets concerned with accounting wool show that the wool was weighed on its way into the palace (the D tablets: Killen 1964); then it was weighed out again for particular objects to be manufactured (the Lc tablets: Killen 1966; 1968a).

The recipients of these allotments of wool seem to have worked in groups or "workshops," some closely connected with the palaces and others much farther away (Killen 1966, 108; Olivier 1967, 83-84; Chadwick 1972, 107). Although we know little about the structure of the groups, it is clear from the personnel tablets that somewhere out there were specialists in spinning who turned the wool (or flax) into yarn for the next stage. Since we have no accounting of yarn, these women may have passed it on directly to the warpers and weavers, who produced the required textiles and sent them back to the palace. Women listed as spinners also seem to have woven on occasion (Killen 1979, 161 n. 20). A particularly heavy kind of cloth apparently needed no further work, but some of the textiles went on to the fullers, and some were sent by the palace, along with more wool, to workshops that added o-nu-ke (edgings?—see Chapters 12; 15) and perhaps other finishing touches (Killen 1979). Finally the materials were all collected again at the palace stores as completed cloth, to be "consumed" presently as ration, wage, guest-gift, or export item. Perhaps we lack accounting of yarn in our tablets—a noticeable absence—because the Knossos tablets, at least, were preserved for us by conflagration exactly at fleece-collection (molting?) time, so that the spinners would not yet have begun their new year's work; or it may be because, once the wool had been sent out of the palace for a project, the craftswomen merely passed the partially finished goods around among themselves.

As we have noted, nearly all the textile workers are women. The shepherds at one end of the line are male, and maybe a few of the weavers plus the fullers at the other end; but everyone else is female. And not only do women clearly dominate the textile industry, but clearly also the textile industry dominates the women. If we look through the female personnel tablets at Pylos, for example (Aa, Ab, Ad series), we find that Ventris and Chadwick (1973, 158–62) list corn-grinders, water-carriers, "nurses" (now thought to be cloth-finishers), carders (i.e., combers), spinners, flax-workers, headband(?)-makers, weavers, unassigned workers, and new captives. We form much the same impression from reading Homer, watching the captive women endlessly grind grain, carry wash-water, spin, and weave. Concerning Alkinoos's palace, Homer says:

And fifty serving-women he has in his house:
some grind the apple-colored grain at the mills,
and others weave at the looms and whirl the
    spindles. . . .

(*Od.* 7.103–5)

It may be argued that Homer represents the Iron Age; and not far to the east, at Iron Age Gordion, we find the palace women working in rooms equipped precisely with long rows of grinders and great heaps of loom weights and whorls (see Chapter 3). But the Linear B documents show that the same allocations of work held for Late Bronze Age Aegean women.

The Linear B profession names and accounts also present a distinctive picture of outlying workers tied somehow to the palace organization, and suggest specifically that the tie is a piecework system. That is, although some women (as we see in Homer, who is following the story of a "nobleman") lived and worked in concentrated groups in or around the palace, many others lived scattered about the towns and countryside and did a share of the revenue work wherever they lived. We see this "domestic workshop" system reflected in the distribution of loom weights and spindle whorls, which occur by the hundreds in some of the Late Bronze Age palaces and town mansions, but also in smaller quantities at many a house and farmstead.

Such a domestic system tallies very closely with the way in which textiles were typically manufactured in pre-industrial Europe. On the central Mediterranean island of Malta, which survived chiefly on textile exports from the Neolithic until the last century (McConnell n.d.; 1985), one finds the following description (Bowen-Jones et al. 1961, 124):

In 1861 there still remained almost 9,000 workers occupationally described as spinners and weavers and some 200 beaters and dyers. Ninety-six per cent. of the total were women, and male labour was generally used only in the final stages of cloth preparation. The industry included all processes from the growing of indigenous short staple annual cottons to the manufacture of cloth. The actual operations however were carried out almost entirely by individual workers in their own homes and were linked only by merchants specialising in this trade. In many cases merchants advanced seed to the farmers on a crop-sharing basis. In all cases they bought the picked lint and then distributed quantities by weight to 'out-work' spinners. These would return the yarn, which had been prepared by primitive traditional teasers and spinning wheels, and were paid by weight and fineness of the yarn. The village merchant would store the yarn until he received an order for cloth and would then make similar contracts with domestic weavers.

In Mycenaean times the palace served as link, instead of the merchants; and the fiber was different. Otherwise the picture we have is very much the same. Textile manufacture in northern France and the low countries, early in our own millennium, is also described in this way (see Perroy 1963, 84–90). There the English fleece imported by the merchant was first cleaned and sorted by women called *éliseresses* (choosers), then beaten by men (*batteurs*) to further clean and untangle it, then washed and re-greased (ibid. 84–86). The entrepreneur then took the wool to female carders (*cardeuses*)[1] or combers (*peigneresses*), according to the sort of yarn he wanted, then took it back and distributed it week by week to female spinners (*fileresses*) in carefully weighed units. The yarn thus produced was collected at the end of each week, and after being rewound into the desired skeins or bobbins by yet another group of women (*dévideresses*), it was taken to the weavers in appropriate lots. Practically all the workers, once again, were women and worked in their own homes, whether in town or in the country, being connected only by the entrepreneurs. Similar systems existed in many parts of Europe prior to the Industrial Revolution, especially where the finished textiles were mostly traded abroad rather than consumed locally.

In ancient Egypt we see a rather different system—but again the labor force for textile manufacture is almost exclusively female until the 18th Dynasty. Middle Kingdom tomb paintings and wooden models (see Chapters 2, 3) show women organized into self-contained factories, which produced the whole cloth from start to finish. Excluding overseers, a one-loom work-group is typically shown with one flax-preparer, one spinner,

---

[1] Perroy points out (1963, 86) that carding is never mentioned in the legal regulations before the 14th century A.D., and that when it does finally appear it is obviously being viewed with great distrust. "Tout se passe comme s'il s'agissait d'une technique nouvelle, contre laquelle l'esprit conservateur et traditionaliste de la règlementation nourrissait de grandes préventions" (ibid). This testimony supports the suggestion that our lack of archaeological evidence for carded wool, mentioned in Chapter 2, is not an accident.

13.1   Scenes from Middle Kingdom tomb of Khety (no. 17) at Beni Hasan: men laundering, spinning cord, and weaving mats (left to right, above); women preparing flax, a young boy and two women spinning thread, women weaving (left to right, below). (Newberry 1894, pl. 13)

two weavers to manage the loom together, and perhaps another girl to warp or to help prepare the raw fibers. About half of our representations show shops with 2 looms served by 2 to 4 operators apiece (the extra girls appear to be tending the unwoven part of the warp), 1 to 3 spinners, 3 to 5 flax-preparers, and sometimes 1 or more warpers. Men are shown tending the flax crop and washing the cloth; and occasionally a man or boy spins—e.g., in the tombs of Khety (Fig. 13.1) and Baqt (Fig. 2.5); also in the 6th Dynasty relief fragment (Fig. 2.43), and the 18th Dynasty tomb of Thutnofer (Fig. 3.29)—but probably these male spinners are making cord and rope rather than thread for weaving, since, except for one young boy (see below), they are not part of the weaving scenes.

It is not until the 18th Dynasty that we see some male weavers appearing, and with them a brand new loom—the vertical two-beam "tapestry" loom (see Chapter 3, Figs. 3.29–3.30). Our linen artifacts suggest that the women continued for a long time still to make most of the plain white household linens and garments in the traditional way. Certainly the records indicate that village women were still doing their own household weaving in the 19th Dynasty, for the rascally

overseer Paneb, who lived in the Theban workmen's village at Deir el-Medineh, not only "put several of his subordinates to work for him" but "even their wives had to work for him by weaving cloth" (Janssen 1975, 536; see also Černý 1929, 246). The upright loom, furthermore, required large beams that would have been extremely expensive for the ordinary household; and I have yet to see acceptable evidence of such looms in the workmen's villages (see Chapter 3 for Amarna; for Deir el-Medineh, Bruyère [1939, 49] tells us only that they found "fragments de métiers à tisser" with nary a detail). On the other hand, it would seem to have been primarily men (plus a few women-servants), working on the new loom, who were responsible for the prestigious and expensive new polychrome fabrics that we saw being made for the pharaoh, for the top noblemen (in whose tombs we find the representations), and for the temples—any of whom could have afforded such a loom. Moreover, the first observer of the now-deteriorated paintings at Thebes mentioned that at least one of the men "was engaged in making a piece of cloth with a coloured border" (Wilkinson, quoted by Roth [1913] 1951, 15). To the best of my knowledge, however, we have no indications that the Egyptians were making textiles for a major trade industry in the Bronze Age.

Yet another cloth-production system seems to have obtained in Assyria early in the 2nd millennium, but again it is woman-powered. At that time the Assyrians were actively trading tin and textiles to Anatolia in return especially for gold and silver. Most of our details come from letters sent between Assyrian merchants in Anatolia and their female relatives back home in Aššur. We learn first that these women produced some of the exported cloth in their own households, and also that some of the cloth sent was purchased elsewhere in the city. The merchant Puzur-Aššur writes to his wife(?) Waqartum: "If you want to make one [of the expensive 'Abarnian' cloths], make one like the one I wore(?) there. If you don't manage to make fine textiles, as I hear [it] there are plenty for sale over there. Buy (them) for me and send (them) to me" (Veenhof 1972, 104). The merchants often gave rather precise orders about what they wanted, apparently catering to Anatolian tastes. The same letter also says: "The fine textile, which you sent me—keep producing similar textiles. . . . Let them comb one side of the textile; they should not shear it; its weave should be close. Compared with the previous textile which you sent me, process 1 mina of wool extra (in) each (piece), but keep them thin! . . . A complete (finished?) textile which you make should be nine cubits long and eight cubits wide" (ibid., 104–5). One suspects that the Anatolian customers wrapped their clothing about themselves a little differently from the Assyrians, and so were shopping for a slightly different shape.

We also learn that the women at home were weaving as needed for their own households, and producing for the export trade only in their spare time. Lamassī, the wife of

another merchant, complains: "About the fact that I did not send you the textiles about which you wrote, your heart should not be angry. As the girl has become grown-up, I had to make a pair of heavy textiles for (placing/wearing) on the wagon. Moreover I made (some) for the members of the household and the children. Consequently I did not manage to send you textiles. Whatever textiles I (lit. 'my hand') can manage I will send you with later caravans" (ibid., 115).

The husbands and brothers, however, are only the marketers, not the owners of these particular textiles, as the women make clear in their repeated complaints about delayed payments. The lady Waqartum also writes as follows to her brother, who was apparently to convey to her in a homeward-bound caravan the profits realized for her by her husband: "I have trusted you even like my husband and master. . . . But to-day I mean even less to you than a pawned(?) slave-girl, for to a slave-girl you at least measure out regularly food rations; but I here have to live from my debt(s). . . . The 1 mina of gold, the proceeds (profits) (made by the sale) of my textiles, which my master sent me, you have taken away. . . . [Your firm received from me] in all 15 textiles of good quality. All this is my production, my goods entrusted for (sale with) profit. . . . My gold you have taken! I beg you . . . , send it to me with the first caravan and give me courage!" (ibid., 110). Clearly the women were financing and producing these high-class goods with their own capital and spare energy, using the profits to maintain their households and increase their capital (compare Friedl 1975, 63, concerning West African societies). Veenhof, who has analyzed and explicated these mercantile letters in detail, points out that in several cases the numbers of textiles sent by a single woman are sufficiently large that she could hardly have made them all herself

(Veenhof 1972, 113). Whether the woman bought the rest or oversaw their manufacture by other women in her own household (might she have used some capital to purchase slaves to help?), or some of each, is not clear. We see, however, that buying cloth from other local makers was at least an option.

In any case, the women of a single household seem to have been producing each homemade textile from start to finish, for they began by buying the raw wool. That they generally expected to obtain this wool locally we discover from occasional requests to send wool from Anatolia when the local supply had risen too high in price (ibid., 116).

The men also traded textiles on their own. We have seen one request already to the effect that if the merchant's wife didn't have time to make a particular type of cloth she should buy some for him on the local market. (Note the implications that other Assyrians, of whom we have no record, were manufacturing and locally marketing surplus textiles; that the merchant's wife was free to go to the local market; and that prices for Assyrian textiles were advantageously higher in Anatolia.)

Of textiles within Anatolia, we learn from the correspondence that the Assyrian merchants frequently traded local Anatolian wool—both white and dyed (red is mentioned)—back and forth within Anatolia for metals, and occasionally shipped some locally made red or white cloths back to Aššur (ibid., 130–31). The pack-train drivers sometimes even picked up more textiles during their journey back to Aššur. But clearly the main flow of cloth is in the other direction: virtually every load west is a mixed consignment of textiles and tin.

As with the Linear B texts, we see a cloth industry in Assyria produced by women and distributed in part by men. The chief difference comes in the fact that some of the Assyrian women own and oversee their entire operation and derive direct profits from their efforts; whereas the Mycenaean women of whom we have record are divided up to perform specialized sub-tasks, while the palace owns (and redistributes) the materials of production and the products. It is entirely possible, of course, that there were female Mycenaean householders engaged in private enterprise, but we have no record of them. (A private system seems rather more compatible with what we know of earlier Minoan textiles; see Chapter 15). For the most part, in the other areas of the Near East and in later periods in Assyria (when married women could own no private property: Saporetti 1979), spinning and weaving for the palaces, temples, and wealthy households was done largely by "workshops" of women having the status either of servants or of slaves, e.g., at Lagash in the time of Lugalanda and Urukagina (early 24th century B.C.: Lambert 1961), at Ur during the end of the 3rd Dynasty (ca. 2000 B.C.: T. Jacobsen 1970, 222–23), and at Karana (19th century B.C.: Dalley 1977; 1984, 53–54).

Meanwhile, the cloth consumed by small private households had to be produced largely by the women of the household itself. In the urban societies, making the cloth at home was only one of several options, although a major one. We have seen the Old Assyrian merchants' wives buying textiles upon occasion; and the transactional records from Egypt show that made-up garments in particular frequently changed hands (Janssen 1975, 249–92). How often an Egyptian household set out to *buy* cloth or garments, however, is not entirely clear, for the legal texts show that metal goods and (home-produced) linens were the chief articles used to pay off debts or to trade for something *else* that was wanted, such as slaves (Gardiner 1935, 141–42). (One might surmise, however, that the busy New Kingdom tomb robbers were happy to sell off linens from the tombs to anyone who would buy them; and occasionally we find record of people, even women, commissioning clothes to be woven: Janssen 1975, 270, 276–77, 284.) In the non-urban societies, on the other hand, making the cloth at home was not just the norm but the rule, as we see, for example, by the typical association of textile-making equipment with women of all types in the graves (cf. Chapter 2; also Askarov 1977, 126).

WHY should the making of textiles be so predominantly a female occupation in early societies? Under what circumstances was it not? What, in fact, are the socioeconomic factors at work on textile production?

To begin with, in an article on basic subsistence activities, Judith Brown points out that one obtains a much higher degree of predictability in the division of labor by sex on the basis of one particular observation than on any other factor that has been proposed. That observation is that "nowhere in the world is the rearing of children primarily the responsibility of men, and in only a few societies are women exempted from participation in subsistence activities. If the economic role of women is to be maximized, their responsibilities in child care must be reduced or the economic activity must be such that it can be carried out concurrently with child care" (J. Brown 1970, 1075). After elaborating her data she summarizes by saying that certain "societies are able to draw on womanpower because their subsistence activities are compatible with simultaneous child watching. Such activities have the following characteristics: they do not require rapt concentration and are relatively dull and repetitive; they are easily interruptable and

easily resumed once interrupted; they do not place the child in potential danger; and they do not require the participant to range very far from home" (ibid., 1075–76.) Subsistence activities that fall under these categories include such typically, though not exclusively, female activities as "gathering, hoe agriculture, and [local] trade" (ibid., 1076). They do *not* include "the herding of large animals, the hunting of large game, deep-sea fishing, or plow agriculture" (ibid., 1076). It is not that women are incapable of such activities— societies can be cited in which women participate in any one of these, just as societies can be cited in which men gather, trade locally, etc. But because none of them can be accomplished safely with tots underfoot, societies do not *depend* for them on its women alone (ibid.).

The model gives equally accurate predictions outside the realm of direct subsistence activities. The mine, with its deep holes and falling rocks, and the smithy, with its flying hammers and sparks, are hardly safe playgrounds for little ones. On the other hand, domestic spinning, weaving, fiber preparation, etc. have been found the world around to be ideal for women's chores: they are not dangerous to the children, they can be done at home, and they are repetitious and simple enough to be interrupted and resumed easily around the frequent little crises of child-raising. The listing of so many women in the Linear B accounts as both the mother of thus many children and a member of a given "profession" such as spinner or weaver or corn-grinder points again in this direction. And I have wondered whether the one young boy shown spinning among the Egyptian women is being taught skills that will be useful to him later as a (male) cord-maker, while the women keep an eye on him. Vocational kindergarten, as it were.

So Brown's observation predicts, and in an

intuitively satisfying way, that textile production will generally be women's work. But how, then, are we to understand those recorded cases in which the men were weaving? Are they random flukes, is the model wrong, or are there subsidiary principles of socioeconomics that explain them?

Consider the men we see weaving in Egypt. Throughout the Middle Kingdom, for all the many representations of weaving, it is always women who are shown at the task, using the ancient ground-loom. Then, well into the New Kingdom, we begin to see a few depictions of men weaving—and weaving on a newly introduced vertical loom (see Chapter 3). The two go together—new loom and new type of weaver. At the same time we find several new decorative textile techniques turning up in the Egyptian repertoire—tapestry, warp pick-up, etc. (see Chapter 5). Both the loom and the techniques seem to have come in from Syria or thereabouts, at least partly as the result of Thutmose III bringing home Syrians as war captives to work in his workshops (see Chapter 3) and glorify Pharaoh with expensive and novel luxury fabrics. As time goes on, we see the new techniques trickle down until, by the time of Herodotus and then the Romans, private citizens, both male and female, are producing fancy tapestries for other private, if wealthy, citizens (cf. Carroll 1985, 171–73).

Male weavers existed in classical Athens, too, in this case working in small, private shops in order to sell the resulting clothing in the market, while the women made cloth and clothing for home and personal use (Thompson 1982, 217–19). The buyers must have been either men with cash on hand but no women in their households (presumably a very small minority, from what we know of Athenian life), or any marketgoer who could be snagged by something a little bit more interesting than "homespuns."

We have not far to go for predictive principles. In both cases the womanpower is still being used maximally in the home, where the children are, and for basic subsistence purposes. But the men, who in each case are weaving *in addition* to the women, are weaving either for the luxury of their masters (if they are slaves) or for their own profit (if they are free). Ethnographic surveys show that the making of new goods with prestige value in a community is generally taken on by those members of the society with more power to say who does what and more leisure to experiment, so as to capitalize on both the novelty and the prestige (Sanday 1974, 200–201). Moreover, experimentation with radically new methods (as with the Egyptian vertical loom) is less likely to occur among those already locked into production within a given craft, because they have "little margin for error" (Boulding 1976, 147) and a heavy investment in the old ways. As G. M. Foster puts it (1968, quoted in Boulding 1976, 147), "the reason lies in the nature of the productive process itself which places a premium on strict adherence to tried and proven ways as a means of avoiding economic catastrophe." This principle of conservatism among the production squad surely applied to the Egyptian women who processed flax into fine linen for a myriad of traditional household and funerary uses, leaving the men to pick up and exploit the manufacture on a new loom of the new luxury fabrics (plus whatever else they cared to produce on it).[2] It is interesting that, after a period of obvious

---

[2] We have no direct proof that the new tapestries were being made on the vertical loom. But practical considerations make any other conclusion unlikely. The warp of the horizontal ground-loom is simply too inaccessible for prolonged, detailed work in small areas other than at the very edge. On a vertical loom, however, any desired spot can be made both easy to reach and easy to see—and from a comfortable sitting position.

experimentation with the new techniques, this new class of Egyptian weavers, too, slipped over into conservative production, sticking to the chosen subset of "new" ways for the next two millennia (see Chapter 5).

It seems, then, that we may expect to find men becoming involved with the weaving when something radically new is being added to the technology, and/or when new prestige goods are being developed and exploited fairly rapidly. (A quick glance at the course of the Industrial Revolution will strongly support the model, as will, on the other end of the spectrum, a glance at the Ashanti band-weavers of modern Africa—all male, because the industry came in as new, prestigious, and profitable, all at once.) Otherwise we must expect the women to be doing the spinning and weaving while they tend their children.

ONE of the issues we have raised here, and not for the first time, is that of the social status of textiles. What factors make cloth production a drudgery or a delight, a necessity or a luxury, a duty or a privilege? There are some obvious answers: cold winters can make both clothing and its production a necessity; slavery, serfdom, or taxes can make spinning and weaving a drudgery. Pity the poor weaver, says an Egyptian papyrus, describing—although satirically—a scene strongly reminiscent of the New Kingdom representations of basement weaving-workshops (see Figs. 3.29–3.30):

> The [mat-]weaver in the workshop,
> He is worse off than a woman;
> With knees against his chest,
> He cannot breathe air.
> If he skips a day of weaving,
> He is beaten fifty strokes;

> He gives food to the doorkeeper,
> To let him see the light of day
> (Lichtheim 1973, 188.)

On the other hand, the Assyrian merchants' wives seem from their letters to have gotten some pleasure from their weaving. They were in business for themselves, and thus had some feeling of choice in the matter. Their complaints center not around the work of weaving but around not being paid on time and around the menfolk constantly changing their minds as to what would sell best. It is also clear from the high prices fetched that the women were making prestigious luxury goods. All the more reason to be eager to weave in their precious spare time.

One suspects that the conscripted quotas of the women in the Linear B tablets were harder to bear. But their lot may have been better than that of the women newly captured in raids and wars, and kept under closer surveillance for a while at the palaces. We glimpse this sort of textile worker repeatedly in Homer, we can walk through her working quarters in the palace at Gordion, and we read of her in the war correspondence of Zimri-Lim, king of Mari on the Euphrates, to his wife Šibtu, early in the 2nd millennium B.C.: "I have just sent you some female-weavers. . . . Pick out the *ugbabātum* priestesses and assign [the rest] to the house of female-weavers. From among these female-weavers and from the previous female-weavers choose . . . 30 female-weavers—or however many who are choice (and) attractive . . . —and assign them to [the 'harem']" (Batto 1974, 27). (In his next letter, Zimri-Lim changes his mind, deciding he'd rather pick out his own 'harem,' thank you; ibid., 27–28.[3]) For all their sad plight, however, the king also instructs the queen to or-

---

[3] The exact function of these women, selected for their beauty, is not well understood. At this early period they may have performed exclusively as special singers and dancers rather than providing sexual services (Dalley 1984, 99–100).

der plenty of rations for both the pretty ones and the plain ones "so that their appearance does not worsen" (ibid., 27).

Duty and privilege in cloth-making are much more directly visible in modern peasant societies than in the ancient records—in fact, they are so common in rural societies that one has to assume that they were equally important factors back then, but seldom recorded. By duty here I mean social responsibility rather than forced labor. We see it directly in Penelope's duty to weave a special cloth for her father-in-law's funeral (see Chapter 16), but it is also implied in many texts concerning dowries. Someone had the social duty of preparing a girl for her wedding obligations and needs, often the girl herself, with her mother's help. In modern peasant societies, cloths are often presented by and to both families at a wedding. We have already encountered the woman of Old Assyrian Aššur who had to make a pair of special textiles "for the wagon" because her daughter had "become grown-up" (Veenhof 1972, 115). When, however, we read of one young lady of Old Babylonian times who took to her new house "24 garments and 42 head-dresses, all carefully looked after in individual clothes-chests," plus "burial shrouds ready for her death" (Dalley 1980, 53), we have crept beyond duty into the lap of luxury.

As for the endless offerings to the gods, does weaving cloth for the deity constitute a duty or a privilege? The young, upper-class girls of Athens vied for the privilege of helping to weave the new dress for the statue of Athena (see Chapter 16); and at the same time making the sacred peplos was a solemn duty for the community. Certainly in our own era we see the same double attitude involved in providing sumptuous textiles to dress the altars and officials of the Christian church.

That leaves only delight still to be reckoned. But delight in creation does not show up in economic accounts. Nor do we find it in the representational art of the ancients, since that art generally served a utilitarian purpose (e.g., religion, or the recording of things). We might hope to find it in letters, as we would today; but before the invention of the alphabet, writing was such a complicated business that one generally had to hire a scribe to write and a reader to read any letters sent or received. Under such circumstances one will predictably be rather less than chatty, and get on with whatever business is requiring the trouble and expense of a letter. And so we see it. Literature is less constrained to be business-like; but in the patriarchal societies of the Near East, the literature seldom touches on the affairs and feelings of women, who were the ones making the textiles.

In Homer, on the other hand, who gives us our earliest literary texts from Europe, we catch a glimpse of pleasure. Both Circe and Calypso—those independent European ladies who live alone and run their own homesteads—sing as they weave (*Od.* 10.221ff.; 5.61–62). And Helen, back in Sparta, bloodline queen of all she surveys, sits cheerfully telling stories of Troy and spinning yarns of expensive purple wool (*Od.* 4.120ff.), just like a modern woman enjoying her knitting or her needlepoint while she chats.

We have no linguistic records from central Europe in the Neolithic and Bronze Ages. But the exuberance of the stream of creatively patterned textiles coming out of that area strikes me as a sign of weavers who are having a lot of fun along the way. Scholars have sometimes objected that the early Europeans were too close to subsistence level to have had time and energy to waste on lavishly embellishing their cloth. But the fancy cloth is there. And such an attitude towards textiles, while not entirely predictable, makes sense as the proper interpretation on at least two grounds.

To begin with, what for us constitutes squandering time on unnecessarily fancy utilitarian objects may not have looked that way to these early weavers. In the hustle of our industrial society, it is hard for most of us to conceive of the radical difference between our attitudes toward time and efficiency and those of many non-industrialized societies and individuals. There, time may not be thought of as money—to be "spent," "made," "squandered," or "saved"—but merely as existing. E. C. Clark concludes (1969, 54), for example, that the major stumbling block in trying to industrialize rug-making in Turkey in the 19th century A.D. was that the craftspeople, although skilled and plentiful, had no particular concern "either for time or for systematic work habits." If you need to make an object anyway—such as clothes, towels, rugs—you may as well make something you will *enjoy* making, *enjoy* looking at, *enjoy* using. The shift from such an attitude of enjoyment to one of efficiency has often been remarked upon in Near Eastern ceramics: when the fast potter's wheel was invented, the elaborate and exquisite early decorations were suddenly reduced to the simple and humdrum, i.e., the mass-produced.

Second, pleasure in fancy textiles makes particular sense as a concomitant of the sort of woman-and-fertility-centered, horticultural, even matrilineal societies that we are gradually reconstructing for "Old Europe" (see, e.g., Gimbutas 1982; Barber 1979; Atchity and Barber 1987). That is, if indeed childbearing was one of the occupations of highest priority among the Neolithic European farmers—as is strongly suggested by such artifacts as the steatopygous female figurines emphasizing female fertility (Çatal

Hüyük, Malta, etc.)—so that other activities were aligned around it, then the manufacture of cloth formed a natural (though not absolutely inevitable) by-product of the system. We need only assume, then, that this secondary occupation—also a creative one (see Chapter 16)—received or accrued some of that same lavish respect and time commitment accorded to child-rearing. Certainly there are plenty of hours in the long, snowy winters of central Europe, when crop-growing is impossible, that are available to while away in such pursuits.

Wherever we catch a glimpse of central European fabrics, they are fancy. The Neolithic cloths from Switzerland and Germany, with their weft designs (stripes, triangles, checks, etc.) and elaborated borders, are followed later by the Hallstatt textiles, which pile plaids and checkers on top of zigzag and diamond twills, with embroidery for frosting (see Chapters 4, 7). When such exuberant decoration appears on grungy old rags from the salt mines, well may we regret the huge gaps in our knowledge. We have essentially nothing preserved in Europe between 3000 and 1300 B.C., or at any period in the heart of the Danubian area, where we see the warp-weighted loom blossoming early in the Neolithic (see Chapter 3). Our losses in Greece and Italy are equally great, if the Minoan frescoes bear true witness to the elegance and complexity of the fabrics—which they probably do (see Chapter 15). Our one sizable Bronze Age Italian textile, from Lago di Ledro, is handsomely patterned with woven lozenges (see Fig. 6.4).

One forms the same picture of pride in textiles from the representational art of most of this zone, beginning with the Tisza statuettes (e.g., at Hódmezővásárhely), through the costumed ladies of Vučedol, Cîrna (Fig. 13.2), and Kličevac (see Fig. 13.5) and the Minoan ladies of Petsofá, Hagia Triada,

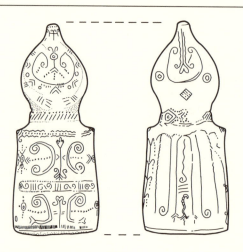

13.2 Clay statuettes from Cîrna, Romania. Bronze Age; 2nd millennium B.C. (After Dumitrescu 1961, pl. 152–53)

Thera, Knossos, etc. (see Chapter 15), to the big-skirted Hallstatt women on the Sopron vase from western Hungary (Fig. 13.3). The Hallstatt urn, moreover, shows the women doing their spinning and weaving to the entertainment of music and dance—a veritable party!

Working parties of just this sort took place regularly right up into our century in Hungary and nearby parts of Europe. The spinning and weaving had to be done, it is true; but these were considered pleasant occupations—much lighter and cooler, for example, than hauling water or raking hay. Young girls looked forward to learning how to spin. In Europe, too, unlike the Near East, looms were and are set up indoors and worked during the long periods of stormy weather and winter darkness, when little else can be done around the farm. A typical Hungarian evening in the villages consisted of a group of women getting together and spinning or embroidering all evening, while the men entertained them with stories, music, songs, and dances. Some of the men might be plying small crafts also, and invariably some of the

girls would drop their work for a bit to add to the entertainment with dancing and games. Singing, talking, and flirting, of course, didn't stop the handwork;[4] and singing makes work easier. The Sopron vase (Fig. 13.3) shows the same tradition 3000 years ago—and most likely it went back another 3000 years. We have other evidence for the communality of textile work, too. The warp-weighted loom was large enough to accommodate two or three weavers working at once, and we have seen both representations and direct proof (in Chapters 3, 6) that several women often shared the labor of a single cloth. Note that such sharing was not necessary to the functioning of the warp-weighted loom. It was done out of choice.

With these deep traditions went a great pride in textile art. I see it as no accident that in Hungary today, and in the Danube Corridor in general, whole museums are given over to handmade textiles (and ceramics) as major art forms, whereas in most of Europe they are counted as marginal art or are totally neglected.[5]

One can trace this continuous pride and

4 I am aware of such customs in several other areas of central Europe and Scandinavia. "Quilting bees" in rural America were also very similar in both economic and social function.

5 Scandinavia is another exception. A sense of celebra-

tion of women's art can be felt most particularly at the folk museums at Kalocsa and Mezőkövesd in Hungary, the costume museum in Belgrade, Jugoslavia, and the Margit Kovacs museums in Szentendre and Györ, Hungary. These last are museums of ceramics created by

13.3 Design on vase from Sopron (Ödenburg), Hungary, showing women spinning and weaving while being entertained. Hallstatt culture; early 1st millennium B.C. See Fig. 2.15 for photo. (Courtesy of Naturhistorisches Museum, Vienna)

interest in textiles in central Europe another way: through the costumes. There is a striking resemblance between the central Ukrainian girl's costume of this century (Fig. 13.4), and the one from Bronze Age Kličevac (Fig. 13.5), right down to the checkered skirt and zigzag edge;[6] between the Austrian dirndl or Serbian chemise with belted

Kovacs that depict the central European peasant woman's world of activity and of feeling—showing, for example, a young girl singing with heart and soul as she spins.

[6] In 1975 I predicted, on the basis of comparative reconstruction from the modern folk costumes, that the proto–Indo-European costume must have looked rather like the modern Ukrainian or central Balkan folk costume stripped of its jackets (and of its trousers, for men) (Barber 1975, 307–19). This costume consists of a white, bast-fiber chemise, decorated at the edges or openings in red and possibly black, with apron-like colored "blanket-wraps" belted over it for the women, and (for either sex) a large colored woolen blanket-wrap thrown over the head and/or shoulders as a mantle.

Later I learned of the rather similar clothing found in a kurgan at Tsarskaja in the Kuban, from the 3rd millennium B.C. (Veselovskij 1898, 37; see Chapter 6). I see in it a strong corroboration of the validity of extending the "comparative method" of linguistics to the reconstruction of other highly structured cultural systems such as forms of dress.

The main feature of that reconstruction that I would change, after ten more years of study, is my estimate of its origin. I now suspect that the belted kilt (belted apron for women) is the basic Indo-European garment, and that the white chemise below it was picked up by some of the Indo-Europeans along their southern territory, where it was creeping northwards from the Mesopotamians. Several Indo-European groups lack it. But the Greeks and probably the Hittites and the Romans picked up both the chemise and the West Semitic name for it: Gk. χιτών (khitōn), Linear B ki-to(-n-), Hitt. kattanipū-, Lat. tunica (< *ctunica?); compare Hebrew kuttoneth, Ugaritic ktn(t), and Akkadian kitinnu 'linen; linen cloth,' kitū 'flax, linen,' which was ultimately borrowed from Sumerian gada (E. Masson 1967, 27–29; Friedrich 1952, 105–6; Chicago Assyrian Dictionary 1956–, K.473–5 kitû). See Chapter 12.

13.4 Modern Ukranian costume. Compare zigzag at bottom, and large checkers on skirt just above, with Fig. 13.5. (Ethnographic Museum, Leningrad)

13.5 Female statuette of clay, front and back, from Kličevac in northeastern Jugoslavia. Bronze Age; 2nd millennium B.C. (M. Hoernes 1898, pl. 4)

jumper and the statuettes from Cîrna (see Fig. 13.2); between the modern Hungarian village costumes, where girls petticoat their skirts out so wide for holidays that they can't sit down, and the voluminous skirts on the Hallstatt vase (see Fig. 13.3).[7] All of these costumes are highly ornate, whether because of the woven textiles, or embroidery, or sewn-on ornaments, or all three. Just as the modern folk costumes serve in cut and detailing to show at a glance the precise village and social class—rich or poor, married or unmarried—to which the wearer belongs, so the Neolithic and Bronze Age costumes undoubtedly did too.

The ethnographic parallels also suggest, however, that hidden within the glee of ornamentation were some more serious purposes. Just as the modern European peasant girl may copy into her textiles designs and colors chosen to serve as blessings, warnings, magical protection and the like, so the ancient ones apparently did as well. For instance, the standard white-red-black color scheme of Slavic folk costumes carries on, half-forgotten, what is clearly an old Indo-European color scheme fraught with social and cosmic significance. Roses, a symbol of protection traceable back at least three millennia (see Chapter 16), and the hooked lozenge, a symbol of female fertility traceable perhaps even to the Palaeolithic cave paintings, cover the sleeves, bodices, and aprons of girls from Russia and Poland in the north to Bulgaria and Greece in the south (Ambroz

[1966] 1967, 22–28 and figs. 1–4).[8] Other symbols are more complicated, but turn up with astonishing regularity. Particularly interesting ones for the women's world include birds, eggs, and snakes or frogs. Birds are repeatedly associated with virginity, the virgin being the as-yet untapped keeper of the awesome power of fertility. We see this association in Athena, the virgin goddess, promoter of Athenian fertility, who has the habit of flying away as a bird (e.g., *Od.* 1.319–20); in the Slavic Rusalki or Vily (willies), the spirits of girls who died unwed and can now help you prosper or kill you, who are portrayed in folk art as girl-headed birds or fish;[9] in the European swan-maidens (white, in Indo-European as in so many other cultures, equals purity, here virginity); in central European bird-shaped cups, bowls, and ladles for (plentiful) food, which go back several thousand years (cf. T. T. Rice 1963, 81 figs. 61–63); and so forth. These birds populate not only Slavic girls' aprons but also early Greek pottery. If we had early Greek clothing we might well find it there too (see Chapter 16). The association of eggs with fertility is still obvious to us today, since it is part of our Easter rituals; and eggs help us to understand how birds got drawn into the fertility symbolism. (See Gimbutas 1982 for long discussions of bird and egg symbols in the European Neolithic.) Snakes and frogs occur as embodiments of the guardian spirit of the household in folklore from Lithuania in the north to Greece in the south, as well as

---

[7] People often think that everyone dresses that way, but some comparative study of dress the world around (e.g., Tilke 1945; Barber 1975) will soon change that idea; and if the reader is concerned that such long continuity is unlikely, he need only return to Chapter 11 and the 20,000-year continuity of the string skirt.

[8] The most amusing (and convincing) example of this symbol of the vulva occurs in medieval Russia, where the plates of iron door-locks were made in the form of a hooked lozenge, with the keyhole in the center (Ambroz [1966] 1967, 24 and fig. 3.6). One had only to insert the

key to participate by analogy in unlocking the fertile storehouse of the biological world.

[9] The Rusalki still appear as bird- and fish-maidens all over carved barn doors, gates, windowsills, and shutters, and they long ornamented the ancient Kievan wedding jewelry (inveighed against by the Christian priests of the time). See, for example, T. T. Rice 1963, 81 figs. 61–63, and Zvrantsev 1969. They occur throughout the folk tales, and can even be recognized in certain dance rituals (see Rybakov [1967] 1968).

among the motifs used in textiles, painting, and even sculpture far back into time (Gimbutas 1958, 23–36; Barber 1979; Gimbutas 1982).[10]

This rich outpouring of textile art in central Europe today is perhaps, then, a direct legacy of 7000 years of central European women pouring their creativity of design into the cloth that they needed to make anyway for a hundred household uses. The situation

is not unique in the world: one sees a similar richness of textiles in parts of Asia, in ancient Peru, among the Navajo—in places and at times that allowed the women some freedom of craft experimentation. But because of the ready perishability of cloth in the European climate, researchers have constantly overlooked this important form of human expression. Clothes may make the man, but women spent their lives making the clothes.

---

[10] A famous example is Phidias's statue of Athena Parthenos, placed in the Parthenon as part of the rebuilding program after the destruction of Athens during the Persian Wars. The war being over, Athena is shown having set her shield down, while at her feet the sacred Athenian "house"-snake has come out to bask in safety once again (cf. Herington 1955, 26).

Recently Mary Kelly has done an interesting study (1987) on the pagan Slavic goddess Berehinia (the "protectress"), who resembles in many striking ways Athena, the Rusalki, and also another group of goddesses of (pre-)Greek mythology, Artemis and the Potnia Theron (Mistress of Animals). Berehinia continues to be represented in Slavic women's embroideries to this day, as an important part of the design, even though in most areas the women have forgotten her significance and even her name.

I was most astounded, then, when I was shown a

piece of 19th-century(?) A.D. Cretan weaving owned by Sophia Kaná, a textile artist and collector in Aghios Nikolaos, Crete, which had, woven into it, the typical repeated motif of a Berehinia-figure—but with snake-like objects in the upraised hands instead of Berehinia's usual triple flowers or birds. The piece apparently dates from before Evans's excavation with Knossos, so it was presumably not influenced by the famous "snake goddesses" found there. In fact, the motif is so stylized that one tends to see it as one more nice geometric design unless someone points out the figure in it: its significance had apparently been forgotten. The motif may somehow have crept into the local repertoire by intermarriage of a Cretan man with a Slavic bride. On the other hand, it just might have survived from Classical times. The figure, with various things in her hands, has been found on a variety of ancient Greek ceramics (see Ambroz [1966] 1967, 29–35 and especially fig. 6).

CHAPTER 14

THE WEIGHT CHASE

A new archaeological research tool now lies at hand. The evidence shows so consistently that women did the spinning and weaving of cloth in early Europe and the Near East (except under some very particular conditions, which we have explored) that we must leave the burden of proof to those who claim that men did this work at a specific time and place. We can then proceed with the strong hypothesis that when we see non-prestigious textile equipment suddenly invading an area, not only men but also women have moved. In short, we now have a way of tracking the movements of women—of whole families rather than just warriors or traders.

For most textile-making equipment in early times was both humble and conservative in the extreme, as we have seen, and can only be imagined to have moved with the user. There are exceptions: spindles made of such precious substances as gold or ivory (e.g., Alaca Höyük, Peratí) may well have been given as gifts by queens and princesses. But simple clay whorls and loom weights had no intrinsic value; they were of value only to the craftswoman for making her thread and her cloth, and they had no reason to travel except with her. In a long or difficult migra-

tion they may even have been left behind and remade at the end of the journey—from local materials but on the old and familiar pattern. We have seen this already in the appearance at Gurob, in Egypt, of a European-style low-whorl spindle made out of local Egyptian materials. We have also looked at the movement of Egyptian fiber-wetting bowls into Palestine in the Late Bronze Age, where they were being made of local clay rather than of Egyptian stone (see Chapter 2 for these examples). Clearly in each case these objects were being made for (and sometimes by) the women so that they could ply their crafts in their accustomed ways.

In this chapter, I will track in more detail some interesting migrations of loom weights, and explore the puzzling trails of some very peculiar spindle whorls, in order to illustrate the potential benefits to archaeologists of this line of inquiry.[1]

It is very clear from mapping Neolithic and Bronze Age loom weights that the warp-weighted loom was born and developed in southeast Europe and perhaps Anatolia in the Neolithic, expanding farther and farther to the north and west in the late Neolithic,

[1] Belief in migrations may not be "fashionable" now among many archaeologists; and certainly migrations have too often been invoked to cover our ignorance. But the direct historical *records* of them (e.g., the Egyptian depictions at Medinet Habu of the Sea Peoples moving with wives, children, and baggage, or Caesar's descrip- tion of the Helvetii, not to mention the more modern migrations of Huns, Tatars, Turks, and American colo- nists) as well as the linguistic evidence make an extreme anti-migration position as senseless as using migration to explain all. This chapter explores what can be deduced if one keeps an open mind.

Bronze, and Iron Ages, but not generally expanding to the south or east, presumably because the inhabitants of those territories already had a practical loom, the ground-loom (see Chapter 3). By 2500 B.C. the line between the two territories seems to run along the east side of the Anatolian plateau and Cilicia, ending at the northeast corner of the Mediterranean.

It is of considerable interest, then, that loom weights suddenly appear in Palestine, far from home, in the Middle Bronze II period. We find them at quite a number of sites, from Megiddo in the north to Tell Beit Mirsim in the south, including Gezer, Shechem, and Tel Mevorakh.[2] The weights are typically made of well-fired clay, standing three to five inches high and tapering towards the top, where there is a transverse hole (Fig. 14.1). Most of these weights are more or less oval or egg-shaped, but a few are more rectangular in section (that is, forming steep, truncated pyramids). In short, most of them are identical in type to the loom weights found all over Anatolia in the Early Bronze Age (Fig. 14.2): at Troy II, Aphrodisias, Alaca Höyük, Alishar, Mersin, etc. (see Chapter 3). In this they differ markedly from the Minoan/Aegean, Balkan, Czech, and Swiss types of the Neolithic and Bronze Ages (see Figs. 3.17–23). We must conclude that the shape of the Palestinian Middle Bronze II weights is neither "ordinary" nor "nondescript" (as many excavators would have it), but quite distinctively Anatolian. The weights are unadorned, and apparently made of local clay; they were not themselves objects of trade. The simplest explanation for their sudden appearance,

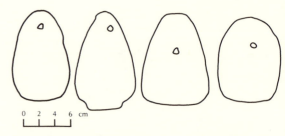

14.1   Typical clay loom weights from Megiddo in the Middle Bronze II period; early 2nd millennium B.C. (After Loud 1948, pl. 169 nos. 2, 5, 11, 13)

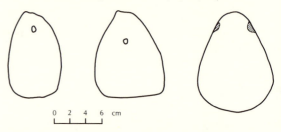

14.2   Typical clay loom weights from Early Bronze Age Anatolia. *Left, middle*: from Alishar (after von der Osten 1937, vol. 1, fig. 99 no. e2103c–d). *Right*: from Mersin. (After Garstang 1953, 173 fig. 112)

therefore, is that some Anatolian women moved with their families to Palestine in noticeable numbers at the beginning of the Middle Bronze II period, and set up housekeeping in their native fashion, which included the domestic weaving of cloth on the warp-weighted loom.

It is curious, however, that there seems to be no trace of these weights in the area between Anatolia and Palestine, namely in Syria (Fig. 14.3);[3] and we are left with a rather interesting four-step problem: (1) A southward movement of people who were descendents of the Early Bronze Age culture of Anatolia must have occurred around the

---

[2] Megiddo XIII–IX: Loud 1948, pl. 169–70, including 26 found together as a set; Tell Beit Mirsim: Albright 1936–37, 56 and pl. 45:1–8; Gezer: MacAlister 1912, 74–75 and fig. 268; Shechem: Albright 1936–37, 56; Tel Mevorakh: E. Stern 1984, 63 and pl. 45:9. Kenyon says (1957, 230–31) that while excavating Middle Bronze Age Jericho she "found a large number of clay loom-weights,

showing that weaving had been carried on above." But unfortunately she gives no description or image of the weights themselves.

[3] My thanks to M. van Loon for suggesting additional bibliography to check, and for the remark that he had not found such weights at his own Bronze Age Syrian sites.

beginning of Middle Bronze II. (2) This movement must have involved considerable numbers of women, who ended up in Palestine. But (3) the route of the migration apparently did not lie overland—unless the excavators have failed to notice and publish their loom weights, or unless the movement was so swift through Syria that essentially no artifacts were left along the way. (4) The alternative is that this mass of people travelled to Palestine from Anatolia by sea.

In addition to the weights, we can add the evidence of the spindle whorls—less diagnostic of origin, but similarly indicative of a new population of cloth-makers. Describing the excavations at Megiddo, Guy states (1938, 170) that "whorls appear not to have been used prior to MB [Middle Bronze] II. . . . The four MB II whorls (Fig. 175:1–4) differ from all other dated specimens in both material and form." Unfortunately, although the excavator found these clay whorls to be notably different from the other Megiddo artifacts, their simple, common shapes (biconical or spherical) and lack of decoration make them impossible to trace backwards in the archaeological literature. But within their Megiddo context it is clear that they are new and different. The simplest hypothesis is that they came in with the immigrant craftswomen who brought the new, Anatolian-style loom weights.

Now, this happens to be the era of the so-called Hyksos migrations, in which various people seem to have been moving to and from various places, but particularly in and through the Palestinian corridor. Evidence for the precise nature of these movements has not been easy to find or to interpret. But this new, rather solid piece of evidence com-

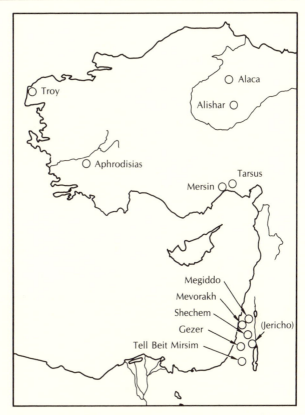

14.3   Map of the distribution of similar loom weights in Early Bronze Age Anatolia and Middle Bronze Age Palestine (see Figs. 14.1–2 for typical weights)

ing from an entirely different quarter may help. It is now worthwhile, for example, to go back and reassess the other, more nebulous kinds of possibly Anatolian data in Middle Bronze Age Palestine, since the loom weights demonstrate that a migration from Anatolia to Palestine (at least) must in fact have occurred in or just before Middle Bronze II. As that event is untangled, some light may be shed on other aspects of the Hyksos problem.[4]

---

[4] Mace insists on the presence of large numbers of loom weights in Egypt: "I find them by the dozen in the ancient town of Lisht (Empire Period)" (Mace 1922, 75). I tracked some of these weights to the Metropolitan Museum of Art; but their shapes and sizes were so miscellaneous that I was not convinced that they were neces-

sarily *loom* weights, nor that they belonged to either of the influxes of loom weights to reach Palestine, as discussed here. That is, I see no evidence yet that the users of either the Middle Bronze II "blob" weights or the Late Bronze III/Early Iron Age donut weights (see below) swept on south into Egypt.

A small trickle of well-fired loom weights of this general type continues down into the Late Bronze Age (cf. MacAlister 1912, 73–74), presumably among the inheritors of the Middle Bronze II intruders' culture. But then, starting at the end of the Bronze Age, we find something new: a profusion of crumbly, ill-fired or merely sun-dried weights that are either donut-shaped or pierced spheres (e.g., at Gezer: MacAlister 1912, 74 and fig. 268d; and at Tell Beit Mirsim: Albright 1936–37, pl. 45 nos. 9–16). Furthermore, at Gezer the excavator remarks that the "large piles of weavers' weights are very often found associated with heaps of grain. The connexion is too common to be accidental" (MacAlister 1912, 75). And the connection may be that, as we have seen several times before, the women were assigned the two chief tasks of weaving and of grinding grain.

Avigail Sheffer, who has studied the whole lot of Palestinian donut-weights, remarks both on their occurrence "in almost every Iron Age excavation" in Israel,[5] and on the "very friable, soft-baked clay" of which they are always made (Sheffer 1981, 81). Worried by the practicality of such soft weights on a loom, she and some local Bedouins made sun-dried replicas of the weights and strung them up on a warp of handspun wool (17 weights on a 24 cm width). Sheffer reports that "the weaving itself was very easy and quick, taking less than an hour to produce a piece of material one metre long. No damage occurred to the loom weights even when the loom had to be moved from place to place" (ibid., 82 and pl. 15).

We see here three noteworthy qualities: the weights are pierced spheres or donuts, they are very crumbly, and they occur in great quantity. In all three of these features they differ markedly from the Middle Bronze Palestinian weights just discussed. But we see exactly these same three features in the roughly contemporary Iron Age loom weights from the women's quarters at Gordion, Turkey (de Vries 1980b, 37–39: about 2300 ill-fired donuts, beside rows of grain-grinders), and in the Late Bronze Age (Unětice) loom weights from Hradčany, Czechoslovakia (Červinka 1946, 141 with fig.: more than 80 soft donuts in one group). Given the differentness of all earlier loom weights, I see these combined similarities as no coincidence. The most reasonable hypothesis at the moment is that this type of loom weight came into Anatolia from the northwest with the Phrygians and/or their allies early in the Iron Age; and that other people of a similar culture, or at least of a similar textile technology, brought the weights to Palestine, presumably as part of the "Sea People" disturbances that marked the close of the Bronze Age and the beginning of the Iron Age. Once again the weight type and its associated craftswomen seem to have reached Palestine chiefly by sea, for although occasional Iron Age weights are reported from Syria, they are few and not demonstrably early. Given the widely scattered Mediterranean sources of those Sea Peoples who

---

[5] She lists in addition Lachish, Samaria, Tell Qasileh, Tell Taʻanach, Beer Sheba, and Nir David (Sheffer 1981, 81–82). Levy and Edelstein (1972, 334 and pl. 23–24) mention finding loom weights at Nir David that had fallen from the loom(s) in rows, but the pictures they provide show the older type of flattened pyramid weights. Maisler (1951, pl. 39.B) shows pictures of the types found at Tell Qasileh from the Israelite Period, including "blobs," spheres, and donuts. Tufnell (1953, 106–8) discusses some of the many weights and half-dozen weaving areas discovered at Lachish, as does Starkey (1936, 188–89), who also mentions finding a charred upright from a loom still in place. Further plans of these areas exist among the excavation day-cards (my thanks to the library of the Archaeological Institute, London, and to the librarian H. M. Bell for helping me find them).

have been fairly securely identified, and knowing for certain from the Egyptian monuments that some of these migrants were travelling as entire families, and many travelling by boat, one can imagine shiploads of migrating families setting sail from the north end of the Aegean or Adriatic, families capable of carrying south-central European weaving technology across the waters.[6]

Once again we find ourselves using the humble loom weights as a source of new but fairly solid evidence for the origin and destination of one component of an exceedingly complex series of people movements. In this instance, the next step is to try to pin down the northern points from which the migrants pushed off—and a better knowledge, from further excavation and charting, of the precise territory of the crumbly donut-weights in Late Bronze Age Europe is the place to start. It could shed much light on the Sea Peoples.

SPINDLE whorls do a rather simple job. They act as little flywheels on the spindle, stabilizing and prolonging the turning of the spindle as the work of twisting the thread is done. There are few practical requirements for their shape: they need to be broad enough to help maintain the momentum; they may be heavy enough to help with drafting but must not be so heavy that they break the thread; and it helps if they are symmetrical about a central axis so as not to introduce an inefficient and irritating wobble into the rotation. In short, anything fancier than a simple round disk or blob with a centered hole is unnecessary. And most spindle whorls the world over are of just these sim-

ple shapes—perhaps with a bit of decoration to make them pretty or auspicious.

So when some spindle whorls turn up that are extremely idiosyncratic in shape, although a bit scattered about in time and space, the simplest conclusion to draw is that they are somehow related to each other.

In the description that follows, I tend to take the spindle whorls from Anau, in western Turkestan, as centrally typical (Fig. 14.4). They first appear at Anau close to or at the beginning of the series of "strange whorls," they include the largest variety of related styles to be found at any one site, and they continue there for millennia—far longer than at any other site.

To begin with, most of the whorls in this group have a scoop out of one end: a trait that in itself is non-functional for spinning. The scoop is often so deep and the whorl so tall that the object looks like a fat clay bullet or rocket nose cone. On less extreme examples, the whorl may look like a miniature thick-walled cup or bowl (one Italian excavator dubbed the type *scodelletta* 'little soup-

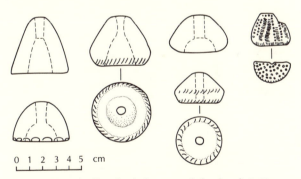

14.4   Clay spindle whorls from Neolithic levels I–II at Anau, in Turkestan. (After Pumpelly 1908, 163 figs. 341, 346, 348, 342, 349, 350)

[6] I am not saying that Sea Peoples came all the way from what is now Czechoslovakia, for I would bet that the loom-weight gap between Czechoslovakia and the coast is more apparent than real. In particular, someone needs to do a thorough job of investigating Jugoslavian loom weights of the Neolithic, Bronze, and Iron Ages,

by visiting all the local museums. (Coverage in the literature is very poor.) Pierced balls, at least, occur in northern Jugoslavia in the Neolithic, as we saw in Chapter 3, and I suspect they continued on there as an indigenous variety.

bowl': Bernabò Brea 1976, 280); or it may resemble half an egg, cut crosswise, with a shallow depression in the middle of the flat end. Such half-eggs typically have a bevelled edge with a particular repertoire of designs incised on the flat and bevelled parts.[7] Those whorls among the key finds of this type that do not have a scoop out of them share the half-egg shape, with the same repertoire of designs on the flat face, and they often have the bevelled edge. Another apparently related or evolved form is a truncated bicone with a scoop out of the truncated face.

The most typical decoration is a sort that I have nicknamed the "sand dollar"—four to seven spokes radiating from the center and made of a stack of fingernail impressions (little moons), or a stack of chevrons, or a "pine tree" (chevrons on a central line), or a row of dots, or occasionally just a line (Fig. 14.5). Often one single spoke of the group is (deliberately?) askew. Frequently the rim is notched; and occasionally sign-like figures occur, especially X's, H's, snakes, and a four-footed animal. These designs are incised, not painted, although painted pottery abounds in the cultures in which the whorls are found and painted whorls occur in other cultures (see below). The incised designs are sometimes filled with white.

There is one more feature that recurs so persistently with these whorls that I take it too as diagnostic: someone, usually the excavator, remarks on the extraordinary quantities of these spindle whorls. Schliemann dug up 8000 such at Troy; in northern Italy they turned up in such numbers that "in the Archaeological Exposition at Turin, 1884, . . . they were twined [in long strings] about the columns, thereby providing a place of storage as well as a place of display" (T. Wilson 1893–94, 968). At Tepe Gawra, where scooped-out whorls turn up suddenly in level VII, the excavator comments that there were as many whorls in that one "comparatively short-lived and unsubstantial" level as in the very thick level that followed it (Speiser 1935, 78).

So we have three correlating features: the unusual group of shapes, the type of decoration, and the unusually large numbers. Each by itself might be an accident of independent invention; but taken as a set, or even taking two out of three, these features seem too strange a group to show anything but "genetic" relationship among the cultural complexes that have them.

The finds are widely scattered, yet not exactly common. Schliemann's hoards at Troy, which he published with such fanfare, first made the whorls famous; but they also occur across the north Mediterranean at various times in the Bronze Age—in Turkey, Greece, northern Italy, and Switzerland.

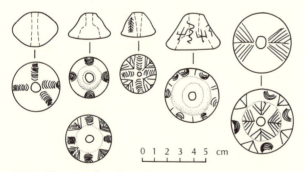

14.5   Clay spindle whorls from level III at Anau, in Turkestan. (After Pumpelly 1908, 165 figs. 370–71, 375, 374, 379, 377)

[7] I am indebted to Jill Carington Smith, whose discussion of the distinctive form and peculiar distribution of this type of whorl in her Ph.D. thesis (1975, 353–89) prompted me to take up the chase. Since unfortunately I have not been able to obtain a copy of her valuable dissertation, which remains unpublished, I have had to do my own dragnet of site reports looking for these whorls, thereby undoubtedly duplicating some of her work, which traced them at sites in Greece, Italy, and Turkey, and at Anau, and suggested a possible origin on the steppes.

The next group to be widely publicized was the huge lot found by Pumpelly at Anau, in western Turkestan (Pumpelly 1908). Others have been excavated from various Neolithic sites in Iran, northern Iraq, and eastern Turkey. Finally, the hollow, notched, and sand-dollared whorls occur in some late Neolithic sites in the Ukraine and southern Poland.

That's a very strange collection of sites and times, at first glance. Can we make any sense out of it?

Since the geography of the problem looks so opaque, let us tackle the problem from another end, beginning with the old structuralist assumption that form and function tend to be related, at least at first—that the peculiar form may hold a key to the solution. Why might the spindle whorls have been made hollow? And why do they occur in such large numbers?

The number question is the easiest to solve. Quite simply, each woman must have possessed many spindles instead of the usual one or two. (I mentioned in Chapter 2 a woman buried in Peru with her collection of 68 tiny cotton-spindles; Liu 1978, 98.) If you have only one or two spindles, you have to unload the spindle as soon as you fill it, before you can do any more spinning. But you must produce many a spindle-full of thread before you are ready to weave a single cloth. The prime reason for having many spindles, then, is to avoid or at least delay rewinding. (We know, by contrast, that the Mesopotamian women skeined their thread off of their spindles, at least for the weft: we see them doing so in the mosaic from Mari; see Chapter 2, fig. 2.18). And we know from the paintings and models that Egyptian women generally rewound likewise.

I can find no cogent technical reason why a spinner might want to delay rewinding. But she could avoid rewinding altogether if she chose to use her spindle as her "shuttle."

Or, to put it the other way, she can save an entire step, namely rewinding, by using the spindle as a "shuttle"—but then she will have to have a lot of spindles available to fill before she starts weaving.

She will also be making some new demands on the shape of her spindle whorl. Now it is no longer just a flywheel: it is going to need a streamlined "nose" to pass easily through the shed without catching on the warp.

The rounded bottoms on many of our peculiar whorls would have served this function well; the extreme nose-cone shape would have served it even better. The hollow shape, moreover, inexplicable within the craft of spinning, now appears to have a reasonable and practical function as a solution to increasing the mass of the whorl without increasing its diameter. If it is to be used on a "shuttle" it will have to be kept narrow enough to pass through the shed. Furthermore, if one is to load the spindle very fully for use as a "shuttle," both the flat and the hollow tops make a rather more efficient surface against which to build the cone of thread than the end of a spherical or sharply biconical whorl.

All in all, the formal and functional details of some of our whorls begin to fit together pretty well, when we make the simple assumption, based on the large numbers, that the spindles were being used also as "shuttles."

The distribution question is not so easy, but plotted against time it shows some intriguing patterns not likely to be the result of chance.

The earliest sites with hollow whorls cluster in Iran and southwest Turkestan between about 5500 and 3500 B.C. (Fig. 14.6): first Cheshmeh Ali, Anau I, and Dalma Tepe, in the north; then spreading out to Altyn-depe, Pisdeli Tepe, Tepe Gawra XIII–XII (and

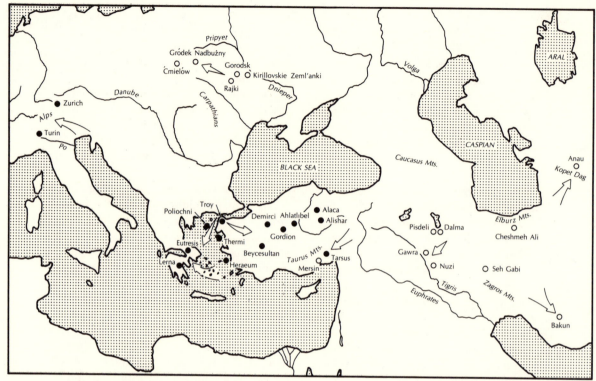

14.6   Map of hollow and "sand-dollar" whorls, in the Neolithic (○) and Bronze Ages (●).   Arrows indicate direction of influx, where ascertainable

XVI?), Nuzi XII–X, Seh Gabi (next to lowest strata), and Bakun B II.[8] In the 4th millennium, cupped whorls turn up in force in levels 12–10 at Mersin, in Cilicia (Garstang 1953, 178 and fig. 116), far to the west of Gawra. They also appear in a curious line of sites across the Ukraine and into Poland (Tripolye and Funnel Beaker cultures; Fig. 14.7), with a demonstrable east-to-west movement and the usual "large quantity"

[8] See Appendix B for the references and technical data. For those not acquainted with Near Eastern archaeology: *tepe* (like *tel(l)* and *höyük* or *hüyük*) simply means "mound," and has been omitted from the map for reasons of space.

[9] The Tripolye sites include Rajki, Gorodsk, and Kiev-Kirillovskie Zemljanki (Passek 1949, 168 and figs. 84, 86, 96). The late Polish Funnel Beaker sites include Gródek Nadbużny (Kowalczyk 1970, 145, 155–56 and fig. 49:7–8; Poklewski 1958, 326 and fig. 15) and Ćmie-

(350 at little Gródek Nadbużny alone: Kowalczyk 1970, 155, 145; cf. Passek 1949, 168). The line runs south of the Pripyet marshes and north of the hill zone, skirting along the northern fringe of the agricultural Tripolye culture during its C2 phase, as though the carriers were foreigners who mingled along the edge as they passed by. Nomadic sheepherders, perhaps?[9]

In the 3rd millennium (Early Bronze Age),

lów (Podkowińska 1950, fig. 35:7–11). The whorls are not the only sign of influence on southeastern Poland from the Tripolye area at this time: see Kowalczyk 1970, 164. Might herders have made the long trek directly from the area of Anau by moving around the east and north sides of the Caspian during particularly wet years, when the usually dry desert is covered with verdant pasture? They might then reach quite naturally, not the shores of the Black Sea, but the area around Kiev.

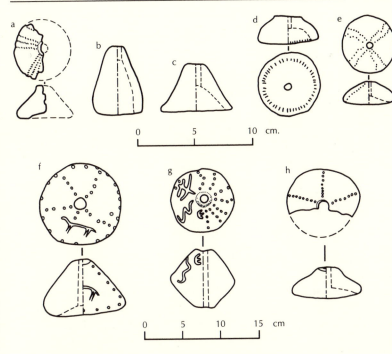

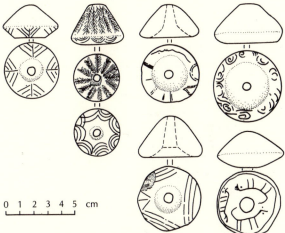

14.7 Late Neolithic spindle whorls from Gródek Nadbużny (a–c) and Ćmielów (d–e) in southeast Poland; and from Rajki and Gorodsk in the Ukraine (f–h). (After Poklewski 1958, pl. 15.9; Kowalczyk 1956, pl. 2.6, 2.4; Podkowińska 1950, pl. 35.7, 35.11; Passek 1949, figs. 86.2, 86.9, and 84.11)

a subtype of these whorls turn up across much of Anatolia—at Troy (Figs. 14.8, 14.9), Beycesultan, Alaca, Alishar, Tarsus, etc.—as well as in the eastern Aegean islands: at Thermi (Lesbos), Poliochni (Lemnos), and the Samian Heraeum (see Appendix B). The movement within Anatolia seems to be a local eddy from northwest to southeast, as though funneling across the straits from Europe. Meanwhile the primacy of whorl shape over decoration becomes muddied, although the huge quantities remain a constant. Had some of the groups of women stopped using spindles as "shuttles" some time back, without relinquishing, for some other reason, the tradition of owning many spindles?

The waters clear a bit, however, when we look farther west, because again we see the westward movement strongly. The copious hollow whorls reach Greece basically in the Middle Bronze period (e.g., Eutresis: Goldman 1931, 198 and pl. 19), the only earlier example being a single whorl with scooped

14.8 Bronze Age whorls dug up at Troy by Schliemann. (After Schliemann [1875] 1968, pl. 33, 40, 31)

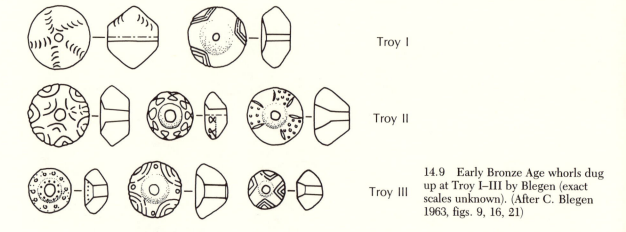

Troy I

Troy II

Troy III

14.9   Early Bronze Age whorls dug up at Troy I–III by Blegen (exact scales unknown). (After C. Blegen 1963, figs. 9, 16, 21)

top found at Lerna IV (Early Bronze III: Carington Smith 1975, 356; Caskey 1955, 37, and pl. 22.1). What is most interesting about the sojourn of these whorls in Greece is that, when and where they and their users are present, virtually no loom weights occur (Carington Smith 1975, 352), although loom weights are frequent enough in both the Early and Late Bronze Ages. It is much harder to believe that the women were spinning enormous quantities of thread but were totally ignorant of weaving, than to believe that they were in the habit of using a different type of loom, one that did not use weights. In the latter case, these people must have originated so far east that they were outside the territory of the warp-weighted loom: that is, east of central Anatolia and Cilicia, and/or east of the Ukraine. Here is yet another kind of proof of the east-to-west movement.

Then, it seems, these cloth-makers picked up and moved still farther west. For as the loom weights begin to reappear in Greece in the Late Bronze Age and the concave whorls disappear, the idiosyncratic spindle whorls turn up in northern Italy and Switzerland. Again there is no doubt of their presence. In the Late Bronze Age pile-dwellings around

Zurich they lie about in profusion, with incised decorations, notched edges, and often with deep hollows, looking if anything even more like those from Anau than do those from Troy II (Fig. 14.10; Ruoff 1981, 253 fig. 3). In fact, one might suppose that there was a direct pipeline across the steppes from Anau into central Europe that supplied Anatolia with modified versions of the whorls by way of Thrace and Troy in the Early Bronze Age, and supplied Switzerland separately with a pristine version more than a millennium later—if it weren't for the fact that there is no other trace of such a supply line at that latitude.

IN chasing the concave whorls, we have raised more questions than we have answered. It is not proven that all the examples cited are truly related to each other; nor is it at all clear that they are not. The case for common origin is greatly strengthened by the correlation of the range of shapes with the style and method of decor and with the persistently large numbers; but it is weakened by a number of rather considerable leaps in time and space. On the side of non-randomness, however, we were able to establish consistent vectors of radiating move-

14.10   Late Bronze Age whorls from Switzerland. (Photo courtesy of Swiss National Museum)

ment within the large (northerly) area where the whorls do occur; and there are broad and archaeologically well-known (southerly) areas of the ancient world where these objects consistently do not occur. Only further excavation and careful reporting of textile-related finds will suffice to make or break the various hypotheses set out here.

It is also possible that we are seeing evidence of people-movements that—like the migrations of the Huns so much later—sometimes moved so far and so fast that they left little behind along the way for an archaeologist to pick up. We know from the political and linguistic repercussions in the literate zone along the Mediterranean that vast movements were in fact taking place somewhere, somehow, in the inner continent during the 3rd and 2nd millennia B.C. Surely if there are any solid clues to such migrations to be picked up, they will be at the two ends of the pipeline, and they will need to be of so humble a sort that we will know they can't be explained as trade. Spindle whorls, as we have said, are only a (non-salable) means to the (salable) end; and they were generally the property of women. If the women were moving as a group, then the whole community was moving.

But people and cultures are complex: textile artifacts were not the only things moving. What really needs to be done is to take the results of this survey of one little artifact and use them to generate new ideas for further work. That to me is the most important result of this exercise we have just gone through: the idea that the textile artifacts are relatively autonomous, and suggest a view of what is going on that is rather independent of the types of archaeological data commonly used. In fact, in putting together this survey I have been at pains to *avoid* other types of evidence (correlations with pottery, metalwork, etc.), just so as not to prejudice the case made by the spindle whorls and loom weights themselves. The weight-chase data have upheld some hypotheses and suggested other quite new ones. If the new ones inspire or irritate other scholars to go out and locate more data, textile or otherwise, that prove or disprove them, I will have done what I set out to do. I have demonstrated the value of paying attention to even the very crudest textile objects.

CHAPTER 15

MINOANS, MYCENAEANS, AND KEFTIU

If, as you wander about in the Theban tombs, you look up from the typical Egyptian wall scenes of feasting and daily life, you are likely to see in the ceiling panels above you a startling array of Aegean-looking scrolls and spirals and even bulls' heads. Archaeologists have long exclaimed over the appearance, without visible means of transport, of these strongly Aegean artistic motifs on Egyptian ceilings; for Aegean pottery—which we know was imported—does not show many of these design elements, let alone the large, all-over patterns. How did the Egyptian artists come by them, and why did they choose to put them on their ceilings?

A few scholars have also noted that the designs in question are of a typical textile variety, and have hazarded the suggestion that the Egyptians had been importing Aegean cloth, now perished, from which they had copied these designs. The patterns are thus of considerable interest to us.

Nor are these the only places in which Egyptian artists have been suspected of depicting Aegean textiles. The small but famous series of tombs in which Aegean-looking gifts are brought to Pharaoh by emissaries sporting long Minoan curls, fancy kilts or loincloths, and elaborate sandals (of a sort still used to this day in Anatolia and the Balkans), under the labels of "people of Keftiu" and/or "people of the Isles in the midst of the Great Green (Sea)," stirred decades of heated debate over the accuracy of the artists and the geographical origins of the people depicted—a debate finally resolved to the satisfaction of most by Vercoutter's monumental study (1956) of the entire series.

Starting from the premise that different tomb owners had different reasons for depicting the foreigners, Vercoutter was able to demonstrate that some of the owners—the viziers—had been concerned with, and would have seen for themselves, both the objects brought from abroad and the people who brought them, whereas others—the temple treasurers and the military men—would probably have seen only the objects and so had copied the bearers somewhat freely from the tombs of the viziers (Vercoutter 1956, 188–98, etc.). The accuracy of the details of the tomb paintings, then, had to be assessed anew for each tomb; and even the viziers may not have been above copying from each other sometimes. But where objects of the same class survive today for comparison (e.g., pottery and some metalwork), it has become clear that the top Egyptian artists were excellent observers of foreign people and things when they wished to be. And Aegean men and goods were among the observed.

Given the material about ancient cloth that we have accumulated here, what can we say about these topics now? What more can we deduce safely about Aegean cloth from the evidence of the representational art—Aegean and/or Egyptian—by building on our direct knowledge of the looms, dyes, fibers, and techniques of the 2nd millennium? Can we assess the degree of Egyptian familiarity with Aegean textiles and how the Egyptians acquired that familiarity? And what else of more general archaeological interest might the study of these textiles and of this international contact add to our understanding of the ancient world?

THE AEGEAN EVIDENCE

For all our stockpiling of evidence, we still have pitifully little direct data about Aegean cloth. But it is enough to give us some solid points on which to anchor our deductions. We know from pottery impressions and small oxidized or carbonized shreds of cloth that weaving was practiced in the Aegean from the Neolithic on down (see Chapter 4, etc.), just as it was everywhere else in southern Europe and the Near East. It is only in the 2nd millennium that preservation is finally good enough for us to glimpse directly any aspects of the lavish decoration that the overall history of European textiles leads us to expect for the Aegean: blue with traces of red at the edge, from a Mycenaean *tholos* burial at Routsi near Pylos (Marinatos 1967b, A16), and five-colored beadwork in a zigzag pattern, from a Mycenaean chamber tomb at Dendra (yellow, brown, black, blue, and white; also some straight blue-and-white; Persson 1931, 106).[1] On the other hand, it is not until the beginning of the Iron Age that we find our first fully preserved examples of cloth, let alone clothing, coming from Greek soil—the tunic and belt from Lefkandi, of the 11th century B.C. (see Chapter 6). Nor do they and the accompanying scraps disappoint us, with their charming variety of weaving and embroidery techniques as well as of designs.

Wherever the fiber is determinable, throughout these millennia, it is linen. We know for certain from the Linear B texts and other artifacts that wool was used extensively in the Bronze Age, but apparently it had an even harder time surviving the ages in the Aegean climate than the linen did—to the point that we see the linen preserved around the very holes left by a completely deteriorated fiber, almost necessarily colored wool, once worked into the same fabrics with it.

We can also glean other definite pieces of information from the Mycenaean Linear B archives, despite the many difficulties of interpreting those texts on account of the heavily ambiguous spelling system. We clearly have reference to several kinds of cloth—even if we aren't sure what they are—and to various grades or degrees of costliness suitable for different estates: "kingly," "for followers"(?), "for guests"(?) (KN Lc525, Ld571, Ld573; Ventris and Chadwick 1973, 315–18; compare Driessen 1984, 53–56), as well as for normal uses. Bands and/or edgings play an important role in the textiles, since we have as many as four different words that seem to refer to them (even if we aren't sure yet exactly how they differ): *onukh-*, *odak-*, *termi-*, and *ampuk-*.

The listed colors for cloth or borders indisputably include white, red, and "purple"

---

[1] Some of the large amount of beadwork at Dendra was seemingly on a belt, which may have been of leather. But compare the beadwork on cloth at Acemhöyük (Turkey) and Murten (Switzerland), and the probable example of gold beadwork on cloth at Early Bronze Age Troy, all described in detail in Chapters 4 and 6. Beading was apparently a popular technique of cloth decoration north of the Mediterranean.

(where we must remember that "purple" may have ranged anywhere from bluish-red to "true purple"—light or dark—to blue), as well as grey at least once (*polios*: KN L587 + 589 + 596; Ventris and Chadwick 1973, 319). And often the description given is *poikilos* 'multicolored, with variegated design.' Of course there are other terms that could be color words but that we don't understand yet. The only recognizable dyestuff mentioned is safflower (see Chapters 10 and 12), which can produce a colorfast red to pink, and also a bright yellow, which, being extremely fugitive, is of no practical commercial value for textile manufacture; but since we have no proof from the texts that either dye was actually used by the Mycenaeans for cloth (rather than for, say, food or medicine, if at all), we must leave it aside. On the other hand, the "purple" can be backed up archaeologically for the earlier Minoans as well, by the heaps of murex shells, crushed for dye extraction, that were associated with Kamares ware in East Crete (see Chapter 10).

We also learn that hard materials were added to some of the textiles at the manufacturing stage: in some cases bronze on linen, presumably to make the sorts of mail-plated shirts of which we have slightly later archaeological examples (KN J693; cf. Ventris and Chadwick 1973, 320, 487–88; see note 11 in Chapter 6); and in one case, perhaps, a substance or object called *pa-ra-ku* is involved, which, although of uncertain translation, must be both hard and precious, given the company it keeps as one of several inlay materials on the furniture tablets (KN L587 + 589 + 596; cf. Ventris and Chadwick 1973, 319).[2] Finally, we hear repeatedly of sewing

and tailors, as well as occasionally of fulling and fullers (e.g., MY Oe129; Ventris and Chadwick 1973, 322).

We know, of course, from both archaeological and reconstructed linguistic evidence that the chief loom in this area was the warp-weighted loom. It is even pictured occasionally in Linear A (see Fig. 3.12), and the shape of the Linear B CLOTH (TELA) ideogram, with three closed edges and one fringed edge, implies its use for most weaving. We also know that this loom requires the weaving of a heading band, which can easily be made multicolored and must be woven on a different loom altogether, a simple band-loom. The Linear B texts suggest that there were even band-loom specialists (*ampuko-worgoi*: PY Ab210, Ad671 [Ventris and Chadwick 1973, 160] and maybe *azetriai*: KN L1568 edge [ibid., 317–18; and see Chapter 12]), a detail that fits nicely with the many words in Linear B for fancy bands and edgings.

All in all, our basic, hard facts about Aegean textiles put the industry squarely within the mainstream of what we have deduced of the overall tradition of textile-making in Europe from the Neolithic to the Iron Age, a tradition rather different from that of Egypt or the Middle East. This observation suggests both some further points of information and some further constraints. In particular, the European tradition is one of exuberantly elaborate patterning, and we must expect the pattern techniques to be predominantly float weaves, with perhaps some patterns from the twill family—the technique so important in Iron Age Europe but already present in Austria in the Late Bronze Age at least (see Chapter 7). Indeed, the set-up of

---

[2] Ventris and Chadwick, having no other resources, suggest by their translation that the cloth is merely the color of *pa-ra-ku*. I wonder, however, whether we are looking at something made into beads or platelets (such as faience or boar's tusk) to be woven into or sewn onto

the cloth itself. We now know that such cloth existed in the Mycenaean world. It might even mean the flat platelets themselves: the Greek stem πλακ- (*plak-*) 'flat object' comes to mind.

the Early Bronze Age loom at Troy, and the large numbers of small loom weights in the finds on Crete and Thera from the 2nd millennium, suggest very strongly that mechanized twill-weaving was already widespread in the Aegean. At what point tapestry and embroidery were taken up remains to be determined.

LET us turn now to the Aegean pictorial representation of its own textile world. Whereas the Egyptians generally portrayed themselves as wearing plain white cloth—pleated, beaded, and bejeweled sometimes, but woven as plain white cloth—the Minoans in particular depicted themselves as wearing multicolored cloth in designs so varied and so elegant as to make the owner of a modern handweaving boutique envious. It has often been doubted that the Minoans were capable of producing such fabric; but our hard data indicate that they had looms and materials entirely equal to the task, as well as a long European tradition of elaborate pattern-weaving behind them. Let us, then, examine the corpus of Aegean textile representations for internal consistency, and for agreement with, amplifications of, and apparent contradictions to our hard data.

We can derive a simple but relevant framework for the sequence and types of cloth depicted by appealing to the general development of Aegean clothing fashions as we see them during the 2nd millennium B.C., this being the first period in which we have representational evidence in the Aegean for either cloth or clothing. The overall scheme that emerges is one of four main phases, of which the middle two are by far the richest and will occupy most of our time and attention.

Very few representations of cloth prior to the Middle Bronze III period have survived, the most notable being the female figurine

15.1   Clay figurine of a woman, from Petsofá, Crete; early 2nd millennium B.C. (Middle Minoan II). (Myres 1902–3, pl. 8)

from Petsofá, with her large, stripe-patterned skirt, open bodice, and exuberant chapeau (Fig. 15.1). Figured frescoes had apparently not yet begun in the Aegean; and I will dub the tiny corpus of other representations of dress *Pre-classical Minoan*. We know almost nothing of the cloth of this period, except to be able to say that the later forms of Minoan dress—open bodice and large skirt for the women, and brief loincloth, cinch-belt, and dagger for the men—were already fairly developed, and presumably so were the textile techniques.

The second cohesive group of cloth and clothing is the one so lavishly illustrated on the monuments of Crete and the nearest islands from Middle Bronze III until the shattering destructions in Late Bronze IB. On all archaeological fronts this is a complex and innovative era, with several sub-periods, and the textiles were undoubtedly evolving rapidly. But in the confused state of our present knowledge I must treat the period as one, and will characterize it as follows: (1) men ordinarily wear a brief loincloth (of a wide variety of shapes, including a sort of mini-kilt, sometimes "flounced" in layers), a tight belt, and light boots (or socks in sandals?), but occasionally they don a great robe or cape; (2) women wear flounced or at least full and ornamented skirts, and tight, short-sleeved, bare-breasted bodices; (3) the women's fabrics are often extremely ornate, the men's much less so; (4) fancy edgings abound, for both sexes; and (5) cloth is frequently cut and tailored. Although this set of fashions extends into the Cyclades, I will call it the *Classical Minoan* period of dress. What we are shown in the monuments is apparently the "festive" form of the women's dress, for special occasions and/or special people, but I see no reason to believe that it is not a natural outgrowth of the local "ordinary" dress forms.

This is not entirely true of the next cluster of representations, a group that appears to show the transitional dress of the period that saw a shift of power from the Minoans to the Mycenaeans, and shows an increasingly archaic ritual dress for women. Hence I will call them the *Transitional/Ritual* styles of dress. The frescoes from which we can draw information date chiefly to Late Minoan II–IIIA on Crete and Late Helladic IIIA–B on the mainland. Ideas about dress seem to have been borrowed in both directions between Crete and the mainland. Presently we will sort out the tangle a bit more; but for now suffice it to say that, despite the general similarity to the old fashions at first glance, there are many subtle differences from before: (1) men now wear substantial kilts (except for bull-leaping), with the old socks and sandals—cinchbelt is optional; (2) women still wear flounced skirts and breast-supporting bodices, but the breasts may be covered; (3) now the women's fabrics are generally rather plain and the men's often very ornate—a complete reversal; (4) fancy edgings continue, but with different patterns prevailing; and (5) some cutting and tailoring persists, but clothes are becoming squarer.

Thoroughly overlapping with the Transitional/Ritual style is another mode of dress that had apparently been hiding from us unrepresented on the mainland for some time, a style I will name the *Native Mycenaean* dress. It was probably worn by all mainlanders who didn't (or when they didn't) have Cretan pretensions: (1) tunic or kilt for the men, and knee-high leggings; (2) all-covering chemise for the women; (3) rather plain fabrics for everyone, stripes and "sprinkles" (of dots, little crosses, dot-rosettes, etc.) being the most common decoration, if any; (4) contrastive but mostly plain edgings; and (5) little or no evidence of cutting or tailoring the garments. One reason I have chosen this name is that the kilt, tunic, and chemise correspond so well to what one would reconstruct for the late proto-Indo-Europeans (Barber 1975) that one must suspect the Greeks of wearing something similar as they entered the southern Balkans. Hence "native" is probably not far from the mark (the tunic/chemise and apron-like wrap around the hips persist even to this day at the core of Balkan folk-wear). Another reason is that a careful assessment of the nature and placement of the gold foil ornaments found in the Shaft Graves at Mycenae shows that a long-sleeved chemise or tunic was already in use there at the start of Late Helladic I (ibid., 316–17).

The chief monuments that we have at the

moment for each of these groups include:[3]

Pre-Classical Minoan Style:
Petsofá: clay figurines (Fig. 15.1)
Phaistos: bowl and fruitstand painted with stylized persons

Classical Minoan Style:
Knossos: Ladies in Blue, Miniature Dress Ornaments (Fig. 15.7), Lady in Red, Priest King, Miniature Fresco (Grandstand and Dancing Floor), fresco fragments of men's loincloths and women's clothes; faience dresses, girdles (Fig. 15.6), and Snake Ladies from the Temple Repository; ivory knot from the Southeast House (Fig. 15.14b)
Mallia: sword hilt with acrobat (Fig. 15.5)
Tylissos: painted steatite figurine
Phylakopí: fresco of person(s) with fishnet (Fig. 15.8)
Pseira: fresco of seated women (Fig. 15.4)
Nirou Khani: fresco of sacred knot (Fig. 15.14e)
Hagia Triada: fresco of woman dancing in shrine garden (Color Plate 2)
Miscellaneous female figurines from Crete
Thera: Priestess (Fig. 15.15), Dressing Ladies, Admiral's *ikria*, Maritime Fresco, Saffron Gatherers
[Mycenae: faience Sacred Knots (Fig. 15.14c) and inlaid daggers from Shaft Graves; fresco of top of woman's skirt (Fig. 15.10); Ivory Triad]

Transitional/Ritual Style:
EARLY:
Knossos: Campstool Fresco, La Parisienne (Fig. 15.14a), Dancing Girl, Bull Leapers, Cupbearer(s) (Fig. 15.9), Procession Fresco (see Fig. 15.9), Captain of the Blacks
Hagia Triada: sarcophagus
Thebes: fresco of procession of women
Mycenae: frescoes from Ramp House area
LATE (ritual only?):
Pylos: Tiny Toreador, frescoes of women in ceremonial dress

Tiryns: fresco of procession of women; clay idols
Mycenae: painted limestone plaque, fresco of woman wearing sacred knot (Fig. 15.14d), "New Lady," fresco in Citadel House, fresco of *ikria* (Fig. 15.22)
Voula: pottery sock and sandal
Tanagra: *larnakes*

Native Mycenaean Style:
Tiryns: frescoes of women in chariots, frescoes of men
Pylos: frescoes of men
Mycenae: fresco in Citadel House, clay idol, Warrior Vase (Fig. 16.8), re-used painted stele (Fig. 16.9)
Cyprus: imported chariot craters (see Fig. 16.10)
Phylakopí: clay idol
Miscellaneous clay idols

Now that we have established a general frame of reference, we can go back and look in detail at the most interesting features of the actual textiles depicted. Since nothing from the first period gives us any details, only hints of existence, we shall start with the second period, the Classical Minoan. It is this period that gives us the most extensive representations of Aegean cloth that we have.

In some ways the easiest group of cloth representations to deal with is that from Thera, because it is homogeneous. It is firmly and fairly narrowly datable, since the excavated houses at Akrotiri were all destroyed simultaneously by the massive eruption of the Theran volcano early in the 15th century B.C., and the houses in question had not been there terribly long. The cloth depicted shows the following designs:

Stripe: solid or dashed, broad or narrow;
Plaid or *Diaper:* formed by single thin stripe

---

[3] Those entries put in brackets do not quite fit the definition as classified. The objects listed here from the Shaft Graves were not found in Crete, but they were either imported or made under strong Minoan influence and are contemporary with the Classical Minoan objects and frescoes. The same is probably true of the Ivory Triad. The fresco fragment, on the other hand, is assumed to be rather later, yet its type of textile places it here. Is it archaizing, or misdated?

A set of bibliographical references for all these monuments can be found in Appendix C.

(solid or dashed) in squares, often with filler—dot or small cross;

Scatter Figure: polka dots, splayed dittoes, lilies (Saffron Gatherers);

Strip Figure: lozenges with an inner "tooth" on each side, with or without a tiny cross in each outer triangle (Saffron Gatherers);

Grid/Rapport Figure (see also "Plaid"):

(a) 4-petaled flower rapport (Priestess) (Fig. 15.2, 15.15)

(b) 4-pointed star rapport, inside partial grid of dots (Saffron Gatherer carrying necklace).

Note that the last two patterns, the 4-petaled flower rapport and the 4-pointed star rapport, can be drawn in such a way that the patterns cannot be distinguished: it is a toss-up as to which design is figure and which is ground (Fig. 15.2). In the above examples, the painter has pretty clearly made a choice; but we will see that this sort of playfulness with designs is typical of the Minoan decorative artist.[4]

The patterns of the edgings are generally made up of the dot, stripe (running the length of the edging), bar (running across the

15.2   Rapport pattern composed of either 4-pointed stars inside circles, as at left, or 4-petaled flowers, as at right (compare Fig. 15.15)

edging), diagonal, and zigzag, but often these elements are combined into more interesting patterns: zigzags alternating with bars, zigzag with a dot in each resulting triangle, zigzag with alternating fillers of dot and stripes. One saffron gatherer's headband, though badly damaged, appears to have a design formed from a row of cirles, each centered with a dot (Marinatos 1976, pl. 66), but the design may have been still more complicated. The seated saffron gatherer, on the other hand, has a "yo-yo" pattern (Fig. 15.3) on some of her narrow bands, the center of the yo-yo being a striped lens or oval.[5]

15.3   Simple "yo-yo" pattern with oval fillers, and an indication (dotted line) of how the yo-yo can be put into rapport with other such lines to form an extended pattern

On the whole, the Theran textiles all look readily—even easily—weavable. To imitate most of these designs, the techniques of choice would be supplemental-warp float for the bands and supplemental weft for the larger cloths, possibly in double-faced or even double-cloth techniques. Stripes and true plaids require only an appropriate change of color in the warp and/or weft, not a change of weave.[6] The scattered figures could be produced with a supplementary weft or by simple embroidery. In short,

---

[4] The very same star/petal illusion occurs repeatedly, much earlier, at Tell Halaf, far to the east in northern Mesopotamia. See, for example, H. Schmidt 1943, 52 fig. 27 for a bowl covered with the same design. I keep wondering whether the similarity is purely accidental or whether it is warning us of much older diffusions of textiles and their patterns.

[5] It is not entirely clear whether either this or the "toothed lozenge" described above should be classed as edgings or strip figures. I have gone by their apparent use—the yo-yo as a belt(?) and the lozenge as a flounce—but who knows how they were woven! The

same problem recurs presently, among the other Classical Minoan motifs, where it is not even always clear how they were used, since some of the frescoes are so fragmentary.

[6] The various plaid/diaper designs continue to puzzle me as to which direction they were woven in. The saffron gatherer on the cover of Marinatos 1976, for example, wears a bodice of material that looks, on the face of it, like a diagonal diaper pattern done with supplemental weft. Created in this manner, the lines would typically appear dotted, and the cross in the center would be a convenient, even necessary, trick to catch the floats

these depictions of cloth form a believable and internally fairly consistent group, from the point of view of a weaver. With that as an anchor, let us move into the main body of Cretan material.

It is instructive to begin by looking in detail at two of the most elaborate and attractive Minoan representations of female dress: one from the tiny coastal isle of Pseira, in the north, and the other from the sprawling villa at Hagia Triada, in the south. In the Pseira fresco (Fig. 15.4), one surviving sleeve shows a grid of circles with something inside, and an edging of a row of rosettes. Another sleeve (if it ever existed as such: Maria Shaw is currently reviewing the evidence) is edged with a row of plain dots and shows nested pairs of zigzag bands opposed so as to make lozenges, with a 4-pointed star at the center of each lozenge, and all the ground space filled in with dotted rosettes. As if the fancy bodice weren't enough, the skirt material sports an elaborate "yo-yo" pattern, in which alternate rows are filled with an interlaced knot and a four-spiral cluster edged with large bead-like dots. The dancing woman from Hagia Triada (see Color Plate 2), of whom we have only the bottom two-thirds, has a delicately flounced and divided skirt composed of twin layers of colored squares alternating with a wide layer of figured and edged material. Interlocked quatrefoils, some filled and some plain, make up the main design in red, white, and blue, while

15.4   Relief fresco depicting a seated woman (the left arm may come from a depiction of another woman). Island of Pseira, just north of Crete; mid-2nd millennium B.C. (Late Minoan I). (Seager 1910, pl. 5; courtesy of the University Museum, University of Pennsylvania)

just where they would become intolerably long. Done as an 8-thread pattern, floats would never jump more than 3 threads.

But the bodice is so tight that if the girl has cut it on the straight of the fabric, she will hardly be able to move her arms. She will be much more comfortable if she has started from a plaid and cut on the bias. (In reconstructing the cut of the Snake Ladies' costume, Sandra Rosenbaum [pers. comm. 1988] also concluded that the fabric must have been cut on the bias.) It is very easy to weave exactly the same pattern square to the fabric (also 8-count), using a single thread to form a dotted plaid

stripe each way, and a supplemental thread (whether weft or embroidery) only for the cross.

In favor of this latter suggestion is the much greater efficiency of the plaid (everything is mechanized except the two "stitches" of the cross). In favor of the former method is the fact that the presence of the cross is motivated by the structure of the cloth. How to choose? These and other counterbalanced problems seem to arise with each group of plaid/diaper representations one analyzes. I wonder if the weavers were so skilled that they were using both techniques—here one and there the other, as the occasion suited them. Richard Ellis has pointed out to me (pers. comm. 1987) that the 7th century B.C. textiles from the Gordion city mound showed just this sort of trick of using two techniques to achieve the same sort of pattern at two different angles.

the edging shows snail-shell spirals on a white ground between two thin red stripes.

What a mind-boggling array of complicated textiles! And yet, on the whole, the designs are merely variations and elaborations of what we see on Thera: major organization into grids and interlocks, with elements of stripes, zigzags, yo-yos, dots, circles, stars, and petals, differently arranged. The additions are chiefly the spiral, knot, and quatrefoil, the histories of which will become clearer presently. And all of them, to one familiar with the pottery and glyptic motifs, seem utterly Minoan.

If we now summarize the larger textiles on all the Cretan representations down to the destruction during Late Minoan IB, we find:

Stripe: broad or narrow (Snake Ladies, faience dresses, Tylissos figurine, Miniature Fresco, Priest King, etc.)

Plaid or *Diaper:* formed by single thin stripe in squares (Knossos ivory knot, Shaft Grave knots, Miniature Fresco)

Zigzag: (Nirou Khani knot, Knossos fragments of women's clothes; Miniature Dress Ornaments; Pseira lady)

Scatter Figure: polka dots (Snake Lady, Tylissos figurine)

Strip Figure:
crocus frieze (faience dress and belt)
frieze of sphinxes, griffins, and bull's heads (Miniature Dress Ornaments)
frieze of hanging flutes? (Miniature Dress Ornaments)
lozenge chain (Snake Lady)
barred or toothed stripe (Knossos fragment of women's clothes)

Repeated Strip Figure:
triangles and dots between rows of dots (Knossos fragments of men's loincloths)

dotted rosettes, spirals, or zigzags (Knossos fragments of men's loincloths)
3-prong ("anvil") interlock (Mallia acrobat)

Grid/Rapport/Nested Figure:
grid of circles (Pseira lady, Ivory Triad)
lozenge network, half-filled with stripes (Ladies in Blue, Snake Ladies, Lady in Red)
tricurved arch network, with solid and dotted arch fillers (Ladies in Blue)
quatrefoil interlock (Hagia Triada Dancer)
petal rapports (Ivory Triad)
S-spiral chains with 4-pointed stars between rows (Snake Lady)
opposing nested zigzags with 4-pointed stars between and scattered dot rosettes and spirals (Pseira Lady)
yo-yo rapport, filled with 4-pointed star and snowflake (faience girdle)
yo-yo rapport, filled with spiral cluster and interlaced knot (Pseira lady)
nested chevrons (zigzags?) filled with dotted spirals (Knossos fragment of men's clothes)

Unitary Figure:
crocus patch (faience dress)
birds on rocks (Phylakopí fisher).

And for the edgings we find the usual dots, bars, zigzags (sometimes, as with the Ladies in Blue, of the slightly curved "flame" variety; sometimes with dots[7]), plus circles, lozenges, and rosettes. We also find rows of snail-shell spirals (e.g., Hagia Triada Dancer, Ladies in Blue) and chains of S-spirals (Snake Lady), as well as a chain of 4-petaled flowers (Mallia acrobat, Fig. 15.5).

In comparison with the Theran repertoire, the Cretan list is mostly only an expansion of sub-varieties, which could be produced by the same techniques. But it is interesting where the expansion comes: precisely in the

---

[7] There are two rather different types of zigzags on the edgings, and they suggest rather different production techniques to me as a weaver. The one composed of thin, straight lines (as on the Theran girls, and on the Dancing Girl from Knossos in the next period) looks like the sort of thing one would do by picking up a contrastingly colored supplementary warp for a single shed at a time, as needed, in a regular geometric pattern. The

curved zigzag, however, is formed with a much wider band; and both the curve and the width indicate that the pattern threads (warp or weft) floated over several ground threads at once. The spiral edgings are easily woven in the same technique, as I discovered by trial and error in attempting to reproduce them, long before I knew that this was the chief method attested in prehistoric Europe for pattern weaving.

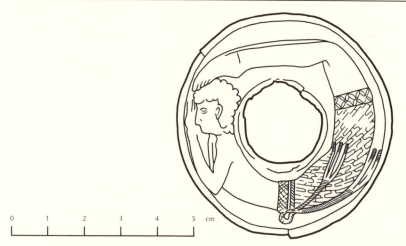

0   1   2   3   4   5 cm

15.5   Acrobat engraved on the gold-covered pommel of a sword, from the Old Palace at Mallia, Crete; mid-2nd millennium B.C. (Middle Minoan III). Note kilt with interlock pattern and 4-petaled edging. (Iraklion Museum, no. 636; drawing by M. Stone)

most difficult and time-consuming types, the most complex and least geometric designs. It is probably the difference between the amount of luxury affordable at the center of the culture and at the periphery. In any case we see extremely elaborate build-ups of fairly simple and familiar elements into repetitive strips, chains, grids, and rapports. This same principle was present on Thera, in the grids of 4-petaled flowers swapping with 4-pointed stars.

The one really new category is that of the "unitary" figures: the crocus patch and the birds on the rocks. To these we can add the related friezes of crocus flowers (Fig. 15.6), sphinxes, bulls' heads, etc. (Fig. 15.7). Such things can be produced in textile art, and in quite a variety of ways. The most famous way is with tapestry technique, but one could also imagine weft supplement of the sort done by the Neolithic Swiss, or embroidery (any design whatsoever can be embroi-

15.6   Faience plaques of dresses and belts, decorated with crocuses and a yo-yo pattern, from the Temple Repository, Knossos, Crete; mid-2nd millennium B.C. (Evans 1921, 506 fig. 364; by permission of Mark Paterson on behalf of the Sir Arthur Evans Trust)

dered), or even sewing on appliqué patches. All of these methods would be very time-consuming, of course.

Another possibility, therefore, is that the rare examples of a single pictorial design covering most of a textile were inventions of the painters, and were intended not to show an actual textile, or type of textile, but to identify a deity or divine principle for the beholder of the painting. Yet another possibility is that ritual clothing, intended to be worn only once for a special event, was itself painted with such a design. If it were never to be washed, there would be no problem; or if it were to be repainted with a different scene for the next festival, again no problem. But we mustn't count on the saving of time as an important factor. Such considerations as enormous time and effort did not faze the ancient Peruvian textile workers: we know that large numbers of women worked in relays to produce a single mantle embroidered with hundreds of tiny figures all over it (see Paul 1985). And a single Persian rug may take years to produce.

It is possible, however, that the sphinxes cavorting among the Miniature Dress Ornaments (Fig. 15.7) are trying to tell us something. They are female sphinxes, of the Syrian type, rather than male ones of the Egyptian type. Their griffin companions, too, are natives of Syria, and both make their earliest appearance in Crete precisely here on these dresses (Frankfort 1936–37, 116–17). So we would seem to be dealing in this case with figured cloth imported from Syria. By an almost uncanny coincidence, one of the few and precious relics of polychrome cloth from Pharaonic Egypt also has female sphinxes on it (see Figs. 5.10–5.11), and also points to Syria as the source both of many of its motifs and of its mode of manufacture, embroidery. This is the tunic of Tutankhamon that we discussed at length in Chapter

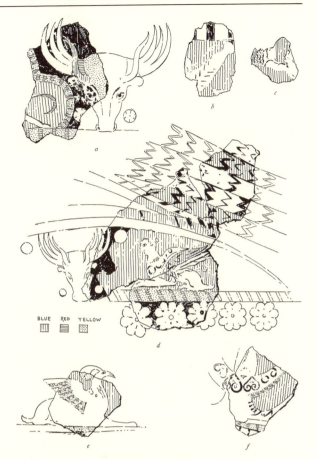

15.7 Miniature ornaments, including sphinxes, griffins, and bulls' heads, apparently adorning women's clothing. Fresco from Knossos; mid-2nd millennium B.C. (Late Minoan I). (Evans 1930, 41 fig. 25; by permission of Mark Paterson on behalf of the Sir Arthur Evans Trust)

5, which must have been made specifically for him, since it has his name embroidered on it, but which must have been produced by foreigners (slaves? well-wishers?) since it is largely covered with Syrian motifs carried out in a non-Egyptian art form, embroidery. The tunic is some two centuries later in date than the Minoan frescoes, but we also know that the Syrians had already been in the business of exporting fancy and expensive textiles for a millennium.

Most of the other textile figures that confront us in the Cretan paintings, however, have strongly Minoan connotations: saffron crocuses, bulls' heads, etc. So if the idea of figured textiles was imported, it was picked up quickly by the Minoans—just as they picked up the idea of figured frescoes abruptly from the Egyptians at about the same time (Shaw 1967; Immerwahr 1989). In fact, all these arts show signs of mixing, for the shapes of the crocus clumps on their little humped pads, both in Minoan frescoes of scenery (Cameron 1968, fig. 12) and on the faience models of dresses (see Fig. 15.6), look rather strongly like Egyptian frescoes of papyrus clumps on humped pads. Similarly, one might point to the Phylakopí dress with birds and rocks on it (Fig. 15.8), the Knossian fresco showing a frieze of partridges among rocks (Evans 1928, pt. 1 fig. 52 and frontispiece), and the much earlier Egyptian fresco frieze of geese from a tomb at Meydum, now in Cairo. The Knossos frieze in particular has always struck me as looking singularly like tapestry.

Regardless of the exact status of these fanciest cloths, it is clear that the tradition of elaborate textiles was already in full flower by the beginning of what I have called the Classical Minoan period of production. There is no question that adequate techniques were available, and that all the designs depicted are possible textile designs, especially within a weft-float tradition. Indeed, our appeals to the Swiss Neolithic cloths for relevant technique are telling us that the Minoans *could* have been doing this sort of thing for a millennium and a half already. We shouldn't be surprised at evidence that they may have become good at it by so late a date.

When we turn to the next time period, after the disasters of Late Minoan IB, we see some changes in who wears what. The men

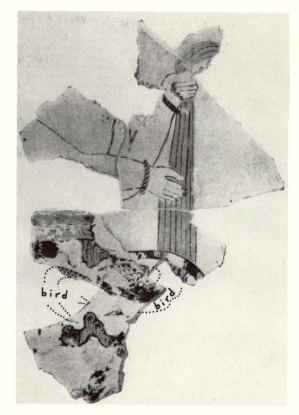

15.8   Person, probably female, holding a fishnet(?) and wearing a skirt decorated with birds and rocks. Phylakopí, island of Melos; mid-2nd millennium B.C. (Based on Atkinson et al. 1904, fig. 61)

at Knossos turn to sumptuous pointed and tassled kilts, in place of the brief loincloths common earlier. On the cloth itself we see the same elegant patterns we had seen before on the women. The interlock patterns are even more in evidence, with the Cupbearer and the men in the Procession Frescoes at Knossos providing several splendid new examples (Fig. 15.9).

By contrast, the women's cloth (but not cut of clothing) becomes rather plainer. The central woman in the Knossos Procession Fresco still wears exceedingly elaborate textiles; and it seems probable on grounds of

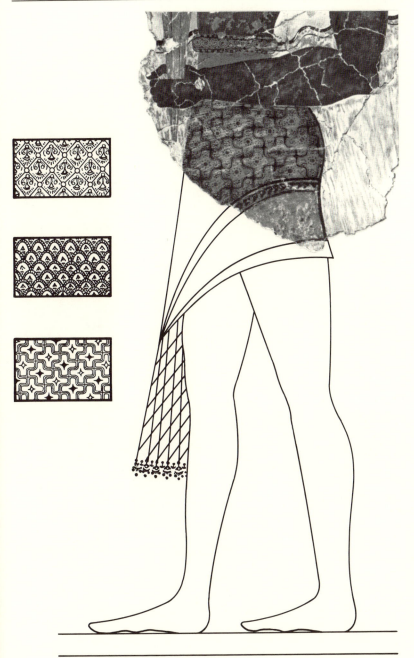

15.9 Fresco of a cupbearer wearing a pointed kilt ornamented with a pattern of interlocking quatrefoils. The tassel and other cloth patterns (in boxes) are drawn from similar kilts in the Procession Fresco. Knossos; mid-2nd millennium B.C. (Composite drawing by M. Stone around photo courtesy of Iraklion Museum)

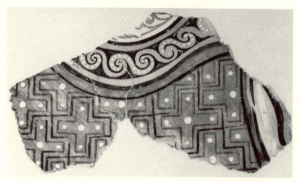

15.10   Fresco fragment of a woman's skirt, from Mycenae, Greece; mid- to late 2nd millennium B.C. (Late Helladic III). (Rodenwaldt 1919, pl. 9)

the style of the cloth that the early fresco lady from Mycenae (Fig. 15.10) should be dated no later than this era, since the 4-pronged interlock pattern clearly belongs to this group. But the Theban procession figures already show significantly plainer cloth on their dresses. Among the edgings, the zigzag and rosette continue in popularity, and are joined by two new companions: the rosette divided by a triglyph (Knossos Procession Fresco), and the four-color barred band (the interesting properties of which we will explore shortly).

For the Cretans, this women's dress with the flounced skirt and open-fronted bodice was traditional, but for the Mycenaeans it was borrowed, lock, stock, and barrel, and it contrasts sharply with the much more conservative "native" dress, based on the all-covering chemise. As time passes, only the women—on both Crete and the mainland—retain the Cretan forms, and apparently only for certain festive or ritual occasions. In one case we even see both styles in the same fresco: that found in the Citadel House at Mycenae. The flounced Minoan style clearly persisted here and there for several more centuries (e.g., on the Tanagra *larnakes*), much as Elizabethan courtiers' huge lace col-

lars and pointed corsets persist today in the folk costumes of Brittany. The Minoan bodice may even have "genetic reflexes" in some of the more southerly Greek folk costumes today.

The men on the mainland, however, appear to have been quite as plain as the women in native attire. In fact, of the Native Mycenaean style there is remarkably little to say, since the frescoes show the cloth itself as becoming mostly quite plain (Fig. 15.11),

15.11   Fresco of ladies wearing chemises and driving a chariot. Note the barred pattern on the wheel rim and on the border of the fresco. Tiryns, Greece; late 2nd millennium B.C. (Late Helladic IIIB). (Rodenwaldt 1912, 98 fig. 40)

edged with increasingly plain bands of a contrasting color (although bars, zigzags, circles, and rosettes continue). Stripes and small, simple scatter figures persist, as in the great procession scene on the Vestibule wall at Pylos (M. L. Lang 1969, pl. 119–20). Occasionally one sees an ornate band depicted, as with Pylos lady no. 50Hnws (ibid., pl. 31 and D), who boasts rows of zigzags, circles, and four-color barred bands. But as Mabel Lang concludes from her study of all the Pylos frescoes, the Late Helladic IIIB artists had inherited a variety of earlier painting styles and motifs, which they drew upon at will (ibid., 221–27). If elaborate cloth and clothing persisted, it may have been only for deities and royalty, and/or only for state occasions, much as we revert to 19th-century long gowns and tails for royal encounters and for weddings, or to medieval garb for academic and religious processions. In short, a stagnant holdover, not a growing tradition. If a school of elaborate weaving was still alive and evolving—and there is some evidence, discussed in the next chapter, that it was—it was doing so elsewhere in the culture and did not get depicted in the palace frescoes.

OUT of this rather considerable corpus of material, there are three types of cloth that strike me as particularly interesting. The first of these is the four-color barred edging that becomes so fashionable in the Late Bronze Age (Fig. 15.12). It consists of two parallel bands, one with alternate bars of yellow and red, the other with bars of blue and black.

The motif occurs most widely in frescoes from the Late Helladic IIIA period, such as on the hem of the center lady in the Procession Fresco at Knossos, on the processional ladies at Tiryns (both on the bodice edge and on the frame of the picture), and in numerous stray fragments from Tiryns. It also appears slightly earlier(?) as the border of the

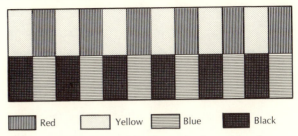

Red　　　Yellow　　　Blue　　　Black

15.12　Simplest form of the four-color barred band, a common Mycenaean edge pattern for both clothing and frescoes

famous Knossos fresco showing two women and a man, all clad in brief loincloths, doing acrobatics across the back of a charging bull. (This fresco is now generally dated to Late Minoan II or IIIA.) The border of the Hagia Triada sarcophagus, which is dated firmly to Late Minoan IIIA, consists of a slightly elaborated version of the four-color barred band on either side of a typical Transitional/Ritual style rosette band. Several examples occur on clothing shown in the Pylos frescoes, in Late Helladic IIIB.

In order to familiarize myself thoroughly with the textile motifs represented in the frescoes, I have acquired the habit of handcoloring copies of them for myself. About the seventh or eighth time I found myself coloring this particular motif, I began to muse on its frequency as a border pattern, and it occurred to me that it would be very easy to weave using a common belt-weaving trick. In order to make a belt very strong, one often resorts to using so many warp threads so close together that the weft does not show at all; it merely binds the warp together without being exposed to wear. By making all the even threads one color and all the odd threads another, with each change of shed the unwoven part of the belt appears to change color entirely, like magic (since the threads of the opposite color are entirely hidden below: turn the whole thing over and you see just the reverse coloration). Intrigued, and tired of paperwork, I raided my yarn chest and set up two such warps side by side, one with red and yellow alternating, and the other with blue and black alternating, then knitted myself a set of heddles over a pencil and started to weave. Within minutes I had an exact replica of the four-color barred edging growing on my makeshift loom.

As I wove, I became aware of a persistent image in my head of a picture from Marta Hoffmann's book on the warp-weighted loom (Fig. 15.13), a picture of an old Lappish woman sitting on the floor weaving the heading band for her loom, with the future warp stretched out on a frame on her left and the heading band growing on the bandloom on her right. The band was about the same width as mine and had the same design on it: a double band of bars. I had never stopped to think about her pattern before. The weave corresponded exactly to mine, except that

she was pulling her weft through the shed in pairs, that is, in loops to form the future warp. So I tried pulling my weft through the same way, and soon had an elegant little model of a warp with a heading band. It corresponds exactly to the weave of the many heading bands we have from the Swiss Neolithic and Danish Bronze Age sites, and to the color pattern of the four-color barred edging of the frescoes.

It is a simple step, then, to the hypothesis that the four-colored barred edging is shown so often on textiles because it occurred there in real life. It seems to have been particularly popular among the Mycenaean Greeks (for whom we have virtually no textile representations prior to Late Helladic IIIA: they may have come by it much earlier for all we know). It also seems reasonable that the fresco painters, seeing this border design all around them on people of note, picked it up as a handy border design for frescoes. As a

15.13 Lappish woman making a warp (large Z-shape) and its heading band (lower left) for her warp-weighted loom, in 1955. She is pulling a loop of thread from the ball beside her right knee (it has already gone through the shed in the heading band) to make it long enough to slip over her warping posts. Note barred pattern on heading band. (Hoffmann [1964] 1974, 66 fig. 26)

15.14 Representations of Minoan "sacred knots": (a) fresco of a girl (nicknamed "La Parisienne") wearing a knot, from the palace at Knossos (after Evans, Cameron, and Hood 1967, back cover; courtesy of Gregg International Publishers); (b) ivory carving, from the Southeast House, Knossos (courtesy of Iraklion Museum); (c) faience pieces from Shaft Grave IV, Mycenae (courtesy of National Museum, Athens); (d) fresco fragment from Mycenae (after Rodenwaldt 1921, fig. 26); (e) fresco fragments from Nirou Khani, Crete (after Xanthoudides 1922, 11 fig. 9) (Drawings by M. Stone)

Mycenaean favorite, this multicolored edging would certainly answer well to the Linear B phrase *poikilonukha*.[8]

The second type of cloth that catches my attention is the group associated with the "sacred knot" (Fig. 15.14). The most famous

[8] In Linear B, *poikilo-* means roughly "multicolored," and *onukh-* (lit. "claw") refers to edgings (see Chapters 12 and 13).

This is not to say that the convention of painting multicolored borders around the Aegean frescoes comes exclusively from textiles. Maria Shaw has plausibly suggested (1967, 107–9) that the Minoans may have picked up the idea from the multicolored barred band often used as a frame by the Egyptian painters. But the Egyptian band, while rather similar in overall impression, is quite different in detail. Why? One can easily imagine a Minoan returning from Egypt and describing (or himself attempting to imitate) the impressive Egyptian wall-paintings, with their vast procession scenes of red men

representation is the painting nicknamed "La Parisienne" from the palace at Knossos. At the back of her neck this lively girl wears a long, narrow scarf knotted into a loop, with the fringed tails flying out behind. The material of the scarf is shown as blue with slim

and white women. When it came to imitating at such remove, however, the hazily remembered impression of a border of colored bars, it would be quite natural to cast about at home for a local model, hitting upon, in this case, a frequent textile edging. Thus the border may legitimately come from *both* an Egyptian prototype and a specific Aegean textile model. Once the design was translated into paint, of course, it no longer had to conform to the exigencies of weaving, and was free to evolve on its own as a fresco border.

One more point. Philologists have heretofore found it puzzling that the only objects in Linear B to receive the epithet *poikilonukh-* are textiles and chariot wheels. Is it coincidence that the rim of the chariot wheel on the

red and black stripes that continue out to the ends of the fringes. Our other representations of the "sacred knot" are mostly of the knotted scarf alone, apparently a badge of office or a sacred object in itself:

(1) a carved ivory piece from the Southeast House at Knossos—plaid (one thin stripe each way), with a plain bar just above the fringed ends;
(2) a fresco from Nirou Khani, with a herringbone pattern (ends not preserved);
(3) several pieces of faience, representing three or more knots, from Shaft Grave IV, Mycenae (which contained three women and two men)—in plaid, with two to four thin stripes each way; fringed at one end; and
(4) a fresco fragment from Mycenae of a woman wearing the scarf, with a small ditto pattern, and a zigzag near the ends (tips not preserved).

What I find striking is that this group, unlike most of the rest of the Aegean depictions of textiles, matches so closely the repertoire of cloth we find in the salt mines of Hallstatt and Hallein: stripes, plaids, and perhaps even a herringbone twill. I have no answer as to why that should be. I see two major possibilities. Either, as we continue to excavate, we will be finding more and more connections between the Aegean and Central Europe in the 2nd millennium B.C. (remember that the earliest fancy textiles from the salt mines go back into the Bronze Age); or else we must reckon with the sacred knots as archaistic in their fabric, using only(?) the types of cloth that were in use in the Aegean when the cult began at some distant point in

the past—perhaps the early 3rd millennium, when we find our first evidence of the manufacture of twill. Again, as with the four-color barred edging, I have the strong impression that the graphic artists were representing pretty nearly what they were seeing. And why shouldn't they?

The third group of Aegean textiles that intrigue me is the set with interlocking patterns. These include:

Interlocks Conceived in Strips and/or Grids:
   3-pronged "anvil" interlock (Mallia acrobat; Fig. 15.5)
   yo-yo rapport (Pseira lady; Fig. 15.3–15.4)
   spiral chain (Knossos snake lady)
   4-petaled flower rapport = 4-pointed star rapport (Theran ladies; Fig. 15.2, 15.15)
Complex Interlocks:
   4-pronged "cross" interlock = swastika rapport:
      with 5 dots inside (Mycenae lady; Fig. 15.10)
      with 5 dotted rosettes inside (Knossos Cupbearer; Fig. 15.9)
      with 4-pointed star inside (Knossos Procession Fresco; Fig. 15.9)
   4-pronged "quatrefoil" interlock (Hagia Triada lady, perhaps also Knossos Procession Fresco;[9] see Color Plate 2).

Right from our first evidence for the nature of Minoan textiles we see this sort of playfulness with design elements: the Mallia acrobat (Fig. 15.5) is dated to Middle Minoan IIIb, and the Pseira (Fig. 15.4) and Hagia Triada (Color Plate 2) ladies are placed there or in Late Minoan I. The characteristic is

---

Tiryns fresco of two women driving a chariot (see Fig. 15.11) is decorated with the familiar blue and black half of the barred edging? One can dismiss the likeness as coincidence—the accident of reducing things to paint. But one could also hunt for other possible reasons for the similarity—e.g., that the actual rims were typically painted with this pattern; or that some sort of rim clamps ("claws"?—*onukhes*) made a pattern of this sort on the wheels, and the name was extended to other things with a similar pattern, such as textile edgings. In fact, the spoked wheels recently found in the Hallstatt

burial at Hochdorf have just such rim-clamps at just such intervals (see photos in Biel 1987, 28–29).

[9] Evans restored the dress of the central female of the Procession Fresco with a quatrefoil interlock pattern (Evans 1928, suppl. pl. 26.14). But the edge of the fragment runs right along the top edge of the border design, and I cannot tell whether he could see enough of the pattern above to restore it accurately, or whether, as with so much else in that fresco, he merely went on probabilities.

equally evident in the pottery. Close parallels to the Pseiran yo-yo design occur on Kamares ware vases (see Walberg's type 16.5–11: Walberg 1976, fig. 44), among others on a handsome Middle Minoan II cup (Warren 1975, 75). Spiral chains and rapports occur constantly on the pots, not to mention the stone carving and the frescoes, to the point that they are considered the hallmark of Aegean decorative art. Already in the Early Bronze Age in the Cyclades, they crawl all over the "frying pans" in elaborate rapport patterns; and they occur in simpler designs on the mainland in the Neolithic.

The optical illusion that converts the 4-petaled flower rapport into the 4-pointed star rapport (see Fig. 15.2) is also a typical Minoan trick. One sees again and again in pottery and frescoes the tendency to play with space, to make figure of ground and ground of figure. We have a 4-petaled flower rapport on the dress of a young priestess from Thera (Fig. 15.15): clearly the painter, at least, was thinking of it as composed of petals because of where he (or she?) chose to break the pattern. One has to think hard to "flip" the pattern optically into its other possibility, the 4-pointed star motif. But having made it obvious by the alignment that we were to see petals on the dress, the artist also couldn't resist drawing our attention to the other possibility by audaciously drawing her earring as a 4-pointed star within a circle. The design occurs again on the dress of one of the saffron gatherers, and was clearly painted by laying down petal-shaped ovals of dark paint on the light ground; but then the painter painted a gridwork of white dots over these ovals so as to frame the 4-pointed star shapes in between. When we look at it now we see stars in a network. The painter of the women in the House of the Ladies went a step further, however, and lifted the stars out of the interstices of the net and put them at the juncture

points! How such patterns may have been woven is another question; presumably the basis there was the square or diagonal grid.

This playful attitude towards space reaches its climax in the continuous interlocking of pronged shapes. The most magnificent of these is the design on the skirt of the lady depicted in a garden, at Hagia Triada (see Color Plate 2). Executed in red, white, and blue, it is a stunning example of Minoan decorative artistry. But it is not alone: slightly simpler versions occur on the lady from Mycenae (Fig. 15.10) and on several of the kilts in the Procession and Cupbearer Frescoes at Knossos (Fig. 15.9). A handsome trefoil version has recently been found carved on an al-

15.15 Fresco of the "priestess" from the West House at Akrotiri, island of Thera, mid-2nd millennium B.C. Note reversal of pattern on the sleeves and earring (compare Fig. 15.2). (Courtesy of National Museum, Athens)

abaster vase in the Unexplored Mansion at Knossos, which was destroyed at the end of Late Minoan II (Popham 1984, 234, and pl. 215.5, 216.7, 229.7), while a simple 3-pronged version that fits into a strip occurs on the kilt of the Middle Minoan IIIB acrobat from Mallia (Fig. 15.5; also Kantor 1947, pl. 10 for yet others).

We could add to this list of repetitive textile patterns the grids of circles, stars, rosettes, and hearts, as well as the various network patterns with straight or wavy sides, filled with every manner of bric-a-brac (see Fig. 15.9). All in all, one gets the impression that the Minoans loved best to wear these small, all-over designs. We will undoubtedly see more of them as we continue to excavate.

It is also worth noting that these designs which flourish so in the Classical Minoan style take their last fling on the men's kilts during the Transitional/Ritual style used at court, and then disappear from view. One wonders if the Mycenaeans cheerfully bought up and wore the sumptuous Minoan fabrics as they began to take over affairs on Crete, but then allowed the local native industry to fade in the face of the sorts of quotas we see in the Linear B accounts and mass production we see in the pottery.

A word about color. The dominant colors used for cloth in the frescoes are red, blue, yellow (or tawny), and white, with a little black. Green is conspicuously absent. It is used in other parts of the frescoes upon occasion, but not for cloth. From a technical point of view that is not surprising, for the color was probably achievable in textiles at that time only by double-dyeing (just as in the frescoes it was usually, though not al-ways, a combination of blue and yellow paint). The process involved first immersing the batch of wool in the one color, say blue, until it was the right shade to neither overwhelm nor be overwhelmed by the other color (yellow); and then dyeing the wool again in a dyebath of the other color. Later, in the Iron Age, the Hallstatt people learned that they could make green all at once by using a yellow plant dye with iron mordant (see Chapter 7): the iron, in reacting with the dye chemicals, fixes the dye but turns it green at the same time. In the Bronze Age, however, presumably such technology was not available; and the Minoans perhaps had not yet discovered the principle of double-dyeing. At any rate, green we do not find.

Our survey of pictorial evidence for textiles in the Aegean implies strongly that cloth with elaborate and colorful designs of small, repetitive figures was a specialty of the Minoans, from well before Middle Minoan III (such expertise was not developed overnight) down at least into Late Minoan IIIA. We see nothing in the designs depicted on the larger cloth that could not be produced by supplementary-weft techniques, which we know from the Swiss Neolithic linen to have been perfected in Europe long since, although other techniques for some of them could be imagined. For the elegant edgings, simple warp-faced and warp-float techniques would suffice, both of which are also well attested. The Mycenaeans, on the other hand, seem to have preferred rather plain cloth with much simpler edgings for daily wear—at least, once they went beyond their pretensions to Cretan fashions.

THE EGYPTIAN EVIDENCE

We now turn back to the Egyptian material. In order to provide some sort of understandable framework for the detailed argu-ments to follow, I shall begin with a quick overview of Egyptian-Aegean relations as they appear to us at the moment.

We know from the combined archaeological and literary records[10] that Minoan contact with Egypt, however much earlier it may have begun, flourished off and on from the Middle Kingdom, early in the 2nd millennium, down into the New Kingdom, and most especially during the reign of Queen Hatshepsut (ca. 1504–1482 B.C.), who apparently received official Minoan embassies at court. Although the detailed correlation to Minoan archaeological periods is vehemently disputed, we are safe in saying that this large period corresponds approximately to Middle Minoan plus a little bit of Late Minoan. No indisputably Late Minoan II pottery has been found in Egypt (Kemp and Merrillees 1980, 245), although Late Minoan IB probably has, if it has been reliably distinguished from the Late Helladic IIA sherds (ibid., 226, 232).

Late in the reign of Hatshepsut's stepson and successor, Thutmose III (1482–1450), we see evidence, discussed below, that the Mycenaeans had either joined or replaced the Minoans in a major expedition to the Egyptian court at Thebes. The pottery problems just mentioned imply that this ought to correspond to Late Helladic II and/or Late Minoan IB. For from then on, Minoans and Minoan artifacts effectively disappear from the Egyptian scene.

After a short hiatus of maybe thirty years, during which time no one at the Egyptian court, at least, seems to have laid eyes on Aegean people of either sort, trade with the Mycenaeans flourishes again, reaching its peak during the reigns of Amenhotep III (1417–1379) and his son Akhenaton (1379–1362). The Aegean influence at both of their courts is considerable, and the imported pottery excavated at their sites is chiefly Late Helladic IIIA (at Amarna, 98 percent late IIIA2: Hankey and Warren 1974, 147).

During the next two dynasties, the Aegean trade clearly continues, for we have Late Helladic IIIB pottery throughout the long and stable reign of Rameses II (1304–1238). But Aegean influence at court was minimal, no embassies are recorded, and the last we hear of Aegean people is in the rather one-sided accounts of the battle of Rameses III, in his Year 8 (ca. 1190 B.C.), against the infamous Sea Peoples, who seem to have included some folk of Mycenaean culture among them. Then we learn nothing more.

Surviving Egyptian representations of official Aegean emissaries occur entirely within the reigns of Hatshepsut and Thutmose III, a short space of 54 years. We will ignore all the other "possibly Aegean" figures—mostly either generic prisoners or representatives of the four corners of the world—that Vercoutter (1956) seems to have demonstrated to be either copies of the emissary paintings or fairly free inventions (in the tombs of Puyemre, Amenemopet [= Imenemipet], Kenamun, Amenemheb, and Ineni [= Anena]). That leaves us with five tombs.

The earliest of these is the tomb of Senmut (Thebes no. 71), officially priest of Amon and

---

[10] The chief studies from which this framework has been compiled are Kemp and Merrillees 1980, which sorts out the Minoan pottery in Egypt; Hankey and Warren 1974, which pulls together the Aegean and Near Eastern imported artifacts relevant to cross-dating; and Vercoutter 1956, which sorts out both the literary and the graphic evidence for Minoans and Mycenaeans in Egypt. The reader is hereby directed to these sources for details. Many aspects of the difficult problems involved in Egyptian-Aegean relations are irrelevant to an analysis of the textile trade, such as, for example, the year-dates. I have used some current "standard" dates,

those of the *Cambridge Ancient History* (1970–), not because I have anything to say on the subject of absolute chronology, but in order to make the framework more graspable to the uninitiated. (For the same reason I ignore the fact that Thutmose III technically ruled with Hatshepsut during the twenty years in which she alone wielded the power, and treat him for rhetorical purposes as having followed her.) On the other hand, I believe that the textile material has some independent information to add on the subject of cross-dating in the Late Bronze Age, as will appear below.

chief steward under Queen Hatshepsut. In modern parlance he was the queen's finance minister and the chief architect of her public works (her temple at Deir el-Bahari being one of the most felicitous pieces of architecture in all of ancient Egypt), as well as the person who, more than anyone else, it seems, helped Hatshepsut manage her power and keep her hold on the throne. As such, Senmut was a prime victim of the unpleasant attentions of Thutmose III, who defaced every trace he could find of his hated stepmother and her flunkies as soon as he finally regained his throne in 1482. Senmut had died in Year 19 of Hatshepsut's reign, about 1485 B.C.

Senmut's tomb contained two things of interest to us. One is a painting of an embassy of Aegean people who wear Minoan-style loincloths, codpieces, cinchbelts, and hairdos, and who are bringing typically Aegean-looking vessels as gifts, presumably to Hatshepsut (Fig. 15.16). Unfortunately, Thutmose's destruction crew and other more recent accidents of fate have destroyed most of the precious scene: parts of three Aegean ambassadors remain today, and parts of two more were recorded in the last century (by Hay: H. R. Hall 1909–10, pl. 14). In two or three cases the loincloth was plain (one of

them bright red) with a fancy edging. In another case the belt and/or loincloth has bands of sawtooth alternating with bands of dots or bars, all done in red, white, and blue. As Hatshepsut's favorite, Senmut was presumably present at the reception of the Aegean embassy, and he seems to have counted it among the more memorable sights of his life at court.

The other article for our attention is the handsomely adorned cloth found tied upside down on the back of a mummified horse (Fig. 5.9). The band that decorates it has the honor of being the earliest pattern-woven cloth known from Egypt after the all-white towel looped in a zigzag design and the scrap with little blue stripes at the edge, both from the 11th Dynasty, centuries earlier (see Chapter 5). The geometric pattern here is quite complicated, worked out in red, brown, and yellow with a warp-float technique.

Chronologically, the next tomb to show Aegean emissaries is that of Antef (Thebes no. 155), who was Chief Herald under Hatshepsut, and who was politically adroit or innocuous enough to keep that post into the early reign of Thutmose III. Unfortunately, this register of the scene is mostly gone (although the register of Syrian ambassadors

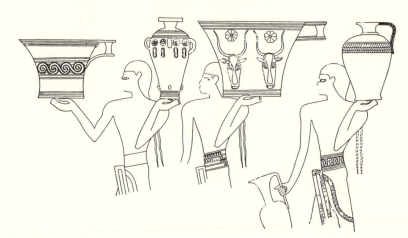

15.16   Minoan ambassadors to the Egyptian court at Thebes, from the tomb of Senmut (Th 71), early 15th century B.C. Note codpieces, long hair, and yo-yo and barred-band patterns. (Davies 1926, fig. 2; courtesy of the Metropolitan Museum of Art)

just below is well preserved), so we see only the remains of one prostrate emissary wearing a Minoan-style loincloth, and behind him the distinctive sandals of a second Minoan (Säve-Söderbergh 1957, pl. 13). As Chief Herald, Antef, too, apparently assisted at the reception of these embassies. It would be wonderful to know if the Aegean presentation was the selfsame event as that shown by Senmut, but that is beyond us. In Antef's tomb, too, there is a second thing to catch our interest: the painted ceiling (see Color Plate 3). That will be described presently.

Third comes the tomb of Useramon (or Amenuser; Thebes no. 131), who was vizier—in effect, prime minister—during the early years of Thutmose III. His tomb was finished shortly before Year 28 (that is, 1476 B.C., since Thutmose counted his regnal years from the date when he was officially designated pharaoh as a very young child, with Hatshepsut as his regent). This scene is far better preserved, and we can count a total of 16 fully or partly visible Aegean visitors. Like those in Senmut's tomb, they wear Minoan loincloths (Fig. 15.17) with prominent codpieces and carry Minoan-style vessels. The fabrics are shown either as plain or with small, busy designs on them that can no longer be made out with any accuracy. As in Antef's tomb, the men wear elaborate sandals with brightly colored socks or booties inside. They also sport brightly colored, prominent belts, but not so obviously cinched in as those in Senmut's tomb. Either the wasp waists of the Minoan men did not impress this artist so much, or he felt more bound by the Egyptian canon of proportions for the "proper" human figure. Once again, the clothing is shown as exclusively red, white, and blue.

Fourth comes the celebrated tomb of Rekhmire (Thebes no. 100), nephew of Useramon and next holder of the office of Vizier. Rekhmire kept that office through the

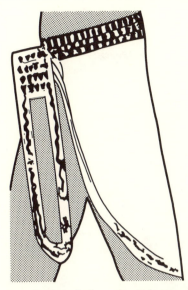

15.17   Loincloth on the 12th porter, tomb of Useramon (Th 131); early 15th century B.C. Textile pattern is red on white. (After Vercoutter 1956, pl. 16.137)

rest of Thutmose's long and energetic reign, and briefly into that of the following pharaoh, Amenhotep II (1450–1425). Like most officials, he began his tomb almost immediately upon becoming important, so as to be as ready as possible for the next world at all times. Among the scenes he ordered painted was one of the reception of the foreign embassies, 16 Aegeans among them clad in Minoan-style loincloths and codpieces (Fig. 15.18). A number of years later, however—and we wish we knew how many—the vizier went to the trouble of having this group of figures, and only this group, partially repainted. What was altered was the style of clothing: each and every loincloth was erased and a pointed kilt painted over it. Fortunately for us, the expungers did not do a very complete job and we can make out some of the original paint. The old cloth patterns again seem to have been mostly small, all-over designs, whereas the new ones are invariably in strips or zones, some vertical,

15.18 Kilts of two Aegean ambassadors to the Egyptian court at Thebes: leader on right, fourth emissary on left. Tomb of Rekhmire (Th 100); early 15th century B.C. Note traces of the original loincloth and codpiece (cf. Figs. 15.16–17), repainted with kilts. (Vercoutter 1956, pl. 21.162 and 19.156)

some horizontal. Again the predominant colors are red, white, and blue, with only two exceptions (other than the pair wearing yellow and black-spotted leopard skins, nos. 5 and 14). Man 9 seems to have a mostly yellow kilt, and Man 4 has one small yellow panel among the hodgepodge of designs on his.

This is the first of the tombs to have a linguistic label on the Aegean visitors: they are said to be princes from the Keftiu country—consistently a designation for Crete—and the "Islands in the Midst of the Great Green (Sea)" (Vercoutter 1956, 57, 133–34). It has been cogently argued that the people of the Islands were indeed specifically the Mycenaeans—as one would expect from all considerations other than the term "Islanders"—

but that the Egyptians first encountered northerners of this culture during the initial period of Mycenaean expansion, when such islands as Rhodes and then Cyprus were the jumping-off points for further travel (ibid., 154–56). That most of the crew and even the entrepreneurs should have been the islanders, born and bred to life in a boat, rather than the mainlanders ("tamers of horses"), seems fairly reasonable.

The last of the tombs showing Aegean emissaries is that of Menkheperraseneb (Thebes no. 86). This man, eldest son of Rekhmire, was High Priest of Amon under Thutmose III and Amenhotep II—that is, he administered the treasury where the tribute was stored. As such, he would have seen as much as he wanted of the objects brought by such embassies, but may or may not have been present at the reception itself. At any rate, Vercoutter shows (ibid., 283–84) that most of the twelve Aegean people shown in Menkheperraseneb's tomb (Fig. 15.19) seem to be free copies and rearrangements of parts of the figures in Rekhmire's tomb, to which he would have had access, whereas the objects portrayed are often new and different— including textiles!—but are quite believably Aegean. Clearly, the visit depicted is the same one recorded by Rekhmire in the repainted version.

The following structure emerges. During the reigns of Hatshepsut and Thutmose III, the court at Thebes received at least two official embassies of Minoans, who wore the usual Minoan loincloth with cinchbelt and fancy boots. The Egyptian artists who recorded the scenes were enormously impressed by the prominent "codpieces" that hung down in front;[11] they also perceived the Minoans as wearing exclusively red, white, and blue, and generally depicted the cloth as having a small, curly, all-over pattern and a fancy edging. At some time during Rekh-

15.19   First five Aegean ambassadors to the Theban court, from the tomb of Menkheperraseneb (Th 86); mid-15th century B.C. Note the kilts, and the stylized "bolt of cloth" over the arms of the 1st and 4th porters. (Davies and Davies 1933, pl. 5; courtesy of the Committee of the Egypt Exploration Society)

[11] These appendages have been much discussed: they may indeed represent codpieces, or more simply, as Vercoutter plausibly suggests (1956, 253–56 and fig. 33), the end-flap of the loincloth that has been brought forward between the legs and then caught up under the belt so as to fall down in a showy cascade in the front. That explanation is the only one that satisfactorily accounts for the fancy edging, which is always the same as that on the main body of the cloth. The artists of Senmut's tomb obviously didn't quite understand what they were trying to draw, whereas Useramon's artists understood it much better. This point, incidentally, demonstrates clearly that Useramon was not copying from Senmut, and that another opportunity to scrutinize the Minoans in person had occurred in the meanwhile. For a detailed discussion of the Minoan loincloth, see Sapouna-Sakellaraki 1971.

mire's term of office, however, the Egyptians received another official Aegean embassy at court; but these men were wearing elaborate paneled, pointed, and tasseled kilts, along with the usual belts, booties, and long curly hair. Then there were apparently no more embassies from the Aegean.

The cloth in these kilts was perceived as quite different from that in the earlier loincloths. In several cases it consists of patterned stripes running vertically, in a few cases horizontally, the end stripe down the overlapping edge at the front of the kilt being a little wider, fancier, stiffer, and longer than the other stripes, with a tassel—if any— emerging from the bottom end of this stripe. Such an arrangement accords remarkably well with what we know of making cloth on the warp-weighted loom: the heading band is necessarily different from the body, and stiffer; and it results in a fringe of its own narrow warp at one or both ends, which are corners of the final cloth. The stiffness (and tassel) could also be accounted for by assuming that some of the bands along the front overlap and the bottom edges of the kilts had been sewn onto the kilt afterwards. The other general type of Aegean kilt depicted by Rekhmire's artists is made of panels that virtually had to have been sewn together to form the garment, if we are to believe the artist at all, since on a single kilt some panels run vertically, some horizontally, and each has a wildly different pattern from the others—a real feat to weave all in one piece, but easy to weave separately and sew together. The very first emissary in Rekhmire's group has an additional embellishment: a fringe all

the way around the bottom of his kilt, which suggests that this kilt was woven the other way—from top to bottom rather than side to side. If the fringe truly belongs with that kilt pattern, it means that an elaborated side-selvedge formed the overlap edge, and the figured stripes were woven vertically on the loom rather than horizontally (not my choice of how to do it most efficiently!). In this, however, it corresponds to the way in which a very similar kilt elsewhere must have been woven: the pointed kilt on the King's Gate figure at Boğazköy (Fig. 15.20). Here the figured stripes run horizontally on the kilt, but the fringe runs down the overlap edge. In other words, here too the patterned stripes must have been woven vertically on the loom—or the fringed edge woven separately and sewn on.

Mycenaean men wore either the kilt or the tunic, never the loincloth. The Minoans on Crete seldom wore anything but the loincloth (or a great, stiff robe) until just the time when the Mycenaeans arrived on their island. Is it coincidence that the only other ethnic group to turn up wearing a kilt in the middle of the 2nd millennium is the Hittites, who are the only other Indo-Europeans around at this point besides the Mycenaeans? I think not. I strongly suspect that the kilt came to the Aegean with the Mycenaeans as an Indo-European garment (cf. Barber 1975), and that it travelled to Egypt with Mycenaean or heavily Mycenaeanized emissaries.[12]

Before we leap, however, to the tempting conclusion that the change of dress in Rekhmire's tomb is the same as that recorded in

[12] There is at least one early representation of a kilt, and a tasseled one at that, from within the purely Minoan world: on the sword hilt from Mallia (see Fig. 15.5). Perhaps this surprisingly short-haired acrobat is a foreigner, like the seven youths imported to Knossos from Athens in the Theseus legend. On the other hand, the design on his kilt is a typically Minoan one. Perhaps the Mi-

noans were already picking up the kilt from across the sea.

Note too that a series of textile ideograms in Linear B has been identified as referring to cloth intended for kilts (Duhoux 1974). Some of the variants show a warp fringe, others show a double line (heavy or applied border?) at one or both ends or along one long side. Some

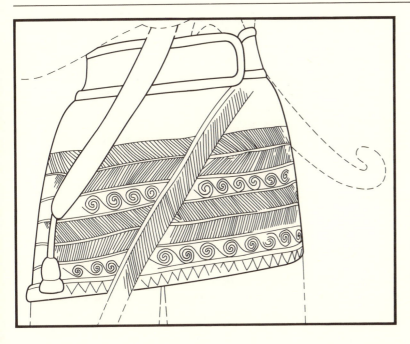

15.20   Kilt worn by a male in martial dress, from a Hittite relief on the King's Gate at Boğazköy, in central Turkey; 3rd quarter of the 2nd millennium B.C. Compare the elongated front corner and figure-striped cloth with the kilts in Figs. 15.18–19. (Museum of Anatolian Civilizations, Ankara)

the Knossos frescoes, and thus is nicely synchronous, we must stop and look carefully: the textile match is not so neat. Why don't either the Minoan or Mycenaean frescoes of kilts show these elaborate stripes and panels? The Egyptian artists may not have had the time to record in explicit detail the pattern on each and every kilt, as the visitors paraded past. But they clearly did have enough time to record a reasonably accurate impression. Their perception that these emissaries wore striped and paneled kilts, entirely different from those of any other race they knew, came from observation. So who was wearing them? Are we to take the fresco's label, Keftiu (Minoans) and Islanders, at face value? Mycenae is not on an island. Later the label of "Islanders" clearly came to refer

to the Mycenaeans in general; but this is one of the earliest uses (Vercoutter 1956, 127–34), and therefore ought to be more literal. Was this the particular costume of Rhodes and perhaps Cyprus, the islands from which Mycenaean maritime expansion into the East Mediterranean pushed off? We shall find reason to return to this question presently.

The question of colors is also puzzling. Egyptian artists normally used red, yellow, blue, green, black, and white freely in their paintings. That they chose never to use green for their portrayal of Aegean clothing matches exactly what we found in the Aegean frescoes of clothing. But the persistent lack of yellow on the textiles until Rekhmire's tomb, where yellow is used even then on only two of the 13 kilts (although freely

also show the "ingot" shape that would produce the long points in front, while others have a median line lengthways, suggesting folding at the waist. (See ibid., 117 for all relevant diagrams.) The ideograms are frequently surcharged with WE, written out once as *we-a₂-no*

(*weanós*: ibid., 119–21), which comes from the basic Indo-European root for clothing (Lat. *vestis*, etc.). It suggests that to the Mycenaeans the kilt was somehow the most basic form of clothing, other types (like the tunic) having other, special names.

used on the two leopard skins, as well as elsewhere in the scenes), does not correspond. Certainly by Late Minoan I, at Thera and on Crete, yellow was in plentiful supply. But it is also clear that the Egyptians *perceived* the earlier contingents of Aegean people as wearing only red, white, and blue; and their observations are otherwise sufficiently accurate—especially for overall characteristics like this—that I have to believe that for some reason they saw only red, white, and blue cloth. This reduced color scheme will turn up again to haunt us.[13]

THUS armed, we can now turn our attention back to the Egyptian ceiling designs, which, as we have mentioned, sometimes include motifs that look both very Aegean and very "textile" in nature.

The motif most often cited under this heading is the spiral, characteristic of the Aegean since the Early Bronze Age at least. The chronological list of occurrences of spirals on tomb ceilings, given in Table 15.1, begins with a few of the Middle Kingdom, then jumps to the 18th Dynasty, ending with a few in the 19th, 20th, and 21st.[14] All these have spirals—but no two ceilings are exactly the same, and a few are wildly different from

any others. Another motif that is cited as Aegean-looking is the design of a bull's head with a rosette between its horns, much as we see it in three dimensions in the famous bull's head *rhyton* from Mycenae. As it happens, the Egyptians for some reason always chose to combine these rosetted bulls' heads with spiral motifs, wherever we have them; so listing the tombs with spiral ceiling-patterns nets the bulls too—in the tombs of Neferhotep, Inherkha, and Imiseba.

Spirals occur so freely on Aegean pottery, which we know was imported, that one might at first wonder if textiles need to be dragged into the explanation. And bulls' heads were sometimes used as an artistic motif in both Syria and Egypt quite independently of the Aegean, it seems. So neither of these designs will clinch our textile case immediately.

But the third motif cited occurs only once in all Egypt: a quatrefoil interlock almost identical in form to that on the skirt of the Hagia Triada dancer. It differs only in its colors (using the usual Egyptian six-color scheme instead of being limited to red, white, and blue) and in the inclusion of a skinny quatrefoil inside every, rather than every other, large quatrefoil. We have seen

---

[13] I have been quite puzzled by this discrepancy. Two fairly simple possibilities are (1) that the Minoan yellow dyes were too fugitive to withstand the voyage, and (2) that the Minoans hadn't yet begun to use yellow dye at the time of the earliest embassies. But I feel quite unsatisfied by either.

There is a third possibility, which I had suppressed in my head until I read the recent cogent analyses (from new data) of the Theran fresco of the Saffron Gatherers as being a depiction of a specifically female ritual, probably connected with puberty (N. Marinatos 1984, 62–72; Immerwahr 1989, ch. 4). Saffron is above all else a potent and beautiful yellow dye, and here it is connected specifically with women (it is also a medicine for menstrual ills). Did the original Minoan culture—before it became diluted with Mycenaeans—reserve yellow cloth specifically for a particular class of women and their associates? Is that why the Egyptians didn't see Aegean men wearing yellow textiles until the very end? The re-

striction of the later Homeric and Classical epithets and descriptions involving yellow clothing to women, especially young women like Iphigenia, Athena, and the Muses, would also seem to go back into this Bronze Age stratum. And the Knossos Cupbearer, with his bright yellow kilt, may have been serving the goddess of such affairs, or he may, as a wearer of the northern kilt, have belonged to another culture that didn't care yet about this tradition but enjoyed the locally made, sumptuous cloth.

[14] Table 15.1 is only as comprehensive as I could make it from the literature available to me. There may well be more examples. "Th" refers to Thebes, as numbered by Gardiner and Weigall 1913 (q.v. for titles and dates), and, for Th 359, by Bruyère 1933. For a list of the sources I used for each of these tombs, as well as for all the other tombs cited in this chapter as having probable Aegean connections, see Appendix D.

TABLE 15.1
Egyptian Tombs with Spiral Decor

Tomb	Owner's Name and Chief Title	Period
Assiut	Hepzefa (Hapdjefai), nomarch (see Fig. 15.23)	12th Dynasty
Qau 18	Wahka II (B)	12th Dynasty
Th 21	User, royal scribe and steward	Thutmose I–II
Th 81	Ineni (Anena), overseer of granary	Amenhotep I–Thutmose III
Th 67	Hapuseneb, high priest of Amon (see Fig. 15.21)	Hatshepsut
Th 39	Puyemre, priest of Amon	Hatshepsut–Thutmose III
Th 155	Antef, great herald (see Color Plate 3)	Hatshepsut–Thutmose III
Th 82	Amenemhet, scribe to Useramon, overseer of weavers of Amon (see Color Plate 3)	Thutmose III
Th 87	Minnakht, overseer of granaries	Thutmose III
Th 251	Amenmose, royal scribe	Thutmose III
Th 262	[name lost], overseer of fields	Thutmose III?
Th 17	Nebamun, royal scribe and physician	Amenhotep II?
Th 78	Haremhab, royal scribe	Thutmose IV–Amenhotep III
Th 90	Nebamun, standard-bearer, captain of police	Thutmose IV–Amenhotep III
Th 226	[name lost], royal scribe	Amenhotep III
Th 40	Huy, vizier	Tutankhamon
Th 181	Nebamun and Ipuky, sculptors	late 18th Dynasty
Amarna 49	Ay, first vizier, then pharaoh	Akhenaton–Ay
Th 50	Neferhotep, "divine father"	Ay–Haremhab
Th 19	Amenmose, priest	Rameses I–Seti I
Th 51	Userhet, mortuary priest	Seti I
Th 16	Panehesy, priest	Rameses II
Th 45	Dhutemhab, overseer of weavers of Amon (tomb usurped from Dhout: time of Amenhotep II)	Rameses II
Th 359	Inherkha (Anherkhawi, Khai-inheret), chief of public works	Rameses III
Th 65	Imiseba, chief of temple-scribes	Rameses IX–X
Th 68	Nesipanoferher, priest of Amon	Herihor

that these interlock patterns show a long and natural development in Crete in the Middle Minoan period, where they are entirely at home with other aspects of the local decorative arts, whereas in Egypt this design is isolated. It occurs on the soffit or "ceiling" of a doorway in the tomb of one Amenemhet, a high functionary during the early reign of Thutmose III, the tomb having been completed about Year 28, i.e., ca. 1476 B.C. (Nina Davies and A. Gardiner 1915, 1; see Color Plate 3). Pottery correlations indicate that the early reign of Thutmose III should fall at about the end of Late Minoan IB (Hankey and Warren 1974, 146), that is, about the time the Hagia Triada fresco was being destroyed, not painted initially. So every consideration brings us to the conclusion that the Egyptian artist borrowed the pattern from the Aegean world, and almost certainly from the world of textiles, since the design occurs in Crete mostly in frescoes of textiles.

The plot thickens when we investigate Amenemhet's background. According to the inscriptions in his tomb, he was scribe and chief steward to Useramon, that same powerful vizier who officiated at the reception of an embassy of Minoans to the court of Thutmose III; moreover, he had also inherited the important and honorable post of "head of the weavers of Amon" (Davies and Gardiner 1915, 8). As Useramon's scribe, Amenemhet was thus in a prime position to see and record whatever Useramon was doing, including entertaining Minoans; and as head of the weaving shops that made luxury cloth for the highest priests of the realm, he certainly had technical knowledge and interest in textiles—probably far beyond any other high official in the land. If anyone had both interest in and access to fancy imported textiles, it should be Amenemhet. Maybe it is not so surprising, then, to find such an exact replica of a typical Minoan textile pattern, and one

of the loveliest they ever invented, reproduced in his tomb. Nor is it the only typically Aegean design there: another of his eight ceiling patterns is a handsome diagonally running spiral, not quite like any other found in the tombs, and hence not likely to have been copied from them. Are we to imagine Useramon rewarding his faithful helper with the particularly suitable gift of a couple of magnificent and curiously wrought textiles, perhaps out of the largesse that we see the pharaoh showering onto his vizier?

HAVING established to near certainty that at least one Minoan textile found its way to Egypt and was copied onto a ceiling, we now must go back and take the other ceiling designs more seriously. For, as Smith's Law says, "What did happen, can happen." Let us begin by investigating the nature of Egyptian treatment of ceilings in general.

From the time that tomb ceilings begin regularly to receive decoration at all, in the 12th Dynasty, until the late 19th or early 20th Dynasty (when scenes of importance to the funeral rites finally creep up to that heretofore unimportant surface), the ceiling designs fall into four categories. They show sky, with or without stars (e.g., Th 362: Davies 1933, 9; cf. Frankfort 1929, 59; or the great star chart in Senmut's unfinished tomb under the temple of Deir el-Bahari: Hayes 1959, 112); or birds in flight, as if startled up from a swamp thicket (e.g., Th 50, tomb of Neferhotep: Davies 1933, pl. 56; or Th 31, that of Khons, with crickets and ducklings all in a flap: Davies 1948, pl. 19); or a grape arbor, viewed as if from directly underneath, with the leaves and clusters of grapes hanging down among the grid of wooden staves (e.g., Th 359, tomb of Inherkha: Bruyère 1933, pl. 5; or Th 16 Panehesy); or a repetitive polychrome design framed by architectural strips painted yellow to imitate wood.

It is the origin of this last group that interests us. But note, meanwhile, that all of the other categories of ceiling designs represent things that one normally sees overhead.

The earliest and most common repetitive designs throughout the entire period are checkers, zigzags, and lozenges: the normal Egyptian mat patterns. One sees handsome representations of these mats elsewhere in the tombs, where their function as mats is clear: for example, forming the shade-giving wall of a pavilion behind Urarna, a nobleman of the 5th Dynasty (Davies 1901, pl. 15), or covering the magnificent wall and awnings around a sacred door painted on a 12th Dynasty wooden coffin (Terrace 1968, pl. 2–3). Most of these same designs occur already as painted wall decoration in a 1st Dynasty tomb at Saqqara (no. 3121: W. B. Emery 1949, pl. 50), where they presumably also represent mats. That is, the making of elaborately patterned, polychrome mats was a native Egyptian art going back to the earliest dynasties and probably much earlier.

Why mat patterns on the ceiling, then? One reason is that mats were often laid on poles across the rafters in the houses, in order to prevent the mud of the roof from crumbling down onto the occupants (W. S. Smith 1958, 171 and fig. 60). In these cases, when one looked up one would indeed see mats. Fancy mats are painted in just this position on the expensive plaster ceilings of some of the rooms of Amenhotep III's palace at Malkata, in imitation of the cheaper roofing. Since the tombs were fashioned of stone or brick, the tomb architects, too, took up this strategy of painting the decoration on.

Another common source of mats overhead was the outdoor pavilion erected to provide shade from the hot tropical sun. We see such pavilions, with checkered mat coverings over a flat or gently sloping grid-like framework of yellow wooden beams, both on land and on boats—for example, in the 12th Dynasty tomb of Antefoker (Th 60: Davies 1920, pl. 20, 30). The constructional details of these pavilions can be seen especially clearly on a 12th Dynasty model boat now in the British Museum (no. 9525: Glanville 1972, 15 and fig. 14).

In 1929, Ludwig Borchardt pointed out evidence of another type of pavilion, following some excavation at Luxor. He noticed, high up along a wall that belonged simultaneously to the Medinet Habu temple and to the palace of Rameses III, a series of beam holes in arcs of 3, 5, or 7 (L. Borchardt 1929, 111 and fig. 1). If one placed into them the ends of rafters that were suitably supported at the other end, and threw some sort of floppy covering over each group, one would produce a series of barrel-vaulted tents or pavilions of varying sizes, the largest in the middle. Borchardt went on to show that this arrangement answers very closely to a ceiling, for example, in the small Ramesside tomb of Irinefer, a barrel vault with rafters indicated as running both lengthwise at the apex and crosswise in the middle, with a pillar to support both at the crossing (ibid., 111 and fig. 2). In the tombs, all of this is sculpted in mud, plaster, or stone, of course, and then painted yellow to imitate wood with blue-painted hieroglyphs carved into it. The empty panels between are painted with repetitive polychrome patterns, many of which are the old, traditional mat patterns that we have been discussing, but some of which are not. (We shall discuss those in a moment.) It seems entirely reasonable that, in real life, large and elegantly woven mats should have been used to cover such pavilions, so arranged that the guests would be able to view and enjoy the bright decorations; but one could also imagine other coverings being used—rugs, for example, or even leather. (Leather would have the disadvantage of not letting any air through; yet we possess the fragmentary remains of a colorful leather canopy that belonged to the 21st Dynasty princess Isimkheb: Brugsch 1889.)

One of the most dazzling arrays of decorated ceiling panels in a barrel-vaulted tomb occurs in that of Inherkha (or Anherkhawi, or Khai-inheret, depending on how one reads his name), no. 359 at Deir el-Medineh (Bruyère 1933, 32–35 and pl. 3–5). Here we find the ceiling divided into 8 compartments: 4 on either side of a central yellow rafter, with 3 yellow cross-rafters making the remaining divisions. Within its frame of yellow rafters, each panel has a border that looks like a fringe, or perhaps a set of lashings, on all four sides (compare the fringe hanging down from the top of the lower canopy on the funeral barque of Neferhotep: Davies 1933, pl. 22). Within that border the panels contain (as one moves down one side of the room and back up the other):

(1) concentric rectangles of rosettes (there is only one other similar ceiling, in Th 68 Nesipanoferher [L. Borchardt 1929, fig. 9, and Jéquier 1911, pl. 32]; but compare the ceiling of the side chamber of the *tholos* tomb at Orchomenos in Greece: Marinatos and Hirmer 1960, pl. 161; Stubbings 1973, fig. 38);

(2) an S- and C-spiral rapport enclosing rosetted bulls' heads (for the bull plus spiral motif, see also five other ceilings discussed below);

(3) a bead network (or 4-petal rapport) with rosettes in the interstices (an increasingly common pattern in the 18th Dynasty, first found without rosettes in the Middle Kingdom, e.g., at el-Bersheh: Newberry n.d., 11 fig. 1);

(4) alternating wide and narrow stripes, the wide stripes filled alternately with rosettes or running spirals (compare several similar but not identical panels in Th 68 Nesipanoferher: Jéquier 1911, pl. 34, 35, 37);

(5) a stylized grape-arbor pattern;

(6) a diagonally running spiral rapport, with glyphs in the interstices;

(7) a bead network with rosettes, virtually identical to no. 3;

(8) a C-spiral rapport (Kantor [1947, pl. 4–5] gives numerous Aegean examples in various media, and Egyptian examples, all on scarabs, except one that is apparently a ceiling design and published by Champollion without provenance).

All of these designs give the immediate impression of rugs; and with the exception of the grape arbor, all are more easily explained as textile, leatherwork, or perhaps beadwork patterns than anything else. But those, too, are reasonable things to hang overhead on a pavilion for decoration as well as for shade.

Having demonstrated that every category of design shown on Egyptian tomb ceilings until very late is derived from things that Egyptians could see overhead, and that the repetitive designs among them derive from mats, cloth, and whatever else one might cover an outdoor pavilion with, we are in an even stronger position than before in maintaining that Amenemhet, the scribe of Useramon and overseer of the temple weavers, was copying a textile when he put a distinctively Minoan textile pattern on his ceiling.

This entire line of argument suggests, in fact, that all the spiral and other such designs that are not easily ascribed to matting should have their origin in textiles and similar arts (that is, arts that produce large, floppy coverings). Yet our textile studies have given us every reason to believe that the ancient Egyptians never wove such things—at least not until the late 18th Dynasty at the very earliest, since we see their exploratory first attempts under Amenhotep II and Thutmose IV (see Chapter 5). It would be very easy at this point, then, to jump to the conclusion that all spiral ceilings before the late 18th Dynasty were therefore copies of specifically Aegean textiles. But the case isn't so simple.

When Helene Kantor drew together the material known in 1947 for Aegean-Egyptian relations, she pointed out five occurrences in Egypt of a very distinctive type of pattern, in

15.21 Ceiling pattern from the tomb of
Hapuseneb (Th 67), composed of spirals ending in
a vertical "bud"; early 15th century B.C. (After
Jéquier 1911, pl. 28.43; and Kantor 1947, pl. 11B)

which the curl of a spiral ends in a vertical
bud or palmette (as in Fig. 15.21). The motif
is perfectly at home in the Aegean, but again
isolated as a tiny group in Egypt. Three of
the Egyptian examples are from tomb ceilings: Th 67 Hapuseneb (Hatshepsut's reign),
Th 251 Amenmose (Thutmose III's reign),
and a fragment from Th 262 (Thutmose III's
reign).[15] A fourth example is on the cabin of

Queen Hatshepsut's boat, as painted on the
wall of her temple at Deir el-Bahari; and the
fifth is tooled on the leather of the chariot
found in the tomb of Maherpra, a high official under Amenhotep II (see Daressy 1902,
pl. 22 no. 24147).

Here, then, we have proof positive that
some of the Aegean-type designs had to do
with leather—another commodity that survives not at all in the Aegean. As a weaver,
such evidence relieves my mind; for although I could readily see weaving the version of the pattern with a simple bud in the
center, as shown by Hatshepsut and her
priest Hapuseneb, I would hate to have to
weave (or repeatedly embroider) the detailed palmettes of the fancier version. The
design is not impossible to produce on a
loom, it just isn't the sort of pattern that
evolves naturally and easily in that medium,
at least not without a drawloom. Were the
Minoans and/or Mycenaeans also exporting
tooled leather?[16]

Once we entertain the notion of leather, it
behooves us to notice such objects of appli-
quéed leather as the canopy of Princess Isimkheb, and the horsecloth shown among
the New Year's gifts in the tomb of Kenamun
(Th 93), chief steward of Amenhotep II (Da-

[15] Norman Davies (1922a, 51) says he found the pieces
of this last fragment on the floor of "a certain tomb,"
along with a number of other handsome but heteroge-
neous fragments; and "found, after industrious inquiry
among the older guards, that they did not come from
this tomb at all, or one of its period, but had been laid
there temporarily by an inspector and forgotten on his
removal from the district." In a footnote he adds: "I have
since found that this shell-like design (from Tomb 162)
occurs again in the contemporary tomb, No. 251, and
also in an archaizing tomb, No. 160." (Tomb 160 is
Saite, so I have not considered it in this chapter.) One
would assume from these statements either that Davies
later determined that the fragments with the shell or
spiral pattern derived originally from the nameless tomb
Th 162, or that Th 162 was the tomb on whose floor he
found the fragments originally.

But apparently Davies got his own notes a bit mixed,
as well, as I learned upon pursuing the attribution. Ac-

cording to information kindly supplied me by Marsha
Hill of the Metropolitan Museum of Art (pers. comm.
1986), "following recent work on the Davies' tracings
and notebooks housed in the Griffiths Institute, it seems
that the pattern fragment was found by Davies stored in
tomb 16 and considered by him as probably from tomb
262 (he himself had confused the numbers of tombs 162
and 262)." I will therefore refer to it as from Th 262,
which Engelbach (1924, 18) and Porter and Moss
(1960–, 344) attribute to the reign of Thutmose III.

[16] Spirals and rosettes also occur all over the chariot
of Yuaa and Thuiu, the parents of Queen Tiy (see Quibell 1908, 65–67 and pl. 51–54: no. 51188). The walls of
this chariot are made mostly of molded and gilded plaster; the chariot also shows no signs of wear and therefore
was presumably only a funeral gift (ibid., 65–67). A well-
used little chair from the same tomb also has a spiral
pattern on the edges (no. 51112: ibid., 52–53 and pl.
36). Both objects may have had leather prototypes.

vies 1930, pl. 22). The overall pattern of rosettes and stars on the latter, if not identical to anything on the ceilings, nonetheless suggests another possible source of at least a few of these designs. And there is nothing to indicate that the Egyptians did not make the leather horsecloth themselves. In short, we may have to reckon with ceiling patterns from leather covers for canopies and pavilions, in addition to those from mats and textiles. And they too may be either imported or native.

We must also reckon with Hatshepsut's boat. It is only the first of a considerable series of boat cabins with spiral designs on the sides. The chief group that I have encountered includes: two model boats from the tomb of Amenhotep II (nos. 5089, 5091: Daressy 1902, 258–60 and pl. 51), and wall paintings in the tombs of Kenamun (Th 93: Davies 1930, pl. 42), Nebamun and Ipukhy (Th 181: Nina Davies 1936, pl. 63), and Neferhotep (Th 50: Davies 1933, pl. 22 and—different boat—pl. 43). All of these show close variants of a design that is slightly different from Hatshepsut's: a simple spiral rapport with a rosette in the enclosed quadrilateral, and a polychrome barred edging around the whole. (In general, the spiral is yellow, its center green, the diagonal rows of quadrilateral spaces alternately red and blue with contrasting rosettes.) Apparently the pattern became a favorite, for we then find versions of it on the tomb ceilings of Huy, vizier to Tutankhamon (Th 40), of Userhet (Th 51; Rameses I), and of Dhutemhab (Th 45; late Rameses II); and on the ceiling of a chapel of

Rameses II at Deir el-Medineh (Bruyère 1948, 123 fig. 67).[17]

Since it was readily visible to the public eye on boats and chapels, we are not forced to postulate continual imports of such a pattern. But we may still wonder how the design got onto the boats of Hatshepsut and Amenhotep II in the first place. Are we supposed to be reminded of the colorful deckshelters, or *ikria* (Fig. 15.22), apparently of

15.22　Fragments of fresco depicting windshelters (*ikria*) covered with patterned cloth, for the deck of a boat. Mycenae; mid- to late 2nd millennium B.C. (Late Helladic III). (Shaw 1980, fig. 4; courtesy of *American Journal of Archaeology*)

---

[17] The pattern also has a forerunner in the design that occurs first in the tomb of User, a royal scribe and steward under Thutmose I and II (Th 21), then again in the tomb of Nebamun, a high functionary who served principally under Thutmose IV (Th 90). In both cases, the curved quadrilateral space between the spirals has been broken up into four triangular corner pieces surrounding the central rosette. A version in which the spiral rapport has disintegrated into disconnected spirals in a square grid occurs in the tomb of Puyemre, a priest of Amon under Thutmose III (Th 39). In all three tombs, the triangles filling in the quadrilaterals show the same alternation of color in diagonal rows between red and green that we see later between red and blue; the spirals are yellow, and their centers are green. Such idiosyncratic similarities are not due to chance.

textiles, leather, and perhaps felt, that we see depicted on boats as well as separately at Thera and Mycenae (Shaw 1980; 1982)? Did the Aegean sailors give the Egyptians a new idea for a particularly handsome and elegant form of cabin, originally of furlable textiles, but perhaps eventually shifted to painted wood? Is this a part of what we are to understand by the expression "Keftiu boats" in the Egyptian shipyard lists (Vercoutter 1956, 54)?

WHATEVER the precise answers to these questions, we are finding that the probability of importations of perishable manufactured goods from the Aegean is multiplying in all directions: not just textiles, now, but leather and maybe even boat parts. But we are also refining our understanding to the point where we can distinguish the reflections of textiles among them with some confidence. It is time, then, to go back and pick out the most obvious and interesting Aegean textiles among the ceilings and see what we can add to our knowledge of the craft.

There is an important change, however, in the kind of representation we find around the reign of Amenhotep III, which will also affect our interpretations. The earlier pieces seem to stand out from each other as few in number and quite distinct in character; but later the designs begin to smear together, as though either a lot of rough copying were going on, or else a great many imports of approximately but not exactly the same design were flooding the market. Strictly within the evidence of the paintings, I find it hard to make a choice; but the great increase in imported Aegean pottery during the reigns of Amenhotep III and Akhenaton suggests that increased trade—of textiles along with the pottery—is at least partly responsible.

The later group, then, in its homogeneity, is probably telling us what the average bolt of imported Aegean cloth looked like during that period. (Again we seem to be getting hints of the Mycenaean tendency towards a simplified and uniform "mass" production.) The earlier group, however, is probably telling us what the cream of the crop looked like: the pieces selected by the emissaries as most likely to win Pharaoh's favor, or selected by the early merchants as most likely to win customers abroad. Some of the earlier ceilings, in fact, are so idiosyncratic that it is almost impossible to believe that the artists were not sitting there copying the master's favorite pavilions. In one very early case, the tomb of Hepzefa at Assiut (Fig. 15.23), the artist has crammed in six patterns in a way that makes hash of the architecture, as if he had to fit them all in at any cost. But viewed on its own, the ceiling looks like six odd-sized rectangles of cloth stitched together to make a large piece. One senses the same pride and pleasure in personal ownership that is evident in the pets sometimes pictured under the master's and mistress's chairs—here a pet monkey, there a pet goose. The pets were clearly a real and treasured part of daily life; handsome canopy tops, a conspicuous symbol of status, luxury, and taste, may have been just as real and just as carefully copied for the next world.

We have one other curious bit of evidence for the cloth- and mat-covered pavilion, in a set of wooden linen-chests from the 18th Dynasty tomb of Kha that are painted with all-over designs remarkably similar to those on some of the ceilings (Schiaparelli 1927, figs. 109–12). Each of these four oblong boxes has a lid like a low-pitched, gabled roof (with different designs on each of the faces), making it look like a small house or pavilion. On three of the boxes, the back side is painted with a simple checker pattern, the short sides with either that pattern or other all-over designs, and the front with a scene of

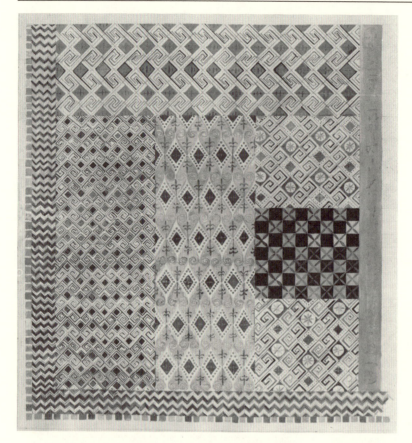

15.23 Part of the painted ceiling in the 12th Dynasty tomb of Hepzefa, at Assiut; early 2nd millennium B.C. Note the "wrought-iron fence" motif of interlocked hearts in the center panel. (Photo of an early drawing by Baroness von Bissing; courtesy of Hans-Wolfgang Müller)

the lord and lady dining with the aid of a servant. The illusion is quite strong that the people are sitting inside the box/pavilion. The fourth chest has textile-type patterns on all four sides. Using patterns from textiles for the outside of a linen-chest seems peculiarly appropriate.

The earliest ceilings to show Aegean-type designs are actually from the height of the Middle Kingdom, including that from the tomb of the nomarch Hepzefa (see Shaw 1970)—from an era of trade rather than of official embassies. The spirals occur in a heart shape that is mirrored again at the apex to form what I nickname the "wrought-iron fence" motif. This motif is then offset, and interlocked at the spirals (how Minoan a

trick!) to spring another row of fencework, and so forth. The space within the heart is occupied by a palmette, while the space between groups contains a solid diamond framed with dots. Two other ceiling designs in the tomb are composed of squared spirals, or meanders. Maria Shaw has cleverly shown that one of these is the squared counterpart of the spiral heart, hence closely related (ibid., 29 and pl. 6.18–19), while the other contains as an element the dot-surrounded diamond. Since meanders were as uncommon as spirals in Egypt, one must suspect them also of being imports (see Kantor 1947, pl. 6 for other examples), whether piggyback on cloth or on mats.

Mats? Did the Minoans also make fancy

mats? Or had they simply acquired a technique of weaving other than weft-float, perhaps one like double-cloth that would make "squaring the circle" a natural transformation of the design?

The "wrought-iron fence" motif turns up again, diamonds, palmettes, and all: on a doorway in the tomb of Ukhhotep at Meir (12th Dynasty, under Amenemhet II); on the ceiling of the tomb of Antef (see Color Plate 3), the Great Herald of Hatshepsut who depicted Aegean emissaries on his walls (see above); and on the kilt of the third Aegean visitor in the tomb of Menkheperraseneb, who served under Thutmose III and Amenhotep II (see Fig. 15.19). A very similar motif (with rosettes instead of diamonds, and no palmettes) was painted on the ceiling of a barrel-vaulted room among a group of private houses at Thebes—perhaps a small chapel—from the time of Thutmose IV (Anthes 1943, 15–16 and pl. 6e). The latest example that I know of is an unfinished version on the ceiling of the tomb of Amenmose (Th 19), a priest who must have died during the reign of Seti I, early in the 19th Dynasty. Here the diamonds have been made over into the sort of concentric lozenges typical of Egyptian tomb ceilings, and the palmettes have disintegrated into equally typically

Egyptian dotted quatrefoils, such as decorate the next ceiling panel in the same tomb.

The simplest hypothesis is that one or more textiles with this design came into Egypt in the 12th Dynasty, presumably from Crete (Middle Minoan I/II?), where spirals, rapports, and interlocks are at home;[18] and that a second importation occurred from the same general source at the time of Antef (Late Minoan IB?).[19] Menkheperraseneb's depiction presumably represents yet a third sighting of this motif (Late Minoan IIIA?), this time on a stranger's clothing. The chapel from the time of Thutmose IV must show yet another importation, co-occurring, as we shall see, with the earliest known representation of the bull-and-spiral motif; whereas the 19th Dynasty example would seem to be an Egyptianized rendering of one of the earlier examples.

There is something else of note in Menkheperraseneb's tomb, on the ceiling (Color Plate 3). There are no spirals here; in fact, the design might be passed over very easily as being the familiar old mat pattern of lozenges and zigzags, except for three things. First, the design is the only ceiling pattern I know of in Egypt that is exclusively red, white, and blue—exactly like the Keftiu kilts. Second, the bands forming the zigzags

[18] Arthur Evans (1928, 745 figs. 480–81) shows several scarabs, from the 12th Dynasty on, with spirals in mirrored heart-shapes; but no other details correspond. He also shows a similar motif labelled "on kilt of man of Keftiu, Rekhmara Tomb"—but there is nothing like it in Rekhmire's tomb today. It is evidently the Menkheperraseneb kilt pattern turned upside-down.

Evans, in fact, would see the "wrought-iron fence" motif as Egyptian, whereas I see the design as relatively isolated in Egypt and find in the Bronze Age Aegean a whole host of family members, in the form of heart-spirals, if not the exact design itself. Walberg, for instance, shows many such hearts on Middle Minoan pottery, including occasional mirrored hearts (Walberg 1983, pl. 30—note especially 3(i)6, 3(iii)1, 3(iii)7; Walberg 1976, 181 fig. 36—note especially 3.5, 3.6—and 193 fig. 48.i.11); Popham shows it on Late Minoan II pottery (Popham 1970, pl. 7.c; Popham 1984, pl. 166 nos. 56,

58, 59). The heart-shaped spirals are also depicted on textiles: on the skirt of the seventh lady in the Knossos Procession Fresco (Evans 1928, suppl. pl. 25). And for interesting later Aegean evidence of specifically blue point-to-point hearts, see Chapter 16 and Fig. 16.11.

[19] Antef's tomb contains not only this ceiling motif, but also, the reader will recall, one of the depictions of Aegean foreigners, and two more suspiciously Aegean-looking ceiling motifs: a heart-shaped meander, and a unique labyrinth pattern.

A further curious tie among the earlier "wrought-iron" motifs is that the heart-shaped spirals are apparently blue in each case: Ukhhotep, Wahka, Antef, and Hepzefa. (My warm thanks to H. W. Müller for providing me with a color picture of this last.) Menkheperraseneb's is black, and no colors are given for the chapel. In most of the other spiral patterns in Egypt, the spirals are yellow or white.

and lozenges look unusually thin: the proportions are quite different from the usual Egyptian ones. Third, this main design has an edging (unusual at this period, though not unheard of) that is also entirely in red, white, and blue; and the edging is also composed of lozenges, right up until those lozenges unceremoniously turn into zigzags. A most un-Egyptian irregularity!

There is only one other example that I know of in which such a change of design occurs in midstream: the belt band from Lefkandi (see above and Chapter 7), where zigzags become diamonds by way of chevrons. There the shift is undoubtedly the happy result of boredom interacting with the particular weaving technique; but in paint one is not restricted by what the warp will do, nor does the work progress so slowly. So why that particular change? The zigzags on the ceiling edge are also of an unusual type for Egypt: a single line zigzags continuously, with little nests of tents inside each resulting triangle. This is exactly the form we see suddenly filling up Late Minoan IIIA pottery (Popham 1984, pl. 171.4 plus many closely related variants). It also occurs on the kilt of the fifth Aegean porter in Menkheperraseneb's tomb, alternating with a band of chevrons (see Fig. 15.19; Vercoutter 1956, 267 fig. 61, and pl. 22.169), and twice in closely related forms on the fourth kilt in Rekhmire's tomb (see Fig. 15.18 left; and see the sixth in Menkheperraseneb's, which is a rough equivalent thereof). In fact, a comparison of Popham's newly excavated horde of Late Minoan IIIA pottery (Popham 1984) with the kilts in the tombs of Rekhmire and Menkheperraseneb reveals an astonishing number of parallel motifs.

Menkheperraseneb's Aegean visitors are a problem in themselves. Many of them, as Vercoutter has pointed out (1956, 266 etc.), look as though they are merely reversed copies or amalgamations of the porters in his father's tomb. Now, as overseer of the Treasury of Amon, Menkheperraseneb was in a good position to study the objects brought to Thebes by the embassies and left behind to be stored in the temple, even if he was perhaps not invited to the reception itself. But it is also just conceivable that the reason his pictorial record is so similar to that of his father, yet also noticeably different, is that the son was in fact at the reception, that each of the two men recorded the same event independently, and that the different scribes and artists in their respective retinues simply noticed and emphasized different things. The kilt with the "wrought-iron fence" pattern and the red, white, and blue ceiling, both absent from Rekhmire's tomb, would seem to resurrect the younger man's credibility somewhat. Menkheperraseneb's tomb is also the only one to bother to show the Aegean visitors bringing textiles over their arms (along with the celebrated metal vases). His paintings show four such porters.

Leaving the era of the embassies and picking our way with care into the later group of ceilings, we find that the most interesting design is that in which a bull's head with a rosette between its horns occurs among running spirals. The earliest example we have is on the ceiling of that same barrel-vaulted chapel that contained the "wrought-iron fence" motif, from the time of Thutmose IV (Anthes 1943, pl. 6). The next example comes from the ceiling of the robing room of Amenhotep III, in his palace at Malkata, near Thebes (Fig. 15.24; Frankfort 1929, pl. 13; W. S. Smith 1958, 169 and pl. 121A). (This palace has long been a source of discussion on account of its many apparent ties with Aegean art.) And finally we have the ceiling designs from three rather late Theban tombs: Th 50 Neferhotep, Th 359 Inherkha, and Th 65 Imiseba.

15.24   Ceiling fresco from the robing room of the palace of Amenhotep III at Malkata, Thebes, showing a spiral rapport and bulls' heads; early 14th century B.C. (Photograph courtesy of the Metropolitan Museum of Art; Rogers Fund, 1911: no. 11.215.451)

Each design is significantly different—there is no question here of copying directly either from each other or from the same single source. The chapel ceiling has a horizontal row of mournful-looking bulls' heads between vertically running S-spirals, each bull having a disc or rosette filling the space between the incurving horns. Each bull's head occupies the space of two spirals. In Amenhotep's robing room, however, each bull's head (with a rosette filling the space between horns) is set diagonally within the quadrilateral spaces left by a spiral rapport. As with the spiral rapport patterns on the boats, these spaces are contrastively colored: in other words, it is the same pattern we discussed earlier on the boats, only with rosetted bulls' heads in place of plain rosettes.

Neferhotep's design is wildly different. C-, S-, heart-, and eyeglass-spirals are complexly interlocked into a square grid; the rosetted bulls' heads are set square in the large red mushroom-shaped interstitial spaces, and grasshoppers crouch in the slim, blue, diagonal spaces. The bulls, unlike before, have their eyes on the sides of their skulls (rather than on the front); and they have blotchy hide-marks down their noses, but no nostrils are shown. (Another elaborate ceiling design in the same tomb also is based on a rather similar spiral rapport, but with rosettes and hieroglyphs in the interspaces.)

Inherkha's pattern, on the other hand, harks back to the form in the chapel, with rows of bulls' heads set between vertically running S-spirals. But here the spirals are reversed each time (so that they mirror their neighbors), the horns are vestigial supports for great discs above, and a peculiar fan is painted below each nose—whether to represent a great snort of breath or a mythical beard of the sort that bulls wear in Mesopotamian monuments, or just to fill up the space utterly. Imiseba's pattern is different again, with a proportionately rather small bull's head with a small disc between the horns, set in a field framed by interlocked spirals with a banana-like element in the small interspaces.

Where are these coming from? Bulls' heads with rosettes on the forehead occur in Aegean art earlier than anything here (e.g., the silver-and-gold *rhyton* from Shaft Grave IV at Mycenae, 16th century B.C.: Marinatos and Hirmer 1960, pl. 175; cf., more subtly, a steatite *rhyton* from the Rhyton Well at Mycenae: Wace 1919–21, pl. 13.1D). W. S. Smith has pointed out (1965, 32–33 and pl. 52) that an even closer parallel occurs on the two 14th-century silver wishbone-handled bowls from Enkomi in Cyprus and Dendra in Greece (Buchholz and Karageorghis 1973, 459 and pl. 4: no. 1684; Persson 1931, pl. 1, 12–15). On both cups the horns curve down, and on the Enkomi cup the rosettes occur below rather than above the bulls; but that may be largely a function of the shape of the space to be decorated. The forms of the heads are extremely similar. (On the Dendra cup the "rosettes" appear, as on one of the *rhyta*, as a swirl of hair on the bull's forehead—between the horns in that sense.) Closer still is a cup with a row of bulls' heads with rosettes between the horns, depicted among the precious "gifts" brought to Egypt by the Keftiu themselves at the time of Senmut (Fig. 15.16; Vercoutter 1956, pl. 35.231). Smith also points out a rather less similar Ugaritic Hathor-head with spiral curls and a small disc between the horns, as well as a constellation vaguely similar to our

bulls and spirals in a mural at Nuzi (W. S. Smith 1965, 33 and pl. 51)—a bull's head motif with a little crossed circle between the horns and some curly plant-like designs on either side. The artists seem here to have been drawing from an international fund of motifs which makes our design rather harder to trace.

It is noteworthy that all of the Egyptian bull-and-spiral ceilings occur relatively late in the Egyptian series: from Thutmose IV on—that is, after the court embassies are over and the Minoans are no longer on the scene. So if they are Aegean, these patterns must be Mycenaean or "Mycenaeanized," and they may even be Syrian. They also occur at precisely the time when we see little in the way of fancy textile motifs depicted in the Greek mainland palaces. Again we must ask: if the Mycenaeans themselves were not making such things, then who was? The people of Rhodes, or Cyprus, or some other Mycenaeanized outpost?

We receive a fresh shower of representations of Aegean-type designs at the close of the Bronze Age, with such tombs as Th 359 Inherkha and Th 68 Nesipanoferher. We have already discussed at length the eight-rug paneled ceiling of Inherkha, who was chief architect to Rameses III. The ceiling of Nesipanoferher, priest of Amon under Herihor of the 21st Dynasty, is no less varied and no less full of spirals. If anything, these panels appear the most rug-like of the lot. After that, there is nothing more, other than isolated late copies and reworkings.

OUR ultimate deduction concerning the Egyptians' knowledge of Aegean textiles is that they knew quite a lot. They seem to have received a variety of handsome Minoan textiles during the 12th and early 18th Dynasties in particular, and to have viewed the wearers and bearers of such textiles at least twice at the Theban court in the early 15th century B.C., under Hatshepsut and Thutmose III. The Egyptian observers recorded a Minoan preference for red and blue dyes, and for complicated all-over patterns. We can even use the Egyptian evidence to name some favorites: the running and rapport spiral—including the "wrought-iron fence" variant—and the quatrefoil interlock.

Then, as Minoan pottery gives way to Mycenaean, we find that Minoan-style cloth gives way to some other sorts of Aegean-looking textiles. We have called them "Mycenaean" by convention, but we have also

seen some reasons to doubt the precision of this term. At any rate, loincloths are replaced by kilts in the last Aegean embassy to Thebes, and new patterns of cloth turn up: figured panels and stripes (including the "tented" zigzag) on the kilts, bull's head patterns, and increasingly baroque spiral rapports. These textile imports appear to continue down to the era of the Sea Peoples, early in the 12th century B.C.

Our final task will be to integrate into this picture a few other sources bearing on textiles while we deal with a few last problems.

SOME OTHER EVIDENCE

From approximately the 12th through the 18th Dynasties, in the Faiyum, the Egyptians seem to have been in contact with the Minoans in a way quite different than momentary bouts of trade or tribute. It is not at all clear what is happening there, despite the massive work of Kemp and Merrillees (1980) in reviewing all the previous excavations in the area and all the Minoan and possibly Minoan pottery there. The center of activity seems to be el-Lahun (ancient Rehone; ibid., 15), which lies on one of the Faiyum waterways and was probably an important docking site. Close around it lie the other sites with a high incidence of Minoan artifacts: Gurob, Kahun, and el-Haraga.

It is in a modest grave at Gurob that Brunton and Engelbach found the low-whorl spindle we discussed in Chapter 2: of European—presumably Aegean—form, but made of local Egyptian materials (see Fig. 2.32; Brunton and Engelbach 1927, pl. 13.8). The only simple explanation for its presence is that some European women were living in Gurob more or less permanently, and doing their own spinning. If they were also weav-

ing according to their own custom, their products may have been the source of some of the Aegean designs we see in Egypt. That is, it is not necessarily the case that everything was imported from across the Mediterranean. Some of the people may have moved too.

Next door in 12th Dynasty Kahun, meanwhile, someone had left behind something equally un-Egyptian for Petrie and his team to find: a "handful of weaver's waste" of spun wool in three different colors (Petrie, Griffith, and Newberry 1890, 28). We have no reason to believe that the Egyptians were skilled in either weaving or dyeing wool at this time, or were even raising the appropriate types of sheep (those depicted are all of the hairy varieties); yet the presence of cut-off ends from a loom virtually proves that the weaving had taken place right there in Kahun. So now we can be virtually certain that foreigners, presumably women and probably Aegean, were busy weaving in the Faiyum in the 12th Dynasty according to their own foreign customs and with some of their own foreign materials.[20] We get a surprise, however,

---

[20] I have long been puzzled as to why the Minoans should turn up in such force precisely in the Faiyum. One would think that the Minoans, being of necessity

ship-travellers, would end up with a "colony" along the Nile somewhere, or on the Mediterranean shore. (By "colony" I envisage only something similar to the Greek

when we look at the colors: they are red, blue, and green! So *someone* knew how to make green dye.

We find more evidence later of these northern-style textile crafts being plied in Egypt: specifically, some more spun and unspun, colored and uncolored wools found at Amarna (Frankfort and Pendlebury 1933, 18; Pendlebury et al. 1951, 109). Indeed, we see all sorts of hints that Akhenaton and his family enjoyed bright and cheery textiles quite different from the traditional white Egyptian linen: the geometrically figured sashes that the king wears as he drives his chariot or leans out of the window (Davies 1903, pl. 17; Davies 1905, pl. 35), or the fat red cushions, patterned with tiny blue and yellow diamonds, that the family lounges on in the boudoir (in the famous Princess Fresco, now in the Ashmolean Museum: Frankfort 1929, 16 fig. 12) or leans on in the Window of Appearances (Davies 1905, pl. 35). Akhenaton's successor(s) used the same window cushion, according to Neferhotep (Davies 1933, pl. 9); and we possess a long, tapering sash similar to Akhenaton's that belonged to Rameses III (see Chapters 3, 5, and Fig. 3.34).

There is no guarantee that these particular textiles were Aegean, however. The Syrians, and many others as well, are shown wearing elaborate cloth by this time; three splendid

examples of ornate Syrians are those presenting tribute to Tutankhamon in the tomb of Huy (Th 40; Nina Davies and A. Gardiner 1926, pl. 19–20), those grovelling at the feet of Amenhotep III in Tomb Th 58 (Nina Davies 1936, III pl. 60), and the faience inlays of prisoners discussed below. As with the Minoans, we tend to see tiny all-over designs on the cloth, but mostly dots, rosettes, and skinny quatrefoils.

On the other hand, we have some guarantees that Syrian textiles were well known in Egypt by the mid-18th Dynasty. We have already discussed at length the gala tunic of Tutankhamon (Chapter 5 and Figs. 5.10–11), with its wide embroidered band of mixed Egyptian and Syrian motifs, clearly produced specifically for that pharaoh (his cartouche is part of the decor), but by foreign craftspeople. We have mentioned (Chapter 5) Thutmose III's records of bringing home foreign textiles and workers as part of the booty from the sack of Megiddo. And we have discussed the introduction into Egypt of both the tapestry loom (Chapter 3) and tapestry technique (Chapter 5; see Color Plate 1): both apparently from Syria, and both presumably about this time.[21] Tapestry technique caught on and embroidery was largely rejected in Egypt; but we learn something valuable about how the Syrians were

---

"colony" we have today in Chicago or the Spanish Basque "colony" in Idaho: when anyone else back home decides to go off to the New World, he heads for Uncle Nick in Chicago or Uncle Jaime in Boise simply because they are already there and can help him get started, and so the crowd grows.) Recently a student of mine, John Yohannes, was doing some serious map-study of Egypt with this question in mind and noticed that there is a trench running southeast from the Mediterranean coast all the way to the ridge immediately northwest of the Faiyum. Is it possible that this was still an open waterway around 2000 B.C., and that the Minoans, sailing eastward along the coast after crossing directly to Libya from Crete, found their way up it to a point much closer to the Faiyum than to any other part of Egypt, so that they considered this their "home base" from then on? A

small amount of judicious geological fieldwork of the sort done recently at Troy (Kraft, Kayan, and Erol 1980) could answer this question.

[21] In assessing the textiles from the tomb of Thutmose IV, it is important to notice the number of heirlooms there. One cloth bears the cartouche of Amenhotep II—and so do at least five of the vases; one cloth bears the name of Thutmose III, and so does one of the vases (Carter and Newberry 1904, 18–19, 143–44). All of this gives me the feeling that the big textile innovations had more or less stopped by the time of Thutmose IV, and now people were coasting, and consolidating the gains in technique. Thutmose IV had nothing better to show than what his father and grandfather had left him. The piece with Thutmose III's name shows that its weavers had not yet decided how best to negotiate the edge of a

producing their textiles around 1450 B.C. At the moment it seems unlikely that southern European women practiced either tapestry or embroidery yet (though they may have been learning these arts from the same sources at about the same time). As for the other weaving method that turns up in Egypt in this millennium—namely, warp-patterning of narrow bands—the source is harder to pinpoint. We know, at least, that the Europeans had the technique long before Sen-

mut's horsecloth (see Fig. 5.9) was made; and we can see that by the time of Rameses' girdle such work was being done in Egypt itself, since the pattern on the latter consists of *ankh* signs (see Fig. 3.34).

By the time of the Ramesside pharaohs, too, the inhabitants of Syria and Palestine had enlarged their repertoire of cloth made for wearing. A series of brightly colored faience tiles from the Egyptian palaces at Tell el-Yahudiyeh (Fig. 15.25), Kantir (see Fig.

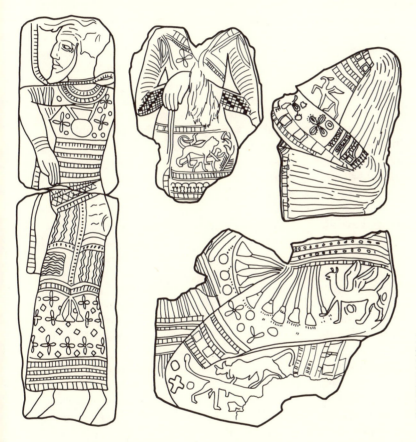

15.25 Fragments of faience tiles of foreigners, from a 20th Dynasty Egyptian palace at Tell el-Yahudiyeh; 12th century B.C. Note panels and beasts on kilts, and compare Figs. 15.7, 15.18, 15.26, and 16.5. (After Wallis 1900, pl. 5–6)

tapestry color-field (see Chapter 5, and Color Plate 1), and were still experimenting. By the time they wove the cloth for Amenhotep II, they had chosen the slit technique and were becoming rather ambitious in their designs. Tutankhamon's tapestries many years later show

no further innovations of technique—but they are done with extreme skill. This is one reason why I put the "watershed" line dividing Egyptian attitudes towards textiles somewhere in this part of the 18th Dynasty.

15.26), and Medinet Habu (Hayes 1937; Wallis 1900; Daressy 1910) shows us what these new fashions were; and they include both some decorated versions of the old Syrian spirally wrapped gown and an elaborate kilt, often paneled or friezed with amazing beasts, and often sporting a tassel at the extra-long (i.e., pointed) front corner.

I have complained before about the paneled kilt. The first hint of trouble came when we discovered that the kilts of the clearly Aegean emissaries shown by Rekhmire and Menkheperraseneb, with their elaborately figured panels and stripes, did not match the textiles of the kilts shown in Mycenaean frescoes. The kilts shown in the last frescoes at Knossos certainly have an elaborate tassel in the right spot, and dip down in the front; but the textile motifs are the little, curly, all-over designs characteristic of the Minoans; and although they may have a wide bottom border, the kilts are not composed of panels. The Mycenaean mainlanders, on the other hand, show themselves wearing tunics at least as often as kilts, and the cloth in both cases is exceedingly plain: frequently edged and occasionally fringed, but never constructed of fancily decorated stripes or panels. We pointed a finger inquiringly at Rhodes and Cyprus, the Mycenaean stepping-stones to the east Mediterranean, on the basis of Rekhmire's inscription. Now we have another pointer to the east for such kilts, in the faience tiles. What is going on?

First, Rhodes and Cyprus. We have little direct evidence from either of these islands about cloth or clothing, except for some non-detailed bronze figurines of kilted males, and two ivory mirror handles from Cyprus (Late Bronze III; Buchholz and Karageorghis 1973, pl. 480–81: nos. 1747–48) showing heroic male combatants wearing knee-length kilts decorated with wide ornamental bands. They look not unlike some of those in the tombs of Rekhmire and Menkheperraseneb. For the rest we must content ourselves with the general archaeological picture. That means pottery.

Pottery in Bronze Age Europe and the Near East seldom looks so much as though it were copied off of textiles as does the Mycenaean pottery of Rhodes, Cyprus, and the other Mycenaean or "Mycenaeanized" islands and seaports. The friezes of chariot riders (see Fig. 16.10), friezes of wild animals, panels of ornate birds and geometric motifs, and the little fillers are all typically "textile" in shape and busy treatment. Remember that in a textile you can only deal with one row of weft at a time; so construction in strips or panels is a necessity. You can choose, of course, to ignore this natural division in the overall design you wish to create: you can make a huge tapestry of a single tableau, as with the French gobelins. But the path of least resistance in weaving is to plan the decoration in manageable strips or friezes, especially if you are attempting "representational" art rather than merely trying to cover the cloth with a pleasing pattern. In other words—to sort this out—it looks as though some weavers in the Mycenaean world had begun to depict real objects (e.g., birds and animals) and even scenes (e.g., chariot processions), making them quite naturally into friezes and panels; and the potters had followed suit, taking forms directly from the weavers. For remember, too, that a pot-painter is *not* tied to strip-shaped space the way the weaver is, and in fact is normally confronted with complexly curved and non-linear surfaces that may be covered in any order whatsoever.

The filler ornaments, too, are the sorts of things a weaver working with floating weft will come up with in order to reduce the length of the floats. (Long floats snag easily, and add nothing to either the beauty or the practicality of the fabric.) Fillers, of course, can have other sources in art; but in weaving they are sometimes a necessity.[22]

Technical analyses have demonstrated that all the Mycenaean-looking pottery on Rhodes in the Late Helladic IIIA and IIIB periods was in fact imported from the mainland, and specifically from the Argolid (Mee 1982, 81–89), and that in Cyprus at least the chariot craters (see Fig. 16.10), along with much else, were imports from there too (Catling and Millett 1965). So if we are looking to Rhodes and Cyprus for such fancy textiles as may have inspired this pottery, we will need to look right back to the mainland, to the Argolid, where we thought all the textiles were plain. So once again: who was wearing the paneled and tasseled kilt?

When it comes right down to it, we really don't have a very complete picture of Argolid male fashions in Late Helladic III. The frescoes that we happen to have from the Argolid show men hunting or peaceably driving chariots. If only a particular class wore the kilt, perhaps the right scenes didn't happen to be preserved. Where we see the kilt is on the warriors at Pylos, and on the men portrayed in the Knossos processions and the Egyptian tribute-bearing scenes—on men who may have worn them as "messengers" or "sailors" or both.[23]

As a matter of fact, the Egyptians show us large quantities of warriors and sailors wearing the pointed kilt at the very end of this period. In the reliefs depicting Rameses III's battles against the Libyans and the Sea Peoples, it seems as though most of the enemies, especially among the Sea Peoples, as well as half the Egyptian allies are wearing it (see Sandars 1985, figs. 14, 74–77, 79–84, 86, 87, 90 right, 93). The kilt seems, in fact, to have become the basic garb for war and/or travel throughout the Mediterranean—outside Egypt—and the different ethnic types of kilt-wearers can be distinguished only by their hats and hairdos, noses, beards, and jewelry, when at all. The reliefs themselves do not show enough detail for us to see what patterns, if any, occurred on the garments; we see only the division of the kilts into panels or registers, the pointed front, and sometimes the stylized triple tassel. For such patterns we have to go back to the much more elaborate and purposely colorful representa-

---

[22] Note that only in weaving does the craftsperson have to create the "blank" spaces at the same time as the "filled" ones. The weaver's considerations of sequence and existence are crucial aspects of any discussion of textile art, and are often overlooked by historians of ancient art.

[23] Fashions in kilts may be worth paying attention to. Both Evans (1928, 745) and Vercoutter (1956, 64–67) complain that the silly Egyptians labelled as "king of the Keftiu" a figure who looks much more like a Syrian in both coiffure, skin color, and style of kilt: to Vercoutter this is one more sign that Menkheperraseneb's scene was a freely and carelessly invented pastiche. I'm not so sure. The kilted Keftiu in the lower row (where the "king" is) alternate with people in clearly and typically Syrian dress, while their own kilts mostly show special features associated with the Levant and Anatolia (the half-circle at the waist, the peculiar placement of the border, the slanted fringe, the color scheme). In fact, there are very close parallels to some of these details on the ivories from Ugarit (W. S. Smith 1965, fig. 55, 57).

I am coming to feel, therefore, that Menkheperraseneb's second row represents a different boatload of strangers—Keftiu and coastal Semites travelling together, who may even have arrived at the Theban court at a rather later date than the people of the upper row (since the types in this lower row do not occur in Rekhmire's tomb). That is, perhaps the combining of Cretan, Anatolian, and Levantine cultural traits was actually occurring at this time in Ugarit, on Cyprus, and/or on the south coast of Anatolia (e.g., in Pamphylia, which means "All Races"), rather than only in the heads of "careless" Egyptian artists. (Compare the cargo mixed from very similar sources in the 14th century B.C. shipwreck recently found at Ulu Burun, off the south coast of Turkey: Bass 1987.) Perhaps some group of Minoans, displaced eastward by the geological and political catastrophes of which we have ample evidence, had chosen a useful easterner to be their leader in exile. Having resurrected this king's claim to some authenticity by means of his followers' kilts, however, I will leave him as prey for the historians.

15.26   Fragments of faience tile depicting a red-skinned captive wearing a friezed kilt; from the palace of Rameses II at Kantir; 13th century B.C. (Hayes 1937, pl. 8; courtesy of the Metropolitan Museum of Art)

tions of prisoners and generic enemies on the faience tiles.

What we see are friezes of creatures. Some are of bulls or of wild goats(?) among flowery fillers (Fig. 15.26), remarkably like those on the pottery of Argos and its export markets in Late Helladic IIIB, of the whole sub-Mycenaean world in Late Helladic IIIC, and on into archaic Classical times in Ionia (see Fig. 16.5). One beast, however, seems to be a rhinoceros, and others are Syrian-looking griffins (see Fig. 15.25). So the Syrians themselves have had a hand in this. But the owner of the "wild goat" kilt is shown with red skin (Fig. 15.26; Hayes 1937, 26), a convention

used by the Egyptians only for themselves (males) and for the people from the Keftiu and the Islands of the north—not for Syrians, Palestinians, Hittites, or any others. So despite the fact that this man wears his kilt over a long white tunic, in the fashion of so many people of the Levant, he is evidently perceived as being of Aegean blood.

The only sense I can make of all these facts is that the Mycenaeans and the Syrians had been very busy mixing up new textile ideas together during the time between the deaths of Thutmose III and Rameses II (certainly the traceable spread of Mycenaean pottery makes this probable); and that in the course of swapping techniques, fashions, motifs, and even people back and forth, they had all by various routes come to the point of making and sometimes wearing friezed and/or paneled kilts, some of which were handsomely decorated in a new Animal Style. To judge from the styles, it would even seem possible that tapestry technique had finally made its way to the Aegean, alongside the native weft-float methods. Looking back at the frieze on the bottom of Tutankhamon's tunic, one can suspect the Syrians, at least, of making some of their figures in embroidery as well as tapestry; and that technique too may have reached the Aegean, as we saw from the frescoes of miniature ornaments.

We have one more strong hint at Mycenae that cloths friezed with representational subjects were indeed being manufactured for Mycenaean use: one of the *ikria* or deck-shelters (see Fig. 15.22) painted in a room on the Citadel there consists of friezes of very Aegean nautilus shells between familiar bands of lozenges (Shaw 1980, fig. 4 and pl. 26 fig. 1). Maria Shaw shows by her parallels that such figured screens were almost certainly woven of cloth originally.

Within this context of figured cloth, the late ceiling patterns that show representations of bulls' heads, and the striped patterns that involve running spirals, seem even more plausibly to have come out of an Aegean/Syr- ian textile *koiné*, at the very least, if not strictly from the Aegean.

CONCLUSIONS

No matter which way we have turned, we have found the evidence strong for a lively Bronze Age Aegean textile industry and a lively trade with Egypt during most of the 2nd millennium B.C. We saw that the Aegean representations of cloth, found chiefly in the frescoes, accorded well with what we knew of European cloth from direct archaeological evidence; and we saw that Minoan cloth in particular was highly ornate. By the time we were done, we had even isolated several of the favorite Minoan patterns: the spiral band and rapport, the four-lobed interlock, and the "wrought-iron fence" motif with its filler of dot-edged diamonds.

We concluded from the evidence that the Egyptians were well acquainted with this cloth. They observed it during the 18th Dynasty on the persons of the Aegean ambassadors to the Theban court, and among the "gifts" brought by those emissaries. We also deduced step by step that wealthy Egyptian noblemen were using Aegean rugs as brightly decorative and even ostentatious canopy-covers from Middle Minoan/Middle Kingdom times (early 2nd millenium) to perhaps as late as the collapse of Bronze Age so- cieties ca. 1200 B.C. It is for this reason, apparently, that we find so many Aegean textile-type motifs on the tomb-ceilings of particular classes of the Egyptian nobility. The Egyptian representations, once recognized, even added to our stock of information about the Aegean textiles—concerning motifs, colors, uses, and dating.

Aegean merchant-sailors spread these textiles liberally about the East Mediterranean while bringing fresh ideas and techniques back to Greece and Crete. We can see the return-cargo of ideas in the frescoes in particular. We found we could follow the sequence of Aegean carriers both by the changes in style of clothing among the emissaries and captives shown by the Egyptians, and by the continuing parallels to the textile patterns in the Aegean pottery motifs. Finally, toward the close of the 2nd millennium the entire Aegean culture plunged deep into a Dark Age, along with Egypt, the Levant, and the East Mediterranean trade. What may have happened then is a puzzle for the next chapter, to be taken in its own right and on its own evidence.

CHAPTER 16

AND PENELOPE?

Readers of the *Odyssey* will remember that Penelope held her importunate suitors at bay for over three years while she wove a funerary cloth for her father-in-law—unraveling secretly at night what she wove each day. One of the suitors recounts it thus:

Setting up a large loom in the palace, she wove
A delicate and very large [warp]. And then she
   said to us:
"Young men, my suitors since divine Odysseus
   has died,
Wait, although you are pressing for marriage
   with me, until this cloth
I have finished—lest my yarns perish, wasted:
This funeral cloth for the hero Laertes, which is
   for whenever
Deadly fate shall bring him down in death that
   lays us low—
Lest any of the Achaian women in the province
   should fault me
That one who has acquired so much lies without
   his cloth."
Thus she spoke; and the manly spirit within us
   was persuaded.
Then during the day she would weave on the
   great loom,
But at night she would take it out again, having
   set torches near.
Thus for three years she escaped detection in her
   trick, and persuaded the Achaians.
But when the fourth year came and the seasons
   arrived,

Then one of her women told, who knew clearly;
And we came upon her as she was unraveling her
   great warp.
So she had to finish it up, and not willingly, but
   by force.

                    (*Od.* 2.94–110)

Handweavers, however, will quickly calculate that a simple shroud or winding sheet—the usual assumption—would take only two or three weeks to weave on the available loom (cf. Geijer 1977, 54). Even if Penelope did not already have her yarns (which she complains might spoil if not used), and had not already set up her warp (implied but not stated explicitly), and even if she made an unnecessarily long sheet, the operation should still not have lasted more than a few months. Why, then, do the impatient suitors patiently twiddle their thumbs for over three years before finding that something is wrong? Have we jumped to an unwarranted conclusion as to what she was weaving?

The words used by Homer for her web are *pharos* ($\phi\tilde{\alpha}\rho\text{o}\varsigma$: l. 97) and *speiron* ($\sigma\pi\epsilon\tilde{\iota}\rho\text{o}\nu$: l. 102), both of which terms refer to a large, rectangle of cloth exactly as it comes off of the loom.[1] The contexts of the words differ

---

[1] *Pharos* occurs in Linear B in the plural, *pa-we-a₂* "pieces of cloth." See Ventris and Chadwick 1973, 313–14 for discussion. After a great deal of reading of Greek (from all periods prior to 400 B.C.) with textiles in mind, I have the strong impression that a *pharos* was archetypically an uncut unit of heavy woolen cloth, with its three closed edges and one cut edge (see Chapters 3, 6, 7, etc.), directly usable as a cloak, blanket, or woman's peplos.

elsewhere: a *pharos* typically served as a woman's dress, appropriately draped and belted (e.g., *Od.* 5.230), whereas a *speiron* typically served as a sail (e.g., *Od.* 5.318). Penelope's *pharos* is further described only as *tapheion* (ταφεῖον) "funerary." All we are told, then, is that Penelope is making a "funerary cloth"—possibly but by no means necessarily a shroud or winding sheet, in the Christian or ancient Egyptian sense of a simple cloth used to wrap up the body.

What other sort of function might a large, uncut rectangle of cloth have served at a Greek funeral? What sort of cloth might a woman have needed at least a couple of years to weave? And why was a queen to be found weaving at all, when that was exactly the wearisome task that female slaves were brought home to perform (cf. *Od.* 5.103–5)?

The basic answer to the second question is immediately obvious to the handweaver: any kind of non-mechanized pattern weaving, such as tapestry or pile carpeting, takes that kind of time. From our survey of the development of weave types, we can see that pile carpeting is very unlikely, whereas by late Mycenaean times tapestry was already being produced in Egypt and had probably been in use in Anatolia and Syria for over a millennium. Given the long history of trade among the three areas, we would be unwise to assume that the late Mycenaean Greeks did *not* know of tapestry. Alternatively, or in addition, the Greeks might well have used the old European technique of supplementary weft, in the fashion of the Swiss pile-dwellers, for extremely elaborate and time-consuming, though not necessarily geometric, designs. Either would take this kind of time.[2]

Can we discover anything further about the production of elaborately figured cloths by either Mycenaean or Archaic Greek women, especially highborn ones? Can we discover a special relationship between such cloths and Greek funerary practices? As a matter of fact, yes. Once we look at the subject this way, armed with what we now know about the history of textiles, we will see that positive evidence lies all about us.

---

[2] Whether the actual technique was tapestry or supplementary weft, the point is that only some such elaborate and non-mechanized pattern technique would take so long to do. For simplicity's sake, although we cannot be sure which of these two choices to make, I will refer to this pattern weaving as "tapestry," in quotation marks. We have found quite a few tapestry fragments and occasional embroidery from the Hellenistic and Roman periods (see below). (The Hellenistic fragments from Noin Ula in Mongolia are described casually as "embroidered" [Schaefer 1943; Yetts 1926], and the one I have seen myself clearly is; but I can find no attempt at a careful analysis of all the textile techniques, only of motifs; and a figured piece in at least one of the photographs [Schaefer 1943, fig. 1] looks for all the world as though it contains inwoven patterns that are also not tapestry.)

That the technique involved was not embroidery at this early date is suggested both by the direct evidence we have amassed for who knew what techniques when, and by the ancient tradition that the Greeks learned the art of embroidery from the Phrygians (Pliny, *Nat. Hist.* 8.74.196), that is, well within the Iron Age. We could even add the simple fact that Homer, Euripides, etc. *say* that the women producing fancy cloth were weaving on their looms—not embroidering in their laps. This is a point to remember when reading the usual translations of Greek texts. Alan Wace pointed out many years ago that most translators, unaware of the subtleties of textile manufacture, regularly mistranslate ποικίλος (*poikilos*) and its derivatives and synonyms as "embroidered," when applied to cloth, although the contexts make it quite clear that a weaving technique is intended (Wace 1948).

Linguistically, the word *poikilos* is interesting to this discussion, because it is derived from an Indo-European root for any sort of figured design, being cognate with Latin *pingo, pictus* 'draw, paint'; Russian *pisat'* 'paint, draw, write,' *pëstryj* 'multicolored'; Lithuanian *piešti* 'draw, write'; Sanskrit *piṃśáti* 'adorn,' *péśa-* 'shape, color, decoration'; Old Persian *ni-pišta-* 'drawn'; Tocharian A *piktsi* 'to paint, write'; Old High German *fēh* and Old English *fāh* 'variegated'; Old Norse *fā* 'to paint'; Gothic *filu-faihs* 'varied' (cf. Vasmer [1950–58] 1964–73, 3.266; Kluge 1975, 189; Schulze 1934, 257–61). In fact, it seems to be the basic Indo-European root for graphic and pictorial arts. Within Greek, *poikilos* seems to refer to objects that have a varicolored or variegated design, but are specifically made by human craft (Bolling 1958, 275–80).

FIGURED CLOTH IN GREECE

Let us begin with Euripides' *Ion*. Since the plot hinges on the recognition of the hero by means of his baby blanket, the play is rife with textile motifs. In the pivotal scene, Ion questions Creusa about what she put into the basket with her abandoned infant, to see if it matches what is in the basket Ion holds:

CREUSA: Take a look: a cloth which I myself wove while still a child.

ION: Of what sort? The weavings of maidens are varied.

CREUSA: Not a finished piece, but a sort of sampler of the shuttle.[3]

ION: Having what design? You won't fool me with this.

CREUSA: For one thing, a Gorgon is on the central warps of the robe . . .

ION: O Zeus, what fate is tracking us down?

CREUSA: . . . and it is bordered with snakes, like an aegis.

ION: Indeed that is the cloth!

(*Ion* 1417–23)

Euripides presents it as quite natural and common that a young girl, even (or especially?) a princess, should be practicing "tapestry-work" on her loom, learning to weave such pictorial designs as Gorgons and snakes.

But we are given more. Braced by the scene just recounted, we need not be overwhelmed by the astonishing wealth of "tapestries" Euripides has Ion choose for the banquet pavilion he is asked to set up:

Taking sacred textiles from the treasuries,
He made a shelter—wonders for men to see.
First he threw over the roof-pole coverings of robes,
The dedication of Zeus's son, which Herakles
Had brought to the god as spoils of the Amazons.

(*Ion* 1141–45)

These "tapestries" from the north, we are told at great length, depicted sun, moon, and the constellations of stars—most appropriate for the ceiling. For the sides of the tent he chose other "barbarian" (i.e., non-Greek) "tapestries" depicting battles, hunts, and hybrid monsters; and at the entrance he hung a weaving of "Cecrops twisting with coils near his daughters—an offering of one of the Athenians" (*Ion* 1163–65).

We need not, of course, believe that each and every one of these "tapestries" existed; obviously Euripides had a lot of fun designing an artistically satisfying tent. But we can distill from this scene the general premises (a) that large and elaborate pictorial cloths were not unknown; (b) that one place they were typically stored was in temple treasuries—we mustn't forget that Greek temples, like many cathedrals, doubled as the art museums of the day, reckoning their wealth as much in the assemblage of rare objects as in gold and silver; and (c) that these "tapestries" came from both the Greek and the "barbarian" worlds. Furthermore, when a "tapestry" is indicated as made by a Greek, it is also described as depicting elements of a myth. Was that typical of Greek "tapestries"? It certainly was of other forms of Greek art, such as vase painting and relief sculpture.

But, the skeptic may say, is not the entire notion of figured "tapestries" as temple offerings merely a happy conceit of the poet as he works out his weaving motif to the fullest?

No. We know from scattered sources that such "tapestries" *were* woven expressly for the temples. The most famous case is that of

---

[3] Literally, a pin-beater (κερκίς, *kerkis*), which, as we saw, might have had weft wrapped around it, but which served the very important function of beating the weft home and straightening the warp. In fact, if one were weaving true tapestry, the large sword-beater would be useless and the small pin-beater would be the weapon of choice for hitting home the short stretches of different colored wefts, the tails of which would hang down loose (or in a butterfly) rather than being on any sort of bobbin. (As we saw also, the true shuttle was not yet invented, and the weft could not be thrown from side to side of the loom as Wace would have it [Wace 1948, 55].)

16.1   The folded peplos of Athena, on the Parthenon frieze; mid-5th century B.C. Note ribbed edge, lower right. (Photo courtesy of Trustees of the British Museum)

the peplos made at regular intervals to dress the statue of Athena Polias that stood in the Erechtheum on the acropolis at Athens. It is the presentation of this garment that forms the subject of the great marble frieze around the Parthenon (Fig. 16.1). One can see the peplos being folded up by a priest on the east end of the building. Although the painted decoration is gone, the ribbing of the heading band—the trademark of the warp-weighted loom—was sculpted into the marble and shows quite clearly.

Every year the Athenians held a festival of thanksgiving to Athena, their patroness; and every fourth year they held a particularly large version of the festival—the Great Panathenaia. The celebrations included athletic events, the most unusual of which were a torch race (Parke 1977, 37, 45, 171–72) and the Pyrrhic dance (according to legend the dance done by Athena to celebrate a victory of the gods over the giants: ibid., 36), as well as a huge procession through the city to bring Athena her new dress (see Pfuhl 1900; Deubner 1932; Davison 1958; Mommsen

1968, 116–205; etc.). During the procession, the peplos was apparently displayed to the public by being strung up like a sail on poles on top of a ship cart (Mommsen 1968, 188–96). Plutarch, in his *Life of Demetrios*, tells of a catastrophe that occurred at this moment in the ritual, in the last decade of the 4th century B.C. The Athenians, it seems, in order to honor Demetrios for saving the city from some enemies, had extravagantly voted that he be given an altar as "Demetrios the Savior" and be "woven into" Athena's garment (ἐνυφαίνεσθαι τῷ πέπλῳ, *enuphainesthai tōi peplōi*), "along with Athena and Zeus"; but during the Panathenaia, as the procession was carrying the peplos through the Kerameikos, a squall hit, and it ripped the sacred garment through the middle (Plutarch, *Demetrios* 10.5, 12.3). Plutarch drily remarks that the deity thus expressed its opinion of the Athenians' doings.

We deduce from this bit of history that the sacred peplos was indeed decorated with an inwoven design, which always included at least the figures of Athena and Zeus. From the context one also deduces that the point of resemblance that made it seem appropriate specifically to add Demetrios to the peplos was that each of the three was viewed in some way as a savior figure.

From Euripides' *Hecuba* we learn more of the traditional design. The captive women who form the Chorus wonder aloud whether they will be taken off to Athens: "In the city of Pallas shall I yoke horses to the beautiful Athenian chariots in the saffron [κροκέῳ, *krokeōi*] peplos, figuring it [ποικίλλουσ', *poikillous'*] with craftful [and intricate—δαιδαλέαισι, *daidaleaisi*] flower-dyed wefts [ἀνθοκρόκοισι πήναις, *anthokrokoisi pēnais*]—or [weave] the race of Titans which Zeus son of Kronos puts to bed with a fiery bolt?" (*Hec.* 466–74). Evidently the peplos contained a group of chariots and/or the terrible Huge Ones as well as Zeus and Athena.

In the *Republic* (2.378c) Plato remarks that one should neither tell nor weave Gigantomachies; and Euripides has Iphigenia bewail that she will never weave Athena and the Titans like other ladies (*Iph. Taur.* 222–24).[4] The references almost have to be to Athena's peplos—precisely because the authors act as though everyone will instantly recognize

what "tapestry" is meant. So we glean the additional information that one didn't weave just any old giants but specifically the Battle of the Gods and the Giants in which the gods, led by Zeus and Athena, put down a terrifying and nearly catastrophic insurrection of those awesome monsters who rumble around where they have been chained under the earth, and who occasionally escape and erupt forth to challenge the gentle order of the gods.[5] As leaders in the battle against them, Zeus and Athena certainly belong in the scene, and also fill the role of the saviors of Athens—like the unfortunate Demetrios. The pieces of the puzzle are beginning to fit together. The other half-dozen surviving passages that describe or refer to the peplos and its design (quoted by Pfuhl 1900, 12 n. 71) simply confirm the presence of the Gigantomachy and hint at the inclusion somewhere of Athenian warriors, possibly as a sort of honor guard.

From ancient sources we also learn that it was the duty of two of the Arrephoroi, child priestesses of Athena, chosen each year from the noble class, and the Ergastinai, the priestesses who would do the actual weaving, to set up the warp (διάζονται, *diazon-*

---

[4] She speaks of weaving on the ἱστοῖς καλλιφθόγγοις: "lovely-sounding looms." Warp-weighted looms do not "whisper" or "whir," as the translators would have it. They clank. In fact, if the 40 to 100 clay weights on them hang freely, they make so much noise every time one moves the heddle bar that modern experimenters have started to wonder if certain features on the weights were added to make them quieter! (Cf. Carington Smith 1975, 93.) On the other hand, in moderation the sound of the clay weights is rather pleasant, in the manner of wind chimes.

[5] Classicists will note a discrepancy, in these various references, between Titans and Giants, who, our myth books tell us, are different races of divinities. In fact, when all the ancient references to the peplos and Panathenaia have been considered, there are about as many uses of "Giant" as of "Titan." In short, the Classical Greeks themselves didn't bother with much of a distinction here. Both the Giants and the Titans are particularly huge, both move mountains and shake the earth, etc. The crucial point is that both types of divinity rep-

resented the same forces of nature, vulcanism, so there was no need to distinguish them rigorously.

This sort of "inconsistency"—two deities for the same thing—drives us crazy, but was not of concern to the ancients: not because they were stupid but because they weren't looking at the world with consistency in mind. Consistency only becomes a useful premise or principle when sufficient data to demonstrate its widespread existence has been stockpiled, through mass literacy over a long time. Alphabetic literacy began to take hold in earnest only in the late 5th century B.C. Prior to that watershed, "explanation" takes the form principally of analogical description—what we call "myth" (and consider quaint, "off the wall," and utterly benighted). With cause-and-effect explanation, one principle explains a whole set of phenomena, so consistency is a central notion. But with analogical "explanation," the more analogies the better. (We have called it the Multiple Aspects Principle, in a forthcoming work on "myth principles"; meanwhile see Frankfort and Frankfort 1949; and P. T. Barber 1988.)

tai) for the peplos some nine months before the presentation (sources quoted by Deubner 1932, 31 n. 6, 31 n. 9; cf. Herington 1955, 33; Parke 1977, 38, 43, 93). Now, we know that the statue that the peplos was destined to dress was not large: it was an ancient *xoanon* of olive wood (Herington 1955, 17), sufficiently small that when the Athenians were fleeing the Persians in great haste in 480 B.C., they were nonetheless able to snatch up this statue and run off to Salamis with it (Plutarch, *Themistocles* 10.7). It was almost certainly little more than "life-size."[6] So the peplos that dressed it was almost certainly about life-size also—that is, 4 to 5 feet wide (to go around the body once) and 5 to 7 feet long (the extra length was used to belt it up into a fold above the sash, and sometimes to turn over at the neck as a sort of bib that could double as a hood if pulled up from behind). These are also the most convenient and normal dimensions for a cloth on the warp-weighted loom, as we have seen.

If it takes two or three girls (about as many as can weave on such a loom at once) the better part of one year to weave such a "tapestry," working full-time, how long does it take one girl? The better part of two or three years; and it won't be so much fun, because she hasn't anyone to talk with or pass the weft to. It will take even longer if she has to manage a large household and bring up a child at the same time—like Penelope.

Under such circumstances, Penelope's suitors seem not to have been so far off in their reckoning.

We find numerous representations in Greek art of what look like tapestry figures. The artist of the handsome Chiusi vase (see Fig. 3.26) has depicted a row of "tapestry" figures right on Penelope's loom; she sits dejectedly in front of it, talking with Telemachos. On a red-figure cup by Makron, ca. 490 B.C. (Fig. 16.2), Demeter wears a cloak with bands of leaping dolphins, winged runners, and chariot racers; and the Euthydikos

16.2   Demeter wearing a cloak with friezes of dolphins, chariots, and winged runners. Cup by Makron, ca. 490 B.C. (Photo courtesy of Trustees of the British Museum; no. E-140)

---

[6] The ancient Greeks were smaller than we are, on the average; so their life-size looks a bit small to us. On the other hand, deities were portrayed a little bigger than humans; so deities tend to look properly life-size to us. For the peplos, the difference is probably only a matter of inches anyhow. (I do not believe, with David Lewis [1979–80], that the woolen peplos clothed Phidias's huge statue. One needs to consider the difficulty of dressing the body, under both the Aegis and all those curls, and the near impossibility of getting the drapery to hang the same way each time for all those later copyists.)

Kore (Akr. no. 686), desecrated by the Persians in 480 B.C., wore a friezed robe displaying a band of chariots with horses and riders still partially discernible across shoulder and chest, done in red and black on a light ground (H. Schrader 1939, 79 and fig. 44). And in the Archaic period, numerous women are shown wearing peploi covered with figured friezes, both on small statuettes of painted clay (e.g., Akropolis find no. 15148) and on vases. That these ladies, where named, are always either goddesses or princesses is only to be expected, for economic reasons: the enormous amount of time required to weave such a large "tapestry" would make it too expensive for anyone else to own. On the famous François Vase painted by Kleitias (Fig. 16.3), we see such ladies arriving for the wedding of Thetis and Peleus. Some wear peploi with all-over patterns; others, like Hera, have donned their best "tapestries" (see Ridgway 1984, 36–38, for the problems of making such dresses), which are shown composed of half-a-dozen narrow, horizontal friezes of people, chariots, horses,

and other animals (real or imagined)—just like the vase they are painted on (Fig. 16.4). One feels for a moment that one has glanced into a set of "infinite mirrors," that frieze within frieze might go on forever. One gets exactly the same impression from vases by Sophilos, such as the magnificent *dinos* in London or the sherds in Athens. The only variation that we see in the form of these pictorial depictions on textiles is in some much simpler garments on which the "tapestry" figures form a ladder of picture boxes down the center front of the garment, while the rest is virtually plain (e.g., Cecchetti 1972, pl. 26 no. 69). (This would be a somewhat cheaper dress.) If huge, single-scened gobelins were made, we find no trace.

Clearly we do best to imagine the Gigantomachy and other subjects on Athena's fancy peplos as arranged in stacked friezes, much as we see such things depicted by Kleitias and Sophilos. A rare surviving tapestry from late Roman Egypt shows just such an arrangement, although the friezes alternately depict animals and winged, haloed

16.3 Detail of the François vase (Fig. 16.4), showing goddesses attending a wedding. Note the dress friezed with scenes much like this one. (Furtwängler 1904, pl. 1–2; by permission fee)

16.4 François vase, by Athenians Kleitias and Ergotimos, decorated with friezes of mythological stories; ca. 570 B.C. (Archaeological Museum, Florence; no. 4209. Courtesy of Gabinetto Fotografico Soprintendenza Archeologica della Toscana)

cherubs (Greene 1955, pl. 9). This piece is more relevant than it may seem at first glance, because the loose packing suggested to the conservator that it was made on a warp-weighted loom (hence not by Egyptians), which, if correct, would demonstrate directly that such tapestries *were* made on warp-weighted looms (ibid., 14, 16). Fragments of figured tapestry of a similar date, from Egypt, show friezes of combats, dancing, hunting, foliage, birds, and animals (Kendrick 1920, esp. nos. 20, 21, 90, 91, 101, 102).

POTTERS AND WEAVERS

Clearly also the friezes on the "tapestries" and the friezes on the vases are closely related. Which came first, in this train of reflections? Making narrow friezes is a simple and natural solution to the problems of keeping track of a storytelling design on a loom. After all, the weaver can only create one little row at a time. Dividing a vase up into stacked registers, on the other hand, is not an *obvious* way to treat an already fully created surface; and the poor viewer must keep turning the vase round and round to follow the bands and their stories. Could it be that old, figured textiles with mytho-histories were the sources from which the less-destructible arts—vases, terracottas, and later sculptured reliefs—were deriving their forms and concepts in archaic Greece? (Presently, of course, the influence would inevitably have become reciprocal and the arts would have continued to develop together.)

We could appeal to wall-painting as the place where the Greek tendency toward friezes began, and as a source for artistic carryover from the Bronze Age: handsome, strip-shaped wall paintings of Homeric subjects (Troilos, the Chimaera, chariot-riders, etc.) have recently been uncovered in southwestern Turkey, near Elmalı (Mellink 1976). Perhaps the vase painters began by copying from frescoes? But that does not explain the peculiar shapes of the figures in the Greek "Geometric" period, when Greek art first begins to re-emerge from the dark. These figures appear to have been influenced specifically by the quirks of producing cloth, as we shall see.

Lack of direct proof is not proof of nonexistence. I am fully aware that because the textiles have not survived, I cannot prove my case. But by the same token neither can the case be disproved. There is much interesting secondary evidence awaiting consideration, once we move away from the bias that only vases survived and therefore only vases existed.

To a weaver, early Greek vases look like textiles from the start. One can even divide

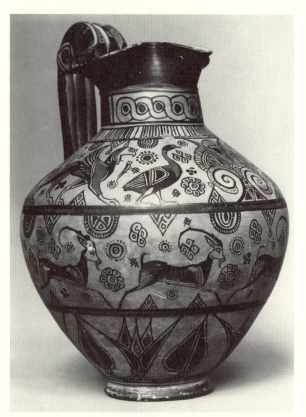

16.5   East Greek vase of "wild goat" style, from Rhodes, ca. 630–620 B.C. Note filler ornaments. (Photo courtesy of Museum of Fine Arts, Boston; no. 03.90; gift of Mrs. S. T. Morse)

the Corinthian Orientalizing resembles a supplementary-weft "float catch" (or "overshot") technique.[7] In Attica, in fact, the vase decorations look as if they had textile influence from the time of Kleitias and Sophilos right back to the early Geometric vases. At least some historians of Greek art have felt the same way. Bernhard Schweitzer, for example, says (1971, 30):

The Geometric style is without doubt entirely a pottery style, as it has come down to us. But a series of phenomena suggest that it developed alongside a lost textile art and that this may even have been the origin of Geometric art before 900 B.C. The early history of the meander in the tenth century can probably not be explained satisfactorily without the hypothesis that its roots lay in textile work. Surface ornaments such as the checkerboard, saw-tooth and lozenge patterns seem to be developed directly from weaving techniques. . . . Geometric decoration is made up of decorative bands, seams and borders. . . . Surely the character of the abstract surface style of decoration used in Early Geometric, clinging more and more to the tectonic structure of the vessel, like a garment, is best explained as being associated with a flourishing textile industry?[8]

Particularly of note are the huge pottery grave-markers and the funeral amphorae from the early 8th century, including the so-called Dipylon vases, which appear as the first known pieces of monumental art after the "dark age" that separates the late Mycenaean Greeks from the archaic Classical Greeks. These giant funerary vases are covered top to bottom with bands of busy decoration, the chief registers of which often depict a funeral (Fig. 16.6). The dead man is laid out in the center on a bier, with a pat-

them fairly readily into three or four groups, according to what kinds of textile techniques they seem to be imitating. For example, the Attic Geometric (see Fig. 16.7) and the main East Greek styles (Fig. 16.5) look like supplementary-weft "float pick-up" (or "undershot"), Attic Archaic looks like tapestry, and

[7] For the East Greek "scattered flower" style, which will not be discussed much here, compare the dresses on the Akropolis Kore no. 675, on the statue of Phrasikleia (in the National Museum in Athens; Ridgway 1984, fig. 9), etc., with the early Christian curtain from Akhmim (ancient Panopolis), now in the Royal Ontario Museum, which shows colored wool tapestry inserted into a white linen field (Gervers 1977b). Compare also the

scatter-flower textiles depicted occasionally by the Minoans, e.g., in the Saffron Gatherers fresco on Thera (see Chapter 15).

[8] Borrowing textile motifs into other media is not uncommon elsewhere either: medieval Russian architecture, for example, is full of decorative motifs borrowed from the peasant embroidery and vice versa.

16.6   Late Geometric Attic funerary vase, showing mourning (neck), animals (shoulder and lower belly), and chariots and warriors (belly). Note meanders around the mourning scene. (Walters Art Gallery, Baltimore; no. 48.2231)

other such typical weaving designs, with an occasional band of repeated animals or chariots.

Sometimes, as on a huge crater now in New York (Fig. 16.7), we see a bit more. Again the peripheral registers are filled with meanders and other typical weaving patterns—some of which we actually have in our meagre stock of early Greek textile remains—and again the main register depicts the *prothesis*: the dead man laid out on his bier with mourners all around. In this case, however, we see the family: one member seated on a chair at the foot, and little children on this person's lap and up on the bier itself.[9] An occasional bird or beast fills in underfoot. We deduce from the treatment of the chair legs (and the legs of the horses below) that the four legs under the bier are all intended to belong to the bier itself (not to a second table underneath, as our own type of perspective would suggest). The elegant geometric pattern under the body is then most easily interpreted as a patterned cloth covering the bier. Certainly it would be easy enough to weave. As before, another patterned textile hangs(?) above the body. In the large register below the funeral, we see a row or procession of charioteers and footsoldiers. (The perspective that shows us four legs on the bier and all twelve legs on the three horses pulling the chariot also gives us the two wheels of the chariot side by side, instead of in ocular perspective. It is not a wagon. On still other vases we do see four-wheeled wagons carrying the dead man on his bier to the grave—the *ekphora*.)

Are these warriors mourners, or an honor guard for the funeral, or participants in funeral games (like those of Patroklos)—or

terned cloth above (is it the roof of a pavilion to keep the sun off, or has a blanket over the corpse been lifted for a moment for us to see and understand?), while all around, the mourners are lamenting. In the simplest scenes, this is all we see. The numerous minor registers are filled with meanders and

<hr>

[9] Kurtz and Boardman suggest that these particular small figures "are not necessarily children, nor need their position be interpreted literally" (1971, 59). That one or both are indeed children and literally on the bier,

however, is suggested quite strongly by the clay model of a funeral cart from Vari that is discussed below. There, a small child modelled in clay is physically right up on the bier.

16.7 Attic Geometric funeral crater, with friezes of mourning and chariot-riding. Note filler ornaments and geometric bands. (The Metropolitan Museum of Art; Rogers Fund, 1914: no. 14.130.14)

even all of the above? Or are they just a random filling ornament? We can't be certain. But they seem to have textile descendents in the charioteers on Athena's peplos and on the dresses depicted on Kleitias's vase. And they have ancestors prior to the great blackout of the dark age.

Of a shape very similar to the Geometric crater we have just been inspecting is a large Mycenaean bowl known as the Warrior Vase, from about 1200 B.C. (Fig. 16.8). Its one large register is painted with a line of foot-soldiers who are evidently just marching off to war, for behind them a woman stands with her hands to her head in a typical gesture of mourning or distress. Under the handle skulks a stray bird or two. There are differences in dress, equipment, and stylization, certainly; but the conception of arrangement into a frieze is strikingly similar. The similarity increases when we look at the design painted onto a roughly contemporary grave stele from Mycenae (Fig. 16.9). This particular stone was originally carved for a much earlier shaft grave; but late in the Mycenaean period it was retrieved, plastered over, and painted with at least three stacked registers of figures. The topmost, which is largely missing, seems to have shown a person seated on a chair, with something or someone in front of him or her. The next register shows a line of marching soldiers, almost exactly as in the Warrior Vase, while the bottom register presents a row of four deer (with a stray hedgehog tucked in), very much like those in the minor bands of the Geometric vases, and like those of the archaic East Greek vases friezed with wild goats and other such creatures (see Fig. 16.5).

Furthermore, during the Late Bronze Age we find that one of the chief sorts of pottery is decorated with a register of people in chariots—the so-called Chariot Craters (Fig. 16.10). Most of these have been found in Cyprus, but it has recently been shown that

16.8 "Warrior Vase" from Mycenae, ca. 1200 B.C., showing a frieze of soldiers in fringed tunics setting out, while a woman in a long gown (far left) mourns. (National Museum, Athens)

16.9 Painted grave stele from Mycenae, ca. 1200 B.C., showing a frieze of animals (below), soldiers (middle register: compare Fig. 16.8), and a throne scene (top, broken). Compare registers of later funeral vases (Figs. 16.6–7). (National Museum, Athens; copy by M. Stone)

16.10 "Chariot crater" found in Cyprus, but made in Greece; late 13th century B.C. (Late Cypriot III). Note filler ornaments. (Courtesy of Trustees of the British Museum; no. 1925.11-1.3)

they were manufactured in mainland Greece (Catling and Millett 1965), where a few have turned up as well (e.g., at Tiryns: Slenczka 1974). Although some have "clean" backgrounds, and in this are reminiscent of the Mycenaean frescoes of chariots (see Chapter 15 and Fig. 15.11), others have their background spaces well filled already with quantities of miscellaneous ornaments. It is as though Mycenaean weavers and painters both began copying from the new frescoes, but the textile medium required fillers to keep the floats from becoming too long, and this ornamented style gradually came to be copied by the vase painters too.

One can trace much the same history for the animal friezes on pottery. They, too, start in Mycenaean times looking rather like frescoes (cf. the Mycenaean stele in Fig. 16.9), develop heavily stylized forms and abundant filler ornaments (some of the Chariot-style vases have animals instead of chariots), and then disappear from view during the dark age to reappear in Geometric times still more stylized and angular in form. The

evidence of the kilts and the *ikria*, discussed in Chapter 15 (see Figs. 15.22, 15.25–26), gives added weight to the implication that the animal friezes were popular on Late Mycenaean textiles, at least in some areas.

Everything—people, animals, and fillers—seems to shift from rounded in the Mycenaean era to squared or angular in the Attic Geometric period, only to round out again gradually in Archaic art. Everything, that is, except the meander—that hallmark of Greek art—which stayed square once it attained that form: it almost certainly arose as a squared version of the running spiral, the central characteristic of earlier Aegean art. Now, curving lines are about as easy to produce as angular ones when one is painting. But most techniques of weaving restrict one rather heavily in this regard. Either curves are easy and certain straight lines are difficult, or vice versa. The changes in shape we have observed can be explained rather simply by shifts in weaving technique, but not by any other structural explanation that I know of.[10]

[10] The part that weaving may have played in the development of the Greek meander is of particular interest to me because of a practical experience I had. Early in my textile research I had noticed the frequent occurrence of running spirals, so characteristic of Bronze Age Aegean art, on the borders of Minoan garments in the frescoes; and the frequent occurrence of meanders, so characteristic of Classical Greece, on the borders of Archaic Greek garments, especially on the *korai* buried on the Akropolis in the clean-up after the Persian destruction of 480 B.C. In order to learn better how these designs might have been produced, I experimented with weaving the two patterns (along with some other common ones from each period) in as many techniques as I could. It soon became clear that one could make running spirals quickly and easily with floated supplementary weft—"overshot" technique. But the curves of the spirals and of the other Minoan patterns (e.g., the interlocking quatrefoil) were virtually impossible to make in the other techniques I knew: I kept finding myself forced to square the circles; that is, I kept coming out with square meanders where I was trying for round spirals. Did the meander in fact develop this way? Was it created from the running spiral by a simple change of

dominant weaving technique?

On the other hand, the best technique I could find for making handsome meanders was to weave double-cloth with contrasting light and dark weft. But (because my warp was plain white) I couldn't seem to get rid of a bit of white warp showing at intervals along the edge of the meander. I realized it was a necessary and unavoidable evil of the technique, and relegated the experiment to the reject pile. Then one day, as I was looking at the paint remaining on the *korai* in the Akropolis Museum, and admiring the well-preserved meander along the border of the *chiton* worn by Kore no. 594, I noticed that the artist had painted little white ticks all along the edge of the girl's meander, exactly as they appeared in my own weaving. I drew two immediate conclusions: (1) that my guess as to technique had been correct, and (2) that I had killed once and for all the argument put forward by many art historians that the painters simply made up designs to paint onto statues and vases so they would look pretty, whereas Greek clothing was actually plain. There is no way that an artist "thought up" that imperfection in the weaving: he was looking at real cloth.

East Greek pottery from Ionia and the islands shows the textile influence just as strongly as Attic, fillers and all, but without the reduction to angular stick-figures that suggest a change of weaving technique in Attica. Particularly prominent in the East Greek style are the rows and rows of wild animals that we had seen on the kilts of the eastern Mycenaeans (Chapter 15). It is as though the Mycenaean tradition were being preserved more directly here. This in turn fits well with the Greeks' own folk memory of what happened at the end of the Bronze Age: the children and grandchildren of the Trojan War heroes fled eastward during the political breakdown and chaos that included the "Dorian Invasion," joining their civilized compatriots across the water. Presumably they took with them whatever they could carry, including such cloth and clothing as they could manage.

In discussing the vases of the local proto-Geometric period (just after 1000 B.C.) found at Karphi in Crete, Mercy Seiradaki comments that their style, with its peculiar motifs, "is more reminiscent of the L. M. II Palace style [15th century B.C.] than anything else, but the lapse of time between the two makes this comparison seem foolish" (Seiradaki 1960, 31; cf. Benson 1970, 151 n. 4). She resolves her dilemma by noting the striking resemblance of the style to textile art.

It is easy to imagine that when some evacuation of the old Minoan centres took place owing to invasion . . . the warmest, most imperishable, and most ornate coverings would have been taken along, as safeguards against the cold and reminders of ancient magnificence. At Karphi new ones would also have been made very soon, presumably on the old patterns, if the place was anything like as cold then as now. Possibly the most cherished of the originals and certainly copies of copies could easily have survived over the necessary number of years. What more likely than that the pot-painters, lacking their customary models, should have turned to their grandmothers' handiwork for inspiration, particularly if there was a precedent for doing so?

(Seiradaki 1960, 37)

We could imagine just the same scenario for the wealthy Mycenaeans fleeing to Ionia.

Elsewhere in Crete, at Fortetsa, vases from the Geometric and Orientalizing periods have turned up in some numbers, again covered with strongly textile motifs arranged in horizontal bands (Fig. 16.11; Brock 1957, esp. color pl. 117–30). But what is equally striking about these funeral pithoi is their color scheme. Unlike the usual Greek vase painted with black and a little white on red,

16.11 Pithos from Tomb II at Fortetsa, near Knossos, painted in red and blue on white; early 1st millennium B.C. Compare heart motifs with Color Plate 3. (Brock 1957, pl. 119 no. 1021)

these vases are painted with red and blue on a creamy white. The Egyptian observation that the Cretans preferred their textiles red, white, and blue (see Chapter 15) thereby receives another strong confirmation, as does the theory that the potters were deliberately copying textiles. Moreover, to clinch the whole matter, one of the dominant motifs on the Fortetsa vases is the blue pattern we nicknamed the "wrought-iron fence," when we deduced that it must have been a popular Cretan textile pattern from the Middle Bronze Age onwards (see Chapter 15, Figs. 15.19, 15.23, and Color Plate 3).

Surely all these striking similarities between the art of the period just before the dark age and the art of the period just after can't be entirely accidental. It is simpler to hypothesize that the artistic conventions of depicting funeral scenes, filler ornaments, and friezes of charioteers, warriors, goats, and other animals, were hiding out during the dark age in the perishable medium of textiles, which in turn was influencing the form. Thus the case for the continuous existence of storytelling "tapestries" since the Bronze Age becomes stronger and stronger.

CLOTH TO MARK HISTORY AND RITUAL

It is worth noting that the reason (in addition to the almost universal loss of paint on sculpture) that we tend to think of Classical Greek clothing as plain, and therefore think that the Greeks didn't know how to make fancy cloth, is that clothing apparently *was* fairly plain in the Golden Age of Athens, late in the 5th century. But it had not been so in the preceding centuries, as both the many anti-sumptuary laws and my arguments from the visual arts demonstrate. It is noticeable that the representation of elaborate figured or heavily patterned clothing on anyone but deities tails off rather rapidly on the vases (where the paint is best preserved) at just about the time of the two Persian Wars (490–480 B.C.). Anyone, that is, who is Greek. Quaint Amazons and effeminate, trousered Persians are shown wearing elaborately ornamented cloth. I sense a strong political message here: that anyone who wears luxurious and expensive clothing, rather than rough and ready plain-weave, must be a Persian sympathizer. Social pressure of that sort could quickly kill a fashion that no amount of anti-sumptuary legislation had been able to dent.

Whatever *we* think, however, clearly *Homer* believed that women were weaving figured "tapestries" long before his time. He tells us so, flat out. In the third book of the *Iliad* (125–27) he describes Helen at her loom as she "wove in the many struggles of the horse-taming Trojans and bronze-armored Achaeans." What could be clearer than that? And in Book 22 (440–41) he describes Andromache weaving multicolored roses.

Roses? George Melville Bolling has shown from the scholiasts and lexicographers that the *throna* (θρόνα) which Andromache is weaving are magical flowers, and almost certainly roses (ῥόδα, *rhoda*)—that age-old European protective talisman that peasant girls of central Europe still weave and embroider all over their clothes. Bolling describes the situation thus:

A scholiast on Theocr., 2, 59 says that "Homer" used θρόνα = ῥόδα. His remark implies that he believed three things of which only the last could be learned from Homer: (1) That different flowers secured different blessings for their wearers; (2) that roses brought back one's man safe and sound to those who wore them; (3) that Andromache's most intense wish was for the safety of Hector. The only line of which the scholiast could have been speaking is X441, and if we follow him, we see that the whole passage X437–46 is a unit and most pathetic. Andromache in her ignorance that her husband has stayed outside the fortification is weaving a charm for his protection and ordering her maids to prepare for him a hot bath that he will never enjoy. Immediately (X447 ff.) the wailing of the Trojans reveals what has happened. It must have been a wish to make his audience sympathize with Andromache that made the poet break for once his *tabu* on θρόνα.

(Bolling 1958, 281)

As with Euripides' pavilion, the precise content of the weaving design was almost certainly made up by the poet to gain a particular artistic effect. But in neither case would the scene have worked if the idea of figured weaving hadn't been thoroughly familiar to both singer and listener. The scene with Helen in the *Iliad* provides yet another example. Helen, we are told, is busy weaving the battles between Greeks and Trojans when the divine messenger Iris comes, in the form of one of Priam's daughters, expressly to tell her that battling is not what is going on outside. She should stop weaving and go out on the wall to see for herself that now everyone is sitting and waiting for a single combat between Helen's two husbands, Paris and Menelaos (*Il.* 3.121–38). Is the single combat, then, to be the next frieze-scene in Helen's "tapestry"? Is she weaving a chronicle? That is certainly what Aristarchus, an Alexandrian scholar of the 2nd century B.C., believed when he wrote that "from this cloth divine Homer took most of his story of the Trojan war" (scholia on *Il.* 3.125; cf. Perry 1898, 175, 240).

Among illiterate and proto-literate cultures of the world, it is not unusual for the history of the clan or social group to be carefully recorded in a series of images, often more mnemonic than explicit, each of which encapsulates the most important event of a period of time. The Dakota Indians, for example, recorded the passage of each year in this way, painting the chosen mnemonic device sequentially onto a precious buffalo robe (see K. Davis 1974 for color photo and references).

The Mycenaeans, of course, were not totally illiterate: they had their linear script for accounts. But its ill-suitedness to the language presented large numbers of potential ambiguities to the reader, and hence the script was best confined—as apparently happened—to the making of records of severely limited vocabulary and content that would be read chiefly by the person who wrote them and read only soon after being written. Certainly literacy was so restricted that it died out quickly in the upheavals that ushered in the Iron Age and the "dark age," in the 12th century B.C. If true literacy was confined, then, largely to economic accounts, it does not seem unnatural for the Mycenaean and sub-Mycenaean Greeks to have found some other mnemonic device for jogging their memories with respect to their clan histories. After all, what was more important to an Indo-European than his *kleos*, or renown? Brunhilde weaving Siegfried's exploits in the *Niebelungenlied*, the great Viking tapestries of the Oseberg funeral ship (Krafft 1956), and the battle of William the Conqueror and King Harold on the Bayeux Tapestry (ironically, an embroidery!) are all witnesses to how Indo-European women of different times and cultures have taken up textile techniques to perpetuate the fame and history of their clan.

Even if we don't wish to go so far yet as to postulate actual history on the textiles—Helen's woven warriors as well as Athena's charioteers may have been generalized rather than specific—we need not shy from the idea of ritual textiles full of important iconography. Folk textiles the world over are replete with designs symbolizing fertility, protection, power, lineage, blessings, curses, magic, and the future, as well as the past. Recently I accidentally happened upon a picture of an Indonesian textile that reminded me so strongly of Geometric Greek vases that I pursued its origin. It turned out to belong to a class of ritual textiles from Sumatra (Fig. 16.12; compare Fig. 16.13), made in float technique (with overshot supplementary weft). These cloths, which are of various shapes and sizes, are used during important "life-crisis ceremonies," such as marriage, childbirth, and death:

The *tampan* [ritual cloths] identified the nexus of ritual concern and by their very presence delineated a ritual sphere. . . . The bride sits on one . . . during specific times in the wedding ceremony. . . . In the south [of Sumatra] the handles of the funeral bier were wrapped with *tampan*, and on the Krui coast the head of the deceased person rested on one . . . while the body was washed. The *tampan* even entered house-consecration ceremonies, for one was tied to the ridge pole during the ritual and stayed there for the life of the house. . . . These textiles became ritual markers, serving to differentiate ceremonial occasions from everyday routine.

(Kahlenberg 1977, 28)

16.12 *Tampan* (ceremonial cloth) from Indonesia, South Sumatra: a so-called ship cloth, woven in supplementary-weft technique; late 19th to early 20th century A.D. (Courtesy of the Los Angeles County Museum of Art; Costume Council Fund)

16.13 *Prothesis* scene from an Attic Geometric funeral pitcher. Compare the triangular shoulders and chevron- and diamond-shaped fillers with the ship cloth, Fig. 16.12. (Photo courtesy of Trustees of the British Museum; no. 1912.5-22.1)

Anyone, it seems, could have and use a *tampan*, whereas "only the senior representatives of the patrilineal descent groups" could use the variants called *palepai* and *tatibin*, which differed in shape rather than in subject matter. The *palepai* was hung as a "backdrop to the principal person" in each ceremony—wedding, funeral, naming the newborn, etc. The designs on some are of "ships carrying trees, shrines, and people . . . , while in others a simple geometric shape is repeated in narrow studied rows. Still other compositions are so literal they seem to be a graphic rendering of a story or myth. . . ." Lately, the making of these cloths has died out to such an extent that the cloths given as "gifts" at these ceremonies are later quietly returned for future "giving," and the significance of the designs is no longer entirely understood (ibid.).

The nearby Batak tribes are more active in the use and manufacture of their forms of ritual cloths. Their *ragidup*, while not pictorial, is particularly interesting because the numerous registers of ancient geometric de-

signs on its end panels are considered to represent the life and fortune of the person for whom it was made, and are used to foretell that person's life (Gittinger 1975, 18–22). Indeed, the woven piece, created by women over a period of time on a peculiar circular warp, is considered a direct metaphor for time and for what a lifetime produces, i.e., the cycle of a new generation—hence fertility and creation (ibid., 22–23). The most important *ragidup* is that given to a girl pregnant for the first time: it is her "soul cloth" and the "guardian of her well being," which she carefully preserves, and "its inherent revitalizing and protective powers are sought in the time of childbirth . . . and in cases of her or her child's illness" (ibid., 23). In fact, her whole family is felt to draw strength in time of crisis from this cloth. It has been bestowed on her by her own (female/child-bearing/creating/weaving) side of the family—the man's side of the family never bestows textiles in the gift-exchanges (ibid., 22–25). In such a crisis as the death of an elder, dozens of ritual textiles are bestowed by the woman's family, to shore up the sagging "vital force" (a fundamental concept of this culture) with generative power; and "one of these, a *ragidup*, finally covers the body in burial" (ibid., 24).

Such birth-to-death uses of textiles are not uncommon around the world. There is no guarantee, of course, that the Aegean attitude toward textiles was identical to the Indonesian; in fact, it is virtually certain that they differed. But the Indonesian example gives us some highly useful ideas of what kinds of attitudes can develop. The idea of magical power over life and death being housed in an independent object is certainly not foreign to the Greek world. Just the same sort of thinking occurs in such stories as that of Meleagros, whose mother Althaia carefully preserved a stick of firewood that was said to contain somehow her son's life-powers or life-span. When she became angry with him, the story goes, she hurled it onto the fire, and as it was consumed he died.

In Batak lore, the cloth obtains its symbolic power for creation and fertility because "in the very process of weaving the woman creates a new object—a united whole—from seemingly disparate elements" (Gittinger 1975, 22–23). Again we see a not-unsimilar metaphor, differently worked out, in the Indo-European myth of the Fates (Gmc. *Norns*, Lat. *Parcae*, Gk. *Moirai*), who create a person's life-thread out of a pile of amorphous fluff as they spin. The frequent portrayal of Aphrodite as a celestial spinner, a female creating something—whether thread or new life—out of next to nothing, draws from the same idea (cf. Suhr 1969). Let us ponder again a naive onlooker's description, alluded to in Chapter 2, of an African woman spinning goat hair on a grass stalk: "she

twisted some hair round it and continued to twist, while a thread *as if by magic* grew out of the mass of hair continually fed into it" (Crowfoot 1931, 11; emphasis mine).

It seems that the creation of thread symbolized the creation of life and a life-span in Greek mytho-explanatory thought. The weaving metaphors, however, are reserved for how one works out the details of what happens in that life: "But come, weave a plan . . . ," says Athena (*Od.* 13.386); "weave a trick," says her devotee Odysseus (*Od.* 5.386); "weaving a plan," says Penelope (*Od.* 4.739). Is this metaphor yet another indicator of a then-common cultural use of textiles—to designate somehow what happened, or will happen, or should happen, in the owner's life?[11]

Gradually we are picking up a consistent set of clues as to why so many queens in Greek mytho-history are carrying out the wearisome task of weaving. The maids and the slaves undoubtedly wove the masses of sheets, towels, blankets, tunics, cloaks, and dresses for the household. Some of them, if the owners were lucky, were even skilled enough to weave ornamented ones for fancier occasions, for trade, and for gift-giving (cf. Wace 1948, 51). But the queen (and princesses) may have had the special job of weaving certain iconographically important pieces, using costly materials such as Helen's purple-dyed yarns (*Od.* 4.135) plus their own relative leisure; and the iconography may have included mytho-history, as well (perhaps) as talismans and other magical or apotropaic signs. It is just conceivable that the scattered birds, hedgehogs, crickets, and other stray creatures (see Figs. 16.6–7 and 16.9) that creep into the background of so many of the monuments discussed above,

---

[11] My thanks to Kenneth Atchity for producing this idea and tossing around with me many others, over the last decade, about the role of weaving in Homer—to the place where often neither of us is sure who thought up

what. For a rather different discussion of Homer and weaving, oriented towards literary criticism and anthropology, see Atchity and Barber 1987 (written in that form just after this chapter was initially composed).

both Mycenaean and later, have some significance of this kind. I am reminded of the creatures that populate Chinese dishes and textiles: to name a few, ducks for faithfulness, herons for longevity, and the goldfish at the bottom of the bowl to insure that there will always be a wealth of food to fill the vessel. All those engaging hedgehogs must have *something* to say for themselves.

What we learn of Helen, of Andromache, and of the "little successors of the Bronze Age princesses" weaving on the Akropolis (as Simon calls them: 1983, 67)—the two young Athenian girls who were chosen to help make Athena's figured peplos—all fits together. And Penelope? Surely she is one of their company, and felt socially obliged (or excused) to spend some years weaving an iconographically important cloth for Laertes' funeral. All we need to discover now is more exactly how such a figured textile fit into a Greek funeral.

FIGURED FUNERAL CLOTHS

We have already drawn some of our visual evidence for the existence of "tapestry" from funeral monuments—the Geometric vases and the re-used Mycenaean tombstone. But there is more. Already in the late Mycenaean period we find sarcophagi made of clay and painted with funeral scenes. The most elegant and famous of these is the early one from Hagia Triada, but a whole series of others of the same general shape, very crudely painted, have been found at Tanagra in Boiotia. The most typical scenes on them show lines of mourning women, in both Native Mycenaean and Ritual Minoan dress (see Chapter 15 for these terms), lines of men or animals, fabulous or mythical scenes and figures, chariots, and even sometimes the *prothesis*—accompanied by running spirals, just as the Geometric funeral vases are accompanied by running meanders.[12] Most of the scenes are bordered with a checker pattern, echoed in the checkered funeral cloths on the Geometric vases.

At Vari in Attica, furthermore, a clay model of a funeral cart was found that dates to the early 7th century B.C. (see Karouzou 1980, 135 bottom for color photo). It consists of a four-wheeled cart carrying the bier, which is covered with an ornamented cloth. The cart is accompanied by four mourning women and a child (who has crawled up on top of the pall), and is led by a man. Kurtz and Boardman (1971, 78) tell us that on the model "the cloth is a lid, which when lifted reveals a clay figure of the dead." One is reminded of the cloth that seems to hang above the body in the funeral scenes on the Geometric vases. It would also seem to correspond to the uppermost of the two cloths laid over Patroklos during his *prothesis*:

And laying him on a bed they covered him with
  a linen sheet [λιτί]
From head to feet, and over that a pale blanket
  [φάρει]
                              Il. 18.352–53)

We might add that Greek inscriptions and laws of the 5th century B.C. restrict a funeral to two or three cloths at most: (1) a *strōma* (στρῶμα), presumably the 'spread' that covered the bier under the body; (2) an *enduma* (ἔνδυμα) or 'wrap,' presumably around the body itself; and (3) an *epiblēma* (ἐπίβλημα) or 'throw,' over the whole works (Kurtz and Boardman 1971, 200–201).

Of greatest interest, however, is that the clay "cloth" (*epiblēma*?) that covers the body

---

[12] For people and animals: Spyropoulos 1969, pl. 5, 13a, 14; Spyropoulos 1971, pl. 17, 18b; Spyropoulos 1973, pl. 11. For chariots: Ahlberg 1971, pl. 67a. For

prothesis: Spyropoulos 1969, pl. 14a; Spyropoulos 1970, pl. 48a; and perhaps Spyropoulos 1973, pl. 10b.

on the model, as well as that which covers the bier itself (*strōma*?), are both decorated with friezes of battling warriors and such. (Unfortunately, the paint is in such poor condition that one cannot discern the subject matter more exactly.) We deduce that the all-important "funeral cloth" that Penelope weaves is most likely an ostentatious cover to lay over the dead man (or possibly the bier under him, though that would seem less critical, because less visible). Perhaps that same cloth, raised to display the deceased during a phase of the *prothesis*, also served as the roof of a shade-giving pavilion—a "tapestry" pavilion like Ion's.[13]

What happened to this cloth after the body was carried to the grave or pyre? The 5th-century anti-sumptuary legislation demands that the coverlets be plain white and be brought home again (ibid.), as though neither of these things were always so. Presumably the cover cloths were often buried or burned—a form of the conspicuous consumption of wealth so common at funerals. Neither burial in Greek soil nor burning is conducive to preservation of cloths, however. We therefore can expect little archaeological trace of them, especially during the first centuries of the Iron Age, when cremations were much more common than inhumations (ibid., 36, 54, 71).

But we are lucky. The dry climate of the Crimean area has preserved for us a few pieces of textile from the burials of Greek colonists up there. In one of these (see Figs. 7.11, 16.15), laid over the sarcophagus like a flag over a veteran's coffin, lay the remains of a huge cloth decorated in black, red, and buff (like vases) with six stacked friezes of mytho-historical figures: warriors, horses and chariots, deities such as Athena and Nike, heroines such as Phaidra and Jocasta,

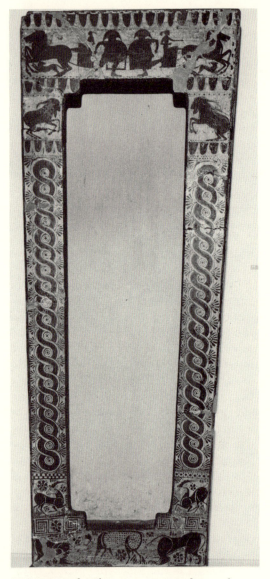

16.14 Lip of a Clazomenian sarcophagus, from the east coast of the Aegean; ca. 500 B.C. (Photo courtesy of Kestner Museum, Hannover; no. 1897.12)

[13] The Bronze Age Aegean people may have used fancy cloths as pavilion covers for themselves, in addition to selling them to the Egyptians. See Chapter 15.

and heroes like Mopsos (Stefani 1878–79; Gertsiger [1972] 1975). The date is early 4th century B.C.

The technique is neither tapestry nor supplementary weft, although from the same tomb came bits of an elegant tapestry of ducks and stag heads, woven in yellow, green, and black on a dark cherry-red ground (see Fig. 7.12; Gertsiger 1973, 78–80, 89 no. 4). The great pall is painted. But Herodotus explains to us that painting fabrics with colorfast dyes was a speciality of the east end of the Black Sea (Hdt. 1.203; see Chapter 10). Apparently we have the cheap and flashy substitute for tapestry of a social climber. Nonetheless, it demonstrates indisputably that cloths covered with mythohistory sometimes went to the grave with wealthy Greeks.

The position of the cloth draped over the top of the open coffin suggests the origin of the decoration on the Clazomenian sarcophagi (Fig. 16.14). These large and handsome clay coffins are decorated across their wide, flat top lips with just the same sorts of friezes of warriors, chariots, animals, and fillers that we have been discussing, done in the full (not stick-like) style of the East Greek pottery (Cook 1974; Cook 1981). In at least one case a complete lid has survived, and it too is covered with similar friezes of chariots, mythical animals, and warriors, surrounded by a border of meander-cross with stars—a pattern that Cook could find elsewhere almost only on representations of textiles (Cook 1981, 85, 94–95, 107 and pl. 39–46). Again one must wonder whether the painted version, however elegant, was a cheaper substitute for a time-consuming and therefore expensive cover-tapestry showing the appropriate mythical scenes needed for "proper" burial. Perhaps relative cheapness in achieving a symbolic end was the spur behind the production of the Tanagra sarcophagi, too.

And why should Mopsos, of all people, turn up on a cloth from the Crimea (Fig. 16.15, Fig. 7.11)? Scholars have scratched their heads over the inclusion of this obscure prophet from Asia Minor. Was he claimed as an ancestor by the family of the deceased? For that matter, why Phaidra and Jocasta? What dictated the choice of deities and events? We will probably never know in de-

16.15 Detail of one of the friezes from the resist-painted pall found in Kurgan 6 of the Seven Brothers, near the ancient Greek colony of Pantikapaion (now Kertch) in the Crimea (see Fig. 7.11); early 4th century B.C. Note the horses and chariot or cart (right) and the name "Mopsos" (top center). (Gertsiger 1973, fig. 3)

tail, but it seems reasonable that they were the deities, heroes, and events that held particular significance for the owner of the cloth. That the cloth was precious, and not new when laid into the tomb, is suggested by the careful mend that it contains. An heirloom, perhaps, despite the simple method of manufacture.

The Antiquity of the Tradition

Andromache's and Helen's weaving designs had particular significance for their makers. Penelope's cloth for Laertes presumably had too. Perhaps it showed his patron deity and the exploits of himself and his ancestors: a fitting tribute to a hero at his death, a eulogy on cloth. Homer seems to have imagined it thus. But have we any more evidence that such "tapestries" really go back to the age of the Trojan War—to the real Penelope and Helen? Did Homer merely extrapolate his own (8th century) experience back—and take it too far? Or did storytelling cloths of Mycenaean and later origin exist as heirlooms among highborn Attic and Ionic families and in temple treasuries—in both cases to be seen on special occasions (including funerals, at times), waiting, as it were, to rekindle the art again once circumstances permitted?

We may not wish to trust a possibly gullible Alexandrian writer concerning Helen; but the details that Penelope alternately wove and unraveled a web for a very long time would seem to be an old part of the story as Homer inherited it. Homer doesn't explain them much; he seems to assume that everyone knows the tale.

The peplos of Athena Polias, however, gives us one more clue. This garment has the advantage that it was a real object, and displayed a known subject on it. Why the Battle of Gods and Giants? Surely not just whimsy. This same subject holds the place of honor on other central pieces of Athenian art, such as the metopes on the front of the Parthenon, and before that the sculpture on the front of the pre-Persian temple.

From the story of "Demetrios the Savior" we got the impression, strengthened elsewhere, that the subject of the peplos had to do with those who had saved Athens, Athena and Zeus being foremost because of their parts in the Gigantomachies. The peplos would seem to be an offering to the goddess specifically in thanks for saving her people from the terrible threat of the Huge Ones—and a repeated reminder to her never to let them escape again.

In order to understand the original significance of this offering and what it therefore suggests about textile history, we need to understand the source of the myth so closely associated with it. Hesiod describes one of these awesome battles thus:

Terribly the boundless sea resounded all about,
And the earth roared hugely, and broad Heaven groaned,
And high Olympus shook from its very foundation
Under the rush of the immortals, and the heavy quaking reached
To murky Tartarus—the arduous pounding of feet
And of mighty bombarding, in the unspeakable uproar;
For thus they hurled their grievous missiles at each other.
The cry of both sides reached the starry heaven
As they shouted, and they rushed together with a great war-cry.
. . . The life-giving earth roared all about
As it burned, and the vast forest crackled hugely all around with fire.
And the whole land seethed, as did the stream of Ocean
And the barren sea; and the hot fumes surrounded
The earthborn Titans, and an indescribable flame

reached up to the divine Upper Air
And blinded their eyes (strong though they
were)—
A flashing beam of thunder and lightning.
And prodigious heat took hold of Chaos. And it
seemed,
To look with the eyes and to hear the sound with
one's ears,
As though earth and broad heaven above were
Coming together; for so great a crash would have
risen
From earth on the one hand being overturned,
and heaven on the other falling down from
above:
Such a crash was there from the gods coming
together in strife.
                    (*Theogony* 678–86, 693–705)

Those who have worked extensively with myths generated from catastrophe agree that this particular story is a roughly but rationally decipherable, metaphoric account of a volcanic eruption (cf. Rose 1959, 44–45), and most likely, at least in part, of the cataclysmic destruction of Thera that occurred in the 15th century B.C., which was one of the largest and loudest eruptions the human race has ever witnessed (cf. Luce 1969, 58–95, esp. 74–84). Surely this eruption above all others would call forth relief at salvation and a desire never to have to go through such cosmic terror again. Athens, after all, had had a ringside seat. Giants, Titans and such, as metaphors for and personifications of the volcanic forces, are therefore exactly appropriate symbols to commemorate such an awesome event.

The Greeks themselved placed the origins of their festival back in Mycenaean times: some parts were ascribed to Theseus and some to the earlier indigenous inhabitants, who were said to have set it up in honor of the death of a giant named Asterios ("Bright One" or "Glitterer"), although some of the games were established much later (see Da-

vison 1958, 32–35, for full references). Theseus, of course, is the main culture-hero of Athens, and as such tends to attract all "origins" to himself; but as destroyer of the power of Minos (destroyed, in fact, in the 15th century), and as one whose young son was killed on the coast near Athens by a gigantic tidal wave (metaphorically the Bull from the Sea), he has as much right as anyone to be assumed to have witnessed the destructive power of Thera. Geologically and archaeologically we know that Thera had made trouble several times shortly before its violent collapse, but was then quiet for many centuries afterwards. So we may be seeing a festival combining thanks for salvation from two successive upheavals, both no later than the Bronze Age, or perhaps Greek and non-Greek "genetic reflexes" of the same one.

Are we, then, to imagine the ruler of Athens (whether Theseus or another) desperately and solemnly vowing to Athena—as the volcano across the way was blowing its heart out in an eruption that would make Mount Saint Helens, Kilaueia, and even Krakatoa look small—that if the divine Protectress would save him and his people from this unimaginably devastating monster, he would provide her with the finest he could offer: huge sacrifices, the most expensive of new dresses, and a grand celebration and victory dance in her honor, every year in perpetuity?

Athens, unlike many an Aegean site, survived the disaster. That would have been proof enough that Athena and Zeus had cared about and saved their people. To commemorate the event symbolically in dance, in fire rituals, and through the age-old local craft of weaving—especially when Athena was the particular patroness of weaving—does not seem so strange.[14] Once again we

---

[14] The theory that this great Athenian festival goes far back into prehistory and has some of its principal origins in local vulcanism has the added advantage that it makes

sense of the peculiar features of the festival. The easy interpretation of the apparently fast and vigorous Pyrrhic Dance as originally a Fire Dance makes sense (Gk.

are led to the commemoration of mytho-history on textiles, and once again well within the Late Bronze Age. That is, for the thank-offering of a peplos figured with a giganto-machy to make sense, it must go back to that period; and the ritual must have been carried right on through the dark age, in however impoverished a form.

We have thus demonstrated the credibility of each point that, if untrue, would destroy our hypothesis that Penelope was weaving an ornate, figured "tapestry" for important ritual use at Laertes' funeral, instead of a simple shroud: that ornate, figured cloths existed and were woven in Greece; that they sometimes included mytho-historical scenes; that they were produced especially by high-born ladies; that a cloth of the suggested size and complexity would take one woman about the amount of time allotted by Homer, namely two or three years (whereas a plain shroud, within that technology, would take two or three weeks); that ornate cloth was associated with the burial rituals; that mytho-history was associated with at least some burial cloths; and that both the tradition and the capability of making friezed, figured cloth went well back into the Late Bronze Age—that is, pre-dated the destruction of Troy. Along the way we have also shown that

painted clay was an alternative—and cheaper—carrier of the iconography requisite for an elegant burial (luckily for us, since clay survives so much better than cloth); that weaving patterns were copied onto pottery in the Aegean during the Late Bronze Age and Early Iron Age; and that in Greek religious thought (as in many other cultures) a magical power over life and death could reside in an independent object such as thread or cloth, giving it the potential for particular importance at a time of danger or death.

One of the most interesting points to come out of this study, however, is the implication that heirloom "tapestries" recording the earlier mytho-history of the Greeks may have survived from Mycenaean times through the Dark Age into the Archaic Greek period when Homer lived. Such a survival might help to explain the astonishing tenacity and detailedness of some of the Greek traditions. That is, Homer and the other bards may have had considerable help in remembering the content of their epics.

Could they indeed have glanced up at the patron's palace walls and seen hanging there a graphic reminder of the episodes in their songs, among the scenes on precious heirloom "tapestries"—of Troy—Helen—and Penelope?

---

pyr- 'fire'); the several torch races (quite unusual among non-Attic Greek games: see Parke 1977) and the general association of Hephaistos with the event become understandable; and the association with the cosmic battle against Giants and/or Titans falls into place among like company.

Once again I would inveigh against underestimating the longevity of folk traditions. Parke (1977) and other classicists persist in treating all Greek ritual as no older than the oldest known reference, typically 6th century. On the contrary, it seems to me that the burden of proof is upon them to demonstrate that these traditions are so

young! I do not believe for a moment (with Davison 1958, 25–26) that the peplos ritual was probably borrowed from Hera at Olympia in the 6th century (although aspects of the ceremony may have been "modernized" from that quarter). Since both goddesses were Aegean, it is much more likely in light of our textile data that the ceremonies for dressing both go back independently to the heyday of Old European weaving—the Bronze Age or even the Neolithic. All that is new with Athena's dress, even in the 15th century, I suspect, is the subject matter on it.

Almost nothing has survived out of the enormous mass of textiles produced between 7000 B.C. (when we get our first proof of existence) and the middle of the 1st millennium B.C. (where this book stops). But the relentless pursuit of evidence has allowed us to glimpse both the quantity and the magnificence of what we have lost. Even the tiniest and humblest scraps of data were found to contribute serious information.

Careful attention to method, too, has allowed us to deduce a remarkable amount about the nature and economic importance of the industry and its products. Here, traditional academic divisions into separate disciplines broke down in the attempt to integrate and make sense of what we were handling. Archaeology, biology, linguistics, ethnology, philology, chemistry, art history, and literature each held an honored place in some part of the work.

But one thing stands out above all, beyond both the methods and the subject matter. Repeatedly we have found ourselves documenting the astonishing longevity of traditional ways of doing things—not only traditions dictated by the state of the technology, but also purely cultural constructs. Indeed, cultural habits lasting centuries or even a millennium began to pale in comparison to those of ten to twenty thousand years' duration. And textiles have clearly figured among the most long-lived.

APPENDICES

THE LOOM WEIGHTS:
DATA TABLE AND ITS BIBLIOGRAPHY
FOR CHAPTER 3

Following are the data I have collected on excavated groups of weights that may represent looms or stored sets for looms. Since stray weights occur often, I have required for an entry a minimum of 4 weights to have been found together. Note that vocabulary for weight shapes is misleadingly limited! Abbreviations for period are:

Neol. = Neolithic	Chalc. = Chalcolithic	
EN = Early Neolithic	EB = Early Bronze	
MN = Middle Neolithic	MB = Middle Bronze	
LN = Late Neolithic	LB = Late Bronze	

I have chosen this "cultural" dating system for the earlier eras to allow the table to slide as we change our views of absolute dates. These periods represent somewhat different absolute dates in different areas, with the central European phases running somewhat later than the Greek and Anatolian, but the difference is nowhere near so great by the newer calibration of carbon-14 dating as all but the most recent books indicate. In the later periods, historical dates become available. All dates of course are B.C. An asterisk (*) denotes that a drawn plan or a photo of the individual weights in situ exists.

Site	Period	No. of Weights	Shape	Weight	Loom Width
1. Tiszajenő, Hungary*	EN	8+	truncated pyramid	—	185 cm
2. Szolnok-Szanda, Hungary	EN	20+; 20+	truncated pyramid	—	—
3. Kisköre, Hungary*	EN	about 20	truncated pyramid	—	—
4. Dévaványa-Sártó, Hungary	Neol.	about 30	truncated pyramid	—	—
5. Franchthi Cave, Greece	MN	5+	sphere	100+ g	—
6a. Knossos, Crete	MN–LN	7	box	200–300 g	—
6b. Knossos, Crete	MN–LN	13	box	350–635 g	—
7. Aszód, Hungary	LN	32	truncated pyramid	—	—
8a. Robenhausen, Switzerland	LN	about 12	cone	—	40–50 cm
8b. Robenhausen, Switzerland	LN	"typ. 10–12"	cone	—	—

Site	Period	No. of Weights	Shape	Weight	Loom Width
9. Zurich/Utoquai, Switzerland*	LN	about 6	cone	—	—
10. Zurich/Rentenanstalt, Switzerland	LN	6	cone	500–1000 g	—
11. Gródek Nadbużny, Poland	LN	5; 3	cylinder; sphere	—	—
12. Salcuţa, Romania*	LN	28	cone; truncated pyramid; box; crescent	—	—
13. Slatina, Bulgaria	LN	6; 4	truncated pyramid; disc	—	—
14. Gomolava, Jugoslavia*	LN	9; 15	sphere; donut	—	120 cm
15a. Alishar, Turkey	Chalc.	9; 5	truncated egg	—	—
15b. Alishar, Turkey*	EB	18	truncated egg	—	—
16. Mersin, Turkey	EB	5+	egg	2+ lbs.	—
17. Troy, Turkey*	EB II	44 (18 + 24 + 2)	truncated egg	—	110 cm
18. Aphrodisias, Turkey*	EB II–III	10–13	truncated pyramid	—	130–140 cm
19. Myrtos, Crete	EB II	9+	sphere; disc	—	—
20. Aghia Irini, Kea, Greece	EB III	16	egg	168–211 g	—
21. Hradčany, Czechoslovakia	2nd mill.	80+	donut, pyramid	—	—
22. Megiddo, Israel	MB II	26	egg	—	—
23. Tell Beit Mirsim	MB II	12+	egg	—	—
24. Jericho, Israel	MB	"large number"	—	—	—
25a. Gezer, Israel	MB–LB	30	truncated egg	—	—
25b. Gezer, Israel	LB	25; 7	sphere	—	—
26a. Knossos, Crete	MB III–LB I	ca. 55	sphere	130–800 g	—
26b. Knossos, Crete	MB III?	400+	"flat"	—	—
27. Arkhanes, Crete	MB III–LB I	22; 25	sphere +	—	—
28. Kythera, Greece	LB I	6+	disc	ca. 140 g	—
29a. Thera, Greece	LB I	ca. 30	disc	—	—
29b. Thera, Greece	LBI	130; 65	disc	—	—
29c. Thera, Greece	LBI	"hundreds"	disc	80–275 g	—
30. Palaikastro, Crete	LB I–II	71; big hoard	cube; sphere	—	—
31. Enkomi, Cyprus*	LB	6+; 5; 4; 7	cone	—	—
32. Nir David, Israel*	10th c.	"10, 20, 50"	egg?	—	—
33. Tell Qasileh, Israel	Iron Age		donut	—	—

Site	Period	No. of Weights	Shape	Weight	Loom Width
34. Beer Sheba, Israel	Iron Age		donut	—	—
35a. Alishar, Turkey	9th–8th c.	30	donut	—	—
35b. Alishar, Turkey	9th–8th c.	2 hoards	donut	—	—
36. Gordion, Turkey	690	21; 75; 130; 300; 450; 500; 800	donut	—	159 cm
37. Tell Beit Mirsim	7th c.	97+; "scores of basketfuls"	donut	—	—
38. Niemitz, Germany	4th c.	14	truncated pyramid	—	60 cm
39. Campello, Alicante, Spain	ca. 400	50	donut; drum; truncated pyramid	200–1000 g	—
40. Monte Loffa, Italy	end 1st mill.	49	—	—	—
41a. Gezer, Israel	early 1st mill.	7+	donut	—	—
41b. Gezer, Israel	Hellenistic	87	pyramid	—	—

Comments and Bibliography or Source

1. Tiszajenő, Hung.: in a heap between two posts; Selmeczi 1969, 18–19; Raczky, pers. comm. 1984
2. Szolnok-Szanda, Hung.: on house floors; Kalicz and Raczky, pers. comm. 1984
3. Kisköre, Hung.: on house floor; National Museum, Budapest
4. Dévaványa-Sártó, Hung.: Raczky, pers. comm. 1984
5. Franchthi Cave, Gr.: Carington Smith 1975, 136–38
6. Knossos, Crete: (a–b) J. D. Evans 1964, 180, 235
7. Aszód, Hung.: Kalicz, pers. comm. 1984
8. Robenhausen, Switz.: (a) Heierli 1887, 426; (b) groups in several rooms; Messikommer 1913, 71; Keller [1866] 1878, 514 and pl. 38
9. Zurich/Utoquai, Switz.: Swiss National Museum
10. Zurich/Rentenanstalt, Switz.: Swiss National Museum
11. Gródek Nadbużny, Pol.: Kowalczyk 1956, 39, 36, and pl. 2.18–20
12. Salcuţa, Rom.: other uses for some shapes? Berciu 1961, 179–81
13. Slatina, Bulg.: Petkov 1965, 50
14. Gomolava, Jug.: Tringham and Brukner, pers. comm. 1982
15. Alishar, Tk.: (a) "several nests"; von der Osten 1937, I. 42, 93 and figs. 44, 99; (b) on floor beside circular structure; von der Osten 1937, I.214, figs. 224, 279
16. Mersin, Tk.: in weaver's house; Garstang 1953, 173 and figs. 110, 112, and pl. 26
17. Troy, Tk.: lying in several parallel rows; Blegen et al. 1950, 350–53 and figs. 369, 461
18. Aphrodisias, Tk.: all pointing north; Kadish 1971, 136 and fig. 11, pl. 30 fig. 36
19. Myrtos, Crete: Warren 1972, 52–54 and fig. 21; 220–22 and fig. 96
20. Aghia Irini, Kea, Gr.: Carington Smith 1975, 233–34
21. Hradčany, Czech.: piled 7–8 deep by wall, ill-fired; Červinka 1946, 141
22. Megiddo, Isr.: Loud 1948, pl. 170 and plan 400
23. Tell Beit Mirsim, Isr.: Albright 1936–37, 56 and pl. 45.1–8
24. Jericho, Isr.: fallen from above; Kenyon 1957, 230–31
25. Gezer, Isr.: (a) together in room; (b) pile in house; some in jar; MacAlister 1912, 74–75 and fig. 268 a–c
26. Knossos, Crete: (a) on floor; stored in tub?

Catling et al. 1979, 15–16, 61–65; (*b*) in a heap; Evans 1901–2, 24

27. Arkhanes, Crete: Sakellarakis 1977, 170
28. Kythera, Gr.: Coldstream and Huxley 1973, 59–60, 207, and pl. 59
29. Thera, Gr.: (*a*) in and around jar; Marinatos 1968a, 23–24; (*b*) fallen; Marinatos 1968b, pl. 116; Marinatos 1971, 27; (*c*) fallen; Doumas and Tzakhili, pers. comm. 1983–84
30. Palaikastro, Crete: Dawkins 1903–4, 207
31. Enkomi, Cyprus: Dikaios 1971, 647, 664–65, 736–37, 756–57, and plans 251, 256
32. Nir David, Isr.: alabaster set, in rows; Levy and Edelstein 1972, 334 and pl. 24.1; Carington Smith 1975, 102
33. Tell Qasileh, Isr.: Sheffer 1981, 81
34. Beer Sheba, Isr.: lying in six rows; Carington Smith 1975, 105; Sheffer 1981, 81
35. Alishar, Tk.: von der Osten 1937, II.312 and fig. 507; 345, 450 and fig. 396
36. Gordion, Tk.: set of 21 in use; others stored; ill-fired; de Vries 1980b, 37–39; R. S. Young 1962, 165
37. Tell Beit Mirsim: loom uprights too; Albright 1941–43, 56, 62; Albright 1936–37, 56 and pl. 45.9–16
38. Niemitz, Gmy.: Jentsch 1886, 584 and fig.
39. Campello, Alicante, Sp.: in heap in closet of Iberian house; Castro-Curel, pers. comm. 1984.
40. Monte Loffa, It.: Barfield 1971, 141
41. Gezer, Isr.: MacAlister 1912, 74–75 and fig. 268 d–e

THE HOLLOW WHORLS:
LIST AND ITS BIBLIOGRAPHY
FOR CHAPTER 14

The data for the early Near Eastern sites with hollow whorls are:

Anau I–III: the entire range of shapes and designs described: Pumpelly 1908, 163–70 and pl. 42–44; seen at the Peabody Museum, Harvard (my thanks to Una MacDowell for her help).

Altyn-depe 15–7: similar to Anau, less variety: V. M. Masson 1981, 14–15.

Cheshmeh Ali: nose-cone and cupped types: courtesy of R. Dyson, M. de Schauensee, M. Voigt and the University Museum, University of Pennsylvania.

Dalma Tepe: nose-cone and cupped whorls: seen at the University Museum, Philadelphia, courtesy of M. Voigt.

Gawra XIII–XII: cupped, notched, and incised whorls (one with a four–legged horned animal) in quantity: Tobler 1950, 168 and pl. 85, 155; single whorl with "concave base" in earlier level XVI, of only 2 whorls in that level: Tobler 1950, 168 and fig. 24).

Nuzi XII–X: cupped and beveled type, "ever-present": Starr 1939, 361 and pl. 39Q.

Pisdeli Tepe: whorls "identical" to Anau I (not illustrated): Dyson and Young 1960, 26; cupped whorls: seen at the University Museum, Philadelphia, courtesy of M. Voigt.

Seh Gabi: nose-cone type "occurred in large numbers" in next to lowest strata: T. C. Young 1971, 9 and fig. 15:12–16; cupped, decorated whorls also occur later: Hamlin 1974, 276 top left.

Tall-i-Bakun B II: "concave-based whorls" (not illustrated): McCown 1942, 4; nose-cone type: Egami and Masuda 1962, fig. 21:20.

I have not found evidence of these whorls farther west during the Neolithic or Eneolithic, either in central Anatolia (Çatal Hüyük, Çatal Hüyük West, Can Hasan, Suberde), or in East Anatolia/Trans-Caucasia (Korucu Tepe, Pulur, Karaz, Kültepe/Nakhichevan, Geoy Tepe, Yanik Tepe), or in northern Mesopotamia (Hassuna, Nineveh, Shimshara, Tepe Giyan). Nor have I found them in other northeastern sites (e.g., Belt Cave, Hotu Cave, Tureng Tepe, Shah Tepe, Djeitun, Namazga); nor to the west, south, or east of Bakun (Ali Kosh, Tepe Yahyā, surveys of Baluchistan and Sistan).

But note that literature alone is somewhat misleading, for the words "hollow" or "concave" cover a wide variety of shapes. Among the sites with whorls so described, there are at least two major types that are not what we want. The whorls from Sialk (McCown 1942, 4 and fig. 1:2; Ghirshman 1938, pl. 52:1, 4), Tall-i-Gap (Egami and Sono 1962, fig. 32:1–6 and pl. 40:10–15), Djaffarabad (Dollfus 1975, 192 and fig. 54:7–9), Djowi (Le Breton 1957, fig. 18.5), and some other early sites nearby in Iran are indeed concave, but more like flaring, thin-walled cups or skirts, painted on the outside with splashy designs. They are much bigger and thinner-walled than ours, they are painted rather than incised, and they occur in very small numbers. Geographically they form a group within south-central Iran in the 6th and 5th millennia, and scholars of that area and period may find them a useful diagnostic, but they do not belong with the group we are tracking. Tepe Sabz, in the Deh Luran plain, is interesting in having both the "painted skirts" and one prick-marked hollow whorl of our type (Hole, Flannery, and Neely 1969, figs. 89a–d and 90f).

A second type occurs at Tepe Hissar, where the "miniature cup shape" mentioned by E. F. Schmidt (1937, 117) turned out to be broad and flat with a little rim, like a modern ashtray, when I inspected the whorls at the University Museum, Philadelphia (courtesy of R. Dyson and M. de Schauensee)—again utterly different from ours.

The data for the Bronze Age Anatolian and island sites are:

Ahlatlıbel: Koşay 1934, 60–69.
Alaca Höyük: hard to decipher the exact sequence from the publications, but for Early Bronze Age see esp. Koşay 1951, 150–51 and pl. 113 and 115 (but not 114, which is wrongly labelled).
Alishar: for Early Bronze see E. F. Schmidt 1932, 48 and figs. 57–58; numerous stone whorls (ibid., 50 and figs. 59–61; von der Osten 1937, 185–89 and figs. 188–90) attest clearly the presence here of another textile tradition as well. For Middle Bronze, see E. F. Schmidt 1932, 124–27 and figs. 153–56; Schmidt also found a carved bone shaft similar to the Levantine spindles of a slightly later period (see Chapter 2). For the Hittite Old Kingdom period, see E. F. Schmidt 1932, 203–6, esp. fig. 262. (It is hard to reconcile Schmidt's Alishar publications with either the Alaca material or Goldman's comparison to Tarsus. Given Schmidt's frequent complaint that spindle whorls were constantly turning up in the "wrong" strata (both too high and too low), I tend to lean on Goldman's firsthand assessment, which does reconcile most of the data—see *Tarsus* below.)

Beycesultan: Lloyd and Mellaart 1962, 277–78 and figs. F.5, F.6—see esp. level VII (Early Bronze III).
Demirci Hüyük: Bittel and Otto 1939, 27.
Gordion, Hittite cemetery: Mellink 1956, pl. 24.
Heraeum: Milojčić 1961, pl. 23:5–8, 32:6.
Poliochni: Bernabò Brea 1976, pl. 226–33, for "yellow" period. Contrast the very different whorls in other periods, in Bernabò Brea 1964.
Tarsus: Goldman 1956, 328–34 and pl. 446–50.
Thermi: Lamb 1936, 161–62 and fig. 47; for shape note esp. no. 25.

Note too that a new wave of cup-shaped whorls hits Tepe Gawra in Level VII, dated ca. 3000 B.C., after five levels of absence (Speiser 1935, 78). That may be telling us something about the source of the cupped whorls in this period—though the message is not clear.

None of these lists is exhaustive, but I hope they are representative. Much of the excavated material, especially from the north and east, is incompletely published and/or difficult to obtain in U.S. libraries, not to mention hard to ferret out of unindexed literature. For relative chronologies of the Near Eastern sites I have relied heavily on H. L. Thomas 1967, and on material kindly supplied by Mary Voigt.

My sincere thanks to the staff of the Peabody Museum, Harvard University, for allowing me to inspect and weigh the whorls that Pumpelly brought back from Anau; and to René Wyss of the Swiss National Museum, Zurich, for letting me inspect and weigh many of the Late Bronze Age Swiss whorls. In both cases the whorls range considerably in size and weight: at Anau a fairly even spread from 12 to 40 g, with a scattering on up to 90 g; and at Zurich a fairly even spread from 15 to 57g, with a scattering up to 80 g. That is, the bulk of the Anau whorls range from ½ to 1½ oz., while those from Late Bronze Switzerland range from ½ to 2 oz.—not much difference. (Ounces are a more suitable form of measurement here, since differences of 5 or 10 grams—less than ½ ounce—aren't noticeable to someone spinning heavy wool or flax). This range is suitable for spinning either flax or wool, although the low end seems light for draft-spinning long flax. There was no significant difference at Anau by level: the range and distribution for Level I and for Level III were essentially the same, and although the whorls known for certain to have come from Level II were all about 40 grams, there were only three of them—not much of a sample.

AEGEAN REPRESENTATIONS OF CLOTH: LIST AND ITS BIBLIOGRAPHY FOR CHAPTER 15

To avoid excessive references in the text, I present here, in one convenient spot, a set of bibliographical references for the chief Aegean monuments discussed in Chapter 15. (I have tried to choose the clearest pictures, rather than always the original publication; and I have included color photos where I know of them and where color is useful.) For brevity, I use two abbreviations: *KnFA* for Evans, Cameron, and Hood 1967 (*Knossos Fresco Atlas and Catalogue*), and *PM* I–IV for Evans's *Palace of Minos* (Vol. 1—1921; Vol. 2—1928; Vol. 3—1930; Vol. 4—1935).

Pre-Classical Minoan:

Petsofá figurines: Myres 1902–3, pl. 8; Sapouna-Sakellaraki 1971, figs. 1–2; Marinatos and Hirmer 1960, pl. 15

bowl and fruitstand, Phaistos: Gesell 1985, figs. 39–40

Classical Minoan:

Ladies in Blue: *PM* I fig. 397; *PM* II.2, fig. 457

Miniature Dress Ornaments: *PM* III, figs. 23, 25; *PM* I, fig. 400; *KnFA*, pl. E.3

Lady in Red: Cameron 1971, cover ill.

Priest King (Prince of Lilies): *PM* II.2, frontispiece

Miniature Fresco: *PM* III, pl. 16–18, figs. 28–36

fragments of men's clothing: *PM* II.2, fig. 485; *PM* III, figs. 20?, 220; *KnFA*, pl. E.2; Sapouna-Sakellaraki 1971, pl. Γ–F.

fragments of women's clothing: *PM* II.2, figs. 430–31; *PM* III, figs. 20?, 21–22, 27

Temple Repository dresses: *PM* I, fig. 364; Bossert 1937, pl. 245

Snake Ladies: *PM* I, figs. 359–61, 382; Marinatos and Hirmer 1960, pl. XXIV, 70

ivory knot, Southeast House pillar crypt: *PM* I, fig. 308

Mallia acrobat: Marinatos and Hirmer 1960, pl. 69

Tylissos figurine: *PM* III, fig. 293

Phylakopí person(s) with fishnet: Atkinson et al. 1904, fig. 61; *PM* III, fig. 26

Pseira ladies: Seager 1910, pl. 5; *PM* II.2, fig. 458

Nirou Khani knots: Xanthoudides 1922, fig. 9; *PM* II.1, fig. 168

Hagia Triada dancer: Halbherr 1903, pl. 10; *PM* II.2, fig. 459a; Rodenwaldt 1919, fig. 11

miscellaneous female figurines: *PM* IV, figs. 14–17, 149–50, suppl. pl. 44

Thera, Priestess: Marinatos 1972, pl. J–K, 100–101

Thera, Dressing Ladies: Marinatos 1972, pl. F–H, 96–97

Thera, *ikria*: Shaw 1982; Marinatos 1972, pl. I, 98

Thera, Maritime Fresco: Marinatos 1974, fig. 5, endplate, etc.; Doumas n.d., pl. 18, 20–21

Thera, Saffron Gatherers: Marinatos 1976, pl. A–K, 58–66

Shaft Grave knots: Schliemann 1880b, figs. 351–52; *PM* I, fig. 309

Shaft Grave daggers (hunters): Marinatos and Hirmer 1960, pl. XXXV–XXXVIII

Mycenae fragment of woman's skirt: Rodenwaldt 1919, pl. 9

Ivory Triad: Marinatos and Hirmer 1960, pl. 218–19

Transitional/Ritual:

Campstool Fresco: *PM* IV, pl. 31

La Parisienne: *PM* IV, pl. 31; *KnFA*, pl. F.1 and back cover; Marinatos and Hirmer 1960, pl. XVI

Dancing Girl: *PM* III, fig. 40; *KnFA*, pl. F.2

Bull Leapers: *PM* III, fig. 144, pl. 21; Marinatos and Hirmer 1960, pl. XVII

Cupbearer(s): *PM* II.2, pl. 12, figs. 452, 456e; *PM* III, fig. 194; Marinatos and Hirmer 1960, pl. XV

Procession Fresco: *PM* II.2, suppl. pl. 25–27, fig. 456a–d; Sapouna-Sakellaraki 1971, pl. B, 41

Captain of the Blacks: *PM* II.2, pl. 13

Hagia Triada sarcophagus: Paribeni 1908; Long 1974; Marinatos and Hirmer 1960, pl. XXVII–XXX

Thebes procession of women: Reusch 1956

Mycenae, Ramp House fresco dump: Lamb 1919–21, pl. 7–8

Tiny Toreador, Pylos: M. L. Lang 1969, pl. 124 (36H105)

Pylos women: M. L. Lang 1969, pl. 119, 121, 127–28, M–O, etc.

Tiryns procession of women: Marinatos and Hirmer 1960, pl. XI, 226; Rodenwaldt 1912, figs. 27–39

Tiryns idols: Iakovides 1983, pl. 14–15

Mycenae, limestone plaque: Tsountas and Manatt [1897] 1969, pl. 20; *PM* III, fig. 88

Mycenae, lady with sacred knot: Rodenwaldt 1921, fig. 26

Mycenae, New Lady: Warren 1975, 123 right

Mycenae, Citadel House ladies: Taylour 1969, fig. 2; French 1981, figs. 12–14

Mycenae, painted *ikria*: Shaw 1980

Voula pottery sock and sandal: Marinatos and Hirmer 1960, pl. 236

Tanagra *larnakes*: Warren 1975, 132; Spyropoulos 1969, pl. 5a

Native Mycenaean:

Tiryns, women in chariots: Rodenwaldt 1912, fig. 40, pl. 12

Tiryns, frescoes of men: Rodenwaldt 1912, pl. 1, 11

Pylos, frescoes of men: M. L. Lang 1969, pl. 119–26, 129, M–N, etc.

Mycenae, Citadel House ladies: Taylour 1969, fig. 2; Warren 1975, 131 left; French 1981, figs. 12–14

Mycenae idol: Warren 1975, 131 right

Warrior Vase: Marinatos and Hirmer 1960, pl. 232–33

Mycenae, re-used stele: Bossert 1937, pl. 45

chariot craters: Karageorghis 1976, pl. 121, 123, 127–29

Phylakopí idol: C. Renfrew 1985, fig. 6.4

miscellaneous idols: Gesell 1985, fig. 46

Minoan glyptic art, of course, is full of evidence for the forms of Minoan dress (e.g., *PM* I, fig. 500), but its scale is so small that it cannot give us details about the textiles themselves.

EGYPTIAN TOMBS WITH AEGEAN DATA: LIST AND ITS BIBLIOGRAPHY FOR CHAPTER 15

To avoid excessive references in the text, and to make the bibliography as convenient as possible to those interested in pursuing these matters, I append here a list of the sources I used for all tombs cited in Chapter 15 as having probable Aegean connections. The Theban ones are listed in order of their tomb numbers (as given by Gardiner and Weigall 1913 and Bruyère 1933) for easy reference; the page and plate references in parentheses are specifically for the ceilings. The reader is hereby directed to these sources for all tombs in Chapter 15 that are not separately noted:

Amarna 49 Ay: Davies 1908 (pl. 23)
Assiut 1 Hepzefa: W. S. Smith 1965 (pl. 167); Shaw 1970
Meir B.4 Ukhhotep: Blackman 1915 (door: 15 and pl. 9, 28)
Qau 18 Wahka II (or B): Petrie 1930 (pl. 1)
Th 16 Panehesy: Baud and Drioton 1932 (9 fig. 1); Jéquier 1911 (pl. 19.32)
Th 17 Nebamun: Säve-Söderbergh 1957 (30)
Th 19 Amenmose: Foucart 1935 (pl. 35)
Th 21 User: Davies 1913 (22 and pl. 20.2)
Th 39 Puyemre: Davies 1922b (pl. 29)
Th 40 Huy: Nina Davies and A. Gardiner 1926 (pl. 1)
Th 45 Dhout/Dhutemhab: Davies 1948 (pl. 9)
Th 50 Neferhotep: Davies 1933 (pl. 57); Lange and Hirmer 1968 (color pl. 45); Nina Davies 1936 (pl. 84)
Th 51 Userhet: Davies 1927 (5 and pl. 18)
Th 65 Imiseba: Porter and Moss 1960–, 1.129–32; Prisse d'Avennes 1878 (pl. 33 upper)

Th 67 Hapuseneb: Jéquier 1911 (pl. 28.43)
Th 68 Nesipanoferher: L. Borchardt 1929 (fig. 9); Jéquier 1911 (pl. 31–37)
Th 71 Senmut: H. R. Hall 1909–10; Davies 1926; Vercoutter 1956
Th 78 Haremhab: Brack and Brack 1980 (17 and pl. 53)
Th 81 Inena (An[e]na): Nina Davies 1963; Jéquier 1911 (pl. 20, 25.38)
Th 82 Amenemhet: Nina Davies and A. Gardiner 1915 (12–13 and pl. 32)
Th 86 Menkheperraseneb: Davies and Davies 1933 (2 and pl. 30.B); Vercoutter 1956
Th 87 Minnakht: L. Borchardt 1929 (fig. 8)
Th 90 Nebamun: Davies and Davies 1923 (pl. 30)
Th 93 Kenamun: Davies 1930
Th 100 Rekhmire: Davies 1943; Vercoutter 1956
Th 131 Useramon: Davies 1926; Vercoutter 1956
Th 155 Antef: Säve-Söderbergh 1957 (pl. 19)
Th 162: see Th 262, and note 15 in Chapter 15
Th 181 "two sculptors": Davies 1925 (21–22 and pl. 30)
Th 226 [name lost]: Davies and Davies 1933 (40 and pl. 30.c)
Th 251 Amenmose: Davies 1922a (51 n.1)
Th 262 [name lost]: Davies 1922a (51 and fig. 1); see note 15 in Chapter 15
Th 359 Inherkha (=Anherkhawi, Khai-inheret): Bruyère 1933 (32–35 and pl. 3–6).

Jéquier (1911) also shows spirals in the following tombs: Th 79 Menkheper (pl. 11.21), Th 85 Amenemheb (pl. 10.19), Th 92 Suemnut (pl. 18.31)—all dated to Thutmose III– Amenhotep II. Jéquier is sufficiently inaccurate that I have used him only as a last resort in my research.

To minimize typesetting difficulties, Greek and Georgian have been transliterated, Cyrillic, Japanese, and Hebrew transcribed. The systems will be clear to those who know the languages. Germanic umlauted vowels (*ä, ö, ü*) have been alphabetized according to the plain letter, and the alternate spelling *aa* has been used for *å*.

Aakerström, Aake. 1978. "Mycenean Problems." *Opuscula Atheniensia* 12: 19–86.

Aaström, Paul. 1957. *The Middle Cypriote Bronze Age* (Lund).

———. 1964. "Remains of Ancient Cloth from Cyprus." *Opuscula Atheniensia* 5: 111–14.

———. 1972. *Swedish Cyprus Expedition*, vol. 4, pt. 1D (Lund).

Abibullaev, O. A. 1959. "Raskopki kholma Kjul'-tepe bliz Nakhichevani v 1955 g." *Materialy i Issledovanija po Arkheologii SSSR* 67: 431–52.

———. 1963. "Nekotorye itogi izuchenija kholma Kjul'-tepe v Azerbajdzhane." *Sovetskaja Arkheologija* 1963 no. 3: 157–68.

———. 1965. "Ostatki zhilishch vo vtorom sloje poselenija Kjul'-tepe, okolo Nakhichevani." *Materialy i Issledovanija po Arkheologii SSSR* 125: 40–64.

Abrahams, David H., and Sidney M. Edelstein. 1964. "A New Method for the Analysis of Ancient Dyed Textiles." *American Dyestuff Reporter* 53: 19–25.

Abrahams, Ethel B. 1908. *Greek Dress* (London).

Acar, Belkis. 1975. *Kilim ve Düz Dokuma Yaygılar* (Istanbul).

Adovasio, J. M. 1975–77. "The Textile and Basketry Impressions from Jarmo." *Paleorient* 3: 223–30.

———. 1983. "Appendix: Notes on the Textile and Basketry Impressions from Jarmo." In L. S. Braidwood et al. 1983, 425–26.

Ahlberg, Gudrun. 1971. *Prothesis and Ekphora in Greek Geometric Art* (Göteborg).

Aitchison, J. M. 1963. "Homeric [anthos]." *Glotta* 41: 271–78.

Åkerström. See Aakerström.

Albright, W. F. 1936–37. *The Excavation of Tell Beit Mirsim, II: The Bronze Age. Annual of the American Schools of Oriental Research* 17.

———. 1941–43. *The Excavation of Tell Beit Mirsim. Annual of the American Schools of Oriental Research* 21–22.

———. 1960. *The Archaeology of Palestine* (Harmondsworth).

Aldred, Cyril. 1965. *Egypt to the End of the Old Kingdom* (New York).

Alexiou, Stylianos. 1960. "New Light on Minoan Dating; Early Minoan Tombs at Lebena." *Illustrated London News* 237 (Aug. 6): 255–57.

Allchin, F. R. 1969. "Early Cultivated Plants in India and Pakistan." In Ucko and Dimbleby 1969, 323–29.

Allchin, F. R., and Norman Hammond. 1978. *The Archaeology of Afghanistan* (London/New York).

Ambroz, A. K. [1966] 1967. "On the Symbolism of Russian Peasant Embroidery of Archaic Type." *Soviet Anthropology and Archaeology* 6.2: 22–36.

Amiet, Pierre. 1961. *La Glyptique mésopotamienne archaïque* (Paris).

———. 1966. *Elam* (Paris).

Amiran, Ruth B. K. 1957. "Tell el-Yahudiyeh Ware in Syria." *Israel Exploration Journal* 7: 93–97.

Anati, Emmanuel. 1960a. "La Grande Roche de Naquane." *Archives de l'Institut de Paléontologie Humaine* 31.

———. 1960b. "Prehistoric Art in the Alps." *Scientific American* 202 (Jan.): 52–60.

———. [1960] 1961. *Camonica Valley*. Translated by L. Asher (New York).

Anatolian Civilisations: Istanbul. 1983. Exh. cat. (Istanbul).

Andersson, J. G. 1923. "An Early Chinese Culture." *Bulletin of the Geological Survey of China* 5.1: 1–68.

Andreev, G. I. 1965. "Prjaslitsa s Poberezh'ja Primor'ja." *Materialy i Issledovanija po Arkheologii SSSR* 130: 186–90.

Anthes, Rudolf. 1943. "Die deutschen Grabungen auf der Westseite von Theben in den Jahren 1911 und 1913." *Mitteilungen des deutschen archäologischen Instituts, Abt. Kairo* 12: 1–66.

Ap'ak'idze, A., G. Gobejišvili, A. Kalandaze, and G. Lomt'at'ize. 1955. *Mc'xet'a I* (Tbilisi; Russian trans., 1958).

Arik, Remzi Oguz. 1937. *Les Fouilles d'Alaca Höyük, 1935* (Ankara).

Arne, T. J. 1945. *Excavations at Shah Tepe, Iran* (Stockholm).

Artamonov, M. I. 1941. "Materialy po Arkheologii Kabardino-Balkarii." *Materialy i Issledovanija po Arkheologii SSSR* 3.

———. 1965. "Frozen Tombs of the Scythians." *Scientific American* 212.5 (May): 100–109.

Askarov, Akhmadali. 1973. *Sappalitepa* (Tashkent).

———. 1977. *Drevnezemledel'cheskaja kul'tura epokhi bronzy juga Uzbekistana* (Tashkent).

Assaf, Ali Abou. 1968. "Tell-'Aschtara in Südsyrien." *Annales Archéologiques Arabes Syriennes* 18: 103–22.

Åström. See Aaström.

Atchity, Kenneth, and E.J.W. Barber. 1987. "Greek Princes and Aegean Princesses." In Atchity, ed., *Critical Essays on Homer*, pp. 15–36 (Boston).

Atkinson, Thomas D., R. C. Bosanquet, C. C. Edgar, A. J. Evans, D. G. Hogarth, D. Mackenzie, C. Smith, and B. F. Welch. 1904. *Excavations at Phylakopi in Melos* (London).

Avi-Yonah, Michael, ed. 1975. *Encyclopedia of Archaeological Excavations in the Holy Land* (London).

Äyräpää, Aarne. 1950. "Die ältesten steinzeitlichen Funde aus Finnland." *Acta Archaeologica* 21: 1–43.

Backer, Stanley. 1972. "Yarn." *Scientific American* 227 (Dec.): 46–56.

Badawy, Alexander. 1968. *A History of Egyptian Architecture* (Berkeley).

Bailey, K. C. 1932. *The Elder Pliny's Chapters on Chemical Subjects* (London).

Baity, Elizabeth C. 1942. *Man Is a Weaver* (New York).

Bar-Adon, Pessaḥ. 1971. *The Cave of the Treasure* [in Hebrew] (Jerusalem).

———. [1971] 1980. *The Cave of the Treasure.* English translation (Jerusalem).

Baranyovits, F.L.C. 1978. "Cochineal Carmine: An Ancient Dye with a Modern Role" *Endeavor* 2.2: 85–92.

Barber, E.J.W. 1975. "The Proto-Indo-European Notion of Cloth and Clothing" *Journal of Indo-European Studies* 3: 294–320.

———. 1979. "Greek Kings and Aegean Queens: A Multidisciplinary Study in Disentanglement." Paper delivered at the International Conference on the Transformation of European Culture 4000–2000 B.C.; Dubrovnik.

———. 1982. "New Kingdom Egyptian Textiles." *American Journal of Archaeology* 86: 442–45.

———. 1983. "Chinese Silk in the West before 400 B.C." Paper delivered at the Irene Emery Roundtable on Museum Textiles, Indianapolis.

Barber, Paul T. 1988. *Vampires, Burial, and Death: Folklore and Reality* (New Haven).

Barfield, Lawrence. 1971. *Northern Italy before Rome* (London).

Barker, A. F. 1936. "An Historical Introduction to the Third Method of Yarn Spinning." *Journal of the Textile Institute* 27: 98–110.

Barker, A. W. 1922. "Domestic Costumes of the Athenian Woman in the Fifth and Fourth Centuries B.C." *American Journal of Archaeology* 26: 410–25.

Baroja, Julio Caro. 1957. *España Primitiva y Romana* (Barcelona).

Barrelet, Marie-Thérèse. 1977. "Un Inventaire de Kar-Tukulti-Ninurta: textiles décorés assyriens et autres." *Revue d'Assyriologie* 71: 51–92.

Barrois, A. G. 1939. *Manuel d'archéologie biblique 1* (Paris).

Bar-Yosef, Ofer. 1985. *A Cave in the Desert: Naḥal Ḥemar* (Jerusalem).

Bass, George F. 1985. "The Ulu Burun Shipwreck." In *VII. Kazı Sonuçları Toplantısı* (Ankara), 619–35.

———. 1987. "Oldest Known Shipwreck Reveals Bronze Age Splendors." *National Geographic* 172 (Dec.): 693–733.

Bateman, Alan M. 1942. *Economic Mineral Deposits* (New York).

Battaglia, R. 1943. "La Palafitta del Lago di Ledro nel Trentino." *Memorie del Museo di Storia Naturale della Venezia Tridentina* 7.

Batto, B. F. 1974. *Studies on Women at Mari* (Baltimore).

Baud, Marcel, and Étienne Drioton. 1932. *Tombes thébaines: Nécropole de Dirâ' Abû'n-Nága: Le Tombeau de Panehsy* (Cairo).

Baumgartel, E. 1947. *The Cultures of Prehistoric Egypt.* 2 vols. (London).

Bazin, Marcel, and Christian Bromberger. 1982. *Gilan et Azarbayjan oriental: Cartes et documents ethnographiques* (Paris).

Beazley, J. D. 1956. *Attic Black-figure Vase Painters* (Oxford).

———. 1964. *The Development of Attic Black-Figure* (Berkeley).

Beck, Horace C. [1936] 1976. "The Magical Properties of Beads." *The Bead Journal* 2: 32–36.

Beckwith, John. 1954. "Textile Fragments from Classical Antiquity." *Illustrated London News* 224 (Jan. 23): 114–15.

Bedini, Alessandro. 1976. "Tomba CI." In *Civiltà del Lazio Primitivo* (Rome), 287–88.

Bejlekchi, V. S. 1978. *Rannij Eneolit Nizov'ev Pruta i Dunaja* (Moldavian SSSR).

Bellinger, Louisa. 1950. "Textile Analysis: Early Techniques in Egypt and the Near East." *The Textile Museum: Workshop Notes,* no. 2.

———. 1959a. "Craft Habits, Part I: Loom Types Suggested by Weaving Details." *The Textile Museum: Workshop Notes,* no. 19.

———. 1959b. "Craft Habits, Part II: Spinning and Fibers in Warp Yarns." *The Textile Museum: Workshop Notes,* no. 20.

———. 1961. "Repeats in Silk Weaving in the Near East." *The Textile Museum: Workshop Notes,* no. 24.

———. 1962. "Textiles from Gordion." *The Bulletin of the Needle and Bobbin Club* 46: 4–33.

———. 1963. "Basic Habits of Textile Fibers." In G. Thomson, ed., *Recent Advances in Conservation,* pp. 192–94 (London).

———. 1965. "The History of Threads: Natural Fibers and Filaments." In *Threads of History; Catalog of American Federation of Fine Arts,* 20–43.

Ben-Dor, I. 1936. "Pottery of the Middle and Late Neolithic Periods." *Annals of Archaeology and Anthropology, Liverpool* 23: 67–100.

Benson, J. L. 1970. *Horse, Bird and Man* (Amherst).

Benveniste, Emile. 1954. "Problèmes sémantiques de la reconstruction." *Word* 10: 251–64.

———. [1966] 1971. *Problems in General Semantics.* Translated by M. E. Meeks (Miami).

Bequignon, Y. 1933. "Un Nouveau Vase du peintre Sophilos." *Monuments et Mémoires de la Fondation Eugène Piot* 33: 43–66.

Berciu, D. 1961. *Contribuţii la Problemele Neoliticului în Romînia in Lumina Noilor Cercetări* (Bucharest).

———. 1967. *Romania before Burebista* (London).

Beresford, William. 1909. *Memorials of Old Staffordshire* (London).

Berlin, Brent, and Paul Kay. 1969. *Basic Color Terms: Their Universality and Evolution* (Los Angeles).

Bernabò Brea, L. 1964. *Poliochni, Città Preistorica nell'Isola di Lemnos.* Vol. 1 (Rome).

———. 1976. *Poliochni, Città Preistorica nell'Isola di Lemnos.* Vol. 2 (Rome).

Betancourt, Philip P. 1976. "The End of the Greek Bronze Age." *Antiquity* 50: 40–47.

Bieber, Margarete. 1973. "Charakter und Unterschiede der griechischen und römischen Kleidung." *Archäologischer Anzeiger* 1973: 425–47.

Biel, Jörg. 1980. "Treasure from a Celtic Tomb." *National Geographic* 157 (March): 429–38.

———. 1981. "The Late Hallstatt Chieftain's Grave at Hochdorf." *Antiquity* 55: 16–18.

———. 1987. "A Celtic Grave in Hochdorf, Germany." *Archaeology* 40.6: 22–29.

Bittel, Kurt. 1937. *Boğazköy, die Kleinfunde der Grabungen 1906–1912* (Leipzig).

Bittel, Kurt, and Heinz Otto. 1939. *Demirci-Hüyük* (Berlin).

Björck, Gudmund. 1954. "Pour le vocabulaire des tablettes 'à bannieres' de Knossos." *Eranos* 52: 271–75.

Blackman, Aylward M. 1915. *The Rock Tombs of Meir III* (London).

Blegen, Carl W. 1921. *Korakou, A Prehistoric Settlement near Corinth* (Boston and New York).

———. 1928. *Zygouries* (Cambridge, Mass.).

———. 1963. *Troy and the Trojans* (New York).

Blegen, Carl, John Caskey, Marion Rawson, and Jerome Sperling. 1950. *Troy: General Introduction: The First and Second Settlements.* Vol. 1 (Princeton).

Blegen, Elizabeth Pierce. 1935. "News Items

from Athens." *American Journal of Archaeology* 39: 131–36.

Bloesch, H., and B. Mühletaler. 1967. "Stoffreste aus spätgeometrischen Gräbern . . . von Eretria." *Antike Kunst* 10: 130–32.

Blümner, Hugo. 1877. "Denkmäler-Nachlese zur Technologie." *Archäologische Zeitung* 35: 51–55.

———. [1912] 1969. *Technologie und Terminologie der Gewerbe und Künste bei Griechen und Römern* (Hildesheim).

Boardman, John. 1964. *Greek Art* (New York).

———. 1970. "Travelling Rugs." *Antiquity* 44: 143–44.

———. 1977. "The Parthenon Frieze—Another View." In *Festschrift für Frank Brommer* (Mainz), 39–49.

———. 1983. "Symbol and Story in Geometric Art." In W. Moon 1983, 15–36.

Bocquet, Aimé. 1979. "Lake-Bottom Archaeology." *Scientific American* 240 (Feb.): 56–64.

Bökönyi, Sandor. 1969. "Archaeological Problems and Methods of Recognizing Animal Domestication." In Ucko and Dimbleby 1969, 219–29.

———. 1974. *History of Domestic Mammals in Central and Eastern Europe*. Translated by L. Halápy and R. Tringham (Budapest).

Bökönyi, Sandor, Robert J. Braidwood, and Charles A. Reed. 1973. "Earliest Animal Domestication Dated?" *Science* 182: 1161.

Bolling, George Melville. 1958. "*Poikilos* and *Throna*." *American Journal of Philology* 79: 275–82.

Bonfante, Larissa. 1975. *Etruscan Dress* (Baltimore).

———. 1985. "Etruscan Textiles." *American Journal of Archeology* 89: 325–26.

Borchardt, Jürgen. 1972. *Homerische Helme* (Mainz).

Borchardt, Ludwig. 1911. "Ausgrabungen in Tell el-Amarna 1911." *Mitteilungen der deutschen Orientgesellschaft* 46: 1–32.

———. 1929. "Die Entstehung der Teppichbemalung an altägyptischen Decken und Gewölben." *Zeitschrift für Bauwesen* 79.5: 111–15.

Bordaz, Jacques. 1968. "The Suberde Excavations." *Türk Arkeoloji Dergisi* 17.2: 43–71.

Born, W. 1941. "Textile Ornaments of Ancient Asiatic and Mediterranean Civilizations." *CIBA Review* 37 (Jan.): 1327–29.

Bosanquet, R. C. 1896–97. "Notes from the Cyclades, III: Textile Impressions on Aegean Pottery." *Annual of the British School at Athens* 3: 61–63.

———. 1901–2. "Excavations at Petras." *Annual of the British School at Athens* 8: 282–85.

———. 1902–3. "Excavations at Palaikastro II:1–4." *Annual of the British School at Athens* 9: 274–89.

———. 1904. "Some 'Late Minoan' Vases Found in Greece." *Journal of Hellenic Studies* 24: 317–29.

Bosanquet, R. C., and R. M. Dawkins. 1923. *The Unpublished Objects from the Palaikastro Excavations* (Annual of the British School at Athens, suppl. 1; London).

Bossert, Helmuth T. 1937. *Altkreta* (Berlin).

———. 1942. *Altanatolien* (Berlin).

Boulding, Elise. 1976. *The Underside of History* (Boulder).

Bowen-Jones, H., J. C. Dewdney, and W. B. Fisher, eds. 1961. *Malta, Background for Development* (Durham).

Bowyer, D. 1972. "Appendix X. Chromatography Analyses for Lipids in Clay." In Warren 1972, 330–31.

Brack, Annelies, and Artur Brack. 1980. *Das Grab des Haremhab: Theben Nr. 78* (Mainz).

Braidwood, Linda S., et al. 1983. *Prehistoric Archaeology along the Zagros Flanks* (Chicago).

Braidwood, Robert J. 1937. *Mounds in the Plain of Antioch* (Chicago).

———. 1952. "From Cave to Village." *Scientific American* 187.4 (Oct.) 61–66.

———. 1974. *Prehistoric Men*. 8th ed. (Chicago).

Braidwood, Robert J., and Linda Braidwood. 1959. *Excavations in the Plain of Antioch*. Oriental Institute Publications 61 (Chicago).

Braidwood, Robert J., and B. Howe. 1960. *Prehistoric Investigations in Iraqi Kurdistan* (Chicago).

Braidwood, Robert J., and Gordon R. Wiley. 1962. *Courses toward Urban Life* (Chicago).

Brandenstein, W. 1936. *Die erste "indogermanische" Wanderung* (Vienna).

Brandford, Joan Segal. 1978. "Appendix A: The Textiles [at Magdalenska Gora]." In Hencken 1978, 301–10.

Brandt, Karl. 1935. "Neuerkenntnisse zu vor- und frühgeschichtlichen Webstuhlen." *Prähistorische Zeitschrift* 26: 87–101.

Branigan, Keith. 1966. "Prehistoric Relations between Italy and the Aegean." *Bullettino di Pa-*

lentologia Italiana, n.s. 17: 97–109.

———. 1969. "The Genesis of the Household Goddess." *Studi Mycenei ed Egeo-Anatolici* 8.

———. 1970a. *The Foundations of Palatial Crete* (London).

———. 1970b. *The Tombs of Mesara* (London).

Breasted, James H. 1906. *Ancient Records of Egypt II* (Chicago).

Brewster, Ethel H. 1917. *Roman Craftsmen and Tradesmen of the Early Empire* (Menasha, Wis.).

Brice, W. C. 1961. *Inscriptions in the Minoan Linear Script of Class A* (Oxford).

British Museum: A Guide to the Antiquities of the Bronze Age (London, 1920).

Britnell, William J. 1977. "How Upright Was the Warp-weighted Loom?" *Antiquity* 51: 238–39.

Brjusov, A. Ja. 1951. "Svajnoje Poselenije na R. Modlone." *Materialy i Issledovanija po Arkheologii SSSR* 20: 7–76.

Brock, J. K. 1957. *Fortetsa, Early Greek Tombs near Knossos* (Cambridge).

Broholm, H. C. 1938. "Nye Fund fra den Aeldste Bronzealder." *Aarbøger* 1938: 65–85.

———. 1943–49. *Danmarks Bronzealder* (Copenhagen).

Broholm, H. C. and M. Hald. 1935. "Danske Bronzealders Dragter." *Nordiske Fortidsminder* 2.5/6 (Copenhagen): 215–347.

———. 1939. "Skrydstrupfundet." *Nordiske Fortidsminder* 3.2 (Copenhagen).

———. 1962. *Bronzealderens Dragt* (Copenhagen).

Broneer, O. 1948. "The Dorian Invasion: What Happened at Athens." *American Journal of Archaeology* 52: 111–14.

Brönsted, J. 1950. "Bronze Age Clothing Preserved in Danish Graves." *Archaeology* 3: 16–21.

Bronze Age of Serbia (Belgrade, 1972).

Broudy, Eric. 1979. *The Book of Looms* (New York).

Brown, A. C. 1980. *Ancient Italy before the Romans* (Oxford).

Brown, Judith. 1970. "A Note on the Division of Labor by Sex." *American Anthropologist* 72: 1073–78.

Brown, K. S. 1980. "Near Eastern Textile Decoration." Ph.D. thesis, University of Pennsylvania.

Brugsch, Emil. 1889. *Le Tente funéraire de la Princesse Isimkheb* (Cairo).

Bruin, Frans. 1967. "Royal Purple and the Dye Industries of the Mycenaeans and Phoenicians." In *American University of Beirut Festival Book* (Beirut), 295–325.

Brunello, Franco. 1968. *L'Arte della Tintura nella storia dell'umanita* (Vincenza).

Brunton, Guy. 1937. *Mostagedda and the Tasian Culture* (London).

Brunton, Guy, and G. Caton-Thompson. 1928. *The Badarian Civilisation and Predynastic Remains near Badari* (London).

Brunton, Guy, and R. Engelbach. 1927. *Gurob* (London).

Bruyère, Bernard. 1933. *Fouilles de Deir el Médineh, vol. 8.3 (1930)* (Cairo).

———. 1937. *Fouilles de Deir el Médineh, vol. 15 (1934–35)* (Cairo).

———. 1939. *Fouilles de Deir el Médineh, vol. 16 (1934–35)* (Cairo).

———. 1948. *Fouilles de Deir el Médineh, vol. 20 (1935–40)* (Cairo).

Buchanan, Briggs. 1981. *Early Near Eastern Seals in the Yale Babylonian Collection* (New Haven).

Buchholz, H.-G., and V. Karageorghis. 1973. *Prehistoric Greece and Cyprus* (New York).

Buck, Carl D. 1945. *A Dictionary of Selected Synonyms in the Principal Indo-European Languages* (Chicago).

Buck, Carl D., and W. Petersen. 1945. *A Reverse Index of Greek Nouns and Adjectives* (Chicago).

Buck, Peter H. 1964. *Arts and Crafts of Hawaii V: Clothing* (Honolulu).

Budge, G.A. Wallis. 1920. *An Egyptian Hieroglyphic Dictionary* (London).

Buhl, Marie-Louise. 1983. *Sūkās VII* (Copenhagen).

Bukowski, Zbigniew. 1960. "Remarks on the Function of Button-like Ornaments of the Lusatian Culture." *Arkheologia Polski* 5: [200?]–244.

———. 1977. *The Scythian Influence in the Area of Lusatian Culture* (Wrocław).

Bulleid, Arthur, and H. St. George Gray. 1911. *The Glastonbury Lake Village* (Glastonbury).

Burkett, Mary E. 1977. "An Early Date for the Origin of Felt." *Anatolian Studies* 27: 111–15.

Burlington Fine Arts Club: Catalogue of an Exhibition of Ancient Egyptian Art (London, 1922).

Burney, C. A. 1958. "Eastern Anatolia in the

Chalcolithic and Early Bronze Age." *Anatolian Studies* 8: 157–209.

———. 1962. "Excavations at Yanik Tepe, Azerbaijan, 1961." *Iraq* 24: 134–49.

Burney, C. A., and D. M. Lang. 1971. *The Peoples of the Hills: Ancient Ararat and the Caucasus* (London).

Burnham, Harold B. 1964. "The World's Oldest Textiles." *Meeting Place: Journal of the Royal Ontario Museum* 1: 105–8.

———. 1965. "Çatal Hüyük—The Textiles and Twined Fabrics." *Anatolian Studies* 15: 169–74.

Bursch, F. C. 1936. "Gravformen van het Noorden." *Oudheidkundige Mededeelingen*, n.r. 17: 53–72.

Burt, Ben. 1977. *Museum of Mankind: Discovering Other Cultures: Weaving* (London).

Burton-Brown, Theodore. 1951. *Excavations in Azerbaijan, 1948* (London).

Butterworth, E.A.S. 1966. *Some Traces of the Pre-Olympian World in Greek Literature and Myth* (Berlin).

Cadogan, Gerald. 1976. *Palaces of Minoan Crete* (London and New York).

Çambel, Halet, and Robert J. Braidwood. 1970. "An Early Farming Village in Turkey." *Scientific American* 222 (March): 50–56.

Cambridge Ancient History (Cambridge, 1970–).

Cameron, M.A.S. 1968. "Unpublished Paintings from the 'House of the Frescoes' at Knossos." *Annual of the British School at Athens* 63: 1–31.

———. 1971. "The Lady in Red; A Complementary Figure to the Ladies in Blue." *Archaeology* 24: 35–43.

Campbell Thompson, R. 1934. "An Assyrian Chemist's Vade-mecum." *Journal of the Royal Asiatic Society* 1934, 771–85.

Campbell Thompson, R., and M.E.L. Mallowan. 1933. "The British Museum Excavations at Nineveh, 1931–32." *Annals of Archaeology and Anthropology, Liverpool* 20: 71–186.

Carington Smith, Jill. 1975. "Spinning, Weaving and Textile Manufacture in Prehistoric Crete." Ph.D. thesis, University of Tasmania (Hobart).

———. 1977. "Cloth and Mat Impressions [Keos]." In John E. Coleman, *Keos I: Kephala, a Late Neolithic Settlement and Cemetery*, pp. 114–25 (Princeton).

Carroll, Diane Lee. 1965. "Patterned Textiles in Greek Art." Ph.D. thesis, University of California at Los Angeles.

———. 1973. "An Etruscan Textile in Newark." *American Journal of Archaeology* 77: 334–36.

———. 1985. "Dating the Foot-Powered Loom: The Coptic Evidence." *American Journal of Archaeology* 89: 168–73.

Carter, Howard. 1932. "Embroidery and Its Probable Evolution." *Embroidery* 1 (Dec.): 7–10.

———. 1933. *The Tomb of Tut-ankh-Amen III* (New York).

Carter, Howard, and Harry Burton. 1929. "A Bleating-Ibex Vase; and a 'Gala-Robe' . . . ." *Illustrated London News* 175 (Aug. 3): 196–97.

Carter, Howard, and A. C. Mace. 1923. *The Tomb of Tut-ankh-Amen I* (New York and London).

Carter, Howard, and Percy E. Newberry. 1904. *Catalogue général des antiquités égyptiennes: The Tomb of Thoutmosis IV* (Westminster).

Caskey, John L. 1955. "Excavations at Lerna, 1954." *Hesperia* 24: 25–49.

———. 1956. "Excavations at Lerna, 1955." *Hesperia* 25: 147–73.

Cassau, A. 1935. "Ein Feuersteindolch mit Holzgriff und Lederscheide aus Wiepenkathen, Kreis Stade." *Mannus* 27: 199–207.

Castro Curel, Zaida. 1980. "Fusayolas Ibéricas, antecedentes y empleo." *Cypsela* 3: 127–46.

———. 1983–84. "Notas Sobre la Problemática del Tejido en la Península Ibérica." *Kalathos* 3–4: 95–110.

Catling, E. A., H. W. Catling, and D. Smyth. 1979. "Knossos 1975: Middle Minoan III and Late Minoan I Houses. . . ." *Annual of the British School at Athens* 74: 1–80.

Catling, H. W., and A. Millett. 1965. "A Study in the Composition Patterns of Mycenaean Pictorial Pottery." *Annual of the British School at Athens* 60: 212–24.

Caton-Thompson, G., and E. W. Gardner. 1934. *The Desert Fayum* (London).

Cecchetti, Paola Colafrancheschi. 1972. "Decorazione dei Costumi nei Vasi Attici a Figure Nere." *Studi Miscellanei* 19.

Černý, Jaroslav. 1929. "Papyrus Salt 124 (British Museum 10055)." *Journal of Egyptian Archaeology* 15: 243–58.

Červinka, I. L. 1946. "Hradčany (okr. Prostejov)." *Vlastenecky Spolek Musejni v Olomouci: Časopis* 55: 138ff.

Chadwick, John. 1972. "The Mycenaean Documents." In McDonald and Rapp 1972, 100–116.

Chang, Kwang-Chih. 1977. *The Archaeology of Ancient China* (London).

Chantraine, Pierre. 1968–80. *Dictionnaire étymologique de la langue grecque* (Paris).

Chantre, Ernest. 1898. *Recherches archéologiques dans l'Asie occidentale: Mission en Cappadoce* (Paris).

Chaplin, Raymond E. 1969. "The Use of Nonmorphological Criteria in the Study of Animal Domestication. . . ." In Ucko and Dimbleby 1969, 231–46.

Charbonneaux, Jean, Roland Martin, and François Villard. 1971. *Archaic Greek Art* (New York).

Cheng Te-k'un. 1960. *Archaeology in China II: Shang China* (Cambridge).

Chicago Assyrian Dictionary 1956– (Chicago).

Childe, V. Gordon. 1929. *The Danube in Prehistory* (Oxford).

———. 1931. *Skara Brae, a Pictish Village in Orkney* (London).

Clark, C. R. 1944. "Egyptian Weaving in 2000 B.C." *Bulletin of the Metropolitan Museum of Art*, n.s. 3: 24–29.

Clark, E. C. 1969. "The Emergence of Textile Manufacturing Entrepreneurs in Turkey, 1804–1968." Ph.D. thesis, Princeton University.

Clark, Grahame, and Stuart Piggott. 1965. *Prehistoric Societies* (New York).

Clark, J.G.D. 1936. *The Mesolithic Settlement of Northern Europe* (Cambridge).

———. 1947. "Sheep and Swine in the Husbandry of Prehistoric Europe." *Antiquity* 21: 122–36.

———. 1952. *Prehistoric Europe, the Economic Basis* (London).

Clark, Louise. 1983. "Notes on Small Textile Frames Pictured on Greek Vases." *American Journal of Archaeology* 87: 91–96.

———. 1984. "Small Textile Frames: An Addendum." *American Journal of Archaeology* 88: 65.

Clayton, Ellis. 1939. *Identification of Dyes on Textile Fibres* (Bradford, Yorkshire).

Coffey, G. 1907. "Two Finds of Late Bronze Age Objects." *Proceedings of the Royal Irish Academy* 26: 119–24.

Coldstream, J. N., and G. L. Huxley. 1973. *Kythera* (Park Ridge, N.J.).

Cole, Sonia. 1970. *The Neolithic Revolution* (London).

Coles, John M., and Eric S. Higgs. 1969. *The Archaeology of Early Man* (London).

Colini, G. A. 1898. "Il sepolcreto di Remedello Sotto nel Bresciano e il periodo eneolitico in Italia." *Bullettino di Paletnologia Italiana* (= *Preistoria*) 24: 1–47.

Collinder, Björn. 1977. *Fenno-Ugric Vocabulary* (Hamburg).

Collingwood, Peter. 1974. *The Techniques of Sprang* (London and New York).

Collingwood, W. G. 1910. "An Exploration of the Circle on Banniside Moor, Coniston." *Cumberland and Westmoreland Antiquarian and Archaeological Society*, n.s. 10: 342–53.

Compte-Rendu de la Commission Impériale Archéologique [French/German-language edition of a portion of *Otchët Imperatorskoj Arkheologicheskoj Kommissii*, q.v.].

Comşa, Eugene. 1954. "Consideraţii cu privire la evolutia culturii Boian." *Studii şi Cercetări de Istorie Veche* 5: 361–98.

Contenau, Georges, and Roman Ghirshman. 1935. *Fouilles du Tepe-Giyan* (Paris).

Contenson, Henri de. 1971. "Tell-Ramad, A Village of Syria of the 7th and 6th Millennia B.C." *Archaeology* 24 (June): 278–85.

Cook, R. M. 1960. *Greek Painted Pottery* (London).

———. 1974. "Old Smyrna: The Clazomenian Sarcophagi." *Annual of the British School at Athens* 69: 55–60.

———. 1981. *Clazomenian Sarcophagi* (Mainz).

Čop, Bojan. 1956. "Notes d'étymologie et de grammaire hittites III." *Linguistica* 2 [= *Slavistična revija* 9]: 19–40.

Coren, Stanley, and Clare Porac. 1977. "Fifty Centuries of Right-Handedness: The Historical Record." *Science* 198: 631–32.

Corpus Vasorum Antiquorum: Robinson Collection (Cambridge, Mass., 1934–37).

Cotte, J., and C. Cotte. 1916. "Examen d'un pâte préhistorique." *Comptes Rendus de l'Académie des Sciences* 162: 762–64.

———. 1918. "Le Kermès dans l'antiquité." *Revue Archéologique* 7: 92–112.

Cranstone, B.A.L. 1969. "Animal Husbandry: The Evidence from Ethnography." In Ucko and Dimbleby 1969, 247–64.

Cross, Dorothy. 1937. *Movable Property in the Nuzi Documents* (New Haven).

Crowfoot, Elisabeth. 1960. "Appendix A: Textiles, Matting and Basketry [Jericho]." In Kenyon 1960, 519–26.

———. 1964. "Appendix G: Textiles, Matting and Basketry [Jericho]." In Kenyon 1964, 662–64.

Crowfoot, Grace M. 1931. *Methods of Hand Spinning in Egypt and the Sudan*. Bankfield Museum Notes, ser. 2, no. 12 (Halifax).

———. 1933. "A Textile from the Hood Collection of Egyptian Antiquities." *Ancient Egypt* 1933: 43–45.

———. 1936–37. "Of the Warp-weighted Loom." *Annual of the British School at Athens* 37: 36–47.

———. 1941. "The Vertical Loom in Palestine and Syria." *Palestine Exploration Quarterly* 1941: 141–51.

———. 1951. "Linen Textiles from the Cave of Ain Feshkha in the Jordan Valley." *Palestine Exploration Quarterly* 1951: 5–31.

———. 1954. "Textiles, Basketry, and Mats." In Singer, Holmyard, and Hall 1954, 413–51.

Crowfoot, Grace M., and Norman de Garis Davies. 1941. "The Tunic of Tutʻankamūn." *Journal of Egyptian Archaeology* 27: 113–30.

Crowfoot, Grace M., and H. Ling Roth. 1923. "Were the Ancient Egyptians Conversant with Tablet-Weaving?" *Annals of Archaeology and Anthropology, Liverpool* 10: 7–20.

Cuadrado Diaz, Emerito. 1961. "Die iberische Siedlung von el Cigarralejo bei Murcia." *Jahrbuch des römisch-germanischen Zentralmuseums Mainz* 8: 26–37.

Dalley, Stephanie. 1977. "Old Babylonian Trade in Textiles at Tell al Rimah." *Iraq* 39: 155–59.

———. 1980. "Old Babylonian Dowries." *Iraq* 42: 53–74.

———. 1984. *Mari and Karana* (London).

Dalman, Gustaf. 1937. *Arbeit und Sitte in Palästina 5: Webstoff, Spinnen, Weben, Kleidung* (Gutersloh).

Daremberg, Charles Victor, and Edmond Saglio. 1877–1919. *Dictionaire des antiquités grecques et romaines* (Paris).

Daressy, G. 1902. *Catalogue général des antiquités égyptiennes, 3: Fouilles de la Vallée des Rois* (Cairo).

———. 1910. "Plaquettes emaillées de Medinet-Habou." *Annales du Service des Antiquités de l'Égypte* 11: 49–63.

Davidson, Gladys R. 1952. *Corinth 12: The Minor Objects* (Princeton).

Davidson, Gladys R., and Dorothy B. Thompson. 1943. *Small Objects from the Pnyx: I. Hesperia*, suppl. 7 (Baltimore).

Davies, Nina. 1936. *Ancient Egyptian Painting*. Vol. 3 (Chicago).

———. 1963. *Private Tombs at Thebes, 4: Scenes from Some Theban Tombs* (Oxford).

Davies, Nina, and Alan Gardiner. 1915. *The Tomb of Amenemhēt* (London).

———. 1926. *The Tomb of Huy* (London).

Davies, Norman de Garis. 1901. *Rock Tombs of Sheikh Saïd* (London).

———. 1903. *The Rock Tombs of El Amarna*. Vol. 1 (London).

———. 1905. *The Rock Tombs of El Amarna*. Vol. 2 (London).

———. 1908. *The Rock Tombs of El Amarna*. Vol. 6 (London).

———. 1913. *Five Theban Tombs*. Archaeological Survey of Egypt Memoir 21 (London).

———. 1913–14. "A Foreign Type from a Theban Tomb." *Annals of Archaeology and Anthropology, Liverpool* 6: 84–86.

———. 1917. *The Tomb of Nakht at Thebes* (New York).

———. 1920. *The Tomb of Antefoker . . .* (London).

———. 1922a. "The Egyptian Expedition 1921–1922: The Graphic Work of the Expedition." *Bulletin of the Metropolitan Museum of Art* 17 (Dec.): pt. 2, 50–56.

———. 1922b. *The Tomb of Puyemrê at Thebes* (New York).

———. 1925. *The Tomb of Two Sculptors at Thebes* (New York).

———. 1926. "The Egyptian Expedition 1924–1925: The Graphic Work of the Expedition." *Bulletin of Metropolitan Museum of Art* 21 (March): pt. 2, 41–45.

———. 1927. *Two Ramesside Tombs at Thebes* (New York).

———. 1929. "The Townhouse in Ancient Egypt." *Metropolitan Museum Studies* 1.2: 233–55.

———. 1930. *The Tomb of Ken-amūn at Thebes* (New York).

———. 1933. *The Tomb of Nefer-hotep at Thebes* (New York).

———. 1941. *The Tomb of the Vizier Ramose* (London).

———. 1943. *The Tomb of Rekhmirê* (New York).

———. 1948. *Seven Private Tombs at Ḳurnah* (London).

Davies, Norman de Garis, and Nina Davies. 1923. *The Tombs of Two Officials of Tuthmosis the Fourth* (London).

———. 1933. *The Tomb of Menkheperrasonb, Amenmosĕ, and Another* (London).

Davies, Oliver. 1950. *Excavations at Island MacHugh* (Belfast).

Davis, Jack L. 1984. "Cultural Innovation and the Minoan Thalassocracy at Ayia Irini, Keos." In Hägg and Marinatos 1984, 159–66.

Davis, Kingsley, 1974. "The Migrations of Human Populations." *Scientific American* 231 (Sept.): 92–105.

Davison, J. A. 1958. "Notes on the Panathenaia." *Journal of Hellenic Studies* 78: 23–42.

Dawkins, R. M. 1903–4. "Excavations at Palaikastro, III." *Annual of the British School at Athens* 10: 192–226.

Degen, B. E. 1941. "Kurgany v Kabardinskom Parke g. Nal'chika." In Artamonov 1941, 213–316.

De Góngora y Martinez, M. 1868. *Antigüedades prehistóricas de Andalucía* (Madrid).

De Jonghe, Daniel. 1985. "Linnen doeken en mummiewindsels van het Oude en het Middenrijk." *Bulletin des Musées Royales d'Art et d'Histoire* 56: 5–33.

Delougaz, Pinhas. 1952. *Pottery from the Diyala Region*. Oriental Institute Publications 63 (Chicago).

Delougaz, Pinhas, and Helene Kantor. 1972. "New Evidence for the Prehistoric and Proto-literate . . . of Khuzestan." *Vth International Congress of Iranian Art and Archaeology* (Tehran): 14–33.

Demakopoulou, K. 1971. "A Mycenaean Pictorial Vase of the Fifteenth Century B.C. from Laconia." *Annual of the British School at Athens* 66: 95–100.

Deubner, L. A. 1932. *Attische Feste* (Berlin).

Dever, William G. 1970. "The 'Middle-Bronze I' Period in Syria and Palestine" In James A. Sanders, ed., *Near Eastern Archaeology in the 20th Century*, pp. 132–63 (Garden City, N.Y.).

Devlet, M. A. 1971. "Arkheologicheskie Raskopki v Todzhe v 1970 g." *Uchënye Zapiski Tuvinskoj ASSR, Kyzyl* 15: 250–63.

De Vries, Keith, ed. 1980a. *From Athens to Gordion: The Papers of a Memorial Symposium for Rodney S. Young* (Philadelphia).

———. 1980b. "The Greeks and Phrygians in the Early Iron Age." In de Vries 1980a, 33–49.

Dietrich, B. C. 1975. "The Dorian Hyacinthia: A Survival from the Bronze Age." *Kadmos* 14: 133–42.

Dikaios, Porphyrios. 1940. "The Excavations at Vounous-Bellapais in Cyprus, 1931–2." *Archaeologia* 88: 1–174.

———. 1953. *Khirokitia* (Oxford).

———. 1969a. *Enkomi: Excavations 1948–58*. Vol. 1 (Mainz).

———. 1969b. *Enkomi: Excavations 1948–58*. Vol. 3 (Mainz).

———. 1971. *Enkomi: Excavations 1948–58*. Vol. 2 (Mainz).

Dimand, M. 1924. *Die Ornamentik der ägyptischen Wollwirkereien* (Leipzig).

Dollfus, G. 1975. "Les Fouilles à Djaffarabad de 1972 à 1974: Djaffarabad, périodes I et II." *Délégation Archéologique Française en Iran* 5: 11–222.

Dolukhanov, Paul M. 1979. *Ecology and Economy in Neolithic Eastern Europe* (London).

Dörpfeld, W. 1902. *Troja und Ilion* (Athens).

Dossin, Georges. 1939. "Les Archives économiques du palais de Mari." *Syria* 20: 97–113.

Dothan, Trude K. 1963. "Spinning Bowls." *Israel Exploration Journal* 13: 97–112.

———. 1979. *Excavations at the Cemetery of Deir El-Balah. Qedem* 10 (Jerusalem).

———. 1982a. "A Lost Outpost of Ancient Egypt." *National Geographic* 162 (Dec.): 739–69.

———. 1982b. *The Philistines and Their Material Culture* (New Haven).

Doumas, Christos. N.d. *Santorini: The Prehistoric City of Akroteri* (Athens [ca. 1980]).

———. 1983. *Thera, Pompeii of the Ancient Aegean* (New York).

Douskos, Iris. 1980. "The Crocuses of Santorini." In Christos Doumas, ed., *Thera and the Aegean World, II*, pp. 141–46 (London).

Dragomir, Ion T. 1983. *Eneoliticul din sud-estul României* (Bucharest).

Driessen, J. 1984. "Some Military Aspects of the Aegean in the Late XV and Early XIV Centuries B.C.: I." *Annual of the British School at Athens* 79: 49–56.

Duerst, J. Ulrich. 1908. "Animal Remains from the Excavations at Anau." In Pumpelly 1908, 339–442.

Duhoux, Yves. 1974. "Idéogrammes textiles du

Linéaire B: *146, *160, *165 et *166." *Minos* 15: 116–32.

Du Mesnil du Buisson, Comte. 1927. "Les ruines d'el Mishrife (l'ancienne Qatna): 2e campagne de fouilles." *Syria* 8: 277ff.

Dumitrescu, V. 1961. *Necropola de Incinerație din Epoca Bronzului de la Cîrna* (Bucharest).

———. 1965. "Principalele rezultate ale primelor două companii . . . de la Căscioarele." *Studii și Cercetări de Istorie Veche* 16: 215–37.

Durrant, A. 1976. "Flax." In N. W. Simmonds, ed., *Evolution of Crop Plants*, pp. 190–93. (London and New York).

Dyson, Robert H., Jr. 1964. "Sciences Meet in Ancient Hasanlu." *Natural History* 73.8: 16–25.

———. 1969. "A Decade in Iran." *Expedition* 11 (Winter): 39–47.

Dyson, Robert H., Jr., and T. Cuyler Young, Jr. 1960. "The Solduz Valley, Iran: Pisdeli Tepe." *Antiquity* 34: 19–28.

Eakle, James K. 1950. "Purple as a Divine and Royal Attribute in Ancient Times." M.A. thesis, University of California at Berkeley.

Edgar, M.C.C. 1911. *Catalogue général des antiquités égyptiennes du musée du Caire 56: Greek Vases* (Cairo).

Edgerton, William F. 1933. *The Thutmosid Succession* (Chicago).

Edwards, Michael. 1983. *Excavations in Azerbaijan (N-W Iran) 1: Haftavan, Period VI* (Oxford).

Efimenko, P. P. 1958. *Kostenki I* (Moscow and Leningrad).

Egami, Namio, Shinji Fukai, and Seiichi Masuda. 1966. *Dailaman II: The Excavations at Noruzmahale and Khoramrud* (Tokyo).

Egami, Namio, and Seiichi Masuda. 1962. *Marv-Dasht I: The Excavations at Tall-i-Bakun* (Tokyo).

Egami, Namio, and Toshihiko Sono. 1962. *Marv-Dasht II: The Excavation at Tall-i-Gap in 1959* (Tokyo).

Ellis, Richard. 1981. "Appendix V: [Gordion] Textiles." In Rodney S. Young, *Gordion Excavations: Final Reports I*, pp. 294–310 (Philadelphia).

Ember, M. 1952. "Die Textilabdrücke auf den Toszeger Gefässen." *Acta Archaeologica* 2: 139–42.

Emery, Irene. 1966. *The Primary Structures of Fabrics* (Washington, D.C.).

Emery, Walter B. 1949. *Excavations at Saqqara: Great Tombs of the First Dynasty* (Cairo).

Engelbach, R. 1924. *A Supplement to the Topographical Catalogue of the Private Tombs of Thebes* (Cairo).

Erman, Adolf. 1955. *Wörterbuch der ägyptischen Sprache I* (Berlin).

Errera, I. 1916. *Collection d'anciennes étoffes égyptiennes* (Brussels).

Etienne, Mona. 1977. "Women and Men, Cloth and Colonization." *Cahiers d'études africaines* 18: 41–64.

Evans, Sir Arthur J. 1901–2. "Knossos Excavations, 1902." *Annual of the British School at Athens* 8: 1–124.

———. 1902–3. "The Palace of Knossos." *Annual of the British School at Athens* 9: 1–153.

———. 1909–52. *Scripta Minoa* (Oxford).

———. 1921. *The Palace of Minos*. Vol. 1 (London).

———. 1928. *The Palace of Minos*. Vol. 2 (London).

———. 1930. *The Palace of Minos*. Vol. 3 (London).

———. 1935. *The Palace of Minos*. Vol. 4 (London).

Evans, Sir Arthur J., Mark Cameron, and Sinclair Hood. 1967. *Knossos Fresco Atlas and Catalogue* (Farnborough).

Evans, J. D. 1964. "Excavations in the Neolithic Settlement of Knossos, 1957–60, Part I." *Annual of the British School at Athens* 59: 132–240.

Evans, J. D., and Colin Renfrew. 1968. *Excavations at Saliagos near Antiparos. Annual of the British School at Athens*. suppl. 5 (Oxford).

Evans, Lady Maria M. 1893. *Chapters on Greek Dress* (London).

Evans, Robert K. 1974. "Craft Specialization in the East Balkans in the Chalcolithic." Ph.D. thesis, University of California at Los Angeles.

Fannin, Allen. 1970. *Handspinning: Art and Technique* (New York).

Farina, Giulio. 1929. *La Pittura Egiziana* (Milan).

Faure, P. 1968. "Toponymes creto-myceniens dans une liste de Amenophis III." *Kadmos* 16: 138–49.

Faxon, Harriet. 1932. "A Model of an Ancient Greek Loom." *Bulletin of the Metropolitan Museum of Art* 27: 70–71.

Firth, Cecil M., and Battiscombe Gunn. 1926.

Excavations at Saqqara: Teti Pyramid Cemeteries I (Cairo).

Fitzgerald, Gerald M. 1931. *Beth Shan Excavations III* (Philadelphia).

Flannery, K. V. 1965. "The Ecology of Early Food Production in Mesopotamia." *Science* 147: 1247–56.

Flattery, David S., and Martin Schwartz. 1988. *Haoma and Harmaline* (Berkeley).

Fogelberg, Julie M., and Arthur Kendall. 1937. "Chalcolithic Textile Fragments." In Von der Osten 1937, 3:334–35.

Folsom, Robert S. 1968. *Handbook of Greek Pottery* (Greenwich, Conn.).

Forbes, R. J. 1956. *Studies in Ancient Technology IV* (Leiden).

Formozov, A. A. 1965. *Kamennyj Vek i Eneolit Prikuban'ja* (Moscow).

Fořtová-Šámalová, Pavla. 1952. "The Egyptian Ornament." *Archiv Orientální* 20: 231–49.

Fossey, John M. 1981. *Khostia 1980* (Montreal).

Foster, Ellen D. 1976. "The Flax Impost at Pylos and Mycenaean Landholding." *Minos* 17: 67–121.

Foucart, George. 1935. *Tombes thébaines: Nécropole de Dirâʿ Abû'n-Nága: Le Tombeau d'Amonmos* (Cairo).

Fouqué, F. 1879. *Santorin et ses éruptions* (Paris).

Frankfort, Henri. 1929. *The Mural Paintings of El-ʿAmarneh* (London).

———. 1936–37. "Notes on the Cretan Griffin." *Annual of the British School at Athens* 37: 106–22.

Frankfort, Henri, and H. A. Frankfort. 1949. "Myth and Reality." In Henri Frankfort, Mrs. H. A. Frankfort, John A. Wilson, and Thorkild Jacobsen, *Before Philosophy*, pp. 11–36 (Baltimore).

Frankfort, Henri, and J.D.S. Pendlebury. 1933. *The City of Akhenaten II* (London).

Franz, Leonard. 1927. "Eine niederösterreichische Urnenzeichnung." *IPEK: Jahrbuch für prähistorische und ethnographische Kunst* 3: 96ff.

French, Elizabeth. 1981. "Cult Places at Mycenae." In Hägg and Marinatos 1981, 41–48.

Friedl, Ernestine. 1975. *Women and Men: An Anthropological View* (New York).

Friedrich, Johannes. 1952. *Hethitisches Wörterbuch* (Heidelberg).

Frisk, Hjalmar. 1960–72. *Griechisches etymologisches Wörterbuch* (Heidelberg).

From the Lands of the Scythians. Exh. cat. (New York, 1975).

Furry, Margaret S., and Bess M. Viemont. 1935. *Home Dyeing with Natural Dyes* (Washington, D.C.).

Furtwängler, Adolf. 1904. *Griechische Vasenmalerei.* Vol. 1 (Munich).

———. 1932. *Griechische Vasenmalerei.* Vol. 3 (Munich).

Furumark, Arne. 1941a. *The Chronology of Mycenaean Pottery* (Stockholm).

———. 1941b. *Mycenaean Pottery* (Stockholm).

Fyfe, Theodore. 1902–3. "Painted Plaster Decoration at Knossos." *Annual of the British School at Athens* 10: 107–31.

Galanopoulos, A. G., and E. Bacon. 1969. *Atlantis* (London).

Gallus, Sándor. 1934. "A Soproni burgstall alakos urnái." *Archaeologia Hungarica* 13: 1ff.

Garašanin, D., and M. Garašanin. 1979. *Supska* (Belgrade).

Gardiner, Alan H. 1935. "A Lawsuit Arising from the Purchase of Two Slaves." *Journal of Egyptian Archaeology* 21: 140–46.

———. 1947. *Ancient Egyptian Onomastica* (Oxford).

———. 1957. *Egyptian Grammar.* 3rd ed. (Oxford).

Gardiner, Alan, and A.E.P. Weigall. 1913. *A Topographical Catalogue of the Private Tombs of Thebes* (London).

Gardner, Ernest Arthur. 1897. *A Catalogue of the Greek Vases in the Fitzwilliam Museum, Cambridge* (Cambridge).

Garstang, John. 1953. *Prehistoric Mersin: Yümük Tepe in Southern Turkey* (Oxford).

Gastaldi, B. 1865. *Lake Habitations and Prehistoric Remains in the Turbaries . . . of . . . Italy.* Translated by C. H. Chambers (London).

Gaul, J. H. 1948. *The Neolithic Period in Bulgaria. American School of Prehistoric Research Bulletin* 16 (Cambridge, Mass.).

Geijer, Agnes. 1938. *Birka III: Die Textilfunde* (Uppsala).

———. [1972] 1979. *A History of Textile Art.* Translated by R. Tanner (London).

———. 1977. "The Loom Representation on the Chiusi Vase." In Gervers 1977a, 52–55.

Gejvall, Nils-Gustaf. 1969. *Lerna, Vol. 1: The Fauna* (Princeton).

General Introductory Guide to the Egyptian Col-

lections in the British Museum (London, 1964).

Gertsiger [Gerziger], Dora. [1972] 1975. "Eine Decke aus dem sechsten Grab der 'Sieben Brüder.' " Antike Kunst 18: 51–55. Translated by J. Aphonkin.

———. 1973. "Antichnye Tkani v Sobranii Ermitazha." Pamjatniki Antichnogo Prikladnogo Iskusstva 1973: 71–100.

Gervers, Veronika. 1973. "Methods of Traditional Felt-Making in Anatolia and Iran." Bulletin de liaison du CIETA 38 (July): 152–63.

———. 1977a, ed. Studies in Textile History (Toronto).

———. 1977b. "An Early Christian Curtain in the Royal Ontario Museum." In Gervers 1977a, 56–81.

———. 1978. "A Nomadic Mantle in Europe." Textile History 9: 9–34.

Gesell, Geraldine C. 1985. Town, Palace, and House Cult in Minoan Crete (Göteborg).

Ghirshman, Roman. 1938. Fouilles de Sialk près de Kashan 1933, 1934, 1937. Vol. 1 (Paris).

Gimbutas, Marija. 1956. The Prehistory of Eastern Europe (Cambridge, Mass.).

———. 1958. Ancient Symbolism in Lithuanian Folk Art (Philadelphia).

———. 1977. "Gold Treasure at Varna." Archaeology 30: 44–51.

———. 1982. The Goddesses and Gods of Old Europe (Berkeley).

Gipper, Helmut. 1964. "Purpur." Glotta 42: 39–69.

Gittinger, Mattiebelle. 1975. "Selected Batak Textiles: Technique and Function." Textile Museum Journal 4.2: 13–26.

Glanville, S.R.K. 1972. Wooden Model Boats (London).

Glare, P.G.W. 1976. Oxford Latin Dictionary (Oxford).

Glob, P. V. [1970] 1974. The Mound People: Danish Bronze-Age Man Preserved. Translated by J. Bulman (Ithaca, N.Y.).

Glory, A. 1959. "Débris de corde paléolithique à la Grotte de Lascaux." Mémoires de la Société Préhistorique Française 5: 135–69.

Glotz, G. 1925. The Aegean Civilization (New York).

Godart, Louis. 1972. "Les Tablettes de la série Co de Cnossos." Minos 12: 418–24.

Godart, Louis, J. T. Killen, and J.-P. Olivier. 1979. "Un Sixième Fragment de tablette en Linéaire B de Tirynthe." Archäologischer Anzeiger 1979: 450–58.

Godwin, H. 1967. "The Ancient Cultivation of Hemp." Antiquity 41: 42–48.

Goldman, Hetty. 1931. Excavations at Eutresis in Boeotia (Cambridge, Mass.).

———. 1956. Excavations at Gözlü Kule; Tarsus: II (Princeton).

Gophna, Ram, and Etan Ayalon. 1980. "Survey of the Central Coastal Plain, 1978–1979." Tel Aviv 7: 147–50.

Gophna, Ram, and Pirhiya Beck. 1981. "The Rural Aspect of the Settlement Pattern of the Coastal Plain. . . ." Tel Aviv 8: 45–80.

Gorodtsov, V. A. 1910. Bytovaja Arkheologija (Moscow).

Götze, A. 1902. "Die Kleingeräte aus Metall, Stein, Knochen, u.s.w." In Dörpfeld 1902, 320–423.

———. 1908. "Über Brettchenweberei in Altertum." Zeitschrift für Ethnologie 40: 481–500.

Govi, Christiana Morigi. 1971. "Il Tintinnabulo della 'Tomba degli ori' dell'arsenale militare di Bologna." Archeologia Classica 23: 211–35.

Graef, Botho, and Ernest Langlotz. 1925. Die antiken Vasen von der Akropolis zu Athen, I (Berlin).

Granger-Taylor, Hero, and John Peter Wild. 1981. "Some Ancient Silk from the Crimea in the British Museum." Antiquaries Journal 61: 302–6.

Grant, Elihu, and G. Ernest Wright. 1931–39. Ain Shems Excavations (Haverford).

Gray, Dorothea. 1974. "Seewesen." Archaeologia Homerica I, G.

Grbić, Miodrag. 1960. Porodin (Bitolj).

Green, M. W. 1980. "Animal Husbandry at Uruk in the Archaic Period." Journal of Near Eastern Studies 39: 1–36.

Greene, Francina S. 1955. "The Cleaning and Mounting of a Large Wool Tapestry." Studies in Conservation 2: 1–16.

Greenewalt, Crawford H., Jr. 1971. "An Exhibitionist from Sardis." In D. G. Mitten, J. G. Pedley, and J. A. Scott, eds. Studies Presented to G.M.A. Hanfmann, pp. 29–46 (Mainz).

Greenewalt, Crawford H., Jr., and Lawrence J. Majewski. 1980. "Lydian Textiles." In de Vries 1980a, 133–47.

Greiss, Elhamy M. 1955. "Anatomical Identification of Plant Remains and Other Materials from el Omari. . . ." L'Institut d'Égypte, Bulletin 36: 227–35.

Greppin, J.A.C. 1981. "Gk. [mallós] 'fleece, lock of wool.' " *Glotta* 59: 70–75.

Griffith, F. L. 1896. *Beni Hasan*. Vol. 3 (London).

———. 1898. *Beni Hasan*. Vol. 4 (London).

Griffith, F. L., and Grace M. Crowfoot. 1934. "On the Early Use of Cotton in the Nile Valley." *Journal of Egyptian Archaeology* 20: 5–12.

Gross, Victor. 1883. *Les Protohelvètes* (Paris).

Gullberg, Elsa, and Paul Aaström. 1970. *The Thread of Ariadne* (Göteborg).

Guy, Philip L.O. 1938. *The Megiddo Tombs*. Oriental Institute Publications 33 (Chicago).

Hägg, Inga. 1967–68. "Some Notes on the Origin of the Peplos-Type Dress in Scandinavia." *Tor* 1967–68: 81–127.

Hägg, Robin, and Nanno Marinatos, eds. 1981. *Sanctuaries and Cults in the Aegean Bronze Age* (Lund).

———. 1984. *The Minoan Thalassocracy* (Stockholm).

Hägg, Robin, and Franciska Sieurin. 1982. "On the Origin of the Wooden Coffin in Late Bronze Age Greece." *Annual of the British School of Archaeology* 77: 177–86.

Haines, R. C. 1956. "Where a Goddess of Love and War Was Worshipped 4000 Years Ago." *Illustrated London News* 229 (Aug. 18): 266–69.

Halbherr, Federico. 1903. "Resti dell' Età Micenea: Scoperti ad Haghia Triada presso Phaestos." *Monumenti Antichi* 13: cols. 5–74.

Hald, Margrethe. 1942. "The Nettle as a Culture Plant" *Folk-Liv* 6: 28–49.

———. 1946. "Ancient Textile Techniques in Egypt and Scandinavia." *Acta Archaeologica* 17: 49–98.

———. 1950. *Olddanske Tekstiler* (Copenhagen).

Hald, Margrethe, and H. C. Broholm. 1940. *Costumes of the Bronze Age in Denmark* (Copenhagen).

Haley, J. B., and Carl Blegen. 1928. "The Coming of the Greeks." *American Journal of Archaeology* 32: 141–54.

Hall, H. R. 1909–10. "An Addition to the Senmut-Fresco." *Annual of the British School at Athens* 16: 254–57.

———. 1914. "The Relations of Aegean With Egyptian Art." *Journal of Egyptian Archaeology* 1: 110–18, 197–206.

———. 1927. "Keftiu." In S. Casson, ed., *Essays in Aegean Archaeology (Evans Festschrift)*, pp. 31–41 (Oxford).

Hall, Rosalind. 1980a. "A Pair of Linen Sleeves from Gurob." *Göttinger Miszellen* 40: 29–38.

———. 1980b. "A Mohair Dress in the Petrie Museum." *Göttinger Miszellen* 41: 51–58.

———. 1981a. "Two Linen Dresses from the Fifth Dynasty Site of Deshasheh Now in . . . London." *Journal of Egyptian Archaeology* 67: 168–71.

———. 1981b. "Fishing-net Dresses in the Petrie Museum." *Göttinger Miszellen* 42: 37–43.

———. 1981c. "The Pharaonic *mss* Tunic as a Smock?" *Göttinger Miszellen* 43: 29–37.

———. 1982a. "Garments in the Petrie Museum of Egyptian Archaeology." *Textile History* 13: 27–45.

———. 1982b. "Textiles in the Petrie Museum of Egyptian Archaeology." *Conservation News* 17 (March): 11–12.

———. 1985. " 'The Cast-off Garment of Yesterday': Dresses Reversed in Life and Death." *Bulletin de l'Institut Français d'Archéologie Orientale* 85: 235–43.

———. 1986. "Stopfen und Nähen." In *Realexikon der Ägyptologie* 6 (Wiesbaden): 66–67.

Hall, Rosalind, and Lidia Pedrini. 1984. "A Pleated Linen Dress from a Sixth Dynasty Tomb at Gebelein Now in . . . Turin." *Journal of Egyptian Archaeology* 70: 136–39.

Hallager, Erik. 1977. *The Mycenaean Palace at Knossos: Evidence for Final Destruction in the IIIB Period* (Stockholm).

Hallo, William W. 1979. "Obiter Dicta Ad SET." In Marvin A. Powell Jr. and Ronald H. Sack, eds., *Studies in Honor of Tom B. Jones*, pp. 1–13 (Kevelaer).

Hamčenko, Sergei. 1926. "Sposterezhennja nad danymy doslidiv Trypil's'koï kul'tury 1909–1913 rr." In V. Kozlovska, ed., *Trypil's'ka Kul'tura na Ukraini I*, pp. 31–41 (Kiev).

Hamlin, Carol. 1974. "Seh Gabi, 1973." *Archaeology* 27: 274–77.

Hammond, H. B. 1845. *The History of Silk, Cotton, Linen, Wool, . . .* (New York).

Hamp, Eric P. 1982. "[Mallos]: A Clarification." *Glotta* 60: 61–62.

Hančar, Franz. 1937. *Urgeschichte Kaukasiens von den Anfängen seiner Besiedlung . . .* (Vienna).

Hanfmann, G.M.A. 1948. "Archaeology in Homeric Asia Minor." *American Journal of Archaeology* 52: 135–55.

Hankey, Vronwy. 1973. "The Aegean Deposit at el Amarna." *Acts of the International Archae-*

ological Symposium, "The Mycenaeans in the Eastern Mediterranean" (Nicosia) 128–36.

————. 1974. "A Late Bronze Age Temple at Amman." *Levant* 6: 131–59.

Hankey, Vronwy, and Peter Warren. 1974. "The Absolute Chronology of the Aegean Late Bronze Age." *Bulletin of the Institute of Classical Studies* 21: 142–52.

Hansen, Donald P. 1970. "A Proto-Elamite Silver Figurine in the Metropolitan Museum of Art." *Metropolitan Museum Journal* 3: 5–26.

Harlan, Jack R. 1956. *Theory and Dynamics of Grassland Agriculture* (Princeton).

Harrison, Evelyn B. 1977. "Notes on Daedalic Dress." *Journal of the Walters Art Gallery* 36: 37–48.

Hatting, Tove. 1983. "Osteological Investigations on *Ovis Aries* L." *Videnskabelige Meddelelser fra Dansk Naturhistorisk Forening* 144: 115–35.

Hawkes, H. B. 1908. *Gournia, Vasiliki, and Other Prehistoric Sites on the Isthmus of Hierapetra . . .* (Philadelphia).

Hawkes, Jacquetta. 1968. *Dawn of the Gods* (New York).

Hawkes, J. G. 1969. "The Ecological Background of Plant Domestication." In Ucko and Dimbleby 1969, 17–29.

Hawke-Smith, C. F. 1976. "The Knossos Frescoes: A Revised Chronology." *Annual of the British School at Athens* 71: 65–76.

Hayes, W. C. 1937. *Glazed Tiles from a Palace of Ramesses II at Ḳanṭîr* (New York).

————. 1953. *The Scepter of Egypt I* (New York).

————. 1955. *A Papyrus of the Late Middle Kingdom* (Brooklyn).

————. 1959. *The Scepter of Egypt II* (Cambridge, Mass.).

Haynes, A. E. 1975. "Twill Weaving on the Warp Weighted Loom." *Textile History* 6: 156–64.

Hazzidakis, J. 1921. *Tylissos à l'epoque minoenne* (Paris).

Heichelheim, Fritz M. [1938] 1958. *An Ancient Economic History.* Translated by J. Stevens (Leiden).

Heierli, Jakob. 1887. "Die Anfänge der Weberei." *Anzeiger für schweizerische Alterthumskunde* 2–3: 423–28.

Helbaek, H. 1959. "Notes on the Evolution and History of *Linum*." *Kuml. Aarhus* 1959: 103–29.

————. 1960. "The Palaeoethnobotany of the Near East and Europe." In Braidwood and Howe 1960, 99–118.

————. 1963. "Textiles from Çatal Hüyük." *Archaeology* 67: 39–46.

————. 1969. "Plant Collecting, Dry-farming and Irrigation Agriculture in Prehistoric Deh Luran." In Hole, Flannery, and Neely 1969, 383–426.

————. 1970. "The Plant Husbandry of Hacılar." In Mellaart 1970, 189–244.

Helck, W. 1979. *Die Beziehungen Ägyptens und Vorderasiens . . .* (Darmstadt).

Heltzer, M. 1978. *Goods, Prices and the Organization of Trade in Ugarit* (Wiesbaden).

————. 1982. *The Internal Organization of the Kingdom of Ugarit* (Wiesbaden).

Hencken, Hugh. 1968. *Tarquinia and Etruscan Origins* (London).

————. 1978. "The Iron Age Cemetery of Magdalenska Gora in Slovenia." *American School of Prehistoric Research, Bulletin* 32.

Henneburg, A. v. 1932. "Die altägyptischen Gewebe des ethnographischen Museums in Trocadero." *Bulletin du Musée d'Ethnographie du Trocadero* (July): 3–17.

Henshall, Audrey S. 1950. "Textiles and Weaving Appliances in Prehistoric Britain." *Prehistoric Society: Proceedings* 10: 130–62.

Herington, C. J. 1955. *Athena Parthenos and Athena Polias* (Manchester).

Herity, Michael, and George Eogen. 1977. *Ireland in Prehistory* (London).

Hess, Katharine P. 1958. *Textile Fibers and Their Use.* 6th ed. (Chicago).

Heurtley, W. A. 1939. *Prehistoric Macedonia* (Cambridge).

Heurtley, W. A., and R. W. Hutchinson. 1925–26. "Report on the Excavations at the Toumba and Tables of Vardaroftsa, Macedonia." *Annual of the British School at Athens* 27: 1–66.

Heurtley, W. A., and C.A.R. Radford. 1928–30. "Report on the Excavations at the Toumba of Saratse, Macedonia." *Annual of the British School at Athens* 30: 113–50.

Heyn, A.N.J. 1954. *Fiber Microscopy* (New York).

Higgins, R. A. 1954. *Catalogue of the Terracottas, British Museum* (London).

————. 1967. *Greek Terracottas* (London).

Higham, C.F.W. 1968. "Trends in Prehistoric European Caprovine Husbandry." *Man*, n.s. 3: 64–75.

Hilzheimer, Max. 1941. *Animal Remains from Tell Asmar* (Chicago).

Ho, P. T. 1975. *The Cradle of the East* (Chicago).

Hochberg, Bette. 1979. *Spin Span Spun: Fact and Folklore for Spinners* (Santa Cruz, Calif.).

———. 1980. *Handspindles* (Santa Cruz, Calif.).

Hodson, F. R. 1964. "Cultural Grouping within the British Pre-Roman Iron Age." *Prehistoric Society: Proceedings* 30: 99–110.

Hoernes, M. 1898. *Urgeschichte der bildenden Kunst in Europa* (Vienna).

Hoernes, Rudolf. 1891. "Ausgrabungen bei Ödenburg." *Mitteilungen der anthropologischen Gesellschaft, Wien* 21: [71–78].

Hofenk-de Graaff, J. H. 1972. "L'Analyse des matières colorantes dans les textiles anciens." *Bulletin de Liaison du CIETA* 35: 12–21.

Hoffmann, Marta [1964] 1974. *The Warp-Weighted Loom* (Oslo).

———. 1977. "Manndalen Revisited: Traditional Weaving in an Old Lappish Community. . . ." In Gervers 1977a, 149–59.

Hoffmann, Marta, and Harold B. Burnham. 1973. "Prehistory of Textiles in the Old World." *Viking* 37: 49–76.

Hoffmann, Marta, and R. Traetteberg. 1959. "Teglefunnet." *Stavanger Museums Aarbok* 1959: 41–60.

Hoffmann, Michael. 1979. *Egypt before the Pharaohs* (New York).

Hogarth, D. G. 1899–1900. "The Dictaean Cave." *Annual of the British School at Athens* 6: 94–116.

———. 1900–1901. "Excavations at Zakro, Crete." *Annual of the British School at Athens* 7: 121–49.

Hole, Frank. 1977. *Studies in the Archaeological History of the Deh Luran Plain* (Ann Arbor).

Hole, Frank, and Kent V. Flannery. 1962. "Excavations at Ali Kosh, Iran, 1961." *Iranica Antiqua* 2: 97–148.

Hole, Frank, K. V. Flannery, and J. A. Neely. 1969. *Prehistory and Ecology in the Deh Luran Plain* (Ann Arbor).

Hood, Sinclair. 1971. *The Minoans* (London).

Hooper, Luther. 1914. "The Loom and Spindle: Past, Present, and Future." *Annual Report of the Smithsonian Institution, 1914*: 629–78.

Hoopes, Johannes. 1905. *Waldbäume und Kulturpflanzen im germanischen Altertum* (Strassburg).

Hopf, Maria. 1961. "Pflanzenfunde aus Lerna/Argolis." *Der Züchter: Zeitschrift für theoret. und angewandte Genetik* 31: 239–47.

———. 1962. "Nützpflanzen vom Lernaischen Golf." *Jahrbuch des römisch-germanischen Zentralmuseums Mainz* 9: 1–19.

Horsfall, Ronald S., and L. G. Lawrie. 1949. *The Dyeing of Textile Fibres.* 2nd ed. (London).

Houston, Mary G. 1920. *Ancient Egyptian, Mesopotamian, and Persian Costumes* (London).

Huebner, Julius. 1909. "The Examination of Some Ancient Egyptian Textiles." *Journal of the Society of Dyers and Colourists* 25: 223–26.

Hundt, H.-J. 1959. "Vorgeschichtliche Gewebe aus dem Hallstätter Salzberg." *Jahrbuch des römisch-germanischen Zentralmuseums Mainz* 6: 66–100.

———. 1960. "Vorgeschichtliche Gewebe aus dem Hallstätter Salzberg." *Jahrbuch des römisch-germanischen Zentralmuseums Mainz* 7: 126–50.

———. 1961. "Neunzehn Textilreste aus dem Dürrnberg in Hallein." *Jahrbuch des römisch-germanischen Zentralmuseums Mainz* 8: 7–25.

———. 1962. "Textilreste aus dem Hohmichele." In Gustav Riek, *Der Hohmichele, ein Fürstengrabhügel der späten Hallstattzeit bei der Heuneburg,* pp. 119–214 (Berlin).

———. 1967. "Vorgeschichtliche Gewebe aus dem Hallstätter Salzberg." *Jahrbuch des römisch-germanischen Zentralmuseums Mainz* 14: 38–67.

———. 1968. "Die verkohlten Reste von Geweben, Geflechten, . . . aus Grab 200 von Cigarralejo." *Madrider Mitteilungen* 9: 187–205.

———. 1969. "Über vorgeschichtliche Seidenfunde." *Jahrbuch des römisch-germanischen Zentralmuseums Mainz* 16: 59–71.

———. 1970. "Gewebefunde aus Hallstatt; Webkunst und Tracht in der Hallstattzeit." In *Krieger und Salzherren: Halstattkultur im Ostalpenraum* (Mainz), 53–71.

———. 1974. "Die Textilreste aus den Gräbern vom Dürrnberg." In Fritz Moosleitner, Ludwig Pauli, and Ernst Penninger, *Der Dürrnberg bei Hallein,* 2: 135–42 (Munich).

Hurry, J. B. 1930. *The Woad Plant and Its Dye* (London).

Hutchinson, Sir Joseph, J.G.D. Clark, E. M. Jope, and R. Riley, eds., 1977. *The Early History of Agriculture: A Joint Symposium* (Oxford).

Hutchinson, R. W. 1962. *Prehistoric Crete* (Baltimore).

Huxley, G. L., and J. N. Coldstream. 1966. "Kythera, First Minoan Colony." *Illustrated London News* 249 (Aug. 27): 28–29.

Iakovides, Spiros E. 1969. *Perati, to Nekrotapheion* (Athens).

———. 1980. *Excavations of the Necropolis at Perati* (Los Angeles).

———. 1983. *Late Hellandic Citadels on Mainland Greece* (Leiden).

Immerwahr, Sara A. 1971. *The Athenian Agora XIII: The Neolithic and Bronze Ages* (Princeton).

———. 1983. "The People in the Frescoes." In Olga Krzyszkowska and L. Nixon, ed., *Minoan Society: Proceedings of the Cambridge Colloquium, 1981,* pp. 143–53 (Cambridge).

———. 1985. "A Possible Influence of Egyptian Art in the Creation of Minoan Wall Painting." In *L'Iconographie minoenne, Bulletin de Correspondance Hellénique,* suppl. 11, 41–50.

———. 1989. *Aegean Painting in the Bronze Age* (University Park, Pa.).

Indreko, Richard. 1948. *Die mittlere Steinzeit in Estland* (Stockholm).

Ingholt, Harald. 1940–50. *Rapport préliminaire sur sept campagnes de fouilles à Hama, 1932–38, 1940. Arkaeologisk-Kunsthistoriske Meddelelser* 3 (Copenhagen).

Iten-Maritz, J. 1975. *Der anatolische Teppich* (Munich).

Jacobsen, Thorkild. 1970. *Toward the Image of Tammuz and Other Essays* (Cambridge, Mass.).

Jacobsen, T. W. 1969. "Franchthi Cave." *Archaeology* 22: 4–9.

Jacobsthal, E. 1898. "Schnurbänder." *Verhandlungen der Berliner Gesellschaft für Anthropologie . . .* 30: 332–38.

James, Frances W. 1966. *The Iron Age at Beth Shan* (Philadelphia).

Janssen, J. J. 1975. *Commodity Prices from the Ramessid Period* (Leiden).

Jarman, M. R. 1972. "Appendix VI. The [Myrtos] Fauna." In Warren 1972, 318–20.

Jarman, M. R., G. N. Bailey, and H. N. Jarman. 1982. *Early European Agriculture* (Cambridge).

Jażdżewski, Konrad. 1936. *Kultura Puharów Lejkowatych* (Poznan).

———. 1965. *Poland* (New York).

Jehasse, Jean, and Lorrence Jehasse. 1973. *La Nécropole préromaine d'Aléria* (Paris).

Jenkins, Ian, and Dyfri Williams. 1985. "Sprang Hair Nets: Their Manufacture and Use in Ancient Greece." *American Journal of Archaeology* 89: 411–18.

Jenny, Wilhelm A. 1928. "Schamiramalti." *Prähistorische Zeitschrift* 19: 280–304.

Jensen, L. B. 1963. "Royal Purple of Tyre." *Journal of Near Eastern Studies* 22: 104–18.

Jentsch, Hugo. 1886. "Das heilige Land bei Niemitzsch, Kreis Guben." *Verhandlungen der Berliner Gesellschaft für Anthropologie . . .* 18: 583–96.

Jéquier, Gustave. 1911. *Décoration égyptienne: Plafonds et frises végétales du Nouvel Empire thébain* (Paris).

Jidejian, Nina. 1968. *Byblos through the Ages* (Beirut).

Johl, C. H. 1964. *Altägyptische Webestühle und Brettchenweberei in Altägypten* (Hildesheim).

Johnson, Rubellite K., and Bryce G. Decker. 1980. "Implications of the Distribution of Names for Cotton (*Gossypium* spp.) in the Indo-Pacific." *Asian Perspectives* 23.2: 249–307.

Jones, Marilyn. 1982. "The Madder Saga." *Shuttle, Spindle, and Dyepot* 13.2: 28–39.

Jørgensen, Lise Bender. 1984. "North European Textile Production and Trade in the 1st Millenium A.D." *Journal of Danish Archaeology* 3: 124–34.

Joseph, Brian D. 1982. "The Source of Ancient Greek [tolúpe]." *Glotta* 60: 230–34.

Jucker, Ines. 1963. "Frauenfest in Korinth." *Antike Kunst* 6: A.2.47–61.

Kadish, Barbara. 1969. "Excavations of Prehistoric Remains at Aphrodisias, 1967." *American Journal of Archaeology* 73: 49–65.

———. 1971. "Excavations of Prehistoric Remains at Aphrodisias, 1968 and 1969." *American Journal of Archaeology* 75: 121–40.

Kahlenberg, Mary H. 1977. *Textile Traditions of Indonesia* (Los Angeles).

Kalicz, Nándor. 1970. *Clay Gods: The Neolithic Period and Copper Age in Hungary* (Budapest).

Kalligas, Petros. 1984–85. "Anaskaphes sto Leukanti Euboias 1981–1984." *Arkheios Euboikon Meleton* 1984–5: 253–69.

Kâmil, Turhan. 1982. *Yortan Cemetery in the*

Early Bronze Age of Western Anatolia (Oxford).

Kantor, Helene J. 1947. *The Aegean and the Orient in the Second Millennium B.C.* (Bloomington, Ind.).

Karageorghis, V. 1956. "Two Mycenaean Bull-Craters in the G.G. Pierides Collection, Cyprus." *American Journal of Archaeology* 60: 143–49.

———. 1976. *The Civilization of Prehistoric Cyprus* (Athens).

Karaulašvili, Ts. 1979. "Peasant Methods of Preparation of Cloth at Kakheti" [in Georgian]. *Vestnik Gosudarstvennogo Muzeja Gruzii* 34B: 32ff.

Kardara, Chrysoula. 1961. "Dyeing and Weaving Works at Isthmia." *American Journal of Archaeology* 65: 261–66.

"Karmin." 1924. *Farbe und Lack*: 411–12 etc.

Karo, Georg. 1930. *Schachtgräber von Mykenai* (Munich).

Karouzou, Semni. 1980. *National Museum [of Greece]: Illustrated Guide . . .* (Athens).

Keightley, David N., ed. 1983. *The Origins of Chinese Civilization* (Berkeley).

Keller, Ferdinand. [1866] 1878. *The Lake Dwellings of Switzerland and Other Parts of Europe.* 2nd ed. (London).

Kelly, Mary. 1987. "Embroidery for the Goddess." *Threads Magazine* June/July 1987: 26–29.

Kemp, Barry J. 1984. *Amarna Reports, 1* (London).

Kemp, Barry J., and Robert S. Merrillees. 1980. *Minoan Pottery in Second Millennium Egypt* (Mainz).

Kempinski, Aharon, and Michael Avi-Yonah. 1979. *Syria Palestine II* (Geneva).

Kendrick, A. F. 1917. "Woven Fabrics from Egypt." *The Burlington Magazine* 31 (Jan.–Dec.).

———. 1920. *Catalogue of Textiles from Burying Grounds in Egypt.* Vol. 1 (London).

Kenyon, Kathleen M. 1957. *Digging up Jericho* (London).

———. 1960. *Excavations at Jericho, I: Tombs Excavated in 1952–4* (London).

———. 1964. *Jericho II* (London).

Keramopoulos, A. D. 1917. "Thebaïka." *Arkhaiologikon Deltion* 3.

Keuls, Eva C. 1983. "Attic Vase Painting and the Home Textile Industry." In W. Moon 1983, 209–30.

Khazanov, A. M. 1978. "Characteristic Features of Nomadic Communities in the Eurasian Steppes." In Wolfgang Weissleder, *The Nomadic Alternative*, pp. 119–26 (The Hague).

Khlopin, I. N. 1982. "The Manufacture of Pile Carpets in Bronze Age Central Asia." *Hali* 5.2: 116–18.

Kierstead, Sallie P. 1950. *Natural Dyes* (Boston).

Killen, J. T. 1962. "The Wool Ideogram in Linear B Texts." *Hermathena* 96: 38–72.

———. 1963. "Some Adjuncts to the SHEEP Ideogram on Knossos Tablets" *Eranos* 61: 69–93.

———. 1964. "The Wool Industry of Crete in the Late Bronze Age." *Annual of the British School at Athens* 59: 1–15.

———. 1966. "The Knossos Lc (Cloth) Tablets." *University of London Institute of Classical Studies* 13: 105–9.

———. 1968a. "The Knossos *o-pi* Tablets." In *Atti e memorie del 1.o congresso internazionale di Micenologia* (Rome), 636–43.

———. 1968b. "Minoan Woolgathering: A Reply I." *Kadmos* 7: 105–23.

———. 1969. "Minoan Woolgathering: A Reply II." *Kadmos* 8: 23–38.

———. 1972. "Two Notes on the Knossos Ak Tablets." *Minos* 12: 423–40.

———. 1974. "A Problem in the Knossos Lc(1) (Cloth) Tablets." *Hermathena* 118: 82–90.

———. 1979. "The Knossos Ld(1) Tablets." In *Colloquium Mycenaeum* (Neuchâtel), 151–81.

———. 1981. "Some Puzzles in a Mycenae Personnel Record." *Živa Antika* 31: 37–45.

Kimakowitz-Winnicki, M. von. 1910. *Spinn- und Webewerkzeuge* (Würtzburg).

Kimmig, W. 1940. "Ein Keltenschild in Ägypten." *Germania* 24: 106–11.

Kirby, R. H. 1963. *Vegetable Fibers* (London).

Kissel, M. L. 1918. *Yarn and Cloth-Making—An Economic Survey* (New York).

Kitchen, K. A. 1966. "Aegean Place Names in a List of Amenophis III." *Bulletin: American Schools of Oriental Research* 181: 23–24.

Klima, Bohuslav. 1963. *Dolní Věstonice* (Prague).

Klose, O. 1926. "Ein buntes Gewebe aus dem prähistorischen Salzbergwerke auf dem Dürrnberge. . . ." *Mitteilungen der anthropologischen Gesellschaft in Wien* 56: 346–50.

Kluge, Friedrich. 1975. *Etymologisches Wörterbuch der deutschen Sprache* (Berlin).

Knobel, E. B., W. W. Midgley, J. G. Milne, M. A. Murray, and W.M.F. Petrie. 1911. *His-*

torical Studies. British School of Archaeology in Egypt 19 (London).

Knowles, P. F. 1955. "Safflower—Production, Processing, and Utilization." *Economic Botany* 9: 273–99.

Koch, P.-A. 1963. *Microscopic and Chemical Testing of Textiles.* Translated by J. W. Hooper (London).

Koeppel, Robert, Alexis Mallon, and Rene Neuville. 1934. *Teleilat Ghassul I* (Rome).

Kohl, Philip L. 1981. *The Bronze Age Civilisation of Cental Asia* (Armonk, N.Y.).

———. 1982. "Implications of Recent Evidence for the Prehistory of N.E. Iran and S.W. Turkmenistan." *Iranica Antiqua* 17: 1–20.

Kökten, Kiliç, Nimet Özgüç, and Tahsin Özgüç. 1945. "Türk Tarih Kurumu Adına Yapılan Samsun Bölgesi Kazıları Hakkinda Ilk Kısa Rapor." *Türk Tarih Kurumu: Belleten* 9.35: 361–400.

Kordysh, Neonila. 1951. "Notes on Weaving in the Tripillyan Culture of the Ukraine." *Annals of the Ukrainian Academy of Arts and Sciences in the U.S.* 1.2: 98–112.

Koridze, D. 1955. *Tbilisis arkeologiuri dzeglebi* (Tbilisi).

Korobkova, G. F. 1962. "Otpechatki Tkanej na Keramike." In Zadneprovskij 1962, 231–34.

Koşay, Hâmit Z. 1934. "Ahlatlıbel Hafriyati." *Türk Tarih, Arkeologya ve Etnografya Dergisi* 2: 3–101.

———. 1941. *Pazarlı* (Ankara).

———. 1951. *Les Fouilles d'Alaca Höyük, 1937–1939* (Ankara).

———. 1959. "Erzurum-Karaz Kazısı Raporu." *Türk Tarih Kurumu: Belleten* 23: 349–413.

———. 1973. *Alaca Höyük Excavations, 1963–1967* (Ankara).

———. 1976. *Keban Project: Pulur Excavations 1968–1970* (Ankara).

Kostrzewski, Józef. 1936. "A Unique Discovery: A Fortified Polish Village of about 600 B.C." *Illustrated London News* 189 (August 8): 243–45.

———. 1938. *Gród prasłowiański w Biskupinie* (Poznan).

———. [1947] 1949. *Les Origines de la civilisation polonaise.* Translated by B. Hamel (Paris).

———. 1955. *Wielkopolska w Pradziejach* (Warsaw).

Kowalczyk, Jan. 1956. "Osada Kultury Pucharów Lejkowatych w Miecjs. Gródek Nadbużny." *Wiadomości Archeologiczne* 23: 23–48.

———. 1969. "Początki neolitu na zeiemiach polskich." *Wiadomości Archeologiczne* 34: 3–69.

———. 1970. "The Funnel Beaker Culture." In Wiślański 1970, 144–77.

Krafft, Sofie. 1956. *Pictorial Weavings from the Viking Age* (Oslo).

Kraft, John C., Ilhan Kayan, and Oğuz Erol. 1980. "Geomorphic Reconstructions in the Environs of Ancient Troy." *Science* 209: 776–82.

Kretschmer, Paul. 1896. *Einleitung in die Geschichte der griechischen Sprache* (Göttingen).

Kuftin, B. A. 1950a. *Arkheologicheskie izyskanija v Rionskoj Nizmenosti . . .* (Tbilisi).

———. 1950b. *Materiali k arkheologij Kolkhidi II* (Tbilisi).

Kuhn, Dieter. 1977. *Literaturverzeichnis zur Textilkunde Chinas und zur allgemeinen Webtechnologie* (Wiesbaden).

———. 1979–80. "The Spindle-wheel: A Chou Chinese Invention." *Early China* 5: 14–24.

———. 1982. "The Silk-Workshops of the Shang Dynasty (16th–11th C. B.C.)." In *Explorations in the History of Science and Technology in China* (Shanghai) 367–408.

———. 1987. *Spinning and Reeling. Science and Civilisation in China,* ed. J. Needham, vol. 5.9 (Cambridge).

Kujala, Viljo. 1947–48. "Antrean Korpilahden kivikautisen verkon kuituaines." *Suomen Museo* 54–55: 24–27.

Kurdian, H. 1941. "Kirmiz." *Journal of the American Oriental Society* 61: 105–7.

Kurtz, Donna C., and John Boardman. 1971. *Greek Burial Customs* (London).

Kuschke, A. 1962. "Bericht über eine Sondage im Palastgarten von Ugarit-Ras Shamra." In C.F.A. Schaeffer 1962, 256ff., 292ff.

Kushnareva, K. Kh. 1959. "Poselenie Epokhi Bronzy na Kholme Uzerlik-tepe okolo Agdama." *Materialy i Issledovanija po Arkheologii SSSR* 6: 388–430.

Kushnareva, K. Kh., and T. N. Chubinishvili. 1970. *Drevnie Kul'tury Juzhnovo Kavkaza* (Leningrad).

Kyrle, G. 1918. "Der prähistorische Bergbaubetrieb in den Salzburger Alpen." *Österreichische Kunsttopographie* 17: 1–70.

LaBaume, W. 1933. "Der stehende Webstuhl." *Prähistorische Zeitschrift* 24: 301–4.

———. 1955. *Die Entwicklung des Textilhandwerks in Alteuropa* (Bonn).

Lacaisne, Z. 1912. "Note sur des tissus recouvrant des haches de cuivre." *Mémoires de la Délégation en Perse* 13: 163–64.

Lacy, A. D. 1967. *Greek Pottery in the Bronze Age* (London).

Lamb, Winifred. 1919–21. "Excavations at Mycenae: III—Frescoes from the Ramp House." *Annual of the British School at Athens* 24: 89–99.

———. 1936. *Excavations at Thermi in Lesbos* (Cambridge).

———. 1937. *Excavations at Kusura near Afyon Karahisar*. Vol. 1 (Oxford).

———. 1938. *Excavations at Kusura near Afyon Karahisar*. Vol. 2 (Oxford).

Lamberg-Karlovsky, C. C. 1970. "Excavations at Tepe Yahyā, Southeastern Iran, 1967–1969." *Bulletin of the American Journal of Prehistoric Research* 27.

———. 1971. "The Proto-Elamite Settlement at Tepe Yahyā." *Iran* 9: 87–96.

Lambert, M. 1961. "Recherches sur la vie ouvrière: Les Ateliers de tissage de Lagash." *Archiv Orientálni* 29: 422–43.

Lamon, R. S., and G. M. Shipton. 1939. *Megiddo I* (Chicago).

Landercy, Mathilde. 1933. "La Destination de la [kerkís] dans le tissage en Grèce au IV. siècle." *L'Antiquité Classique* 2: 357–62.

Landi, Sheila, and Rosalind M. Hall. 1979. "The Discovery and Conservation of an Ancient Egyptian Linen Tunic." *Studies in Conservation* 24: 141–51.

Lane, George. 1931. *Words for Clothing in the Principal Indo-European Languages* (Baltimore).

Lang, Mabel L. 1969. *The Palace of Nestor at Pylos in Western Messenia, vol. II: The Frescoes* (Princeton).

Lang, Margarete. 1908. *Die Bestimmung des Onos oder Epinetron* (Berlin).

Lange, Kurt, and Max Hirmer. 1968. *Egypt* (London).

Langewis, Laurens, and Frits A. Wagner. 1964. *Decorative Art in Indonesian Textiles* (Amsterdam).

Langlotz, Ernst, and Max Hirmer. 1965. *Ancient Greek Sculpture of Southern Italy and Sicily* (New York).

Lansing, Ambrose, and W. C. Hayes. 1937. "The Egyptian Expedition 1935–1936: The Museum's Excavations at Thebes." *Bulletin of the Metropolitian Museum of Art* 32 (January): pt. 2, 4–39.

Lapp, Paul W., and Nancy L. Lapp. eds. 1974. *Discoveries in the Wâdî ed-Dâliyeh. Annual of the American Schools of Oriental Research* 41 (Cambridge, Mass.).

Lasareff, M. Victor. 1958. "Les Collections de tissus anciens dans les musées de l'URSS." *Bulletin de liaison du CIETA* July 1958: 38–46.

Laufer, Berthold. 1930. "The Early History of Felt." *American Anthropologist* 32: 1–18.

Leakey, Richard E. 1981. *The Making of Mankind* (New York).

Le Breton, L. 1957. "The Early Periods at Susa, Mesopotamian Relations." *Iraq* 19: 79–123.

Leggett, W. F. 1944. *Ancient and Medieval Dyes* (Brooklyn).

———. 1949. *The Story of Silk* (New York).

Leipen, Neda. 1977. "Classical Tradition in Early Christian Art: A Textile Fragment. . . ." In Gervers 1977a, 168–77.

Leix, Alfred. 1938. "Ancient Egypt, Land of Linen." *CIBA Review* 12 (August): 397ff.

Lempese, Angelike. 1970. "Anaskaphikai ereunai eis Anatoliken Kreten." *Praktika tes Arkhaiologikes Etaireias* 1970: 257–97.

Leroi-Gourhan, André. 1943. *L'Homme et la matière* (Paris).

———. 1968. *The Art of Prehistoric Man in Western Europe* (London).

Leroi-Gourhan, Arlette. 1982. "The Archaeology of Lascaux Cave." *Scientific American* 246 (June): 104–12.

Le Rouzic, Zacharie. N.d. *Carnac, les monuments mégalithiques* (Quimper, ca. 1908).

Leumann, Manu. 1964. "Lateinische Laut- und Formenlehre 1955–1962." *Glotta* 42: 69–120.

Levi, Doro. 1935. *Il Museo Civico di Chiusi* (Rome).

Levin, M., and S. Horowitz. 1961. "Textile Remains from the Caves of Nahal Hever." *'Atiqot* 3: 163–64.

Levy, S., and G. Edelstein. 1972. "Cinq Années de fouilles à Tel 'Amal (Nir David)." *Revue Biblique* 79: 325–67.

Lewis, C. T., and C. Short. 1958. *A Latin Dictionary* (Oxford).

Lewis, D. M. 1979–80. "Athena's Robe." *Scripta Classica Israelica* 5: 28–29.

Lewy, Heinrich. 1895. *Die semitischen Fremdwörter im Griechischen* (Berlin).

Li, Chi. 1977. *Anyang* (Seattle).

Li, Hui-lin. 1974a. "The Origin and Use of Cannabis in Eastern Asia. . . ." *Economic Botany* 28: 293–301.

———. 1974b. "An Archaeological and Historical Account of Cannabis in China." *Economic Botany* 28: 437–39.

———. 1983. "The Domestication of Plants in China: Ecogeographical Considerations." In Keightley 1983, 21–64.

Lichtheim, Miriam. 1973. *Ancient Egyptian Literature*. Vol. 1: *The Old and Middle Kingdoms* (Berkeley and Los Angeles).

Liddell, Henry George, Robert Scott, and H. S. Jones. 1968. *A Greek-English Lexicon* (Oxford).

Liu, Robert K. 1978. "Spindle Whorls Part I: Some Comments and Speculations." *The Bead Journal* 3: 87–103.

Lloyd, Seton. 1943. "Tell Uqair." *Journal of Near Eastern Studies* 2: 131–58.

Lloyd, Seton, and James Mellaart. 1962. *Beycesultan* (London).

Lolling, H., R. Bohn, A. Furtwängler, and U. Köhler. 1880. *Das Kuppelgrab bei Menidi* (Athens).

Lomborg, Ebbe. 1981. "Et tøjstykke fra Hvidegaardsfundet." In *Det Skabende Menneske: Festschrift til P.V. Glob* (Copenhagen), 64–84.

Long, Charlotte. 1974. *The Ayia Triadha Sarcophagus* (Göteborg).

Loret, Victor. 1930. "Deux Racines tinctoriales de l'Égypte ancienne: Orcanette et garance." *Kemi* 3: 23–32.

Lorimer, H. C. 1950. *Homer and the Monuments* (London).

Loud, Gordon. 1948. *Megiddo II*. Oriental Institute Publications 62 (Chicago).

Lucas, A., and J. R. Harris. 1962. *Ancient Egyptian Materials and Industries*. 4th ed. (London).

Luce, J. V. 1969. *Lost Atlantis* (New York).

Lutz, Henry F. 1923. *Textiles and Costumes among the Peoples of the Ancient Near East* (Leipzig).

Lydekker, R. 1912. *The Sheep and Its Cousins* (London).

MacAlister, R.A.S. [1911] 1965. *The Philistines* (Chicago).

———. 1912. *The Excavation of Gezer, II* (London).

McConnell, Brian E. N.d. *From Bobbins to Bronze: Exchange, Textile Production, and Chiefdoms in the Maltese Archipelago* (unpublished ms., 1984).

———. 1985. "Malta's Megalithic Temples and Foreign Exchange." *American Journal of Archaeology* 89: 341 [abstract].

McCown, Donald E. 1942. *The Comparative Stratigraphy of Early Iran* (Chicago).

McDonald, William A. 1967. *Progress into the Past* (New York and London).

———. 1972. "Excavations at Nichoria in Messenia: 1969–71." *Hesperia* 41: 218–73.

McDonald, William A., and George R. Rapp, Jr. 1972. *The Minnesota Messinia Expedition* (Minneapolis).

Mace, Arthur C. 1921. "Excavations at Lisht." *Bulletin of the Metropolitan Museum of Art* 16 (November): pt. 2, 5–19.

———. 1922. "Loom Weights in Egypt." *Ancient Egypt* 7: 75–76.

McGready, A. G. 1968. "Egyptian Words in the Greek Vocabulary." *Glotta* 46: 247–54.

Mackay, Ernest. 1925. *Excavations at the "A" Cemetery at Kish* (Chicago).

———. 1931. *Report on Excavations at Jemdet Nasr, Iraq* (Chicago).

———. 1935. *Indus Civilisation* (London).

McLaughlin, Barbara K. 1981. "New Evidence on the Mechanics of Loom Weights." *American Journal of Archaeology* 85: 79–81.

Mailey, Jean E. 1970. "Suggestions Concerning the Ground of the Ch'u Silk Ms. . . ." In Noel Barnard, ed., *Early Chinese Art and Its Possible Influence in the Pacific Basin*, 1.103–12 (New York).

Maisler, B. 1951. "The Excavations at Tell Qasîle." *Israel Exploration Journal* 1: 194–218.

Maiti, R. K. 1979. "A Study of the Microscopic Structure of the Fiber Strands of . . . Bast Fibers. . . ." *Economic Botany* 33: 78–87.

Makarenko, N. 1933. *Marijupil's"kij Mogil"nik* (Kiev).

———. 1934. "Neolithic Man on the Shores of the Sea of Azov." *Eurasia Septentrionalis Antiqua* 9: 133–51.

Mallowan, Max E. L. 1933. "The Prehistoric Sondage of Nineveh. . . ." *Annals of Archaeology and Anthropology, Liverpool* 20: 71–186.

———. 1970. "The Development of Cities from Al-'Ubaid to the End of Uruk 5." In *Cambridge Ancient History* I.1 (Cambridge), 327–462.

Marcade, Jean-Claude. 1969. *Au Musée de Delos* (Paris).

Marinatos, Nanno. 1984. *Art and Religion in Thera* (Athens).

Marinatos, Spyridon. 1957. "A Magnificent Find of Homeric Gold and Gems from an Unplundered Tomb . . . at Nestor's Pylos." *Illustrated London News* 230 (April 6): 540–43.

———. 1967a. "Anaskaphai Theras." *Praktika tes Arkhaiologikes Etaireias* 1967: 124–50.

———. 1967b. "Kleidung, Haar- und Barttracht." *Archaeologia Homerica* 1 A'-B'.

———. 1968a. *Excavations at Thera I* (Athens).

———. 1968b. "Anaskaphai Theras II." *Praktika tes Arkhaiologikes Etaireias* 1968: 87–127.

———. 1968c. "Mycenaean Culture within the Frame of Mediterranean Anthropology and Archaeology." In *Atti e Memorie del 1.o congresso internazionale di Micenologia 1968* (Rome) 277–96.

———. 1969a. *Excavations at Thera II* (Athens).

———. 1969b. "Anaskaphai Theras III." *Praktika tes Arkhaiologikes Etaireias* 1969: 147–92.

———. 1970. *Excavations at Thera III* (Athens).

———. 1971. *Excavations at Thera IV* (Athens).

———. 1972. *Excavations at Thera V* (Athens).

———. 1974. *Excavations at Thera VI* (Athens).

———. 1976. *Excavations at Thera VII* (Athens).

Marinatos, Spyridon, and Max Hirmer. 1960. *Crete and Mycenae* (New York).

Markovin, V. I. 1960. "Kul'tura Plemen Severnogo Kavkaza v Epokhu Bronzy (II tys. do n.e.)." *Materialy i Issledovanija po Arkheologii SSSR* 93.

Marshall, J. [1931] 1973. *Mohenjo-daro and the Indus Civilization* (Delhi).

Masson, Emilia. 1967. *Recherches sur les plus anciens emprunts sémitiques en Grec* (Paris).

Masson, V. M. 1981. *Altyn-depe* (Leningrad).

Masson, V. M., and V. I. Sarianidi. 1981. *Central Asia: Turkmenia before the Achaeminids.* Translated by R. Tringham (London).

Masurel, Hubert. 1984a. "Les Premiers Tissus." *Archéologia* 188 (March): 46–55.

———. 1984b. "Les Tissus à l'age du fer." *Archéologia* 189 (April): 43–55.

Matisoff, James A. 1978. *Variational Semantics in Tibeto-Burman* (Philadelphia).

Matthiae, Paolo. 1980. *Ebla, An Empire Rediscovered.* Translated by C. Holme (London).

Matz, F. 1928. *Die frühkretischen Siegel* (Berlin).

Mayrhofer, Manfred. 1953–80. *Kurzgefasstes etymologisches Wörterbuch des Altindischen* (Heidelberg).

Mecquenem, R. de. 1905. "Offrandes de fondation du temple de Chouchinak." In *Mémoires de la Délégation Scientifique Française en Perse* 7 (Paris), 61–130.

Mee, C. 1982. *Rhodes in the Bronze Age* (Warminster).

Meissner, Bruno. 1932–33. "[QNBR']." *Archiv für Orientforschung* 8: 225.

Meister, W. 1936. "Zur Geschichte des Filzteppichs im ersten Jahrtausend." *Ostasiatische Zeitschrift* 22: 56–61.

Melena, José L. 1975. *Studies on Some Mycenaean Inscriptions. Minos,* suppl. 5 (Salamanca).

Melida, José R. 1929. *Arqueologia Española* (Barcelona).

Mell, C. D. 1932a. "A Brief Historical Sketch of Dyer's Broom." *Textile Colorist and Converter* 54: 26–28.

———. 1932b. "The History and Economic Uses of Safflower." *Textile Colorist and Converter* 54: 97–99.

———. 1932c. "A Brief Historical Account Concerning Woad." *Textile Colorist and Converter* 54: 166–68, 202.

———. 1932d. "A Brief Historical Account of Madder." *Textile Colorist and Converter* 54: 241–44.

———. 1932e. "A Brief Historical Account of Weld." *Textile Colorist and Converter* 54: 335–37, 343.

Mellaart, James. 1959. "The Royal Treasure of Dorak." *Illustrated London News* 235 (November 28): 754 and suppl. pl. I–III.

———. 1961. "Excavations at Hacılar: Fourth Preliminary Report." *Anatolian Studies* 2: 37–77.

———. 1962. "Excavations at Çatal Hüyük." *Anatolian Studies* 12: 41–65.

———. 1963a. "Çatal Hüyük in Anatolia: Excavations which Revolutionise. . . ." *Illustrated London News* 242 (February 9): 196–98.

———. 1963b. "Excavations at Çatal Hüyük, 1962." *Anatolian Studies* 13: 43–103.

Mellaart, James. 1965. "Çatal Hüyük West." *Anatolian Studies* 15: 135–56.

———. 1966. "Excavations at Çatal Hüyük, 1965." *Anatolian Studies* 16: 165–91.

———. 1967. *Çatal Hüyük, A Neolithic Town in Anatolia* (London and New York).

———. 1970. *Excavations at Hacılar* (Edinburgh).

———. 1978. *The Archaeology of Ancient Turkey* (Totowa, N.J.).

———. 1979. "Egyptian and Near Eastern Chronology: A Dilemma?" *Antiquity* 53: 6–18.

Mellink, Machteld J. 1956. *A Hittite Cemetery at Gordion* (Philadelphia).

———. 1969. "Excavations at Karataş-Semayük in Lycia, 1968." *American Journal of Archaeology* 73: 319–31.

———. 1976. "Local, Phrygian, and Greek Traits in Northern Lycia." *Revue Archéologique* 1976 no. 1: 21–34.

Merpert, Nicolai, and Rauf Munchajev. 1969. "Excavations at Yarim Tepe." *Sumer* 25: 125–32.

Merrillees, R. S. 1974. *Trade and Transcendence in the Bronze Age Levant* (Göteborg).

Messerschmidt, Franz. 1935. *Bronzezeit und frühe Eisenzeit in Italien* (Berlin and Leipzig).

Messikommer, H. 1913. *Die Pfahlbauten von Robenhausen* (Zurich).

Michell, H. 1955. "Coccus or kermes." *Classical Review*, n.s. 5: 246.

Midgley, T. 1928. "The Textiles and Matting [Badari]." In Brunton and Caton-Thompson 1928, 64–67.

———. 1937. "Notes on the Badarian Cloth and Matting." In Brunton 1937, 61–63.

Midgley, W. W. 1911. "Linen of the IIIrd Dynasty." In Knobel, Midgley, Milne, Murray, and Petrie 1911, 37–39.

———. 1915. "Reports on Early Linen." In Petrie and Mackay 1915, 48–51.

Mikov, V. 1959. "The Prehistoric Mound of Karanovo." *Archaeology* 12: 88–98.

Milgram, Jacob. 1981. "The Tassel and the Tallith." *4th Annual Rabbi Louis Feinberg Memorial Lectures in Judaic Studies*, University of Cincinnati, April 7.

Milojčić, Vladimir. 1961. *Samos: Band I: Die prähistorische Siedlung unter dem Heraion* (Bonn).

Milojčić, Vladimir, J. Boessneck, and M. Hopf. 1962. *Die deutschen Ausgrabungen auf der Argissa-Magula in Thessalien I* (Bonn).

Moeller, Walter O. 1970. "The Felt Shops of Pompeii." *American Journal of Archaeology* 74: 200.

———. 1976. *The Wool Trade of Ancient Pompeii* (Leiden).

Mommsen, A. 1968. *Heortologie* (Amsterdam).

Montelius, Oscar. 1895–1910. *La Civilisation primitive en Italie* (Stockholm).

Montell, G. 1941. "Spinning Tools and Methods in Asia." In Sylwan 1941, 109–25.

Montet, Pierre. 1925. *Les Scènes de la vie privée dans les tombeaux égyptiens de l'ancien empire* (Strasbourg).

Moon, Brenda. 1961. "Mycenaean Civilisation Publications, 1956–60." *University of London Institute of Classical Studies Bulletin*, suppl. 12.

Moon, Warren, ed. 1983. *Ancient Greek Art and Iconography* (Madison, Wis.).

Moorey, P.R.S. 1967. "Some Ancient Metal Belts: Their Antecedents and Relatives." *Iran* 5: 83–98.

———. 1980. *Cemeteries of the First Millennium B.C. at Deve Hüyük, near Carchemish . . .* (Oxford).

Moreschini, A. Q. 1984. *Le formazioni nominali greche in -nth-* (Rome).

Morgan, Jacques Jean Marie de. 1925–27. *La Préhistoire orientale*, Vols. 1–3 (Paris).

Morise, Y. 1928. "Wild Silk in Manchuria." *China Journal of Science and Arts, Shanghai* 8: 238–45.

Mortensen, Peder. 1970. *Tell Shimshara: The Hassuna Period* (Copenhagen).

Moser, Henri. 1885. *A travers l'Asie centrale* (Paris).

Mountjoy, P. A. 1986. *Mycenaean Decorated Pottery* (Göteborg).

Moussa, Ahmed, and Hartwig Altenmüller. 1977. *Das Grab des Nianchnum und Chnumhotep* (Mainz).

Moussa, Ahmed, and Friedrich Junge. 1975. *Two Tombs of Craftsmen* (Mainz).

Müller-Karpe, H. 1966. *Handbuch der Vorgeschichte*. Vol. 1 (Munich).

———. 1968. *Handbuch der Vorgeschichte*. Vol. 2 (Munich).

———. 1974. *Handbuch der Vorgeschichte*. Vol. 3 (Munich).

———. 1980. *Handbuch der Vorgeschichte*. Vol. 4 (Munich).

Munksgaard, Elisabeth. 1974a. *Oldtidsdragter* (Copenhagen).

———. 1974b. "Kipervævning fra Haastrup." *Fynske Minder 1974*: 115–26.

———. 1979. "Det saakaldte kohorn fra Øksenbjerg, omspundet med hør." *Aarbøger* 1979: 5–10.

Murray, Caroline, and Peter Warren. 1976. "*Po-ni-ki-jo* among the Dye-plants of Minoan Crete." *Kadmos* 15: 40–60.

Murray, W. H. 1973. *The Islands of Western Scotland* (London).

Mylonas, George. 1929. *Excavations at Olynthus Part I: The Neolithic Settlement* (Baltimore).

———. 1953. "Anaskaphe nekrotapheiou Eleusinos." *Praktika tes Arkhaiologikes Etaireias* 1953: 77–84.

———. 1959. *Agios Kosmas* (Princeton).

———. 1973. *Ho Taphikos Kyklos B' ton Mykenon* (Athens).

———. 1980. *To Ergon tes Arkhaiologikes Etaireias kata to 1979* (Athens).

Myres, John L. 1902–3. "Excavations at Palaikastro. II.13: The Sanctuary-Site of Petsofa." *Annual of the British School at Athens* 9: 356–87.

———. 1950. "Minoan Dress." *Man* 1950: 1–6.

Myres, John L., and K. T. Frost. 1915. "The Historical Background of the Trojan War." *Klio* 14: 446–67.

Nahlik, A. 1956. "W sprawie rozwoju krosna tkackiego." *Kwartalnik Historii Kultury Materialnei* 4: 518–40.

Naville, Edouard, H. R. Hall, and E. R. Ayrton. 1907. *The XIth Dynasty Temple at Deir el-Bahari* (London).

Negahban, Ezat O. 1964. *A Preliminary Report on Marlik Excavation* (Tehran).

Neumann, Erich. 1955. *The Great Mother* (New York).

Neustupný, Evžen, and Jiří Neustupný. 1961. *Czechoslovakia before the Slavs* (London).

Newberry, P. E. 1893. *Beni Hasan*. Vol. 1 (London).

———. 1894. *Beni Hasan*. Vol. 2 (London).

———. N.d. *El Bersheh I* (London).

Nielsen, Karen-Hanne. 1971. "Tilskæring." *Skalk* 1971 no. 5, 13–15.

Nilsson, Martin P. [1906] 1957. *Griechische Feste von religiöser Bedeutung* (Leipzig).

———. [1927] 1950. *The Minoan-Mycenaean Religion and Its Survival in Greek Religion* (Lund).

Oettinger, Norbert. 1976. *Die militärischen Eide der Hethiter. Studien zu den Boğazköy-Texten* 22 (Wiesbaden).

Olivier, J. P. 1967. "La Série Dn de Cnossos." *Studia Micenei ed Egeo-Anatolici* 2: 71–93.

———. 1972. "La Série Dn de Cnossos reconsidérée." *Minos* 13: 22–28.

Olschki, Leonardo 1949. *The Myth of Felt* (Berkeley).

O'Neale, Lila M., and Dorothy F. Durrell. 1945. "An Analysis of the Central Asian Silks Excavated by Sir Aurel Stein." *Southwestern Journal of Anthropology, Albuquerque* 1.3: 392–446.

Oppenheim, A. L. 1967. "Essay on Overland Trade in the First Millennium B.C." *Journal of Cuneiform Studies* 21: 236–54.

Orlandos, Anastasios. 1935. "The Discovery of Painted Pinakes near Corinth." *American Journal of Archaeology* 39: 5.

Orth, F. 1922. "Der Werdegang wichtiger Erfindungen auf dem Gebiete der Spinnerei und Weberei." *Beitrage zur Geschichte der Technik und Industrie* 12: 61–108.

Otchët Imperatorskoj Arkheologicheskoj Kommissii [19th-century Russian annual publication with some authorless, titleless articles; see *Compte-Rendu de la Commission Impériale Archéologique*].

Otte, M. 1978. *La Préhistoire à travers les collections du Musée Curtius de Liège* (Liège).

Özgüç, Nimet. 1966. "Excavations at Acemhöyük." *Anatolia-Anadolu* 10: 29–52.

Özgüç, Tahsin. 1948. *Die Bestattungsbräuche im vorgeschichtlichen Anatolien* (Ankara).

———. 1978. *Excavations at Masat Höyük and Investigations in Its Vicinity, I* (Ankara).

Özgüç, Tahsin, and Mahmut Akok. 1958. *Horoztepe* (Ankara).

Page, Denys. 1959. *History and the Homeric Iliad* (Berkeley).

Palmer, L. R. 1965. *Mycenaeans and Minoans* (London).

Papademetrios, Ioannes. 1951. "Anaskaphe en Mykenais." *Praktika tes en Athenais Arkhaiologikes Etaireias* 1951: 192–203.

Papagianni, Maria. 1981. "Leukanti: o arkhaioteros ellenikos naos." *Takhydromos* (July 16, 1981): 28–30.

Paribeni, Roberto. 1908. "Il Sarcofago dipinto di Haghia Triada." *Monumenti Antichi* 19: cols. 5–86.

Parish, W. F. 1936. "Origin of Textiles and the Wheel." *Rayon Textile Monthly* 17: 567–70.

Parke, H. W. 1977. *Festivals of the Athenians* (London).

Parrot, André. 1937. "Les peintures du palais de Mari." *Syria* 18: 325–54.

———. 1962. "Les Fouilles de Mari, 12e campagne (automne 1961)." *Syria* 39: 151–79.

Passek, Tatiana S. 1949. "Periodizatsija Tripol'skikh Poselenij." *Materialy i Issledovanija po Arkheologii SSSR* 10.

Pasternak, Y. 1963. "The Neolithic Age." In *The Ukraine: A Concise Encyclopedia* (Toronto) 532–37.

Paul, Anne. 1985. "Unfinished Paracas Garments." *American Journal of Archaeology* 89: 345 [abstract].

Payne, Sebastian. 1973. "Kill-off Patterns in Sheep and Goats: The Mandibles from Asvan Kale." *Anatolian Studies* 23: 281–303.

———. 1985. "Animal Bones from Aşıklı Hüyük." *Anatolian Studies* 35: 109–22.

Peet, Thomas Eric. 1909. *The Stone and Bronze Ages in Italy and Sicily* (Oxford).

Peet, Thomas Eric, and Sir C. Leonard Woolley. 1923. *Tel El-Amarna, The City of Akhenaten.* Egypt Exploration Society Memoir 38 (London).

Pelliot, Paul. 1959. *Notes on Marco Polo* (Paris).

Pelon, Olivier. 1966. "Maison d'Hagia Varvara et architecture domestique à Mallia." *Bulletin de Correspondance Hellénique* 90: 552–85.

Pendlebury, H. W., J.D.S. Pendlebury, and M. B. Money-Coutts. 1935–36. "Excavations in the Plain of Lasithi I. The Plain of Trapeza." *Annual of the British School at Athens* 36: 5–131.

———. 1937–38. "Excavations in the Plain of Lasithi II." *Annual of the British School at Athens* 38: 1–56.

Pendlebury, J.D.S. 1930. *Aegyptiaca* (Cambridge).

———. 1935. *Tell el Amarna* (London).

———. 1951. "Egypt and the Aegean." In George Mylonas, ed., *Studies Presented to David Moore Robinson, I* 184–97 (St. Louis).

Pendlebury, J.D.S., T. E. Peet, C. L. Woolley, and H. Frankfort. 1951. *The City of Akhenaten III* (London).

Perini, Renato. 1967–69. "Una decorazione su tessuto della palafitta di Ledro." *Preistoria Alpina* 5: 224–29. [Same as *Natura Alpina* 21 (1970): 28–32.]

Perkins, D. 1964a. "The Fauna from the Prehistoric Levels of Shanidar Cave and Zawi Chemi Shanidar." In *INQUA Report of the VI International Congress on Quaternary, Warsaw 1961* (Lodz), 2: 565–71.

———. 1964b. "Prehistoric Fauna from Shanidar, Iraq." *Science* 144: 1565–66.

———. 1964c. "Zawi Chemi Shanidar, A Post-Pleistocene Village Site in Northern Iraq." In *INQUA Report of the VI International Congress on Quaternary, Warsaw 1961* (Lodz), 4: 405–12.

Pernice, E. 1897. "Die korinthischen Pinakes im Antiquarium der königl. Museen." *Jahrbuch des deutschen archäologischen Instituts* 12: 9–48.

Pernier, Luigi. 1910. "Vestigia di una Città Ellenica Arcaica in Creta." *Memorie dell' Istituto Lombardo di Scienze e Lettere* 22.

———. 1935. *Il Palazzo Minoico di Festos I* (n.p.).

Pernier, Luigi, and Luisa Banti. 1947. *Guida degli Scavi Italiani in Creta* (Rome).

Peroni, Renato. 1971. *L'Età del Bronzo nella Penisola Italiana* (Florence).

Perroy, Edouard. 1963. *Le Travail dans les régions du nord du XIe au début du XIVe siècle* (Paris).

Perry, Walter Copland. 1898. *The Women of Homer* (New York).

Persson, Axel W. 1931. *The Royal Tombs at Dendra near Midea* (Lund).

Peter, Irmgard. 1976. *Textilien aus Ägypten* (Zurich).

Petersen, Glenn. 1982. "Ponapean Matriliny: Production, Exchange, and the Ties That Bind." *American Ethnologist* 9: 129–44.

Petkov, Nedelcho. 1959. "Neolitichno selishche pri s. Slatina." *Arkheologija* 1–2: 100–101.

———. 1965. "Praistoricheski pletki i tŭkani ot Sofijskoto pole i blizkite mu okolnosti." *Arkheologija* 7: 45–57.

Petrie, W.M.F. 1891. *Illahun, Kahun, and Gurob* (London).

———. 1894. *Tell el Amarna* (London).

———. 1898. *Deshasheh* (London).

———. 1917. *Tools and Weapons* (London).

———. 1920. *Prehistoric Egypt* (London).

———. 1927. *Objects of Daily Use* (London).

———. 1930. *Antaeopolis: The Tombs of Qau* (London).

Petrie, W.M.F., F. L. Griffith, and P. E. Newberry. 1890. *Kahun, Gurob, and Hawara* (London).

Petrie, W.M.F., and E. Mackay. 1915. *Heliopolis, Kafr Ammar, and Shurafa* (London).

Petrie, W.M.F., E. Mackay, and G. Wainwright. 1910. *Meydum and Memphis (III)* (London).

Pettinato, Giovanni. 1981. *The Archives of Ebla* (Garden City, N.Y.).

Pfister, R. 1934–40. *Les Textiles de Palmyre* (Paris).

———. 1937. "Les Textiles du tombeau de Toutankhamon." *Revue des arts asiatiques* 11: 207–18.

———. 1951. *Textiles de Halabiyeh (Zenobia)* (Paris).

Pfister, R., and L. Bellinger. 1945. *The Excavations at Dura Europus: Final Report 4, Part II: The Textiles* (New Haven).

Pfuhl, E. 1900. *De Atheniensium pompis sacris* (Berlin).

———. 1940. *Tausend Jahre griechischer Malerei* (Munich).

Phillips, Patricia. 1975. *Early Farmers of West Mediterranean Europe* (London).

Picard-Schmitter, M. T. 1967. "Deux métiers horizontaux utilisés en Égypte vers 2000 avant J.C." *Bulletin de liaison du CIETA* 26 (July): 13–39.

Pieridou, A. 1967. "Pieces of Cloth from Early and Middle Cypriote Periods." *Report of the Department of Antiquities, Cyprus*: 25–29.

Piggott, Stuart, Glyn Daniel and Charles McBurney. 1973. *France before the Romans* (London).

Pilar, Manuela do. 1968. "Lisières et franges de toiles égyptiennes." *Bulletin de liaison du CIETA* 28: 97–114.

Pinner, Robert. 1982a. "The Earliest Carpets." *Hali* 5.2: 110–15.

———. 1982b. "Decorative Designs on Prehistoric Turkmenian Ceramics." *Hali* 5.2: 118–19.

Plamenevskaja, O. L. 1975. "Nekotorye dannye o tkanjakh iz kurgana Arzhan." *Uchënye Zapiski Tuvinskoj ASSR, Kyzyl* 17: 199–206.

Platon, Nicholas. 1962. "Anaskaphe Zakrou." *Praktika tes Arkhaiologikes Etaireias* 1962, 142–68.

———. 1971. *Zakros: The Discovery of a Lost Palace of Ancient Crete* (New York).

Ploss, Emil Ernst. 1967. *Ein Buch von alten Farben* (Munich).

Podkowińska, Zofia. 1950. "The Neolithic Settlement on Gawroniec Hill at Ćmielów (Opatów

District)." *Wiadomości Archeologiczne* 17: 94–146.

Poklewski, Tadeusz. 1958. "Osada Kultury Pucharów Leikowatych w Gródku Nadbużnym." *Archeologia Polski* 2: 286–328.

Pomerance, Harriet. 1966. "Weaving of Crete." *Craft Horizons* 25 (September-October): 32–35 and 51–55.

Pomeroy, Sarah B. 1975. *Goddesses, Whores, Wives, and Slaves: Women in Classical Antiquity* (New York).

Ponting, K. G. 1976. "Indigo and Woad." *Folk Life* 14: 75–88.

Popham, Mervyn R. 1970. *The Destruction of the Palace at Knossos* (Göteborg).

———. 1980. "Cretan Sites Occupied between c. 1450 and 1400 B.C." *Annual of the British School at Athens* 75: 163–67.

———. 1984. *The Minoan Unexplored Mansion at Knossos. Annual of the British School at Athens*, suppl. 17 (London).

Popham, Mervyn R., L. H. Sackett, and P. G. Themelis. 1979–80. *Lefkandi I: The Iron Age* (London).

Popham, Mervyn R., E. Touloupa, and L. H. Sackett. 1982. "The Hero of Lefkandi." *Antiquity* 56: 169–74.

Porada, Edith. 1965. *The Art of Ancient Iran* (New York).

———. 1969. "Iranian Art and Archaeology: A Report of the 5th International Congress, 1968." *Archaeology* 22 (January): 54–65.

Porter, Bertha, and Rosalind L. B. Moss. 1960–. *Topographical Bibliography of Ancient Egyptian Hieroglyphic Texts. . . .* 2nd ed. (Oxford).

Post, Lennart von, Emelie von Walterstorff, and Sune Lindqvist. 1925. *Bronsaaldersmanteln fraan Gerumsberget i Västergötland* (Stockholm).

Postgate, J. N., and J. A. Moon. 1982. "Excavations at Abu Salabikh, 1981." *Iraq* 44: 103–36.

Pottier, Edmond. 1908. "La Chouette d'Athéné." *Bulletin de Correspondance Hellénique* 32: 535–48.

Pottier, Edmond, and Salomon Reinach. 1888. *La Nécropole de Myrina* (Paris).

Prag, Kay. 1974. "The Intermediate Early Bronze-Middle Bronze Age." *Levant* 6: 69–116.

Praistorija Jugoslavenskih Zemalja III: Eneolitsko Doba (Sarajevo, 1979).

Prisse d'Avennes, A. C. 1878. *Histoire de l'art égyptien* (Paris).

Pritchard, James B. 1969. *Ancient Near Eastern Texts*. 3rd ed. (Princeton).

———. 1978. *Recovering Sarepta, A Phoenician City* (Princeton).

Protonotariou-Deilaki, E. 1969. "Tholotos Taphos Kazarmas." *Athens Annals of Archaeology (Arkhaiologika Analekta ex Athenon)* 2: 3–6.

Protsch, Reiner, and Rainer Berger. 1973. "Earliest Radiocarbon Dates for Domesticated Animals." *Science* 179: 235–39.

Puhvel, Jaan. 1976. "The Origins of Greek *kosmos* and Latin *mundus*." *American Journal of Philology* 97: 154–67.

———. 1977. " 'Basket' in Greek and Hittite." *American Journal of Philology* 98: 150–52.

———. 1981. " 'Spider' and 'Mole' in Hittite." In Yoel L. Arbeitman and Allan R. Bomhard, eds., *Bono Homini Donum: Essays in Historical Linguistics*, pp. 237–42 (Amsterdam).

———. 1983. "Homeric Questions and Hittite Answers." *American Journal of Philology* 104: 217–27.

Pulleyblank, E. G. 1983. "The Chinese and Their Neighbors in Prehistoric and Early Historic Times." In Keightley 1983, 411–66.

Pumpelly, Raphael, ed. 1908. *Explorations in Turkestan; Expedition of 1904* (Washington, D.C.).

Quagliati, Q. 1904. "Pisticci: tombe lucane con ceramiche greche." *Notizie degli Scavi di Antichità* 1: 196–208.

Quibell, J. E. 1908. *Catalogue général des antiquités égyptiennes: Tomb of Yuaa and Thuiu* (Cairo).

———. 1913. *Excavations at Saqqara V (1911–12): The Tomb of Hesy* (Cairo).

Quiring, H. 1945–47. "Vorphönizischer Königspurpur und *uqnû*-Stein." *Forschung und Fortschritte* 21–23: 98–99.

Raban, Avner. 1983. "The Biblical Port of Akko on Israel's Coast." *Archaeology* 36: 60–61.

Rachlin, Carol King. 1955. "The Rubber Mold Technic for the Study of Textile-impressed Pottery." *American Antiquity* 20: 394–96.

Raczky, Pál. 1976. "A Körös Kultúra Leletei Tiszajenőn." *Archeologiai Értesítő* 103: 171–89.

Radmilli, A. M. 1962. *Guida della preistoria italiana* (Florence).

Rapp, George, Jr., and S. E. Aschenbrenner.
1978. *Excavations at Nichoria in SW Greece I* (Minneapolis).

Rau, Wilhelm. 1970. "Weben und Flechten im vedischen Indien." *Akademie der Wissenschaften und der Literatur* 11.

Reed, Charles A. 1960. "Review of the Archaeological Evidence on Animal Domestication in the Prehistoric Near East." In Braidwood and Howe 1960, 119–145.

———. 1961. "Osteological Evidences for Prehistoric Domestication in Southwest Asia." *Zeitschrift für Tierzüchtung und Züchtungsbiologie* 76: 31–38.

———. 1977. *Origins of Agriculture* (The Hague).

Rees, Alwyn, and Brinley Rees. 1961. *Celtic Heritage* (London).

Reese, David S. 1980. "Industrial Exploitation of Murex Shells. . . ." *Libyan Studies* 11: 79–93.

Reisner, George A. 1923. *Excavations at Kerma IV* (Cambridge, Mass.).

Renfrew, Colin. 1972. *The Emergence of Civilisation: The Cyclades and the Aegean in the 3rd Millennium B.C.* (London).

———. 1985. *The Archaeology of Cult: The Sanctuary at Phylakopi* (London).

Renfrew, Jane. 1973. *Palaeoethnobotany* (New York).

Reusch, Helga. 1956. *Die zeichnerische Rekonstruktion des Frauenfrieses in böotischen Theben* (Berlin).

Rice, James W. 1963. "The Conservation of Historic Textile Colorants." *Textile Museum Journal* 1.2: 55–61.

Rice, Tamara Talbot. 1963. *A Concise History of Russian Art* (New York).

Richter, G.M.A. 1929. "Silk in Greece." *American Journal of Archaeology* 33: 27–33.

———. 1931. "A Stand by Kleitias and an Athenian Jug." *Bulletin of the Metropolitan Museum of Art* 26: 289–94.

———. 1945. "Greek Painting: Four Newly Acquired Vases." *Bulletin of the Metropolitan Museum of Art*, n.s. 3: 166–71.

———. 1965. *Handbook of Greek Art* (London).

Richter, G.M.A., and Alison Franz. 1968. *Korai* (London).

Ridgway, Brunilde S. 1977. "The Peplos Kore, Akropolis 679." *Journal of the Walters Art Gallery* 36: 49–61.

———. 1984. "The Fashion of the Elgin Kore."

J. Paul Getty Museum Journal 12: 29–58.

Riefstahl, Elizabeth. 1944. *Patterned Textiles in Pharaonic Egypt* (Brooklyn).

———. 1964. *Thebes in the Time of Amunhotep III* (Norman, Okla.).

Riefstahl, Elizabeth, and Suzanne Chapman. 1970. "A Note on Ancient Fashions." *Boston Museum Bulletin* 68: 244–59.

Riegl, Alois. 1889. *Die ägyptischen Textilfunde im k.k. österreichischen Museum* (Vienna).

Riis, P. J. 1948. *Hama, fouilles et recherches 1931–8 II.3: Les Cimitières à crémation* (Copenhagen).

Rimantienė, R. 1979. *Šventoji: Narvos kultūros gyvenietės* (Vilnius).

Ripinsky, Michael. 1983. "Camel Ancestry and Domestication in Egypt and the Sahara." *Archaeology* 36.3 (May–June): 21–27.

Robert, Carl. 1900. "Die Fusswaschung des Odysseus auf zwei Reliefs des fünften Jahrhunderts." *Athenische Mitteilungen* 25: 325–38.

Robertson, M. 1959. *Greek Painting* (Geneva).

Robinson, David M. 1941. *Excavations at Olynthus X* (Baltimore).

Robinson, Fred C. 1967. "European Clothing Names and the Etymology of *girl*." In W. W. Arndt, P. W. Brosman, F. E. Coenan, and W. P. Friedrich, eds., *Studies in Historical Linguistics in Honor of George Sherman Lane*, pp. 233–40 (Chapel Hill).

Robinson, Stuart. 1969. *A History of Dyed Textiles* (Cambridge, Mass.).

Rodden, Robert J. 1962. "Excavations at the Early Neolithic Site at Nea Nikomedeia, Greek Macedonia." *Prehistoric Society: Proceedings* 28: 267–88.

———. 1964. "A European Link with Chatal Huyuk: Uncovering a 7th Millennium Settlement, Part II." *Illustrated London News* 244 (April 18): 604–7.

Rodenwaldt, Gerhart. 1912. *Die Fresken des Palastes. Tiryns II* (Athens).

———. 1919. "Mykenische Studien I: Die Fussböden des Megarons von Mykenai." *Jahrbuch des deutschen archäologischen Instituts, Berlin* 34.

———. 1921. *Der Fries des Megarons von Mykenai* (Halle).

Roebuck, Carl Angus. 1969. *The Muses at Work: Arts, Crafts and Professions in Ancient Greece and Rome* (Cambridge, Mass.).

Rose, H. J. 1959. *A Handbook of Greek Mythology* (New York).

Rosenfeld, Hans-Friedrich. 1958. *Wort- und Sachstudien: Untersuchungen zur Terminologie des Aufzugs . . .* (Berlin).

Rostovtzeff, M. I. [1918] 1922. *Iranians and Greeks in South Russia* (Oxford).

———. 1941. *The Social and Economic History of the Hellenistic World II* (Oxford).

Roth, Henry Ling. [1913] 1951. *Ancient Egyptian and Greek Looms*. 2nd ed. (Halifax).

———. [1918] 1977. *Studies in Primitive Looms* (Carlton, Bedford; 1918 ed. Halifax).

Roth, Henry Ling, and Grace M. Crowfoot. 1921. "Models of Egyptian Looms." *Ancient Egypt* 4: 97–101.

Rouse, W.H.D. 1902. *Greek Votive Offerings* (Cambridge).

Rowe, L. E. 1908. "Egyptian Portraiture of the XX Dynasty." *Bulletin of the Museum of Fine Arts, Boston* 6: 47–50.

Rudenko, S. I. 1953. *Kul'tura naselenija gornogo Altaja v Skifskoe vremja* (Moscow).

———. 1968. *Drevnejshie v mire khudozhestvennye kovry i tkani* (Moscow).

———. 1970. *Frozen Tombs of Siberia*. Translated and updated by M. W. Thompson (Berkeley). [Original edition: Rudenko 1953.]

Rudolph, Richard C. 1978. *Chinese Archaeological Abstracts* (Los Angeles).

Ruoff, Eeva. 1981. "Stein- und bronzezeitliche Textilfunde aus dem Kanton Zürich." *Helvetia Archeologica* 12: 252–64.

Rybakov, B. A. [1967] 1968. "The Rusalii and the God Simargl-Pereplut." *Soviet Anthropology and Archaeology* 6.4: 34–59.

Ryder, M. L. 1962. "The Origin of Felt-making and Spinning." *Antiquity* 36: 304.

———. 1964a. "The Origin of Spinning." *Antiquity* 38: 293–94.

———. 1964b. "Fleece Evolution in Domestic Sheep." *Nature* 204: 555–59.

———. 1965. "Report of Textiles from Çatal Hüyük." *Anatolian Studies* 15: 175–76.

———. 1968. "The Origin of Spinning." *Textile History* 1: 73–82.

———. 1969a. "Changes in the Fleece of Sheep Following Domestication." In Ucko and Dimbleby 1969, 495–521.

———. 1969b. *Animal Bones in Archaeology* (Oxford and Edinburgh).

———. 1972. "Wool of the 14th Century B.C.

from Tell el-Amarna, Egypt." *Nature* 240 (December): 355–56.

———. 1974. "Wools from Antiquity." *Textile History* 5: 100–110.

———. 1977. "Some Miscellaneous Ancient Fleece Remains." *Journal of Archaeological Science* 4: 177–81.

———. 1983. *Sheep and Man* (London).

Ryder, M. L., and J. W. Hedges. 1973. "Some Ancient Scythian Wool from the Crimea." *Nature* 242: 480.

Säflund, Gösta. 1939. *Le Terremare della provincie di Modena . . .* (Lund).

Sakellarakis, Ioannes. 1974. "Anaskaphe Arkhanon." *Praktika tes Arkhaiologikes Etaireias 1974*: 207–12.

———. 1977. "Anaskaphai. Krete. Phourni Arkhanon." *Ergon tes Arkhaiologikes Etaireias 1977*: 166–74.

Saltzman, Max, A. M. Keay, and Jack Christensen. 1963. "The Identification of Colorants in Ancient Textiles." *Dyestuffs* 44: 241–51.

Sandars, N. K. 1985. *The Sea Peoples: Warriors of the Ancient Mediterranean* (London).

Sanday, Peggy R. 1974. "Female Status in the Public Domain." In M. Rosaldo and L. Lamphere, eds., *Woman, Culture, and Society*, pp. 189–206, 334–35 (Stanford).

Saporetti, Claudio. 1979. *The Status of Women in the Middle Assyrian Period*. Translated by B. Boltze-Jordan (Malibu).

Sapouna-Sakellaraki, Ephe. 1971. *Minoikon Zoma* (Athens).

Sarianidi, V. I. 1976. "Bactria in the Bronze Age." *Soviet Anthropology and Archaeology* 15: 49–83.

Sauer, Carl. 1952. *Agricultural Origins and Dispersals* (New York).

Sauter, Marc-R. 1976. *Switzerland from Earliest Times to the Roman Conquest* (London and Boulder).

Säve-Söderbergh, Torgny. 1957. *Four Eighteenth Dynasty Tombs* (Oxford).

Scamuzzi, Ernesto. 1965. *Egyptian Art in the Egyptian Museum of Turin* (New York).

Schachermeyr, F. 1960. "Das Keftiu-Problem." *Jahreshefte des österreichischen archäologischen Instituts Wien* 45: 44–68.

Schaefer, Gustav. 1938. "The Loom of Ancient Egypt." *CIBA Review* 16 (December): 546–49.

———. 1945. "On the History of Flax Cultivation." *CIBA Review* 49 (April): 1766–67.

Schaefer, H. 1943. "Hellenistic Textiles in Northern Mongolia." *American Journal of Archaeology* 47: 266–77.

Schaeffer, C.F.A. 1931. "Les Fouilles de Minetel-Beida et de Ras Shamra: 2e campagne." *Syria* 12: 1–14.

———. 1939. *Ugaritica I* (Paris, 1939).

———. 1951. "Une Industrie d'Ugarit: la pourpre." *Annales Archéologiques de la Syrie* 1.ii: 188–92.

———. 1952. *Enkomi-Alasia I* (Paris).

———. 1962. *Ugaritica IV* (Paris).

Schaeffer, Judith. 1975. "The Costume of the Korai—A Reinterpretation." *American Journal of Archaeology* 79: 149 [title only].

Schaeffer-Forrer, C.F.A. 1978. "Ex Occidente Ars." In *Ugaritica VII* (Paris), 475–551.

Scheil, V. 1921. "Notules." *Revue d'Assyriologie* 18: 95–100.

Schiaparelli, E. 1923. *Esplorazione della "Valle delle Regine." Relazione sui Lavori della Missione archeologica Italiana in Egitto* 1 (Turin).

———. 1927. *La Tomba intatta dell' Architetto Cha. Relazione sui Lavori della Missione archeologica in Egitto* 2 (Turin).

Schick, Tamar. 1986. "Perishable Remains from the Naḥal Ḥemar Cave." *Journal of the Israel Prehistoric Society* 19: 84–86 and 95*–97*.

Schlabow, Karl. 1937. *Germanische Tuchmacher der Bronzezeit* (Neumünster).

———. 1957. "L'Art du tissage dans l'Europe du nord aux périodes du bronze et du fer." *Bulletin de Liaison du CIETA* July 1957: 13–16.

———. 1958. "Textilien und Leder [Schwarza]." In Rudolf Feustel, *Bronzezeitliche Hügelgräberkultur im Gebiet von Schwarza (Südthüringen)*, pp. 28–38 (Weimar).

———. 1959. "Beiträge zur Erforschung der jungsteinzeitlichen und bronzezeitlichen Gewebetechnik. . . ." *Jahresschrift für mitteldeutsche Vorgeschichte* 43: 101–20.

———. 1965. *Der Thorsberger Prachtmantel* (Neumünster).

———. 1970. "Textileindrücke auf Tongefässen der Jungsteinzeit." In *Fundamenta Reihe A,2: Frühe Menschheit und Umwelt* (Cologne) 419–22.

———. 1974. "Vor- und frühgeschichtliche Textilfunde aus den nördlichen Niederlanden." *Palaeohistoria* 16: 171–221.

———. 1976. *Textilfunde der Eisenzeit in Norddeutschland* (Neumünster).

Schliemann, Heinrich. [1875] 1968. *Troy and Its Remains* (New York).

———. 1880a. *Ilios: The City and Country of the Trojans* (London).

———. 1880b. *Mycenae* (New York).

———. [1880] 1885. *Ilios, ville et pays des Troyens*. Translated by E. Egger, with extra appendices (Paris).

Schmidt, Erich F. 1932. *The Alishar Hüyük, Seasons of 1928 and 1929, Part I* (Chicago).

———. 1935. "The Persian Expedition at Rayy." *Bulletin of the University Museum of Pennsylvania* 5: 41–49.

———. 1937. *Excavations at Tepe Hissar, Damghan* (Philadelphia).

Schmidt, Hubert. 1902a. *Heinrich Schliemanns Sammlung trojanischer Altertümer* (Berlin).

———. 1902b. "Die Spinnwirtel aus Thon." In Dörpfeld 1902, 424–28.

———. 1943. *Tell Halaf I: Die prähistorischen Funde* (Berlin).

Schmidt, Karl Horst. 1967. "Die Stellung des Keltischen in frühgeschichtlicher Zeit." *Glotta* 44: 151–67.

Schmidt, R. R. 1945. *Die Burg Vučedol* (Zagreb).

Schmitter, M.-T. 1939. "Chine ou Proche-Orient? (Découvertes des fragments de tissus)." *Revue Archéologique* 6.13: 73–102.

Schneider, James. 1978. "Peacocks and Penguins: The Political Economy of European Cloth and Color." *American Ethnologist* 5: 413–47.

Schrader, Hans. 1939. *Die archaischen Marmorbildwerke der Akropolis* (Frankfurt).

Schrader, O. 1886. *Linguistisch-historische Forschungen zur Handelsgeschichte und Warenkunde* (Jena).

Schrader, Walter. 1961. *Alte Seidenstoffe Asiens* (Braunschweig).

Schuette, Marie. 1956. "Tablet Weaving." *CIBA Review* 117 (November): 1–29.

Schuette, Marie, and Sigrid Müller-Christensen. [1956] 1964. *A Pictorial History of Embroidery*. Translated by D. King (London).

Schultes, R. E. 1970. "Random Thoughts and Queries on the Botany of *Cannabis*." In C.R.B. Joyce and S. H. Curry, eds., *The Botany and Chemistry of Cannabis*, pp. 11–38 (London).

Schulze, Wilhelm. 1934. *Kleine Schriften* (Göttingen).

Schwartz, Martin. 1980. "The Etymon of *snake*, *snail*, and *sneak* in the Light of Indo-Iranian." In K. Klar, M. Langdon, and S. Silver, eds., *American Indian and Indo-European Studies*, pp. 461–67 (The Hague).

Schweitzer, Bernhard. 1971. *Greek Geometric Art* (London).

Seager, Richard B. 1910. *Excavations on the Island of Pseira* (Philadelphia).

Seibert, Ilse. 1974. *Women in the Ancient Near East* (New York).

Seiradaki, Mercy. 1960. "Pottery from Karphi." *Annual of the British School at Athens* 55: 1–37.

Selmeczi, L. 1969. "Das Wohnhaus der Körös-Gruppe von Tiszajenő." *Évkönyve, A Móra Ferenc Múzeum* 1969 no. 2: 17–22.

7000 Years of Iranian Art (Washington, D.C., 1964–65).

Shaw, Maria C. 1967. "An Evaluation of Possible Affinities between Egyptian and Minoan Wall Paintings." Ph.D. thesis, Bryn Mawr College.

———. 1970. "Ceiling Patterns from the Tomb of Hepzefa." *American Journal of Archaeology* 74: 25–30.

———. 1980. "Painted 'Ikria' at Mycenae?" *American Journal of Archaeology* 84: 167–79.

———. 1982. "Ship Cabins of the Bronze Age Aegean." *International Journal of Nautical Archaeology* . . . 11: 53–58.

Sheffer, Avigail. 1976. "Comparative Analysis of a 'Negev Ware' Textile Impression from Tel Masos." *Tel Aviv* 3: 81–88.

———. 1981. "The Use of Perforated Clay Balls on the Warp-weighted Loom." *Tel Aviv* 8: 81–83.

Sherratt, Andrew. 1981. "Plough and Pastoralism: Aspects of the Secondary Products Revolution." In I. Hodder, G. Isaac, and N. Hammond, eds., *Pattern of the Past: Studies in Honour of David Clarke*, pp. 261–305 (Cambridge).

Sidorov, A. 1930. "O vitie voloknistych veshchestv." *Izvestija Gosudarstvennaja Akademija Istorii Materialnoj Kul'tury* 6.5: 5–12.

Simon, Erika. 1983. *Festivals of Attica* (Madison, Wisc.).

Simpson, R. Hope. 1965. *Gazetteer and Atlas of Mycenaean Sites* (London).

Singer, Charles, E. J. Holmyard, and A. R. Hall, eds. 1954. *A History of Technology, Vol. I: From Early Times to Fall of Ancient Empires* (New York and London).

Singh, Purushottam. 1974. *Neolithic Cultures of Western Asia* (London and New York).

Sinitsyn, I. V. 1948. "Pamjatniki predskifskoj epokhi v stepjakh nizhnego povolzh'ja." *Sovetskaja Arkheologija* 10: 148–60.

Siret, Henri, and Louis Siret. 1887. *Les Premiers Ages du métal dans le sud-est de l'Espagne* (Brussels).

Siu, Ralph G. H. 1951. *Microbial Decomposition of Cellulose* (New York).

Six, J. 1919. "Altgriechische 'durchbrochene Arbeit.'" *Jahresheft des östereichischen archäologischen Instituts* 19–20: 162–66.

Skowronski, Hella, and Mary Reddy. 1974. *Sprang* (New York).

Slenczka, Eberhard. 1974. *Figürliche bemalte Mykenische Keramik aus Tiryns. Tiryns VII* (Mainz).

Smith, Leslie. 1982. "Textiles." In *Egypt's Golden Age: The Art of Living in the New Kingdom*, exh. cat. (Boston), 180–84.

Smith, Sydney. 1945. "Middle Minoan I–II and Babylonian Chronology." *American Journal of Archaeology* 49: 1–24.

Smith, W. Stevenson. 1935. "The Old Kingdom Linen List." *Zeitschrift für ägyptische Sprache* 71: 134–49.

———. 1958. *The Art and Architecture of Ancient Egypt* (Harmondsworth).

———. 1965. *Interconnections in the Ancient Near East* (New Haven and London).

Snodgrass, A. M. 1967. *Arms and Armour of the Greeks* (London).

Solovjev, L. N. 1950. "Selitsy s tekstil'noj keramikoj iz poberezh'ja Zapadnoj Gruzii." *Sovetskaja Arkheologija* 14: 265–305.

Specht, F. 1939. "Sprachliches Urheimat der Indogermanen." *Zeitschrift für vergleichende Sprachforschung* 66: 1–74.

Specht, W. 1959. "Kriminaltechnisches Gutachten über Garnproben der Gewebe 18 und 19." In Hundt 1959, 97–100.

Speiser, E. A. 1931–32. "Ethnic Movements in the Near East in the Second Millennium B.C.: The Hurrians. . . ." *Annual of the American Schools of Oriental Research* 13: 13–54.

———. 1935. *Excavations at Tepe Gawra* (Philadelphia).

Spyropoulos, Th. G. 1969. "Anaskaphe mykenaikou nekrotapheiou Tanagras." *Praktika tes Arkhaiologikes Etaireias* 1969: 5–15.

———. 1970. "Anaskaphe mykenaikou nekrotapheiou Tanagras." *Praktika tes Arkhaiologikes Etaireias* 1970: 29–36.

———. 1971. "Anaskaphe mykenaikou nekrotapheiou Tanagras." *Praktika tes Arkhaiologikes Etaireias* 1971: 7–14.

———. 1973. "Anaskaphe mykenaikes Tanagras." *Praktika tes Arkhaiologikes Etaireias* 1973: 11–21.

Spyropoulos, T., and John Chadwick. 1975. *The Thebes Tablets II. Minos*, suppl. 4 (Salamanca).

Stalio, B., and R. Galović. 1955. *Narodni Muzej, Beograd: Praistorija II: Katalog Keramike* (Belgrade).

Starkey, J. L. 1936. "Excavations at Tell ed-Duweir, 1935–6." *Palestine Exploration Fund Quarterly Statement* 1936: 178–89.

Starr, Richard F.S. 1939. *Nuzi. Report on the Excavations at Yorgan Tepe near Kirkuk, I* (Cambridge, Mass.).

Staub, Johannes. 1864. *Die Pfahlbauten in den Schweizer-Seen* (Zurich).

Staudigel, Otfried. 1975. "Tablet-weaving and the Technique of the Rameses-girdle." *Bulletin de liaison du CIETA* 41–42: 71–100.

Stein, Sir Mark Aurel. 1921. *Serindia* (Oxford).

Steinkeller, P. 1980. "Mattresses and Felt in Early Mesopotamia." *Oriens Antiquus* 19: 79–100.

Steinmann, A. 1937. "Les 'Tissus à jonques' du sud de Sumatra." *Revue des Arts Asiatiques* 11: 122–37.

Stephani, Ludolf. 1878–79. "Erklärung einiger Kunstwerke der kaiserlichen Ermitage. . . ." *Compte-Rendu de la Commission Impériale Archéologique* 1878-79.

Stephens, Ferris J. 1931. "The Ancient Significance of Sisith." *Journal of Biblical Literature* 50: 59–70.

Stern, Ephraim. 1984. *Excavations at Tel Mevorakh: Part Two: The Bronze Age. Qedem 18* (Jerusalem).

Stern, Philip Van Doren. 1969. *Prehistoric Europe* (New York).

Stewart, Andrew. 1983. "Stesichoros and the François Vase." In Moon 1983, 53–74.

Stewart, Eleanor, and James Stewart. 1950. *Vounous 1937–38* (Lund).

Stewart, Robert B. 1976. "Paleoethnobotanical Report—Çayönü 1972." *Economic Botany* 30: 219–25.

Stol, M. 1983. "Leder(industrie)." In *Reallexikon der Assyriologie und vorderasiatischen Archäologie* (Berlin), 527–43.

Strommenger, Eva. 1970. "Die Grabungen in Habuba Kabira-Süd." *Mitteilungen der deutschen*

Orientgesellschaft 102: 59–81.

Stubbings, Frank. 1951. *Mycenaean Pottery from the Levant* (Cambridge).

———. 1973. *Prehistoric Greece* (New York).

Suhr, Elmer G. 1969. *The Spinning Aphrodite* (New York).

Sulimirski, T. 1950. "The Problem of the Survival of the Tripolye Culture." *Prehistoric Society: Proceedings*, ser. 2, vol. 16: 42–51.

Swindler, Mary H. 1929. *Ancient Painting* (New Haven).

Sylwan, Vivi. 1924. "Die Technik der ägyptischen Wollwirkereien." In Dimand 1924, 22–28.

———. 1937. "Silk from the Yin Dynasty." *Bulletin of the Museum of Far Eastern Antiquities* 9: 119–26.

———. 1941. *Woollen Textiles of the Lou-lan People* (Stockholm).

———. 1949. *Investigation of Silk from Edsengol and Lop-Nor* (Stockholm).

Tallgren, A. M. 1926. "La Pontide préscythique après l'introduction des métaux." *Eurasia Septentrionalis Antiqua* 2.

———. 1930. "Caucasian Monuments: The Kazbek Treasure." *Eurasia Septentrionalis Antiqua* 5: 109–82.

———. 1934. "Sur les monuments mégalithiques du caucase occidentale." *Eurasia Septentrionalis Antiqua* 9: 1–46.

Tarasov, L. M. 1965. "Paleoliticheskaja Stojanka Gagarino." *Materialy i Issledovanija po Arkheologii SSSR* 131: 111–40.

Taylour, Lord William. 1958. *Mycenaean Pottery in Italy* (Cambridge).

———. 1969. "Mycenae, 1968." *Antiquity* 43: 91–97.

———. 1970. "New Light on Mycenaean Religion." *Antiquity* 44: 270–79.

Terrace, Edward L.B. 1968. *Egyptian Paintings of the Middle Kingdom* (New York).

Textiele bodemvondsten (Amsterdam, 1981).

Theocharis, D. 1973. *The Neolithic in Greece* (Athens).

Thomas, Angela P. 1981. *Gurob, A New Kingdom Town* (Warminster).

Thomas, Homer L. 1967. *Near Eastern, Mediterranean, and European Chronology* (Lund).

Thompson, M. W. 1968. "The Horizontal Loom at Novgorod." *Medieval Archaeology* 12: 146–47.

Thompson, Wesley. 1982. "Weaving: A Man's Work." *Classical World* 75: 217–22.

Thomsen, Thomas. 1935. "Egekistefundet fra Egtved." *Nordiske Fortidsminder* 2: 165–201.

Thomson, George. 1978. *The Prehistoric Aegean* (London).

Thomson, W. G. 1973. *A History of Tapestry*. 3rd ed. (East Ardsley, Wakefield, Yorkshire).

Thorburn, W. A. 1976. "Military Origins of Scottish National Dress." *Costume* 10: 29–40.

Thureau-Dangin, F. 1934. "Un Comptoir de laine pourpre à Ugarit d'après une tablette de Ras Shamra." *Syria* 15: 137–46.

Thurstan, Violetta. 1954. *A Short History of Ancient Decorative Textiles*. 2nd ed. (London).

Tidow, Klaus. 1966. "Von Spinnen und Weben und ihrer Darstellung im Textilmuseum Neumünster." *Die Heimat* 73: 168–70.

Tihelka, K. 1960. "Moravský Věteřovský Typ." *Památky archeologické* 51.

Tilke, Max. 1945. *Kostümschnitte und Gewandformen* (Tübingen).

Tobler, Arthur J. 1950. *Excavations at Tepe Gawra* (Philadelphia).

Tolmacheff, V. 1934. "Les Antiquités scythes en Chine." *Eurasia Septentrionalis Antiqua* 9: 256–58.

Tosi, Maurizio. 1968. "Excavations at Shahr-i Sokhta, A Chalcolithic Settlement in the Iranian Sistan." *East and West* 18: 9–66.

Trendall, A. D. 1956. "Archaeology in Sicily and Magna Graecia." *Archaeological Reports 1955*, Supplement, *Journal of Hellenic Studies* 76: 47–62.

Trippett, Frank. 1974. *The First Horsemen* (New York).

Tsountas, Chrestos, and J. Irving Manatt. [1897] 1969. *The Mycenaean Age* (Amsterdam).

Tsuboi, Mieko. 1984. "Hemp-Yarn Wetting Vessel" [in Japanese]. *Senshoku no Bi* [*Textile Art*] 30 (Summer): 148–49.

Tufnell, Olga. 1953. *Lachish III: The Iron Age* (Oxford).

———. 1958. *Lachish IV: The Bronze Age* (London).

Tzakhili-Douskou, Iris. 1982. "Ta poikila Theraika imatia. . . ." *Athens Annals of Archaeology* (*Arkhaiologika Analekta ex Athenon*) 14: 251–64.

Ucko, Peter J., and G. W. Dimbleby. eds. 1969. *The Domestication and Exploitation of Plants and Animals* (Chicago).

Ur- und frühgeschichtliche Archäologie der Schweiz. 1968–79. 6 vols. (Basel).

Uvarova, Praskov'ja S. 1902. *Kollektsii Kavkaz-skogo muzeja, t.5: Arkheologija* (Tiflis).

Valvasor, Johann Weichard. 1689. *Die ehre dess hertzogthums Crain* (Laybach and Nürnberg).

Van Buren, E. D. 1926. *Greek Fictile Revetments in the Archaic Period* (London).

Van den Berghe, Pierre L. 1979. *Human Family Systems: An Evolutionary View* (New York).

Vandier, J. 1952. *Manuel d'archéologie égyptienne 1,2* (Paris).

Van Gennep, Arnold. 1912. "Note sur le tissage aux cartons en Chine." *T'oung Pao* 13: 693–98.

Van Gennep, Arnold, and G. Jéquier. 1916. *Le Tissage aux cartons et son utilisation décorative dans l'Égypte ancienne* (Neuchâtel).

Van Loon, Maurits. 1966. *Urartean Art* (Istanbul).

———. 1969. "New Sites in the Euphrates Valley." *Archaeology* 22 (January): 65–68.

———. 1975. *Korucutepe*. Vol. 1 (Amsterdam).

———. 1978. *Korucutepe*. Vol. 2 (Amsterdam).

———. 1980. *Korucutepe*. Vol. 3 (Amsterdam).

Van Reesema, Elizabeth Siewertsz. 1920. "Old Egyptian Lace." *Bulletin of the Needle and Bobbin Club* 4: 12–18.

———. 1926. *Contribution to the Early History of Textile Technics* (Amsterdam).

Van Selms, A. 1954. *Marriage and Family Life in Ugaritic Literature* (London).

Van Seters, John. 1966. *The Hyksos, A New Investigation* (New Haven).

Vasić, Miloje M. 1902. "La Nécropole de Kličevac." *Revue Archéologique* 40: 172ff.

———. 1932. *Preistoriska Vinča*. Vol. 1 (Belgrade).

———. 1936a. *Preistoriska Vinča*. Vol. 2 (Belgrade).

———. 1936b. *Preistoriska Vinča*. Vol. 3 (Belgrade).

Vasmer, Max. [1950–58] 1964–73. *Etimologicheskij Slovar' Russkogo Jazyka*. Translated from German by O. I. Trubachev (Moscow).

Vaughan, Agnes Carr. 1959. *House of the Double Axe* (Garden City, N.Y.).

Veenhof, Klaas R. 1972. *Aspects of Old Assyrian Trade and Its Terminology* (Leyden).

Ventris, Michael, and John Chadwick. 1973. *Documents in Mycenaean Greek*. 2nd ed. (Cambridge).

Vercoutter, Jean. 1954. *Essai sur les relations entre Égyptiens et Préhellènes* (Paris).

———. 1956. *L'Égypte et le monde égéen préhellénique* (Cairo).

Verkhovskaja, A. S. 1955. "Tekstil'nye Izdelija iz Raskopok Karmir-Blura." In B. B. Piotrovskij, *Karmir-Blur III*, pp. 67–71 (Yerevan).

Vermeule, Emily T. 1975. *The Art of the Shaft Graves of Mycenae* (Cincinnati).

Vermeule, Emily T., and Vassos Karageorghis. 1982. *Mycenaean Pictorial Vase Painting* (Cambridge, Mass.).

Verneau, René. 1906. *Les Grottes de Grimaldi: Vol. 2* (Monaco).

Veselovskij, N. I. 1898. "Kubanskaja oblast': Raskopki." *Russkaja Arkheologicheskaja Kommissija: Otchët*: 29–39.

Vogt, Emil. 1937. *Geflechte und Gewebe der Steinzeit* (Basel).

———. [1946] 1947. "Basketry and Woven Fabrics of the European Stone and Bronze Ages." *CIBA Review* 54: 1938–64.

Vogt, Hans Heinrich. 1973. *Farben und ihre Geschichte* (Stuttgart).

Voigt, Mary M. 1983. *Hajji Firuz Tepe, Iran: The Neolithic Settlement* (Philadelphia).

von der Osten, Hans H. 1934. *Ancient Oriental Seals in the Collection of Mr. Edward T. Newell*. Oriental Institute Publications 22 (Chicago).

———. 1937. *The Alishar Hüyük, Seasons of 1930–32*, Parts 1–3. Oriental Institute Publications 28–30 (Chicago).

Von Stokar, Walter. 1938. *Spinnen und Weben bei den Germanen* (Leipzig).

Vouga, Paul. 1923. *La Tène* (Leipzig).

———. 1934. *Le Néolithique lacustre ancien* (Neuchâtel).

Vydra, Josef. 1954. *Indigo Blue Print in Slovak Folk Art* (Prague).

Wace, Alan J.B. 1919–21. "Excavations at Mycenae: 4—The Rhyton Well." *Annual of the British School at Athens* 24: 200–209.

———. 1921–23. "Excavations at Mycenae: 2, The Granary." *Annual of the British School at Athens* 25: 38–61.

———. 1948. "Weaving or Embroidery?" *American Journal of Archaeology* 52: 51–55.

Wace, Alan J.B., and Sir Arthur Evans. 1931. "Prehistoric Dress." In Leonard Whibley, *Companion to Greek Studies*, 4th ed., pp. 618–24 (New York).

Wace, Alan J.B., and M. Thompson. 1912. *Prehistoric Thessaly* (Cambridge).

Waetzoldt, H. 1972. *Die neo-sumerische Textilindustrie* (Rome).

Wainwright, G. A. 1913. "The Keftiu People of the Egyptian Monuments." *Annals of Archaeology and Anthropology, Liverpool* 6: 24–83.

———. 1920. *Balabish* (London).

Walberg, Gisela. 1976. *Kamares: A Study of the Character of Palatial Middle Minoan Pottery* (Uppsala).

———. 1983. *Provincial Middle Minoan Pottery* (Mainz).

Wallis, Henry. 1900. *Egyptian Ceramic Art* (London).

Walters, H. B. 1893. "Odysseus and Kirke on a Boeotian Vase." *Journal of Hellenic Studies* 13: 77–87.

Ward, William A. 1971. *Egypt and the East Mediterranean World, 2200–1900 B.C.* (Beirut).

Warren, Peter. 1967. "Minoan Stone Vases as Evidence for Minoan Foreign Connections." *Prehistoric Society: Proceedings* 33: 37–56.

———. 1968. "A Textile Town—4500 Years Ago?" *Illustrated London News* 252 (February 17): 25–27.

———. 1969. "Minoan Village on Crete." *Illustrated London News* 254 (February 8): 26–27.

———. 1972. *Myrtos: An Early Bronze Age Settlement in Crete* (Oxford).

———. 1975. *The Aegean Civilizations* (Oxford).

Watson, Burton. 1961. *Records of the Grand Historian of China*. Vol. 2 (New York).

Watson, D.M.S. 1931. "The Animal Bones from Skara Brae." In Childe 1931, 198–204.

Watson, Patty Jo. 1979. *Archaeological Ethnography in Western Iran* (Tuscon).

Weber, Hans. 1969–70. " 'Coae Vestes.' " *Istanbuler Mitteilungen* 19/20: 249–53.

Webster, T.B.L. 1972. *Potter and Patron in Classical Athens* (London).

Weinberg, Gladys Davidson, and Saul S. Weinberg. 1956. "Arachne of Lydia at Corinth." In *The Aegean and the Near East; Studies Presented to Hetty Goldman* (New York), 262–67.

Weinberg, Saul S. 1962. "Prehistoric Elateia." *Hesperia* 31: 158–209.

Weir, Shelagh. 1970. *Spinning and Weaving in Palestine* (London).

Wharton, Edward Ross. 1882. *Etyma Graeca* (London).

Whittle, Alasdair. 1985. *Neolithic Europe: A Survey* (Cambridge).

Wild, John Peter. 1966. " 'Mantus.' " *Zeitschrift für vergleichende Sprachforschung* 80: 247–48.

———. 1967. "Two Technical Terms Used by Roman Tapestry-weavers." *Philologus* 111: 151–55.

———. 1970a. *Textile Manufacture in the Northern Roman Provinces* (Cambridge).

———. 1970b. "Borrowed Names for Borrowed Things?" *Antiquity* 44: 125–30.

———. 1976. "Loanwords and Roman Expansion in North-west Europe." *World Archaeology* 8: 57–64.

———. 1984. "Some Early Silk Finds in Northwest Europe." *Textile Museum Journal* 23: 17–23.

Willets, R. F. 1969. *Everyday Life in Ancient Crete* (New York).

Williams, Bruce. 1975. "Archaeology and Historical Problems of the Second Intermediate Period." Ph.D. thesis, University of Chicago.

Williams, Charles K. II, and Joan E. Fisher. 1973. "Corinth, 1972: The Forum Area." *Hesperia* 42: 1–44.

Wills, Norman T. 1979. *Woad in the Fens*. 3rd ed. (Long Sutton, Lincs.).

Wilson, Lillian. 1930. "The Loom Weights [Olynthus]." In David M. Robinson, *Johns Hopkins University Excavations at Olynthus II*, pp. 118–29 (Baltimore).

Wilson, Thomas. 1893–94. "The Swastika." *Report of the U.S. National Museum* 1893/4: 763–1011.

Windeknecht, Margaret, and Thomas Windeknecht. 1981. "Color-and-Weave on a Light-Dark Sequence." *Shuttle, Spindle, and Dyepot* 48 (Fall): 24–27.

Winlock, H. E. 1920. "The Egyptian Expedition 1918–1920: Excavations at Thebes." *Bulletin of the Metropolitan Museum of Art* 15 (December): pt. 2.

———. 1922. "Heddle-jacks of Middle-Kingdom Looms." *Ancient Egypt* 5: 71–74.

———. 1942. *Excavations at Deir el-Bahri, 1911–31* (New York).

———. 1945. *The Slain Soldiers of Neb-ḥepēt-Rē ʿMentūḥotpe* (New York).

———. 1955. *Models of Daily Life in Ancient Egypt* (Cambridge, Mass.).

Winlock, H. E., and W. E. Crum. 1926–33. *The*

Monastery of Epiphanius at Thebes (New York).

Winter, W. 1958. "Review of Ventris and Chadwick." *American Journal of Philology* 79: 201–8.

Wipszycka, Eva. 1965. *L'Industrie textile dans l'Égypte romaine* (Warsaw and Krakow).

Wiślański, Tadeusz, ed. 1970. *The Neolithic in Poland* (Wrocław).

Woolley, Sir Leonard. 1934. *Ur Excavations 2* (London).

———. 1955. *Alalakh* (Oxford).

Wreszinski, Walter. 1914–39. *Atlas zur altägyptischen Kulturgeschichte* (Leipzig).

Wright, Henry T., ed. 1981. *An Early Town on the Deh Luran Plain: Excavations at Tepe Farukhabad* (Ann Arbor).

Wyatt, W. F. 1968. "Early Greek /y/." *Glotta* 46: 229–37.

Wyss, René. 1969. "Wirtschaft und Technik." In *Ur- und frühgeschichtliche Archäologie der Schweiz II: Jüngere Steinzeit* (Basel), 117–38.

———. 1973. *Wirtschaft und Gesellschaft in der Jungsteinzeit* (Bern).

Xanthoudides, Stephanos A. 1910. "Epinetron." *Athenische Mitteilungen* 35: 323–34.

———. 1922. "Minoikon megaron Nirou." *Arkhaiologike Ephemeris* 1922: 1–25.

———. 1924. *Vaulted Tombs of the Messara* (London).

Yadin, Yigael. 1963. *The Art of Warfare in Biblical Lands*. Translated by M. Pearlman (New York).

Yadin, Yigael, Y. Aharoni, R. Amiran, T. Dothan, I. Dunayevsky, and J. Perrot. 1960. *Hazor II* (Jerusalem).

Yates, James. 1843. *Textrinum Antiquorum: An Account of the Art of Weaving among the Ancients* (London).

Yetts, W. Perceval. 1926. "Discoveries of the Kozlóv Expedition." *Burlington Magazine* 48: 168–84.

Yonge, C. D., and H. Drisler. 1893. *An English-Greek Lexicon* (New York).

Young, D. 1965. "Some Puzzles about Minoan Woolgathering." *Kadmos* 4: 111–22.

Young, Rodney S. 1958. "Gordion Campaign of 1957, Preliminary Report." *American Journal of Archaeology* 62: 139–54.

———. 1962. "The 1961 Campaign at Gordion." *American Journal of Archaeology* 66: 153–68.

Young, Theodore Cuyler, Jr. 1962. "Taking the History of the Hasanlu Area Back Another Five Thousand Years. . . ." *Illustrated London News* 241 (November 3): 707–9.

———. 1971. *Excavations of the Godin Project* (Toronto).

Zadneprovskij, Ju. A. 1962. "Drevnezemledel'cheskaja Kul'tura Fergany." *Materialy i Issledovanija po Arkheologii SSSR* 118.

Zervos, Christian. 1954. *La Civilisation de la Sardaigne* (Paris).

Zeuner, Frederick E. 1963. *A History of Domesticated Animals* (London).

Zindorf, A., S. Horowitz, and R. Blum. 1971. "Textile Remains of Nahal Mishmar." In Bar-Adon 1971, 248–50.

Zisis, V. G. 1955. "Cotton, Linen, and Hempen Textiles from the Fifth century B.C." *Praktika tes Akademeias Athenon* 29: 587–93.

Zvrantsev, M. P. 1969. *Nezhegorodskaja Rez'ba* (Moscow).

Key numbers for the main site maps on pages xxiv–xxviii are given in parentheses immediately after place names: e.g., (A133). A number followed by i refers to an inset. Other pages with maps showing locations are followed by (map). The following abbreviations are used: (def.) = definition; (diag.) = diagram; (etym.) = etymology; n = note; p = picture; t = table.

Aahmesi, 155–56n
Aakerström, A., 174n
Aaström, P., 62–63, 174n
Abarnian cloth, 287
Abghaz coast, 168
Abrahams, D., 237
Abu Salabikh (A133), 57, 63
Abusir, 148
Abydos (C205), 155n
Acar, B., 81
accounts: of sheep flocks, 24–25, 28; of textile workers, 272n, 283; of wool, 24–25, 284. *See also* cuneiform records; Mycenaean Greek accounts
accuracy of Egyptian artists, 311, 337–38, 340, 345, 348, 350, 355n
Acemhöyük (A105), 171–72, 312n
aceramic Neolithic, 10, 12, 51, 80, 130n, 132
Achaemenids, 202
Achaians, 358, 372
acid, 176–77, 184, 216, 228n, 231–32, 235–36, 243
acid dyes, 235 (def.), 236
Acre. *See* Akko
acrobats, 316, 319, 320p, 325, 328, 330, 336, 394
Adaouste (A5), 17, 224, 230, 234
Adovasio, J., 51, 127, 132
Adriatic, 303
Aegean area (A), 35, 54, 59, 63–65, 76, 93, 98, 101, 107, 110, 162, 173, 174n, 203, 226n, 247, 263–64, 276–77, 279–81, 284, 300, 303, 311–57, 370, 376, 378p, 378n, 381–82, Plate 3
Aegean foreigners in Egypt. *See* Egyptian representations: of foreigners; emissaries
Aegean islands, 33, 112, 307, 311, 314, 334, 337, 354, 371, 392. *See also individual island names*
Aegean languages (pre-Hellenic), 260, 264, 266, 269, 271, 277–81, 279t
Aegean motifs in Egypt, 156, 162, 311, 331–57
Aegean pottery in Egypt, 75, 311, 331, 345, 351, 356
Aegean representations of cloth. *See under* Minoan; Mycenaean
Aegean site list of minor textile finds, 174n
Aegean textile color analysis, 330, 347n
Aegean textiles in Egypt. *See under* ceiling designs; emissaries
aegis, 360, 363n
Aeschylus, 268n
Afghanistan, 52
Africa, 15n, 33–34, 117, 229, 234, 238n, 287, 291, 376
Aghia Irini, Keos/Kea (D236), 388–89
Aghia Triadha. *See* Hagia Triada
Aghios Nikolaos Museum, 75n
Ahlatlıbel, 306p (map), 392
Ahlberg, G., 377n
Ainu, 49
Akhenaton, 49n, 113n, 159, 331, 339t, 345, 352
Akhmim, 366n
Akkadian, 231; *baqamu*, 29; *gazazu*, 29; *kinaḫḫu*, 230; *kitinnu*, 255n, 295n; *kitû-*, 255n, 295n; *qanû*, 271; *suratha*, 230; *tabarru*, 230; *takiltu*, 230; *ugbabātum*, 291; *ûqnu*, 231
Akko (Acre) (C170), 229
Akok, M., 61
Akropolis, Athens, 91, 361, 364, 366n, 370n, 377, 380
Akropolis Korai: no. 594, 370n; no. 675, 366n; no. 686, 363–64
Akropolis Museum, 370n
Akrotiri (D241), 102, 124n, 229, 316. *See also* Thera; Theran frescoes
Alaca Höyük (A93), 60–61, 221n, 299–300, 301p (map), 306p (map), 307, 392
Albanian: *kanëp*, 36; *ngjehs*, 254
Albright, W., 229, 237–42, 300, 302, 389–90
Alcibiades, 32
Aldred, C., 148, 155n
Alexandrian scholars, 373, 380
Ali Kosh (A138), 22, 51, 131–32, 391
Alishar (A95), 68, 99, 164, 167, 167p, 212, 300, 300p, 301p (map), 306p (map), 307, 388–90, 392
alkali, 11, 54, 176, 232, 235–36, 281n (etym.)

alkanet, 232, 232n (etym.)
Alkanna tinctoria, 232
Alkinoos, 102, 284
Allchin, F., 32–33
allotments, of materials, 265, 273n, 283–85
Alps (A), 194, 306p (map)
Altaic language family, 37–38
Altai mountains (A inset), 18, 31, 199, 201p, 203, 205–6, 219, 221, Plate 4
Althaia, 376
Altrier, 32
Altyn-depe, 305, 391
alum, 232, 236 (def.), 237–38, 276; mineral sources of, 238n
Amarna (C199), 49n, 70, 71p, 86, 88–89, 221, 286, 331, 339t, 352, 396
Amarna period, 88, 156n, 162
Amarna workmen's village, 88–89
Amasis, 33
Amazons, 360, 372
ambassadors. *See* emissaries
amber, 184, 195
Ambroz, A., 297, 298n
Amenemheb, 331, 396
Amenemhet (scribe), 339t, 340, 342, 396, Plate 3
Amenemhet II (pharaoh), 347
Amenemopet (Imenemipet), 331
Amenhotep I, 339t
Amenhotep II, 113n, 114p, 158, 333–34, 339t, 342–44, 347, 352n, 353n, 396
Amenhotep III, 159, 331, 339t, 341, 345, 348–49, 349p, 352
Amenmose (priest), 339t, 347, 396
Amenmose (royal scribe), 339t, 343, 396
Amenuser. *See* Useramon
Americans, 121n, 122, 299n
Amiet, P., 42, 57p, 83, 84p
ammonia, 236, 238–39, 274
Amon, 158, 331, 334, 339t, 340, 344, 348, 350
Amorgos (D239), 174n
anachronisms, 29, 85n, 171, 261
analogical explanation, 37, 362n, 381. *See also* reversals
Anati, E., 91, 91p
Anatolia, 3, 10, 12, 15–16, 18, 51n, 59–63, 65, 78, 97, 99, 101–2, 113, 124, 127, 132, 164, 166–74, 196–98, 203, 212, 217–18, 221, 230, 238n, 249, 251, 254, 259, 287–88, 299–302, 300p, 301p (map), 307–8, 311, 355n, 359, 387, 391–92
Anau, 303, 303–4pp, 304n, 305, 306p (map), 306n, 308, 391–93
Anchusa tinctoria, 232
Andalucia, 33, 144
Andersson, J., 17
Andes mountains, 81
Andromache, 372–73, 377, 380
Anena. *See* Ineni
Anglo-Indian, *bang*, 37
Anglo-Saxon era, 19, 101, 235n, 277

Anglo-Saxon word-forms. *See* Old English
angular design, 365, 370–71, 374–75pp
Anherkhawi. *See* Inherkha
animal fiber (generic), 176, 202n, 236n. *See also* fur; hair; wool; *individual animals*
animal friezes, 353p, 354, 356, 356p, 363–67, 363p, 366–67pp, 369–72, 369p, 377, 379
Ankara Museum of Anatolian Civilizations, 61, 171, 337p
ankh sign, 120, 120p, 157, 160p, 161 (def.), 353
Antef, 332–33, 339t, 347, 396, Plate 3
Antefoker, 341
Anthes, R., 347–48
anti-sumptuary laws, 372, 377–78
antler, 55
Antrea, 41. *See also* Korpilahti
Aphrodisias (A99), 93, 94p, 101, 103–4, 167n, 300, 301p (map), 388–89
Aphrodite, 257, 376
appendices discussed: A, 101, 104; B, 306n, 307; C, 316n; D, 338n, 339t
appliqué, 162, 200, 219–20, 321
Apremont (A8), 119
Arabia, 33
Arabic, 281n; *al hinna*, 232n; *halfa*, 33; *kanūn* (Syrian), 271; *ras el maghzal* (Egyptian), 53
Arachne, 105, 106p, 198
Aral Sea, 306p (map)
Ararat (A89), 231
archaeolinguistics. *See* linguistic analysis
Archaeological Institute, London, 132n, 302n
Archaic Greek era, 3, 53–54, 69, 70p, 107, 274. *See also* Greek art: Archaic
archil, 232
Argissa Magula (A47), 22
Argolid (D), 174n, 355
Argos, 356
Ariadne, 77, 267
Aristarchus, 373
Aristophanes, 262, 274
Arkhanes (D247), 74, 388–89
Armageddon, 158
Armenia, 202n, 231, 238
Armenian: *kanap'*, 36; *kirmiz*, 231n
armor, 173n, 194, 205n, 220, 298n, 313, 372
Armoy, County Antrim (A10), 30, 112, 195, 196p
Arrephoroi, 362, 377
arsenic, 231
Artamonov, M., 219–20
Artemis, 298n
art history, 247, 355n, 366, 370n, 383
asafoetida, 232
Ashanti, 291
Ashdod, 242
Ashmolean Museum, Oxford, 52n, 68n, 95, 107, 176, 352
Asia (A inset), 17, 30, 36, 38, 215–16, 221, 298; central, 31, 205n, 215, 220–21 (*see also* steppes); eastern, 17–

19, 78, 85n, 215, 253; south-central, 18, 205; south-eastern, 225, 231; southwestern, 23, 157; western, 234

Asia Minor, 29, 69, 203, 232, 379. *See also* Anatolia; Turkey

Askarov, A., 31, 289

asphalt, 130–31

Assiut (C202), 339t, 345, 346p, 396

Aššur (A124), 287–88, 292

Assyria, 33, 212, 231–33, 287–88, 291–92

Assyrian: *gabû*, 238; *isu*, 33; *kuniphu, kunibu*, 38; *mardutu, mardatu*, 212. *See also* Neo-Assyrian

Assyrian botanical gardens, 33

Assyrian chemistry manual, 230, 232–33, 238–39

Assyrians, 33, 38, 171, 202, 212, 230, 232–33, 238–39, 287–88, 291

Assyrian textile trade, 171, 238n, 287–88, 291

Asterios, 381

asymmetrical pile-knot, 202, 202p (diag.)

Aszód (A67), 95, 387, 389

Atchity, K., 293, 376n

Atenists, 64

Athena, 105, 106p, 199, 206, 292, 297, 298n, 338n, 361–62, 361p, 364, 368, 373, 376–78, 380–81, 382n; peplos of, 292, 361–64, 361p, 368, 377, 380–82; Polias, 361, 380; statue of, 292, 298n, 361, 363; weaving contest with Arachne, 105, 106p, 198–99

Athenians, 290, 360–63, 365p, 377, 380

Athens (D228), 32, 68, 204–5, 290, 292, 297, 298n, 336n, 361–64, 372, 380–81; destroyed by Persians, 92n, 363–64, 370n, 380

Atkinson, T., 63n, 107n, 241, 322p, 395

Atlantic coast, 12, 229

Atropos, 263

Attica (D), 18, 33, 63, 64p, 72p, 78, 92n, 205–6, 366, 367–68pp, 370, 371p, 377

Attic dialect, 260, 266, 276

Attic Geometric. *See* Greek Geometric era

Austria, 16, 18, 55, 168, 178, 186, 188p, 191p, 213, 213p, 226n, 295, 313

Avestan, *yāsta*-, 254

awnings. *See* canopy covers; pavilions

Ay, 113n, 339t, 396

Äyräpää, A., 41

Ayrton, E., 149

Babylonians, 32, 118, 212, 238

Babylonian, *sindhu*, 32

Backer, S., 21

backstrap loom, 81, 81p, 86, 106, 117–18, 124, 251n, 253–54, 270

Bacon, E., 102

Badari (C203), 83, 83p, 88, 112, 145

Badarian culture, 15n, 145–46, 151

bags, 30, 33, 49n, 79, 130, 132, 144, 174n, 197, 203

Baity, E., 31

Bakun, 306, 306p (map)

Balabish (C206), 30

balanced weave, 127 (def.), 128p (diag.), 134, 134p, 142, 149, 156–58, 166, 197, 200

Balashova, E., 168n

balcony, for weaving, 106

Balkans, 4p, 69, 173n, 216, 234n, 263, 281, 295n, 300, 311, 315

balls of thread, 10, 45p, 46, 49, 68, 70–73, 106–9, 115, 262, 266, 269, 326p

Baltic language, 36–37, 277

Baluchistan, 391

Bandkeramik culture, 16

band looms, 116–18, 116p, 124, 253–54, 259, 273n, 280, 283, 313, 326, 326p; representations of, 116–17, 116p

bands, 40, 80–81, 116, 118, 137, 156, 157p, 160p, 161–62, 191, 197–98, 210, 251–52, 259, 271–72, 312, 317, 325–27, 326p, 332, 336, 348, 353. *See also* belts; borders; heading band/cord; stripes; tapes

band weaving, 116–18, 124, 135–37, 142, 156, 183, 191, 251, 253–55, 258–59, 273n, 274, 279–81, 283–84, 291, 325–26, 353

Bankfield Museum, Halifax, 84p

Baqt, 44, 45p, 286

Bar-Adon, P., 71n, 86, 165, 165n, 224

Baranyovits, F., 231

Barber, E., 29, 31, 67, 153, 159–60, 169, 173, 255n, 261n, 262, 269, 274, 293, 295n, 297n, 298, 315, 336, 376n

Barber, P., 37, 362n

bards. *See* singers/singing

Barfield, L., 100–101, 100p, 175n, 390

bark. *See* tree bark

Barker, A., 42

Barkova, L., 200n

Baroja, J., 34

barred band pattern, 198, 324–28, 324–26pp, 327–28n, 332p, 344

Barrelet, M.-T., 164, 212

barrel-vaulted ceilings, 341–42, 347–48

Barrois, A., 83n

barrow. *See* burial mounds

Bar-Yosef, O., 12, 25, 51, 130n, 131, 132

Bash-Adar (A148i), 202

basic dyes, 236 (def.)

baskets/basketry, 5, 9, 33, 46n, 51, 70, 70p, 72, 72p, 79, 106, 132, 140, 144, 262, 264–65, 360. *See also* wool-baskets

basket weave, 127 (def.), 127p (diag.), 155, 165, 174n, 188, 210

Basques, 352n

Bass, G., 355n

bast, 11 (def.), 13 (def.), 15, 19–20, 25, 33, 40–41, 44, 49–50, 72–73, 134, 141, 190, 202n, 211, 217, 227, 230, 234, 249, 251–53, 255n, 259, 262, 295n; preparation of, 13, 19, 34, 41; structure of, 13; ultimate fibers of, 13, 20–21, 47–48

Batak tribes, 375–76

Bateman, A., 238n
batik, 225 (def.). *See also* resist-dyeing
Battaglia, R., 174
battle, of gods and giants, 361–62, 364, 380–82
Batto, B., 291–92
Battonya Parazstanya, 95
Baud, M., 396
Baumgartel, E., 83n
Bavaria, 178
Bayeux Tapestry, 373
Bazin, M., 61
beading, 39, 93, 140p, 140–41, 154–55, 156n, 162, 171–73, 195, 312, 314, 342
beads, 51–52, 55, 130, 141, 155, 171–72, 174, 184, 200, 223, 313; woven in, 155, 172
beaters: for cleaning, 239, 274, 285; for weft, 83–84, 85 (def.), 86, 89, 92n, 273–74
beating fibers, 13–14, 215–16, 262–63
beating weft up, 84–86, 92, 92p, 113, 205n, 253, 269, 273–74, 278t, 279–80, 280t, 360n
Beckwith, J., 206
Bedini, A., 195
Bedouins, 44p, 56, 81, 302
Beer Sheba (C186), 302n, 388, 390
Behringen (B153), 218
beige, 190
Belgrade, 294n; State Folk Ensemble of, 258p
Bell, H., 132n, 302n
Bellinger, L., 13, 18, 47–48, 50, 53n, 66, 68, 197–98, 211, 219, 231
Belt Cave (A141), 22, 391
belt-hooks, 132
belts, 30, 40, 69, 80–81, 118–21, 120p, 144, 155–56, 159, 172, 178–80, 179p, 183–84, 195, 196p, 200, 217, 224, 252–55, 257–59, 281, 295, 312, 317, 319, 320p, 325, 332–33, 336, 348, 352, 359, 363; words for, 254. *See also* bands; clothing: girdle/sash
benches, for weaving, 105
Beni Hasan (C197), 44, 45p, 48, 74p, 84, 84p, 151, 286p
Benson, J., 371
Benveniste, E., 261n
Berciu, D., 97, 389
Berehinia, 298n
Beresford, W., 234–35n
Berger, R., 22–23
Berlin, B., 230
Bernabò Brea, L., 303–4, 392
berries, as source of dye, 232–33
Bethel, 242
Beth Shan (Shean) (C174), 63, 71p
Beth Shemesh, 242
Beycesultan (A100), 59n, 217, 221n, 251, 306p (map), 307, 392
bias cut, 318n
Bible, 50, 72, 229–30. *See also* Chronicles; Exodus; Joshua; Old Testament
Biel, J., 32, 204

bier cloths, 218, 366–67, 374, 377–78
birds, as symbols/spirits, 203, 297, 298n, 367–68, 376–77
Birka, 119
Bittel, K., 392
bitumen. *See* asphalt
Björkö, 119
black, 3, 11, 21, 29–30, 146, 155, 158–59, 165, 169–70, 169p, 172, 190, 195, 196p, 202, 206–8, 224–26, 230, 231n, 234n, 295n, 297, 312, 325–26, 325p, 328, 330, 334, 337, 347n, 364, 371, 378–79
Blackman, A., 396
Black Sea (A), 18, 92n, 168, 173n, 203, 205–6, 238n, 251, 306p (map), 306n, 379
blankets, 150, 155, 159, 174, 178p, 197, 200, 218–19, 225, 275, 358n, 360, 367, 376–78
bleaching, 14–15, 39, 216
Blegen, C., 54, 93, 93p, 103, 118, 171–72, 266, 278, 308p, 389
Bloesch, H., 197n
blue, 17, 49n, 119, 149, 154–56, 158–59, 166, 170–72, 174, 190, 195, 224–25, 227, 230, 233–35, 237, 312–13, 316, 318, 325–30, 325p, 332–35, 337–38, 341, 344, 347–49, 351–52, 371p, 372
Blum, R., 165
Blumner, H., 46, 70p
Boardman, J., 367n, 377–78
boar's tusk, 173n, 205n, 220, 313
boat cabins, spiral designs on, 343–45, 349
boats, 15, 34, 205, 218n, 301, 303, 334, 341–45, 344p, 349, 351–52n, 355n, 361, 373, 374p, 375; ethnic mixture on, 355n
bobbins, 54, 70, 77p, 80, 85, 89–91, 105, 107–8, 108p, 112, 116p, 178p, 192, 267, 273, 285, 360n. *See also* shuttles; spools
Boehmeria spp., 19, 73. *See also* ramie
Boğazköy (A94), 336, 337p
Boiotia (D), 92n, 112, 377
Bökönyi, S., 22–24, 26n, 28–29
Bolling, G., 359n, 372–73
Bologna (A36), 116, 265p, 269p
Bombyx spp., 30–31, 203
bone, 43, 51, 62–63, 107, 117–18, 132, 176
bones, 10–11, 22, 25–28, 76, 81, 132, 140, 167, 169, 172, 174, 223, 240; of sheep, 10, 22, 25–28, 240
Bonfante, L., 194–95, 224
Bonsanquet, R., 228–29
Book of the Dead, 12p
Borchardt, J., 173n, 220
Borchardt, L., 341–42, 396
borders, 32, 118–19, 122, 134–37, 158, 170, 180, 189, 191–92, 194–95, 197, 204, 210–14, 224, 272–73n, 283, 286, 312–13, 315, 317–19, 320p, 324p, 325–28, 330, 332, 335, 344, 348, 352, 354, 355n, 361p, 366, 370, 377, Plate 2, Plate 3; applied, 137, 148–49, 152, 156, 160–62, 191, 197, 200, 272–73n, 283–84, 336; closing, 117–18, 129, 135–37, 136p, 142, 180, 254, 273n, 283; independently shed, 118, 135, 191, 213,

254; side, 118. *See also* heading band/cord; selvedges

Borno (A33), 176

borrowed fashions, 315, 324, 330, 356, 382n

borrowed technology, 76, 113, 158, 160–62, 290, 322, 327n, 356–57

borrowed words. *See* linguistic borrowing

Borum Eshøj (B164), 122, 123p, 177–78, 179–80pp, 182–83, 195

Bosanquet, R., 35, 74

Bossert, H., 394–95

Boston Museum of Fine Arts, 149, 155n, 366p

botanical evidence. *See* palaeobiology

Boulding, E., 290

Bowen-Jones, H., 285

bows, for fluffing wool, 22

Bowyer, D., 240

Brack, A., and A. Brack, 396

braids/braiding, 137, 142, 200, 206

Braidwood, L., 51

Braidwood, R., 22, 25, 27n, 51, 79

brakes, for flax, 13, 14p

braking. *See* brakes; breaking

breaking, of flax, 13 (def.); of warp-threads, 148–49

Breasted, J., 158

Brice, W., 92p

brides, 292, 298n, 374

Britain, 99, 101, 113, 184–86, 195, 234n, 238, 277, 285

British Museum, 12p, 44p, 46p, 49n, 52n, 65p, 69, 224, 272p, 341, 361p, 363p, 364, 369p, 375p

Britons, 234

Brittany, 324

Brjusov, A., 144n

brocade, 10, 138p, 139–40, 139p, 142, 144, 159 (def.), 189, 224, 237n, 268n. *See also* supplementary weft

Brock, J., 371

Broholm, H., 105, 176–78, 180, 182–83, 217

Bromberger, C., 61

Bronze Age, 20, 25n, 28–30, 31, 33, 34p (map), 35, 40, 55, 59n, 60, 65, 68–69, 73, 84, 86, 98, 101, 110, 112–13, 115, 116p, 123p, 141–44, 163–85, 192–95, 197, 211, 214, 218, 220n, 222, 225, 226n, 231n, 235n, 241, 255–58, 263–64, 266, 269–70, 280–81, 287, 292–93, 294p, 295, 296p, 297, 299–302, 303n, 304, 306–7pp, 311–57, 365, 370p, 377, 378n, 380–82, 387–88, 392; Early, 54, 60p, 61–62, 68, 73, 76, 93, 94p, 101, 104p, 107, 110, 113, 121–22, 142, 166n, 168, 170–71, 173–74nn, 175p, 176, 183–85, 193–94, 210, 217, 221, 239, 281, 288, 300, 300–301pp, 306, 308, 308p, 312, 314, 329, 338, 387–88, 392; Late, 50, 62–63, 64p, 71, 91, 107, 112, 124n, 166, 172–74, 185, 186, 191p, 192–93, 195, 218, 224, 229, 242, 256p, 281, 284–85, 299, 301n, 302–3, 308–9, 309p, 313, 315, 325, 331n, 350–51, 353–55, 357, 369–71, 369p, 382, 387–88, 391; Middle, 68, 74, 107n, 124, 165, 174n, 184, 224, 229, 281, 300–302, 300–301pp, 307, 314, 372, 387–88, 392; in Scandinavia, 19, 29, 113, 122, 176–83, 191, 193, 255, 258

Bronze Age sheep breeds, 22n, 24–25

bronze on linen, 313. *For other uses, see* metal

broom, 16, 228

Broudy, E., 85n, 112, 115–17, 125, 213

Brown, J., 289

brown, 21, 29, 154, 156, 158, 172, 177, 188p, 190, 191p, 200, 204, 217, 224–25, 230–33, 312, 332

Brugsch, E., 342

Bruin, F., 229

Brukner, B., 98n, 99, 144n, 389

Brunello, F., 223–24, 231–32, 234–35

Brunhilde, 373

Brunton, G., 65, 83n, 145, 351

Bruyère, B., 286, 338n, 340, 342, 344, 396

Buccellati, G., 68n, 166n

Buchanan, B., 57p

Buchholz, H.-G., 350, 354

Buck, P., 155

Budge, W., 53p

buff, 3, 21, 29, 226, 378

buffalo robes, with year-chronicles, 373

Bukowski, Z., 121

Bulgaria, 97–98, 144, 173n, 297, 388–89

Bulgarian, *konop*, 36

bull-and-spiral design, 338, 342, 347–50, 349p

Bull from the Sea, 381

bull-leaping, 315–16, 325, 395

bull's head design, 173, 311, 319–20, 321p, 322, 332p, 335p, 338, 342, 347–51, 349p, 357; rhyta in, 335p, 349, 350

burial mounds, 3, 177, 181, 184, 197, 199, 217–19, 221, 234n. *See also* kurgans

Buriat: *ulhan, ylteneg*, 38

Burkett, M., 215–17, 220n

Burlington Fine Arts Club, 156

Burnham, H., 11, 51, 66–67, 99, 127–29, 130n

Burt, B., 155

Burton, H., 159

buttons, 200

buying/selling textiles, 287–90

Byzantine era, 32

cabins. *See* boat cabins

Caesar, 228, 234, 299n

Cairo, 49n, 151, 158, 322, Plate 1. *See also* Egyptian Museum

Cairo Agricultural Museum, 49n

calcium salts, as mordant/developer, 227, 237

Calypso, 105, 292

Çambel, H., 22

Cambridge Ancient History, 331n

Cambridge University Museum of Archaeology and Anthropology, 64

camels, 30, 42

Cameron, M., 322, 327p, 394–95

Camonica Valley (A34), 91, 91p

Campbell Thompson, R., 230, 232–33, 238

Campello, Alicante, 389–90

Canaanites, 229
cane, 264, 271 (etym.)
Can Hasan, 391
Cannabis spp., 15, 17–18, 38
canopy covers, 173n, 342, 344–45, 357, 378n
Capra, 23
captives, as craftworkers, 4, 158, 162, 284, 288, 290–91, 321, 352, 359, 376
caravans, 205n, 287–88
carbonate of soda, as mordant/developer, 233, 238
carbonized remains. *See* preservation: by carbonization
carbon stain, 153
Carchemish, 63
carded yarn. *See* woolen yarn
cards/carding, 20, 22, 26n, 261, 264, 285
card weaving. *See* tablet weaving
Carington Smith, J., 97n, 98–100, 105, 109–10, 174n, 241, 304n, 308, 362n, 389–90
carminic acid, 231
Carpathians (A), 306p (map)
carpets. *See* pile rugs; rugs
carpet-weaving technique, 49n
Carroll, D., 85, 125, 194, 290
Carter, H., 155–59, 162, 352n, Plate 1
Carthamus tinctoria, 227, 232
cashmere, 22
Căsioarele (A53), 97
Caskey, J., 308
Caspian Sea (A), 171n, 212, 306p (map), 306n
Cassau, A., 183, 217
castration, 26–28
Castro-Curel, Z., 176n, 390
casts. *See* impressions; pseudomorphs
Çatal Hüyük (A104), 10–11, 25, 41, 47n, 51, 59, 61, 66, 79, 81, 88, 98–99, 101, 116, 124–25, 127–30, 128–29pp, 132, 144, 167, 210, 216–17, 220n, 223, 225, 249, 252p (map), 254–55, 293, 391
Çatal Hüyük West, 391
Catling, H., 100n, 355, 370, 389
Caton-Thompson, G., 10, 44, 48, 67, 83n, 145
cat's cradle, 122
Caucasus (A), 121–22, 121p, 144n, 164, 168–70, 194, 206, 211–13, 226, 230, 231n, 237n, 239, 251, 254, 255n, 259, 306p (map); connections with Hallstatt, 122, 164, 168–70, 194, 212–13
caulking, 130–32
Cave of the Treasure. *See* Naḥal Mishmar
cave sites, 12, 20, 33–34, 39–40, 68–69, 85, 99–100, 130–31, 165, 224, 230, 234, 297
Çayönü Tepesi (A90), 11, 22
Cecchetti, P., 364
Cecrops, 360
ceiling designs, 156, 311, 333, 338–50, 343p, 346p, 349p, 356–57, 360, 396, Plate 3; categories of, in Egypt, 340; copying textiles, in Egypt, 311, 338–40, 342, 345–50, 356–57, Plate 3; copying textiles, in Greece, 342; copying wooden frames, 340–42
cellulose, 72, 215, 236n

Celtic, *glas-*, 235nn
Celtic culture, 186, 220n, 226n, 234–35nn
Celts, 186, 234. *See also* Proto-Celts
central workshop system, 158, 284, 288, 291
Černý, J., 286
Červinka, I., 101, 101p, 302, 389
Chadwick, J., 232, 238, 260, 261n, 262, 264–65, 270, 272n, 278, 283–84, 312–13, 358n
chain figures, 319–20, 328–29
Chalcolithic, 23, 59n, 68, 71n, 86, 98, 99, 124, 164–65, 167, 210, 224, 387–88
Champollion, J., 342
Chang, K., 31
Chantraine, P., 261n
Chaos, 381
Chaplin, R., 26n
Charavines, France, 175
chariot craters, 316, 355, 369–70, 369p, 395
chariots/carts, 170, 206, 207p, 316, 324p, 327–28n, 343, 352, 354–55, 361–65, 363–65pp, 367–70, 367–69pp, 372–73, 377–79, 379p, 395
cheap substitutes, 159, 227, 364, 379, 382
checker pattern, 139p, 140, 142, 143p, 176, 190, 191p, 192, 198, 206, 213, 213p, 293, 295, 296p, 341, 345, 366, 377. *See also* plaid
chemical testing, 11, 16, 32, 136, 227, 234, 236–37
chemistry, of dyes, 223, 225, 227, 235–39
Cheng, T., 31
Cheremis: *kene, kine*, 37
Cheshmeh Ali, 305, 306p (map), 391
chests, for cloth/clothing, 292, 345–46
chevron/zigzag. *See* zigzag/chevron/diamond pattern
Chicago Assyrian Dictionary, 29, 33, 38, 255n, 261n, 295n
Chicago Museum of Natural History, 23
childbearing, 257, 293, 374–75
child care and textile production, 114p, 286p, 289–91, 293, 363
children, 114p, 121n, 122, 141, 167, 265, 286–87, 286p, 289–94, 299n, 360, 362–63, 367, 375, 377
Chimaera, 365
China, 17–18, 30–32, 38, 69, 80–81, 81p, 199, 203–4, 212, 215
Chinagrass, 19. *See also* ramie
Chinese culture, 17–18, 31–32, 38, 200, 203–5, 205n, 221, 252, 377
Chinese language, 38, 278; *má*, 38
Chiusi (A37), 92n, 107–8, 108–9n, 108p, 363
Chnemhotep. *See* Khnumhotep
Choga Mish (A136), 56, 57p
Christensen, Jack, 227
Christensen, Julie, 168n
Christian culture, 292, 297, 359–60, 366n
chromatography, 227, 237
Chronicles, 230
chronicles in pictures, 373–74, 376, 382
Chuvash, *kantăr*, 37
Cigarralejo (A3), 119, 122

Cilicia, 300, 306, 308
cinchbelts, 314–15, 323p, 332–33, 332p, 335
Circe, 292
Cîrna (A56), 293, 294p, 296
Citadel House, Mycenae, 316, 324, 356, 395
clan history, 234n
Clark, C., 84
Clark, E., 293
Clark, G., 39
Clark, J.G.D., 20, 28, 39, 41, 176, 184, 217
Clark, L., 109n, 124
Classical era, 15, 34, 53, 69, 110, 164, 196, 198, 229, 231n, 260, 263, 338n, 356
Classical Greek. See entries under Greek
Classical Minoan Dress, 315 (def.), 316, 318–22, 330, 394
Clazomenae (D234), 379
Clazomenian sarcophagi, 378p, 379
cleaning, 47, 220n, 238–39, 252–62, 283, 285
clipping wool/hair, 29–30, 49n, 261–62, 283
clogs for weaving, 105, 106p
cloth, 5 (def.); as booty, 231, 289, 352, 360; cut up for museums, 148; earliest known, 25; elasticity in, 122, 124n, 140; length of, 105–6, 287, 363; over sarcophagus, 3, 199, 206, 207p, 378–80; width of, 80–82, 85–86, 103–5, 118, 124, 127, 134, 183, 185, 193, 195, 251, 253, 287, 363
cloth beam, 82 (def.), 84, 86, 89–90, 92, 103n, 106, 109, 111p, 113, 129, 180, 253, 270, 270p, 280t; rollable, 106, 108p, 115, 270
clothing, 15, 34, 39, 49n, 144, 146, 148, 152–56, 159, 166, 169, 172–74, 177–78, 182–84, 189, 189p, 192, 194–95, 197, 202n, 204, 205n, 211, 215, 218–19, 221, 225, 231n, 232, 233n, 236, 254–58, 261n, 273, 286–92, 295n, 314–16, 318–19, 321–22, 324–25, 325p, 332–37, 347–48, 352–56, 366, 370n, 372; apron, 40, 231, 258p, 295n, 296p, 297, 315; blanket-wrap, 295n, 315; blouse, 178, 182–83, 183p, 217–18; bodice, 297, 314–15, 317n, 318, 324–25; as booty, 158, 205n; burial dress, 145–46, 173, 174n, 177, 195, 207–9, 208p; cap, 33, 39, 122, 144, 172, 182–83, 194, 216n, 218–21, 276; chemise, 32, 169, 189–90, 203–4, 252, 255, 258, 295, 296p, 315, 324, 324p; chiton, 295n, 370n; cloak/cape/mantle, 119, 155, 174, 183, 185, 192–94, 193p, 216 (etym.), 217–18, 262, 295n, 312, 315, 321, 358n, 363, 363p, 376; coat, 200; coat of no seams, 116; codpiece, 332–33, 332–34pp, 335; commissioned, 289; comparative reconstruction of, 255n, 295n; corselet, 33; dirndl, 295; dress, 154, 172, 174, 194, 292, 316, 319, 319p, 322, 324, 329, 359, 361, 366, 369p, 376, 394; festive vs. ordinary, 315, 324; footcloth, 178, 185, 217, 220; girdle/sash, 155, 257–58, 268, 316, 319, 320p; gloves, 159; hairnet, 39–40, 122–23, 123p, 183, 185, 195; hat, 220–21, 268, 276, 314; headband, 39, 124n, 284, 317; headgear, 39, 200, 214, 219, 221, 292, 314; jacket, 295n; jumper, 297; kilt, 148, 154–55, 295n, 311, 315, 320p, 322, 323p, 329–30, 333–37, 334–35pp, 337p, 338n,

347–48, 351, 353p, 354–56, 356p, 370–71; leggings, 315; loincloth, 311, 314–16, 319, 325, 332–33, 332–34pp, 335–36, 335n, 351; oldest extant, 147p; peplos, 268n, 292, 358n, 361–64, 361p, 364–65pp, 368, 377, 380, 382; plain, in Classical Greece, 370p, 372; pre-shaped, 177n; ritual, 315, 321, 324; robe, 197, 205n (etym.), 325, 336, 360, 364, 369p; scarf, 327–28; shawl, 177, 195, 217, 219; shirt, 18, 19n, 147–48, 147p, 169, 200, 252, 261 (etym.), 273, 313; skirt, 155, 164, 182–83, 193, 195, 217, 255, 294, 296p, 297, 314–16, 322p, 324, 324p, 338, 347n, 394; sleeve, 122, 148, 160p, 173, 182, 297, 315, 318, 329p; socks/stockings, 122, 200, 219, 315–16, 333, 335, 395; trousers, 295n, 372; tunic, 33, 121n, 147–48, 147p, 153–55, 159–62, 160–61pp, 173n, 182, 197, 217, 255, 255n (etym.), 274, 274p, 295n, 312, 315, 336, 337n, 354, 356, 376; undergarment, 169, 225; veil, 202; vest, 218; vocabulary of, 205n. See also belts; costume; girdle of Rameses III; helmets; kilts; skirts; string skirts; tunics
clumsiness in weaving, 132, 145, 177–78, 183, 193, 218
Ćmielów, 306p (map), 307p
Coccoidea, 231
Coccus spp., 230n, 231n
cochineal, 231
Cocking, J., 107n
cocoons, 30, 44
Coffey, G., 195, 196p
Coldstream, J., 229, 389
Cole, S., 39
Coles, J., 39
collectors (ancient), 18, 212
Collinder, B., 37
Collingwood, P., 183
Collon, D., 84
colonies: Assyrian, 171; Egyptian, 71, 76, 154; Greek, 3, 92n, 205–9, 378, 379p; Minoan, 351n; Phoenician, 229
color, 108, 109n, 133, 136–37, 139–42, 144, 146, 148–49, 154–55, 157–59, 170, 175, 178, 180, 189–90, 191p, 198, 200, 202–4, 205n, 210–12, 216–17, 219, 223–43, 272n, 275, 286, 295n, 312–13, 317, 319n, 321, 324–28, 330, 337–38, 342, 349, 351–52, 355, 357, 359–60nn, 366, 370n, 371, Plates 1–4; changed by mordants/developers, 233, 235–36; historical order of use of, 225; natural, 13, 16, 21, 30, 165, 189–90, 195; perception of, 230. See also specific colors
colored thread, 49n, 108, 109n, 190, 223, 225, 275. See also dyeing
colorfastness, 206, 225n, 226–27, 231–33, 235–37, 239–40, 313, 321, 330, 338n, 379
Color Plates discussed: Plate 1, 157–58, 352, 353n; Plate 2, 316, 318, 328–29, 338; Plate 3, 333, 338, 339t, 340, 347–48, 371p, 372; Plate 4, 202–3
color restrictions, in Aegean cloth, 330, 337–38, 348, 351
color stripes. See stripes
color symbolism, 297

combs/combing, 13, 20–22, 46, 72, 77, 184, 261–62, 264, 280t, 283–85. *See also* hackling
comparative reconstruction of dress, 169n, 295n, 315, 336
complementary warp patterning, 198 (def.), 199p
complementary weft patterning, 203
Comşa, E., 99
condiments, 232n, 233, 275–76
conservatism, 78. *See also* longevity; survivals; traditions
construction, of space, in weaving, 354, 355n, 365–66, 370
contest of Arachne, 105, 106p
continuous draft. *See* draft-spinning
Cook, R., 379
Čop, B., 266
Copper Age, 28
Coptic era. *See* Egypt: Coptic
copying: between crafts, 171, 220n, 311, 326, 327n, 338, 340–42, 345, 354–55, 357, 365, 366n, 370–72, 382, Plate 3; between Egyptian tomb artists, 311, 331, 335, 340, 347–50, 355n
cord/cordage, 15–16, 20, 33–34, 36, 39–41, 45p, 49–50, 68, 76p, 79, 104, 121–22, 129–32, 165, 180, 185, 204, 223, 225, 255, 263n, 266, 286, 286p, 289
Corded Ware, 121–22
cording, in tablet-weaving, 119, 121, 189, 191
Coren, S., 67
Corinth (D221), 92n, 99, 106p, 240n, 241–42, 366
Corinthian Orientalizing art, 366
correspondence, by merchant families, 287–88, 291
Corsica, 22n
Cortaillod culture, 54, 134
costume: of ancient Europe, 293, 294–95pp, 295, 296p, 297; folk, 169n, 173n, 295, 296p, 297
costume museums, 294n
Cotte, J., and C. Cotte, 17, 224, 227, 230, 234
cotton, 4, 17–18, 21, 30, 32–33, 35, 41, 51–52, 54n, 66–68, 143, 205, 232, 237, 251, 285, 305; dyeing, 33; problems of spinning, 43; reaching Mediterranean, 33
countershed, 82 (def.), 82p, 87, 110, 111p, 112, 117
cover-cloth, at funeral, 3, 199, 206, 207p, 376–80
coverlets. *See* blankets
Cranstone, B., 26
Cratylus, 274
creation, as textile analogue, 44, 293, 298, 375–76
crescentic weights, 97, 100, 100p, 105, 388
Crete (A, D), 35p, 54, 68–69, 70p, 73–77, 91, 92p, 100–101, 104p, 228–29, 232, 239–41, 243, 298n, 313–30, 314p, 320p, 327p, 334, 336, 338, 340, 347, 352n, 355n, 357, 371–72, 387–89, Plate 2; analysis of textiles of, 318–22
Creusa, 360
Crimea (A), 3, 207, 226, 378–79, 379p
Croatians, 173, 224n
crocheting, 121n
Crocus cartwrightianus, 233

crocus pattern, 319–20, 320p, 322
Crocus sativus, 233. *See also* saffron
Cross, D., 28–30
cross-sections, of fibers, 16, 31
Crowfoot, E., 165–66, 224
Crowfoot, G., 16, 33, 42–44, 46, 48–50, 53–54, 56, 69–70, 83n, 87p, 115, 119–21, 152, 156, 159–62, 227, 270–71, 273, 376
Cucuteni (A54), Cucuteni/Tripolye culture, 98, 144, 255, 306
Cueva de los Murciélagos, Andalucia (A1), 33–34, 144
cuneiform records, 24–25, 28–29, 33, 38, 83, 88, 163, 212, 220, 229–32, 235, 238, 261n, 271, 287–88, 291–92
Curcuma longa, 233
cushions, 352
cutout decoration, 200, 219, 219p, 220n
cutting cloth, 178, 182, 218, 315, 318n
Cyclades, 54n, 109, 174n, 241, 315, 329
cylinder seals. *See* seals
Cyprus (A), 62–64, 174n, 228n, 238, 242, 316, 334, 337, 350, 354–55, 369, 369p, 388, 390
Czech: *konopě*, 36; *krasny*, 230n; *kuželovitém*, 101
Czechoslovakia, 99, 101p, 300, 302, 303n, 388–89

Dabaghiyah, 51n
Daga, 44, 45p, 85, 90, 91p, 113n
Dakota Indians, 373
Dalley, S., 171, 288, 291n, 292
Dalma Tepe, 305, 306p (map), 391
Damjanich János Museum, Szolnok, 95p
dance/dancers, 234n, 258, 258n, 291n, 294, 297n, 316, 318, 365, 381, 394–95, Plate 2
Danish: *firskaft*, 187; *høj*, 177; *toskaft*, 187; *vævekile*, 177
Danube (A), 97, 113, 144, 205, 249, 254, 271, 281, 293–94, 306p (map)
Daremberg, C., 69
Daressy, G., 153, 159, 343–44, 354
Darius, 69
darning, 82, 109, 112, 122, 125
Davidson, G., 99
Davies, Nina, 340, 352, 396, Plate 3
Davies, Norman, 45p, 46, 84p, 85–86, 90, 91p, 113n, 114p, 121, 156, 159–62, 227, 332p, 340–44, 352, 396, Plate 3
Davies, O., 195
Davis, K., 373
Davison, G., 361, 381, 382n
Dawkins, R., 35, 74, 389
De Bello Gallico, 234
Debrecen, 95
deccan hemp, 15n
Decima (A42), 195
Decker, B., 32n
deck-shelters, 218n, 344–45, 344p, 356
decoration, for protection, 226n, 297, 298n, 303, 372–76

Degen, B., 121, 121p
de Góngora y Martinez, M., 34, 144
Deh Luran plain, 392
Deibjerg (B160), 119
Deir el-Bahari (C209), 149, 150p, 331, 340, 343
Deir el-Balas (C207), 166
Deir el-Medineh (C211), 71p, 286, 342, 344
de Jonghe, D., 85, 151–52
Delougaz, P., 42p, 56, 57p
Demeter, 363, 363p
Demetrios, 361–62, 380
Demirci Hüyük, 392
Dendra (D219), 172, 174n, 312, 350
Denmark, 19, 40, 101, 105, 116, 116p, 119, 122, 123p,
    126, 141–44, 164, 166n, 176–85, 193, 195, 197, 217–
    18, 254–55, 256p
density, of pile-knots, 201–2
Deny, S., 216n
de Schauensee, M., 391
Desmostachya bipinnata, 33
destruction of fibers/cloth. *See* preservation
detergent, 239, 274
Deubner, L., 361, 363
Dévaványa-Sártó (A71), 94–95, 387, 389
Deve Hüyük (A109), 63, 64p
developers, 226–28, 236 (def.), 237–38, 330
de Vries, K., 102, 219, 302, 390
Dhout, 339t, 396
Dhutemhab (overseer of weavers), 339t, 344, 396
diagonal ribbing, 164, 178–79, 210
diagonal twill. *See* twill
diaper pattern, 206, 316, 317–18n, 319
Dictaean Cave (D248), 68, 69p
Dikaios, P., 174n, 228n, 242, 390
Dimini (A45), 51n, 54n, 220n
Dipylon vases, 366
direction, of weaving, 92, 113, 125, 204–5n, 253, 317–
    18n
disc weights, 98, 102, 104–5, 104p, 271, 280–81, 388
distaffs, 43p, 50 (def.), 54, 56–57, 58p, 63, 69 (def.), 70,
    70p, 76, 78, 107n, 264, 274
division of labor, 4, 283–86, 289–91
Djaffarabad, 391
Djehutihetep, 44, 89–90, 90p
Djeitun, 391
Djowi, 391
Dnieper River (A), 306p (map)
docking sites, for dyes, 236n
dog hair, 30
Dollfus, G., 391
domestication, 9–35, 50, 53n, 203, 215, 233; for meat
    and milk, 23–24; use without, 11–12, 20, 34, 259
domestic production, 286–89
domestic workshop system, 272n, 284–85, 287–88
donut weights, 99, 101–2, 101p, 104, 301–3, 388–89
doorkeepers, 114p, 291
Dorak (A97), 170, 213, 306p (map)
Dorian Invasion, 371

Doric dialect, 266, 267n, 273, 275
Dörpfeld, W., 54
Dothan, T., 70–71, 75, 166
double-cloth, 317, 347, 370n
double-dyeing, 225, 330
double-faced weave, 137, 156–57 (def.), 203, 317, 325–
    26
double vocabulary, 276–82
double-woven borders, 182, 182p, 191
Doumas, C., 229, 389, 394
Douskos, I., 233. *See also* Tzakhili, I.
dowries, 203, 205n, 292
draft-spinning, 41–44 (def.), 46–51 (def.), 53n, 67–68,
    72, 76, 78, 264, 303, 393
dragon's blood, 231n
Drakones (D258), 74, 75p
drawloom, 112, 343
drawstrings, 165
Driessen, J., 312
Driffield, D., 132n
Drioton, E., 396
Drisler, H., 261n
drop-spindles, 43 (def.), 43p, 46, 54–56, 59, 63, 67–68,
    78
drugs, 17–18, 36–38, 219, 275–76
drying, 239–40, 242
Duhoux, Y., 336–37n
Dumitrescu, V., 97, 294p
Duncan, R., 204–5n
Dura Europus, 122, 206
Durrant, A., 13
dyeing, 5, 39, 49n, 164, 184, 189–90, 200, 223–43, 275–
    76, 278t, 285, 288, 376; before spinning, 49n, 225,
    239, 275; before weaving, 190, 225, 229, 239, 275; of
    cotton, 33; earliest evidence for, 223–25, 230; of flax/
    linen, 15, 49n, 133, 211, 217, 236n; heat for, 228, 239–
    40, 242–43; of silk, 204, 275n; as spun thread, 225,
    228n, 239; uneven, 228n, 239; as whole cloth, 225,
    236, 239–40; of wool, 21, 29, 49n, 211, 217, 228–29,
    236n, 239, 241, 242p, 275n, 351. *See also* double-dyeing
dye plants, 223, 226–28, 232–35, 237, 239–40, 275
dye pots, 225, 228–29, 236, 238–43, 241–42pp. *See also*
    tubs
dye recipes, 228–29, 232–33, 238–39
dyer's broom, 228
dyer's equipment, 239
dyer's shops. *See* dye-works
dyes, 17, 175, 184, 223, 226–43, 247, 311, 313, 330,
    338n, 351–52, 379; bonding of, 235–36; colorfast,
    206, 225n, 226–27, 231–33, 235–37, 239–40, 313,
    321, 330, 338n, 379; draining, 240–42, 242p; fugi-
    tive, 227, 232–33, 236; indeterminacy of tests for,
    223, 227; minerals as, 223, 227, 230–31, 239, 275;
    penetration of, 15, 225; vs. pigments, 21, 29; salvag-
    ing, 240, 242, 242p; self-fixing, 235, 236n, 237; syn-
    thetic, 225, 232. *See also* leuco-form; vat-dyes
dye-works, 229, 237–43, 241–42pp
Dyson, R., 202n, 224, 231, 391

Eakle, J., 230
Early Dynastic era, 42p, 57
earnings, from textiles, 265, 284, 287, 291
Easter eggs, 235, 297
Eastern Nettle, 19. *See also* ramie
East Greek style, 366, 366p, 369, 371, 378p, 379
Ebla (A117), 145, 166, 213
Edelstein, G., 243, 302n, 390
Edelstein, S., 237
edgings. *See* borders
Egami, N., 29n, 391
eggs: dyeing, 235, 297; as symbols, 297
Egtved (B159), 178, 180, 181p, 182
Egypt, 3, 10, 33, 41, 44, 63, 68, 71, 75–76, 78, 86, 88,
    115, 119–22, 124–25, 145–62, 163n, 165–66, 170–73,
    186, 189, 194, 198, 200, 203, 210–12, 215, 221, 224–
    27, 230, 232, 235, 237–38, 247, 249, 251, 253, 285,
    288–91, 299, 301n, 303, 311–13, 321–22, 327n, 330–
    57, 359, 365, 372, 378; Coptic, 49, 119, 122, 159–60;
    dynastic/pharaonic (Bronze Age), 10, 20, 44n, 66, 86,
    115, 145–62, 211, 224; Empire, 76, 157–58, 162,
    301n; historical survey of New Kingdom trade to,
    331; Middle Kingdom, 25p, 44, 45p, 74p, 83, 84p,
    85p, 87p, 90, 90–91pp, 149–55, 159, 285–86, 286p,
    290, 331, 338, 342, 346, 351, 357; New Kingdom,
    64, 83, 91, 113, 121, 125, 152–55, 227, 289–91,
    301n, 331–57; Old Kingdom, 76, 152, 232; pre-dy-
    nastic (Neolithic), 10, 15, 20, 25, 44, 110, 132, 145–
    46, 226, 341; Roman, 29n, 70, 122, 159, 162, 226,
    290, 364; Saite, 343n. *See also* Egyptian dynasties
Egypt Exploration Society, 45p, 91p, 114p, 160–61pp
Egyptian Arabic. *See* Arabic
Egyptian dye industry, 224–27, 229–30
Egyptian dynasties: 1st Dynasty, 146–48, 147p, 224,
    341; 3rd Dynasty, 148, 224; 4th Dynasty, 76, 148,
    224; 5th Dynasty, 76, 148–49, 154, 224–25, 235, 341;
    6th Dynasty, 76, 76p, 286; 11th Dynasty, 44, 75,
    149–52, 150p, 164, 332; 12th Dynasty, 44–45, 49n,
    71, 75, 84p, 86, 89, 90p, 224, 227, 232, 236, 238,
    339t, 340–41, 346p, 347, 350–51; 18th Dynasty, 12p,
    44n, 46p, 63–64, 114p, 149–53, 156–62, 198, 224,
    238, 285–86, 331, 338, 339t, 342, 345, 350–52, 353n,
    357, Plate 1, Plate 3; 19th Dynasty, 63–65, 149, 198,
    286, 331, 338, 340, 347; 20th Dynasty, 65, 198, 331,
    338, 340, 353p; 21st Dynasty, 152, 227, 232, 338,
    342, 350; 22nd Dynasty, 119, 122. *See also* Egypt:
    dynastic/pharaonic
Egyptian fibers, 15, 20, 33–34
Egyptian flax, 12–13, 66
Egyptian hieroglyphs: in ceiling designs, 341–42, 349;
    on cloth, 153–54, 154p, 157–58, 160p, 161, 210, 352,
    Plate 1; of hairy sheep, 25p; for *spin*, 53p; of textile
    tools, 53p, 90, 91p
Egyptian language, 10n, 53p, 231, 232n, 235; *idmy,
    insw, insy, inšj*, 230
Egyptian linen, 10–11, 15, 41, 49n, 66–68, 81, 83n,
    119–21, 145–62, 164, 166, 191, 194, 211, 224–25,
    230, 232, 235, 237–38, 288–90; bought/sold, 288–89

Egyptian looms, 82p, 83–91, 83–85pp, 113–15, 249
Egyptian Museum, Cairo, 85, 149, 150p, 152, 154p,
    157p, 158, 160p, 224
Egyptian officials, at receptions, 332–33, 335, 340, 348
Egyptian representations: of flax-growing, 12p; of for-
    eigners, 311, 331–38, 332–35pp, 347–48, 352, 353p,
    355–57, 356p; of hairy sheep, 25p, 49n; of mat-weav-
    ing, 286p; of men spinning cord, 45p, 286p; of men
    washing cloth, 45p, 286p; of spinning, 44, 45p, 48p,
    53, 63–64, 73, 74p, 76, 76p, 85p, 88, 90p, 114p,
    286p, 305; of weaving, 45p, 74p, 81, 83–85, 83–85pp,
    89–90, 90–91p, 110, 113, 113n, 114p, 115, 249, 285–
    86, 286p, 290, 305
Egyptians: ancient, 49n, 53, 67, 81, 86–87, 118, 225,
    237, 314; modern, 46n, 53. *See also* Egypt
Egyptian Second Intermediate Period, 30, 154, 210
Egyptian shipyard lists, 345
Egyptian skin-color conventions, 327n, 355n, 356, 356p
Egyptian spindles and whorls, 45p, 46p, 48p, 52–53n,
    53, 53p, 59, 60, 63–67, 65p, 78
Egyptian temple treasurers, 311, 334, 348
Egyptian texts mentioning textiles, 287–88, 291
Egyptian thread-making, 44–50, 45–48pp, 66–68, 70–
    73, 71p, 74p, 75–78
Egyptian use of wool, 25, 49, 49n, 211, 351
Egyptian workmen's village, 88–89, 286
ekphora, 367
Elam (A), 164
Elamite culture, 25
El Argar (A2), 68, 176n
el-Bersheh (C198), 44, 90p
Elburz mountains, 306p (map)
elephant hair, 30
Eleusis (D227), 197n, 271
el-Gebelein (C215), 145, 226
el-Haraga, 351
Elista, 170p
Elizabethan court costume, 324
el-Lahun (C194), 351
Ellis, R., 18, 90n, 113, 155–56n, 197–98, 199p, 219,
    225, 318n
Elmalı, 365
el-Omari (C189), 25
Elster, E., 51n, 54n
embroidery, 3, 18, 31–32, 121n, 124, 142, 153, 159–62,
    160–61pp, 166, 169, 175n, 177, 183, 183p, 189–90,
    197–200, 203, 206, 208, 209p, 224–25, 257, 275,
    293–94, 297, 298n, 312, 314, 317, 318n, 320–21, 343,
    352–53, 356, 359n, 366n, 372–73; as function of dyed
    thread, 225
embroidery frames, 124
Emery, I., 127n
Emery, W., 341
emissaries to Egyptian court: Aegean, 226n, 311, 331–
    38, 332–35pp, 340, 345, 347–48, 350–51, 354–55,
    357; carrying cloth, 335, 335p, 348; Syrian, 332–33,
    352, 355n
Eneolithic, 144n, 168, 391

Engelbach, R., 65, 343n, 351

England, 18, 101

English, 41, 80, 85, 200n, 205, 216, 231n, 260, 262, 266, 267n, 274–78, 281n; *carmine, crimson,* 231n; *glass,* 235n; *honey,* 233; *library,* 231n; *short,* 261; *thrum,* 274, 274p; *walk, waulk,* 216. *See also* Middle English; Old English; *individual terms for etymologies*

Enkomi (A110), 62–63, 242, 350, 388, 390

entertainment, while working, 4, 105, 178, 292, 294, 295p, 363

Erechtheum, 361

Eretria (D226), 197n

Ergastinai, 362, 377

Ergotimos, 365

Erica, 228

Erman, A., 230

Erol, O., 352n

errors. *See* weaving errors

esparto, 20, 33–35, 125, 144, 176; preparing, 34

Esra, G., 24n

Estonia, 41

Estonian, *kanep,* 36

Ethnographic Museum, Leningrad, 296p

ethnographic parallels, 4, 20, 42–44, 46n, 47, 49–53, 59–61, 67, 72–73, 79–80n, 81, 83n, 96, 101–4, 109–12, 115, 117, 124, 130, 134, 168–69, 178, 216–17, 220–21, 226, 231, 236, 238, 247, 267, 289–98, 311, 324, 326, 372, 374–76, 383

Etruria, 194

Etruscan culture, 69, 92, 116, 116p, 194–95, 265p, 269p

Etruscan pendant, 92, 105–6, 116–17, 116p, 265, 265p, 269, 269p

Etruscan textile tools, 69

Euboia, 197

Eulimene, 206

Euphrates River (A), 56, 166, 171, 291, 306p (map)

Euripides, 264, 269, 359n, 360, 362, 373

Europe, 10, 16–19, 22, 25, 28, 30, 32, 36, 52, 59, 65–67, 69, 78, 82, 88, 92, 101, 110, 116, 122–23, 125, 133, 141, 143, 163, 165n, 166, 168, 172–74, 182, 186, 194, 210–11, 213, 215, 217, 226–27, 230, 233–34, 235n, 249, 254, 256–59, 258p, 268, 281n, 285, 292–97, 299, 307, 313–14, 319n, 330, 351, 354, 357, 359, 387; central, 12, 18–19, 35, 99, 113, 122, 143–44, 164, 168, 173n, 175, 178, 184–85, 192–94, 204, 213, 216–17, 221, 226n, 232, 237n, 239, 243, 254, 275, 293, 294n, 295, 297–98, 303, 308, 328, 372; eastern, 19, 36, 40, 144, 168, 173, 225, 233–34, 299; modern, 48, 53, 72, 162, 178, 233, 234n, 256, 293–97; northern, 19–20, 54, 66, 119, 133, 141–43, 163n, 176, 178, 183, 185, 213, 217, 231–32; southern, 35, 144, 195, 225, 230, 233–34, 263, 299, 303, 312, 353; western, 31, 40, 55, 119, 143–44, 180, 204, 224, 232, 234n, 237n

Euthydikos Kore, 363

Eutresis, 107, 306p (map), 307

Evans, Sir A., 77, 174n, 233, 298n, 320p, 321p, 322, 327p, 328n, 347n, 355n, 389, 394–95

Evans, J., 54, 98, 100, 107, 389

Evans, R., 97n

Evenki, *onokto,* 38

ewes, 26–28, 27t

exchange. *See* gifts; trade

Exodus, 30, 50, 72, 230

expense. *See* luxury cloth

experimentation: ancient, 33, 50, 158–59, 162, 165, 290–91, 298, 352–53n; modern, 24n, 47n, 87, 105, 110, 120, 192, 239, 290–91, 302, 325–26, 362n, 370

exports, 31, 34, 166, 204, 284, 287, 321

faced weaves, 127n (def.), 128p (diag.), 142, 157, 164–66, 168, 179, 184, 188, 194, 197, 200, 210–11, 217, 251, 253

factory method, of cloth production, 285–86

faience, 162, 171–72, 173n, 195, 235n, 313, 316, 319, 320p, 322, 327p, 328, 352–54, 353p, 356, 356p

Fairbanks, G., 261n, 264–65

fairytales, 19n. *See also* legends

Faiyum (C), 10, 15, 44, 48, 49n, 64, 65p, 67–68, 145, 146p, 220n, 351, 352n

Faiyum Neolithic linen, 10, 15, 48, 67–68, 132, 145, 146p

Fannin, A., 42

Farina, G., 146

Faroe sheep, 177

Fars River, 169p

Fates, 263, 376

fat-tailed sheep, 24–25

feather pattern, 155

feathers, 155, 164, 261

felt, 5, 20, 22–24, 200, 202–3, 215–22, 219p, 251–53, 268, 276 (etym.), 278t, 345; as armor, 220; cutting, 218–19; decorating, 216, 219–20; earliest evidence for, 216–17, 251; as insulator, 215, 252; interlocking fibers of, 215–16; invention of, 215, 221–22, 251, 281; kneading, 215–16, 276; knitted, 216n; for liners, 220–21; patterned, 216–17, 218n, 219–20; structure of, 197, 215; tensile weakness of, 220, 251–52; trampling, 216, 276; woven, 197, 216 (def.), 217–19, 221. *See also* fiber felt

felting, 5, 39, 124, 176, 178, 184, 197, 215 (def.), 216–21, 276; accidental, 217–18; methods of, 216, 276; spread of, 221

felt rugs, 217, 219–21

Ferghana, 212

fermentation, 215, 235, 239

Fertile Crescent, 91

fertility symbols, 226n, 257–58, 258p, 293, 297–98, 374–76

fiber felt, 197, 200, 215, 216 (def.), 217–21

fiber plants, indiscriminate words for, 15n, 37

fibers, 5, 9–35, 38, 52, 65, 79, 107n, 132, 174n, 176, 178, 185, 195, 206, 211, 215–16, 230, 235–37, 239,

fibers (*cont.*)
  247, 251–52, 259–64, 266, 275, 283, 285–86, 289, 312; distribution of, 34p, 211, 250p; earliest use for thread, 39–41; effect of length on spinning, 43–44, 52; elasticity of, 20–21, 24n; flexibility of, 9; found unspun, 10, 49n, 70, 224, 352; length of, 9, 21, 30–31, 43–44, 47, 50, 52; misidentification of, 10–11, 19–20, 141; natural twist of, 66–67; slipperiness of, 14, 30, 43; spinning of, 21, 24n, 39–43, 53n, 78; strength of, 9, 14, 21, 24n; tension/torsion on, 21, 24n; thickness of, 15, 20–21
fiber-wetting bowls, 45p, 46n, 48, 70–77, 71p, 73–75pp, 78, 240, 299
fibulae, 195
figured stripes. *See* strip patterns
figurines, 24–25, 40, 40p, 144, 155n, 164, 181, 255–57, 256–57pp, 293, 294p, 296p, 297, 314, 314p, 316, 319, 354, 364, 394–95
filler ornaments, 317–19, 317p, 330, 342, 344n, 354–57, 366–68, 366p, 368–69pp, 370–72, 375p, 379; as function of float weave, 354–55, 374, 374–75pp
finishing cloth, 216, 218, 220n, 221, 239, 273n, 274, 284
Finland, 20, 41, 134
Finnish, 36–37; *kaneppi, hamppu,* 36
Finno-Ugric, 37
fire rituals, in Athens, 361, 381, 381–82n
Firth, C., 76p
Fischer, J., 258n
fish, as symbols/spirits, 297, 377
Fisher, J., 92n
fixatives. *See* mordants
flags, 225n, 273, 378
flame pattern, 319
Flannery, K., 131, 392
Flattery, D., 37
flax, 11–15, 18–20, 25, 35–37, 41, 42, 47, 49–51, 65–68, 72, 76, 80 (etym.), 95, 130, 255n, 262–64, 295n; age of, for fiber, 12–13; brittleness of, 46n, 72; characteristics of, 11–16; chemical weakening of, 11, 13, 15; color of, 13; cultivation of, 12p; distribution maps of, 34p, 250p; early domestication of, 11n, 12, 253, 259; early history of, 11–12, 18; fineness of, 12–13, 15; found unworked, 10; harvesting, 12–13; height of, 15, 18n; identification of, 10–11, 15–16; length of, 47, 50; mangling, 45p, 46; as non-insulator, 14–15, 20; preparing, 4, 13–14, 45p, 46–47, 71–72, 74p, 95, 130, 215, 262, 283–86, 286p, 290; retting, 13, 34, 215, 262; smoothness of, 11, 14, 20, 267; species of, 10–12; spinning of, 41, 44p, 46–50, 48p, 52, 66–68, 70–73, 240, 264, 284, 393; structure of, 13–14; ultimate fibers of, 47; wild ancestors of, 11–12
flax seed, 10, 11n, 12–13. *See also* linseed oil
fleece: cuneiform records of, 24–25; quality of, 24–25, 24p, 26, 29–30; quantity (weight) of, 24–25; terms for, 261–62, 274, 276; trauma to, 26n
float weave, 137 (def.), 138p, 139–40, 156, 168, 175, 189–90, 191p, 192, 197–98, 198p, 210, 253, 268n,

293, 313, 317, 317–19nn, 322, 330, 332, 347–48, 353–54, 356, 366, 370, 374, 374p
flocks. *See* sheep flocks
Florence, 195; Archaeological Museum of, 365p
flounces, 315, 317n, 318, 324
flowers, for dyeing, 232–33, 275, 362
Fogelberg, J., 68, 167
folk costumes, 169n, 173n, 258, 258p, 294n, 295, 296p, 297, 315, 324
folk etymology, 234n
folk museums, 294
food. *See* rations; textile resources
foot tension, 80, 81p
Forbes, R., 16, 29, 32, 40, 43, 107n, 122, 216, 218, 230–35
foreigners, living in Egypt, 49n, 64–65, 158, 162, 321, 351–52. *See also* Egyptian representations: of foreigners; emissaries
Fortetsa (D243), 371–72, 371p
Foster, G., 290
Foucart, G., 396
four-colored barred band. *See* barred band pattern
four-petaled flower patterns, 317, 317p, 319–20, 320p, 328–29, 329p, 342
four-pointed star patterns, 317–20, 317–18pp, 328–29, 329p
four-shaft, 187 (def.), 268
France, 17, 20, 29n, 39–40, 119, 141, 174–75, 186, 224, 230n, 234, 277, 285, 354
Franchthi Cave (D217), 27n, 98–99, 387, 389
François Vase, 364, 364–65p
Frankfort, H. A., 362n
Frankfort, Henri, 321, 340, 348, 352, 362n
Franz, L., 213n
French, E., 395
French, 55, 60, 276–78; *alfa,* 33; *batteurs,* 285; *cardeuses,* 285; *dévideresses,* 285; *éliseresses,* 285; *fileresses,* 285; *librairie,* 231n; *navette,* 85n; *peigneresses,* 285; *plier,* 42n
Freud, S., 184n
friction grooves, 71, 71p, 74, 75p, 86, 88
Friedl, E., 287
Friedrich, J., 295n
friezes, 3, 201, 206, 207p, 272p, 319–20, 322, 353p, 354–56, 356p, 361, 361p, 363–73, 363–69pp, 377–79, 379p
fringe, 10, 30, 83n, 137, 140, 145–49, 152, 152p (diag.), 155, 162, 166, 176–77, 179p, 180–81, 195, 199, 212, 224–25, 258, 258p, 274p, 313, 327–28, 327p, 334p, 336, 342, 354, 355n, 369p; inlaid, 151–52, 152p (diag.), 210; warp, 129, 135–37, 146–47, 151, 154, 180, 195, 196p, 199, 255, 274, 274p, 313, 336; weft, 83n, 128, 146–48, 147p, 151, 156
Frisk, H., 38, 270
frit inlay design, 171
Fritzlar Museum, 141
frogs, as symbols/spirits, 297
From the Lands of the Scythians, 173n

frozen finds. *See* preservation: by freezing
Fukai, S., 29n
fullers' shops, 216, 274, 284
fulling, 39, 178, 216 (def., etym.), 217–18, 220n, 274–75, 277, 280t, 283–84, 313
funeral cloth, 3, 199, 206, 207p, 292, 358–59, 366–67, 374–80, 382
funeral scenes, 146, 366–68, 367–68pp, 372, 375p, 377
Funnel Beaker culture, 141, 306
fur, 169, 177–78, 183, 200, 251, 261
furniture covers, 219–20, 230
Furry, M., 236
Furtwängler, A., 108p, 109n, 364p

Gagarino, upper Don (A77), 256, 257p, 258
Galanopoulos, A., 102
Galicia, 122
Gallic language, 216
Garašanin, D., and M. Garašanin, 134
Gardiner, A., 53p, 90, 91p, 113n, 230, 289, 338n, 340, 352, 396, Plate 3
Gardner, E., 10, 44, 48, 67, 145
Garstang, J., 59n, 132, 300p, 306, 389
Gastaldi, B., 55p
Gaul, J., 98
Gaul, 16, 204n, 234n
gauze weave, 151, 151p (diag.)
Gawra. *See* Tepe Gawra
Geijer, A., 13, 20, 31, 108n, 115, 358
genetic selection, 23, 28
Geniemhet, 44n
Genista, 228
geology, 223, 230, 352n
Geometric era. *See* Greek Geometric era
Georgia (Soviet), 168, 173n, 212
Geoy Tepe, 391
German, 47, 54; *Fahne*, 273; *Filz*, 276; *Garn*, 266; *Hanf*, 36; *heben*, 82; *scheiden*, 82; *Schiffchen*, 85n; *Schnur*, 263n; *Waid*, 235n; *Walke*, 216; *Webstuhl*, 80
Germanic, 36–37, 216, 233, 233n, 235, 274n, 276–77, 376
Germanic peoples, 36
Germany, 12, 16, 18, 32, 47, 101, 103, 123, 134, 142–43, 143p, 176, 184, 186, 195, 203–5, 214, 218, 221, 224–25, 231, 293, 389–90
Gertsiger, D., 206–8, 208n, 226, 379
Gerumsberg, Sweden (A13), 192–94, 193p, 218
Gervers, V., 366n
Gerzean, 49n
Gesell, G., 394–95
Gezer (C177), 300, 301p (map), 302, 388–90
Ghiördes knot, 201, 202p (diag.)
Ghirshman, R., 391
giants, 362, 380–81, 382n
gifts, 60, 162, 205n, 264, 292, 299, 311, 332, 340, 343, 350, 357, 361, 375–76. *See also* guest-gifts
Gigantomachy, 362, 364, 380–82. *See also* battle

Gimbutas, M., 95, 169–70, 173n, 255, 293, 298
giraffe hair, 30
girdle of Rameses III, 118–21, 120p, 156–57, 352–53
girdles. *See* belts; clothing: girdle/sash
Gittinger, M., 375–76
Glanville, S., 341
Glare, P., 265
glass, 235n
glass paste. *See* faience
Glauber's salt, 236
Glob, P., 176–77, 181–82
Globular Amphora culture, 141
Glory, A., 20, 40
Glotz, G., 266, 278
glue/glueing, 20, 49n, 50, 72, 173, 215
goats, 22–23, 25, 26n, 29–30, 41, 43, 50, 240, 253, 259, 356, 366p, 372, 376; hair of, 25, 29–30, 49n, 220, 259, 269, 376
gobelin-style tapestry, 354, 364
Godart, L., 238
Godwin, H., 19
Goldberg bei Nördlingen (A23), 106
Goldman, H., 107, 307, 392
Gomolava (A60), 98–99, 103, 144, 388–89
Goodall, F., 44p
Gordion (A96), 18, 101–3, 113, 197–98, 198p, 218–19, 225, 268n, 284, 291, 302, 318n, 389–90, 392
Gorgons, 360
Gorodsk, 306p (map), 306n, 307p
Gossypium, 32–33
Gothic, 233n; *fana*, 273; *filu-faihs*, 359n; *milip*, 233n; **wizdil-*, 235n
Götze, A., 119, 172
Govi, C., 106, 116, 116p, 265p, 269p
Graef, B., 68, 92n
Graf collection, 119
Granary, Mycenae, 174n
Granger-Taylor, H., 122
Grant, E., 242
grass, 9, 20, 33, 231, 376
Grave Circles, Mycenae, 174n. *See also* Shaft Graves
Gravettian, 39–40, 172
Great Wall of China, 205n
Greco-Roman era. *See* Classical era
Greece, 16, 18, 27n, 31, 33, 54, 64p, 68, 99–101, 106p, 110, 111p, 113, 124, 163n, 173, 194, 196–97, 204–6, 232, 260, 276, 281, 283, 293, 297, 304, 307–8, 312, 324p, 387–89
Greek architectural terms, as borrowings, 281
Greek art: Archaic, 53–54, 69, 70p, 107, 356, 359, 364–66, 369–70, 382; Classical, 3, 69, 107, 108p, 271, 272p, 360, 370n
Greek colonies, 3, 92n, 205–9, 378, 379p
Greek Dark Age, 197, 357, 365–66, 368, 370, 372–73, 382
Greek finds: of cloth, 3, 32–33, 122–23, 197, 197n, 206–9, 271, 367; of textile tools (Classical), 69, 69p
Greek Geometric era, 197n, 365–72, 367–68pp, 371p,

Greek Geometric era (*cont.*)
374, 375p, 377
Greek imports of silk, cotton, 32–33, 204–5
Greek language, 18n, 36–37, 68, 172, 220, 226, 235,
247–48, 260–81, 283, 358n
agathis, 267, 269, 278–79tt
agnuthes, 270p (diag.), 271, 278–80tt
anameruomai, 266
ankistron, 263
anthizein, 275
anthokrokos, 362
anthos, 275
antion, 270, 270p (diag.), 280, 280t
aotos, 262
apostupaz-, 263
askein, 272n
asma, 271, 273n, 278–79tt
atraktos, 107, 263–64, 269, 278–79tt
attomai, 271, 272, 278–80tt
aulos, 263n
baphe, 275, 278–79tt
baptein, 275, 278–79tt
barathron, 262n
belone, 275, 278–79tt
belos, 275
bibroskein, 262n
daidaleos, 362
diasma(ta), 271
diazomai, diezeto, 271–72, 278–80tt, 362–63
dimitos, 268
e(i)rion, 226n, 260, 265–66, 278–79tt
eiros, 260
elakata, 262, 264
elakate, 263–64, 269, 278–79tt
engraphein, 226
ephuphe, 273
epiblema, 377
epimeruomai, 266
epinetron, 77–78, 78p
erea, 260
erebinthos, 267n
etrion, atrion, 273, 278–80tt
exastis, 270p (diag.), 271–72, 272p
harpazein, 266
harpedone, 266
heano-, 257, 337n
helissein, 264, 268–69, 278–79tt
histopodes, 270, 270p (diag.), 278–80tt, 280
histos, 80, 102, 269, 270, 270p (diag.), 280t, 362n
histourgein, 269, 269p
hu-, 275, 278–79tt
humen, 275
huphainein, 80, 226n, 269, 278–80tt, 361
huphan, 269, 278–80tt
illas, 266
isatis, 235n
kairos, 270p (diag.), 271, 280t
kalathos, kalathiskos, 262

kalliphthongos, 362n
kanna, 271
kannabis, 18n, 36
kanon, 112, 267, 270p (diag.), 271, 280t
kassuein, 275
katagma, 262, 266
katamiton, 267
keirein, 261, 274
keleontes, 270, 270p (diag.), 278–80tt
keleos, 270
kentein, 257, 275
kerkis, 273–74, 360n
keskeon, keskion, 262, 280t
khernetis, 265
khiton, 255n, 295n
khorde, 266
kimolia ge, 274
kloster, 263, 266
klothein, 262n, 263, 278–79tt
klotho, 263
knapheus, 274, 277, 280t
knaptein, 274, 277, 280t
knêkos, 232
knekós, 233
krekadia, 273
krekein, 269, 273–74, 278–80tt
kroke, kroka, 107, 266, 270p (diag.), 273
krokeos, 362
krokus, 273–74
ksainein, 262, 274, 280t
laas, 271
laiai, 270p (diag.), 271, 278–80tt
lebinthos, 267n
lenos, 260, 278–79t
linaia, 266
linon, 262, 266, 280t
liti, 377
mallos, 260, 266, 267n, 278–79tt
mallukes, 260, 266–67, 278–79tt
mar-u/i- stem, 266–67, 267n, 277
merins, merintha, 266
merinthia, 266
merinthos, 266, 278–79tt
merisma, merusma, 266
mermith-, 266
meru(g)ma, 266, 269
meruomai, maruomai, 266, 267n, 269, 277, 278–79tt
miainein, 275
mitinoi, 268
mitisasthai, 268
mitos, 266–68, 270p (diag.), 280t
mitra, 268n
Moirai, 376
nake, 276
nakos, 276
nakotiltein, 261, 276
naktos, nakta, 276, 278–79tt
nassein, nattein, 274, 276, 278–79tt

nema, 266
nen, nethein, 263, 278–79tt
netron, 263
neura, 263n, 266
neuron, 263n, 266
ois, 260–61
onos, 77
onukh-, 327–28n. *See also* Linear B: *o-nu-ke*
parairema, 272
parathuris, 281n
peirar, 266
pekein, 261, 278–79tt
pene, 269, 270p (diag.), 273, 278–80tt, 362
penion, 107, 270p (diag.), 273
penisma, 273
penizesthai, penasthai, 268–69, 273
penos, 273
peplos, 268n, 361
pharmakon, 275–76
pharos, 271, 358–59, 377
phoinik-, 232n
pilein, 276, 278–79tt
pilema, 276
pilesis, 276
pilos, 220, 276, 278–79tt
plak-, 313
plekein, 80, 269, 280t
plekte, 266
plinthos, 281n
plokamis, 80
plunein, 226n, 274
poikilos, poikillein, 313, 327, 359n, 362
pokos, 262, 278t
polios, 313
polymitos, 268n
porphyreus, 229
probata, 261
pur, 381–82n
puthein, 262
rhabdos, 274
rhaphis, 275, 278–79tt
rhaptein, 275, 278–79tt
rhegeus, rhogeus, 275
rhegistes, 275
rhegma, 275
rhegos, 275
rhezein, 275, 278–79tt
rhoda, 372
rhodane, 273, 278–80tt
rhodanos, 273
rhumma, 274
sandarake, 231n
seira, 266
sepein, 262
sindon, 32
skoinis, 266
smerinthos, 266
sparton, 266

spasma, 266
spathan, 269, 274, 278–80tt
spathe, 274
speiron, 358–59
sphallo, 264n
sphendone, 264n
sphides, 264n
sphondulos, 263, 280t
spongos, 264n
stemon, 266, 270p (diag.), 273, 278–80tt
stroma, 377–78
st(r)upteria, 276, 280t
stupaz-, 262–63
stuphein, 276–77
stupos, 262, 280t
stuppe, stuppeion, 262–63, 280t
-su-, 275, 278–79tt
tala-, 265
talaros, 70, 265
talasia, 265
talasiourgein, 264–65, 265p, 269
tapheios, 359
termioeis, 274, 274p
*tetramitos, 268
throna, 372–73
tillein, 261, 278–79tt
tolupe, 262, 269, 278–79tt
tolupeuein, 268
trepein, 263
trikhes, 260
trimitos, 268
zone, zostos, 254, 257
Greek legends, 105, 106p, 198, 267–68, 361, 371, 376. *See also* mythology
Greek literature, 16, 31, 32, 68, 107, 220, 338n, 359n, 362
Greek looms (Classical), 107–8, 110–11, 267–74, 270p, 279–81. *See also* Greek representations: of looms
Greek purple industry, 229
Greek representations: of figure-friezed cloth, 108p, 363–64, 363–65pp, 372; of looms, 72p, 92p, 92n, 105–6, 106p, 107, 108p, 108–9n, 110, 111p, 124; of spinning, 53–54, 68–70, 70p, 72, 72p, 264; of weaving, 72p, 92p, 105–7, 106p, 108p, 111p, 112, 363
Greeks: ancient, 3–4, 32, 36, 46n, 70, 102, 112, 123, 206, 220–21, 255n, 260–81, 295n, 315, 358–82; modern, 43p, 69, 324, 351–52n. *See also* Greece; Mycenaeans
Greek use of felt, 220, 276
Greek vase paintings, 46n, 68–69, 70p, 72p, 78p, 92p, 105, 106p, 107–8, 108p, 108–9n, 110, 111p, 112, 124, 264, 271, 297–98, 360, 363–72, 363–68pp, 375p, 378–79
Greek writers. *See* Greek literature *and individual authors*
Green, M., 24, 28, 30
green, 49n, 156n, 158–59, 165, 172, 178, 188p, 190, 191p, 200, 203–4, 207–8, 224–25, 227–28, 230, 235n,

green (*cont.*)
  236–37, 330, 337, 344, 352, 379, Plate 1
Greene, F., 365
Greenewalt, C., 198–99
Greiss, E., 25, 49n
Greppin, J., 260
Grevensvænge (B169), 256p
grey, 13, 21, 29, 148, 178, 203, 312
grid patterns, 317–20, 317–18pp, 328–30, 349
griffins, 161, 161p, 173, 202, 319, 321, 321p, 356
Griffith, F., 25p, 49n, 87, 224, 351
Grimm's Law, 36
Grimstone End, 101
grinders, 102, 239–40, 284, 289, 302. *See also* mashing
  dyes
Gródek Nadbużny (A73), 100p, 306, 306p (map), 307p,
  388–89
grooved sticks. *See* slotted sticks
Gross, V., 55
Grotte des Enfants (A6), 39, 172
ground-loom, 81, 82p (diag.), 83–85pp, 83–91, 90–
  91pp, 105, 113, 124–25, 151, 211, 249, 285–86,
  286p, 290, 300; distribution of, 249–54, 250p, 252p,
  259, 300; origin of, 91, 124, 253–54; representations
  of, 83–85pp, 90–91pp, 151, 286p
ground warp, 140, 153, 156
ground weave, 49n, 137, 140, 159, 164, 190, 210, 366n
ground weft, 137 (def.), 139, 152–53, 156, 159
guest-gifts, 205n, 284, 312
guinea hemp, 15n
Gunn, B., 76p
Gurney, O., 132n
Gurob (C196), 49n, 63–66, 86, 88, 299, 351
gut, 39–40, 266
Guy, P., 62, 301
Györ, 294n

Haastrup (B166), 180, 193
Hacılar (A101), 51n, 59n, 220n
hackles, 13, 14p
hackling, 4, 13 (def.), 41
Hagendrup (B167), 181
Hägg, R., 174n
Hagia Triada (D261), 293, 316, 318–19, 325, 328–29,
  338, 340, 377, 394–95, Plate 2
Haines, R., 164
hair, 9, 20 (def.), 21, 21p, 23, 29–30, 41, 43, 176, 215–
  17, 260–61, 276; goat, 25, 29–30, 49n, 220, 259, 269,
  376; horse, 30, 195, 196p; human, 21, 25, 30, 261
Halbherr, F., 395, Plate 2
Hald, M., 19, 115n, 116, 119, 122, 124, 177–78, 180,
  182–83, 217
Haley, J., 266, 278
halfa, 33
half-basket weave, 134, 135p, 137, 142, 165 (def.), 180,
  187–89, 191, 195, 197, 203, 210, 271
Hall, H., 149, 332, 396

Hall, R., 147–49, 151, 154
Hallein (A63), 186–87, 191p, 192, 328
Hallo, W., 261n
Hallstatt (A62), 186–87, 188p, 192, 212–13, 239, 328
Hallstatt culture, 32, 106, 119, 122, 124, 142, 164, 168,
  173n, 180, 185–96, 203–4, 212–14, 213p, 218, 221,
  224, 228, 234, 239, 294, 295p, 328, 330; connections
  with Caucasus, 122, 164, 168–70, 194, 212–13; urn,
  55, 56p, 69, 92, 109, 112, 173n, 213, 294, 295p, 297
Hama (A114), 62
Hamčenko, S., 16–17
Hamlin, C., 391
Hammond, H., 13, 16, 21
handedness, 67
Han dynasty, 80, 81p
hangings, 141, 174, 197, 200, 219, 367, 377, 382, Plate
  4
Hankey, V., 331, 340
Hannover, 141, 184, 378p
Hansen, D., 25, 164
Hapdjefai. *See* Hepzefa
Hapuseneb, 339t, 343, 343p, 396
Harappa (A146i), 33
Haremhab (pharaoh), 113n, 339t
Haremhab (royal scribe), 339t, 396
Harold of England, 373
Harris, J., 15n, 20, 30, 33, 44n, 225, 227, 234–35, 239
Harz mountains, 141, 176, 184
Hasanlu (A125), 202n, 224
Hassuna (A123), 51, 391
Hathor-head motif, 350
Hatnufer, 151, 153
Hatshepsut, 151, 153, 155n, 156–57, 224, 331–33, 335,
  339t, 343–44, 347, 351, Plate 3
Hatting, T., 27n
Hawaiians, 155
Hawkes, J. G., 18
Hay, R., 332
Hayes, W., 90–91, 125, 149, 151, 153–54, 156, 224,
  340, 354, 356
Haynes, A., 105
heading band/cord, 96, 99, 101, 111p, 116–18, 129
  (def.), 129p (diag.), 130, 134, 135p (diag.), 138p, 142,
  180, 182p, 192, 195, 197, 203–4, 211, 249, 254–55,
  270p, 271–73, 272p, 280, 280t, 283, 313, 326, 326p,
  336, 361, 361p
heading-band makers. *See* warp makers
heart-spirals, 321p, 330, 346, 346p, 347n, 349, 371p
heather, 228
Hebrew, 165n; *hemar*, 131; *kuttoneth*, 255n, 295n; *shazar*, 50, 72; *tavah*, 50
Hebrews, 50, 72
heckling. *See* hackling
Hector, 373
Hecuba, 362
Hecuba, 362
heddle bars, 82p, 83 (def.), 84, 86–88, 91, 105, 107n,
  109–10, 111p, 112–13, 117, 125, 267–68, 270p, 271–

72, 280t, 281, 362n; multiple, 85n, 88n, 105, 110,
112–13, 118, 187, 268; size of, 110–12; slotted, 86–
87; supports for, 87–88, 110, 111p, 112. *See also*
heddle jacks
heddle jacks, 82p, 84 (def.), 87–88, 87p
heddles, 82–83 (def., etym.), 87–88, 109–13, 111p,
116p, 117, 144, 148, 174n, 176, 267–68, 270p, 280t,
281–82, 326; forming, 109, 267, 326; independent,
for pattern, 112, 198, 268n; permanent, 109; rigid,
117 (def.); shelf formed by, 112; of string, 83, 109–
10, 117, 267–68
hedgehogs, 369, 369p, 376–77
Hedges, J., 29
Heidengebirge, 186
Heierli, J., 95, 103, 389
heirloom textiles, 158, 352, 371, 380, 382
Helbaek, H., 10–12, 25, 81, 127, 223
Helen of Troy, 60, 70, 264, 292, 372–73, 376–77, 380,
382
Helladic, Late, 107, 315, 324p, 325–26, 331, 344p,
355–56
Hellenistic era, 240n, 241–42, 359n, 361, 389
helmets, 173n, 205n, 220
Helvetii, 299n
hemp, 15–19, 16p, 33, 35, 36–38 (etym.), 41, 67, 219,
251; coarseness of, 15, 17; compared to flax/linen,
15–16, 18n; dyed, 17; identification of, 15–16, 18;
misidentification of, 15n; multiple use of, 15, 17–18;
narcotic use of, 17–18, 36–38, 219; Neolithic evidence for, 16–18; origin and diffusion of, 16–18;
overuse of name, 15n; preparing, 15, 38, 215; seeds,
16–18; in steppes, 17–18, 251; words for, 36–38
hempen cloth, 17–18, 197, 200, 205
hems/hemming, 129, 148, 151, 154, 159, 160–61pp,
165, 191, 197, 218, 325; rolled, 149, 197
Hencken, H., 70
henna, 227, 232, 232n (etym.)
Henneburg, A., 152, 224
Henshall, A., 30, 112, 185, 195
Hephaistos, 382n
Hepzefa (Hapdjefai), 339t, 345–46, 346p, 347n, 396
Hera, 257–58, 364, 382n
Heraeum, Samos, 306p (map), 307, 392
Herakles, 360
Herihor, 339t, 350
Herington, C., 298n, 363
Hermitage, Leningrad, 173n, 200n, 201, 208n, Plate 4
Herodotus, 15–18, 33, 49n, 53, 69, 206, 226, 229, 269,
290, 379
Herpály, 95
Hesiod, 2, 102, 266, 270, 380–81
Hess, K., 13–15, 31
Hesychius, 107, 260, 263, 266, 269–70, 272
Heurtley, W., 98, 107n
Heyn, A., 21n
Hibiscus spp., 15n
hides, 23, 28, 50, 167, 176–78, 183, 218, 276, 334, 338
hieroglyphs. *See* Egyptian hieroglyphs

Higgs, E., 39
Hill, M., 343n
Hilzheimer, M., 24
Hippomedon, 206
Hirmer, M., 226n, 342, 350, 394–96
Hissar (A142), 57, 58p, 171n
Histeus, 283
Historical Museum, Kiev, 92n, 173n
Hittite, 230–31, 260, 277; *ḫulana*, 260; *kaluti*-, 262n;
karš-, 261; *kattanipu*-, 255n, 295n; *kiš(š)*-, 262; *ta-
rupp*-, 269
Hittite Museum. *See* Ankara Museum of Anatolian Civ-
ilizations
Hittite Old Kingdom, 392
Hittites, 59, 255n, 295n, 337, 356, 392
Ho, P., 17
Hochberg, B., 42–43, 47n, 49n, 51
Hochdorf (A24), 204, 328n
Hódmezővásárhely, 293
Hoenigswald, H., 261n, 274n, 280n
Hoernes, M., 296p
Hoernes, R., 55
Hofenk-de Graaff, J., 237
Hoffmann, M., 67, 92n, 96, 101–7, 109–10, 111p, 116–
17, 119, 122, 125, 129–30, 134, 326
Hogarth, D., 68, 69p, 241
Hohmichele (A25), 32, 119, 189–90, 189p, 203–4
Hole, F., 131, 392
Holland. *See* Netherlands
hollow whorls. *See* spindle whorls: concave
Homer, 70, 112, 172, 173n, 205n, 220, 258, 265, 267,
275, 284, 291–92, 338n, 358, 359n, 365, 372–73,
376n, 380, 382. See also *Iliad; Odyssey*
Homeric Greek, 260, 275
Hood, S., 327p, 394–95
hooked lozenge, 258p, 297
hooks. *See* spindle hooks
Hopf, M., 35
Hopi, 220n, 257n
Horemheb. *See* Haremhab
Horgen culture, 54, 95, 134
horizontal looms, 81–82, 84p, 85n, 125, 213, 251, 253,
268, 290n. *See also* ground-loom
Horowitz, S., 165
Horoztepe (A91), 61
horsecloths, 156, 157p, 200, 202–3, 205n, 219, 219p,
221, 332, 343–44, 353, Plate 4. See also *shabrak*
horsehair, 30, 195, 196p
horsemen, 199, 201p, 202, 205n, 206, 209p, 212, 334,
372
horses, 156, 157p, 200, 202–3, 205n, 206, 208, 209p,
219, 332, 334, 362, 364, 367, 378, 379p
Horsfall, R., 15, 233
horticultural societies, 289, 293
Hotu Cave, 391
household linens, 150–51, 153, 159, 286–90, 376
House of the Ladies, Akrotiri, 329. *See also* Theran
frescoes

Howe, B., 25, 51, 79
höyük, hüyük, 306n
Hradčany, Moravia (A65), 96, 101, 101p, 103–4, 302, 388–89
Hsiung-nu, 205n
Hsi-yin-ts'un, Shansi (A151i), 31
Huang Ti, 31
Huebner, J., 224, 227, 236–38
humic acid, 177
humification, 20, 40
Hundt, H.-J., 21, 31–32, 119, 122, 177n, 180, 188–92, 203–4, 218, 227–28, 237, 239
Hungarians, 220, 294, 297
Hungary, 55, 72, 92, 93–95, 94–95pp, 97–98, 101, 103, 113, 144, 186, 213, 220n, 226n, 294–95, 295p, 297, 387, 389
Huns, 299n, 309
Hunteburg, 192
hunter-gatherers, 79–80n
Hurry, J., 234
Hutchinson, R., 98, 107n
Huxley, G., 229, 389
Huy, 339t, 344, 352, 396
Hyksos migrations, 301

Iakovides, S., 63, 395
iconographically important space, 161–62, 340, 374–76, 382
Idalion, 174n
identification problems, 40, 54, 69, 81, 109, 143; in dyes, 223, 227–28, 237; in fibers, 10–11, 15–20, 25; in representations, 83n, 88; in sheep, 22, 28; in use of weights, 92–93, 97, 97n, 98–99
ikria, 218n, 316, 344–45, 344p, 356, 370, 394–95
Iliad, 112, 172, 205n, 220, 257–58, 265, 267, 372–73, 377
Imenemipet. *See* Amenemopet
Imiseba, 338, 339t, 348, 350, 396
imitation. *See* copying
Immerwahr, S., 322, 338n
imports, 10, 19, 23, 32–33, 165n, 171, 182, 194, 202–5, 235, 238, 249n, 252, 285, 311, 316n, 321–22, 331, 338, 340, 344–47, 346p, 351, 355
impressions: of cloth, 3, 17, 25, 32, 51, 79, 95, 109, 121, 121p, 123, 126–27, 127p, 132, 134, 141, 144, 144n, 165–66, 167n, 168, 170, 170p, 174, 212–13, 259, 312; of loom parts, 102; of seeds, 17; of thread, 25, 121
Incas, 81
India, 15n, 32–33, 38, 43, 52, 66–67, 91, 205, 215–16, 225, 231–32, 237, 251, 253
Indic, 251, 261, 275
indican, 234
indigo, 234 (etym.)
indigo dye, 227, 234–35, 237–38
Indigofera tinctoria, 234
indigo plant, 234–35

Indo-European language, 36–37, 80, 232–33, 247, 254, 255n, 260–81, 337n, 359n
Indo-Europeans, 36, 169n, 186, 221n, 222, 233n, 234n, 254–55, 260, 276–77, 280–81, 295, 297, 315, 336, 373, 376; Mediterranean borrowing group among, 262n, 263–64, 277; western vocabulary conspiracy among, 233–35, 260, 273–74, 276–77
Indo-Iranian, 37, 206, 231n
Indonesia, 374, 374p, 376
Indreko, R., 41
industrial organization, 102, 166, 239–43, 283–91
Industrial Revolution, 4–5, 285, 291
Indus valley (A inset), 237
Ineni (Anena), 331, 339t, 396
infrared spectroscopy, 227, 237
Inherkha (Anherkhawi, Khai-inheret), 10n, 338, 339t, 340, 342, 348–50, 396
inlay technique, 151, 152 (def.), 152p (diag.), 153–54, 153–54pp, 159, 162, 210, 251, Plate 1
inscriptions, on/about textiles, 92p, 95, 153–54, 153–54pp, 157–58, 160p, 161, 194, 229, 304, 352, 354, 377, Plate 1
Institute of Archaeology, London, 132n, 302n
interlaced knot pattern, 318–19, 318p
interlock patterns, 318–19, 320p, 322, 323–24pp, 328–30, 338, 340, 347, 357, Plate 2, Plate 3. *See also* rapport patterns
international style, 350, 355n, 356–57
Iokasta. *See* Jocasta
Iolaos, 206
Ion, 360, 378
Ion, 360
Ionia, 356, 371, 379
Iphigenia, 338n, 362
Iphigenia in Taurus, 362
Ipuky, 339t, 344, 396
Iraklion Museum, 35p, 75n, 77p, 92p, 320p, 323p, 327p
Iran, 12, 29n, 36, 38, 55n, 56–59, 61, 83n, 84, 132, 202, 212, 251, 305, Plate 4; eastern, 24; northern, 22, 57, 58p, 171n, 224; southern, 12, 51, 251, 392
Iranian, 37; *snavarә* -, 263n, 266
Iraq, 12, 27n, 51, 127p, 305. *See also* Mesopotamia
Ireland, 30, 112, 195, 196p, 234n. *See also* Armoy; Island MacHugh
Irgenhausen am Pfäffikersee (A30), 135n, 138–40pp, 139–40, 142, 144, 224
Irinefer, 341
Iris, 373
Irish, *crossáin*, 234n
iron, as mordant/developer, 227–28, 236–39, 330. *For other uses, see* metal
Iron Age, 17–18, 30, 54–55, 59, 62–63, 64p, 69, 71, 92, 99, 101–3, 107n, 112, 116, 121n, 122–24, 150, 152, 166, 171n, 173, 185–209, 214, 224–25, 229, 233, 235n, 238–39, 241, 261, 268, 284, 300, 301n, 302, 303n, 312–13, 318n, 330, 359n, 371–73, 378, 380, 382, 388–89, Plate 4

Iron Age sheep, 22n
Isatis tinctoria, 234
Isimkheb, 342–43
Islamic era, 51
Island MacHugh, County Tyrone (A9), 195
Isles in the Great Green, 311, 334, 337, 356
isolated patterns, vs. traditional, 338, 340, 343, 347n
Israel, 12, 63p, 99, 101, 131p, 224, 229, 241n, 242, 249, 302, 388–90. *See also* Palestine
Israelite period, 302n
Israel Museum, 131p
Istanbul, 37
Italians, 301
Italic, 255n, 261
Italy, 16, 18, 29, 54–55, 91, 97, 99–101, 100p, 108p, 108n, 110, 111p, 113, 123, 163n, 174–75, 175p, 194–95, 293, 304, 308, 389–90
Itanos (D252), 229
Iten-Maritz, J., 109
Itzehoe (B155), 256p
ivory, 43, 62–63, 119, 155–56n, 171, 243, 299, 316, 319, 327p, 328, 354, 355n, 394
Ivory Triad, 316, 319, 394

Jacobsen, Thorkild, 220n, 288
Jacobsen, T. W., 27n
James, F., 63
Janssen, J., 286, 288–89
Japan, 49, 73, 75n
Japanese language, 73, 267n, 278
Jarman, M., 76, 240
Jarmo (A127), 22, 25, 27n, 51, 79, 88, 126, 127p, 132, 210, 252p (map), 253, 258–59
Jehasse, J., and L. Jehasse, 124
Jenkins, I., 122, 124, 269n
Jensen, L., 228n, 229
Jentsch, H., 390
Jéquier, G., 118, 120, 342–43pp, 396
Jericho (C178), 132, 165, 224, 300n, 301p (map), 388–89
Jocasta, 206, 378–79
Johnson, R., 32n
Jones, H., 37, 261, 263–64, 268n, 270, 275
Joseph, B., 269
Joshua, 13
Judaean desert, 12, 30, 71n, 85, 124, 127
Jugoslavia, 98, 100, 144, 226n, 294n, 296p, 303n, 388–89
jute, 16
Jutland, 176

Kabardinski Park, 121
Kadish, B., 93, 94p, 103, 167n, 389
Kafr Ammar (C192), 148
Kahlenberg, M., 374–75
Kahun (C195), 49n, 75, 86, 87p, 88, 224, 351

Kajitani, N., 73n, 150n, 151, 153, 228n
Kakheti, 168
Kalicz, N., 94–95, 389
Kalligas, P., 197n
Kalocsa, 294n
Kamares ware, 75, 228, 313, 316, 329
Kaná, S., 298n
Kanesh (A106), 287–88
Kantir (C187), 353, 356p
Kantor, H., 56, 57p, 330, 342–43pp, 346
Karageorghis, V., 350, 354, 395
Karakalpak, *kenep*, 37
Karana (A121), 288
Karataş (A102), 61, 62p
Karaulašvili, Ts., 168
Karaz, 391
Kardara, C., 240n, 242
Karmir-Blur (A88), 202n, 238
Karouzou, S., 377
Karphi (D249), 371
Ka Ruo, Chang-du County, Tibet (A152i), 17
Kassel, 141
Kato Zakro (D255), 101
Kay, P., 230
Kayan, I., 352n
Kazarma, 174n
Kea. *See* Keos
Keast, D., 242p
Keay, A., 227
Keftiu, 226n, 311, 334, 337, 345, 347, 350, 355n, 356; king of the, 355n
Keftiu boats, 345
Keller, F., 10, 97, 389
Kelly, M., 298n
Kemp, B., 75, 331, 351
kemp, 21 (def.), 21p (diag.), 22, 23–24pp, 24n, 29, 141, 177, 184, 217, 262; as unspinnable, 24n
kenaf, 15n
Kenamun, 331, 343–45, 396
Kendall, A., 68, 167
Kendrick, A., 226, 365
Kenyon, K., 300, 389
Keos (Kea) (D235–36), 109, 112, 174n, 388–89
Kephala, Keos/Kea (D235), 109
Kerameikos, 32, 204, 361
Kerma (A143i), 154–55, 164, 171–72, 211
kermes, 224, 227, 230–32, 231n (etym.), 240, 263
kermesic acid, 231n
Kermesidae, 230
kermes insects, 227, 230
Kermococcus vermilio, 230
Kertch (A79), 3, 122, 206–7, 208–9pp, 226, 379p
Kestner Museum, Hannover, 378p
Kha, 150, 153, 155n, 159, 345
Khai-inheret. *See* Inherkha
Khalkha, *ol(son)*, 38
Khety, 44, 286
Khirokitia, 228n

Khlopin, I., 171n
Khnumhotep (Khnemhotep), 44, 83n, 84, 86, 151
Khons, 340
Khuzistan, 56, 57p
Kiev (A76), 98–99, 297, 306n
Kilaueia, 381
Kilda sheep, 22n
kilims, 171, 217
Killen, J., 26, 28, 238, 260, 272n, 273n, 284
kilts: direction of weaving, 336; vs. loincloths, 322; pan-
    eled, 334, 336–37, 351, 353p, 354–56, 356p; pointed,
    322, 323p, 333, 334–35pp, 336, 337p, 337n, 354–55.
    See also clothing: kilt; tassels
Kimakowitz-Winnicki, M., 95
Kimmerians, 102, 197
Kimmig, W., 220n
Kimolian earth, 274
King's Gate, Boğazköy, 336, 337p
Kirby, R., 13, 15n, 19, 33–34
Kirillovskie Zeml'anki, 306p (map), 306n
Kish (A130), 57, 58p, 60, 63, 166
Kisköre (A72), 94, 387, 389
Kleitias, 364, 365p, 366, 368
kleos, 373
Kličevac (A57), 293, 295, 296p
Klose, O., 188n, 189, 191p
Klotho, 263
Kluge, F., 36, 233n, 235n, 261n, 359n
knee guards, 77–78, 78p
knitting, 20, 121n, 122, 216n, 292
Knossos (D244), 54n, 77, 100, 107, 174n, 228, 272–
    73n, 283–84, 294, 298n, 313, 316, 319, 320–21pp,
    322, 323p, 325, 327–28, 327p, 328–29, 336–37, 338n,
    354–55, 371p, 387–89, 394–95
Knossos frescoes: Bull Leapers, 316, 325, 395; Camp-
    stool Fresco, 316, 395; Captain of the Blacks, 316,
    395; Cupbearer, 316, 322, 323p, 328–29, 338n, 395;
    Dancing Girl, 316, 319n, 395; Ladies in Blue, 316,
    319, 394; Lady in Red, 316, 319, 394; La Parisienne,
    316, 327, 327p, 395; Miniature Dress Ornaments,
    316, 319, 321, 394; Miniature Fresco (Grandstand;
    Dancing Floor), 316, 319, 394; Priest King, 316, 319,
    394; Procession Fresco, 316, 322, 323p, 324–25,
    328–29, 347n, 354–55, 395
knotless netting, 184
knot patterns, 318–19, 318p
knotter, 212
knotting, 12, 49, 67, 68, 73, 130, 140, 140p, 155n, 166,
    170, 181p, 199, 201–2, 201p, 202p (diag.), 211–12,
    215. *See also* sacred knots
Knowles, P., 233n
Koch, P.-A., 16
Kohl, P., 31
Kökten, K., 167n
Kommos (D262), 74, 75n
Kopet Dag, 306p (map)
korai, 363–64, 366n, 370n
Kordysh, N., 16, 98

Korobkova, G., 212
Koropi (D230), 206
Körös culture, 93
Korpilahti, Finland (A14), 20, 41
Korucu Tepe, 391
Koşay, H., 60, 61p, 392
Kostrzewski, J., 85n
Kouphonisi (Leuke) (D256), 228–29
Kovacs, M., 294–95n
Kowalczyk, J., 99, 100p, 306, 307p, 389
Krafft, S., 373
Kraft, J., 352n
Krakatoa, 381
Kreienkopp bei Ditfurt, Kr. Quedlinburg (A17), 141–42
Kronos, 362
Kuban (A), 168–69, 225, 295n
Kuehn, G., 24n
Kuftin, B., 168
Kuhn, D., 17, 69
Kujala, V., 41
Kültepe/Nakhichevan, 391
Kurdian, H., 231
Kurdistan, 12
Kurgan culture, 173n
kurgans, 17–18, 28, 31, 121, 169, 169–70pp, 173n,
    199–203, 201p, 206–8, 207–9pp, 212, 218, 219p, 221,
    225, 295n, 379, Plate 4. *See also* burial mounds
Kurinsky, S., 235n
Kurtz, D., 367n, 377–78
Kyrle, G., 189
Kythera (D), 104, 229, 388–89

LaBaume, W., 117
labor hours. *See* labor-saving devices; time required
labor-saving devices, 43, 50, 89, 109–10, 188–89, 293,
    305, 318n, 321. *See also* cheap substitutes; pattern
    weaving: mechanization of; shedding: mechanical
Lacaisne, Z., 133
Lachesis, 263
Lachish (C183), 165, 302n
lac-insects, 230–31
Laertes, 358, 377, 380, 382
Lagash (A131), 164, 288
Lago di Ledro (A35), 175, 175p, 226, 293
Lagozza (A32), 100, 100p
lake dwellings. *See* pile dwellings
Lake Ladoga (A16), 41
Lamassī, 287
Lamb, W., 107n, 392, 395
Lambert, M., 288
Landercy, M., 273–74
Landi, S., 147–49, 151, 154
Lane, G., 205n
Lang, M., 325, 395
Lange, K., 396
Langlotz, E., 68, 92n
lanolin, 21, 240

Lansing, A., 156
Lapps, 39, 109, 116, 326, 326p
larnakes. See sarcophagi
Lascaux (A7), 20, 40–41
Latakia (A115), 229
La Tène (A27), 29n, 122
La Tène culture, 101, 119, 186, 192, 194, 204
Latin, 80, 215, 233, 234n, 235, 260, 276–77
  alvus, 263n
  cannabis, 36
  fallo, 264n
  fides, 264n
  funda, 264n
  fungus, 264n
  fusus, 263
  haru-, 266
  lana, 233n, 260
  liciare, licinae, licinus, licium, 268
  lutum, 233n
  nervus, 263n, 266
  pannus, 273
  Parcae, 376
  pecten, pectere, 261
  pendere, 265
  pensum, 265
  pilleus, 276
  pilus, 276
  pingo, pictus, 359n
  plecto, 80
  praetextae, 194
  sandaraca, 231n
  suere, 275
  terminus, 274
  texere, 5
  torquere, 263
  trilicarius, 268
  tunica, 255n, 295n
  vervex, 260
  vestis, 337n
  vitrum, 234n, 235n
Lattrigen, 14p
Latvian: *kaṇepe,* 36; *knàbt,* 274; *krekls,* 273
Laufer, B., 215–16, 221–22
lavender (color), 224
Lawrie, L., 15, 233
Lawsonia sp., 227, 232
laze rod, 84 (def.), 113
Leakey, R., 80n
leather, 156n, 172, 176, 184, 199–200, 218n, 219–20,
  283, 312n, 341–45
Le Breton, L., 84p, 391
Leek, North Staffordshire, 234n
Lefkandi (D225), 197, 312, 348
legends, 17, 31, 297. *See also* Greek legends
Leggett, W., 30, 32
Lehmann-Filhes, 119
Lemnos, 307
Lempese, A., 74

Lerna, 35, 306p (map), 308
Leroi-Gourhan, André, 40
Leroi-Gourhan, Arlette, 40
Lesbos, 307
Lespugue (A4), 40, 40p, 256
leuco-form, of dye, 228, 234
Leuke. *See* Kouphonisi
Leumann, M., 264n
Levant, 62, 64, 163, 165–66, 224, 228–30, 232, 237,
  355n, 356, 392
leveling agent, 235–36
Levi, D., 224
Levy, S., 243, 302n, 390
Lewis, C., 261n
Lewis, D., 363n
Li, C., 31
Li, H., 17, 38
Libya, 352n
Libyans, 355
lice, 189
lichens, 232, 235, 238
Lichtheim, M., 291
Liddell, H., 37, 261, 263–64, 268n, 270, 275
Life of Demetrios, 361
life-span symbols, 375–76, 382. *See also* thread of des-
  tiny
Lille Dragshøj (B156), 182
lime. *See* slaked lime
Lindqvist, S., 137, 192–93, 193p, 218
line, 13 (def.), 14
Linear A, 77, 91, 92p, 313
Linear B, 77, 173n, 231, 238, 260, 267n, 275, 283–84,
  288–89, 291, 312–13, 330, 336n, 373
  a-ke-ti-ri-ja, 272–73n
  a-pu-k- (ampuk-), 312
  a-pu-ko-wo-ko (ampukoworgoi), 313
  a-ra-ka-te-ja, 264, 283
  a-ze-ti-ri-ja, 272–73n, 283, 313
  CLOTH (TELA), 313
  i-te-ja(-o), 270, 283
  i-te-u, i-te-we, 270, 283
  ka-na-ko, 232n
  ka-na-pe-u, 274, 283
  ki-to(-n-), 255n, 295n
  ku-pi-ri-jo, 238
  MA + RU, 260, 266, 267n
  ne-ki-ri-de, 272n
  o-da-k- (odak-), 312
  o-nu-ke (onukh-), 272–73n, 284, 312, 327–28n
  o-nu-ke-ja, 283
  pa-ma-ko, 275n
  pa-ra-ku, 313
  pa-we-a₂, 358n
  pe-ki-ti-ra₂, 262, 283
  pe-ko-to, 262
  po-ki-ro-nu-ka (poikilonukha), 327
  po-me, 283
  po-ni-ki-jo, 232n

Linear B (*cont.*)
  po-ri-w- (*polios*), 313
  ra-pi-ti-ra₂, 283
  ra-pte(-re), 283
  ri-ne-ja, 283
  ta-ra-si-ja, 265, 283
  te-mi- (termi-), 265, 283, 312
  tu-ru-pte-ri-ja, 276
  we-a₂-no, 337n
  WE surcharge, 337n
  we-we-e-a, 260
linen, 49n, 68, 72, 76–78, 81, 131p, 133–43, 134–40pp, 145–62, 165, 171–72, 174–76, 175p, 190, 197, 206, 220n, 224, 240, 255n, 262 (etym.), 264, 266–67, 271, 280t, 295n, 312–13, 366n, 377, Plate 1; absorbency of, 14; beating, 14; bleaching, 14–15; characteristics of, 14–15; difficulty in dyeing, 15, 49n, 211; distribution of, 211, 250p, 251; dyed, 17; dyeing, 15, 49n, 133, 211, 217, 236n; Egyptian vs. European, 194. *See also* Faiyum Neolithic linen; flax; Swiss Neolithic cloth
linen-chests. *See* chests
linguistic analysis: of cotton, 32n; of dyes, 230–35; of felting, 215–16, 222; of Greek textile terms, 260–81; of hemp, 36–38
linguistic borrowing, 36–38, 204n, 215–16, 231n, 235n, 255n, 264, 266, 269–71, 273n, 274–82, 295n; in contiguous areas, 233, 235, 255n, 260, 263–64, 269, 276n, 277, 295n; layers of, 37, 264n, 275–82, 278–80tt. *See also* double vocabulary; loan words
linguistic evidence, 205n, 230, 299n, 309, 334
linguistic reconstruction, 36–38, 80, 169n, 233–35nn, 247–48, 254–55, 260–82, 295n, 313
linguistic sequence-dating, 261, 264
linings, 220–21
linseed bread, 12
linseed oil, 11n, 12. *See also* flax seed
lint, 14, 285
Linum spp., 10–12
Lipari Islands (A): Lipara, 238n
Lisht (C191), 115, 301n
literacy, effects of, 163n, 292, 362n, 373
literary evidence, 18, 221, 228n, 229, 292, 309, 331, 345, 376, 383; Biblical, 50, 72, 230 (*see also individual books of Bible*); Classical, 231n (*see also* Greek literature; *individual authors*)
Lithuania, 20, 41, 134, 297
Lithuanian: *gelonìs*, 275; *júosta, júostas*, 254; *kanãpès*, 36; *lañktis*, 264; *leñkti*, 264; *pèšti*, 261; *piẽšti*, 359n; *snaujis-*, 263n; *veȓpti*, 275n; *žarnà*, 266
litmus, 232
Liu, R., 52, 54n, 62, 305
Liverpool Museum, 118, 120p, 156–57
llamas, 26
Lloyd, S., 59n, 132n, 217, 392
loan translation, 281n
loan words: from common source, 262n, 263, 267, 274, 276n, 277, 295n; morphological restructuring of, 266, 277; phonological restructuring of, 266–67; with *r/l* confusion, 267n, 269, 277
local manufacture, by/for foreigners, 49n, 65, 158, 162, 206, 299–300, 321
Locray, Switzerland, 55
Loden coats, 178, 216
Long, C., 395
longevity, of tradition, 65, 71n, 76, 78, 145, 159, 162, 171, 173n, 186, 201, 213–14, 234n, 257–58, 260, 291, 294–98, 303, 382n, 383. *See also* conservatism; survivals; tradition
looms, 2, 5 (def.), 10, 80–125, 80 (def., etym.), 130, 134, 167, 176, 183, 204, 205n, 211, 222, 240, 247, 249–55, 269–70, 279–81, 284–86, 294, 311, 314, 351, 359n, 363, 372; distribution of, 124–25, 249–53, 250p, 252p, 308; evolution of, 80–82, 124–25, 213, 253–55, 258; movement around, 81–82, 105, 290n; not yet found, 88–89, 116, 124, 130n, 205n, 213, 249, 308; placement of, in house, 89, 94p, 103, 106, 254 (*see also* upper floors); preserved, 85–86, 92, 93p, 101–2, 110, 286, 302n, 313–14; relation to pattern weaving, 105, 126, 192, 211–12; replacement parts for, 83–84, 88n, 104; width of, 80–81, 86, 98, 101–5, 178, 254, 387–89. *See also* ground-loom; posts; vertical two-beam loom; warp-weighted loom
loom uprights. *See* posts
loom weights, 51, 82, 92–106, 93–96pp, 98p, 100–101pp, 104p, 108–9n, 109–10, 111p, 115, 130, 134, 171, 174, 240–43, 249, 253, 270–72, 270p, 278t, 280, 280t, 281–82, 284–85, 299–303, 300p, 310, 314, 387–90; attaching, 96, 104, 130, 180; balancing, 96, 130, 168, 272; blackout of, in Greece, 308; control bar for, 104–5, 362n; decorated, 95; distribution of, *see under* warp-weighted loom; earliest, 93–94, 249, 254; experiments with, 105, 302, 362n; fallen from above, 101–2, 240–42, 300, 389; field stones as, 96, 109–10, 130n, 253, 271; grooved, 104–5, 104p; identifying function of, 92–93, 97–100, 97n, 301n; inequality in, 96, 101, 101p, 118; moving down warp, 106; noise of, 105, 362n; quantity of, 92–95, 97–104, 254, 300–301nn, 302, 387–90; in rows, 93, 93–94pp, 95, 97n, 98, 101–3, 110, 118, 389–90; in sets, 93–101, 104, 118, 242, 300n, 302, 387–90; shape of, 94–95, 97–102, 98p, 100–101pp, 271, 280–81, 300, 301n, 302, 387–90; storage of, 99, 101–2, 104, 389–90; stringholes in, 93, 94p, 95–102, 104, 300; weight of, 95–97, 99–100, 103–4, 117–18, 387–89. (*See also* crescentic weights; disc weights; donut weights
looped bowls. *See* fiber-wetting bowls
Loret, V., 232
Los Angeles County Museum of Art, 374p
Los Angeles County Zoo, 24
Loud, G., 300, 389
Lucas, A., 15n, 20, 30, 33, 44n, 225, 227, 234–35, 239
Luce, J., 102, 381
Lugalanda, 288
Lund, 119
Lüscherz am Bielersee (A26), 14p, 135n, 136p

Lutz, H., 158
Luxembourg, 32, 205n
Luxor (C214), 341
luxury cloth, 31, 155, 158–59, 166, 171–72, 173n, 189–
    90, 195, 197–98, 204–5, 212, 219, 227, 229, 240, 252,
    262, 286–87, 290–92, 312, 320–21, 330, 338n, 340,
    345, 357, 364, 371–72, 376, 378–79; shift in sex of
    users of, 315, 322, 324
Lydekker, R., 22
Lydia (A), Lydians, 198–200
lye, 19
Lygeum spartum, 33
Lysistrata, 262
Lysistrata, 262, 274

MacAlister, R., 300, 302, 389–90
McConnell, B., 285
McCown, D., 391
MacDowell, U., 391
MacGillivray, J., 100n
Mackay, E., 57, 58p, 148
Mace, A., 115, 155, 162, 301n
Macedonia, 98, 238n
Macedonians, 173n
macramé, 155n
madder, 223, 227, 232, 236–38
Madjar, 155n
Maeder, E., 214
Magdalenian, 39
Magdeburg, 141
magic, 19n, 44, 47, 184n, 225, 257, 297, 325, 372–74,
    376, 382
Maglemosian, 41
maguey, 52
Maherpra, 153, 343
Maikop (A82), 173n
mail plating, 313
Maisler, E., 302n
Majewski, L., 198–99
Makarenko, N., 173n, 231n
Makron, 363, 363p
Malkata (C213), 341, 348, 349p
Mallia (D250), 316, 319, 320p, 328, 330, 336n, 394
Mallory, J., 16
mallow, 15n, 32
Malta (A), 285, 293
Maltese cross, 162
Manatt, J., 395
Manchu, *olo*, *xunta*, 38
mangling flax, 45p, 46
mantle, 216 (etym.). *See also* clothing: cloak
Maori, 49, 155
maps: of fiber use, 34p, 250p; of loom types, 250p,
    252p, 301p; of loom weights, 301p; of sites, xxiv,
    xxvi, xxviii, xxx, 252p, 301p, 306p; of spindle whorls,
    306p; of textile zones, 250p
Maraş (A108), 59

Margit Kovacs Museums, 294n
Mari (A119), 56–57, 171, 212, 291, 305
marijuana, 15
Marinatos, N., 312, 317, 338n
Marinatos, S., 102, 124n, 174, 225, 226n, 233, 281n,
    342, 350, 389, 394–95
Marinković, K., 226n
Maritime Fresco, Thera, 218n
Mariupol (Marijupil') (A78), 173n, 231n
markets, for textiles, 287–88, 290
Marlik (A140), 55n, 59
Marshall, J., 32, 232
Martkopi (A87), 168, 212
mashing dyes, 226, 239–40
Masson, E., 295n
Masson, V., 391
mass production, effect on designs, 293, 330, 345
Masuda, S., 29n, 391
Masurel, H., 175, 194
Matisoff, J., 261n
mat looms, 5n, 83n, 286p, 291
matrilineal societies, 293
mats/matting, 5, 9, 33, 51, 79, 131–32, 140, 144, 170,
    174, 212, 216–17, 225, 276, 286p, 291, 341–42, 344–
    47; on Egyptian ceilings, 341–42, 344–45
Matthiae, P., 125, 166
Mchedlishvili, G., 168n
meander pattern, 171, 197–98, 198p, 202–3, 206, 346–
    47, 346p, 366–67, 367–68pp, 370, 370n, 377, 379,
    Plate 3; development of, 346–47, 366, 370n
mechanization. *See under* pattern weaving; shedding
Mecquenem, R., 119
Medes, 202, 221
medicine, 38, 232n, 234, 313, 338n
medieval period, 69, 78, 85n, 97, 113, 125, 213–14,
    268n, 285, 297n, 325, 366n
Medinet Habu, 299n, 341, 354
Mediterranean Sea, 123, 228n, 229, 238, 285, 337, 351;
    coast of, 11–12, 33, 173, 229, 233n, 309, 351–52n;
    countries around, 18, 30, 32, 65, 85n, 159, 163, 206,
    233, 267n, 302, 355; east end of, 112, 116, 173–74,
    230, 232n, 300, 337, 354, 357; area north of, 15, 16,
    33, 47, 49n, 54–55, 69, 91, 99, 124–25, 171, 173,
    300, 304, 309, 312n
medulla, 21n, 24n
Mee, C., 355
Megiddo (C171), 62–63, 158, 166, 300–301, 300p, 301p
    (map), 352, 388–89
Meilen Rohrenhaab (A31), 55
Meir (C200), 347, 396
Meissner, B., 38
Meister, W., 216, 220
Meketre, 75, 84, 85p, 87, 89
Meleagros, 376
Melida, J., 34
Mell, C., 232–33, 234n
Mellaart, J., 10–11, 25, 47n, 51n, 59n, 79, 98–99, 128–
    29, 130n, 132, 170, 216–17, 220n, 223, 255, 392

Mellink, M., 62, 365, 392

Melos (D240), 63n, 238n, 241, 322p

men, 4, 39, 45p, 60, 76, 76p, 113, 114p, 115, 141, 169, 173n, 177, 258, 283–92, 286p, 294, 295n, 298–99, 311, 314–16, 319, 322, 323p, 324–25, 328, 331–38, 332–35pp, 337p, 339t, 340–57, 353p, 356p, 358, 372, 375, 377, 394–95; as weavers, 4, 83, 113, 114p, 115, 270, 283–84, 286, 286p, 290–91, 299

mending, 3, 129, 154, 159, 380. See also patches

Menelaos, 373

Menkheper, 396

Menkheperraseneb, 334–35, 335p, 347–48, 354, 355n, 396, Plate 3

Mentuhotep II, 149–50

merchants, 18, 205n, 260, 285, 287–88, 291, 299, 345, 357

Meriones, 220

Merrillees, R., 75, 331, 351

Mersin (A107), 59n, 132, 167, 300, 300p, 301p (map), 306, 306p (map), 388–89

Merzifon (A92), 61

Mesolithic, 20, 37, 41, 133–34, 177, 249

Mesopotamia, 25, 28, 42, 57p, 59–61, 67, 69, 71n, 81, 83, 88, 90, 119, 122, 124, 132, 163–66, 210–12, 220, 224, 230, 233, 237, 251, 255n, 261n, 295n, 317n, 350, 391

Mesopotamian accounts, 28, 88. See also cuneiform records

Mesopotamian representations: of spinning, 57p, 90; of warping, 56, 57p, 84p; of weaving, 81, 83, 84p, 90, 249

Messikommer, H., 10, 97, 142, 389

Messikommer, J., 95, 97

metal, 3, 10, 30, 32, 35, 37, 43, 57–63, 68–70, 81, 92, 93, 121, 121p, 132–33, 162, 164, 167n, 168–74, 176n, 181, 184, 186, 192, 194–95, 197, 199–200, 204, 205n, 206, 219, 220n, 221–22, 227–28, 231–32, 236, 238–39, 255, 256p, 264–65, 287–88, 297n, 299, 310, 311–13, 315–16, 320p, 348, 350, 354, 360, 372

metallic thread, 33, 171, 195, 200, 206

Metropolitan Museum of Art, 74p, 78p, 85p, 90, 150p, 151, 151p, 153p, 153n, 157p, 224, 228n, 301n, 332p, 343n, 349p, 356p, 367, 368p; lekythos, 72, 72p, 92p, 105–7, 110, 112, 178, 264–65, 271, 274

Mevorakh. See Tel Mevorakh

Meydum (C193), 148, 224, 322

Mezőkövesd, 294n

Michelsberg culture, 54

Midas, 102

Middle Ages. See medieval period

Middle Babylonian era, 212

Middle East, 43, 51, 56, 63, 65, 78, 113, 133, 211, 215, 232, 239, 249, 313

Middle English, welde, wold, 233n

Middle Low German, walde, 233n

Midgley, T., 15n, 48, 145, 148

Midgley, W., 146, 148, 224

migration, 76, 221, 251, 281, 299–310, 355n, 374; un-

traceable, 301, 309

Millett, A., 355, 370

Miločić, 392

minerals. See alum; dyes; mordants

Minet el-Beida (A116), 229

Minnakht, 339t, 396

Minoan clothing types, 314–16

Minoan era: Early, 74–76, 104p, 239–41; Late, 77, 77p, 122n, 174n, 315, 318p, 319, 321p, 322, 325, 328, 330–31, 338, 340, 347–48, 350, 371, Plate 2; Middle, 35p, 74–75, 228–29, 314p, 320p, 328–31, 340, 347, 357

Minoan hairdo, 311, 332, 332p, 336, 355n

Minoan pottery, in Egypt, 75, 331, 338, 351

Minoan purple industry, 228–29

Minoan representations of cloth, 314–25, 314p, 318p, 320–23pp, 327–30, 327p, 329p, 357, 366n, 394–95

Minoans, 98, 104–5, 228, 241, 271, 281, 288, 293, 300, 311, 313–33, 335–37, 338n, 340, 343, 346, 351–52, 354, 355n, 357, 366n, 370n, 371, 395

Minos, 381

misdating, 25n, 149, 156n, 194, 316n, 324

missing threads. See preservation: differential

missing vocabulary, 260, 262–63, 268, 281–82

mistranslations, 97n, 231n, 260–62, 264, 359n, 362n

Mitanni, 162

mnemonic records on cloth, 373, 382

Modern Greek, 270; parathuro, 281n; rizari, 232

Moeller, W., 216, 239, 260

mohair, 25, 197

Mohenjo-Daro (A145i), 32, 232, 237

Moirai, 376. See also Fates

molluscs. See purple-snails

molting, 21, 24, 29, 41, 42, 261–62, 283–84

Mommsen, A., 361

Mongol, oloson, olasun, 38

Mongolia (A inset), 42, 199, 359

Montell, G., 42

Monte Loffa, 101, 389–90

Montet, P., 13

Moon, J., 57

Moorey, R., 64p

Moors, 234n

Mopsos, 206, 379, 379p

Moravia, 101

mordants, 226 (def.), 227–28, 232–33, 235–39 (def., etym.), 242, 261, 276–77, 280t; acid and basic, 236; metallic, 227–28, 233, 236–39; varying effects of, 233, 235, 238. See also alum

Mordvins, 173n

Moreschini, A., 266, 267n

Morris dance, 234n

Mortensen, P., 51, 132

mosaics, 56–57, 57p, 171, 205n, 305

Moss, R., 343n, 396

Mostagedda (C201), 145

motifs, copied across media. See copying: between crafts

Mouflon, 22
mound burials. *See* burial mounds; kurgans
Mound People, 177, 217–18, 221, 254
Mount St. Helens, 381
Mühletaler, B., 197n
mulberry, 15n, 31
Muldbjerg (B161), 177, 182–83
Müller, H.-W., 346p, 347n
Müller-Karpe, H., 44n
multiple uses, of textile resources, 11n, 12, 17–19, 23–
    24, 26–28, 27t, 36, 38, 223, 228–29, 232–33, 313
mummy wrappings. *See* shrouds
Munksgaard, E., 116, 119, 122, 143, 180–81, 193, 225n
murex, 223, 228–29, 235, 238, 240, 242; chemical com-
    position of, 235; treated with lemon juice, 228n
Murex spp., 228–29; shells of, 223, 228–29, 240, 242,
    313
Murray, C., 232n
Murray, W., 216
Murten (A28), 135n, 140, 140p, 174, 312n
Musée de l'Homme, Paris, 40p
Musée du Louvre, 58p, 155n
Museo Tridentino di Scienze Naturali, 175p
Muses, 338n
museums for textiles, 294, 360
music/musicians, 234n, 273, 291n, 294, 295p, 319
musk ox hair, 30
Mycenae (D220), 172, 174n, 200, 226n, 274p, 313,
    315–16, 324, 324p, 327p, 328–29, 337–38, 344p, 345,
    350, 356, 368, 369p, 377, 394–95
Mycenaean copying, of Cretan fashion, 315, 324–25,
    330
Mycenaean Greek. *See* Linear B
Mycenaean Greek accounts, 28, 232–33, 260, 264, 272–
    73n, 275, 283, 312–13, 327–28n, 330, 373
Mycenaeanized people, 336, 350, 354
Mycenaean representations, of cloth, 316, 324–27,
    324p, 327p, 354, 357, 395
Mycenaeans, 62–63, 173, 200, 225, 233, 260, 264, 271,
    274–76, 274p, 281n, 283–84, 289, 291, 311–13, 315–
    16, 324–28, 330–31, 334, 336–37, 338n, 343, 345,
    350–51, 354–56, 359, 366, 368–71, 369p, 373, 377,
    380–82
Mycenaean textile production system, 272–73n, 283–
    85, 330
Mylonas, G., 100, 174n, 270
Myres, J., 314p
Myrtos (D257), 73–76, 104, 104p, 239–41, 388–89
mytho-history, of cloth, 3, 206, 207p, 360–62, 365, 373,
    376, 378–80, 379p, 382
mythology, 3, 31, 105, 106p, 206, 231n, 257–58, 263,
    297, 360–65, 362n, 363–65pp, 373, 375–82; inconsis-
    tency in, 362n. *See also* fairytales; legends

Naḥal Ḥemar (C181), 12, 25, 30, 41, 51, 68, 127, 130–
    32, 144
Naḥal Mishmar (C180), 71n, 85–86, 88, 116, 165, 210,

224, 249
Nalchik (A85), 121, 121p
Namazga, 171n, 391
Nanai, *onokto, xontaxa*, 38
nap, 153, 216, 273, 274 (etym.)
Naquane, Camonica Valley (A34), 91, 91p
narcotics. *See* drugs; hemp
Narva culture, 20
National Museum, Athens, 64p, 173, 174n, 197n,
    274p, 327p, 329p, 366n, 369p
National Museum, Budapest, 94
National Museum, Copenhagen, 19, 116p, 123, 178–
    79pp, 181–83pp, 183, 256p
Native Mycenaean Dress, 315 (def.), 316, 324, 369p,
    377, 395
Natufian, 132
Natural History. See Pliny the Elder
natural shed, 82 (def.). *See also* sheds
Naturhistorisches Museum, Vienna, 55, 56p, 188p,
    256p, 295p
Navajo, 298
Naville, E., 149
Nea Nikomedeia (A48), 27n, 51, 54n, 107n
Near East, 25, 29n, 35, 52–54, 56–59, 61, 66, 69, 87,
    108, 115, 125, 131, 163, 166, 186, 212, 214, 217,
    226, 230, 234, 235n, 254, 259, 263, 268n, 288, 292–
    94, 299, 306n, 312, 331n, 354, 391–92
Nebamun (royal scribe and physician), 339t, 396
Nebamun (sculptor), 339t, 344, 396
Nebamun (standard bearer), 339t, 344n, 396
needle-made fabrics, 12, 177
needles, 39, 51, 140, 153, 177, 263n (etym.), 275, 278t
needlework, 140, 153, 182, 213, 249
Neely, J., 392
Neferhotep, 113, 338, 339t, 340, 342, 344, 348–49,
    352, 396
Neferronpet, 90, 113, 114p
Negahban, E., 59p
Negev Ware, 166
Negidal, *xontaxa*, 38
Neo-Assyrian, *qunnabu*, 38
Neo-Assyrian art, 202
Neo-Babylonian texts, 238
Neolithic, 10–13, 15–18, 22n, 25, 27–28, 31, 33–35, 47,
    54–56, 59, 61, 76, 84, 91, 95p, 97–99, 107, 113,
    122n, 125, 126–48, 173n, 175–76, 184, 195, 214,
    222–24, 226–27, 230–31, 234, 249, 253–57, 256p,
    259, 281, 285, 292–93, 297, 299–300, 303n, 303–4pp,
    305–6, 306p, 312–13, 329, 382n, 387, 391–93; Early,
    22, 27, 38, 51, 68, 79, 80n, 88, 91, 93–94, 94p, 97–
    99, 98p, 103, 107, 113, 116, 123–24, 126–34, 127–
    29pp, 131p, 228n, 249, 387 (*see also* aceramic Neo-
    lithic); Late, 20, 23, 28, 54n, 59n, 81, 83, 83p, 95,
    97–100, 100p, 103, 107, 109–10, 113, 116, 134–41,
    143p, 144, 173–74nn, 175, 210–11, 217, 224, 234,
    249, 281, 299, 305, 307p, 387–88 (*see also* Swiss Neo-
    lithic); Middle, 27, 54n, 91, 95, 98–101, 113, 141,
    173, 387

Neolithic cloth, 126–44. *See also* Faiyum Neolithic linen; Swiss Neolithic cloth
Neolithic linen industry, 10–15, 127–32
Neolithic representation of weaving, 81, 83, 83p
Neolithic sheep, 22–23, 27–28
Neolithic use of fibers, 16–18, 23, 25n, 28, 31, 33–34, 38
Neo-Sumerian, 24, 231; *kunibu*, 38
Neo-Sumerians, 24, 29, 88n
Nesipanoferher, 339t, 342, 350, 396
nested figures, 318–19, 348
Netherlands, 184, 214, 221, 224, 285
nets/netting, 17, 20, 37, 41, 65, 68, 90, 91p, 95p, 97n, 98, 100, 128, 130, 132, 134, 140, 140p, 142, 154–55, 177, 182–84, 183p, 213, 224, 249, 259, 263n (etym.), 266, 316, 322–23pp, 394
nettle, 16, 19–20, 35, 37, 67, 73, 263n (etym.); preparing, 19, 73
network patterns: Aegean, 319, 323p, 329–30; Egyptian, 342
Neustupný, E., and J. Neustupný, 99
Newberry, P., 44, 45p, 49n, 80p, 87, 157–59, 224, 285p, 342, 351, 352n, Plate 1
New World, 22, 26, 52, 54n, 81, 125, 215, 220n, 228n, 231, 294n, 298, 352n
Niebelungenlied, 373
Nielsen, K.-H., 183, 218
Niemitz(sch), Kr. Gubin (A20), 101, 103, 389–90
Nike, 378
Nile (A), 154, 351n
Nine Bows and Captives design, 159
Nineveh (A122), 51n, 391
Nippur, 164
Nir David [= Tel 'Amal] (C173), 243, 302n, 388, 390
Nirou Khani (D246), 316, 319, 327p, 328, 394
Noin Ula, 359
noise: of preparing flax, 262–63; of weaving, 88, 105, 273, 362n
nomads, 17–18, 31, 79n, 109, 199, 205n, 212, 215, 220–22, 251, 306
non-industrialized societies, 285, 292
Norman, J., 38n
Norns, 376
Norway, 122
notched sticks. *See* slotted sticks
novelties in the economy, 290–91
-nth-formant, 266, 277–79, 281n
Nucella spp., 228
Nuzi, 212, 230, 306, 306p (map), 350, 391
Ny Carlsberg Glyptotek, Copenhagen, 44

oak balls, 236
Ochamchira (A86), 168
ochre, 223–24, 231
Ödenburg. *See* Sopron
Odysseus, 108p, 205n, 220, 266, 358, 376
Odyssey, 60, 70, 102, 105, 205n, 264, 266, 284, 292,

297, 358–59, 376
oil, 11, 12n, 38, 232, 236
Øksenbjerg, 143
Olbia, 92n
Ølby (B168), 182
Old Assyrians. *See* Assyrians
Old Babylonian era, 212, 220, 288, 292
Old Chinese, *mrar*, 38
Old Church Slavic: *plet-*, 80; *poyasŭ*, 254
Old English: *fāh*, 359n; *fana*, 273; *hænep*, 36; *hnoppa*, 274; *hnoppian*, 274; *hrægel*, 273; *wād*, 235n; *wealcan*, 216
Old European cultures, 113, 255, 281, 293, 382n
Old French, 80
Old High German: *fēh*, 359n; *filz*, 276
Old Irish, *cír*, 262
Old Norse: *fā*, 359n; *hampr*, 36; *hræll*, 273
Old Persian, *ni-pišta-*, 359n
Old Prussian, *knapios*, 36
Old Russian, 215; *česati*, 262; *runó*, *rŭvati*, 261
Old Testament, 221, 230
Old Turkic, *käntir*, 37
Olivier, J.-P., 238, 284
Olschki, L., 221
Olympia, 382n
Olympus, 380
Olynthus (A49), 69p, 100
onions, 38, 233
Oppenheim, A., 33, 38, 230, 235, 238
opposing spin, 178, 180, 197. *See also* shadow plaid; shadow stripes
optical illusion, 164, 179–80, 191, 194, 317, 317p, 329, 329p
orange, 225, 231–33
Orchomenos (D222), 342
Orestes, 264
Orestes, 264
Orient. *See* Asia: eastern
Oriental Institute, University of Chicago, 57p, 122, 127p, 167p, 167n
Orientalizing art, 366, 371
Orkney Islands, 28
ornamentation. *See* decoration
Orochi, *onokto*, 38
orseille, 232
Orth, F., 47
Orvieto (A38), 46, 70p
Oseberg Ship, 20, 119, 373
Otchët Imperatorskoj Arkheologicheskoj Kommissii, 173n
Otto, H., 392
outlying textile workers, 284–85
overseers, of weavers, 74p, 113, 285, 286p, 288, 339t, 340, 342
overshot technique. *See* float weave
Ovis spp., 22–24, 23–25pp
Oxford Universal Dictionary, 216
oxidizing, of leuco-base dyes, 228, 234–35

Özgüç, N., 167n
Özgüç, T., 61, 167n
ozone as bleach, 15

Pachypasa, 32
pads, 197, 217–21
Paeonians, 69
painted cloth, 146, 159, 206, 207p, 218n, 226, 237n, 321, 379
painted skin, 175, 226, 232, 234
painted stele (re-used), from Mycenae, 316, 368–70, 369p, 377, 395
palaces, 107, 171, 212, 284–85, 288, 291, 325, 327, 348–50, 349p, 353, 353p, 358, 382
palaeobiology, 11, 223, 383
palaeobotany, 10–12, 16–19, 35, 38, 223, 232–34
Palaeolithic, 17, 20, 22, 38, 40–41, 40p, 44, 50, 78, 79, 172, 231, 249, 255–59, 297
Palaikastro (D253), 35p, 74, 228, 388–89
Paleoskoutella, 174n
palepai, 375
Palestine, 3, 15, 30, 50, 63, 71, 74p, 76, 85, 113, 124–25, 145, 158, 163n, 165–66, 210–11, 221, 229, 235, 237, 241, 243, 249n, 251, 299–302, 301p (map), 353. *See also* Israel
palmette motif, 160p, 161, 161p, 343, 346–47
palm fiber, 20, 33
Palmyra, 206
Pamphylia (A), 355n
Panathenaia, 361–62, 381–82
Paneb, 286
Panehesy, 339t, 340, 396
panels, made independently, 160–62, 160–61pp, 336
Panopolis, 366n
Pan-p'o (A150i), 17
Pantikapaion (A79), 3, 206, 379p. *See also* Kertch
Papademetrios, I., 174n
Papagianni, M., 197n
paper, 34, 215
papyrus, 12p, 20, 215, 291, 322
Papyrus Holmiensis, 229
Parcae, 376
Paribeni, R., 395
Paris (Alexander), 373
Parke, H., 361, 363, 382n
Parrot, A., 56, 57p
Parthenon, 271, 272p, 298n, 361p, 380
Parthians, 29n, 202
passage graves, 141
Passek, T., 306, 307p
Pasternak, Y., 144n
pasting. *See* glue/glueing
patches, 190
Paterson, M., 320p, 321p
Patroklos, 367, 377
patterned cloth: geometric, 3, 31n, 120, 120p, 136–37, 136p, 139p, 139–40, 142–43, 143p, 149, 153, 155–59,

170–72, 175–76, 187–94, 197–200, 198–99p, 202–4, 206, 208, 208p, 218–19, 293, 316–20, 332, 351–52, 354, 359, 364–66, 371–72, 375, Plate 2, Plate 4; representational, 3, 157–59, 161–62, 200–203, 201p, 206–8, 207–9pp, 212, 226, 258, 319–20, 353p, 354, 356, 359–65, 372–80, 382, Plate 1, Plate 4. *See also* pattern weaving; plaid; stripes
pattern heddles, 198, 199p, 268n
pattern weaving, 31, 109n, 118–21, 125–26, 132–34, 144, 149–54, 156–59, 161–214, 218, 268n, 281, 290, 292–93, 312–14, 332, 359–62, 375–76, 382; developmental areas of, 210–14; mechanization of, 110, 112–13, 118, 168, 187, 212, 314, 318n, 359; relation to loom type, 105, 126, 192, 211–12
Paul, A., 321
pavilions, 341–46, 360, 367, 373, 378
Pavlovskii kurgans (A80), 207, 209p
payment, cloth as, 204, 288–89
Payne, S., 22, 26, 30
Pazyryk (A149i), 17–18, 28–29, 31, 169, 199–203, 201p, 205n, 219, 219p, 220n, Plate 4
Peabody Museum, Harvard, 391–92
peasants, 4, 43, 46, 68, 69, 168, 178, 216, 226n, 228n, 231, 277, 292, 295n, 297, 319–22, 366n, 372
pedigreed objects, 205n, 220
Pedrini, L., 148
Peet, T., 70, 86, 88–89
pegs: for ground-loom, 83, 89; for warping, 85p, 89, 90p, 116p, 116–17, 269p
Peleus, 364
Peloponnese (D), 172
Pendlebury, J., 30, 49n, 352
Penelope, 107, 108p, 292, 358–59, 363, 376–78, 380, 382
peplos of Athena. *See under* Athena
Perati (D233), 63, 64p, 299
Perini, R., 175
Perkins, D., 27n
Pernier, L., 70p
Peroni, R., 175–76, 226
Perroy, E., 285
Perry, W., 373
Persia, 231. *See also* Iran
Persian destruction of Athens, 92n, 363–64, 370n, 380
Persian language, 37
Persian pile-knot, 202, 202p (diag.)
Persian Red Sheep, 23p
Persian rugs, 125, 201–2, 321
Persians, 59, 69, 202, 221, 363–64, 372
Persian Wars, 229, 298n, 363–64, 370n, 372
perspective in drawing, 83, 84p, 86, 113n, 115, 117, 367
Persson, A., 172, 174n, 312, 350
Peru, 54n, 298, 305, 321
pestles. *See* grinders
Petkov, N., 98, 98p, 144, 389
Petrie, W.M.F., 29n, 49n, 63–65, 75, 85n, 86–87, 148, 224, 351, 396

Petrie Museum, London, 48, 68, 87p, 146p, 147, 147p
Petsofa (D254), 293, 314, 314p, 316
Pevestorf, 141
Pfister, R., 152, 156, 159, 162, 224, 227, 231–32, 237–38
Pfuhl, E., 361–62
Pfyn culture, 95, 134
Phaidra, 206, 378–79
Phaistos (D260), 74, 75n, 316, 394
Phidias, 298n, 363n
Philistines, 166, 224, 227
Phoenician colonies, 229
Phoenician red, 229
Phoenicians, 229, 232n, 238
Phrasikleia, 366n
Phrygia (A), 199
Phrygians, 18, 102, 197–98, 198p, 218–19, 221, 302, 359n
Phylakopi (D240), 63, 107n, 241, 316, 319, 322, 322p, 394–95
Picard-Schmitter, M., 81, 84
pick (of weft), 81 (def.)
piecework system, 284–85
Piggott, S., 39
pigments, 21, 29, 223, 231
pile-cutting knives, 171n, 212
pile dwellings: in France, 141, 175; in Italy, 54–55, 55p, 175; in Late Bronze Age Switzerland, 308. See also Swiss Neolithic pile dwellings
pile-knots, 170, 201–2, 202p (diag.), 211
pile rugs, 108, 125, 155, 171n, 199–202, 201p, 211–12, 359; origin of, 171n, 212–13
pile weave, 140, 150, 155, 164, 170, 194, 200–202, 210–11
pin-beaters, 107, 116p, 273–74, 279, 280t, 360n
pink, 149, 158–59, 232, 237, 313, Plate 1
Pinner, R., 171n
pins, 61, 63, 109n, 121, 121p, 168, 195
pintadera, 226
pipeline effect, 205, 301, 308–9. See also Hallstatt culture: connections with Caucasus
Pisdeli Tepe, 305, 306p (map), 391
Pisticci (A44), 92n, 110, 111p
plaid, 142, 169, 169p, 186, 188p, 190, 192–94, 211, 213–14, 218, 225, 293, 316–17, 318n, 319, 328
plain weave, 12, 31n, 105, 110, 127 (def.), 127p (diag.), 129–30, 132, 134, 134p, 137, 140, 142, 144–46, 149, 157–59, 164–66, 167n, 168, 174–79, 180p, 184–85, 187, 190, 192–93, 195, 197, 199–201, 203–4, 206, 210–11, 218, 268, 271
plaiting, 5 (def.), 30, 33, 51, 79–80 (etym.), 122, 127n, 144, 156n, 167n, 182p, 254 (etym.), 269, 280t
plant fiber. See vegetable fiber
platelets, 155, 162, 172–73, 173n, 200, 313n, 315
platforms, 45p, 46, 56, 57p, 105–6, 240, 269p
platform shoes for weaving, 105, 106p
Plato, 68, 263–64, 274, 362
Platon, N., 101

pleats, 147–48, 147p, 155n, 314
plied thread. See plying
Pliny the Elder, 13–14, 21, 29, 34, 39, 194, 198, 216, 225–26, 231n, 234, 236, 238, 359n
plucking wool, 21, 24, 29–30, 49n, 261, 265, 274, 276, 278t
plunder. See cloth: as booty; clothing: as booty; raids/raiding
Plutarch, 361, 363
plying, 40, 42, 42n (def., etym.), 47–50, 48p, 52, 53n, 59, 62, 67–68, 72, 148, 204
Podkowińska, Z., 306n, 307p
Poggio della Sala, 194
Poklewski, T., 306n, 307p
Poland, 99, 100p, 121n, 234n, 249, 297, 305–6, 307p, 388–89
Poliochni, 306p (map), 307, 392
Polish grains, 231
pollen, 17, 19, 184
polychromy, development of, 225, 237, 243. See also color
Polynesia, 215
Polynesians, 155
pomegranate, 233
Pompeii (A43), 39, 216, 239
Ponting, K., 235
Pontus, 238n. See also Black Sea
Popham, M., 174n, 197–98, 330, 347–48
Porac, C., 67
Porada, E., 58
Po River, 306p (map)
Porter, B., 343n, 396
Post, L., 137, 192–93, 193p, 218
Postgate, J., 57
posts, for loom support, 88–89, 93–94, 93–94pp, 103, 108, 110, 111p, 242, 270, 270p, 278t, 280, 280t, 286, 302n, 389–90
potash, 238 (def.), 241
Potnia Theron (Mistress of Animals), 298n
potsherds, as spindle whorls, 54, 59–60
pounders, for dyes, 239
power, contained in objects, 374–76, 382
power shift, from Minoans to Mycenaeans, 315, 334, 336–37, 338n
pre-Celtic people of Britain, 234n
pre-Classical Minoan dress, 314 (def.), 316, 394
pre-industrial (recent) economies, 4p, 285, 293
pre-pottery era. See aceramic Neolithic
preservation: in acid groundwater, 176; in alkaline lake silt, 54, 126, 176; in anaerobic conditions, 3, 176; of animal matter, 176; of bones, 28, 176; by carbonization, 10, 16, 54, 107, 141–42, 172, 174n, 189, 202n, 210, 217, 223, 302n, 312; in clay, 79 (see also impressions); by desiccation, 3, 49n, 81, 85, 131p, 145, 147, 189, 197, 199, 378; differential, 142, 176, 184, 204, 217, 312, 365; by freezing, 3, 199–200, 201p, 219, Plate 3; by metal/oxidation, 31–32, 132, 144n, 164, 167n, 174, 189, 197, 199, 205n, 206, 210, 312 (see

also pseudomorphs); in peatbogs, 30, 105, 122, 126, 184, 192, 195, 196p, 217; poor areas for, 79, 132, 142, 144, 163–64, 168, 173, 194, 220, 293, 343, 378; in salt, 186, 189, 192, 199; of vegetable matter, 142, 176; by waterlogging, 3, 199
pre-Shang dynasty era, 31
prestige objects, 204, 205n, 290–91, 299
Priam, 373
prices, for cloth, 288–89, 291
Princess Fresco, Amarna, 352
Prinias (D259), 69, 70p
printed textile patterns, 175, 226
Pripyet River/Marshes (A), 306, 306p (map)
Prisse d'Avennes, 396
Pritchard, J., 229
private enterprise, 287–88, 290
problems of evidence, 3, 39, 53–55, 71n, 79, 80n, 81, 89, 99–100, 109n, 116, 122n, 126, 133, 141, 143, 163–64, 166, 168, 173–74, 176, 184, 188, 204, 223, 227, 259, 277. *See also* identification problems
production of cloth for sale, 287–90
profits from textile sales, 287–88, 290–91
protection symbols. *See* decoration
prothesis, 367, 367–68pp, 375p, 377–78
Proto-Celts, 239, 275
Proto-Elamite era, 25, 164
Proto-Germanic forms, 36, 235n
Proto-Indo-European forms, 80, 233n, 254, 263n, 280n
Proto-Indo-Europeans. *See* Indo-Europeans
Protoliterate era, 56
Protonotariou-Deilaki, E., 174n
Protsch, R., 22–23
Pseira (D250), 316, 318, 318p, 319, 328–29, 394
pseudomorphs, 31–32, 133 (def.), 133p, 144n, 164, 174, 194, 205n. *See also* preservation: by metal/oxidation
puberty rites, 338n
Puhvel, J., 261–62, 263n, 265, 268
pulling wool. *See* plucking wool
Pulur, 391
Pumpelly, R., 303p, 305, 391–92
Punica granatum, 233
purple, 70, 169, 194, 198, 204, 208, 219, 224–25, 228–31, 242–43, 292, 312–13, 376; range of hues designated by, 230, 313
purple-fisher, 229
purple-snails, 228–29, 238
Purpura spp., 228–29
Puyemre, 331, 339t, 344n, 396
Puzur-Aššur, 287
Pylos (D216), 174, 238, 273n, 283–84, 312–13, 316, 325, 355
Pyrenees, 40, 234n
Pyrrhic dance, 361, 381n

Qau (C204), 154, 339t, 396
Quagliati, Q., 111p

quatrefoil interlocks, 318–19, 323p, 328–29, 338, 340, 351, 357, 370, Plates 2–3
querns. *See* grinders
Quibell, J., 343n
Quiring, H., 230–31

Raban, A., 229
rabbit hair, 30
Rabensburg (A64), 213, 213p
Raczky, P., 94, 98, 389
radiocarbon dates, 10, 12, 16, 68, 130n, 387
ragidup, 375–76
rags, 109n, 144, 174, 186, 189–90, 192, 204, 228n, 293
raids/raiding, 4, 93, 102, 149, 158, 197, 205n, 231, 291, 352
Rajki, 306p (map), 306n, 307p
Rameses I, 339t, 344
Rameses II, 64, 113n, 114p, 331, 339t, 344, 356, 356p
Rameses III, 118, 120, 120p, 156, 331, 339t, 341, 350, 352–53, 355
Rameses IX, 339t
Rameses X, 339t
ramie, 16–17, 19
Ramose, 151, 153
Ramp House, Mycenae, 316, 395
rams, 26–27, 27t, 37, 260
Random House English Dictionary, 261n
rapport patterns, 317, 317–18pp, 319–20, 320p, 328–29, 342, 344, 346–49, 346p, 349p, 351, 357, 370n. *See also* interlock patterns
Ras al 'Amiya (A129), 51n
Ras Shamra. *See* Ugarit
rations, 284, 287, 292
Rau, W., 251n, 260–61, 275
realgar, 231
red, 3, 17, 49n, 65, 146, 155–56, 158–59, 164–66, 169–70, 174, 184, 190, 198, 200, 202–3, 206–8, 208p, 223–27, 229–33, 236–37, 275, 288, 295n, 297, 312–14, 316, 318–19, 325–30, 325p, 332–35, 333p, 337–38, 344, 347–49, 351–52, 356, 364, 371–72, 371p, 378–79, Plate 4
reddish/ruddy color, 21, 29, 156, 201, 225, 227, 230–31
red ochre, 223–24, 231
red-white-blue Aegean patterns, 318, 329–30, 332–35, 337–38, 347–48, 351, 371–72, 371p, Plates 2–3
re-dyeing cloth, 236, 321
Reed, C., 22–23, 25
reed (on loom), 85n, 86, 152, 273
reed (plant), 9, 20, 79, 117, 264, 271
reeled silk, 31 (def.)
reels, 91, 107, 264, 273 (etym.)
Rees, A., and B. Rees, 234n
Reese, D., 228–29
Rehone. *See* el-Lahun
reindeer, 37
Reisner, G., 154–55
Rekhmara. *See* Rekhmire

Rekhmire, 333–37, 334p, 347n, 348, 354–55n, 396;
tomb of, and repainting of embassy scene, 333, 334p,
335
Renfrew, C., 54n, 98, 174n, 395
Renfrew, J., 12, 16
Rentenanstalt, Zurich, 95, 388–89
repp. *See* ribbing
Republic, 68, 263, 362
Reseda luteola, 233
reserve dyeing. *See* resist-dyeing
reserve printing, 226n. *See also* resist-dyeing
resin, 52, 175, 226
resist-dyeing, 175, 206, 207p, 225 (def.), 226, 379p
respinning, 48, 72, 107n, 204
restrictions, on weaving shapes, 354, 365, 370
retting, 13 (def., etym.), 34, 41, 46, 50, 51, 73, 215,
262
Reusch, H., 395
reversals (symbolic), 37–38, 156, 332
reweaving, 32, 204, 358, 380
rewinding, 54n, 77, 97n, 285, 305
Rhodes (A), 78, 334, 337, 350, 354–55, 366p
Rhone River (A), 100, 230
ribbing, 117, 134–37, 140, 164, 180, 187, 189–91, 195,
197, 210, 271–72, 272p, 361, 361p. *See also* diagonal
ribbing
ribbons. *See* bands
Rice, J., 235–36
Rice, T., 297
Richter, G., 32
Ridgway, B., 109n, 364, 366n
Riefstahl, E., 119, 148–49, 152–56, 159, 224
Riegl, A., 122
Rietzmeck, Kr. Rosslau (A19), 141
Riis, P., 62
Rimantienė, R., 20, 41
rim clamps, 328n
Ripinsky, M., 30
ritual cloths, 292, 373–76, 374p, 380, 382
Robenhausen am Pfäffikersee (A30), 14p, 97, 135p,
135n, 137–38pp, 224, 387, 389
Robert, C., 107, 108p
robing room of Malkata palace, 348–49, 349p
Robinson, D., 69
Robinson, S., 223, 225–26, 229, 236
rock drawings, 91, 91p, 176
Rodden, R., 27n, 51, 54n, 107n
Rodenwaldt, G., 324p, 327p, 394–95
rolags, 70, 72 (def.), 72p
roller beams. *See* cloth beam: rollable
Roman era, 3, 29n, 49, 70, 77, 86, 101, 122, 125, 165n,
204, 208, 221, 225–26, 238–39, 268n, 290, 359n. *See
also* Egypt: Roman
Romania, 16, 16p, 18, 97–98, 294p, 388–89
Romans, 16, 36, 39, 50, 125, 194, 204n, 221, 268, 295n
Rome (A42) 16, 116, 195, 233n
roof, as site for textile work, 13, 89. *See also* loom
weights: fallen from above; upper floors

rope. *See* cord/cordage
Rose, H., 381
Rosenbaum, S., 318n
Rosenfeld, H.-F., 213
roses, as protection symbol, 297, 372–73
rosette pattern, 158–59, 199–201, 206, 212, 315, 318–
19, 324–25, 328, 330, 338, 342, 343n, 344, 347–50,
349p, 352, Plate 1
Roswinkel (A16), 184, 224
Roth, H. L., 44, 46, 48–49, 81, 84–86, 87p, 109, 112–
13, 119–20, 123, 151, 286
Routsi, near Pylos (D216), 174, 225, 312
roves, 70, 72 (def.), 72p, 78p, 262–64, 266
Royal Cemetery of Ur, 60, 164, 224
Royal Ontario Museum, 366n
royal purple. *See* purple
Rubia tinctorum, 227, 232
Rudenko, S., 18, 31, 200–203, 219–20
rugs, 108, 125, 155, 170–71, 170p, 198–202, 201p, 211–
14, 217, 219, 221, 252, 275, 293, 321, 341–42, 350,
357
run-off, 89, 240
Ruoff, E., 308
Rusalki, 297, 298n
rushes, 217
Russia, 173n, 234, 297
Russian, 200n, 270; *kistej*, 169; *konoplja*, 36; *krasnyj,
krasivyj*, 230n; *pëstryj*, 359n; *pisat'*, 359n; *pukho-
vaja*, 169; *schast'e*, 3; *(tkatskij) stanok*, 80; *vojlok*, 215
Russians, 3, 199, 297, 366n
Rybakov, B., 297n
Ryder, M., 11, 21–22, 25, 27n, 28–30, 41, 49n, 52, 66,
79, 141

S-. *See* S-plied; S-spun; S-twist
Sackett, L., 197–98
sacks. *See* bags
sacred knots (Aegean), 316, 319, 327–28, 327p, 394–95
sacred textiles, 292, 360–63, 361p, 380
saddle cloths. *See* horsecloths
safflower, 227, 232–33, 236, 275, 313; two dyes from,
232–33, 313
saffron, 124n, 233, 316, 322, 338n, 362. See also *Crocus cartwrightianus*; crocus pattern; *Crocus sativus*
Saglio, E., 96
Sahure, 148
sailors, 206, 345, 355, 357
sails, 15, 359, 361
Saint John's Blood, 231
Saint Petersburg, 3
Sakellarakis, I., 389
Salamis, 363
Salcuţa (A55), 97, 388–89
Saliagos (D237), 54n, 98
saliva, as spinning agent, 46n, 49n, 72
salt mines, 186, 188p, 189, 191p, 194, 204, 293, 328
salts, in dyeing, 236–38

saltwater, effect on fibers, 15, 34, 228n
Saltzman, M., 227, 230n
Salzburg, 186
Samaria, 302n
Samos, 33, 307, 392
sandals, of Aegean men, 311, 315–16, 333, 335–36, 395
Sandars, N., 355
Sanday, P., 290
Sanskrit, 260; *apave*, 251n; *bhaṅgá-*, *śaṇá-*, 37; *kacchū-*, 262; *kāñcaná-*, 233; *kṛṇắti*, 261; *lu-*, 261; *mahāra-jana*, 275; *péśa-*, 359n; *piṃśáti*, 359n; *prave*, 251n; *rjayati*, 275; *rájayati*, 275; *ubhnắti*, 80
Sapalli-tepa (A147i), 31
Saporetti, C., 288
Sapouna-Sakellaraki, E., 335n, 394–95
Saqqara (C190), 44n, 149, 341
sarcophagi, 3, 206–8, 207p, 316, 324–25, 377–79, 378p, 395
sarcophagus cover, 3, 199, 206, 207p, 378–80
Sardinia (A), 22n, 238n
Sarepta, 229
Sargon II, 231
Sasso di Furbara (A40), 194
Sato, P. 73n
Säve-Söderbergh, T., 333, 396, Plate 3
Scamuzzi, E., 145–46, 226
Scandinavia, 19, 29, 42, 96, 101, 103–6, 109–13, 111p, 113, 119–20, 122, 134, 143, 176, 180–81, 191, 193, 213, 221, 234n, 249, 255, 258, 271, 294n
scatter figures, 315, 317, 319, 325, 366n
Schaefer, G., 115
Schaefer, H., 359n
Schaeffer, C.F.A., 62–63, 229, 243
Schaffis am Bielersee (A26), 135n, 136p
Scheil, V., 38
Schiaparelli, E., 150, 153, 155, 156n, 159, 345
Schick, T., 12, 25, 30, 68, 130n
Schlabow, K., 119, 123, 134, 141–43, 176, 178–80, 184, 192, 204, 217, 224
Schleswig, 256p
Schliemann, H., 54, 70, 107, 172–73, 174n, 304, 307n, 395
Schmidt, E., 58, 392
Schmidt, H., 172, 317n
scholiasts, 372–73
Schrader, H., 364
Schrader, O., 275n
Schuette, M., 119
Schultes, R., 16–18, 38
Schulze, W., 359n
Schwartz, C., 27n
Schwartz, M., 37, 263n
Schwarza, Thuringia (A22), 184, 217
Schweitzer, B., 366
Schweizerisches Landesmuseum. *See* Swiss National Museum
scodelletta whorls, 303–4
Scorodorma foetidum, 232

Scotland, 28, 216
Scott, R., 37, 261, 263–64, 268n, 270, 275
Scottish, 186
scutching, 13 (def.), 46, 262, 280t, 282–83
Scythians, 17–18, 36–37, 173n, 206, 208n
Seager, R., 318p, 395
seals, 56, 57p, 84p, 88, 90, 92p, 249
seams, 146, 148, 154, 159, 165, 182, 200
Sea Peoples, 299n, 302–3, 331, 351, 355
Searle, 16
seasonal re-use, 236, 241, 321
seed fiber, 32
seeds, 10, 31–32, 140–41, 172, 174, 232–34, 285
Seh Gabi, 306, 306p (map), 391
Sehna pile-knot, 202, 202p (diag.)
Seiradaki, M., 371
selection, for genetic traits, 23, 28
Selevac (A59), 98–99
Selmeczi, L., 94, 94p, 103, 389
selvages. *See* selvedges
selvedges, 9 (def., etym.), 48, 96, 101, 115, 130n, 145–46, 149, 151, 154, 165, 178, 180, 183, 192, 195, 197, 199, 254, 271, 313, 336, 358n; construction of, 128–29, 128p, 135, 135p, 146, 165, 182, 182p, 191
semantic re-analysis, 205n, 230n, 231n, 232–33, 235n, 261, 265, 268, 271–72, 274
semantic reconstruction, 235n, 260–83, 359n; frame for, 260, 261n
Semitic, 261n, 270, 271, 281
Semitic culture, 29n, 163
Senmut, 151, 156, 157p, 331–33, 335n, 340, 350, 353, 396
Sennacherib, 33
sequins. *See* platelets
Serbia, 258, 258p, 295
sericin, 31
Servia, 98
Sesklo (A46), 51n, 54n, 93, 220n
Sesklo culture, 93
Seti I, 339t, 347
Seven Brothers (Sem' Brat'ev), Taman' (A81), 3, 206–7, 208p, 379p
sewing, 4, 37, 39, 126, 129–30, 137, 140, 148–49, 152, 154–56, 157p, 158–62, 160–61pp, 165–66, 171–74, 177, 182–83, 188n, 190–91, 193, 195, 197, 199–200, 202, 205n, 220, 259, 263n, 275 (etym.), 278t, 283, 313, 321, 336, 345, Plate 4. *See also* stitches/stitching
shabrak, 202 (def.), 203, 219p, Plate 4
shadow languages, 281
shadow plaid, 142, 189–90, 193, 210
shadow stripes, 142, 178–80 (def.), 179–80pp, 189–91, 193–94, 210
Shaft Graves, Mycenae, 173, 174n, 200, 315–16, 319, 327p, 328, 350, 369, 394
Shah Tepe, 171n, 391
Shang dynasty, 31, 205n
Shaw, M., 74, 75n, 218n, 318, 322, 327n, 344–46, 356, 394–95

shearing sheep, 4, 21, 29, 141, 261–62, 265
shearing textile surface, 202, 216, 274, 287
shears, 29, 261 (etym.)
Shechem, 300, 301p (map)
shed bar, 82 (def.), 84, 85n, 86, 88, 91, 103, 105, 110,
    111p, 112–13, 117, 125, 187, 268, 270p, 271, 280t,
    281; interference by, 86, 110
shedding: mechanical, 103, 109–10, 112–13, 118–19,
    125, 143–44, 176, 281; order of, 96; of the warp, 90,
    96, 110, 134–35, 167–68, 180, 187, 192, 271–72
sheds, 82 (def., etym.), 83, 88, 96, 103, 105, 110, 111p,
    113, 117–18, 125, 148, 251n; changing, 84, 86–88,
    117, 148, 178, 267, 271, 274, 325; downward-open-
    ing, 204n; independently controlled, 118, 182; multi-
    ple, 167–68, 187, 268 (see also heddle bars: multi-
    ple); simultaneous, 119; size of, 85n, 86, 88, 112,
    305.
Sheen, Harlington, 234n
sheep, 20–30, 41, 43, 50, 53n, 141, 260–62, 276, 277n,
    283, 351; age of, 25–28, 27t, 240; bones of, 10, 22,
    25–28, 240; classification of, 22; combing for wool,
    261–62, 283–84; early domestication of, 22–24, 50,
    253, 259; early fleece records for, 24–25, 261n; in
    Egypt, 25, 25p, 49n, 351; in Europe, 22–23, 30; fe-
    ral, 22n; genetics of, 24, 28–29; hairy, 23, 25p, 28–
    29, 49n, 351; horns of, 27–28; kempy, 23–24, 23p,
    217 (see also kemp); molting of, 21, 24, 29, 41, 42,
    261–62, 283–84; origin and diffusion of, 22–23, 30;
    plucking, 21, 24, 29–30, 261–62; representations of,
    24–25, 25p, 35p, 49n; sex of, 24p, 25–28, 27t; shear-
    ing, 4, 21, 29, 261–62; slaughter patterns for, 26–28,
    27t; species of, 22–25, 23–25pp, 30, 177, 261n (see
    also Ovis spp.); used for meat, 23–24, 26–28, 27t;
    used for milk, 23–24, 26–27, 27t; wild, 21–24, 28–29;
    woolly, 22–25, 28–29, 35, 50, 68, 217, 251, 259
sheep flocks: composition of, 25–28; records of, 24–25,
    28, 35p; tending, 4, 35p, 306
Sheffer, A., 166, 224, 227, 235, 302, 390
shells, as source of purple dye, 228–29, 313
shepherds, 35p, 283–84, 306
Sherratt, A., 68n, 95n, 176n
Shih Chi, 31, 205n
Shimony, C., 130n
Shimshara (A126), 51, 132, 391
ship-cloths, 374p, 375, 375p
ships. See boats
Short, C., 261n
shrinking, 216n
shrouds, 148–49, 153p, 156, 174n, 185, 194, 224, 227,
    232, 236, 292, 358–59, 377, 382. See also clothing:
    burial dress
shuttles, 85, 85n (def., etym.), 90, 107, 178, 273, 305,
    360n; thrown, 85n, 107n. See also bobbins
Sialk, 391
Šibtu, 291
Sidon (A113), 228n, 229
Siegfried, 373
Sieurin, F., 174n

sieves, 240–41
Siivertsi, Lithuania, 41
Si Ling-chi, 31
silk, 9, 17–18, 30–33, 35, 41, 44, 48, 189–90, 189p,
    203–5; as bribe, 31, 205n; broken, 9, 30–31; chemical
    tests for, 31; in China, 30–32, 203; cross-sections of,
    31; domestic, 30–32; dyeing, 204; embroidered, 31–
    32, 203–4; embroidery with, 189–90, 189p, 203–4; in
    Europe, 31–32, 203–5; as gift, 205n; in Greece, 30–
    32, 204; in Hallstatt tombs, 31–32, 203–4; legends
    about, 31; length of, 9, 30–31, 44; patterned, 31,
    203, 205n; reeled, 31 (def.), 32, 44; rewoven, 32,
    204; slipperiness of, 30, 204n; spun, 31–32; tablet-
    woven, 32; unraveling, 204; wild, 30–33
Silk Road, 205n
silkworms, 30–31
sinew, 39–40, 200, 263n, 266
singers/singing, 234n, 291n, 292, 294, 295n, 373, 382
Singh, P., 51
Sinitsyn, I., 169, 170p
Sinkiang, 205n
Sinskaja, 18
Šipintsi (Schipenitz; Zaval'e) (A74), 256p
Sistan, 391
Sitagroi (A50), 51n, 54n, 99, 174n
Six, J., 123–24
sizing, 220n
Skara Brae (A11), 28
skeins/skeining, 57, 57p, 77, 106, 225, 229n, 266, 269,
    285, 305
skin decoration, 175, 226, 226n, 232, 234
skins. See hides
skirts: divided, 318. See also clothing: skirt; flounces
Skrydstrup (B157), 122, 178, 182–83, 183p
slaked lime, 227, 237–38; storage jars of, 237
Slatina (A51), 98, 98p, 388–89
slaves. See captives
Slavic language, 36–37, 261–62, 276–77
Slavs, 36, 169, 295–97, 298n
Slenczka, E., 370
slotted sticks, 86, 88
Slovakia, 226n
slubbed yarn, 148
Smith, L., 155n
Smith, W., 230, 341, 348, 350, 355n, 396
Smith's Law, 340
Snake Ladies (Knossos), 298n, 316, 318n, 319, 328, 394
snakes, 169, 297, 298n, 304, 360
Snodgrass, A., 174n
soap, 238, 274
Soay sheep, 22n, 30
soffit pattern, 340, Plate 3
Solovjev, L., 168
Solutrean, 40
Sophilos, 364, 366
Sopron (A66), 55, 56p, 69, 92, 106, 109, 112, 173n,
    213, 294, 295p
Sorte Muld, 101

Sottosengia, 101
soumak. *See* weft wrapping
Southeast House, Knossos, 316, 327p, 328, 394
Soviet Union. *See* USSR
spacing cords, 84, 84p, 105, 112, 130, 180, 255
Spain, 29, 33–34, 68, 119, 125, 144, 174, 176, 186, 229, 238, 389–90
Spanish, *librería*, 231n
Sparta, 292
Specht, W., 228
spectroscopy, 227, 237
Speiser, E., 304, 392
spelling variants, 10n
sphinxes, 161, 161p, 173, 319–21, 321p
spices. *See* condiments
spiders, 2, 198
spindle hooks, 42, 53, 57, 58p, 60, 68–69, 69p, 263
spindles, 42–44, 43p, 45p, 48, 48p, 51–65, 55–65pp, 67–68, 70p, 78, 89, 97n, 107, 172, 243, 247, 263–64, 269, 278t, 284, 299, 305; finger-flicked, 43, 60, 67, 78; with flywheel, 43, 78, 303, 305; hand-held, 43–44, 44p, 46, 56, 59–60, 63, 67, 78; heads of, 53, 55, 60–61, 63n; high-whorl, 43 (def.), 46, 46p, 53 (def.), 53p, 55n, 56, 58–59, 58–59pp, 60, 64–65, 67, 78; low-whorl, 43 (def.), 53 (def.), 54–55, 63–65, 67–68, 78, 299, 351; materials for, 43, 60–62, 299; middle-whorl, 53 (def.), 60–61, 60–61pp, 63; supported, 33, 43, 52; suspended, 42–43 (*see also* drop-spindles); thigh-rolled, 43, 45p, 46, 60, 63, 67, 78; thread groove on, 46p, 53, 55n, 58–60, 58–59pp, 63–64, 66; toe-twirled, 43, 60; with two whorls, 58, 58p, 61–62, 62p; upside down, 46p, 53, 55n, 58–59, 59p, 66; as weft bobbins, 305, 307; weight of, 33, 43, 52, 55p, 59 (*see also* spindle whorls: weight of)
spindle shafts, 43, 51–55, 58–63, 107, 263–64
spindle whorls, 10, 43, 43p, 46p, 51–55, 55p, 59–62, 78, 89, 93, 102, 240, 242–43, 263, 280t, 284–85, 299, 301, 303–10, 303–4pp, 306–9pp, 391–93; Aegean site list for, 54n, 392; Anatolian site list for, 59n, 392; bevelled, 304, 391; concave, 303–9, 303–4pp, 306p (map), 307–9pp, 391–93; decorated, 55, 63, 303–8, 391–92; distinguished from beads/weights, 51–52, 54–55; effect on twist, 53; function of form in, 51–53, 305; hole in, 51–52, 303; "inscribed," 304, 304p, 307p; in large numbers, 35, 54, 54n, 304–8, 391–92; Neolithic site list for, 51n, 391; non-functionality in form of, 303; padding for, 52, 58; painted, 304, 391–92; sand-dollar, 304–5, 304p, 306p (map), 307–8pp; shape of, 52–53, 60–62, 301, 303–8, 391–93; size of, 51–52, 303, 391; with streamlined nose, 303, 305, 391; Trojan, 35, 54, 304, 307–8pp; weight of, 51–53, 64, 303, 392–93 (*see also* spindles: weight of)
spinning, 4, 9 (def.), 10, 18, 20–24, 26n, 28, 30–33, 37, 39–78, 41 (def., etym.), 95, 100, 107n, 134, 216, 222, 251–52, 262–66, 275, 278t, 283–86, 286p, 289, 291–92, 294, 295n, 299, 305, 308, 351–52, 376, 393; direction of, 65–68 (*see also* S-spun, Z-spun); earliest evidence for, 39–40; European representations of, 4p, 53–55, 56p, 69–70, 70p, 72, 72p, 78, 78p, 265p, 295p; fiber length and, 43–44, 50, 52, 56, 393; into fine thread, 42, 52, 77, 141; and handedness, 67; as metaphor, 376; with multiple spindles, 45p, 46, 48p, 74p; Near Eastern representations of, 57–58, 57–59pp; with no spindle, 41–42, 44; origins of, 9, 39–41, 50, 249; quantitative relation of to weaving, 305; speed of, 42; while travelling, 4, 4p, 69. *See also* Egyptian representations: of spinning; tension: in spinning
spinning-bowl. *See* fiber-wetting bowl
spinning-stick, 42–43, 42p
spinning wheel, 69, 72–73, 78
spiral motifs, 156, 173, 202–3, 208, 220, 311, 318–19, 324p, 328–29, 332p, 337p, 338, 339t, 340, 342–44, 343p, 346–51, 346p, 349p, 357, 370, 377, 396, Plates 2–4; weaving of, 370n
Spitzes Hoch bei Latdorf, Kr. Bernburg (A18), 141–42, 143p, 224
splices/splicing, 41, 45p, 46–51, 47p, 71, 73, 74p, 76, 85p, 145, 240; staggered, 47n, 48
S-plied, 67–68, 145, 164
spool knitting, 121n
spools, 107, 112, 269, 270p, 273. *See also* bobbins
sprang, 120, 122–24 (def.), 134, 141–42, 183, 269n
sprinkle patterns. *See* scatter figures
Spyropoulos, T., 377n, 395
Square-Mouthed Pottery culture, 100
S-spun, 49n, 65–66 (def.), 66p, 67–68, 78, 142, 178–79, 180p, 182, 184, 191
Ssu-ma Ch'ien, 31, 205n
Staffordshire, 234n
stages of cloth production, 272–73n, 283–85
staining, 13, 136, 153, 153p, 160, 177, 204, 228–29, 231–33, 243, 275
stamps, 175, 226
Starčevo culture, 93
Starkey, J., 302n
Starr, R., 87, 230, 391
status cloth/clothing, 257–58, 287, 291–92, 297, 328, 345
Staub, J., 55
Staudigel, O., 119–21, 156
Steinkeller, P., 220
stench, of dye-works, 239–40
Stephani, L., 206–7, 208–9pp, 226
steppes (Eurasian), 17–19, 31, 124, 169, 196, 205–6, 211–13, 218, 220–22, 251–52, 255n, 281, 304n, 308–9. *See also* Asia
Stern, E., 300
Stewart, E., and J. Stewart, 63
Stewart, R., 11n
Stipa tenacissima, 33
stitches/stitching, 165, 176, 182, 200, 220, 253–54; binding, 165; buttonhole, 182–83; chain, 121n, 160, 162, 183, 203; figure-eight, 135; hem, 165; overcast, 129, 190, 197; running, 129, 160, 165, 190, 200; stem, 190; straight, 197; twining, 135, 166, 182–83;

stitches/stitching (*cont.*)
    whipping, 148, 156, 158, 160, 165, 182
Stol, M., 232
Stone, M. (artist), xxiv, xxvi, xxviii, xxx, 12p, 14p, 21p,
    34p, 40p, 42–43pp, 47p, 53p, 55p, 57–60pp, 62–
    66pp, 69p, 71p, 73p, 75p, 81p, 87p, 91–92pp, 94p,
    98p, 100–101pp, 111p, 118p, 127–28pp, 135p, 151–
    52pp, 177p, 180p, 187p, 202p, 209p, 213p, 241–
    42pp, 250p, 252p, 256–57pp, 270p, 294p, 300–
    301pp, 303–4pp, 306–8pp, 317p, 320p, 322–23pp,
    325p, 327p, 333p, 337p, 343p, 353p, 369p, Plate 3
storage jars: for dye chemicals, 237–39, 242; for loom
    weights, 102
Store Arden (B163), 122
storytelling, 205n, 292, 294, 365, 372–73, 375–76, 380
strata of vocabulary. *See* linguistic borrowing: layers of
Stratigraphic Museum, Knossos, 107n
sticks, 14
string skirts, 40, 40p, 179–82, 255–59, 256–58pp, 297n
stringy body-parts, 39, 263n, 266, 275
strip construction, of cloth, 354
stripes, 133, 133–34pp, 136p, 137, 138p, 139–40, 140p,
    142, 148–49, 154, 154p, 155n, 157, 162, 164–65,
    169–70, 178, 188p, 189–90, 191p, 192–93, 197–98,
    198p, 203–4, 210, 224–25, 235, 293, 314, 316–17,
    318n, 319, 325, 328, 342, Plate 1. *See also* shadow
    stripes; strip patterns; texture stripes
strip patterns, 317, 319–20, 328, 330, 333, 334–35pp,
    336–37, 337p, 351, 354, 357
Strommenger, E., 71
Strongylos (D238), 238n
structure, of wool/hair/kemp, 21p, 24n
Stubbings, F., 342
Stubdrup (B162), 176
stuffing (dye pots), 236
Stuttgart, 32, 204
S-twist, 40, 58p, 65–66 (def.), 66p (diag.), 67
Suberde, 51n, 391
sub-Mycenaean era, 356, 373
Sudan (A inset), 43–44, 49, 91, 154, 211
Suemnut, 396
Suhr, E., 376
Sukoró, 95
Sumatra, 374, 374p
Sumbar valley, 171n
Sumerian, 24, 38; *aslag*, 220n; *GIŠ.gada*, 255n, 295n;
    šag₄-TAG, 220; *túg-du₈(-a)*, 220; *udu-*, 24–25. *See*
    also Neo-Sumerian
Sumerians, 220–21. *See also* Neo-Sumerians
supplementary warp, 152, 152p, 154, 197, 317, 319n
supplementary weft, 10, 134p, 136–37, 136p, 138p,
    139–40, 140p, 142, 151–56, 152p, 155n, 159–60, 164,
    210, 253, 317, 318n, 320, 330, 359n, 366, 370p, 374,
    374p, 379; discontinuous, 159. *See also* brocade; in-
    lay technique
Suppliants, 268n
Supska, 134
survivals, 48–51, 68, 76, 78, 213–14, 251, 256–58,

298n, 324–25, 382
Susa (A135), 58, 83, 84p, 90, 119, 132, 133p, 164, 249
Šventoji (A15), 20, 41
swans, 219, 297
Sweden, 192, 193p, 216n, 218, 228, 239
Swiss National Museum, Zurich, 14p, 55p, 95n, 134p,
    137–40pp, 309p, 392
Swiss Neolithic cloth, 10, 15, 25, 41, 47n, 68, 81, 97,
    110, 117, 119, 122n, 134–41, 174–75, 180, 182, 191–
    92, 195, 214, 224–25, 237n, 254, 273n, 283, 320,
    322, 330, 359; dating of, 10
Swiss Neolithic looms, 95–97, 96p, 99–101, 103, 134
Swiss Neolithic pile dwellings, 10, 13, 14p, 54–55, 55p,
    81, 95–97, 96p, 99–101, 103, 122n, 134–35, 139–40,
    142, 144, 172, 174, 194, 359
Switzerland, 12, 16, 18, 99–101, 103, 113, 122, 134–
    39pp, 142–44, 176, 186, 191, 194–95, 213–14, 224,
    249, 293, 300, 304, 308, 309p, 312n, 387–89, 392
sword-beaters, 89, 274, 280, 280t, 360n
Sylwan, V., 31, 205n
symmetrical pile-knot, 201, 202p (diag.)
Syria 12, 62–63, 68, 83n, 113, 121n, 122, 124–25, 158,
    161–62, 166, 203, 205n, 210–13, 229, 243, 249n, 251,
    254, 271, 290, 301–2, 321, 331, 338, 350, 352–53,
    359
Syrian Arabic. *See* Arabic
Syrian artisans, 158, 162, 352–53
Syrian motifs, 161, 321, 350, 352, 356
Syrians, 290, 321, 352, 355n, 356
Syrian spirally wrapped gown, 354
Székesfehérvár, 95
Szentendre, 294n
Szolnok (A69), 94, 95p
Szolnok-Szanda (A70), 94, 387, 389

tabby weave, 127n. *See* plain weave
tablets: construction of, 118–19, 118p, 157; finds of,
    119; number of in deck, 118–19, 204
tablet weaving, 32, 118–22, 118p, 120–21pp, 126, 157,
    178, 189, 203–4, 211, 252p, 254
tablet-woven cloth: finds of, 119–22, 120–21pp, 157,
    168, 189p, 191, 203–4; recognizing, 119
tailors/tailoring, 218, 313, 315, 318n
Tall-i-Bakun, 391
Tall-i-Gap, 391
Taman' peninsula, 206, 208p
tampan, 374, 374p
tan, 165, 202, 206
Tanagra (D224), 316, 324, 377, 379, 395
tannin, 153, 177, 232, 236, 238
tapa cloth, 5, 215
tapered weave, 120p, 156, 352
tapes, 81, 128p, 129, 137, 165, 197, 254. *See also*
    bands
tapestry, 3, 49n, 108, 108p, 124–25, 157 (def.), 158–59,
    166, 168, 170–71, 202, 207, 208p, 253, 286, 290,
    314, 320, 322, 352–54, 356, 359, 360n, 363–66, 373,

379, Plate 1; dovetailed, 158 (def.), 159, 166, 202, Plate 1, Plate 4; made on warp-weighted loom, 365; origins of, 166, 211–13, 253; slit, 158 (def.), 159–60, 162, 166, 198, 202–3, 353n, Plate 1, Plate 4; as weasel word, 359n
tapestry frames, 123
tapestry loom. *See* vertical two-beam loom
tar. *See* asphalt
Tarasov, L., 256, 257p
Tarim Basin, 205n
Tarkhan (C192), 146–48, 147p, 224
Tarquinia (A39), 194
Tarsus, 301p (map), 306p (map), 307, 392
tartans, 186, 216
Tasian culture, 145
tassels, 30, 164, 169, 255, 257, 320p, 322, 323p, 334p, 336, 353p, 354–55
Tatars, 299n
tatibin, 375
Taurus (A), 306p (map)
tawny, 29, 330
Taylour, Lord W., 395
teasing, 216, 274, 285, 287
technological layers, in vocabulary, 37. *See also* linguistic borrowing
Tegle, Norway (A12), 122
Teheran, 59
Tehuti-hetep. *See* Djehutihetep
Tekeköy, 167n
Tel 'Amal, 243
Teleilat Ghassul (C179), 165
Telemachos, 109n, 205n, 363
tel(l), 306n
Tell Agrab (A128), 42
Tell Beit Mirsim (C182), 237–38, 240n, 241–42, 241–42pp, 300, 301p (map), 302, 388–90
Tell el-'Ajjul (C184), 71p
Tell el-Yahudiyeh (C188), 353, 353p
Tell en-Nasbeh, 242
Tell Halaf (A120), 317n
Tell Jemmeh (C185), 71p
Tell Jerishe (C175), 71p
Tell Mor, 242
Tell Qasileh (C176), 166, 224, 302n, 388, 390
Tell Ta'anach (C172), 302n
Tel Masos, 166
Tel Mevorakh, 300, 301p (map)
template, in weaving, 150, 152, 271
Temple of Amon: craftworkers in, 158, 339t, 340; Treasury of, 334, 348
Temple Repository, Knossos, 316, 320p, 394
temples, as textile treasuries, 334, 348, 360, 380
temple weavers. *See* central workshop system; Temple of Amon
tension: in spinning, 21, 24n, 42, 46, 52, 70, 72–73, 75n, 77; in weaving, 5, 80, 82, 87, 92, 115, 117, 124–25, 136–37, 177, 177p, 193, 195, 211–12, 253
tents, 215, 219, 221, 281n, 341, 360

tepe, 306n
Tepe Gawra, 304–6, 306p (map), 391
Tepe Giyan, 391
Tepe Hissar (A142), 392
Tepe Sabz (A137), 392
Tepe Sarab (A139), 22, 24
Tepe Yahyā (A144i), 51, 132, 391
Terek River (A), 168
Terqa (A118), 68, 166
Terrace, E., 341
Terremare, 55, 55p, 174
tests: chemical, 11, 16, 32; by direction of twist, 16
textile, 5 (etym.)
textile installations, 240–41. *See also* weaver's workshops
textile resources, other uses of. *See* multiple uses
textured cloth, 132–33, 142, 145–46, 150, 155n, 166, 168, 190, 197, 199–200, 203–4
texture stripes, 133, 133p, 142, 148–49, 158, 165, 184, 189
Thais spp., 228
Theban tombs, of nobles (C210): numbering of, 113n, 338n, 339t, 343n, 396; Thebes 16, 339t, 340, 343n, 396; Thebes 17, 339t, 396; Thebes 19, 339t, 347, 396; Thebes 21, 339t, 344n, 396; Thebes 31, 340; Thebes 39, 339t, 344n, 396; Thebes 40, 339t, 344, 352, 396; Thebes 45, 339t, 344, 396; Thebes 50, 113n, 339t, 340, 344, 348, 396; Thebes 51, 339t, 344, 396; Thebes 58, 352; Thebes 65, 339t, 348, 396; Thebes 67, 339t, 343, 343p, 396; Thebes 68, 339t, 342, 350, 396; Thebes 71, 331–32, 332p, 396; Thebes 78, 339t, 396; Thebes 79, 396; Thebes 81, 339t, 396; Thebes 82, 339t, 396, Plate 3; Thebes 85, 396; Thebes 86, 334–35, 335p, 396, Plate 3; Thebes 87, 339t, 396; Thebes 90, 339t, 344n, 396; Thebes 92, 396; Thebes 93, 343–44, 396; Thebes 100, 333–34, 334p, 396; Thebes 103, 45p, 91p, 113p; Thebes 104, 44n, 113n, 114p; Thebes 131, 333, 333p, 396; Thebes 133, 113n, 114p; Thebes 155, 332–33, 339t, 396, Plate 3; Thebes 160, 343n; Thebes 162, 343n, 396; Thebes 181, 339t, 344, 396; Thebes 226, 339t, 396; Thebes 251, 339t, 343, 396; Thebes 262, 339t, 343, 396; Thebes 359, 338n, 339t, 340, 342, 348, 350, 396; Thebes 362, 340
Thebes, Egypt (C208–14), 12p, 44, 45p, 91p, 113, 114p, 155n, 156, 157p, 286, 311, 331–35, 332–35pp, 338n, 339t, 340, 342–44, 347–48, 349p, 350–52, 355n, 357, 396, Plate 3. *See also* Theban tombs
Thebes, Greece (D223), 316, 324, 395
Themelis, P., 198
Themistocles, 363
Theocritus, 372
Theogony, 380–81
Thera (D241), 102, 105, 124n, 218n, 228n, 229, 233, 281n, 294, 314, 316–17, 319–20, 329, 329p, 338, 345, 366n, 381, 388–89, 394; analysis of textile representations on, 316–18, 319n
Theran frescoes (Akrotiri): Admiral's *ikria* (West

Theran frescoes (Akrotiri) (*cont.*)
  House), 316, 344–45, 394; Dressing Ladies (House of
  the Ladies), 316, 329, 394; Maritime Fresco (West
  House), 218n, 316, 344–45, 394; Priestess (West
  House), 316–17, 329, 329p, 394; Saffron Gatherers
  (Xeste 3), 124n, 233, 316–17, 329, 338n, 366n, 394
Thermi, 107n, 306p (map), 307, 392
Theseus, 267–68, 336n, 381
Thessaly, 22–23, 54, 92n, 107, 108p
Thetis, 364
thin-layer chromatography, 237
Thomas, A., 63, 86
Thomas, H., 171n, 392
Thompson, M., 54n, 99–100
Thompson, W., 290
Thomsen, T., 181
Thorsberg, 119, 192
Thrace, 18, 205, 308
Thracians, 16, 18, 36
thread: found as such, 10, 54–55, 68, 70, 95, 107, 172;
  terms for, 265–69, 278t, 282. *See* spinning; splices/
  splicing; twisting; warp; weft
thread count, 127, 132, 146, 148–49, 156, 164, 182,
  192, 197n, 318n
thread of destiny, 263, 376, 382
Thureau-Danguin, F., 229
Thuringia, 184
Thurstan, V., 55
Thutmose I, 339t, 344n
Thutmose II, 339t, 344n
Thutmose III, 64, 155n, 157–58, 162, 290, 331–35,
  339t, 340, 343, 344n, 347, 351–52, 356, 396, Plate 1
Thutmose IV, 113n, 114p, 157–59, 162, 339t, 342,
  344n, 347–48, 350, 352n, Plate 1
Thutnofer, 113, 114p, 286
Tibet (A inset), 17–18, 216n
Tibetan language, 38
tie-dyeing, 225 (def.). *See also* resist-dyeing
Tigris River (A), 259, 306p (map)
Tilke, M., 297n
time required, 4–5, 168, 292–93, 305, 320–21, 343,
  358–59, 363, 379, 382
tin, as mordant, 236, 238. *For other uses see* metal
Tiryns (D218), 238, 316, 324p, 325, 328n, 370
Tiszajenő (A68), 93–94, 94p, 103, 387, 389
Tisza River (A), 95, 99, 101, 249, 254, 293
Titans, 362, 380–81, 382n
Tiy, 343n
Tobler, A., 391
Tocharian A: *kärṣt-*, 261; *piktsi*, 359n
Tocharian B, *ṣñor*, 263n
Tomb of the Slain Soldiers, 149, 151n, 152
Tomb of the Two Brothers, 227
Tong En-Zheng, 17
tools: for textiles (finds of), 13, 14p, 50, 69, 69p; for
  working flax, 13, 14p. *See also individual tools*
topping (dyes), 236
torch races, 361, 382n

Touloupa, E., 197
tow, 13 (def.), 14, 52, 262
towels, 149, 152, 164, 332, 376
townhouse industry, 114p, 285
toxic dyes/mordants, 231n, 238–39
trade, 18, 35, 204–6, 221, 229, 237–38, 250p, 255n,
  285, 287–89, 299, 300, 309, 311–12, 331, 345–46,
  351, 355n, 357, 359, 376
traditions, 35, 49n, 63, 65, 67, 69, 73, 76, 130, 145,
  154, 159, 162, 167, 171n, 173n, 180, 210–14, 226–28,
  233n, 237n, 251, 285n, 286, 290–91, 294, 299–310,
  324, 341, 359n, 362, 380–83; miscopied, 194. *See
  also* conservatism; longevity; survivals
Trakhones (D229), 18, 33, 205
Trans-Caucasia, 391
Transitional/Ritual Aegean Dress, 315 (def.), 316, 322,
  324–25, 330, 377, 395
Trans-Jordan, 43
treadle looms, 85n, 125, 213, 268
Treasure Horizon, 221
Treasury of Amon, 334, 348
tree bark, 9, 20, 41, 49, 232, 236
trenches, for loom weights, 56p, 106, 295p
Tri Brata, Lower Volga Basin (A84), 169, 170p
trimming surface, of cloth, 202, 216, 274, 287
Trindhøj (B158), 177, 178p, 180, 182–83
Tringham, R., 98, 144n, 389
triple basket weave, 127p (diag.), 132, 167
Tripolye (A75), 17, 98, 306
Tripolye culture. *See under* Cucuteni
Trippett, F., 220
Troilos, 365
Trojans, 372–73
Trojan War, 257, 371, 373, 380, 382
Troy (A98), 3, 35, 54–55, 60, 93, 93p, 96, 101, 103–4,
  110, 118, 171–72, 174n, 292, 300, 301p (map), 304,
  306p (map), 307–8pp, 308, 312n, 314, 352n, 382,
  388–89
true weaving. *See* weaving: true
Tsangli, 54n
Tsani, 54n, 99
Tsarskaja (Novosvobodnaja), Kuban (A83), 168, 169p,
  225, 295n
Tsountas, C., 395
Tsuboi, M., 73
tubes, for skirt strings, 181–82, 255
tubs, 239–42; serving multiple functions, 241. *See also*
  dye pots
tubular cloth, 115–16
tubular selvedge, 182, 182p, 191
tubular warp, 126
Tufnell, O., 165, 302n
Tukulti-Ninurta I, 212
tumuli. *See* burial mounds; kurgans
Tungus, 38
tunics, of Tutankhamon, 153–54, 154p, 159–62, 160–
  61pp, 321, 352
Tunisia, 43

Tureng Tepe, 391

Turin, 304, 306p (map)

Turkestan, 303, 303–4pp, 305

Turkey, 10–11, 18, 51, 61p, 62p, 64p, 68, 93, 99, 101, 128p, 132, 170–71, 176p, 198p, 211–13, 217, 225, 254, 293, 302, 304–5, 312n, 337p, 355n, 365, 388–90. *See also* Anatolia

Turkic: *kendyr, kendir,* 18, 37; *ojlyk,* 215

Turkish: *benk,* 37; *höyük, hüyük,* 306; *kenevir,* 37; *tepe,* 306

Turkish pile-knot, 201, 202p (diag.)

Turkmenia, 171n, 212

Turks, 81, 293, 299n

turmeric, 233, 238

Tutankhamon, 33, 121n, 152–53, 154p, 155–56, 159–62, 172, 227, 232, 237–38, 321, 339t, 344, 352, 353n, 356

Tutankhaten, 162

Tuva, 37

tweed, 186–87 (etym.)

twill, 31n, 105, 110, 132, 144, 164, 167–68, 175, 186–95, 187 (def., etym.), 187p (diag.), 188p, 193p, 196p, 202, 210–14, 218, 268 (etym.), 282, 313–14, 328, Plate 4; development of, 190–91, 193–94, 211; diagonal, 164, 168, 187 (def.), 187p (diag.), 191, 193, 212, 218, 293, Plate 4; diamond/lozenge, 156n, 187 (def.), 187p (diag.), 188; felted, 218; goose-eye, 193, 193p; herringbone, 30, 187 (def.), 187p (diag.), 188, 190–91, 194–95, 212, 293, 328; not confined to wool, 190, 211–12; origins of, 211–12; phasing with color, 190, 193; phasing with shadow stripe, 190, 194; pointed, 187 (def.), 187p (diag.), 188, 190, 193–94, 293; statistics on types of, 188, 190; *3/1,* 203; *2/1,* 167–68, 195; *2/2,* 167, 167p, 187 (def.), 187p (diag.), 194, 200, 212, 267–68

twining, 12, 34, 72, 125, 128–30, 128p (diag.), 129p, 130–32, 131p, 137, 139–40, 144, 151, 166n, 176, 180–83, 201, 210, 255. *See also* weft twining

twist: added, 45p, 46–48, 54n, 70–73, 74p, 76; amount of, 31–32, 43, 53; as characteristic of fibers, 16, 20

twisting (to make thread), 9, 24, 31–32, 39–44, 47, 49–51, 68, 72, 78, 79, 148, 180, 258, 263n, 264, 303, 376

twist test, for fibers, 16

two-beam looms, 82, 113, 113p, 114–16, 122, 125, 129, 156, 158, 177n, 180, 187, 211–13, 213p, 252, 270, 286. *See also* ground-loom; vertical looms

two-shaft, 187 (def.)

Tylissos (D242), 316, 319, 394

Tyre (A112), 229

Tyrian purple, 229

Tzakhili, I., 389. *See also* Douskos, I.

Ugarit (Ras Shamra) (A116), 212, 229, 231, 242, 350, 355n

Ugaritic, 229–31; *ktn(t),* 295n

Ukhhotep, 347, 396

Ukraine, 17–18, 98, 144n, 205, 225, 231n, 256p, 295,

296p, 305–6, 307p, 308

Ulchi, *onokto, xuntaxa,* 38

ultimate fibers. *See under* bast; flax

Ulu Burun (A103), 355n

Unas, 149, 224, 237

undershot technique. *See* float weave

Unětice culture, 101, 302

Unexplored Mansion, Knossos, 174n, 330

unitary representations, on Minoan dress, 319–20, 320p, 322, 322p

University College, London, 48p, 65p, 68, 82p, 87p, 146–47p. *See also* Petrie Museum

University Museum, Philadelphia, 58p, 198–99pp, 318p, 391–92

unraveling silk, 204

Unterteutschenthal (A21), 176, 184, 217

upper floors, for textile work, 13, 89, 101–2, 105–6, 240–42, 300, 389

uprights. *See* posts

Ur (A134), 60, 164, 166, 224, 261n, 288

Ur III texts, 261n

Uralic, 37

Urarna, 341

urban economy, 288–89. *See also* townhouse industry

urine, textile uses of, 239

Urtica spp., 19

Uruk (A132), 24, 238

Urukagina, 288

User, 339t, 344n, 396

Useramon (Amenuser), 333, 335, 339t, 340, 342, 396

Userhet, 339t, 344, 396

USSR, 144n, 199, 256

Utoquai-Färberstrasse, Zurich, 95, 96p, 388–89

Uzbekistan, 31

Vaalermoor, 192

Valeri, A., 109n

Valley of the Kings (C208), 159

Valley of the Queens (C212), 156n

Valvasor, J., 4p

Vandier, J., 83n

van Gennep, A., 118, 120

van Loon, M., 300

van Reesema, E., 119–20, 122–24

Vardaroftsa, 107n

Vari (D230), 367n, 377

Varna (A52), 173n

Vasmer, M., 36, 215, 261n, 359n

vat-dyes, 225, 235. *See also* leuco-form

Veenhof, K., 238n, 287–88, 292

vegetable dyes. *See* dye plants

vegetable fiber, 9, 11, 14–15, 20, 24, 34p, 40–41, 54, 66, 131, 169, 176, 184–85, 215, 236. *See also* individual plants

Vehnemoor, 192

Veii (A41), 194

Ventris, M., 232, 238, 260, 261n, 262, 264–65, 270,

Ventris, M. (*cont.*)
    272n, 283–84, 312–13, 358n
Venus figures, 40, 40p, 255–58, 257p
Vercoutter, J., 226n, 311, 331, 333p, 334–35, 337, 345, 348, 350, 355n, 396
Verkhovskaja, A., 202n, 238
Verneau, R., 39, 172
Verona, 101
vertical looms, 81, 82 (def.), 83n, 88–89, 103, 113–16, 114p, 125, 156, 158, 212–13, 251n, 252–54, 286, 290. *See also* two-beam looms; warp-weighted loom
vertical two-beam loom, 82, 113, 114p, 115, 125, 156, 158, 212–13, 252, 286, 290, 352; origin of, 213; representations of, 113, 114p, 115–16, 213p
Veselovskij, N., 169, 225, 255n, 295n
Vestal Virgins, 233n
Victoria and Albert Museum, London, 156
Viemont, B., 236
Vikings, 119, 373
Viking tapestries, 373
Villanovan culture, 194
Vily, 297
Vinča (A58), 95, 134, 255
Vinča-Pločnik culture, 134
Vindonissa, 122
vinegar, 235–36
virgin spirits, 297
Vogt, E., 10, 13, 14p, 55, 68, 81, 106, 116, 118, 135–36, 138–41
Vogul, *polna*, 37
Voigt, M., 391
Vojvodina, 98
volcanic eruption, 316, 355n, 362, 380–82
Voldtofte (B165), 19
Volga River (A), 169, 170p, 213, 306p (map)
von Bissing, Baroness, 346p
von der Osten, H., 57p, 99, 167, 300p, 389, 390, 392
von Stokar, W., 184, 224, 227, 234
Vouga, P., 29n
Voula (D230), 316, 395
Vounous (A111), 63, 174n
Vučedol (A61), 293
Vulgar Latin, *can(n)abum, canaba*, 36
Vydra, J., 226n

Wace, A., 54n, 99–100, 174n, 350, 359n, 360n, 376
Waetzoldt, H., 24–26, 28–29, 84, 88n, 125, 220n
wages. *See* earnings
Wah, 150–51, 153
Wahka II (B), 339t, 347n, 396
Wainwright, G., 30
waisted weights, 98
Walberg, G., 329, 347n
Wales, 234n
wall hangings, 197, 200, 382, Plate 4. *See also* hangings
Wallis, H., 353p, 354
Walters Art Gallery, Baltimore, 367p

Walterstorff, E., 137, 192–93, 193p, 218
Waqartum, 287
Ward, W., 230
Wardle, T., 234n
Warka period, representations of sheep in, 25
warp, 5 (def.), 9, 79, 81–83, 88, 92n, 109–10, 111p, 112–13, 116–19, 124, 127–29, 134, 135p, 152, 158, 179–81, 184, 191p, 195, 202, 210–12, 253, 255, 266–68, 270–74, 270p, 278t, 279, 283–84, 286, 326, 326p, 358, 360, 365, 370n; bunched, 80, 92, 104, 115, 135, 142, 195, 253; circular, 90, 115, 375; continuous, 90, 115–16, 177n; cut ends of, 129, 274, 274p, 358n; distinguishing from weft, 5n, 79, 127, 128p, 133, 188, 192; hidden, 128p (diag.), 142, 156–57, 164–65, 325 (*see also* faced weaves; weft-faced weave); lengthening, 105–6; paired, 127, 127p, 134, 135p, 148–49, 152, 155, 165, 210, 212, 268 (*see also* half-basket weave); separating threads of, 106–7, 112, 273, 360n; spacing, 84, 87–88, 130, 211, 271 (*see also* loom weights: control bar for); spiral, 115–16; spreading, 80, 86, 89, 130, 253; storing extra, 105n, 106, 115–16; strain/friction on, 43, 110, 112, 211–12, 267; thread for, 43, 73n, 89, 156, 267–68; tubular, 115–16, 116p; tying on, 80, 90p, 96, 117, 129, 192, 211, 217; used as weft, 116p, 117, 134–37, 136p, 142, 192, 273n; weight per thread, 96. *See also* heading band/cord; shedding: of the warp
warp beam, 80–81, 84, 86, 89–90, 113, 115, 253, 270; proportional to cloth beam, 86
warp-faced weave, 127 (def.), 128p, 137, 142, 156–57, 157p, 159–62, 164, 178–79, 179–80pp, 180, 184, 198, 210, 330
warp-float pattern, 175, 190, 197–98, 198p, 268n, 330, 332, 348, 353
warping, 57p, 84, 84p, 85p, 89–90, 90p, 96, 109, 116p, 180, 269p, 271–72, 280, 280t, 283–84, 286; frames for, 56, 57p, 89–90, 91p, 114p, 116–17, 116p, 213p, 269p, 283, 326, 326p; pegs for, 85p, 89, 90p, 116–17, 116p, 269p
warp makers, 85p, 89, 90–91pp, 272–73n, 283–84
warp pick-up technique, 31n, 156 (def.), 290, 319n. *See also* warp-float pattern
warp-weighted loom, 72p, 82 (def.), 83, 91–113, 91–92pp, 106p, 108p, 111p (diag.), 115–17, 124–25, 129–30, 134–35, 142–44, 165n, 166, 180–81, 192, 195, 197, 204n, 211, 213, 228, 240, 243, 255, 267–68, 270–74, 270p (diag.), 279, 280t, 281, 283, 293–94, 300, 308, 313, 326, 326p, 336, 358, 361, 362n, 387–90; dismantling, 101–2, 270; distribution of, 97–101, 113, 249–54, 250p, 252p, 259, 299–303, 301p, 308; importation to Palestine, 300–303; origin of, 99, 101, 113, 124, 253–54, 258; representations of, 91–92, 91–92pp, 92n, 105–10, 106p, 108p, 111p, 112, 269p, 295p, 313; side view, 110, 111p; uprightness of, 92, 103, 110, 111p, 253; warping up, 96, 192
warp weights, 115, 117. *See also* loom weights
Warren, P., 74, 75p, 76, 104p, 226n, 232n, 239–41, 329, 331, 340, 389, 395

warrior costume, in Late Bronze Age, 354–55
Warrior Vase (Mycenae), 274p, 316, 368–69, 369p, 395
Wartberg culture, 141
washing, 45p, 66, 204, 215–16, 235, 239–41, 257, 262, 274, 284–86, 286p, 321, 374
water channels, 239–41
waterproofing. *See* weatherproofing
Watson, B., 31, 205n
Watson, D., 27–28
Watson, P., 83n
wattle, 79
wax, 52, 225–26
Wayland, H., 168n
weatherproofing, 178, 211–12, 216–18, 220–21, 252
weaver's marks, 151, 151p, 153, 153p
weaver's practices, reconstruction of, 192, 279–81, 318–19nn, 325–26
weaver's waste, 49n, 224, 351
weaver's workshops, 44n, 73, 85p, 89, 102, 106, 114p, 130n, 272n, 284–86, 288, 290–91, 302n, 389. *See also* Egyptian representations: of weaving
weaving, 5 (def.), 80 (etym.), 254 (etym.); antiquity of, 3–4, 79–80, 88, 124; direction of, 92, 113, 125 (*see also* beating weft up; sheds: downward-opening); earliest evidence for, 34, 51, 79, 88, 126–32, 127p, 210, 252p, 253, 258–59; as metaphor, 375–76; origins of, 9–10, 79–80, 126–27, 131–32, 249, 253, 258–59; vs. painting, 354, 365–66, 370; representations of, 45p, 56p, 72p, 74p, 81, 83–85, 83–85pp, 90–92pp, 106p, 108p, 111p, 114p, 116p, 119, 213p, 269p, 295p; with several weavers, 81–82, 84, 84p, 87, 105–6, 113, 178, 178p, 251, 269p, 286, 286p, 294, 363; true, 5 (def.), 9, 79–80, 125, 127n, 130, 132, 134. *See also* loom weights: fallen from above; upper floors
weaving errors, 109, 112–13, 119–21, 148, 174n, 177–78, 183, 198, 199p, 218, 254, 268n
weaving materials, 9, 79–80; flexibility of, 9, 79–80. *See also* fibers; spinning
weaving swords. *See* beaters; sword-beaters
weaving technique, shift of, 347, 370–71
weaving wedges, 177–78, 177p, 193
web, 2, 80 (etym.), 198, 273
Weber, H., 32
weed plants, 18–19
weft, 5 (def.), 9 (etym.), 79, 80 (etym.), 111p, 116–19, 127–29, 135p, 156–58, 203, 210, 251n, 266–69, 270p, 273–74, 278t, 279, 280t, 281; beaded, 155, 172; beating in, 84, 92, 112, 205n, 211, 267; becoming warp, 152, 152p (diag.), 326, 326p; crossed, 105, 178, 178p, 180; deformed, 158; distinguishing from warp, 5n, 79, 127, 128p, 133, 188, 192; hidden, 127, 128p, 142, 156, 164–65, 179, 203, 325 (*see also* faced weaves; warp-faced weave); length of, 9; multiple, 119; paired, 48, 127, 127p, 134, 135p, 136–37, 136p, 138p, 148, 152, 155, 165, 187, 210, 268, 326 (*see also* half-basket weave; twill); slippage of, 9; storage of, 84–85, 106–9, 192, 360n; straightness of, 115n, 177, 177p; thread for, 43, 48, 73n, 79, 159, 267, 305; ways

of inserting, 9, 82, 84–85, 109, 112, 119, 125, 187, 254, 360n
weft-faced weave, 127n, 128p (diag.), 156–58, 164–66, 195, 199–200, 202–3, 212
weft floats, 137, 138p, 139, 293, 319n, 322, 347, 354, 356, 366, 370n, 374, 374p
weft looping, 83n, 149 (def.), 150, 150p, 152, 154, 155n, 159, 164, 194, 197–98, 200, 202n, 210, 332
weft loops, as selvedge/fringe, 83n, 148, 151–52, 156, 255
weft pick-up, 366. *See also* float weave; supplementary weft
weft twining, 128 (def.), 128p (diag.), 129p, 130–32, 131p, 144, 166n, 210. *See also* twining
weft wrapping, 128 (def.), 128p (diag.), 198
Weigall, A., 113n, 338n, 396
weighing wool, 70, 72p, 265, 283–85, 287
weights, found at dye-works, 240–42. *See also* loom weights, *and under* spindles; spindle whorls
Weinberg, S., and G. Weinberg, 105, 106p
Weir, S., 43
weld, 223, 233, 233n (etym.)
Welker, M., 106p
Welsh, *cnaif*, 274
West House, Akrotiri, 329p. *See also* Theran frescoes
West Semites, 228, 295n, 355n, 356. *See also* Canaanites; Hebrews; Syrians
wethers, 26–28, 27t, 37 (def.), 26–28
wetting, 42, 46, 49n, 66, 70p, 72–73, 75n, 76, 215–17, 226, 262. *See also* fiber-wetting bowls; washing
Wharton, E., 264
wheels, 170, 170p, 206, 265, 293, 324p, 327–28n, 367, 377
whey, 216
white, 17, 21, 29, 33, 119, 133, 146, 153, 155, 157–59, 166, 171–72, 177, 190, 195, 198, 200, 202, 204, 207–8, 211, 217, 224–26, 230, 234, 237, 252, 255n, 258, 272n, 286, 288, 295n, 297, 312, 314, 318–19, 329–30, 332–35, 333p, 337–38, 347–48, 351, 356, 366n, 370n, 371–72, 371p, 378
Whitehouse, H., 52
whorls. *See* spindle whorls
width. *See under* cloth; looms
Wiepenkathen, Kr. Hamburg (B154), 184
Wild, J., 32, 204n, 216, 260, 268n
wild ancestors, of flax, 11–12
wild fiber. *See* wild resources
wild goat frieze, 356, 366p, 369, 372
wild resources, use of, 11–12, 20, 34, 259
Wilkinson, J., 286
William the Conqueror, 373
Williams, C., 92n
Williams, D., 122, 124, 269n
willies, 297
Wilson, T., 304
Windeknecht, M., and T. Windeknecht, 142
winders, 77, 77p
Window of Appearances, 352

windproofing. *See* weatherproofing
wind-shelters, on boats, 218n, 344–45, 344p, 356
Winlock, H., 44, 82, 84, 87, 89, 122, 149, 152
Winter, W., 275n
Wipszycka, E., 268n
wishbone-handled cups, with bull's heads, 350
woad, 223, 227, 234–35, 235n (etym.)
women, 31, 39, 53, 60, 97, 141, 156, 162, 173, 177, 180–83, 185, 202–3, 205n, 213, 213p, 226n, 233n, 255–58, 256–58pp, 264, 310, 322p, 331–32, 338n, 342–43, 346, 351, 358–60, 364, 368, 373, 375–77, 394–95, Plate 2; as captives, 4, 162, 205n, 284, 287–88, 291, 359, 362 (*see also* captives); clothing of, 40, 65, 169, 177, 180–83, 185, 189, 189p, 194, 208, 214, 233n, 255–58, 256–58pp, 268n, 314–19, 314p, 318p, 321p, 322, 322p, 324–29, 324p, 327p, 329p, 338n, 347n, 359, 364, 369p, Plate 2; as craftworkers, 2, 4, 4p, 43–50, 54–59, 56p, 69–70, 72–73, 74p, 77–78, 78p, 81, 83–86, 89–90, 96, 102, 105, 106p, 109–10, 112–13, 116p, 171, 228n, 231, 251n, 262, 264–65, 265p, 267, 269p, 270, 273n, 274–75, 283–302, 305, 307–10, 326, 326p, 351, 353, 358–60, 362–63, 371–73, 376–77; graves of, textile tools in, 60, 65, 171n, 289, 305; highborn, making cloth, 292, 358–60, 362, 376–77, 382; as independent agents, 287–89, 291–92; migrations of, 76, 299–303, 307–10; privileged to wear yellow, 233n, 338n; textile professions of, 262, 264, 270, 272–73n, 283–84, 289; work quarters of, 102, 284–85
wooden framework (Egyptian), 340–42
Woodhouse, J., 231n
woof, 79, 80 (etym.)
wool, 20–30, 24p, 33, 35–37, 41, 43, 49–50, 52, 53n, 65–67, 70, 70p, 72, 77–78, 107, 142, 176–77, 180, 184–85, 189–90, 200, 215–22, 224, 233n (etym.), 238, 240–41, 249, 259, 260 (etym.), 261–67, 272–73n, 274, 275n, 276, 278t, 283–85, 287, 292, 312, 351–52, 366n; against the skin, 20, 252; before Bronze Age, not proved, 25n, 141; buying, 288; catchiness of, 20, 117, 215, 267; characteristics of, 20–21; combing vs. carding, 20, 261; development of whiteness in, 29; distribution of, 34p, 211, 250p, 251, 253; dyed, 49n, 70, 224, 351–52, 366n, Plate 4; dyeing, 21, 29, 49n, 211, 217, 228, 235–36, 239, 241, 330, 351; earliest remains of, 25, 49n; early use of, 23–24, 28, 49n; in economy, 24–25, 27–28, 49n, 240; Egyptian use of, 25, 49n; elasticity of, 20–21; fibers of, 9, 20–21, 29; fine, 21 (def.), 29–30; greasing, 285; identification of, 10–11; as insulator, 20, 215; kinkiness of, 20, 66; length of, 21, 43–44, 49, 52, 56; medium, 21 (def.), 30, 49n; natural colors of, 21, 29; preparing, 21–22, 41, 46n, 72, 265, 265p, 283; quality of, 141, 184, 262, 284; scales on fibers of, 11, 20–21, 25, 215, 216n; spinning of, 20–21, 24n, 41, 43–44, 43–44pp, 49–50, 66–67, 283–84, 393; structure of, 21p (diag.), 21n, 24n; thickness (grade) of, 21; weaving, 96, 142, 351. *See also* fleece
wool-baskets, 70, 70p, 72, 72p, 262, 264–65, 265p

woolen cloth, 25n, 28–30, 49n, 96, 105, 119, 141, 165–66, 168, 171, 176, 178, 184, 188–95, 188–89pp, 191p, 193p, 197, 200–203, 206–8, 207–8pp, 219, 224, 262, 274–75, 358n, 363n, Plate 4
woolen garments, 32, 178, 181p, 183p, 189, 193, 217, 295n
woolen warp, 117, 202n, 211, 267
woolen yarn, 20 (def.), 22
wool fibers, 141, 164
Woolley, C. L., 70, 86, 88–89, 164, 224
woolliness, 23–25, 29–30
wool-workers, 72
workers' quarters, 88–89, 286, 291, 302
working-bees, 178, 294
Works and Days, 2, 102, 266, 270
workshops. *See* dye-works; weaver's workshops
workshop system, 272n, 284
worsted yarn, 20 (def.), 22, 49n, 224, 261 (def.)
Wreszinski, W., 151
Wright, G., 242
wrought-iron fence motif, 346–48, 346p, 351, 357, 371p, 372, Plate 3; color scheme of, 347n
Wyss, R., 13, 47n, 95n, 392

Xanthoudides, S., 75, 78, 327p, 395
Xeste 3, Akrotiri, 124n. *See also* Theran frescoes

Yablonsky, G., 216n
yaks, 216n
Yale Babylonian Collection, 57p
Yang-Shao culture, 17, 31
Yanik Tepe, 391
Yarim Tepe, 51n
yarn, 266 (etym.). *See also* spinning; thread; woolen yarn; worsted yarn
yellow, 13, 29, 155–56, 158, 165, 169–70, 169p, 172, 190, 191p, 198, 207–8, 211, 224–25, 227–28, 231–33, 236–37, 239, 312–13, 325–26, 325p, 330, 332, 334, 337–38, 340–42, 344, 347n, 352, 379; worn by women, 233n, 338n, 362
Yetts, W., 359n
Yin-Shang. *See* Shang dynasty
Yohannes, J., 352n
Yonge, C., 261n
Young, R., 102, 219, 390
Young, T., 391
yo-yo pattern, 317–19, 317–18pp, 320p, 328–29, 332p
Yuaa and Thuiu, 343n
Yunnan, China, 81

Z-. *See* Z-plied; Z-spun; Z-twist
Zafer Papoura (D245), 174n
Zagreb mummy wrapping, 194
Zagros mountains (A), 306p (map)
Zawi Chemi Shanidar, 22, 27n

Zeuner, F., 22–24, 27
Zeus, 257–58, 360–62, 380–81
zigzag/chevron/diamond pattern, 197, 347–48, Plate 3; tented (LM IIIA pattern), 348, 351, Plate 3
Zimri-Lim, 281
Zindorf, A., 165
Ziryene *piš*, 37
Zisis, V., 18, 33, 205

zones of textile development, 131–32, 210–11, 249–54, 250p, 258–59, 313
Z-plied, 40, 68, 184
Z-spun, 66 (def.), 66p, 67–68, 78, 142, 145, 146p, 164, 178, 182, 184, 190–91, 194, 206
Z-twist, 65–66 (def.), 66p (diag.), 67
Zurich (A29), 95, 306p (map), 308, 388–89
Zvrantsev, M., 297n